Dictionary of Literary Biography

Documentary Series

12 *Southern Women Writers: Flannery O'Connor, Katherine Anne Porter, Eudora Welty,* edited by Mary Ann Wimsatt and Karen L. Rood (1994)

13 *The House of Scribner, 1846-1904,* edited by John Delaney (1996)

14 *Four Women Writers for Children, 1868-1918,* edited by Caroline C. Hunt (1996)

15 *American Expatriate Writers: Paris in the Twenties,* edited by Matthew J. Bruccoli and Robert W. Trogdon (1997)

16 *The House of Scribner, 1905-1930,* edited by John Delaney (1997)

17 *The House of Scribner, 1931-1984,* edited by John Delaney (1998)

18 *British Poets of The Great War: Sassoon, Graves, Owen,* edited by Patrick Quinn (1999)

19 *James Dickey,* edited by Judith S. Baughman (1999)

See also DLB 210

Yearbooks

1980 edited by Karen L. Rood, Jean W. Ross, and Richard Ziegfeld (1981)

1981 edited by Karen L. Rood, Jean W. Ross, and Richard Ziegfeld (1982)

1982 edited by Richard Ziegfeld; associate editors: Jean W. Ross and Lynne C. Zeigler (1983)

1983 edited by Mary Bruccoli and Jean W. Ross; associate editor: Richard Ziegfeld (1984)

1984 edited by Jean W. Ross (1985)

1985 edited by Jean W. Ross (1986)

1986 edited by J. M. Brook (1987)

1987 edited by J. M. Brook (1988)

1988 edited by J. M. Brook (1989)

1989 edited by J. M. Brook (1990)

1990 edited by James W. Hipp (1991)

1991 edited by James W. Hipp (1992)

1992 edited by James W. Hipp (1993)

1993 edited by James W. Hipp, contributing editor George Garrett (1994)

1994 edited by James W. Hipp, contributing editor George Garrett (1995)

1995 edited by James W. Hipp, contributing editor George Garrett (1996)

1996 edited by Samuel W. Bruce and L. Kay Webster, contributing editor George Garrett (1997)

1997 edited by Matthew J. Bruccoli and George Garrett, with the assistance of L. Kay Webster (1998)

1998 edited by Matthew J. Bruccoli, contributing editor George Garrett, with the assistance of D. W. Thomas (1999)

Concise Series

Concise Dictionary of American Literary Biography, 7 volumes (1988-1999): *The New Consciousness, 1941-1968; Colonization to the American Renaissance, 1640-1865; Realism, Naturalism, and Local Color, 1865-1917; The Twenties, 1917-1929; The Age of Maturity, 1929-1941; Broadening Views, 1968-1988; Supplement: Modern Writers, 1900–1998.*

Concise Dictionary of British Literary Biography, 8 volumes (1991-1992): *Writers of the Middle Ages and Renaissance Before 1660; Writers of the Restoration and Eighteenth Century, 1660-1789; Writers of the Romantic Period, 1789-1832; Victorian Writers, 1832-1890; Late-Victorian and Edwardian Writers, 1890-1914; Modern Writers, 1914-1945; Writers After World War II, 1945-1960; Contemporary Writers, 1960 to Present.*

Concise Dictionary of World Literary Biography, 20 volumes projected (1999-   ): *Ancient Greek and Roman Writers.*

Dictionary of Literary Biography® • Volume Two Hundred Eleven

Ancient Roman Writers

Dictionary of Literary Biography® • Volume Two Hundred Eleven

Ancient Roman Writers

Edited by
Ward W. Briggs
University of South Carolina

A Bruccoli Clark Layman Book
The Gale Group
Detroit • San Francisco • London • Boston • Woodbridge, Conn.

Printed in the United States of America

The paper used in this publication meets the minimum requirements
of American National Standard for Information Sciences–Permanence
Paper for Printed Library Materials, ANSI Z39.48-1984. ∞™

Library of Congress Cataloging-in-Publication Data

Ancient Roman writers / edited by Ward W. Briggs.
    p. cm.–(Dictionary of literary biography: v. 211)
"A Bruccoli Clark Layman book."
Includes bibliographical references and index.
ISBN 0-7876-3105-1 (alk. paper)
1. Authors, Latin–Biography–Dictionaries. 2. Latin literature–Bio-bibliography–Dictionaries. 3.Rome–
In literature–Dictionaries. 4. Latin literature–Dictionaries. I. Briggs, Ward W. II. Series.
PA6013.A53 1999
870.9'0109'03–dc21   99–33325
[B]   CIP

10 9 8 7 6 5 4 3 2 1

Contents

Contents

Plan of the Series

The advisory board, the editors, and the publisher of the *Dictionary of Literary Biography* are joined in endorsing Mark Twain's declaration. The literature of a nation provides an inexhaustible resource of permanent worth. We intend to make literature and its creators better understood and more accessible to students and the reading public, while satisfying the standards of teachers and scholars.

To meet these requirements, *literary biography* has been construed in terms of the author's achievement. The most important thing about a writer is his writing. Accordingly, the entries in *DLB* are career biographies, tracing the development of the author's canon and the evolution of his reputation.

The purpose of *DLB* is not only to provide reliable information in a convenient format but also to place the figures in the larger perspective of literary history and to offer appraisals of their accomplishments by qualified scholars.

The publication plan for *DLB* resulted from two years of preparation. The project was proposed to Bruccoli Clark by Frederick G. Ruffner, president of the Gale Research Company, in November 1975. After specimen entries were prepared and typeset, an advisory board was formed to refine the entry format and develop the series rationale. In meetings held during 1976, the publisher, series editors, and advisory board approved the scheme for a comprehensive biographical dictionary of persons who contributed to North American literature. Editorial work on the first volume began in January 1977, and it was published in 1978. In order to make *DLB* more than a reference tool and to compile volumes that individually have claim to status as literary history, it was decided to organize volumes by

topic, period, or genre. Each of these freestanding volumes provides a biographical-bibliographical guide and overview for a particular area of literature. We are convinced that this organization—as opposed to a single alphabet method—constitutes a valuable innovation in the presentation of reference material. The volume plan necessarily requires many decisions for the placement and treatment of authors who might properly be included in two or three volumes. In some instances a major figure will be included in separate volumes, but with different entries emphasizing the aspect of his career appropriate to each volume. Ernest Hemingway, for example, is represented in *American Writers in Paris, 1920–1939* by an entry focusing on his expatriate apprenticeship; he is also in *American Novelists, 1910–1945* with an entry surveying his entire career, as well as in *American Short-Story Writers, 1910–1945, Second Series* with an entry concentrating on his short stories. Each volume includes a cumulative index of the subject authors and articles. Comprehensive indexes to the entire series are planned.

Since 1981 the series has been further augmented by the *DLB Yearbooks,* which update published entries and add new entries to keep the *DLB* current with contemporary activity. There have also been *DLB Documentary Series* volumes which provide biographical and critical source materials for figures whose work is judged to have particular interest for students. One of these companion volumes is devoted entirely to Tennessee Williams.

We define literature as the *intellectual commerce of a nation:* not merely as belles lettres but as that ample and complex process by which ideas are generated, shaped, and transmitted. *DLB* entries are not limited to "creative writers" but extend to other figures who in their time and in their way influenced the mind of a people. Thus the series encompasses historians, journalists, publishers, book collectors, and screenwriters. By this means readers of *DLB* may be aided to perceive literature not as cult scripture in the keeping of intellectual high priests but firmly positioned at the center of a nation's life.

DLB includes the major writers appropriate to each volume and those standing in the ranks behind them. Scholarly and critical counsel has been sought in deciding which minor figures to include and how full their entries should be. Wherever possible, useful references are made to figures who do not warrant separate entries.

Each *DLB* volume has an expert volume editor responsible for planning the volume, selecting the figures for inclusion, and assigning the entries. Volume editors are also responsible for preparing, where appropriate, appendices surveying the major periodicals and literary and intellectual movements for their volumes, as well as lists of further readings. Work on the series as a whole is coordinated at the Bruccoli Clark Layman editorial center in Columbia, South Carolina, where the editorial staff is responsible for accuracy and utility of the published volumes.

One feature that distinguishes *DLB* is the illustration policy—its concern with the iconography of literature. Just as an author is influenced by his surroundings, so is the reader's understanding of the author enhanced by a knowledge of his environment. Therefore *DLB* volumes include not only drawings, paintings, and photographs of authors, often depicting them at various stages in their careers, but also illustrations of their families and places where they lived. Title pages are regularly reproduced in facsimile along with dust jackets for modern authors. The dust jackets are a special feature of *DLB* because they often document better than anything else the way in which an author's work was perceived in its own time. Specimens of the writers' manuscripts and letters are included when feasible.

Samuel Johnson rightly decreed that "The chief glory of every people arises from its authors." The purpose of the *Dictionary of Literary Biography* is to compile literary history in the surest way available to us—by accurate and comprehensive treatment of the lives and work of those who contributed to it.

The *DLB* Advisory Board

Introduction

Then, in the arts, where there can be no progress, only blossoming or sterility, the Imperial flowers, it must be admitted, are few. The poets, for example, who are still widely read with both admiration and pleasure are Lucretius, Catullus, Virgil, Horace, Propertius, Ovid. All of them grew up under the Republic, and the youngest of them is dead by A.D. 17. After them, who is there? Seneca (d. 65), Martial (c. 104), Juvenal (c. 140); readable, but hectic, strained, and basically unpleasant. Then nobody for two hundred years. In the fourth and fifth centuries, a mysterious little masterpiece, the *Pervigilium Veneris,* and some poets, Pagan and Christian, like Prudentius, Ausonius, Paulinus of Nola, Claudian, who wrote one or two nice pieces, but are very minor figures. Finally, in the sixth century after the West has fallen, one really remarkable poet, Maximian. The list is not long. *—W. H. Auden*[1]

When one thinks of the heritage from the ancients, the names of various forms of government come to mind: aristocracy, oligarchy, tyranny, and especially democracy. Then come the classification of scientific investigation in astronomy, biology, and medicine; the orders of architecture and the great marble buildings designed to last for centuries; statuary and painting; anthropomorphic religion; and finally, the notion that the world can be understood not by superstition but by rational inquiry and analysis. Many people will also think of the beginnings of literature: epic, tragedy, comedy, lyric poetry, and pastoral poetry. Elegy, history, oratory, and philosophy may be added. To many, these are the most obvious, dramatic, and interesting of the legacies from the ancient word, and they are all Greek.

Americans have not always thought highly of the Romans. Though the Founding Fathers modeled the American constitution on the "mixed" government of Rome drawn from the model of the Roman Republic—largely as defined by Polybius and more specifically in Joseph Addison's *Cato* (1713), gave themselves the names of noble Romans of the Republic, and portrayed themselves in statuary as Caesar or Brutus, as the nineteenth century dawned, a reaction against the Roman-influenced Enlightenment and the dominance of the Roman Catholic Church set in. A general movement toward independence (evidenced by revolutions in America, France, and Greece) in this period led many to embrace Hellenism with nearly unbridled enthusiasm. By the middle of the nineteenth century, the Romantic Movement in the arts coupled with new discoveries on mainland Greece and the growth of scientific classical scholarship had made Greek literature, architecture, and philosophy all the rage. Shelley could claim, "We are all Greeks," and Emerson could call Plato "an American genius." The romance of Greek life that so attracted the Romantics makes pedestrian the everyday, often unseen legacies of Roman engineers, planners, civil servants, and administrators. Readers today may often feel as does the exasperated Roman "Reg," in *Monty Python's Life of Brian* (1979):

> All right . . . all right . . . but apart from better sanitation and medicine and education and irrigation and public health and roads and a freshwater system and baths and public order . . . what *have* the Romans *done* for us?

Following the Civil War, the American South, which had viewed itself as a confederation of free and independent states more like the cities of Boeotia than the dependent demes of Attica, viewed the North not as the noble old Roman Republic but as the monolithic and impersonal Roman Empire. Basil L. Gildersleeve, America's greatest classical scholar and an editor of the Boeotian poet Pindar, was one of many who viewed the postbellum North with a jaundiced eye:

> A more canting, lying, thievish race than the Roman was never suffered by the Master of history to run so long a career on His footstool; and the sympathies of every generous soul must always be with their antagonists, whether these antagonists were nations or individuals. . . . In all the wearisome annals of the Republic there is but one great man, and him they killed; in all their verse-manufactory there is but one great poet, and he wasted his talents on the dullest of themes and died a maniac; and moreover, it must be remembered that both Caesar and Lucretius belong to the period of transition from the Republic to the Empire.[2]

In the latter part of the nineteenth century the powerful and impersonal Roman state was portrayed as the antagonist not of freethinking Greece but of sancti-monious individualized Christians such as Ben-Hur or Marcus Vinicius. To distinguish Rome as inferior to modern civilizations, authors and movie directors por-trayed the Romans as gluttonous, immoral, slave-own-ing Sybarites who took unnatural delight in the wholesale slaughter of innocents in the arena. In part this view reflects the attitudes of enlightened authors of the time, such as Seneca, Tacitus, and other imperial historians. Part derives from the desire to ennoble the struggles of early Christianity, and part owes to the desire to plant some salacious ticket- and book-selling sex and violence while pursuing more pious themes.

Though Latin studies were ascendant once again after World War I, the legacy of the Romantic days continues to esteem the originality, creativity, and spon-taneity, and to render the emulative, refining, practical efforts of the Romans somehow inferior to the accom-plishments of the Greeks. Popular culture has yet to portray (except, perhaps, metaphorically in Westerns) the ideal that most of the Roman authors in this volume adhered to: the noble, honest life of the old Roman Republic. Athens and the other states of Greece had experienced either tyranny or democracy. Their high-minded experiments in civic representation had flamed out, to be replaced with oppression and autoc-racy. The story of Roman history with which this vol-ume is concerned is the struggle between the orders called patrician and plebeian. The greatness of Rome lies in part in the flexible confection of democracy and oligarchy that in varying proportions lasted for a thou-sand years.

When Romans first began to write histories of the founding of their city in the third century B.C. (some five centuries after the event), two problems confronted them. The initial settlement on the Palatine Hill on the banks of the Tiber River grew to include the seven hills–the Aventine (the religious center), the Caelian, the Capitoline (the political center), the Esquiline, the Palatine (the residential area), the Quirinal, and the Viminal. The settlement may already have existed when Troy fell in 1184 B.C., but in order to connect this small colony of Alba Longa with the dominant culture of the period of its founding, the Romans established that the Trojan prince Aeneas escaped the fall of Troy and with the aid of his divine mother, Venus, estab-lished a Trojan presence in the "new world" of Italy. To meet the difficulty of Rome's relation to Alba Longa, Aeneas's son Ascanius was declared the first of the Alban kings, who ruled the area from the late twelfth to the eighth centuries B.C. According to Livy, the last of these kings, Amulius, murdered the male progeny of his brother Numitor, rightful heir to the throne, and forced his only daughter, Rhea Silvia, to become a Vestal Virgin, insuring that she would have no offspring. Raped by Mars, Rhea produced twin sons, Romulus and Remus. Amulius ordered them drowned in the Tiber, but the Tiber cast them back. A royal shepherd raised the boys to maturity. As adults, they took deadly revenge on Amulius and founded the city of Rome on the spot where they had been thrown ashore. The year is generally given as 753 B.C. The city was named after Romulus when a flight of birds flew in a direction propitious to him, not his brother. In a sub-sequent quarrel, Romulus killed Remus.

Romulus was the first of seven Roman kings. Though he was deified after his death, mixed reputa-tions attend the kings who followed him: Numa Pompi-lius (reigned 715–673 B.C.), Tullus Hostilius (673–642 B.C.), Ancus Marcius (642–616 B.C.), Tarquinius Priscus (616–579 B.C.), Servius Tullius (578–535 B.C.), and Tarquinius Superbus (534–510 B.C.). These kings, probably imposed from without, were popularly elected, and a senate composed of *patres* (elders) advised them. Rome expanded its base first when Tullus Hosti-lius conquered Alba Longa, then when Ancus Martius founded the colony of Ostia at the mouth of the Tiber. The Tarquin kings were clearly Etruscans, a people who managed a confederacy of central Italian states whose influence was at its height from 620 to 500 B.C. Servius Tullius bounded Rome by a great wall that is named after him and imposed a class structure based on wealth and property rather than birth that was to last until the Empire. Though Tarquinius Superbus was benignly productive, his son's rape of Lucretia, the wife of a kinsman, and her subsequent suicide led to the expulsion of the Tarquins in 510 B.C., the reduction of Etruscan influence, and the everlasting Roman repug-nance for the word "king."

With the expulsion of the Tarquins, the Romans established a republic with aristocrats firmly in control. The Senate was now the chief governing body. To avoid the concentration of power in the hands of one man, two consuls (originally called praetors), chosen from the upper classes, took the place of the king. From the beginning of the Republic, the seeds of conflict and ultimate collapse were sown by aristocratic dominance. The struggle to achieve a constitution agreeable to all was not resolved until 287 B.C. The patricians had most of the money and power, while the plebeians were poor and powerless. Nevertheless, they were the majority, with little but their sheer numbers to use as leverage against the aristocrats.

One of the plebeians' chief difficulties was even knowing what the laws were. In 451 B.C., they achieved the publication of the laws on bronze tablets *(Twelve Tables)* only to realize just how disadvantaged they were. Over the next century, plebeians struggled to be allowed to hold the various public offices, but the big prize was eligibility for the consulship (won in 366 B.C.).

The struggle of the orders that is a theme of the republican period centered on the conflict between the desire by the poorest members of the plebeian class for basic rights and the desire of the wealthier members of the class to manage the government. The Hortensian Law (287 B.C.), which, in addition to relieving the debt of the lower classes, established the equality of the *concilia plebis* (assembly of the plebeians) with the old *comitia centuriata* (aristocratic assembly). The ruling class was now composed of wealthy members of both estates, while the condition of the poorest in the society was not substantially improved.

Whatever internal conflicts may have been roiling, there seemed no dispute between the orders on the need for expansion. The Romans gradually defeated all those who attacked after the expulsion of the Tarquins. The great victory over the Latin League (surrounding towns that challenged Rome) at Lake Regillus in 496 B.C., the capture of the Etruscan town of Veii in 396 B.C., and the repulsion of the Gauls who had sacked the city (all but the Capitol, where geese alerted the young defenders to the Gauls' approach) and slaughtered the Senate in 390 B.C. The Latin League was defeated by Rome in 338 B.C., and following an alliance with Neapolis (Naples) in 326 B.C., the neighboring Samnites (from the modern Abruzzi) began the first of three successive wars with Rome, ending in 290 B.C. The Samnites afterward continued to ally themselves with enemies of Rome.

One of the Greek cities (Tarentum) in the south of Italy (Magna Graecia) initiated hostilities with Rome; it invited King Pyrrhus of the Greek city of Epirus to join them. The king won two battles at such unacceptable cost ("Pyrrhic victories") that he sued for peace and was driven out of Italy. When Rome gained control of Tarentum (270 B.C.) it extended citizenship to colonials or Latin rights (by treaty) to those farther from Rome.

By 270 B.C. Rome was one of the two powers (today we might say "superpowers") in the Mediterranean. Its antagonist, Carthage, began a series of three wars (264–241 B.C., 218–202 B.C., and 149–146 B.C.) that concluded with the destruction of Carthage and the preeminence of Rome in the Mediterranean. In addition, the wars took Roman soldiers the length and breadth of the Mediterranean, and the contact with Greece and the resulting appeal of Greek culture so influenced Roman literature, art, and religion (such as they were) that two centuries later Horace declared that captured Greece had taken its rude captor captive (*Epistles* 2.1.156). In fact, Roman literature begins after the first Punic War. The first piece of Roman literature is traditionally the translation of the *Odyssey* into Latin meter in 240 B.C. At this same time Romans were introduced to Greek drama. The first histories of Rome began to be written, mostly in Greek and by generals in the Punic Wars, but this was also the point at which Rome, feeling its supreme power, also felt the need for a sublime pedigree. These historians, looking for a mythical-legendary basis for the Punic Wars, traced the origin of the hostilities to the abandonment of Dido by Aeneas. With the conquest (167 B.C.) and annexation of Macedonia in 146 B.C. (the same year Carthage fell), and the control of most of Spain in 133 B.C., Rome's triumph was complete. Rome suddenly acquired wealth to match its power, resulting in splendid public works but also in alarming personal luxury and decadence. The writers of this period, beginning with Cato the Censor, expressed concern for the lapse in morality as they praised the power that gave Rome its luxury. The conservatives who sensed inevitable decline from a noble Roman past were also alarmed by the intense passion for "all things Greek" that was most keen among the circle of artists and writers that centered on the Scipios in the second century B.C. Cato for a long time resisted learning Greek, and poets like Naevius wrote from a Roman perspective, but the playwrights Pacuvius, Plautus, and Terence all adapted Greek plays in Greek settings. The power, glory, decadence, and sense of cultural inferiority to Greece that developed in this period characterize the literature and character of the Romans to the end of the Empire.

By the dawn of the first century B.C., the Romans had no one to fight but themselves. The social disorder that had existed from the days of the kings and was only partially repaired with the advent of the Republic, now became the political focus of the chief politicians. Generals usurped some senatorial prerogatives in rewarding their soldiers with land and booty. The small family farms were giving way to *latifundia* (large industrial farms), and the rise of the newly wealthy equestrian class competed with the patricians for wealth and power. The provinces were bled for the enrichment of those at Rome, where more and more work was being done by the enormous number of slaves and less by Roman citizens.

Thus at the turn of the century Rome was wealthy enough to dominate the world but was beginning already to rot from within. Luxury, philhellenism, greed toward fellow citizens and allies, unchecked personal ambition, the encroachment of the army upon the Senate, and the absence of an external threat—all contributed to the collapse of authority and unity in the state.

The period was ripe for reform and the two brothers Gracchi–Tiberius Sempronius Gracchus (ca. 164–133 B.C.) and Gaius Sempronius Gracchus (d. 121 B.C.). A popular general among poverty-stricken plebeians, Tiberius proposed a law limiting the amount of land any individual citizen could own, with excess holdings confiscated by the state and redistributed to veterans and other citizens. The antagonized Senate felt this practice would overthrow the republican basis of government in favor of tyranny. Tiberius and many of his men were killed by a mob led by Scipio Nasica in 133 B.C. Gaius returned to Rome on news of his brother's death, and in 123–122 B.C. he proposed more laws aimed at relieving the poor and protecting veterans. Gaius was outspent and outmanned by his enemies. When he died in 121 B.C., his reforms died with him.

With the Gracchi gone, the Senate ineptly managed the war against Jugurtha (112–105 B.C.) until the consul C. Marius (157–86 B.C.) with L. Cornelius Sulla (138–78 B.C.), his quaestor, finally captured and executed Jugurtha in 104 B.C. The social contentions revived, and when the tribune of the plebeians was killed in 90 B.C. for proposing citizenship to Rome's *socii* (allied nations) in Italy, the Social Wars erupted. The conclusion of the wars brought citizenship to all allies south of the Po River. At the same time Mithridates IV of Pontus invaded the provinces of the East. While Sulla dealt with Mithridates (over the objection of the plebeian assembly), Marius marched on Rome and seized power in 87 B.C.

When Sulla led his army to Rome, he inaugurated a half century of civil war that ended only with the ascension of Augustus. The conservative Sulla became dictator by bloody slaughter in 81 B.C. but retired three years later.

In 70 B.C. the second phase of the civil wars began when Marcus Licinius Crassus (d. 53 B.C.), the wealthiest man in Rome, who had the year before put down the revolt of Spartacus, and Gnaeus Pompey (106–48 B.C.), fresh from success in Spain, were co-consuls. Crassus made an alliance with Julius Caesar against Pompey (who was in the East). Cicero's interception of the conspiracy of Catiline in 63 B.C. enhanced the control of the *optimates* (aristocratic party) by diminishing that of the *populares* (popular party), who had conspired against the state.

Caesar returned to Rome from Spain in 60 B.C., and he, frustrated by the Senate's unwillingness to accept his treaty with the East, and Pompey, who was just as frustrated that the Senate would not release the land he had promised to his veterans, joined Crassus in an alliance called the First Triumvirate. Crassus had sufficient wealth, Pompey had sufficient popularity with the people, and Caesar enough political cunning to quickly establish their power over the Senate. Caesar's subsequent conquests of Gaul and Britain (58–51 B.C.) enhanced the Triumvirate's power and popularity, but when Crassus was killed at Carrhae in 53 B.C., the resulting rivalry between Pompey and Caesar led to open civil war when Caesar crossed his army over the Rubicon into Italy in 49 B.C. (Much of the history of this period may be found in the essays on Caesar and Cicero.)

The struggle between these two great leaders was envisioned by many, notably Lucan, as the crucial contention of personal aggrandizement (Caesar) against the wish to restore the Republic (Pompey). The defeat of Pompey at Pharsalus, his murder in 48 B.C. and the death of M. Porcius Cato in 46 B.C. effectively ended the Republic and paved the way for the Empire. When Caesar was assassinated in 44 B.C., the third stage of the "Roman Revolution" began.

The assassins of Caesar hoped to restore the Republic, while Caesar's supporters divided their loyalties between the ambitious Marcus Antonius (Antony, 82–30 B.C.) and the republican Gaius Octavius (Octavian, 63 B.C.–A.D. 14). Octavian defeated Antony's forces at Mutina in 43 B.C. and moved his army to Rome, but he allowed enough of a reconciliation to create a Second Triumvirate composed of himself, Antony, and Marcus Aemilius Lepidus (d. 13/12 B.C.) with the specific intent of defeating the conspirators, chief among them Marcus Junius Brutus (ca. 78–42 B.C.) and Gaius Cassius (d. 42 B.C.). The Second Triumvirate triumphed at Philippi in 42 B.C., confiscated land, and gave it to their veterans (Virgil, *Eclogues*).

With Octavian powerful in Italy and the West and Antony allied in the East with Cleopatra, Lepidus was forced out, and Octavian ultimately defeated Antony at the battle of Actium (Horace, *Odes* 1.37) in 31 B.C., and his suicide in 30 B.C. ended the Republic forever.

Though the end of the civil-war period began what is generally referred to as the Golden Age of Latin Literature, because of the great writers–Virgil, Horace, Livy, Propertius, Tibullus, and Ovid–the chief contribution of this period both to Roman litarary history and to the style of Roman literature to come was rhetoric. The great orator Cato the Censor had inaugurated a tradition of politician-orators at Rome that extended through the Gracchi to Caesar, Cato the Younger, and especially the quintessential practitioner, Cicero. (The influence of rhetoric on Lucretius, Virgil, and Ovid, and particularly on the authors of the Silver Age from Lucan and Seneca to Statius and Juvenal are apparent in the essays on those authors.)

Greek influence continued to prevail in the discovery and adaptation of Greek lyric meters by

Horace, elegy by Tibullus and Propertius, and pastoral and didactic poetry by Virgil. As the accompanying article by Brooks Otis shows, Roman authors had a clear focus on their role in history, their individual identity, and their Romanness in a way their Greek models did not. What the Augustan authors generally shared was the notion that Octavian may have ended the Republic, but he also ended the war and saved Rome from itself.

Octavian was titled Augustus by the Senate in 27 B.C. and began at once to adapt the structure of the state to the needs of Rome's growing empire, though he continued to call himself *princeps* (chief), never *imperator* (emperor). His new government gave power over Italy and some peaceful provinces to the Senate, which also had the power to pass laws and run the courts. Augustus retained control over the army, which returned to the prosecution of foreign wars. The patrician order had suffered great losses in the Civil War, and Augustus replenished their ranks by appointing members to the senatorial and knightly classes. When the Senate was largely composed of men whose rank he himself had raised, the institution seemed ready to accept a single leader who called himself "first among equals" and never assumed a power the Senate did not grant him. The illusion of a republic was maintained in 23 B.C. when Augustus resigned his consulship and was named tribune for life. He now enjoyed the power of a tyrant, implicitly or explicitly commanding virtually every facet of Roman government.

His attempts to restore the old morality (which Ovid ran afoul of) and religion were less successful than his political reforms in this affluent materialistic society. It was Augustus's great plan to stop the eastward advancement of Rome and concentrate on the pacification of Europe. This course, with modifications, determined both the aims and structures of the Empire for three centuries, until its collapse. The consequences of a Romanized Europe, of course, have enormous implications for subsequent Western culture.

Roman authors of this period reflect their gratitude for the relief and tranquillity of Augustan rule. Suddenly the lyric poet Horace and the elegiac Propertius felt free to devote significant portions of their work to politics and the leader. The pastoral-didactic poet Virgil and the elegist Ovid, aware of this man and moment, wrote epic poems with Rome's past and present, embodied in Augustus, at their core.

Rhetoric still maintained its effect on prose and poetry, moving toward the increasingly artificial and complex, which continued to characterize the most common aspect of the style of Silver Latin Literature.

That age begins with the second of the Julio-Claudians, Tiberius (reigned A.D. 14–37), who assumed

power at the death of Augustus in A.D. 14. Lacking the personal and intellectual qualities of Augustus, he at least served as a chatelain, keeping the size of the Empire in check, maintaining power over a far-flung army and permitting the Senate to gain new powers over the popular assembly.

Tiberius lost his temper with Rome and withdrew to Capri, leaving the management of the government in the brutal hands of Lucius Aelius Sejanus, the prefect of the praetorian guard, who re-instituted terror and political intrigue of the worst kind before he was literally torn to pieces by an angry mob. Caligula (reigned A.D. 37–41) continued to assert the emperor's control in the face of an impotent Senate while behaving with an irrationality some ascribed to madness.

Caligula was replaced (by the praetorian guard) with Claudius (reigned A.D. 41–54), the last of the family of Julius Caesar. His fourteen-year reign produced numerous public works, granted citizenship to many, and extended the Empire into Britain in A.D. 43. He attempted to give more power to the Senate but was suspected of trying to restore the Republic (as readers or viewers of *I, Claudius* know) and was presumably poisoned in A.D. 54 by his wife Agrippina to guarantee that her son Nero would become emperor.

The young (sixteen-year-old) Nero governed quite successfully for five years, advised by Seneca the Younger and assisted by Burrus, the prefect of the praetorian guard. Nero's depravities are legendary and are touched upon in the articles on Seneca, Lucan, and Petronius. They include the murder of his wife and mother to facilitate marriage to his mistress, Poppaea, whom he later murdered. After the exile of Seneca and the death of Burrus, the new praetorian prefect, Tigellinus, began the worst part of Nero's reign. Though Nero blamed the accidental Great Fire of 19 June 64 on the Christians, his rebuilding project was successful, as was his campaign against Boudicca in Britain in A.D. 61 and the wars with Parthia. (On the conspiracy of C. Calpurnius Piso, which led to the deaths of Seneca, Lucan, and Petronius, see the essays on those men.) Rebellions and conspiracies ultimately broke out from Judaea to Gaul to Spain, and when Nero was forced to commit suicide in A.D. 68, the Empire was on the precipice of disaster.

Nero's death marked the end of the Julio-Claudian era. Four emperors were proclaimed in A.D. 69 (Galba, Otho, Vitellius, and Vespasian), all of whom were serving outside Rome.

Vespasian inaugurated the Flavian era when he returned to Rome from Judaea in A.D. 70. He, Titus, and Domitian came from the middle class, not from the patrician class, as had the descendants of Julius Caesar. Vespasian restored order in the army and began many public works (such as the Colosseum); he consolidated power further in the emperor at the expense of the Senate. His son Titus, who had managed the siege and destruction of Jerusalem in A.D. 71, succeeded Vespasian upon his death in A.D. 79, the same year that Vesuvius destroyed Pompeii and Herculaneum (killing Pliny the Elder among many others). Titus's younger brother, Domitian, became emperor on his brother's death in A.D. 81; he continued vast public works, began new projects to foster the arts and restore the old morality, and moved the Empire further into Britain. The final years of his rule, however, were a reign of terror against conspirators and traitors real and imagined, until his assassination in A.D. 96. To this era belong Frontinus (his appearance in this era of public works should come as no surprise), Martial, Statius, Pliny the Elder, Quintilian, and Valerius Flaccus.

After Domitian, the tranquil rules of Nerva (reigned A.D. 96–98) and his adoptive son Trajan (A.D. 98–117) brought the political power of the Empire to its highest point and fostered the great literary works of Juvenal, Pliny the Younger, and Tacitus. The subsequent rule of Hadrian (A.D. 117–138) and the Antonines (A.D. 138–192) covered the productions of Apuleius, Aulus Gellius, and Suetonius. To the later generations belongs Ammianus Marcellinus, but, as Auden implies, the great literature was done centuries before the Empire ended.

Rome's pervasive presence in Western culture is apparent. Its domination is evidenced by the massive public buildings that still stand (for example, the Pantheon and the Baths of Caracalla) and are imitated by the architecture of this country's grandest public buildings (for instance, the U.S. Capitol and Penn Station), which feature the Roman arched domes rather than the post-and-lintel constructs of the Greeks. American churches ape the basilica model of Roman public buildings; the U.S. sense of citizenship and notion of the "melting pot," in which citizenship can be extended to anyone worthy of it, regardless of race or class, are as much inheritances as the Latinate vocabulary that is a touchstone of style throughout the varying tastes of the course of English and American literature.

Despite the breadth of Rome's influence, its authors never ceased to feel the superiority of the Greeks in the arts. Cicero famously lamented:

> If anyone thinks that lesser gain of glory is to be gained from Greek verse than from Latin verses, he makes a serious error, because Greek is read in nearly every nation on earth, while Latin is confined within its own boundaries, and narrow boundaries they are. (*Pro Archia*, 23)[3]

Even the greatest poem by Rome's greatest author has as its central identification of its chosen people their inferiority in the arts. In describing to his son Aeneas the nature of the race he will found, Anchises yields to the Greeks' superiority in the plastic arts (by which he means all arts), in legal skill, and in natural science:

> Others will forge the living bronze more pleasingly
> (I do believe it); others will draw lifelike faces from marble;
> They will argue their cases better, and with the rod describe
> the wanderings of the stars and will tell of the rising stars.
> Roman, remember that it has been given to you to rule nations by your power
> (These will be your skills) to combine morality with the peace you impose
> to spare the conquered and to battle down the proud. (*Aeneid*, 6.847–853)[4]

The history of Latin literature, like that of the other arts at Rome, is thus essentially the history of one nation in imitation of another. Rome lacked an organized, common religion, a foundational myth cycle, an heroic tradition, a Bronze-Age history, and modern heroes with whom to build a literature. It borrowed the gods, characters, and subject matter of its nascent literature from the Greeks in all but one respect–history. The Romans invented only one genre, satire, and refined a rough and heavy language with such genius that it could support the gentle lyrics of Horace, the abstract philosophy of Lucretius and Seneca, and the mighty epics of Virgil and Ovid. Several Roman authors saw themselves as the Roman equivalents of the best Greek authors: Horace is the Roman Alcaeus; Virgil is the Roman Theocritus, Hesiod, and Homer; Propertius is the Roman Callimachus; Lucretius is the Roman Epicurus; and Cicero is the Roman Demosthenes.

It is also worth noting that several of these authors were slaves or came from slave families: Livius Andronicus, the first author of Latin literature was a slave, as had been Terence, Tiro (who edited Cicero's letters), Horace's father, and Epictetur. It was the Greek-speaking early freed slaves who taught the Romans to give their literature a stamp of its own within their endemic desire to imitate, or rival, the Greeks.

Is there then no originality to Latin literature? To demonstrate what is most compelling about Roman literature (and to give an antidote to Auden's remarks), this introduction is followed by an essay by Brooks Otis that brilliantly summarizes the distinction between the Roman and the Greek minds, a distinction that lies chiefly in the Roman literature's subjectivity and search for motivations and character in contrast to the objectivity of Greek literature. These traits, he shows, exist in poets and historians of the two cultures and continue past the Classical Age into the age of the early fathers of the Roman Catholic Church.

This volume serves as a companion to *DLB 176: Ancient Greek Authors*. While that volume could well have offered sixty essays on authors about whom there exists enough information to construct bio-bibliographies, this Roman volume might well have stopped at forty. The number of Roman authors for whom sufficient biographical and literary remains exist is surprisingly small.

As the intended audience for this volume is the intelligent nonspecialist, there is a minimum of Latin in the text. English translations of titles and text are given. Dates in the entries are generally consistent with those in the *Cambridge History of Classical Literature* and are noted throughout by the traditional designations of B.C. and A.D. In the rubrics at the beginning of each entry, dates for literary works are specified when they are known or conjectural; some dates may simply be expressed with *"fl."* for *floruit* to indicate the literarily active time of the author's life. There is also a rubric under each author for the *editio princeps*, the first modern publication in book form of the text of the author's work in the original Latin (that is, not in translation or in part), usually in the first five years after the invention of the printing press (1465–1469).

It remains to thank the contributors for their forbearance over the long process of assembling this volume.

–Ward W. Briggs Jr.

---

1. Quoted in "The Fall of Rome" (1966), *Auden Studies,* 3 (1995): 124

2. Quoted in *Soldier and Scholar: Basil Lanneau Gildersleeve and the Civil War,* edited by Ward W. Briggs Jr. (Charlottesville: University of Virginia Press, 1998), p. 121.

3. Nam si quis minorem gloriae fructum putat ex Graecis versibus percipi quam ex Latinis, vehementer errat, propterea quod Graeca leguntur in omnibus fere gentibus, Latina suis finibus, exiguis sane, continentur.

4. Excudent alii spirantia mollius aera / (credo equidem), vivos ducent de marmore voltus; / orabunt causas melius, caelique meatus / describent radio et surgentia sidera dicent: / tu regere imperio populos, Romane, memento / (hae tibi erunt artes) pacique imponere morem / parcere subiectis et debellare superbos.

Acknowledgments

This book was produced by Bruccoli Clark Layman, Inc. Karen L. Rood is senior editor for the *Dictionary of Literary Biography* series. Penelope Hope was the in-house editor.

Production manager is Philip B. Dematteis.

Administrative support was provided by Ann M. Cheschi, Tenesha S. Lee, and Joann Whittaker.

Accountant is Sayra Frances Cox. Assistant accountant is Angi Pleasant.

Copyediting supervisor is Phyllis A. Avant. Senior copyeditor is Thom Harman. The copyediting staff includes Ronald D. Aiken II, Brenda Carol Blanton, Worthy B. Evans, Melissa D. Hinton, William Tobias Mathes, and Michelle L. Whitney. Freelance copyeditors are Brenda Cabra, Rebecca Mayo, Nicole M. Nichols, Raegan E. Quinn, and Jennie Williamson.

Editorial trainee is Carol A. Fairman.

Indexing specialist is Alex Snead.

Layout and graphics supervisor is Janet E. Hill. Graphics staff includes Zoe R. Cook.

Office manager is Kathy Lawler Merlette.

Photography editors are Margo Dowling, Charles Mims, Scott Nemzek, Alison Smith, and Paul Talbot. Digital photographic copy work was performed by Joseph M. Bruccoli.

SGML supervisor is Cory McNair. The SGML staff includes Tim Bedford, Linda Drake, Frank Graham, and Alex Snead.

Systems manager is Marie L. Parker.

Database manager is Javed Nurani. Kimberly Kelly performed data entry.

Typesetting supervisor is Kathleen M. Flanagan. The typesetting staff includes Karla Corley Brown, Mark J. McEwan, Patricia Flanagan Salisbury, and Kathy F. Wooldridge. Freelance typesetter is Delores Plastow.

Walter W. Ross and Steven Gross did library research. They were assisted by the following librarians at the Thomas Cooper Library of the University of South Carolina: Linda Holderfield and the interlibrary-loan staff; reference-department head Virginia Weathers; reference librarians Marilee Birchfield, Stefanie Buck, Stefanie DuBose, Rebecca Feind, Karen Joseph, Donna Lehman, Charlene Loope, Anthony McKissick, Jean Rhyne, and Kwamine Simpson; circulation-department head Caroline Taylor; and acquisitions-searching supervisor David Haggard.

The Uniqueness of Latin Literature

Brooks Otis[1]

ANYONE ATTEMPTING TO DISCUSS Latin literature, and especially the uniqueness of Latin literature, cannot avoid an initial paradox. Nothing, in one sense, could be more familiar; it has for centuries occupied a large, if not inordinately large, place in the curricula of schools and colleges in the Western world. For a long time all educated men were supposed to know at least a little about Caesar or Cicero, Horace or Virgil. But this very familiarity concealed a great deal of ignorance and uncertainty as to just what Latin literature really was. Everybody knew that the Greeks produced a startlingly original literature: our idea of all the great literary genres or forms, "epic, tragedy, comedy, lyric, philosophy, history, oratory," comes from their Greek originators. But the Romans only followed these Greek models: they were, in a very fundamental sense, imitators, copyists of Greek predecessors. What then is uniquely Roman or Latin in Latin literature? The fact that the language is Latin and not Greek? This does not take us very far unless we can also see that the different language conceals or reveals a different spirit, content or point of view.

And here we encounter the paradox. There is no doubt, of course, that the Romans were indeed different from the Greeks. The trouble is that what most people, including the Romans themselves, thought this difference to be, does not seem to have any literary significance. Others, said Virgil, meaning of course the Greeks, will be better sculptors in bronze and marble, better scientists and astronomers: the specific Roman superiority is political, the art of ruling many peoples under one government. Romans, in other words, can minister and legislate better than anyone else, but culture as such is not their forte. Here, to quote Horace,

Greece conquered her fierce Roman conqueror. Rome's originality or uniqueness does not, in this view, extend to its literature.

It is curious how influential this view has been and how resistant to obvious fact. The thesis that Roman is an inferior copy of Greek literature sheds singularly little light on Roman literature as a phenomenon of the Hellenistic world. The great age of Greek poetry, as everybody knows, had virtually ceased by the close of the fifth century B.C.: epic, choral and personal lyric, tragedy and comedy had achieved definitive expression and fallen into obvious decline. Aside from the doubtful case of the so-called "new" comedy, the original genres of the fourth century were prose: history, oratory, the philosophic dialogue. No poet had the standing of Demosthenes, Plato or Aristotle. There was a curious revival of Greek poetry in Alexandria in the middle of the third century B.C., but this was explicitly based on an acknowledgment of its post-classical situation. The old forms were dead: hence the attempt to innovate in style, genre and content, to be deliberately recherché. In any event, poets such as Callimachus and Theocritus were a flash in the pan. The important Hellenistic literature after 250 B.C. was in prose, and even this prose was decidedly inferior to that of the fourth century. Yet Rome in the first century B.C. and in the succeeding century and a quarter not only produced great poets and prose writers with whom no contemporary Greek could be compared, but effectively revived the long moribund epic and lyric poetry of Homer, Alcaeus and Pindar. If this was only imitation, why could Romans imitate when the Greeks could not? And are acknowledged works of genius such as those of Cicero, Sallust, Catullus, Lucretius, Virgil, Horace and Tacitus to be dismissed as imitations only? Clearly, there is here a phenomenon which the imitation theory cannot explain.

This problem did not greatly—or at all—concern the Middle Ages and the Renaissance, or indeed the seventeenth and eighteenth centuries. In these eras Greek literature was either unknown or very greatly overshadowed by Latin, which was then the real *lingua*

1. From *Arion,* 6 (1967): 185–206. This paper was delivered as one of the James Fenton Lectures at the State University of New York at Buffalo in November 1966. (This article in its original form contained no footnotes, translations, or bibliography. I have added translations of some Latin, the full names of scholars, and a list of scholarly works mentioned in the article. –Ed.)

franca of educated Europe. The fifteenth-century Renaissance marked in one sense the revival of Greek, but true awareness of the originality, scope and power of Greek tragedy, lyric and comedy and in some degree of Greek epic and history, was reserved for the late eighteenth and nineteenth centuries. Romantic Hellenism–the Hellenism of Winckelmann, Holderlin and Shelley–was the force that finally broke the educational, intellectual and cultural dominance of Rome. Virgil, Horace and Ovid were now at last seen to be inferior imitators of original Greek poets. Rome was indeed a worthy object of historical and institutional study–there was accordingly Mommsen and the great *corpus* of Latin inscriptions–but Greece was the only proper field for the esthetically motivated scholar. Thus Wolff released an overwhelming flood of Homeric scholarship while Virgil was relatively neglected. A good word, of course, could still be said for Catullus and Lucretius–they had "original" elements that even romantics could recognize–but little indeed for the "imitative" Augustan poets.

Latin literature has thus been under a cloud. It was perhaps not too hard to do at least some justice to Cicero since, after all, his speeches and letters came out of an obviously Roman milieu–the life of politics and the law courts. But this was not true of the poets. A very great deal of nineteenth-century Latin scholarship was in fact a quite simple-minded search for the Greek, particularly the Hellenistic, sources of Roman poetry. It was really only at the very end of the century that scholars such as [Friedrich] Leo and [Eduard] Norden and, most particularly, Richard Heinze began to show in convincing detail that Roman authors did very new and original things with their Greek models. Even this attempt was limited and hesitant. Leo, for example, was the main proponent of the theory that Roman amatory elegy was copied directly and in detail from a Greek model, and Heinze, despite his great services to Horace, advanced a curiously depreciatory theory of his lyrics. It has, in fact, been only in the last three or four decades that such scholars as [Erich] Burck, [Friedrich] Klingner, [Viktor] Pöschl, [Eduard] Fraenkel and [Bengt] Löfstedt have tried to view Livy, Virgil, Horace or Tacitus in what may be called a properly Roman perspective. Nor has this very recent development reached anything like a mature or definitive result. With few exceptions, the research has been directed to particular authors and works and singularly little attention has been paid to the broader problem of Latin literature or even of Latin poetry as a whole. It is certainly true that some scholars (especially Italians) have written interesting histories of Latin literature (Bignone and Rostagni in particular), but generalization has been impressionistic and scattered and mainly subordinated to the detailed treatment of individual authors. Thus the real problem, the problem I briefly alluded to above–how, indeed, Romans between 60 B.C. and A.D. 125 could successfully imitate the classical Greeks in a thoroughly post-classical or Hellenistic age–has been largely neglected. So my topic is still, paradoxically enough, a rather novel one, on which the last word or even the penultimate word has by no means been said.

The Romans, it is clear, were culturally dependent on Greece. Rome was not, like Greece, an originative culture that could or did produce new art forms and new art motifs, an obviously original or self-generated art and literature. Even Greeks, of course, had sources, and we shall learn more of them as we learn more of Minoan and Hittite culture and of the Middle East in general. But it is hardly likely that future discovery will very greatly diminish the force of the "Greek miracle." The century of discovery, for example, whose literary results are now accessible in such a volume as Pritchard's *Near Eastern Texts,* has revealed some motifs and ideas that the Greeks certainly got from Asia, but has in general increased rather than decreased our sense of Greek originality. But Rome was, like the rest of the Mediterranean world, the heir of Greece. Nor did Rome show any particular aptitude for inventing art forms or art motifs of its own. We can speculate, for example, as to what under other circumstances, such as the sudden blotting out of Greek literature in the Persian wars, the native Saturnian meter might have become: in fact, it was hardly possible for an author like Ennius to continue to use it when he had access to the magnificently developed dactylic hexameter of the Greeks. And so for all other meters and genres (satire is at best a partial and obscure exception). More important, Rome also lacked the subject matter of poetry: poetry indeed is the original vehicle of myth–often or usually the myth or myths of a Heroic Age–and Rome was notoriously poor or lacking in myth. Even the somewhat threadbare legends of the first book of Livy or of Ovid's *Fasti* are heavily laced with Greek importations. Rome had no Homer, no Cyclic Epic, no Mycenean background, no Heroic Age. Nor did it have a religion like Greek religion: the notorious utilitarianism of the city of farmers and fighters seems to have kept its gods within very narrow limits that largely excluded the mythopoeic impulse so vigorous in Greece and in other cultures.

All this explains the curiously deceptive character of Roman literature. Its originality is no surface phenomenon. It is hidden, obscured by an elaborate Greek veneer. We can best get at it by considering briefly a few examples and then using them as the stepping stones to a few, necessarily tentative and incomplete, generalizations.

Let us take first the phenomenon of Cicero. As an orator and a writer of treatises on philosophy, politics and rhetoric, he does not seem at first sight so original. He had been preceded by Demosthenes and many other Greek orators, and no one would call him an original philosopher. Yet his letters are certainly unique: nothing like them has come down to us from the Greeks, and this is not merely because analogous collections of Greek letters have not been preserved. Some original letters and many more imaginary letters of famous Greeks such as Philip of Macedon or Plato have come down to us. If we have only a minimum of authentic material, we at least know something of the type or form that Greeks desired in a letter they thought worth reading and preserving. This is strangely different from the letters of Cicero or of other Romans such as Trajan and the younger Pliny. For comparable human documents in Greek, we have to go to Christian times, to the letters of Basil the Great and Gregory of Nazianzus, for example, and even these are very far removed from the kind of thing we get in Cicero. The fact seems to be that Greeks did not care to write or preserve their letters as documents of a concrete, unique moment in a specific personality and a specific milieu. This is why we can realize Cicero, can penetrate his personal history, his day-to-day experience, as we simply cannot realize or penetrate any of the Greeks. There is certainly more here than an accident: Romans valued and so preserved what Greeks, certainly the classical Greeks, did not value or preserve to anything like the same degree.

We can see much the same phenomenon in the poetry of Catullus or Ovid. The early Greek poetry is very fragmentary and the later Greek poetry (such as, for example, that of the Palatine Anthology) is obviously arranged on a quite impersonal basis—by topic rather than by author. Yet there is no evidence that any classical Greek composed a *libellus* or little collection of poems on his personal love-affairs and friendships or even on his political feelings and reactions. The preserved "epigrams" of such Greeks as Plato, Callimachus or Theocritus are either severely impersonal or, if personal, disconnectedly so and without any real context. We think of Catullus with his Lesbia, of Propertius and Cynthia, of Ovid at Tomis, or Martial at Rome: of what Greek poet do we have a similar personal idea, a comparable glimpse into his social, local and temporal milieu? We can explain, perhaps, some of this by the accidents of preservation, but certainly not all of it. Greek personal poetry is moving and emotionally vivid, but it does not give us or seemingly want to give us a real personality, a uniquely subjective mood. Archilochus and Alcaeus were, we know, capable of fierce hates and fierce attachments. But the feeling, as

we deduce it from the fragments, seems bare, the emotion naked rather than personally clothed or, more exactly, clothed in an environment concrete enough to give us the full sense of real persons.

The case of Horace is here very enlightening. Horace's poems fall into two general categories: the poems in deliberately "prosaic" hexameters, the satires and epistles, the "conversations" that of course are meant to allow for the author's *ego,* the personal detail about Maecenas, his father, his Sabine farm, his journey to Brundisium or encounter with the bore; and, quite distinct, the lyric poems in Alcaic, Sapphic, Asclepiadic and other meters, that are avowed imitations of, among others, Alcaeus, Sappho and Pindar. Obviously, the second or "lyric" category is designed to be more formal and more imitative, more responsive to the stock themes of Hellenic and Hellenistic poetry—love, wine, taxation, the seizing of the passing moment and the evanescence of everything mortal—and, at a higher level, more adapted to praise of the great or to solemn moral exhortation. And in so far as Horace claimed to be a poet, he claimed to be a lyric poet, to belong, in other words, to this second category. The first category was, in his own phrase, "mere talk," *sermo merus,* or rhythmical prose.

Yet this is obviously a rather superficial distinction that collapses as soon as we penetrate beneath the formalities of the verse. There are Horatian lyrics that seem to be no more than studies from the Greek, reproductions of vinous or amatory *topoi,* that apparently have no connection with either Horace or Rome or the Augustan era. But these are not characteristic: what is characteristically Horatian is a curious mixture of Greek lyric motif, moral commonplace, philosophic generalization, Roman exhortation and, most curiously, personal reminiscence. Ideas such as the seizing of the present moment (*carpe diem*), the need to relax, to find time for love and wine, the invulnerability of the sage and the poet, the undesirability of caring too much for wealth or political power, the need for an equal or balanced mind (*aequanimitas*), Epicurean *ataraxia* and Stoic *apatheia* each and all are "Horatianized," so to speak, by being exemplified in the poet's own life.

It is, in fact, Horace's own experience that elevates the *jeu d'esprit* into the Pindaric ode and enables him to range the gamut of all moods and themes. Poetic invulnerability does not seem so very serious a matter in the *integer vitae* where Horace's escape from the wolf is made into a sort of warrant for the humming of love ditties in all weathers and places. Nor does it seem at all serious in 1.17 ("Velox amoenum") when Horace entertains the girl Tyndaris under the personal protection of the god Faunus. Yet what could be more solemn than the poetic invulnerability he attributes to himself in the great Ode to Augustus (3.4: "Descende caelo"): he is there a charmed soul, since babyhood the unassailable, untouchable object of the Muses' protection, and thus the peer of Augustus and of the gods who, in virtue of their harmonious wisdom, can triumph over the giants.

Again, we all know the *carpe diem* poems, the exhortations not to neglect love and wine while we have youth or life, poems sometimes associated with the famous Sabine villa and sometimes not. The *topos* is trite indeed, the stock in trade of the second-rate Hellenistic lyric. But how easily can Horace expand this theme to the whole philosophy of *ataraxia* and *apatheia* in the great Maecenas ode (1.29), wherein we also find a marvelous harmony of all his most characteristic ideas: the value of a moderate income as opposed to excessive wealth, his friendship for Maecenas and his proud consciousness of his own independence, and, once again, his divine invulnerability. In each case the poet uses his own life, his Sabine farm, his friends great and small, his big and little escapes from disaster (the flight from Philippi, the tree-fall, the shipwreck), even the local wine of his birthday year, as the thread on which to connect the Greek lyric motifs, the Roman patriotic ideas and the philosophical reflections.

Yet this is surely nothing at all like autobiography. Horace is not so much writing about himself as using himself as a peculiar sort of *dramatis persona*. In the satires and the epistles he is doing much the same thing: in the sixth satire of the second book (the famous "Hoc erat in votis") he starts with the contrast between his life on the Sabine farm and his life in Rome, but this is actually or ostensibly only the prelude to the amusing tale of the city mouse and the country mouse, a tale which seems to point a sound but very commonplace moral. The personal reference, of course, takes the edge off the moral: the cautionary tale is actually related by Horace's rustic neighbor Cervius; its sturdy naïveté is a welcome relief from the smart but boring Roman gossip about politics, gladiators or dancers. The platitudinous and trite moral is thus given, as it were, a peculiar tone or nuance, at once humorous, self-deprecatory and sincere. Horace is very urbane, even sly, always on the watch for his own affectations, his own self-righteousness, but this ever-present sense of himself, of his own role, is really the means by which he effects the shift of tone, the alternation between humor and seriousness, the movement between the prosaic and the poetic, all the devices which ring such extraordinary variations on the relatively few and relatively commonplace themes of his poetry. But all of the themes are transmitted through Horace, or the peculiar Horatian role he happens to assume, and it is this that gives them poetical vitality.

No mistake can be greater than to measure Horace by a romantic standard: he expresses no untrammeled emotion, or sheer passion, but instead a carefully studied and shrewdly calculated self-portrait. Because the motifs and morals of the poems have been already assimilated to the portrait, they achieve a reality and complexity that is vastly disproportionate to their thematic simplicity. Horace's poetry indeed illustrates the Roman paradox: his poetry is so Greek in one sense; so utterly un-Greek in another. Beside its baffling combination of platitude and surprise, triteness and complexity, Greek poetry seems almost primitive, at any rate disarmingly simple.

But we must not think of the Roman writer as concerned only with himself. In Cicero this is nearly or mainly true: in Horace it is rather the using of self-knowledge for an esthetic, essentially impersonal end. What both procedures imply, however, is an essential subjectivity, an introspective habit and perhaps, above all, a psyche that repays introspection. But the introspective habit and the psyche that goes with it are in no sense confined to the Roman author himself. When he creates characters, he describes them in quite the same introspective way. This is why he could show, when he wished, a development of character such as we hardly find at all among the Greeks. Putting it in the simplest possible way: because a Roman was aware of his own psychic development, he was aware of it in others.

Consider, for example, the case of Dido. She is, partially, at least, modeled on the Medea of Apollonius of Rhodes' *Argonautica*. Apollonius' Medea is at once an ingénue (a young girl subjected to the first experience of amatory passion) and a witch, a skilled enchantress. Medea, indeed, is made to fall in love with Jason (Eros shoots her at the combined request of Aphrodite, Hera and Athena) so she can put her magic at Jason's disposal. Only so could he survive the ordeals that beset the Golden Fleece. But once the Fleece is won and Medea goes off with her lover, we largely lose sight of her. Only when Jason, under great pressure from her pursuing brother Apsyrtus, reaches what amounts to a decision to give her up does she really re-enter the plot: then she shows a fury and rage for which we have been quite unprepared. Yet she drops this entirely when Jason relinquishes his plan and, on her advice, ambushes and treacherously kills Apsyrtus, the brother. She again relapses into obscurity until a legalistic quibble of their later host, King Alcinous, forces her to relinquish her virginity and undergo a hasty cave marriage with Jason. There is at no point development or even continuity of character: the long account of her original struggle with love (the struggle of "shame" and "desire") is curiously allowed to lapse into a few isolated and quite incongruous episodes. The *amoureuse,* the witch, the affianced bride are all, as it were, separate individuals without any personal or psychic connection.

Yet Virgil takes every one of these separate Apollonian Medeas and makes each into a phase of a single psychological drama in which a single character, Dido, develops from a noble queen and woman into a veritable incarnation of revenge. Dido is, when Aeneas first meets her, in book 1, a true Diana (as the simile indicates), a heroine who instinctively responds to the hero Aeneas and whose hospitality is but one indication of her open, generous, heroic nature. She is busy, happy, responsible, an *alter Aeneas* who has already made good as he has not. Then we see her in love: her passion is of course fatal (for she cannot hope to hold Aeneas); it is a wound, a lethal wound, a threat to her regal position, her *pietas* (to the dead Sychaeus), and her human dignity. Nevertheless, her passion does not, like Medea's, incongruously lapse into a period of static expectation, of waiting for a proper marriage. The "cave marriage" of *Arg.* 4 becomes in the *Aeneid* a tragic consummation: it is an illicit act of passion that starts a new train of events. Dido's infatuation blinds her judgment: she insists that the guilty affair is a *coniugium* and defies public opinion by openly living with Aeneas. Then, when the inevitable exposure comes, when Aeneas is rudely recalled to his duty, Dido becomes the fury that Medea was when Jason seemed willing to get rid of her. But how different the motivation and action of the fury is! In the *Argonautica* it is a thing of the passing moment that comes and goes without either preparation or result. In the *Aeneid,* it is the inevitable outcome of irrational behavior, the fatal shift from love to jealousy, from erotic passion to frustrated rage. Dido's character is transformed: instead of the rational, generous, heroic queen, we now see a virago, a woman in the throes of fear and vengeance, a sorceress also (for she now sticks at nothing) driven by her impotent remorse and hatred to suicide and a curse on the future, a wish to darken civilization itself. She finally reaches the point of absolute, implacable hostility to Aeneas and all he represents: her cold silence in the underworld is the end of her drama, the pitiless, unforgiving being that the originally generous and noble woman had now become.

It is difficult for us today to understand why Virgil was so concerned to rearrange the incidents (or some of the incidents) of the *Argonautica* into this utterly different story of destructive passion. Yet it is clear that he did in fact make use of Medea's amorousness, her jealous fury, her skill in sorcery, her curious cave marriage; even, strangely enough, her erotic wound. But the main point, of course, is that by seeing Dido from within, by following her emotions and motives, by empathy, sympathy, the constant penetration and reading of her psyche, he makes us see her character in all its tragic transformation and development and so gives dramatic historicity to his epic. Aeneas, too, is not what he had been before he met Dido: she is an experience that, bitter as it was, helped to prepare him for the Roman future he was to witness in the Show of Heroes in *Aeneid* 6. All this is Roman, not Greek. The Greek motifs are all there (even down to curious and seemingly extraneous details such as the cave and its howling bridal nymphs), but they are made to perform a function that has nothing to do with their original meaning.

Now there has been a long and rather semantic debate as to whether this sort of thing, the Dido narrative, for example, is really to be described in terms of "character development" in the modern sense. To some scholars it seems to be almost an axiom that no ancient, Greek or Roman, understood "character development." Such a view seems to me not so much wrong as misleading. If we understand "character development" only as we find it in Shakespeare (in, for example, *Macbeth* or *Hamlet*) or in a modern novel (Stendhal, for example, or Anthony Powell), then obviously Virgil or any ancient does not have it. What we find in Virgil's Dido, in his Turnus and in Aeneas (in all his major characters, in other words) is rather a dramatic change or transformation, a passing, so to speak, of a line beyond which the drives and motives are quite startlingly different from what they were before.

Now to a certain extent this is also true of Greek or any drama: the essence of drama is conflict and change. Achilles gives up his wrath and rejoins the battle, the Furies become the Eumenides; Oedipus is enlightened and changes from confidence to abject despair; Heracles loses his old identity altogether when he emerges from madness to find himself the murderer of his wife and children. But where Virgil, and Romans in general, go beyond the Greeks is in their psychology, their awareness of motive, their capture of thoughts and emotions in transformation. Greek heroes are, as it were, motivated from without: it is what happens to them, not what happens in them, that we see. Here perhaps Dido is not quite so clearly Roman (Roman, that is, as a character conceived and drawn by a Roman author) as Turnus or Aeneas. Greeks also of course depicted women transformed by jealousy (as Phaedra, Deianira, Medea), but no Greek depicted a woman whose character was transformed in the manner of Dido's; no Greek quite encompassed the same kind of debasement, the supersession of a truly heroic and humane psyche by an evil and destructive one that is yet curiously aware of what has happened to it, of its own loss of dignity and of all freedom to act except for self-destruction.

In Turnus, on the other hand, the movement of character is from mere Homeric *aretê*, something quite Achillean, to voluntary acceptance of fate, even of death. As the alternative of death or honor is repeatedly offered, as each disruption of peace terms, each escape from the heat of unfavorable battle leads only to further disaster and the further suffering of his friends, Turnus learns to submit, to forego both his egoism and his safety, to sacrifice himself to others. And so too, of course, Aeneas learns to accept a destiny that begins by destroying all his old allegiances and hopes, continues by cutting off the possibility of love and concludes with the necessity of fighting an unwanted war. He is in fact wholly remotivated by the vision of Rome in the underworld. We realize such remotivation (in both Turnus' and Aeneas' case) only because we see it inside them, so to speak, only because our own introspective activity is empathetically transferred to them. It is this that is Roman, whether we call it "character development" or not. The Greeks did not have it.

The important thing that is common to Cicero, Horace and Virgil is the introspective method and the inward seizure of motive and of psychic movement that this entails. Whether they look into themselves and reveal what they see as Cicero does in his letters, or Horace in his satires and lyrics, or whether they look into others and grasp their psyches by empathy, they are engaged in much the same activity. But this is not merely a technique, a literary procedure. The real point is the different conception of man and of human society that it implies. Greeks by and large saw and wrote objectively. This does not mean of course that they ignored psychic facts or lacked self-insight. But it does mean that they were not personally engaged, not subjectively committed, as Romans were. Romans, we may say, were practical, involved, moralistic and, comparatively speaking, not at all detached or objective observers.

If they had been able to put the unexamined premise of such an attitude into words, they would have arrived at something not too different from one of the main principles of modern existentialism, that is, the principle that the bifurcation of subject and object tends to undermine the sense of subjectivity, to objectify and thus destroy it, since the subject or predicate of a sentence is always destructive of its subject. When I say that "I am an American" or "Helen is a woman," I of course dissolve the "I" or the real Helen in the quite non-subjective categories of *Americanism* or *womanhood*, concepts that contribute to the definition of the thing's objective reality, but quite lose contact with its subjective essence. We can put this less pretentiously, per-

haps, by saying that the Roman attitude is that of someone who says, or rather feels (for he does not usually *say* it): "I am involved with you in my, your and our fate or destiny; it is our unique sense of this that counts. This is why we must exhort, encourage, understand each other for the living of our common life. We are not at all concerned to stand outside of ourselves: that sort of thing is useless or impractical. To the detached, we will of course seem to be only practical, moralistic, incurious. This is because they do not grasp our subjective drive and because perhaps they lack such a drive themselves."

And it is this basic feeling (for it is hardly an idea) that we may find, I think, pre-eminently in the Roman historians. Sallust, Livy or Tacitus are obviously not detached or objective in the sense that Thucydides or Polybius were, and not even, I think, in the sense that Herodotus was. It is clear that Thucydides was, as an Athenian, very much moved by the Peloponnesian War and by such Athenian disasters as the loss of the army and fleet at Syracuse. It has not, I think, been sufficiently observed how his style and attitude change in the passage of the seventh book that describes the final defeat of Demosthenes. But this is, as it were, a hard-wrung concession to the author's emotions, an obvious exception to his avowed objectivity. He is not writing as an Athenian but as an impartial observer, scientifically arranging the facts into generalizations that will be interesting in their own right and a useful guide to future statesmen. We surely can say the same thing of Polybius, the Greek so curious about Rome, so concerned to explain why Rome could conquer the world when Greeks could not do anything of the sort. And Herodotus, though in a sense pre-scientific and not yet quite free of the *mythical* past, was also surely a prodigy of disinterested curiosity: he was involved in, certainly glad of, the Greek victory over the Persians, but he was more concerned to explain it, to understand the civilizations of Egypt and Asia and their difference from Greece.

We may say indeed that Greek *historia* is not at all history in our sense, but a series of problems investigated or classic "cases" examined and analyzed. Thucydides realized that the Peloponnesian War was peculiarly worthy of his attention because it was the best and biggest of wars: his so-called "archaeology" was simply an attempt to demonstrate this. He had no interest in the past for its own sake, but solely in its comparative utility to a historian like himself. He wanted to show that previous wars (like the Trojan War) were too obscure and too limited to be good "subjects" or "problems." This is also true of Polybius' subject (the quick rise of Rome) or Herodotus' (the extraordinary Greek triumph at Marathon, Salamis and Plataea): each has his own intriguing case or problem. There is, of course, some sense of practical utility (statesmen at least can learn a lesson), but essentially what predominates is sheer curiosity: the problems are exciting and interesting in themselves.

How different is the outlook of the Roman historians! Sallust, for example, prefixes an introduction to his *Catilinarian Conspiracy* in which, writing as a Roman, he describes the rise and decline of the Republic in terms that we today think of as almost simplistic moralities. Rome was virtuous and conquered the world: then it became fat, wealthy and, so, corrupt. Catiline is an instance of extreme degeneration. Livy follows his example: he tells us in his preface that Rome's history is one of primitive virtue corrupted, and indicates only too clearly that the whole is meant as a moral lesson to his countrymen. It is easy to dismiss this oversimplified and overmoralized theory, to compare it unfavorably with the objectivity of Thucydides or Polybius, but it is even easier to miss its meaning, its truly Roman point. And this is that Sallust and Livy are Roman, are involved, are subjective and historically concerned, as their Greek models are not. They see Rome, in other words, as a moral *persona,* a social persona of which they are a part and to which therefore they have introspective access. They see it from within, see its development very much as Virgil sees the development of Dido. And because they so see, their technique of narration, their method of description and analysis, their point of view and feeling for history are wholly different.

Obviously I have no space to illustrate my general point (still less to "prove" it!), but I will make, in this connection, a few remarks about the greatest of Roman historians, Cornelius Tacitus. Tacitus' work revolves around the terrible year 69 A.D., the year of the three emperors. Despite the fact that in the preface to his *Histories* he expressed an intention to carry the work beyond Domitian into the happier reigns of Nerva and Trajan, he did not actually do so: instead his last and greatest work, the *Annals,* was designed to come down to the year from which the *Histories* take off, the year 69. Tacitus, in other words, finally relinquished the "more fruitful and less dangerous subject" of Nerva and Trajan ("uberiorem securioremque materiam") to deal with the course and development of despotism, the progressive deterioration that reached one climax in Nero and another in Domitian. My own view is that this was quite intentional, that his subject was really progressive tyranny, with two climaxes. Unfortunately, the loss of the final two books of the *Annals* and of the last seven or nine books of the *Histories* prevents us from following the scheme to its conclusion or even from acquiring any certain knowledge of its most deci-

sive features. All we can be really sure of is that Tacitus' theme is tyranny, its progressive deterioration and its ultimate crisis.

His situation was peculiar and ambiguous: it is plain that his political career was not interrupted even during the terrible reign of Domitian ("dignitatem nostram a Vespasiano inchoatam, a Tito auctam, a Domitiano longius productam" ["My official career owed its beginning to Vespasian, its progress to Titus, and its further advancement to Domitian"–*Histories* 1.1.14]) and reached its apogee in his consulship (under Nerva) of 97. Unlike the good Agricola, he survived and seemingly prospered under tyranny. This fact explains in part his general attitude toward history: in his *Histories* he reprehends alike the flattery and the hatred of historians of the Julio-Claudian emperors. Each attitude distorts, each lacks the historical truth ("incorrupta fides" ["uncorrupted faith"–*Histories* 1.1.16]). But there is more here than a simple disclaimer of bias. Tacitus represents himself as a realist, an avoider of pompous and unfruitful displays of virtue. We can see his position quite clearly from his praise of Agricola, his perceptible distaste for the ostentatious suicide of Seneca and his pointed awareness of the contrast between Lucan's republican rhetoric and cowardly, even dastardly, end. The reign of Domitian, like that of Nero, was a time when sloth was taken for wisdom ("inertia pro sapientia"[–*Agricola* 6.3.5]); yet it was still possible for great men to live under bad emperors ("posse etiam sub malis principibus magnos viros esse" [–*Agricola* 42.5.2]). The days when rebellion paid, when republicanism was a practical cause, had long gone by. Augustus had corrupted everybody. All that the final successful rebellion against Nero really produced was a demonstration that emperors could be made in the provinces as well as in Rome. The year 69 was the bitterest possible commentary on all attempts to "restore" the republic.

Thus abuse is as foolish as supine acquiescence: the good statesman and historian is he who loves virtue without foolish demonstrations of it, who is a patriot within the limits of action permitted by evil emperors or by the occasional interludes of good ones, and in either case knows that his political initiative is mitigated by the degeneration of character that all despotism "whether good or bad" inevitably presupposes and fosters. It was now too late for liberty. What was left was the good life and, quite as important, the good death. All this, however, in no way diminishes the sense of the Roman *persona,* of the social destiny in which Tacitus, like all other Romans, was involved. The Sallustian and Livian theory of Roman history is thus subjected to a peculiar nuance of realistic retrospect, the predicted has happened: the Republic has gone; slavery has replaced liberty. Now one can only live and look back, aware of both the splendor and the limits of virtue.

What is remarkable in Tacitus, therefore, is the sense of greatness under pressure, of virtue almost but not quite facing extinction, of men ever ready to die well but realistically concerned to live well when possible. Always we feel the author's incisive personality, his *parti pris,* his judgment of Roman society, and always we feel his involvement in it. His characters good or bad, Tiberius, Agrippina, Nero, Vitellius or, alternatively, Thrasea Paetus, the soldier Subrius Flavus, or the historian Aulus Cremutius Cordus, are all seen from inside, empathetically. Sometimes this is only a very partial view, a snapshot, so to speak; sometimes it is a step-by-step study in degeneration (as with Tiberius, Sejanus and Nero), though often this amounts only to the transition from hypocrisy to barefaced wickedness. Yet what is most characteristic and most striking are the mass scenes in which the collective soul of whole groups is laid bare: such are the mutiny in Germany under Germanicus, the Piso conspiracy, the occupation of Rome by Vitellius.

The narratives are planned to display a moral, a Tacitean judgment, which is yet represented as a sort of Roman judgment, a judgment in which the specific Roman virtues, despite all the evil and its apparent triumph, somehow impose themselves, even if, as we must particularly note, they impose themselves in a Tacitean way. In his account of the Piso conspiracy he reveals, more clearly than elsewhere, his final assessment of his era. The conspiracy, despite the firmness of the freed woman Epicharis, is revealed by the folly of Flavius Scaevinus and the rapacity of his freedman Milichus. Scaevinus and his associates, Natalis, Senecio, Lucan, etc., are arrested, confronted, and bribed by promises of immunity: they shamelessly betray the others. Only the freed woman Epicharis resists torture and dies without telling any names.

As for the rest, their deaths reveal the men and the times: Piso refuses to make the great gesture or to seize the only hope left, by accosting the troops and the citizens and rousing them to a last-minute attack on the emperor; he prefers to do nothing but await his executioners. Seneca dies with all the ostentatious rhetoric of his essays, dictating philosophy to the very end. But the military tribune, Subrius Flavus, tells Nero the blunt truth and grimly chides the soldiers who make poor job of digging his grave: "Bad discipline still!" ("ne hoc quidem ex disciplina"). Finally there is the unforgettable picture of the hypocrisy of the times. While the city is filled with funerals of the dead conspirators, the Capitol teems with victims sacrificed to the gods in thanks for Nero's salvation and sacrificed by men who have each lost a son, brother, relative or friend in the conspiracy.

They then go on to deck their homes with laurel, grovel before Nero and beslobber his hand with kisses. Courage, honor, dignity have left such a world, yet even so it is redeemed by virtue in unexpected places. Only a freed woman and an army officer really behave well under pressure. There is still the ghost, at least, of Roman discipline.

It is absurd to treat this episode as sheer reporting or merely factual history. Obviously it is arranged with the greatest art: the emphases are deliberate; the narrative succession contrived; each paragraph and each sentence has its place and function. The contrast of Epicharis and Milichus, of Seneca and Flavius, of cowardice and fortitude, of courageous action and what may be called courageous inertia (the mere willingness to die), all are designed. All parts together produce as their total result a peculiarly Tacitean effect: greatness in the midst of degradation, the inability of leaders to lead and the decisive pre-eminence of human dignity over both life and death. Tacitus is anything but a cynic: he is still too involved in his Roman society and destiny to forget the values of courage and discipline or the greatness of the past in the degeneracy of the present. It is not the Senecan gesture but the old military and Roman virtues that finally count.

The important point for our general argument here is Tacitus' sense of the Roman *persona,* his conception of history as something happening to his own Roman soul, as part of his own extended psychic development. In outliving the Republic he has, as it were, outlived himself. But so have all good Romans, since the fatal establishment of despotism by Augustus. Their fate is common: yet one can remain true to tradition, to Roman morality, as one remains, so to speak, true to his dead ancestors. Here history is still a personal possession. The difference between this conception and that of Thucydides, Polybius or Herodotus is surely obvious. None of them were in this sense, to this Tacitean degree, historical at all.

We could go on to enumerate other instances of the same general point. Yet the examples drawn from Cicero, Horace, Virgil and Tacitus (almost certainly the four greatest figures in Latin literature) are enough to suggest, if not to support, my thesis. The Latin letter writer, poet or historian is introspective, introverted, concerned with motive and attitude, with the state of his soul. By empathy he extends his introspection to other individuals and to his society, the Roman *persona.* This is why he gives us what at least closely approaches character development and a sense of history conceived as personal fate or destiny.

The limitations of such an approach to life and literature are, of course, obvious. The object as such is obscured by the subject, by the author, his bias, his

Romanitas, his wholly unreckoning, largely unconscious involvement in himself and his society. At its worst, this approach is apt to produce the tritest and most platitudinous moralizing or the most limited practicality. "Be honest, be brave, show discipline. Leave philosophy, science and abstract thought to the Greeks. No Roman can afford the time for them. The Roman state is the only worthy occupation or preoccupation of a man."

Such a point of view has long been so obvious, to ancients and moderns alike, that its literary or spiritual meaning has been generally, indeed usually, ignored. For it is in no sense a mere negation of culture or of Greek culture in particular, or at least it is not when translated from the parody of it just set forth above into its more basic and fundamental meaning. The Roman was not primarily concerned to study or to create objects extraneous to himself, objects which had no obvious connection with his own psyche, society or history. The Roman had almost nothing of the amazing plastic imagination of the Greeks, the ability to create gods, statues, characters, literary types, architectural units, each with clear-cut outlines, distinct, visual, objective, external. Yet the Roman was, basically, uninterested in such creation because he was interested in something quite different and indeed quite alien to it. This was quite simply himself, his *psyche,* not necessarily his individualistic, egocentric psyche, but still a psyche that he could introspect and empathetically project, a psyche that he could very often identify with his society, with Rome and its history, but a psyche nonetheless that was first and foremost in himself, a subject and not at all an object.

In primitive Rome, or the early republican Rome, this was doubtless a rather unindividuated psyche and the introspection had nothing at all of the modern brooding or "self-analysis" that we often associate with the term. Nor can we really imagine how it would have developed without the immense stimulus of Greek literature, thought and culture. The probability is that it would not have developed: Rome would have had no literature, art or architecture, or would have borrowed these from one or another of the non-Greek cultures. In any event, Rome did undergo Greek influence to an extreme degree. The first result was a crudely Philistine reaction against it or, alternatively, a slavishly imitative acceptance of it. But when eventually the Romans achieved sufficient command of their own language to adapt it to Greek metres, myths, ideas and thought forms, they became also able, as it were, to "deobjectify" or, positively, to *subjectivize* the objective art and literature of the Greeks. The inner self, the introspective approach, the empathetic narrative, the sense of history, thus really entered literature for the first time: the result was nothing less than the opening of a new world, the finding of a new dimension.

For however splendid the Greeks may have been in the creation of objects, they were, relatively speaking, very backward and weak in the penetration of their own psyches. They were extroverts of a singularly radical or extreme type, not, assuredly, extroverts in the sense of Philistines who did not think (the "outer-directed" people of Riesman), but extroverts in the sense of objectivists, of people whose thought is self-transcending even when they think of themselves, for, of course, the Greek psyche was *also* an object to the Greek. The Roman, on the contrary, did not try to objectify his psyche, but rather to think, feel and act for it or for himself: this is why his sense of self, of others, of society and of society-in-time or -history was so different. This is what makes Cicero, Horace, Virgil or Tacitus so fundamentally un-Greek and in this sense unique.

And here lies the answer to the question raised at the very beginning of this paper: how post-classical, Hellenistic Latins could, unlike any Greeks of their time, revive the long-obsolete Greek classics, revive Homer, Alcaeus and Pindar, for example, and produce not just second-rate imitations but imitations that were also original works in their own right. The answer lies precisely in the subjectivity of their approach, their introspective method, their Roman psyche. Because of this, Dido, Turnus and Aeneas are quite new creations; Horace's lyrics are Horatian and not merely Alcaic and Sapphic; Tacitus' history is utterly un-Thucydidean. Roman literature was classically great because of the unique and original Roman spirit moving within the Greek forms. More precisely, Roman literature is what happens when introverts rewrite the work of extroverts.

All this of course cast a long shadow on the future. One of the subjects with which as a scholar I have been especially concerned, and which in fact actually suggested the thesis of this paper to me, is the Greek and Latin Christian literature of the later Empire from about the second to the fifth century A.D. Here, in a sense, the differences are more obvious than in the classical period. Almost anyone can see, for example, that Augustine's *Confessions* is quite unparalleled by any Greek Christian work, even though we do in fact possess an almost exactly contemporary autobiography of a Greek Christian, the long poem *To Himself* of Gregory of Nazianzus. We also, I may remark, possess a relative abundance of authentic letters by Greek and Latin Christians of the period, as well, of course, as all sorts of other writings: sermons, theological treatises, apologies, histories, etc. The documentation is in fact so rich that we can here make accurate comparisons between Greeks and Romans such as the classical literature, because of its state of preservation, does not at all permit.

I think the comparisons fully bear out the general thesis I have been trying to expound. The inward or introspective approach that is so classically (I may say) exemplified in Augustine's *Confessions* is, by and large, characteristically Latin. But the most interesting thing about it in its Christian form is the extent to which it has become "self-conscious" or philosophically articulate. We can see quite easily how such cardinal concepts as god, man, sin, salvation, grace, forgiveness, freedom and predestination both receive a new meaning in Latin Christian thought and, at the same time, bring out the latent meaning of aboriginal Latin concepts. It is through such writers as Augustine, in fact, that Rome or the Latin consciousness becomes a source of new philosophy, the source certainly without which such very recent developments as twentieth-century existentialism would be quite inconceivable. But we can say this also of most Western philosophy from the Schoolmen to Descartes, Kant, Hegel and the analysts of ordinary language.

But this is too large a topic for the end of a paper. To conclude with the usual privilege of an *obiter dictum,* I should like to express my conviction that the strangest thing, perhaps, about Latin Literature today is not its originality, its uniqueness, as I have tried in a merely suggestive way to express it here, but the much stranger incapacity of modern critics and scholars to understand or appreciate its uniqueness. It is not too much to say that we have been, as it were, blinded by the Greeks. Yet there is really no need to minimize the Greeks in order to comprehend the Romans. For a Latin scholar like myself who is professionally employed in trying to produce other Latin scholars, there is at least one hopeful thing about the present situation. This is quite simply the fact that, despite all the antiquity of the subject, all the centuries of Latin study, all the texts and commentaries, all the grammars and dictionaries, all the formidable apparatus of Latin scholarship, the really interesting and essential matter, the critical understanding of Latin literature, is a largely unfinished task,

something that is quite novel, quite in the future. Why this should be, I am not at all sure, and my speculations on it must await another occasion. It is enough for the moment to accept the fact itself.

References:

Ettore Bignone, *Storia della letteratura Latina* (Florence: G.C. Sansoni, 1945–1951);

Erich Burck, *Das Geschichtswerk des Titus Livius* (Heidelberg: Carl Winter, 1992);

Eduard Fraenkel, *Horace* (Oxford: Clarendon Press, 1957);

Richard Heinze, *Die lyrischen Verse des Horaz* (Amsterdam: A. M. Hakkert, 1959);

Heinze, *Virgil's Epische Technik* (Leipzig: Teubner, 1903); *Virgil's Epic Technique,* translated by Hazel and David Harvey and Fred Robertson (London: Bristol Classical Press, 1993);

Friedrich Klingner, *Virgil. Bucolica. Georgica. Aeneis.* (Zurich/Stuttgart: Artemis Verlag, 1967);

Friedrich Leo, *Zu augusteischen Dichtern* (Berlin: Weidmann, 1881);

Einar Löfstedt, "On the Style of Tacitus," *Journal of Roman Studies,* 38 (1948): 1–8;

Löfstedt, *Roman Literary Portraits* (Oxford: Oxford University Press, 1958), 142ff.;

Viktor Pöschl, *Horazische Lyrik* (Heidelberg: Carl Winter, 1970);

James Bennett Pritchard, *Ancient Near Eastern Texts Relating to the Old Testament* (Princeton: Princeton University Press, 1950; volume 2, 1975);

Pritchard, *The Ancient Near East: Supplementary Texts and Pictures relating to the Old Testament* (Princeton: Princeton University Press, 1969);

Augusto Rostagni, *Storia della letteratura latina,* 3 volumes, third edition (Turin: Unione Tipografico–Editrice Torinese, 1964).

A Note on Manuscripts

Not a single authorial manuscript copy of any ancient Greek or Roman writer's work has survived. The medium on which most ancient works were first written was the papyrus sheet, which existed in the form of a roll, sometimes as much as thirty feet long. On this roll the author wrote the text in a series of columns eight to ten inches high, including twenty-five to forty-five lines. All the manuscripts of the classical period, from Homer to Virgil, from Herodotus to Ammianus Marcellinus, have long been lost to the depredations of time, wars, political upheavals, and the religious movements that periodically altered the ancient world. The destruction of the great Alexandrian Library, the main repository of classical texts, in 47 B.C. meant the destruction of the exemplars of many Greek texts, and many Roman texts simply disappeared over time. In any case, all extant classical texts derive from manuscripts that were produced several centuries after the original works were composed.

Although the book (that is, manuscript) trade began to flourish in Athens in the fifth century B.C., there is no record in ancient Greece of a public library in the contemporary sense of that term. Copies of major dramatic works, such as those by Sophocles, were maintained as public records, but the best collections of texts were in private hands. In the fourth century B.C. the Museum at Alexandria maintained librarians who culled and often condensed the vast number of books produced throughout the Greek world. Their replication of manuscripts necessarily introduced errors and variants into the texts and began the notion of distinct manuscript traditions for ancient authors. The other tradition that arose from this practice was the discarding of an older manuscript once a new copy had been made and the discarding of a complete work once its digest had been compiled. The Alexandrians did much to preserve the best literature, but they were also responsible for many significant losses.

From the earliest literary period in Rome, histories and dramatic works were widely copied, the former for scholarly and school use, the latter for production. In the period of philhellenism under the Scipios, books were widely circulated, but how the books were produced and sold is not known with certainty. Unfortu-

nately, scholars and acting companies tended to interpolate alterations to the authors' texts (see in particular the two surviving endings of Plautus's *Poenulus* and Terence's *Andria*). The notion of restoring the author's original words began in 168 B.C. when the grammarian Crates of Mallos, the head of the library in Pergamum, broke his leg while on a diplomatic visit to Rome, and while recuperating, lectured on literature. He began a process of cleansing texts (mostly performed by scholars from Alexandria) that lasted into the reign of Augustus. Literacy grew, and the concomitant desire of the newly literate to read the old masters such as Plautus, Ennius, and even Virgil curiously resulted in the emendation of obscure or unusual words and expressions (words that were often characteristic of their authors), in order to make works readable by a wider audience.

Corrupt copies of Latin (and to a lesser extent Greek) texts proliferated in the early empire. Scholars such as M. Valerius Probus (late first century A.D.) and Quiuntus Asconius Pedianus (9 B.C.–A.D. 76) began three centuries of scholarship commenting upon and correcting the texts of Roman authors. In the next century the oldest writers—Ennius, Cato, and Plautus—became popular again, and their texts were cleansed. The third century began a noteworthy period of scholarship. Great commentators such as Aelius Donatus in the fourth century and Marius Servius Honoratus in the early fifth century not only left behind a wealth of knowledge and understanding of the literature they treated but also helped preserve fragments of authors that might otherwise be utterly lost (particularly Aulus Gellius). The value of these men cannot be overstated. Pamphilus in the first century A.D. compiled a work on language that quoted many ancient authors, as did Hephestion in his books on meter. Athenaeus (A.D. 190) quotes several hundred authors in his *Deipnosophistai* (Sophists at Dinner) who would otherwise be lost.

In the third century there was also a revival of the making of digests, or epitomization. While it would be preferable to have more true copies from this period, the catalogues produced by such epitomes have been helpful in giving us an understanding of the contents of lost works, such as the lost portions of Livy's history.

In the Christian era the Roman school system survived, and pagan texts were used, despite the recriminations of St. Jerome (A.D. 347–420) and St. Augustine (A.D. 354–430). The Christian Church maintained extensive collections of classical works at Rome and elsewhere. Even as the Roman Empire faced its ultimate collapse, there were plenty of copies of the great authors circulating around the known world, but one hundred years after Rome's fall in A.D. 476, from the mid-sixth to mid-eighth centuries, many Latin works were lost. One common form of destruction involved the recycling of expensive parchment by washing or scraping off the previous writing and rewriting over the clean surface. This form of manuscript, with the traces of another beneath, a palimpsest, has allowed the retrieval of portions of Cicero, Plautus, and even the Bible.

Though under attack, classical literature was preserved in the monasteries of Ireland by monks who then established monasteries across Europe for the transmission and reproduction of these texts. When Charlemagne reconstituted the Roman Empire, he appointed Alcuin (A.D. 735–804) the director of his school. Thanks to Alcuin and his training of the monks under his charge, France was instrumental in maintaining texts through the tenth century. Though great Roman (virtually no Greek) authors such as Cicero, Virgil, and the historians were again read in the schools, many poets such as Catullus, Tibullus, and Propertius were unknown. Major works of Seneca the Younger, Tacitus, Livy, and Manilius are also unmentioned in this period. This situation was repaired in the eleventh and twelfth centuries when many of these works existing in only one manuscript were widely copied and disseminated to scholars and libraries. At the dawn of the Renaissance, Latin was the lingua franca of Europe and necessary for a professional career. At the same time, many professionals who had achieved wealth wanted to possess and read their own copies of the ancients, insuring the continuing survival of what ancient literature had already survived. It is from the Byzantine period, the eighth to the fourteenth centuries, that most of the older extant Greek manuscripts derive. By the dawning of the sixteenth century, the basic present-day texts of ancient authors were secure.

Dictionary of Literary Biography® • Volume Two Hundred Eleven

Ancient Roman Writers

Dictionary of Literary Biography

Accius

(ca. 170 B.C. – ca. 80 B.C.)

W. Jeffrey Tatum
Florida State University

MAJOR WORKS–FRAGMENTARY:

DRAMA

Fabulae cothurnatae: *Achilles, Aegisthus, Agamem-nonidae, Alcestis, Alcmeo, Alphesiboea, Amphitryo, Andromeda, Antenoridae, Antigona, Armorum iudicium, Astyanax, Athamas, Atreus* (ca. 135 B.C.), *Bacchae, Chrysippus, Clytaemestra, Deiphobus, Diomedes, Epigoni, Epinausimache, Eurysaces, Hecuba, Hellenes, Io, Medea* or *Argonautae, Melanippus, Meleager, Minos* or *Mino-taurus, Myrmidones, Neoptolemus, Nyctegresia, Oenom-aus, Pelopidae, Persidae, Philocteta Lemnius, Phinidae, Phoenissae, Prometheus, Stasiastae* or *Tropaeum liberi, Telephus, Tereus* (104 B.C.), *Thebais, Troades.*
Fabulae Praetextae: *Aeneadae* or *Decius, Brutus.*

COMMENTARIES

Didascalion libri ix, 9 books;
Parerga, 2 or more books;
Pragmatica, 2 or more books;
Praxidica;
Sotadicon libri.

VERSE

Annales; erotic verse; verses on the dedication of Brutus's temple of Mars in Saturnian meter.

Editio princeps: *Fragmenta Poetarum veterum Latinorum quorum opera non extant,* edited by Robert Estienne (Paris: H. Stephanus, 1564).

Standard editions: *Frammenti dalle tragedie e dalle preteste,* edited by Anna Resta Barrile (Bologna: N. Zanichelli, 1970); dramas: *Tragicorum Romanorum frag-menta,* edited by Otto Ribbeck, third edition (Leipzig: Teubner, 1897), pp. 157–263; *Scaeni-corum Romanorum fragmenta,* volume 1, edited by Alfred Klotz, Otto Seel, and Ludwig Voit (Monaco: R. Oldenbourg, 1953); *Lucii Accii trago-*

ediarum fragmenta, edited by Quirino Franchella (Bologna: Compositori, 1968); *Accius. I frammenti delle tragedie,* edited by Vincenzo D'Anto (Lecce: Milella, 1980); *Poetarum Romanorum veterum reli-quiae,* edited by Ernst Diehl, sixth edition (Berlin: de Gruyter, 1967).

Translation in English: *Remains of Old Latin,* volume 2, translated by Eric Herbert Warmington, Loeb Classical Library (Cambridge, Mass.: Harvard University Press, 1936), pp. 326–606.

Commentary: *The Fragmentary Latin Poets,* edited by Edward Courtney (Oxford: Clarendon Press, 1993), pp. 56–64.

Although in his own day Accius was a towering literary figure, his writings have survived in a condition so highly fragmentary that he is, for the modern scholar, almost irretrievable. He was born around 170 B.C. at Pirsaurum, the son of freedmen parents. His personal circumstances must have been rather like those of Horace, whose father was a freedman who had acquired wealth enough to provide his son with the best education that money could buy. Certainly Accius was superbly educated. In 140 B.C. his first tragedy was produced in Rome, an event that brought the young writer into competition with the preeminent tragedian of the time, Pacuvius. The two men remained on good terms, and an anecdote by Gellius describes Accius reading the first draft of his *Atreus* to the senior poet (Gell. 13. 2. 2). Around 135 B.C. Accius traveled to Pergamum in order to complete his education. Like Alexandria, Pergamum was a center of literary and rhetorical studies, and presumably Accius's advanced capacities for scholarship and his energetic cultivation of his image as a scholar-poet were developed there. Accius returned to

Accius (seated) behind the scenes at a theater (mosiac at Pompeii)

Rome, where he turned his talents to tragedy. He attracted the friendship and patronage of Decimus Iunius Brutus Callaicus, the consul of 138 B.C., whose victorious campaigns in Spain had brought him a triumph in 136 B.C. Accius wrote the triumphal inscription in Saturnians and his *Brutus* in honor of his patron. Soon he was the master of the tragic stage and Rome's leading man of letters.

The genesis of Roman drama is obscure. That the ultimate origins of Roman comedy and tragedy are Greek is evident enough, but the details of how the Romans came to the practice of adapting Greek plays for the Roman stage is irrecoverable. Modern scholars have next to no secure knowledge of early Latin music, song, or dramatic performances. Perhaps the Etruscans played a role: the Latin words for actor and mask, *histrio* and *persona*, are Etruscan, and the Romans believed that their taste for spectacles had been acquired from the Etruscans. Unfortunately, the nature of dramatic composition and performance among the Etruscans is also a matter for speculation, and so these clues cannot take one far. Matters do not become certain (and even here the certainty is regularly exaggerated) until 240 B.C., when in Rome a Greek captive from Terentun, Livius Andronicus, produced a play, in all likelihood a tragedy, adapted from a Greek model. For the Romans this play was the beginning of Latin literature. The implications of its Greekness are regularly appreciated. That drama was the first and the most vital literary form in Rome is too easily overlooked. In fact, down to the time of Lucilius, all the major poets of Rome composed for the stage.

Roman comedy found its inspiration in Greek New Comedy. Roman tragedy, on the other hand, looked to classical models, to fifth-century B.C. Attic tragedy. Aeschylus, Sophocles, and Euripides, who was the Romans' special favorite, were all imitated by Roman tragedians. Roman tragedy, then, like Roman comedy, adopts and adapts Greek plots and Greek settings. The stories are borrowed from Greek mythology (the Trojan cycle appears frequently), and the world of the stage and its inhabitants are, as in comedy, an amalgamation of things foreign and things Roman. At the same time, the tragedians also composed plays with wholly Roman settings, the plots of which came from Roman legend and, more commonly, from the great events of Roman history. One example of this subgenre is Accius's *Brutus,* which tells the story of Junius Brutus's revolt against the Tarquins. This was the founding event of the Roman republic, but it also had contemporary relevance for Accius's audience since it tended to glorify his friend and patron, D. Brutus Callaicus. Tragedy based on the Greek model was called *fabula cothurnata,* after the *cothurni,* or high footwear, worn by Greek tragic actors; tragedy on Roman themes and with Roman settings was called *fabula trabeata* or *praetexta,* after the uniform of Roman magistrates.

Whatever its setting, Roman tragedy celebrated Roman values. The ideology of the Roman aristocracy, with its emphasis on competitive excellence, *virtus,* which was demonstrated in war and in public life, constituted the moral focus of each tragedy. Consequently, Greek heroes do not, on the Roman stage, struggle toward self-knowledge or wrestle with the unfathomable demands of the mysterious cosmos. They exemplify the aristocrat's quest for *virtus,* or they demonstrate the dangers of the perverse noble, whose powers, crafted by nature for military service and the career of the statesman, have been subverted by baser instincts and pernicious temptations—hence, the probable reason for the popularity of the Trojan cycle with its manifold opportunities to display the moral requirements of valor and the consequences of martial failure.

Romans of all classes, and not exclusively the aristocracy, appreciated these themes. Nevertheless, tragedies had to be crowd pleasers. Roman civic religion involved public festivals, including spectacles, in honor of its gods. Dramatic performances formed part of the celebration at four such holidays: the *Ludi Romani* (Roman Games), in honor of Jupiter Greatest and Best, held in September; the *Ludi Megalenses* (Megalensian Games), in honor of the Great Mother, held in April; the *Ludi Apollinares* (Apollonian Games), in honor of Apollo, held in July; and the *Ludi Plebeii* (Plebeian Games), also in honor of Jupiter Greatest and Best, held in November. These games, which included banquets and chariot races as well as drama, played an important role in the public careers of the magistrates who were responsible for their performance (and who supplemented the state's contribution to their funding). Consequently, the presiding magistrates oversaw every aspect of the games carefully. Plays were commissioned that would enhance the magistrate's reputation from every perspective. Thus, the magistrate sought tragedies that conveyed the right moral tone. He also endeavored to find tragedies that would be popular with the Roman people.

Hence, Roman tragedy often included sensational qualities. Certain myths were simply more exciting or provided a more contemporary resonance than did others. Tragedies that dealt with religious and even philosophical topics echoed the complications in Roman life resulting from the steady importation of new peoples, new cults, and new ideas to what was by Accius's day the center of a great empire. More appealing were plots that celebrated accessible Roman virtues, such as tales of tyrannicide, since the people valued their freedom every bit as much as did the aristocracy. But there is no denying the Roman taste for pathos. Their tragedians scoured Greek drama for plots that included shipwrecks, ghosts, madness, deception, betrayal, and outright cruelty. This taste for the horrible has aptly been compared to the violence of Elizabethan drama, with which it has an actual connection. Although his plays were not apparently meant for popular consumption, the tragedies that Seneca composed during the early empire remained within the traditional framework that he inherited from Pacuvius and Accius, with the result that their stories positively relish a level of violence and horror that can shock even modern sensibilities. Seneca's influence on the whole of European tragedy was, of course, considerable.

Roman tragedies were sensational not merely in their plots. Their style was also designed for mass appeal. Roman tragedy, following the precedent of Euripides, was highly rhetorical. In Accius's day, the full and fulsome rhetoric known as the "Asianic" style was widely attractive. This style is characterized by heavy elaboration and rich ornamentation achieved through such rhetorical devices as alliteration, anaphora, assonance, and antithesis. The characters in Roman tragedy do not really converse with one another: they declaim in meter. Latin lacked the various dialects and the ancient literary traditions available to their Attic forbears. Roman tragedians therefore had to engage in linguistic experiments, combining anachronism, religious language, and neologisms. The result pleased the majority of Romans of all classes but was (like the Greek of Aeschylus and Euripides) susceptible to parody and criticism. Plautus and Lucilius alike took

their shots at tragic discourse. At moments, admittedly, the tragedians' striving after effect yielded strange results. For instance, in his *Bacchae* (Bacchanals) Accius turned to Euripides' *Bacchae* for his model. In an early scene in the Greek play, the aged Teiresias and Cadmus go forth to celebrate the new god. The prophet explains that the god does not distinguish the old from the young when he enjoins the Thebans to dance in his honor (*Bacc.* 206–207). In Accius's version Teiresias says that "neither elderliness nor death nor grand-agedness" should prevent mortals from dancing. A late grammarian preserves the line on account of the peculiar word *grandaevitas* (grand-agedness). But what does one make of "death"? The word no doubt adds to the forcefulness of the line but also renders it ridiculous.

Drama, then, was the literary genre that played the most vital role in Roman public life. In the early days, the assignments of author and actor often overlapped (Plautus is a famous example), and, in any case, the status of these writers in Rome, despite the importance of their art, was not especially high. In 207 B.C. the *collegium scribarum histrionumque* (College of Writers and Actors) was established. This organization no doubt facilitated the business of theater in Rome, but it also provided an important literary and intellectual center. At the end of the third century B.C. writers were still *scribae* (scribes) and not yet *poetae* (poets). The careers of Pacuvius and Accius went a long way toward raising the station of the poets who served Rome.

Accius was the most prolific of all the Roman tragedians. The titles of more than forty *cothurnatae* and of two *praetextae* are known. Of the former, at least one, *Nyctegresia* (The Night Watch)—and possibly *Epinausimache* (The Battle at the Ships) as well—was taken directly from an episode in Homer instead of from an existing Greek tragedy. Accius's tragedies were the favorites of his time, and he became the leading literary figure of his time. He held court in the *collegium scribarum histrionumque,* and Valerius Maximus (3. 7. 11) preserves the story of his refusing to stand in the presence of the wit and distinguished orator Julius Caesar Strabo whenever the latter visited the college. Accius expected the college to erect a large statue in his honor, an aspiration that was regarded as humorous, not on account of its pretensions but because of Accius's diminutive stature.

Accius's output was not limited to tragedy. His *Annales,* in at least twenty-seven books, was either an historical epic or, more likely, an etiological epic of a more Hellenistic type. The one long fragment of it that survives explains the origins of the Roman Saturnalia. The clue is tantalizing, and the *Annales* possibly served as a precursor to Ovid's *Fasti* (Annals). Accius's remaining poetry is too poorly preserved to comment upon with confidence. He composed the *Pragmatica* (Principles for Playwrights) in at least two books; these were in trochaic meters and dealt with literary themes. He also composed the *Parerga* (By-Works) and the *Praxidica,* about which little can be said. His *Sotadicon libri* (books of poems in Sotadic meter) may have been erotic (Accius certainly wrote erotic poetry, though its actual meter is not known). More controversial is Accius's *Didascalia* (Records of the Stage), a scholarly work in nine books, chiefly dealing with the history of the theater in Greece and Rome. In this work he made contributions to Roman literary history and philology, and he made suggestions for improving Latin orthography. This work is usually assumed to have been poetic and written in various meters, but some scholars have maintained an alternative view, that it was a prose work that occasionally cited poetry.

Accius lived an extraordinarily long life (the young Cicero was able to converse with him), and he died sometime between 90 and 80 B.C. Accius's work became, along with that of Ennius and Pacuvius, a Latin classic. His plays were constantly reprised on the Roman stage well into Augustan times, and he had many admirers, including Cicero, who quoted him often. Accius's *Thyestes* was especially popular with later readers, and one of its lines, "Let them hate, so long as they fear," was a favorite with Caligula. The success of the works of Pacuvius and Accius, as literature as well as theater, led aristocratic Romans to try their hands at tragic composition—not for the stage but for private reading. Julius Caesar Strabo composed tragedies, as did Varius Rufus, Asinius Pollio, Quintus Cicero, and even Augustus. Ovid's *Medea* was a masterpiece, and the habit of tragic composition was well established in elite circles by the time of the younger Seneca. But composition for the stage seems to have faltered. As is the case in the modern opera scene, getting a hearing for new compositions was difficult, especially when so much was at stake for the sponsor of dramatic events. Though they may seem stilted to modern tastes, the wide appeal of the tragedies of Pacuvius and Accius posed an insurmountable barrier to later generations of playwrights. Tragedy in Rome, as a result, became a purely literary form. The significance of Accius, then, both for his contemporaries and for the subsequent literary history, is clear enough, even if his actual work is, for the most part, lost. Accius mattered both for what he wrote and for who he was: because of him the Roman tradition of the scholar-poet that Ennius had begun continued into the first century A.D. and flourished even into the next generation.

References:

William Beare, *The Roman Stage: A Short History of Latin Drama in the Time of the Republic,* third edition (London, 1964);

H. D. Jocelyn, "The Quotations of Republican Dramatists in Priscian's Treatise *De metris fabularum Terenti,*" *Antichthon,* 1 (1967): 60–69;

Antonius de Rosalia, ed., *Lexicon Accianum* (Hildesheim: Olms, 1982).

Ammianus Marcellinus

(ca. A.D. 330 – ca. A.D. 395)

Ralph W. Mathisen
University of South Carolina

MAJOR WORK: *Res gestae* (History), 31 books, of which 14–31 survive (ca. A.D. 360–395).

Editio princeps: *Historiae libri XIV–XXVI,* edited by Angelus Sabinus (Rome: Georgius Sachsel and Bartholomaeus Golsch, 1474).

Standard editions: *Ammiani Marcellini Rerum gestarum libri qui supersunt,* 2 volumes, edited by Charles Upson Clark (Berlin: Teubner, 1910–1915); *Ammien Marcellin, Histoire,* edited by Edouard Galletier, Jacques Fontaine, and Guy Sabbah (Paris: Les Belles Lettres, 1968–); *Ammiani Marcellini Rerum gestarum libri qui supersunt,* 2 volumes, edited by Wolfgang Seyfarth (Leipzig: Teubner, 1978).

Translation in English: *Ammianus Marcellinus,* 3 volumes, translated by John Carew Rolfe, Loeb Classical Library (Cambridge, Mass.: Harvard University Press, 1935–1940)–source of most of the translations cited below.

Commentaries: *Philological and Historical Commentary on Ammianus Marcellinus XIV,* edited by Pieter de Jonge (Groningen: J. B. Wolters, 1935); *Philological and Historical Commentary on Ammianus Marcellinus XV,* edited by de Jonge (Groningen: J. B. Wolters, 1948–1953); *Römische Geschichte,* 4 volumes, edited by Wolfgang Seyfarth (Berlin: Akademie-Verlag, 1968–1971)–with German translation; *Philological and Historical Commentary on Ammianus Marcellinus XVI,* edited by de Jonge (Groningen: Bouma's Boekhuis, 1972); *Philological and Historical Commentary on Ammianus Marcellinus XVII,* edited by de Jonge (Groningen: Bouma's Boekhuis, 1977); *Historische Kommentar zu Ammianus Marcellinus Buch XX–XXI,* 3 volumes, edited by Joachim Szidat (Wiesbaden: Steiner, 1977–1981); *Philological and Historical Commentary on Ammianus Marcellinus XVIII,* edited by de Jonge (Groningen: Bouma's Boekhuis, 1980); *Philological and Historical Commentary on Ammianus Marcellinus XIX,* edited by de Jonge (Groningen: Bouma's Boekhuis, 1982); *Philological and Historical Commentary on Ammianus*

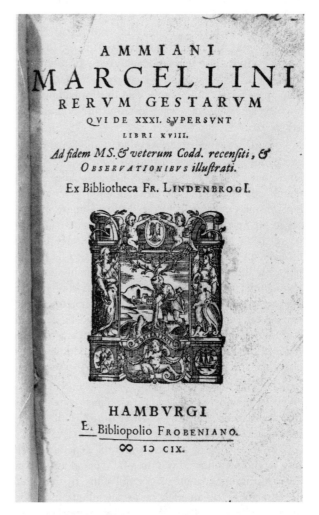

Title page for the 1609 edition of Ammianus Marcellinus's history of Rome after the reign of Domitian (courtesy of the Lilly Library, Indiana University)

Marcellinus XX, edited by Jan den Boeft, Daniel den Hengst, and H. C. Teitler (Groningen: Egbert Forsten, 1987); *Philological and Historical Commentary on Ammianus Marcellinus XXI,* edited by den Boeft, den Hengst, and Teitler (Groningen:

Egbert Forsten, 1991); *Philological and Historical Commentary on Ammianus Marcellinus XXII,* edited by den Boeft (Groningen: E. Forsten, 1995).

Ammianus Marcellinus, who lived from ca. A.D. 330 until ca. A.D. 395, was the last true Roman historian. His *Res gestae* (History) was intended to be a continuation of the historian Cornelius Tacitus, whose own *History* had ended with the reign of Domitian (A.D. 80–96). Ammianus's history was written in thirty-one books and covered the period from the accession of the emperor Nerva in A.D. 96 to the Battle of Adrianople and the death of the emperor Valens in A.D. 378. Of these, only the books commencing with A.D. 353 and dealing with Ammianus's own times (books 14–31) have survived. The thirteen lost books, which covered a period of 258 years, could have provided little more than an overview of the times, and this probability also may explain why they were lost, and the others were preserved.

Little is known about Ammianus and his attitudes except for what survives from his own work. Ammianus characterizes himself as "a former soldier and a Greek" (31.16.9). He generally is thought to have been born in the eastern part of the Roman Empire, probably in the neighborhood of Antioch. Elsewhere (19.8.6) he refers to himself as *ingenuus* (freeborn). He clearly received a traditional classical education, and he probably came from a well-to-do (although probably not aristocratic) background. His religious convictions were likewise traditional. He believed in a supreme being that he referred to as a *numen* or *deus,* and he believed that the world was governed by *fortuna* (luck) and *fatum* (fate). Although he was not a Christian and knew little about Christian beliefs, he was generally tolerant of Christianity.

Ammianus embarked on a military career. His first appearance in history is attested in A.D. 354, during the reign of the emperor Constantius II (A.D. 337–A.D. 361), serving in the east under the general Ursicinus, whom he followed west in A.D. 355 and assisted in the campaign against the usurper Silvanus. By this time, as a member of an elite corps attendant upon the emperor, he had obtained the rather senior rank of "Protector and Domestic." During the years A.D. 357–A.D. 359 (books 18–21) Ammianus was back in the east participating in campaigns against the Sassanid Persians. In the context of the year A.D. 357, moreover, he described himself as *juvenis* (a youngster) (16–10.21). His youth, coupled with his earlier military service, suggests that he may have been born ca. A.D. 330.

The campaigns in which Ammianus served gave him personal experience in many of the events that he reported. In particular, during the course of his discussion of the Persian invasion of Mesopotamia in A.D. 359 Ammianus makes reference to several of his own activities. Ammianus's initial duty was to accompany Ursicinus to Nisibis, a fortress just on the Roman side of the Tigris River. Ammianus reported (18.6.10),

> And when we were within two miles we saw a fine-looking boy, wearing a neck-chain, a child eight years old (as we guessed) and the son of a man of position (as he said), crying in the middle of the highway. . . . I, at the command of my general, who was filled with pity, set the boy before me on my horse and took him back to the city. . . . I set the boy down within a half-open postern gate and with winged speed hastened breathless to our troop, and I was all but taken prisoner . . . . (Rolfe's translation, 1.441)

More substantive from a military standpoint was Ammianus's secret mission inside the Persian Empire (18.6.20–23, 7.1–2):

> There was at that time in Corduene, which was subject to the Persian power, a satrap called, in Latin, Jovinianus, a youth who had secret sympathy with us for the reason that, having been detained in Syria as a hostage and allured by the charm of liberal studies, he felt a burning desire to return to our country. To him I was sent with a centurion of tried loyalty, for the purpose of getting better informed of what was going on, and I reached him over pathless mountains and through steep defiles. After he had seen and recognized me, and received me cordially, I confided to him alone the reason for my presence. . . . (Rolfe, 1.447)

Jovinianus responded by conveying an abundance of military intelligence.

On another occasion Ammianus narrowly escaped capture or death when the Roman forces he was accompanying to the frontier fortress of Amida were ambushed by the Persians. The Roman units eventually were dispersed, and Ammianus added a personal note (18.8.11–13):

> I myself [took] a direction apart from that of my comrades. . . . Finding myself surrounded on all sides by the foremost Persians, I moved ahead at breathless speed and aimed for the city, which . . . could be approached only by a single very narrow ascent. . . . Here, mingled with the Persians . . . we remained motionless until sunrise of the next day, so crowded together that . . . in front of me a soldier with his head cut in two, and split into equal halves by a powerful sword stroke, was pressed on all sides and stood erect like a stump. . . . And when at last I entered the city by a postern gate I found it crowded, since a throng of both sexes had flocked to it from the neighboring countryside. (Rolfe, 1.461–463)

Ammianus then experienced a protracted siege, which finally culminated when the Persians stormed the city. Ammianus escaped in the nick of time. In A.D. 363 Ammianus served in the emperor Julian's campaign against the Persians, but after Julian's death and the accession of Jovian (A.D. 363–A.D. 364), he seems to have left military service and devoted the remainder of his life to intellectual pursuits, and in particular to the researching and writing of his history. He remained in Antioch for several years, at least until ca. A.D. 372. During these years he apparently indulged a desire for travel–visiting Egypt, Greece, and Thrace. In A.D. 375 Ammianus seems still to have been in the east (31.1.2), for he reported that in that year, "At Antioch . . . it became usual that whoever thought that he was suffering wrong shouted without restraint, 'Let Valens be burned alive'" (Rolfe, 3.379).

By the early A.D. 380s Ammianus was in Rome, where he may have been threatened with eviction when "foreigners" were expelled from the city during a famine in A.D. 383/384 (14.6.19). Apparently while there he wrote his history, which seems to have been published in installments–the first fourteen books by the early A.D. 380s, books 15–25 by A.D. 391, and books 26–31 somewhat later. Ammianus then disappears from history, and he may have died ca. A.D. 395.

Ammianus's history is constructed, fundamentally, as a chronological account of events in the eastern and western halves of the Roman Empire. At times, as in the case of his account of Julian's invasion of the Persian Empire, Ammianus remains focused on a sequence of events for several chapters or even books. At other times, however, he skips back and forth, from chapter to chapter, between east and west.

The surviving books of the history commence with book 14, and, on the grounds of the periods they cover, they can be divided into three sections, comprised of books 14–16, 17–26, and 27–31. The first three books deal with the period A.D. 353–A.D. 357, a little more than one year each, and provide coverage of the fall of the Caesar Gallus in A.D. 354 and the accession of the Caesar Julian in the following year. The lengthy descriptions of Gallus's misrule in the east and the purges of the supporters of the defeated usurper Magnentius (A.D. 351–A.D. 353) in the west set the tone for the remainder of the work, one of whose leitmotifs is the problems caused by corrupt or incapable officials. In these books, for example, one first meets the imperial secretary Paulus, nicknamed *Catena* (The Chain) (14.5). Paulus reappears in A.D. 359 in similar circumstances but with a different nickname (19.12):

As if it were prescribed by some ancient custom, in place of civil wars the trumpets sounded for alleged

Constantius II, whom Ammianus compared unfavorably to the emperor Julian (bust in the Palace of the Conservatori, Rome)

cases of treason; and to investigate and punish these there was sent that notary Paulus, often called "Tartareus" [Mr. Perdition]. He was skilled in the work of bloodshed, and just as a trainer of gladiators seeks profit and emolument from the traffic in funerals, so did he from the rack or the executioner. (Rolfe, 1.535)

Ammianus, however, was by no means an opponent of the theory of Roman government, only of its faulty implementation. He praised other officials, such as Ursicinus.

Books 17–26 cover only eight years, less than one year per book. They narrate the activities of Ammianus's hero, the emperor Julian, from A.D. 358 until Julian's death in A.D. 363. The chronological underpinning of these books is provided by wars in the east and west, both civil and foreign. In Gaul, Julian waged successful campaigns against barbarian peoples such as the Alamanni, whereas in the east, Constantius II had scant success against the Persians (books 17–20). In A.D. 361

(book 21) Julian was proclaimed Augustus at Paris, but before the resultant civil war could reach its climax, Constantius died in Asia Minor.

Throughout these books Ammianus contrasts the virtues of Julian with the faults of Constantius. One way in which Ammianus makes the comparison is through the use of another device, the character portrayal. For example, book 16 begins in A.D. 356 with an encomium of Julian:

> Now, whatever I shall tell (and no wordy deceit adorns my tale, but untrammelled faithfulness to fact, based upon clear proofs, composes it) will almost belong to the domain of panegyric. For some law of a higher life seems to have attended this youth from his noble cradle even to his last breath. For with rapid strides he grew so conspicuous at home and abroad that in his foresight he was esteemed a second Titus, the son of Vespasian, in the glorious progress of his wars as very like Trajan, mild as Antoninus Pius, and in searching out the true and perfect reason of things in harmony with Marcus Aurelius, in emulation of whom he molded his conduct and his character. (Rolfe, 1.203)

Julian, therefore, is portrayed as the "good prince" (an epithet, in fact, of Trajan) in marked contrast to the other degenerate officials and rulers Ammianus describes. Julian's emulation of the Roman ideals of the second century, the height of the Roman Empire, stands in clear contrast to their abandonment by senators and officials of his own time.

As for Constantius, a relatively favorable depiction is found in yet another digression on Rome. Ammianus describes the ceremony attendant upon Constantius's famous *adventus* (arrival) in the city in A.D. 357 (16.10):

> Accordingly, being saluted as Augustus with favoring shouts, while hills and shores thundered out the roar, he never stirred, but showed himself as calm and imperturbable as he was commonly seen in the provinces. For he both stooped when passing through lofty gates (although he was very short), and as if his neck were in a vice, he kept the gaze of his eyes straight ahead, and turned his face neither to right nor to left, but (as if he were a manneqin) neither did he nod when the wheel jolted nor was he ever seen to spit, or to wipe or rub his face or nose, or move his hands about. (Rolfe, 1.247)

This portrayal provides another example of Ammianus's skill at recreating a scene.

After reporting Constantius's death, however, Ammianus delivered a more jaundiced postmortem (21.16.1–19):

> Observing, therefore, a true distinction between his good qualities and his defects, it will be fitting to set

forth his good points first. He always maintained the dignity of imperial majesty, and his great and lofty spirit disdained the favor of the populace. He was exceedingly sparing in conferring the higher dignities . . . and he never let the military lift their heads too high. . . . He made great pretensions to learning, but after failing in rhetoric because of dullness of mind, he turned to making verses, but accomplished nothing worthwhile. By a prudent and temperate manner of life and by moderation in eating and drinking he maintained such sound health that he rarely suffered from illnesses. . . . He was content with little sleep when time and circumstances so required. Throughout the entire span of his life he was so extraordinarily chaste that not even a suspicion could be raised against him. . . . let us now come to an enumeration of his defects. . . . if he found any indication, however slight or groundless, of an aspiration to the supreme power, by endless investigations, in which he made no distinction between right and wrong, he easily surpassed the savagery of Caligula, Domitian, and Commodus. . . . in such affairs he showed deadly enmity to justice, although he made a special effort to be considered just and merciful. . . . And, as some right-thinking men believed, it would have been a striking indication of true worth in Constantius if he had renounced his power without bloodshed rather than defended it so mercilessly. . . . although this emperor in foreign wars met with loss and disaster, yet he was elated by his success in civil conflicts and drenched with awful gore from the internal wounds of the state. . . . He was to an excessive degree under the influence of his wives, and the shrill-voiced eunuchs, and certain of the court officials, who applauded his every word, and listened for his "yes" or "no," in order to be able to agree with him. . . . The plain and simple religion of the Christians he obscured by a dotard's superstition, and by subtle and involved discussions about dogma; rather than by seriously trying to make them agree, he aroused many controversies. . . . His bodily appearance and form were as follows: he was rather dark, with bulging eyes and sharp-sighted; his hair was soft and his regularly shaven cheeks were neat and shining; from the meeting of neck and shoulders to the groin he was unusually long, and his legs were very short and bowed, for which reason he was good at running and leaping. (Rolfe, 2.173–185)

Julian then proceeded with an invasion of the Persian Empire (books 22–25), in the course of which, at the age of thirty-two, he was killed (25.3). Ammianus likewise assessed Julian's "virtues and faults," just as he had for Constantius (25.4.1–22):

> He was a man truly to be numbered with the heroic spirits, distinguished for his illustrious deeds and his inborn majesty. . . . In the first place, he was so conspicuous for inviolate chastity that after the loss of his wife it is well known that he never gave a thought to love. . . . Moreover, this kind of self-restraint was made still

greater through his moderation in eating and sleeping. . . . As soon as he had refreshed his body, which was inured to toil, by a brief rest in sleep, he awoke and in person attended to the changing of the guard and pickets, and after these serious duties took refuge in the pursuit of learning. . . . Then there were very many proofs of his wisdom. . . . He was thoroughly skilled in the arts of war and peace, greatly inclined to courtesy, and claiming for himself only so much deference as he thought preserved him from contempt and insolence. He was older in virtue than in years. He gave great attention to the administration of justice. . . . His fortitude is shown by the great number of his battles and by his conduct of wars, as well as by his endurance of excessive cold and heat. . . . His authority was so well established that, being feared as well as deeply loved as one who shared in the dangers and hardships of his men . . . he controlled his men even without pay. . . . And when they were armed and mutinous, he did not fear to address them and threaten to return to private life if they continued to be insubordinate. . . . let me now come to an account of his faults, although they can be summed up briefly. In disposition he was somewhat inconsistent, but he controlled this by the excellent habit of submitting, when he went wrong, to correction. He was somewhat talkative, and very seldom silent; also too much given to the consideration of omens and portents, so that in this respect he seemed to equal the emperor Hadrian. . . . He delighted in the applause of the mob, and desired beyond measure praise for the slightest matters, and the desire for popularity often led him to converse with unworthy men. . . . He was of medium stature. His hair lay smooth as if it had been combed, his beard was shaggy and trimmed so as to end in a point, his eyes were fine and full of fire, an indication of the acuteness of his mind. His eyebrows were handsome, his nose very straight, his mouth somewhat large with a pendulous lip. His neck was thick and somewhat bent, his shoulders large and broad. Moreover, right from top to toe he was a man of straight well-proportioned body frame and as a result was a strong and a good runner (2.503–515).

Ammianus's gentle treatment of his hero's supposed faults stands in sharp contrast to his handling of those of Constantius.

Following Julian's death, Jovian, an army officer, was made emperor. After concluding a hasty peace with the Persians that was "necessary, but shameful," Jovian unexpectedly was found dead in his tent in A.D. 364. Ammianus reveals his opinion of Jovian in his comment: "He took as his model Constantius . . ." (25.5–25.10). Chapter 26 chronicles, in the same year, the accession of Valentinian (A.D. 364–A.D. 375), another army officer, who appointed his brother Valens (A.D. 364–A.D. 378) as coemperor. Valentinian undertook to rule the western part of the empire and allocated the east to Valens.

Valentinian I, whom Ammianus described as cruel and ruthless (statue at Barletta, Italy)

The remaining five books of Ammianus's history, 27–31, cover the years A.D. 365–A.D. 378, or nearly three years per book. That is to say, rather than expanding his coverage as he neared his own times, Ammianus suddenly condensed it. There are several possible reasons. Perhaps Ammianus always had intended to give greater emphasis to the reign of Julian and its aftermath, or perhaps he had some reason to hasten his writing along.

These concluding books have two primary themes: the cruelty of Valentinian and incompetence of Valens and the appearance of various new barbarian peoples on the horizons of the Roman world. Ammianus's accounts of the ruthlessness of Valentinian exemplify his dislike for the abuse of power. In 27.7, Ammianus offers a brief overview of Valentinian's character:

Valentinian was known to be a cruel man, and although in the early part of his reign, in order to lessen his reputation for harshness, he sometimes strove to keep his savage impulses under his mind's control, yet the fault, as yet lurking and postponed, little by little broke forth without restraint and caused the destruction of many men, and was increased by fierce outbreaks of hot anger.... (Rolfe, 3.45–47)

Ammianus then editorializes (27.9) on his, and presumably his audience's, views on how the emperor's power should properly be exercised:

That some princes commit these and similar arbitrary acts with lofty arrogance is because they do not allow their friends the opportunity of dissuading them from unjust designs or deeds, and because of their great power they make their enemies afraid to speak. No correction is possible of the perverse actions of those who believe that what they desire to do must be the highest virtue. (Rolfe, 3.51)

In a subsequent discussion of accusations of poisoning and adultery at Rome in A.D. 371, Valentinian was characterized as "rather a cruel than a strict foe of vices" (28.1.11: Rolfe, 3.95). Reprising Tacitus's views following the death of Domitian (80–96), Ammianus also offered a personal explanation of why such miscarriages of justice had not been reported earlier (28.1.2):

Although, after long consideration of various circumstances, well-grounded dread restrained me from giving a minute account of this series of bloody deeds, yet I shall, relying on the better morals of the present day, set forth briefly such of them as are worthy of notice. (Rolfe, 3.89)

Meanwhile, Ammianus introduces other important players into the narrative: Gratian, the son of Valentinian, named Augustus in A.D. 367; Count Theodosius, the father of the future emperor Theodosius I (A.D. 379–A.D. 395); and, of course, the Goths.

The remaining narrative is interspersed with reports of battles and conspiracies. In the east Valens acted just as cruelly as his brother. Regarding Valens's response to reports of a conspiracy in A.D. 371, Ammianus reported (29.1.17–19),

... it was inexcusable that, with despotic anger, he was swift to assail with malicious persecution guilty and innocent under one and the same law, making no distinction in their deserts, so that while there was still doubt about the crime, the emperor had made up his mind about the penalty, and some learned that they had been condemned to death before knowing that they were under suspicion. This persistent purpose of his increased, spurred on as it was both by his own greed and that of persons who frequented the court at that time, and opened the way to fresh desires, and if any mention of mercy was made—which rarely happened—called it slackness. (Rolfe, 3.197–199)

The purges continued, and Ammianus gave another opinion (29.2.12) of those who did not know how to exercise authority properly:

Yet after these so lamentable events, Valens acted with no more restraint or shame; since excessive power does not reflect that it is unworthy for men of right principles, even to the disadvantage of their enemies, willingly to plunge into crime, and that nothing is so ugly as for a cruel nature to be joined to lofty pride of power. (Rolfe, 3.223)

Valentinian died in A.D. 375; as a result, the empire lost a firm guiding hand, however cruel it may have been, on the helm of the ship of state. Valentinian's death left the ineffectual Valens to deal with the arrival of the Visigoths and their pursuers, the Huns, in A.D. 376. Ammianus's history concludes in A.D. 378 with the disastrous Battle of Adrianople, in which the eastern Roman army was destroyed and Valens was killed. The history ends with a brief discussion of attempts at a Roman recovery after the battle and the optimistic words, "And thus the eastern provinces were saved from great dangers" (31.16.8: Rolfe, 3.505).

There is, however, no discussion of the subsequent history of the empire nor of the accession in A.D. 379 of Theodosius I, who was the reigning emperor when the history was written and read. Perhaps Ammianus decided that it was more politic to write of dead emperors than live ones, or perhaps he found the litany of subsequent Roman defeats too depressing to discuss.

Scholarly opinions about the quality of Ammianus's work have generally been positive. Ernst Stein, for example, called Ammianus "the greatest literary genius that the world has seen between Tacitus and Dante." Edward Gibbon asserted that Ammianus wrote "without prejudices." As for Ammianus, he gave his own views on his history (31.16.9) in a comment at the conclusion of his work:

These events, from the principate of the emperor Nerva to the death of Valens, I, a former soldier and a Greek, have set forth to the measure of my ability, without ever (I believe) consciously venturing to debase through silence or through falsehood a work whose aim was the truth. The rest may be written by abler men, who are in the prime of life and learning. But if they choose to undertake such a task, I advise them to forge their tongues to the loftier style. (Rolfe, 3.505)

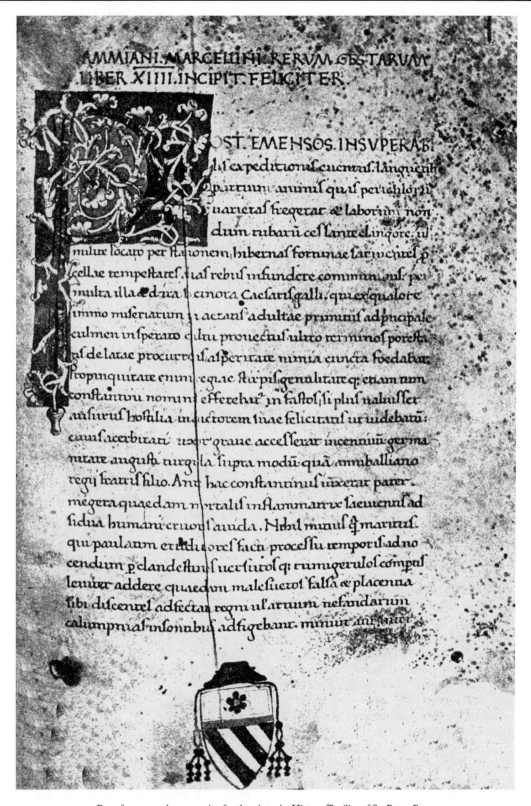

Page from an early manuscript for Ammianus's History (Basilica of St. Peter, Rome;
S. Petr. E 27, f. 1 [XIV, 1(1–3)])

In most regards, Ammianus can be taken at his word. He can rarely be convicted of falsehood, and he can never be accused of taciturnity.

Ammianus certainly is to be admired for his narrative talent. His history is never dull or boring. Contrary to Gibbon's view, however, Ammianus certainly did not write without prejudice. He and his history were products of their times and reflect the social values and intellectual atmosphere of late antiquity in general and the late-Roman aristocracy in particular. Ammianus was an advocate of legitimate government and the reasonable and restrained exercise of authority. For example, he realized that in certain circumstances investigations into accusations of criminal activities, and especially into charges of treason, were necessary. On one occasion (19.12.17) he noted, "For we do not deny that the safety of a lawful prince, the protector and defender of good men, on whom depends the safety of others, ought to be safeguarded by the united diligence of all men . . ." (Rolfe, 1.543). Ammianus also understood, however, that he lived in an imperfect world, and on many occasions he pointed out instances where the ideal system did not function as it should.

In the instance just cited he went on to condemn Constantius for his excessive zeal in the pursuit of traitors:

> It is not seemly, though, for a prince to rejoice beyond measure in such sorrowful events, lest his subjects should seem to be ruled by despotism rather than by lawful power. And the example of Cicero ought to be followed, who, when it was in his power to spare or to harm, as he himself tells us [in a lost work], sought excuses for pardoning rather than opportunities for punishing; and that is the province of a mild and considerate official. (Rolfe, 1.543)

In order to gain further insight into Ammianus's literary method, it is important to understand just who his primary audience was. Ammianus was writing in Rome for an educated senatorial audience. His history probably was presented, moreover, at private readings during the process of composition. If these suppositions are true, Ammianus was quite aware of how his listeners received what he had written: if the response was negative, he might lose the patronage of those who helped to underwrite his efforts.

Consequently, one can understand why every so often Ammianus introduced into the midst of his discussion material that was intended to pique the interest of his listeners. In particular, Ammianus pointedly interjected accounts of what was going on at Rome during the prefecture of one Roman senator or another, including those of Orfitus (A.D. 353–A.D. 355: 14.6), Leontius (A.D. 355–A.D. 356: 15.7), Orfitus for the sec-

ond time (A.D. 357–A.D. 359: 17.4), Tertullus (A.D. 359–A.D. 361: 19.10), Apronianus (A.D. 362–A.D. 364: 26.3), Praetextatus (A.D. 367–A.D. 368: 27.9.8), Olybrius (A.D. 366–A.D. 370: 28.1.1–57), Ampelius (A.D. 371–A.D. 372: 28.1.22), and Claudius (A.D. 374: 29.64).

Ammianus's attempts to keep the attention of his Roman audience also are attested by two quite lengthy digressions on the inhabitants of the city of Rome in which he scathingly lampoons some of the traits and habits of both the Roman aristocracy and the Roman plebeians. The first of these is inserted in the middle of the account of an eastern witch-hunt conducted by Caesar Gallus in A.D. 354. Ammianus offers a lengthy, devastating satire of the faults of the Senate and Roman people titled "Senatus populique Romani vitia." In it he contrasts (14.6.1–26) the industry and seriousness of the Roman past with present-day frivolousness and decadence:

> Some of these men eagerly strive for statues, thinking that by them they can be made immortal, as if they would gain a greater reward from senseless brazen images than from the consciousness of honorable and virtuous conduct. . . . Other men, taking great pride in coaches higher than common and in ostentatious finery of apparel, sweat under heavy cloaks, which they fasten about their necks and bind around their very throats, while the air blows through them because of the excessive lightness of the material; and they lift them up with both hands and wave them with many gestures. . . . I pass over the gluttonous banquets and the various allurements of pleasures, lest I should go too far. . . . In consequence of this state of things, the few houses that were formerly famed for devotion to serious pursuits now teem with the sports of sluggish indolence, reechoing to the sound of singing and the tinkling of flutes and lyres. In short, in place of the philosopher the singer is called in, and in place of the orator the teacher of stagecraft, and while the libraries are shut up forever like tombs, water-organs are manufactured and lyres as large as carriages, and flutes and instruments heavy for gesticulating actors. . . . But of the multitude of lowest condition and greatest poverty some spend the entire night in wineshops . . . or they quarrel with one another in their games at dice, making a disgusting sound by drawing back the breath into their resounding nostrils, or, which is favorite among all amusements . . . they stand open-mouthed, examining minutely the good points or the defects of charioteers and their horses. . . . These and similar things prevent anything memorable or serious from being done in Rome. (Rolfe, 1.41–53).

Perhaps Ammianus felt that he needed something to distract his Roman readers from the mounting body count.

One might wonder, moreover, at how Ammianus's senatorial audience liked hearing itself lampooned in this manner. Clearly they loved it, for in a later book (28.4.1–35) Ammianus reprised his satire, at even greater length:

> First I shall give an account of the delinquencies of the nobles and then of the common people. . . . Some men, distinguished (as they think) by famous fore names, pride themselves beyond measure in being called Reburri, Flavonii, Pagonii, Gereones, and Dalii, along with Tarracii and Pherrasii, and many other equally fine-sounding indications of "eminent ancestry" [a joke: none of these are real names]. . . . Their houses are frequented by idle chatter-boxes, who with various pretenses of approval applaud every word of the man of loftier fortune. . . . Sometimes at their banquets the scales are even called for, in order to weigh the fish, birds, and dormice that are served. . . . Some of them hate learning as they do poison, and read with care only Juvenal and Marius Maximus [an imperial biographer and retailer of court gossip]. . . . a few among them are so strict in punishing offenses that if a slave is slow in bringing the hot water, they condemn him to suffer three hundred lashes. . . . (Rolfe, 3.141–147)

Some commentators have presumed that Ammianus intended these parodies as biting satire, and in some regards they were, but they also were written with tongue firmly planted in cheek, and Ammianus's listeners, who were themselves the butts of the jokes, clearly appreciated the humor and were able to laugh at their own affectations.

Yet, another of Ammianus's Roman digressions (27.3.12–13) tells of a controversy that arose over the papacy and provides some insight into Ammianus's views regarding Christianity:

> Damasus and Ursinus, burning with a superhuman desire of seizing the bishopric, engaged in bitter strife because of their opposing interests; and the supporters of both parties went even so far as conflicts ending in bloodshed and death. . . . And in the struggle Damasus was victorious through the efforts of the party that favored him. It is a well-known fact that in the basilica of Sicininus [now Santa Maria Maggiore], where the assembly of the Christian sect is held, in a single day a hundred and thirty-seven corpses of the slain were found, and that it was only with difficulty that the long-continued frenzy of the people was afterward quelled. (Rolfe, 3.1 9–21)

Although this account paints the Christians in a rather unfavorable light, the pagan Ammianus elsewhere is quite tolerant of them.

These digressions into the nature of the people of Rome mark another aspect of Ammianus's literary method. Like the Greek historian Herodotus, Ammianus was fond of including ethnic and geographical digressions, some of them virtual monographs in their own right, dealing with the peoples or places he was discussing. These, too, undoubtedly were included to provide interesting background information for his listeners. They also are of exceptionally great interest for modern historians.

The descriptions of the senators of Rome can be included in the category of "ethnic excurses," among which one also finds discussions, in other places, of the Isaurians (14.2.1–7), the Saracens (14.3.4–7), the Alamanni (15.4), eunuchs (22.4), the Amazons (22.8.1–49), lawyers (30.4), and the Huns (31.2–3). Other digressions were on geographical topics, including those on "the eastern provinces" (14.8), Amida (18.9), Egypt (22.15–16), the Persian Empire (23.6.1–88, a mini-monograph), Thrace (27.4), and Britain (27.8.4, 18.3.8, referring to lost books). He included other lengthy asides on the topics of, for example, obelisks (17.4), causes of the plague (19.4), astronomy (20.3), military artillery (23.4), and the tides (27.8.4).

As for Ammianus's writing style, he was a Greek (or even a "Hellenized Syrian") writing in Latin, a language that he certainly knew well, but one that was not his native tongue. In some ways, as in his use of curious word orders and long participial phrases, his Greek background shows through. In addition, certain vulgar Latin uses, no doubt acquired in his army experience, also appear. Otherwise, his use of affectation, bombast, and "bewildering ornamental imagery" is to be seen less as a flaw than as an example of the preferred style of his age. Many would no doubt disagree with Rolfe (l.xxiii), who described Ammianus's "style . . . as offensive . . . to the modern reader of his work."

In most cases Ammianus's sources are unknown. He read Cicero, perhaps to improve his style, and Caesar, for information on Gaul. For his own times he is thought to have consulted the works of Eunapius of Sardis and a lost history of the Roman senator Nichomachus Flavianus, but much of the rest of his material seems to have come from his own personal experiences and perhaps from some official sources.

The *Res gestae* of Ammianus Marcellinus is much more than a mere recitation of succeeding events. It provides perceptive insights into the times comparable to those given for earlier periods by such historians as Tacitus and Thucydides, coupled with a narrative ability that might be compared to that of Livy or Herodotus. It is not only informative and singularly entertaining; it also reflects Ammianus's desire to package his material in such a way as to create a perception of the nature of the times: what was good, what was bad; what worked, and what did not. Ammianus knew that he was living during a critical period, and he attempted to convey to his audience his own strong sense that all was not well in the world.

For modern historians, Ammianus provides eye-witness coverage of a momentous period of Roman history and of an Empire under siege. At this time the Empire still was ruled either by a single emperor or by a unified imperial college. The emperors still administered a territory that extended from Spain to the Euphrates and from Britain to Egypt. The empire did face grave difficulties, ranging from external threats to internal corruption and sedition. In Ammianus's world, however, these problems were dealt with as they arose; that the empire would ever collapse was unthinkable. Indeed, the reign of Valentinian I was looked upon as the third "Golden Age," along with the reigns of Augustus (27 B.C.–A.D. 14) and Trajan (A.D. 98–A.D. 117). Yet, at the very end of the work the reader glimpses the beginning of the "barbarian invasions" that ultimately would dismember the western half of the Roman Empire. Even though Ammianus did not live to see the disasters of the fifth century, he may have sensed that they were coming.

Bibliographies and Concordances:

Geoffrey J. D. E. Archbold, *A Concordance to the History of Ammianus Marcellinus* (Toronto: University of Toronto Press, 1980);

Maria Chiabo, *Index verborum Ammiani Marcellini* (Hildesheim, Germany & New York: Olms, 1983);

Giovanni Viansino, *Ammiani Marcellini rerum gestarum lexicon,* 2 volumes (Hildesheim: Olms, 1985).

References:

N. J. E. Austin, *Ammianus on Warfare: An Investigation into Ammianus' Military Knowledge* (Brussels: Latomus, 1979);

Timothy David Barnes, *Ammianus Marcellinus and the Representation of Historical Reality* (Ithaca, N.Y.: Cornell University Press, 1998);

Roger C. Blockley, *Ammianus Marcellinus: A Study of His Historiography and Political Thought* (Brussels: Latomus, 1975);

P. M. Camus, *Ammien Marcellin. Témoin des courants culturels et religieux à la fin du IVe siècle* (Paris: Les Belles Lettres, 1967);

Charles Upson Clark, *The Text Tradition of Ammianus Marcellinus* (New Haven: Yale University Press, 1904);

Gary A. Crump, *Ammianus Marcellinus as a Military Historian* (Wiesbaden: Steiner, 1975);

Jan den Boeft, Daniel den Hengst, and H. C. Teitler, *Cognitio gestorum: The Historiographic Art of Ammianus Marcellinus* (Amsterdam & New York: North-Holland, 1992);

G. Houston, "A Revisionary Note on Ammianus Marcellinus 14.6.18: When Did the Public Libraries of Ancient Rome Close?" *Library Quarterly,* 58 (1988): 258–264;

Arnold H. M. Jones, John Morris, and John Robert Martindale, eds., *The Prosopography of the Later Roman Empire. Volume I. A.D. 260–395* (Cambridge, 1971), pp. 547–548;

John Matthews, *The Roman Empire of Ammianus* (Baltimore: Johns Hopkins University Press, 1989);

Arnaldo Momigliano, "The Lonely Historian Ammianus Marcellinus," *A.S.N.P.,* 4 (1974): 1393–1407;

R. L. Rike, *Apex omnium: Religion in the Res gestae of Ammianus* (Berkeley: University of California Press, 1987);

Henry T. Rowell, *Ammianus Marcellinus, Soldier-Historian of the Late Roman Empire* (Cincinnati: University of Cincinnati, 1964);

Robin Seager, *Ammianus Marcellinus, Seven Studies in His Language and Thought* (Columbia: University of Missouri Press, 1986);

Wolfgang Seyfarth, *Der Codex Fuldensis und der Codex E des Ammianus Marcellinus: Zur Fräge der handschriftlichen Überlieferung des Werkes des letzten römischen Geschichtsschreibers* (Berlin: Akademie-Verlag, 1962);

Ernst Stein, *Geschichte des spätrömischen Reiches vom römischen zum byzantinischen Stuate (284–476 n. Chr.)* (Vienna: L. W. Seidel und Sohn, 1928) 1.331;

Ronald Syme, *Ammianus and the Historia Augusta* (Oxford: Clarendon Press, 1968);

E. A. Thompson, *The Historical Work of Ammianus Marcellinus* (Cambridge: Cambridge University Press, 1947).

Apuleius

(ca. A.D. 125 – post A.D. 164)

Gerald Sandy
University of British Columbia

MAJOR WORKS–EXTANT: *Apulci Platonici pro se de magia* (Apology, A.D. 158–A.D. 159);
Metamorphoses/Asinus Aureus (The Golden Ass, after A.D. 160).

WORK–FRAGMENTARY: *Florida* (ca. A.D. 160–170).

WORK–ATTRIBUTED: *De Deo Socratis,* derived from a separate manuscript tradition (On the God of Socrates).

WORKS–QUESTIONABLE: *De Mundo* (On the Universe);
De Platone et Eius Dogmate (On Plato and His Doctrine);
Peri Hermeneias/De Interpretatione (Logic).

WORK–DOUBTFUL: *Asclepius* (The Herbal).

WORKS–LOST:
UNTITLED WORKS WRITTEN IN BOTH GREEK AND LATIN: epic and lyric poems, comedies, tragedies, riddles, historical accounts of varied topics, orations, and philosophical dialogues (cited in *Florida,* 9).
LANGUAGE OF COMPOSITION UNKNOWN: poems, philosophical dialogues, hymns, music, histories, and satires (cited in *Florida,* 20).
LOST AND FRAGMENTARY WORKS CITED BY LATER WRITERS: Jean Beaujeu, ed., *Opuscules philosophiques (De dieu de Socrate, Platon et sa doctrine, Du monde) et fragments [par] Apulée* (Paris: Les Belles Lettres, 1973), pp. 171–180.
VERSE: *Ludicra* (Diversions)–(cited in *Apology,* 9 and 14); *Anechomenos* (Book of Love); *De proverbiis* (On Proverbs).
PROSE: *Epitoma historiarum* (Epitome of Histories), *De medicinalibus* (On Medical Questions), *De re rustica* (On Agriculture), *De arboribus* (On Trees), *Hermagoras.*
TRANSLATIONS: Plato's *Phaedo* and *Republic.*

Apuleius, portrait on a medallion struck at Rome in the fourth century A.D. (Bibliothèque Nationale de France, Paris)

Manuscripts: The outline at the beginning of this article gives some idea of the complex transmission of the Apuleian body of work. The works listed under the first two headings derive from a single manuscript known as F that was produced at Monte Cassino, Italy, in the eleventh century. (A copy of it in the hand of the famous writer Boccaccio survives.) *De Deo Socratis* and the works under the heading "Works–Questionable" derive from a separate French and German manuscript tradition dating from as early as the first third of the ninth century. It links them less securely to Apuleius, but their Apuleian authorship is attested to by many late-classical and medieval writers. Only the works listed under the first four headings have been discussed in this article. However, the works cited under the heading "Works–Doubtful" convey an impression of the breadth of

Apuleius's interests and activities and the range of his studies and writings in both Greek and Latin.

Editio princeps: *Metamorphoseos Liber ac nonnulla alia opuscula,* edited by J. Andreas De Buxis (Rome, 1469).

Standard editions: *Apulei Opera quae supersunt,* 3 volumes, edited by Rudolph Helm and P. Thomas, third edition (Leipzig: Teubner, 1955–1969); *Les Metamorphoses,* 3 volumes, edited by Donald Struan Robertson, translated by Paul Vallette, (Paris: Les Belles Lettres, 1936–1945); *Apulei Apologia sive Pro se de magia liber,* edited by Harold Edgeworth Butler and Arthur Synge Owen (Oxford: Clarendon Press, 1914; reprinted, Hildesheim: Olms, 1967); *Pro se de magia,* 2 volumes, edited by Vincent Hunink (Amsterdam: J. C. Gieben, 1997); *Apology, Florida,* edited and translated by Paul Vallette (Paris: Les Belles Lettres, 1924); *Opuscules philosophiques [On the God of Socrates, On Plato and His Doctrine, On the Universe],* edited and translated by Jean Beaujeu (Paris: Les Belles Lettres, 1973); *Apulei Platonici Madaurensis De philosophia libri,* edited by Claudio Moreschini (Stuttgart: Teubner, 1991).

Translations in English: *The Golden Ass,* translated by Jack Lindsay (New York: Limited Editions Club, 1932); *The Golden Ass,* translated by Robert Graves (Harmondsworth, U.K.: Penguin, 1950); *Metamorphoses,* 2 volumes, translated by John Arthur Hanson, Loeb Classical Library (Cambridge, Mass. & London: Harvard University Press, 1989); *The Golden Ass,* translated by Patrick Gerard Walsh (Oxford & New York: Clarendon Press, 1994); *Apology and Florida of Apuleius of Medaura,* translated by H. E. Butler (Oxford: Clarendon Press, 1909; reprinted, Westport, Conn.: Greenwood Press, 1970); *The Logic of Apuleius,* translated by David Londey and Carmen Johanson (Leiden: E. J. Brill, 1987).

Commentaries: *L. Apuleii Opera Omnia,* 2 volumes, edited by Gustav Friedrich Hildebrand (Leipzig: C. Cnobloch, 1842; reprinted, Hildesheim: Olms, 1968); *Ad Apulei Madaurensis Metamorphoseon librum primum commentarius exegeticus,* edited by Margaretha Molt (Groningen: M. De Waal, 1938); *Apuleius: A Commentary [Book 1],* edited by A. Scobie (Meisenheim am Glan: Hain, 1975); *Ad Apulei Madaurensis Metamorphoseon librum secundum commentarius exegeticus,* edited by B. J. de Jonge (Groningen: De Waal, 1941); *The Metamorphoses: A Commentary on Book III,* edited by R. T. van der Paardt (Amsterdam: A. M. Hakkert, 1971); *Metamorphoses Book IV.1-27,* edited by Benjamin L. Hijmans Jr. and others (Groningen: Bouma, 1977); *Ad Apulei Madaurensis Metamorphoseon librum quintum commen-*

tarius exegeticus, edited by Jan M. H. Fernhout (Medioburgi: Altorffer, 1949); *Metamorphoses Book IX,* edited by Hijmans and others (Groningen: E. Forsten, 1995); *The Isis-Book: Metamorphoses Book XI,* edited and translated by John Gwyn Griffiths (Leiden: E. J. Brill, 1975); *Apulei Psyche et Cupido,* edited by Louis C. Purser (London: P. H. Lee Warner, 1910; reprinted, New Rochelle, N.Y., 1983); *Cupid and Psyche,* edited by E. J. Kenney (Cambridge: Cambridge University Press, 1990), books 4.28–6.24.

Apuleius Madaurensis, or Apuleius of Madauros, is best known as the author of the Latin novel *Asinus Aureus* (The Golden Ass, after A.D. 160). The "Madaurensis" part of his name refers to his place of birth, Madauros, now known as Mdaurusch in modern Algeria, where St. Augustine also was born. Thus, he was a native of one of the most westerly regions of the Roman Empire. In spite of the prevailing Latin culture of the region, which the Romans called Africa Proconsularis, Apuleius was equally accomplished in both Greek and Latin and the beneficiary of postgraduate studies in Athens. Most of his extant writings are translations or adaptations of Greek works, and he can most profitably be viewed as a transmitter of the intellectual accomplishments of the Greek East to the Latin West.

Most of what is known about Apuleius derives from his *Apulei Apologia pro se de magia liber* (Apology)—the published version of his defense of himself against charges of employing magic to "bewitch" the prosperous widow Pudentilla. The outcome of the trial is not known, but since it was a capital crime to practice magic, and Apuleius can be located in Carthage five or six years after his trial of A.D. 158 or 159, one can safely infer that he was acquitted. St. Augustine reports that certain factions in Oea (modern Tripoli in Libya), where the events for which he was tried were alleged to have occurred, opposed the erection of a statue in Apuleius's honor, and he may have fled this hostile environment to spend the last years of his life in Carthage, the principal city in Africa Proconsularis and the place where he had attended school.

The *Apologia* is a virtuoso performance in the mold of the oratorical road shows of the Greek sophists that were popular in the second and third centuries. It also functions effectively both as a defense against specific criminal charges and as a defense of philosophy. In Apuleius's own words, "I undertake the defense not only of myself but truly that of philosophy as well." The charges, again in Apuleius's words, are, "We accuse him . . . of being a handsome philosopher most eloquent,"—what shame!—"both in Greek and Latin." Approximately the first 25 percent of the speech

Apuleius's birthplace, Madauros (from James Tatum, Apuleius and "The Golden Ass," *1979)*

responds to these accusations. Apuleius characterizes this part of his speech as "necessary appendages to my defense" before he turns to "the crimes themselves." He develops the implication that the ignorant misconstrue the actions of philosophers. He numbers the plaintiffs among the ignorant, of course, repeatedly characterizing them as country bumpkins. He associates himself and the alleged offenses with distinguished philosophers of the distant past. He says that he shares his good looks, for instance, with the philosopher Pythagoras, "who was the first to label himself 'philosopher.'" Above all he aligns himself with Plato, "whose lofty and divine doctrines . . . are scarcely known to the select few of his dedicated followers and not at all to the profane." In this way Apuleius assigns the plaintiffs to the ranks of the profane and enlists with Plato as a codefendant in the age-old battle against popular hostility toward intellectuals, "I shall readily allow . . . myself to be indicted with Plato."

After dealing with marginal issues such as good looks and eloquence, Apuleius confronts the "very charge of [practicing] magic." He uses the same tactic as before, justifying his alleged offenses by citing precedents for them among famous philosophers of the past. Against the charge that he has procured fish for magical

purposes, for example, Apuleius cites the examples of "Aristotle, Theophrastus, Eudemus, Lyco, and the rest of Plato's successors." Like them, he procured fish for scientific investigation and has some of his books, written in both Greek and Latin, entered as evidence in the legal proceedings. Similarly, Apuleius urges the judge to "listen to another equally stupid charge," that of using incantations to bewitch a young male slave and a freeborn woman who were suffering from epilepsy. Nowhere else in the *Apologia* does Apuleius reveal so clearly that his defense is designed as much to confirm his place among his erudite peers as to acquit him of specific criminal charges:

> I shall tell you, [judge] Claudius Maximus, why I investigated the symptom of a ringing sound in the ears [of the alleged victim of my magical incantations]. I do so not so much to exonerate myself in this matter, which you have ruled to be irrelevant to the accusation of an indictable crime, but so as not to pass over in silence anything worthy of your ears or in accord with your learning.

Apuleius then outlines the views on epilepsy expressed by Plato in his *Timaeus*. By Apuleius's own admission his summary of Plato's opinions on epilepsy serves the sole purpose of enlisting the trial judge in the sport of erudite one-upmanship for which their shared cultural background exclusively qualifies them.

The last third of Apuleius's speech revels much less in virtuoso performance as he confronts concrete charges in the same sequence they were made by the plaintiffs. In other words, it conforms more closely to what one would expect in a forensic speech in which the speaker's life is on the line. He manages throughout his defense to give fairly free rein to the declamatory set pieces decreed by his rhetorical schooling, but he has to operate within the constraints of the courtroom.

No such constraints impede flamboyant display in the *Florida,* which almost by definition is epidictic and therefore designed for virtuoso display. This work is a collection of extracts of twenty-three speeches that range in length from five lines to eight pages. Nothing is known of the date when, the purpose for which, or the person by whom they were compiled into an anthology. Those extracts that can be dated belong to a period of approximately ten years after Apuleius's trial and in some cases are linked explicitly to delivery in Carthage. The subjects of several of the speeches are reminiscent of extant speeches delivered by the traveling Greek lecture-tour speakers of the time, known as sophists. Apuleius sometimes acts as spokesman for Carthage and publicly eulogizes the resident proconsul (governor) or publicly wishes the proconsul well as his term of office in Carthage draws to a close. On other occasions the extracts resemble generic speeches that could have been adapted slightly to suit the circumstances of any town visited on the lecture tour, as in the first extract, which appears to be the introduction to a prayer to be delivered publicly at a local shrine. Others are minutely detailed descriptions of places or things—such as a statue that the speaker saw on the island of Samos, India, or a parrot. One speech publicly thanks the people of Carthage for decreeing to honor Apuleius with a statue. Still others provide the audience with lessons in Greek philosophy or Greek drama.

One complete speech dealing with philosophy survives—the work known as *De Deo Socratis* (On the God of Socrates). This work appears to have been at least partially extemporaneous. The Greek version or portion of the discourse that is referred to in the speech has been lost. The "god" of the title is Socrates' personal demon, and the subject is demonology, the fullest and most detailed that has survived from classical antiquity. The discourse, which Apuleius's compatriot St. Augustine criticizes at length in his *De Civitate Dei* (On the City of God), takes as its starting point Plato's description in the *Timaeus* of the supreme being (God) as transcendent and his account in the *Symposium* of the

semidivine demons that bridge the gap between the transcendent Olympian deities and mortals on earth.

Apuleius's other work of Platonist philosophy, *De Platone et Eius Dogmate* (On Plato and His Doctrine), which belongs, along with *De Mundo* (On the Universe) and the *Peri Hermeneias / De Interpretatione* (Logic), to a separate, late manuscript tradition, was intended for the library rather than the speakers' platform. This scholastic compendium of Platonic philosophy at times appears to be based on notes taken by Apuleius during his school days in Athens. The last two philosophical works derive principally from the Aristotelian school. The *Peri Hermeneias* is an imperfectly blended amalgam of Aristotelian, Stoic, and Platonic dialectics. Apuleius in the *Florida* (20) describes dialectics as the only "somewhat bitter drink" of learning that he imbibed in Athens. Aulus Gellius, who probably studied with the same teachers in Athens, describes in his *Attic Nights* (16.8) the difficulty that the subject caused for him, and, like Apuleius, he resorts to multiple sources to try to consolidate his understanding of Aristotelian logic. A final consideration is that the *Peri Hermeneias* may be the otherwise missing third volume of the *On Plato and His Doctrine.* The latter work promises to outline Platonic natural science (physics), ethics, and logic. The first two subjects are treated in its two volumes, but the third subject, logic, is missing. Its absence may imply a projected or lost third volume similar to the *Peri Hermeneias* or the *Peri Hermeneias* itself.

The last of Apuleius's philosophical treatises carries the grand title *De Mundo* (On the Universe). Like all his philosophical works, it is derivative, a free adaptation of a Greek work mistakenly ascribed to Aristotle. Philosophy alone, Apuleius instructs his son, whose name he has substituted for that of Alexander the Great in the original Greek work, is capable of probing the mysteries of the universe just as prophets disclose divine mysteries. Thus, at the outset Apuleius combines physics with divine revelation in anticipation of what he later calls "the culmination . . . of this discourse"—God; he then proceeds to "speak of the entire celestial system," the meteorology, astronomy, and geography of the Greek original, substituting a fervent paean of God, "the regulator of the universe," for the flat, abstract "unifying cause of elements" of the Greek work. The "unmoved prime-mover" is defined at the conclusion of the work in words taken from Plato's *Laws,* "God . . . penetrates the beginning, end, and middle of all things, illuminates them and is conveyed above them in his swift chariot."

Apuleius was above all a compiler and adapter, and these qualities are no less evident in his best-known work, *The Golden Ass,* than in his philosophical adaptations. He acknowledges the Greek source of his novel

The prologue to Apuleius's The Golden Ass *in the earliest extant manuscript for the work, written in the eleventh century at Monte Cassino (Ms. Laur. Plut. 68.2, c. 126; Biblioteca Medicca-Laurenziana, Florence)*

in the opening chapter, "We begin our Grecian tale." (The adjective that Apuleius uses, *Graecanica,* rather than the more customary *Graeca* (Greek), carries the connotation "adapted into Latin" rather than "translated from Greek.") The "Grecian tale," that is, the Greek *Metamorphoses,* no longer survives. However, a two-volume abridgment of its first two volumes has been transmitted in the manuscript tradition of Apuleius's Greek contemporary Lucian, and Photius, the ninth-century patriarch of Constantinople (Istanbul), provides a comparison of the Greek abridgment with the Greek original.

The first sentence of the novel establishes a source that is less direct but no less pervasive, "I would like to stitch together for your benefit various tales written in the Milesian style that you favor." Ancient accounts of Milesian tales almost uniformly characterize them as ribald. One exception to this portrayal occurs in *The Golden Ass.* The passage also shows that Apuleius (or the author of the Greek model) was mindful of the Greek author Aristides of Miletus (hence "Milesian"), who was credited with inventing the narra-

tive tradition in 100 B.C. When in the honeyed tale of Cupid and Psyche the father of Psyche consults the oracle of the "Milesian god," that is, Apollo, at Didyma near Miletus, "Apollo, although an Ionian Greek, gave his prophecy in Latin for the benefit of the compiler of this Milesian tale" (4.36). Only one word of Aristides' collection of *novelle* survives, and the nine short fragments of the Roman historian Sisenna's adaptation or translation of Aristides' work add little. From Ovid, however, the reader learns that both Aristides and Sisenna indulged in ribaldry:

> Aristides associated scandalous Milesian tales with himself. . . . Sisenna translated/adapted Aristides, and he did not suffer because he had woven ribald jests into his story (*Tristia* 2.414 and 433–444).

One can also infer from this passage that Aristides, like the dramatized narrator Lucius in *The Golden Ass,* was an actor in the scandalous events he reported. Finally, Ovid's statement suggests that, as in *The Golden Ass,* the ribald *novelle* were woven into a framing narrative. That Apuleius promises "to stitch together" a medley of Milesian tales for the readers' benefit may not be coincidental. A work attributed to Lucian reveals that Aristides also played the role of delighted recipient of stories told by others in his collection (*Erotes* 1). This narrative pattern occurs frequently in *The Golden Ass*, as in the first inset tale, where the central narrator, as in Chaucer's *Canterbury Tales* or Boccaccio's *Decameron*, represents himself as the beneficiary of a diverting tale told by a traveling companion (1.2–1.20).

Apuleius's version of the story, one of three surviving Latin novels, is the first-person account of the picaresque-like adventures of a young Greek named Lucius. While traveling to Thessaly on business he encounters two other travelers. One of them has just told "off stage" a story about his friend Socrates' disastrous entanglement with the witches for which Thessaly was notorious in antiquity. Lucius insists that the story be repeated for his benefit. The story that follows initiates two of the principal themes of *The Golden Ass*. Lucius describes himself as "thirsty for novelty" and, in order to encourage the storyteller, eager "to know everything or at least most things." This statement prefigures his "ill-starred curiosity," which the priest of the goddess Isis near the conclusion of the novel asserts has been responsible for most of his misfortunes (11.15). The second theme, that of the danger of meddling with witchcraft, provides a preview of the central narrator Lucius's calamitous encounter with a witch.

Lucius continues on his way to Thessaly, where he stays with a couple named Milo and Pamphile. On the morning of the first day of his stay with them he reflects that he is in the very town where Socrates, the subject of the story that he had heard the previous day, died at the hands of lustful witches (2.1). The behavior of his hostess ominously matches the meaning of her name (all-loving) and the reputation of Thessaly as a hotbed of witchcraft, for Pamphile turns out to be a libidinous witch who uses her magical powers to snare lovers and to punish the recalcitrant objects of her passionate desires. Fotis, the brazenly flirtatious maidservant with whom Lucius has a graphically described love affair, invites Lucius to spy on Pamphile's magical transformation of herself into an owl so that she can fly away to her lover without being detected by her husband (3.21). Lucius persuades Fotis to prepare for his use the magical ointment that her mistress had used to transform herself. Fotis proves to be incompetent, however, for when Lucius rubs the ointment on his body and spreads his arms to fly as had Pamphile:

> no down or even a little feather anywhere. Instead, the hair [on my body] became coarse and bristly, my ten-

der skin hardened into hide, at the ends of my palms my fingers lost their individuality and were all squeezed together into hooves, and from the base of my spine a huge tail extended. My face was enormous now, my mouth distended, my nostrils gaping and my lips hanging; my ears also grew grossly bristly and large. (3.24)

Lucius has become a donkey, but

> although I had become a complete donkey and a beast of burden instead of Lucius, I nevertheless retained my human intelligence. (3.26)

Most of the rest of the story depends on the interplay between Lucius's asinine appearance and the retention of his human mental and emotional faculties. Before he has a chance to eat the roses that would restore him to human form, a gang of robbers bursts into his hosts' house and takes him away to use as a pack animal to transport the booty. He passes thereafter from one usually cruel master to another, all the while passing judgment on the depraved behavior of his masters and others that his seemingly dumb asinine guise allows him to witness. An example from book 9 illustrates these narrative dynamics and the tone of the contents. Lucius's master is now a baker, whose wife and her friend exchange two tales of adultery overheard and reported by the asinine narrator. He also becomes involved in the action when his moral sensibilities are outraged by the adultery of the baker's wife and he exposes her lover's hiding place. He then steps off the pages of the novel to underscore the irony of an asinine narrator:

> But perhaps as a scrupulous reader you will criticize my account, reasoning thus: "Although you are a clever little donkey, how could you when confined to the mill know what the women did, as you insist, in secret?" Let me tell you, therefore, how I, though maintaining the appearance of a beast of burden, was curious enough to hear each detail of what was done to destroy the baker. (9.30)

The complex of inset stories and events that revolve around a young woman named Charite comprises almost a third of the novel and highlights other notable features of the narrative. The roots of the complex extend back to book 3 where, as previously mentioned, robbers take the asinine narrator to transport their booty to their hideout. A second gang of robbers joins them, and the two groups proceed to carouse and quarrel like the "semi-bestial Lapiths and Centaurs" of myth. The first group drunkenly boasts of its larcenous success and mocks the other gang's empty-handed return. The second gang defends its honor by insisting that its bolder ventures were more prone to risk, and its members tell three entertaining tales of their failed robberies to prove the point (4.9–21). Bad luck was also a factor: who could have predicted that the bearskin worn as a disguise by the robber Thrasyleon (Brave Lion) would provoke attack by a pack of hunting dogs? "Although he was approaching the last lap of his life, he did not forget us or himself or his habitual courage as he struggled against the gaping jaws of Cerberus himself."

The robbers then break camp and return in the morning with Charite, whom they have kidnapped. The Keystone Cops farce of the robbers' tales now gives way to the famous story of Cupid and Psyche. The longest of the many inset tales and literally the centerpiece of the novel, the tale of Cupid and Psyche was overheard by the asinine narrator as it was being told to comfort Charite by "that crazy and drunken . . . old woman" who served as the robbers' housekeeper. Its first two sentences have the characteristics of a fairy tale: "There were in a certain city a king and queen. They had three lovely daughters." Psyche, the youngest of the three sisters, is so beautiful that mortal men stand in awe of her and worship her as though she were the goddess Venus. The West Wind carries her to a valley, where she enters a palace "built not by human hands but by divine arts." At the end of the day she climbs into bed, and "her unknown husband was soon there and made Psyche his wife." Her sisters, meanwhile, trace her to the palace. They become jealous of her divine husband and wealth and plant the seeds of marital discord by convincing Psyche that her husband is a serpent. When he is asleep, she holds an oil lamp over him to unmask his hidden identity. She sees that her husband is "the handsome god Cupid": "Thus Psyche in her ignorance let herself fall in love with Love." He, however, because she has violated his orders that she not look at him, flies away. While she is searching for him, the goddess Venus learns that her son Cupid has a girlfriend and is all the more outraged that her son "loves Psyche, that sluttish rival to my beauty and contender to my name." She angrily confronts Psyche and insists that she perform certain tasks, the last of which requires that she go to the Underworld to fetch a flask of Proserpina's beauty. Cupid aids her in this task and, "consumed by love," appeals to Jupiter for help against his mother's intransigent vindictiveness. Jupiter ordains that Cupid and Psyche be wed "legally and in accordance with civil law" and "to them was born a child, whom we call Joy."

So ends the tale of Cupid and Psyche, with the asinine narrator expressing regret that he did not have pen and paper to record "such a pretty story." The fairy tale atmosphere of the story, in sharp contrast with the other-

Title page for a 1510 commentary on Apuleius (courtesy of the Lilly Library, Indiana University)

wise prevailing tone of lowlife realism, has raised questions about its sources. Nothing comparable appears in the Greek epitome of the ultimate source of Apuleius's version of the novel, although the epitome does retain the essential framework for such a story—a disturbed young victim of kidnapping and a housekeeper willing to comfort her. Similarities to Western European fairy and folk tales such as *Beauty and the Beast* and *Cinderella* have caught the attention of modern folklorists, but they have not been able to locate a pre-Apuleian narrative tradition that includes the eponymous protagonists and the other Olympian characters. Scholars have also studied closely the iconographic tradition, especially Roman sepulchral art, for clues to the sources of the tale. Again, they have found no parallel narrative pattern. The most likely sources appear to be Plato's *Phaedrus* and *Symposium*. These two dialogues deal with the nature of the soul and love and provide obvious equations: Cupid/Venus = love/Love, Psyche = soul/Soul. The Platonic patterning goes well beyond these obvious equations, however, as when Psyche (Soul) loses her grip on Cupid and, like the souls in Plato's *Phaedrus* that become bloated with evil and fail to ascend to the Plain of Truth, falls back to Earth.

The concluding volume (book 11) of the novel also stands in sharp contrast with the tone of what precedes and with the Greek epitome. The extant Greek version ends on a cynical note when a wealthy woman who has indulged her sexual appetites with the donkey violently expresses her disappointment that his "large . . . trailing symbol of ass[hood]" shrank along with his other asinine attributes when he regained his human form. In Apuleius's version of the story, shame at the prospect of fornicating with a woman at a public festival drives the asinine narrator to flee to the nearby port of Cenchreae, where he prays to the goddess Isis to release him from his intolerable existence. She responds to his prayer and instructs him to take from her priest's hand the roses that will restore his human form. He does so, and Lucius is "reborn." The priest places Lucius's previous experiences *sub specie aeternitatis*:

> Driven like a slave by great suffering of all kinds and buffeted by the mighty storms and tempests of Fortune, you have come at last, Lucius, to the port of Rest and the altar of Mercy. Not your birth nor even your rank nor that branch of learning in which you excel has profited you; but having slipped down into servile pleasures on the uncertain slope of hot-blooded youth, you have reaped the unfortunate reward of your ill-starred curiosity.

Apuleius's novel is difficult to classify. Is it a moral fable, a collection of *fabulae de se* intended to illustrate the dangers of dabbling in witchcraft and giving free rein to youthful lust, as the priest's pronouncement appears to suggest? Or has Apuleius cynically contrived a religious resolution to the preceding ten books of ribald levity in order to find favor with Roman readers who were more prudish than their Greek counterparts? The strangely incomplete last word of the novel contributes to the uncertainty: *obibam* (I continued to go about my business). Is the reader to suppose that Lucius's "business" will be to serve as a celibate member of the College of Pastophori in the ministry of the holy mysteries of Isis and Osiris? Or does the last word signal that he will continue to experience disappointment as he does in books 8 and 9, where the priests of the Syrian Goddess prove to be perverts and thieves?

Similar questions have troubled readers of Apuleius's novel since the time of late classical antiquity. For Macrobius in the fourth century the answer was obvious: the novel was to be relegated to the nursery; Macrobius also expresses disappointment that "Apuleius often dabbled in . . . stories filled with the fic-

tional adventures of lovers." In the fourth-century collection of biographies of Roman emperors known as the *Historia Augusta,* Septimius Severus is reported to have criticized the emperor Clodius Albinus for wasting his time on "old wives' tales and the Punic Milesian Tales of his [compatriot] Apuleius." Another of Apuleius's compatriots, St. Augustine, in a blatant example of identifying the protagonist with the author, could not decide whether Apuleius had been transformed into a donkey or only pretended to have been transformed. (In his *City of God,* St. Augustine also provides a detailed critique of Apuleius's *On the God of Socrates* in defense of the Christian position on the nature of the soul.) Interpretations of *The Golden Ass* as a moral fable began in the late fifth or early sixth century with Fulgentius, who applied a combination of Christian and Neoplatonic allegorical exegesis to the tale of Cupid and Psyche. This allegorizing tendency continued into the Renaissance. William Adlington, in the preface to the first English translation of *The Golden Ass* (1566), also translated Philippus Beroaldus's "scriptoris intentio" (writer's intention) from his commentary of 1500:

> Verily under the wrap of this transformation is taxed the life of mortal man, when as we suffer our mindes so to bee drowned in sensual lusts of the flesh, and the beastly pleasure thereof . . . that we lose wholly the use of reason and vertue. . . . So can we never bee restored to the right figure of ourselves, except we taste and eat the sweet Rose of reason and vertue.

At times Apuleius appears willfully to contribute to the uncertainty that critics have felt about his intentions. For instance, in the episode that immediately precedes the asinine narrator's anguished appeal to the goddess Isis for release from his misery he is to fornicate at a public spectacle with a woman who has been convicted of murder. The spectacle also includes the performance of the salacious pantomime "The Judgment of Paris." The narrator steps off the pages of the novel to deliver a diatribe that takes its theme from Plato's account of Socrates' trial. As in Plato's *Apology,* Palamedes and Ajax are cited as the legendary first victims of the venality of Greek justice. The elevated tone of Platonic discourse gives way in an instant to humorous relief based on the Roman comic playwright Plautus's play *Pseudolus* when a reader is imagined to object, "Look, are we now to endure a donkey philosophizing to us?"

The first printed edition of Apuleius's works (1469) was among the first dozen classical works published during the initial five years of the printing of classical texts (1465–1469). In spite of this priority and possibly because of the uncertainty about his intentions as described above, *The Golden Ass* has had less influence on the development of the novel than one might expect. The first novelists of Western Europe in the early modern period, seventeenth-century French writers such as Georges and Madeleine de Scudéry, turned instead to the ancient Greek novelists for direction. However, *The Golden Ass* was being read in Western Europe even before the age of printing. Petrarch's manuscript of the novel, annotated in his own hand, survives (Vat. Lat. 2193), and he quoted and referred to the novel in some of his works and correspondence. Boccaccio wrote an allegorical version of the tale of Cupid and Psyche and adapted three of the tales of adultery from book 9 of *The Golden Ass* for his *Decameron*. The episodic structure of Apuleius's novel found favor in the sixteenth century with the Spanish authors of two picaresque novels, *Lazarillo de Tormes* (printed, 1553) and *Guzmán de Alfarache* (printed, 1615). The best-known English-language adaptations of *The Golden Ass* are based on the tale of Cupid and Psyche. Thomas Heywood's dramatic version of it, *Loves Mistris, or the Queens Masque* (1636), was popular in the court of James I. Walter Pater's retelling of the tale in *Marius the Epicurean* (1910) continues to be read and to attract scholarly attention.

Bibliographies:

Comprehensive: Carl C. Schlam, "Scholarship on Apuleius since 1938," *Classical World,* 64 (1971): 285–309.

Oratorical Works: Benjamin L. Hijmans Jr., "Apuleius Orator: 'Pro se de Magia' and 'Florida,'" in *Aufstieg und Niedergang der römischen Welt (ANRW)* (Berlin: De Gruyter, 1994), II: 34. 2, pp. 1709–1784 .

Philosophical Works: Hijmans, "Apuleius, Philosophus Platonicus," in *ANRW* (Berlin: De Gruyter, 1987), II, 36. 1, pp. 395–475.

Golden Ass: E. Bowie and S. Harrison, "The Romance of the Novel," *Journal of Roman Studies,* 83 (1993): 159–178;

Gerald Sandy, "Apuleius' 'Metamorphoses' and the Ancient Novel," in *ANRW* (Berlin: De Gruyter, 1994), II: 34. 2, pp. 1511–1574.

References:

Graham Anderson, *Ancient Fiction* (Beckenham, U.K.: Croom Helm, 1984);

John M. Dillon, *The Middle Platonists* (London: Duckworth, 1977);

S. Gersch, *Middle Platonism and Neoplatonism: The Latin Tradition: Publications in Medieval Studies,* 23, 1–2 (Notre Dame, Ind.: University of Notre Dame Press, 1986);

Benjamin L. Hijmans Jr., ed., *Aspects of Apuleius' Golden Ass* (Groningen: Bouma, 1978);

Heinz Hofmann, ed., *Latin Fiction* (London & New York: Routledge, 1999);

Gerald Sandy, *The Greek World of Apuleius* (Leiden: E. J. Brill, 1997);

Carl C. Schlam, *The Metamorphoses of Apuleius* (Chapel Hill: University of North Carolina Press, 1992);

James Tatum, *Apuleius and "The Golden Ass"* (Ithaca, N.Y.: Cornell University Press, 1979);

Patrick Gerard Walsh, *The Roman Novel* (Cambridge: Cambridge University Press, 1970);

John J. Winkler, *Auctor & Actor: A Narratological Reading of Apuleius's "The Golden Ass"* (Berkeley: University of California Press, 1985).

Aulus Gellius

(ca. A.D. 125 – ca. A.D. 180?)

Leofranc Holford-Strevens
Oxford University Press

WORK–EXTANT: *Noctium Atticarum commentariorum libri XX,* commonly called *Noctes Atticae* (Attic Nights, ca. A.D. 180).

Editio princeps: Giovanni Andrea Bussi (Joannes Andreas de Buxis), ed. (Rome: Arnold Pannartz & Conrad Sweynheym, 1469).

Standard editions: *A. Gellii Noctium Atticarum libri XX,* 2 volumes, edited by M. J. Hertz, with the fullest apparatus (Berlin: Wilhelm Hertz, 1883–1885); *A. Gellii Noctium Atticarum libri XX,* 2 volumes, edited by C. Hosius, with parallel passages (Leipzig: Teubner, 1903); *Aulu-Gelle: Les nuits attiques,* 3 volumes, books 1–15 edited by René Marache, books 16–20 edited by Yvette Julien (Paris: Les Belles Lettres, 1967–1998); *A. Gellii Noctes Atticae,* 2 volumes, edited by P. K. Marshall (Oxford: Clarendon Press, 1968; reprinted, with corrections, 1990); *Aulo-Gellio: Le notte attiche,* books 1–13.18, 7 volumes to date, edited by Franco Cavazza (Bologna: Zanichelli, 1985–1996); and *Le Notti Attiche di Aulo Gellio,* 2 volumes, edited by G. Bernardi Perini (Turin: U.T.E.T., 1992; revised, 1996).

Translation in English: *Aulus Gellius,* 3 volumes, translated by John C. Rolfe, Loeb Classical Library (London: Heinemann, 1927; revised, 1946).

The Roman miscellanist Aulus Gellius was the author of the *Noctes Atticae* (ca. A.D. 180?), a collection of mainly brief expositions, based on notes or excerpts he had made in the course of reading about particular topics in a variety of fields such as philosophy, history, and law, but above all, grammar as the Greeks and Romans understood it, the study of language and literature at large. Apart from preserving much information and many literary fragments that would otherwise have been lost, the work bears theoretical and practical witness to the so-called archaizing movement of the second century A.D. and has not lost its capacity to charm readers by its elegance and variety of exposition.

Aulus Gellius (woodcut in Hartman Schedel's Nuremberg Chronicles, *1493)*

In late antiquity and the Middle Ages, Gellius was often known as "Agellius," an attested but very rare name; some humanists maintained that this form, not "A. Gellius," was correct. However, the older manuscripts of the *Noctes Atticae* have "A. Gellii," and in both Servius proper (*Aen.* 5.738) and the expanded commentary (*Geo.* 1.260) the name is spelled out as "Aulus Gellius." Since the mid seventeenth century scholars have agreed that "Aulus Gellius" is the true form; the objection that he was never called "Gellius" alone is falsified by Fronto and a surreptitious citation in the *Historia Augusta.*

Although some scholars have sought to associate the author with the senatorial Gellii of the later Republic, his anecdotes reveal him as a man on the lower reaches of good society, who, though he observes a house fire from the landlord's, not the tenant's point of view (15.1), is always the guest and never the host and who shows a tendency to drop names. When at 16.13.2 he asks rhetorically, "Quotus enim fere *nostrum* est, qui cum ex colonia populi Romani sit . . ." (For how many *of us* are there who, though coming from a colony of the Roman people . . .), Latin usage, stricter than English, implies that he too was among the number; moreover, a provincial *colonia* is a likely milieu for a family sufficiently old-fashioned still not to have adopted a cognomen. In the nineteenth century scholars argued that since Gellius wrote in a style whose other exponents—Fronto, Apuleius, and Tertullian—all came from North Africa, that style was "African Latin" and therefore Gellius too was African; the reasoning is circular, but the conclusion possibly correct, for in 8.13 he discusses a word used by "homines Afri" (people from [the Roman province of] Africa). The word is *cupsones* (apparently meaning "caves"), found elsewhere only in the African St. Augustine and in a thoroughly African context. Since the text of the chapter is lost, however, and since many prominent Romans of the day came from Africa, the argument is uncertain; in any case, Gellius was either born at Rome or taken there as a child.

Of his childhood Gellius mentions nothing; the earliest event in his life that he mentions is his taking the *toga virilis* (a toga of manhood; at age fifteen or later) and choosing for his teacher C. Sulpicius Apollinaris of advanced *grammatica* ("Latin studies" rather than "grammar," 18.4). The only evidence for chronology is in Gellius's own text, especially his anecdotes; since many of them are or may be fictitious, scholars have assumed that, like Cicero and unlike Plato, Gellius took care to locate his characters in the right place at the right time. This is only a working hypothesis, but so far it has not been falsified; on this basis he had become Sulpicius's pupil by A.D. 145 at the latest and the devoted follower of the philosopher Favorinus by A.D. 146. He also studied rhetoric with two of the leading teachers of the time, T. Castricius and Antonius Julianus, and made the acquaintance of the great orator and imperial tutor M. Cornelius Fronto, whom he often visited in his spare time (19.8.1); in order to allow a reasonable time for these studies, a date of birth between A.D. 125 and A.D. 128 seems most likely.

In the course of his studies Gellius spent at least three seasons of a year in Greece (he makes no mention of spring), but possibly more than a year, during which he attended the Pythian Games of A.D. 147 (or perhaps 151). In Athens he studied both rhetoric and philosophy. No names of any rhetors who taught him on a formal basis are known, but he visited Herodes Atticus in his summer retreat at Cephisia (1.2, 18.10); Favorinus and Fronto, both friends of Herodes, may have recom-

mended Gellius, but his talents also spoke for him, though he does not claim to have been part of the inner circle known as the Klepsydrion, or Water Clock (Philostratus, *Vita sophistarum* 585). In philosophy he was a pupil of L. Calvenus Taurus, a Platonist from Berytus (now Beirut), who after initial suspicion that Gellius was interested only in rhetoric, included him in his inner circle of pupils. Gellius's acceptance in this circle was not due to his having any special aptitude for the subject; it was rather perhaps due to solidarity between fellow Romans, for Berytus was highly conscious of its Roman origins and heritage, and Taurus is portrayed in 2.2 as solving a problem of Roman etiquette on purely Roman, not philosophical, lines. While in Athens, Gellius visited the purported cave of Euripides on Salamis (15.20.5) and went to hear the Cynic philosopher Peregrinus (8.3, 12.11), whom, unlike Lucian, he admired; he may have been initiated in the Mysteries, for Eleusis is the setting for the lost grammatical discussion in 8.10.

In 19.12 Gellius reports Herodes' defense of his mourning for an unnamed boy, taken to be his foster son Vibullius Polydeucion; a proposed redating of Polydeucion's death has caused Walter Ameling to set Gellius's visit ca. A.D. 165. The case is not secure; it would, if accepted, require that Gellius made a second visit, for his picture of his student life is that of a young man among young men. When, returning on the night boat from Aegina to Piraeus, he asks the Roman youths to explain the Latin name for the Big Dipper, he begins, "Quin vos opici dicitis mihi" (Why don't you hicks tell me, 2.21.4), using a Greek term for ignorant Italians; only among equals are such insults friendly. On the seventh day of the Athenian months (15.2.3), the young men feasted in honor of the young man's god, Apollo. (They also kept the Roman Saturnalia, with intellectual amusements: 18.2, 18.13.)

On returning to Rome, Gellius buried himself in his books until he was enrolled among the *iudices* available for private cases (at age twenty-five or later); there is no sign that he took any other part in public life. He maintained contact with Sulpicius Apollinaris and Favorinus, of whom the former died in the A.D. 150s and the latter probably ca. A.D. 165; he continued to read and study in his leisure hours, making—or so he says—a list of military terms while riding in a carriage (10.25) and meditating on the preposition *pro* while taking an evening walk at Praeneste (11.3). He reveals nothing of his domestic life beyond the statement in his preface (§1) that his miscellany is intended "liberis meis" (for my children) to read in their leisure time, "negotiorum aliqua interstitione data" (where they get an interval in their affairs); although *liberi* (as he observes in 2.13) may be used of a single child, he may

Palimpsest of Aulus Gellius's Noctes Atticae *in a codex on vellum (sec. V d.C. Scrittura capitale, Biblioteca Apostolica Vaticana; Vat. Pal. Lat. 24, ff. 110v + 109r)*

have obtained dispensation from judicial duties by fathering three children, of whom at least one was an adult and was occupied like any good Roman by *negotia*.

One of several indications that publication took place late in the century is that in stating that Herodes (A.D. 101–177) excelled all contemporary Greek orators (19.12.1), Gellius uses not the imperfect "praestabat" (which might mean only "when I knew him") but the aorist "praestitit," summing up the achievement of one already dead. (Other evidence is given in Leofranc Holford-Strevens, "Chronology," in *Aulus Gellius,* pp. 13–19.) An apparent echo in Apuleius's *Apology* (9.8), sometimes used to support an earlier date, may be due to personal acquaintance either at Rome, as suggested in Holford-Strevens's "Chronology" or in Athens, as suggested in Gerald N. Sandy's "West Meets East: Western Students in Athens in the Mid-Second Century A.D." in volume 5 of *Groningen Colloquia on the Novel;* less likely is a common source. Gellius did not live to fulfill

his intention of adding further books in the future (preface, 23–24).

He called his miscellany *Noctes Atticae* (Attic Nights) because he began to endow his reading notes with literary form (preface 4) during the long winter's nights at Athens. An irritable letter written by Fronto to Claudius Julianus (*Ad amicos* 1.19), governor of Lower Germany ca. A.D. 160, suggests that Gellius already entertained the intention of publishing, though detailed interpretation remains obscure: "Non agnovi ista mea ab Gellio pessime quaeri: credideris admonuisse se edere" (translated something like "I didn't realize that Gellius was after my stuff so badly; you'd have thought he'd have warned me he was publishing"); a later hand has substituted "aptissime" (most appropriately) for "pessime," thus producing a far less plausible sentence. There is no reason to doubt that this reference is to A. Gellius, for G. W. Bowersock has shown that the L. Gellius to whom Arrian dedicated his transcripts of Epictetus was L. Gellius Menander of Corinth. In view of this petulant letter, Gellius's motive for concentrating three of the five Frontonian chapters in the last book but one may have been to emphasize, or even exaggerate, their former intimacy.

The *Noctes Atticae* comprises twenty books, which were probably composed in four hundred chapters; the start of the preface is missing, as are the end of book 20 and all of the eighth book except the chapter headings, preserved only in fifteenth-century manuscripts. When Gellius's text resurfaced in Carolingian times, it had been divided into two parts, one comprising the preface and books 1–7, the other books 9–20; the former is preserved in four medieval manuscripts, none earlier than the twelfth century, and the latter in nine, of which two date from the early ninth century. In addition, there are more than one hundred manuscripts from the fifteenth century, which combine both parts, as did a fourth-century manuscript partially surviving as a palimpsest and a lost manuscript at Louvain.

The length, both of books and of chapters, varies considerably; this unevenness is deliberate on the author's part, accompanying a similar pursuit of variety in subject matter, mode of presentation, and manner of expression, which adds to the charm of the work. Although he professes to have written up his notes in the same chance order as he had made them, this claim is a cliché in programmatic statements about such miscellanies, which were a popular and established genre; there are signs of deliberate disruption, both to the sequence of extracts from the same work (even within a chapter) and to the chronology of Gellius's own life as represented in his reminiscences.

Gellius—like Fronto, Apuleius, and Tertullian—employs a style fashionable in the second century A.D. and often described as "archaizing," although archaism is only one and not always the most prominent feature, and there was never an attempt, as among Greek Atticists and Italian humanists, to reproduce wholesale the language of a bygone age. (Even worse names are "African Latin" and *elocutio novella;* better would be "mannerist.") Under Hadrian, the early authors ignored or mocked by mainstream writers from Horace to Martial had returned to fashion; writing was affected by reading, so that even Suetonius, often said to be free from archaism, employs such expressions as *miscellus* (mixed), previously confined to the agricultural writings of Cato and Varro; *nemo quisquam* (no one at all); and *prosapia* (lineage), a word twice condemned by Quintilian as unusable. Suetonius used such words by osmosis; others used them by choice.

The essence of the style is the search for what Fronto calls "insperata atque inopinata verba" (unlooked for and unexpected words) that nobody would ever

guess (*Epist. M. Caes.* 4.3.3, p. 57); it is necessary to seek out such terms as a recruiter seeks out draft dodgers (*De eloquentia* 2.2, pp. 133–134). A word lifted from an ancient author serves the purpose, provided it can still be understood (both Fronto and Gellius 11.7 warn against obscurity); Gellius combs early Latin authors like Claudius Quadrigarius (17.2), a historian from the first century B.C. who is among his favorite authors, and the early poet Laevius (19.7) for useful words that he can drop into his own writing—and he duly uses some of them along with other words that he discusses elsewhere or that form part of his quotations. Thus, at 19.8.15—the passage that has given modern languages the word-group "classic"—Gellius proposes a search for certain usages in any of the older authors, "id est classicus adsiduusque aliquis scriptor, non proletarius" (that is to say, a first-class, substantial citizen of an author, not one from the lower orders). He discusses *classicus* and *proletarius* at 6.13 and 16.10, respectively, to illustrate passages from Cato the Elder and Ennius; in the latter chapter he also treats *adsiduus* in its legal sense.

The Atticists' desire to use only words attested in good authors has a Latin counterpart in Gellius's concern for the language of "qui ante diui Augusti aetatem pure atque integre locuti sunt" (those who had a pure and sound style before the time of the Divine Augustus, 13.6.4): in 8.2 he and Favorinus exchanged lists of Latin and Greek words in common use but not found in approved authors. Not only does Gellius devote several chapters to such questions, but he also reverts to certain usages still normal or regular in Cicero, but rare after him, such as *septentriones* (north), *supervacaneus* (unnecessary), for later *septentrio, supervacuus* (which was censured by Varro). He construes *plenus* (full of) only with the genitive, never the ablative, a strictness not attained by Cicero himself; makes letter names neuter as in Cicero and Varro, not feminine as in Quintilian; and uses *dies* in the feminine only as in Republican Latin for a limiting day determined in advance (which at 1.25.15–16 he hypercorrectly makes masculine). However, such purism is intermittent: he permits himself Imperial usages such as *iactantia* (boastfulness) or *tamquam* (just as if), introducing a dubious assertion, and post-Silver Latin turns such as *petitu* (at the request of) and *quod* clauses in which classical usage required the accusative and infinitive. He even uses *harenae* (sands) in the plural, contrary to the teaching of 19.8, and *soloecismus* (solecism, syntactical error), despite 5.20.

Moreover, Gellius (unlike Fronto, *De orationibus* 14) has no objection to the coining of new words; when in 18.11 he maintains, against a grammarian's objections, that coinages by the poet Furius Antias are within poets' rights, he may not have only poets in mind. Although words not previously attested can be found in

Fronto, there are far more in Gellius, including such now-familiar words as *positivus* and *retaliare,* and such manifest calques on the Greek as *incongelabilis* (ἄπηκτος, freezeproof) and *inpeccabilis* (ἀναμάρτητος, sinless); first attestation need not be first use, but some at least are likely to be his inventions. He also gives existing words new senses, using *discerniculum* (barrette) for "distinguishing feature," and *genuinus* (inborn) for "authentic" (as in the English "genuine").

Paired or grouped synonyms, favored in Republican Latin, had been used with more restraint in the early Empire but had now come back into fashion; Gellius revels in them even more than did Cato or Cicero. The first sentence of book 1 reports that Plutarch "scite subtiliterque ratiocinatum Pythagoram philosophum dicit in reperienda modulandaque status longitudinisque eius praestantia" (says that the philosopher Pythagoras reasoned astutely and subtly in finding and calculating the preeminence of [Hercules'] stature and height). Gellius is also given to variation: wishing to say that the Spartans prepared two message-sticks equal in thickness and length, he writes "pari crassamento eiusdemque longitudinis" (17.9.7), using different cases, different suffixes, and different words of identity. In one short passage (19.8.11–17) there are six different expressions for using a noun in the singular; in the work as a whole there are six different phrases for visiting a sick friend. Variety, synonymy, archaism, and neologism are all illustrated at pref. 5, where Gellius describes the learning included in his work as "variam et miscellam et quasi confusaneam": the three adjectives all mean "assorted," but the first is in common currency; the second is archaic; and the third, apologized for by "quasi," is found only in this passage, though it has been plausibly conjectured to have appeared in Fronto's works.

In some chapters Gellius simply states what he has to say; in others he presents an idea as the recollection either of a dialogue or of a statement by one of his teachers. Some authors are inclined to take such chapters at face value; others dismiss them all as fictions intended purely to enliven his learned expositions; the latter are closer to the truth. Fiction is certainly to be posited when, as often happens, the narrative is not sustained; it was taken for granted by writers who inserted Gellian material in anecdotal frameworks of their own. Nevertheless, to suppose that Gellius never allowed himself to describe events in his own life is unwise; at the very least, 17.20, in which Taurus's accusation that Gellius is a ῥητορίσκος (little rhetorician) who has come to Athens purely in order to improve his eloquence and still needs to learn that he must perpend not Plato's style but his thought, stimulates him to make a Latin translation of the very passage of Plato

that had occasioned the remark, seems more easily understood as naive self-revelation based on an actual incident than as pure invention wantonly proclaiming lack of interest in philosophy. In general, however, Gellius must be taken as dramatizing a piece of information he has taken from a book; yet, the settings are likely to bear some relation to real experience–if not the particular conversations, then others like them may be supposed to have taken place. In any case, the characters of Gellius's friends and teachers are finely drawn; the fictitious persons are less individual.

The ancient author of dialogues, however, was under no obligation to make his characters express only those opinions, or reveal only those interests, that they did in real life. This fact is particularly relevant to Gellius's representation of Fronto, whose five appearances show him citing Virgil for his careful use of words (2. 26.11,18), professing love of Claudius Quadrigarius (13.29.3), and discussing the Latinity of certain usages (19.8,10,13). Whereas Gellius admires Virgil and provides almost half of all known quotations from Quadrigarius, Fronto's surviving works ignore the poet and barely mention the historian; for all his interest in words and lack of interest in Imperial authors, moreover, Fronto neither accepts nor rejects words according to their attestation. The grammarian judges words by their authority; the writer does so on their merits and reads his favored authors because he expects to find good words in them. On the other hand, in 2.26 the Gellian character Fronto distinguishes between various words for "red" as in *Epist. M. Caes.* 4.3.4–5 where he distinguishes between words for washing and smearing; in 13.29 he identifies the nuance conveyed by saying *multi mortales* instead of *multi homines* for "many people," while warning his hearers not to use the phrase indiscriminately; and at 19.8.18 his injunction that his guests should look for disputed usages in classic authors is said to have been made "ut nobis studium lectitandi in quaerendis rarioribus uerbis exerceret" (in order to develop in his audience the desire to read in the quest for unusual words). All these things are consistent with the Fronto of the letters; Gellius has blended his own concerns and interests with those of the person described. The same may well be true of the chapters concerning Favorinus, especially those dealing with Roman matters.

Whereas earlier scholars had treated every text mentioned by Gellius as a book read, in the second half of the nineteenth century source critics turned him into a mere epigone copying from a handful of previous writers, whom they attempted to identify. Many scholars had their favored author, such as Probus or Favorinus, to whom unattributed material was assigned as a first resource; their contradictory results were listed by

Hosius in the preface to his Teubner text; they even propounded sources for the lost chapters of book 8. In particular, they attempted to ascertain which works of Greek and Latin literature Gellius had read for himself on the basis of criteria used for distinguishing direct and indirect quotation; none of these standards is entirely reliable, not even Ludwig Mercklin's principle that Gellius was likelier to have read works cited by title than those assigned to author alone, nor does it follow, either that if Gellius takes a grammatical example from another scholar, he never read the work from which the latter cited it, or that if he took over a fact from a source, he also took over the writer's comment. Some scholars have also conjectured that when Gellius cites words supposedly spoken by his teachers, he is in fact quoting from their writings; he may often quote their writings, but sometimes he may be recalling things actually heard, at other times fathering on them things they never said at all. More recently there has been a reaction against source criticism that is in some danger of reverting to precritical naïveté: while taking the work as it is remains a valid mode of literary criticism, it is unacceptable in any discourse requiring a base in biographical fact, whether concerning Gellius or others. Besides, another mode of literary criticism seeks to examine the use that Gellius makes of his materials.

Gellius claims to have selected only useful matter for inclusion; the profession of utility is not false but requires a generous interpretation. In 14.6 Gellius says the criterion is to be ethical, but in the preface he says the stated aim is to lead the mind by a short cut to a love of learning and the study of useful arts, or rescue those engaged in their affairs from boorish ignorance of things and words (§12); he gives elementary information on subjects that should be known to a *vir civiliter eruditus* (a man with the education of a citizen; pref. 13), as opposed to the narrow specialist.

Nevertheless, although Gellius expects the grammarian to know law and the lawyer to know grammar, it is grammar (or rather *grammatica*) in which he is at home. He shows the expected interest in unusual words, meanings, and constructions from the older writers; but he pays greater attention to syntax than any extant Latin author before Priscian. He speaks with scorn of half-educated grammarians who lay down prescriptive rules without knowing Early Latin or who rely on reason without regard to authority. He is interested in the textual criticism of Latin authors, often having recourse to allegedly ancient or even original manuscripts. He is well read in Latin literature from Plautus and Cato down to Sallust and Virgil; his most individual quirk is his fondness (already noted) for Claudius Quadrigarius. Unlike Hadrian and even Fronto, he will not hear a word against Cicero; but he takes little inter-

est in the letters (which Fronto preferred to the speeches) and quotes the speeches for their language—on both the grammatical and the rhetorical plane—rather than for their forensic craft. It is symptomatic that Gellius cites Cicero's *Pro Cluentio* (regarded in the schools as his finest work) and *Pro Milone* (also a favorite source of technical examples) only once apiece, and that for grammatical purposes; not being an advocate, Gellius prefers the grander flights of the *Verrines* and the *Philippics* (or as he insists on calling them, the *Antonianae*). Similarly, in 10.3 he finds the plain style of Gaius Gracchus less appealing than the grand style of Cato and Cicero and even essays it himself; however, the negative evidence of his quotations shows him less receptive to high pathos in verse. Gellius does not find Virgil beyond criticism but usually praises him, both for his care with words and for his recondite but unobtrusive erudition. He barely notices Horace and does not notice Ovid at all; he ignores later literature, in the narrow sense, except when in 12.2 he condemns Seneca for scornful comments on Ennius and for his influence on Cicero and Virgil.

In Greek, Gellius has read Homer (which could be taken for granted) and also some Homeric scholarship; he shows some acquaintance with the works of Herodotus and Thucydides, Aeschines' *In Timarchum,* and Demosthenes' *De corona;* most of his philosophical reading was in Greek. He is familiar with two comedies, Aristophanes' *Frogs* and Menander's *Plocion,* but though in 13.19 he claims firsthand knowledge of tragedy (little studied in Imperial Rome), it cannot be proved. Other quotations, particularly of Greek poetry imitated by Virgil, may well come from secondary sources, although that is not to say that his judgments on Virgil's renderings do. In detailed discussions, though not always in passing comments, he approaches any passage of Latin modeled on a Greek original as an exercise in translation and finds it wanting (Amiel D. Vardi, *Diiudicatio*). Translation is a recurrent theme (Leopoldo Gamberale); he himself translates with considerable subtlety (Beall, "Translation"). Gellius's scholarly interests in Greek are often directed to comparison with Latin and do not extend to collating manuscripts; the only manuscript he claims to have consulted in Greece is one of Livius Andronicus's Latin translations, of the *Odyssey,* at the Roman colony of Patrae.

Although Gellius writes about history, law, and philosophy, he is not a historian, a lawyer, or a philosopher. He treats history as a resource for anecdotes and moral lessons; even when in 10.27 he offers the conventional judgment that the second Punic War was a battle for world domination, his real interest is in the colorful story about a diplomatic exchange that preceded it (complete with a scholarly note recording a different

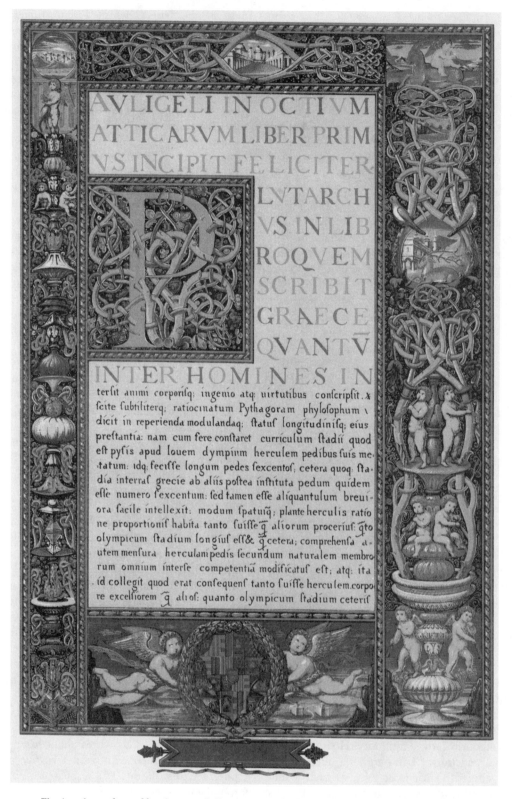

Illuminated page from a fifteenth-century Italian manuscript for Gellius's Noctes Atticae *(British Library)*

version). In fact, he has a particular taste for tales concerning embassies and also for stern punishments in the earlier days of Rome; the former seems to be a hobby for its own sake, but the latter, indulged under humane emperors, suggests dissatisfaction with the trivial cases that came his way.

That Gellius should retail stories of ancient Roman virtue seems so unsurprising that their absence from Fronto and Apuleius is worth recalling, despite the long-standing association between archaic diction and antique virtue. Aware that in the wrong hands the use of archaic words often creates obscurity, Gellius relates in 1.10 that Favorinus rebuked a young man who affected obsolete usages because he admired antiquity for its moral excellence: he should live by ancient morals but use present-day words. The virtuous ancestors, he says, were culturally backward (15.11.3, compare with 15.11.2).

Gellius's legal reading is largely out of date; his favorite authors are Ateius Capito and Masurius Sabinus, who both flourished in the early Principate, and he is more interested in the law as it used to be and in the light that lawyers shed on language and literature than in current legal questions. He reports two of his cases, both of which show dissatisfaction with purely legal norms. In one (12.13), appointed by the consuls with instructions to pronounce a verdict "intra Kalendas" (by the first of the month), he asked Sulpicius Apollinaris whether that included the limiting day; although Sulpicius told him to follow legal authority (according to which it did), the linguistic merits are debated at some length. In the other (14.2), studied in detail by Dieter Nörr, the plaintiff claimed recovery of an undocumented debt. Professional opinion was hostile, but Gellius, inclined to believe him on grounds of moral character, consulted Favorinus, who urged him to find for the better man; but feeling too young and diffident, Gellius declared a *non liquet* (not proven). For Gellius, this was an ethical problem on which legal textbooks had nothing to say; Nörr compares Gellius's desire for guiding principles (§3) with his complaint in 1.3 that neither Theophrastus nor Cicero gives clear rules on the extent to which one might bend strict morality for a friend. These are outsiders' grievances; on the other hand, Gellius expresses contempt for simplistic grammatical rules.

Despite some elementary interest in logic and the natural sciences, Gellius regards as a waste of time philosophy not directed to practical life and professing to find more merit in the words of ancient Romans than in the sayings of philosophers, many of whom do not live up to their words. He is, however, greatly impressed with the moral seriousness, not only of Musonius and Epictetus, but of Peregrinus Proteus, who according to

Lucian was just such a humbug as Gellius ought to have despised. Higher speculation lies outside his range; of Plato's *Timaeus*, on which Taurus had written a commentary, Gellius shows no knowledge, even in Cicero's translation (in which he would have found the Latin equivalents for the Greek proportional terms he calls untranslatable at 18.14). Although the pupil of a Platonist and an Academic, Gellius is more inclined toward Stoicism, though he is uncertain how far its characteristic doctrine of impassibility could or should be taken; but his lack of philosophical commitment allows him both to cite a hostile comment on Epicurus's denial of Providence (9.5.8) and to defend him against Plutarch's logic-chopping (2.8–9).

Gellius is described by St. Augustine (*City of God* 9.4) as "vir elegantissimi eloquii et multae undecumque scientiae" (a man of most exquisite style and much knowledge from all quarters). He is explicitly cited by Lactantius, Servius, Priscian, and St. Gregory of Tours; he was diligently read (though not named) by Nonius Marcellus, Ammianus, and Macrobius, and was known probably to Tertullian and certainly to Minucius Felix, though no echo has been found in St. Jerome or St. Isidore. Gellius was known to Carolingian scholars; many subsequent quotations are taken from florilegia, but some medieval authors clearly knew him at first hand. In the Renaissance he was not only a source of fact but a model for humanistic writing; although his reputation declined when scholars had extracted the information he had to offer and lost sympathy with the Antonines, Gellius's work continued to find devoted readers, often outside the classical profession. His fame spread even to Russia, where in the early eighteenth century a learned circle called its meetings *Noctes Atticae,* and in 1787 the first complete translation of his work into any modern language was published. In recent decades, it has met with renewed interest among scholars, less constrained by canonical classicism.

References:

Walter Ameling, "Aulus Gellius in Athen," *Hermes,* 112 (1984): 484–490;

Gordon Anderson, "Aulus Gellius: A Miscellanist and his World," *Aufstieg und Niedergang der römischen Welt* II, 34, no. 2 (Berlin & New York: De Gruyter, 1994), pp. 1834–1862;

Maria Laura Astarita, *La Cultura nelle: Noctes Atticae* (Catania: Centro di studi sull'antico cristianesimo, Università di Catania, 1993);

Astarita, "Un'evoluzione nei recenti studi su Aulo Gellio," *Bollettino di studi latini,* 25 (1995): 172–188;

Barry Baldwin, *Studies in Aulus Gellius* (Lawrence, Kan.: Coronado Press, 1975);

Stephen Michael Beall, "*Civilis eruditio:* Style and Content in the 'Attic Nights' of Aulus Gellius," dissertation, University of California at Berkeley, 1988;

Beall, "Translation in Aulus Gellius," *Classical Quarterly,* new series 47 (1997): 195–206;

G. W. Bowersock, "A New Inscription of Arrian," *Greek, Roman, and Byzantine Studies,* 8 (1967): 279–280;

Leopoldo Gamberale, *La traduzione in Gellio* (Rome: Edizioni dell'Ateneo, 1969);

Madeleine M. Henry, "On the Aims and Purposes of Aulus Gellius' 'Noctes Atticae,'" *Aufstieg und Niedergang der römischen Welt,* II, 34, no. 2 (Berlin & New York: De Gruyter, 194), pp. 1918–1941;

Leofranc Holford-Strevens, "Analecta Gelliana," *Classical Quarterly,* new series 43 (1993): 292–297;

Holford-Strevens, *Aulus Gellius* (London: Duckworth, 1988; Chapel Hill: University of North Carolina Press, 1989);

Holford-Strevens, "Aulus Gellius: The Non-Visual Portraitist," in *Portraits: Biographical Representation in the Greek and Latin Literature of the Roman Empire,* edited by Mark Edwards and Simon Swain (Oxford: Oxford University Press, 1997), pp. 93–116;

Holford-Strevens, "Elocutio Novella," *Classical Quarterly,* new series 26 (1976): 140–141;

Holford-Strevens, "Fact and Fiction in Aulus Gellius," *Liverpool Classical Monthly,* 7 (May 1982): 65–68;

Holford-Strevens, "Favorinus: The Man of Paradoxes," in *Philosophia Togata II: Plato and Aristotle at Rome,* edited by Jonathan Barnes and Miriam Griffin (Oxford: Oxford University Press, 1997), pp. 188–217;

Holford-Strevens, "More Notes on Aulus Gellius," *Liverpool Classical Monthly,* 9 (December 1984): 146–151;

Holford-Strevens, "Towards a Chronology of Aulus Gellius," *Latomus,* 36 (1977): 93–109;

Marie-Luise Lakmann, *Der Platoniker Taurus in der Darstellung des Aulus Gellius* (Leiden: Brill, 1995);

René Marache, *La Critique littéraire de langue latine et le développement du goût archaïsant au IIe siècle de notre ère* (Rennes: Plihon, 1952);

Marache, *Mots nouveaux et mots archaïques chez Fronton et Aulu-Gelle* (Paris: Presses Universitaires de France, 1957);

Giorgio Maselli, *Lingua e scuola in Gellio grammatico* (Lecce: Milella, 1979);

Ludwig Mercklin, "Die Citiermethode und Quellenbenutzung des A. Gellius in den Noctes Atticae," *Jahrbücher für die classische Philologie,* supplement 3 (1857–1860): 635–710;

Dieter Nörr, "L'esperienza giuridica di Gellio (Noctes Atticae XIV 2)," in *Atti di convegni Lincei 125: Convegno internazionale Filellenismo e tradizionalismo a Roma nei primi due secoli dell'Impero: Roma 27–28 aprile 1995* (Rome: Accademia nazionale dei Lincei, 1996), pp. 33–56;

Paolo Soverini, *Tra retorica e politica in età imperiale* (Bologna: CLUEB, 1988), pp. 201–220;

Amiel D. Vardi, "*Diiudicatio locorum:* Gellius and the History of a Mode in Ancient Comparative Criticism," *Classical Quarterly,* new series 46 (1996): 492–514;

Vardi, "Why *Attic Nights?* or What's in a Name?" *Classical Quarterly,* new series 43 (1993): 298–301;

D. W. T. Vessey, "Aulus Gellius and the Cult of the Past," *Aufstieg und Niedergang der römischen Welt,* II. 34.2 (Berlin & New York: De Gruyter, 1994), pp. 1863–1917;

Marinus A. Wes, *Classics in Russia 1700–1855: Between Two Bronze Horsemen* (Leiden: Brill, 1992), pp. 31–32.

Cato the Elder

(234 B.C. – 149 B.C.)

Ward Briggs
University of South Carolina

MAJOR WORKS–EXTANT: *De agri cultura,* 170 chapters (On Agriculture, ca. 160 B.C.).

MAJOR WORKS–FRAGMENTARY: *Origines,* 7 books (History of Rome from its Beginnings, ca. 169–150 B.C.);

Orationes, (Orations 150; 80 titles and fragments remain, see Malcovati);

Apophthegmata (Memorable Sayings).

MAJOR WORKS–LOST: *De disciplina militari* (On Military Training);

Libri ad filium de agri cultura (Books for His Son on Agriculture);

De medicina (On Medicine);

Carmen de moribus (Poem On Morals).

Editio princeps: *Marci Catonis prisci de re rustica liber,* edited by Georgius Merula (Venice: Nicolaus Jenson, 1472).

Standard editions:

SPEECHES: *Oratorum Romanorum Fragmenta liberae re publicae,* edited by Enrica Malcovati, second edition (Turin: Paravia, 1955), pp. 12–97.

ORIGINES: *Historicorum Romanorum reliquiae,* edited by Hermann W. G. Peter (Leipzig: Teubner, 1906–1914), pp. cxxvii–clxiv, 55–97; *M. Porci Catonis De agri cultura,* 3 volumes, edited by Heinrich Keil (Leipzig: Teubner, 1882–1902); *M. Porci Catonis De agri cultura,* edited by Antonio Mazzarino (Leipzig: Teubner, 1962); *Caton. De l' agriculture,* edited and translated by Raoul Goujard (Paris: Société des Belles Lettres, 1975).

MINOR WORKS: *M. Catonis praeter librum De re rustica quae extant,* edited by Heinrich Jordan (Leipzig: Teubner, 1860).

Translations in English: *Cato the Censor on Farming,* translated by Ernest Brehaut (New York: Columbia University Press, 1933); *Cato and Varro on Agriculture,* translated by William Davis Hooper and Harrison Boyd Ash, Loeb Classical Library (Cambridge, Mass.: Harvard University Press, 1934).

Cato the Elder (bust discovered at Volubilis in North Africa)

Commentaries: Maria Teresa Sblendorio Cugusi, *M. Porci Catonis Orationum Reliquiae* (Turin: Paravia, 1982); *M. Porci Catonis Oratio pro Rhodiensibus,* edited by Gualtiero Calboli (Bologna: Patron, 1978); *M. Porcius Cato, Das Erste Buch der Origines,* edited by W. A. Schroder (Meisenheim am Glan: A. Hain, 1971); *Caton, les Origines,* edited and translated by Martine Chassignet (Paris: Société des Belles Lettres, 1986).

Marcus Porcius Cato was one of the legendary figures of Roman literature and history. He is important to literature as the founder of Roman history and the man who, according to Columella, taught agriculture to speak Latin. What has come down to present-day readers from his *De agri cultura* (ca. 160 B.C.) represents the first surviving piece of Latin prose. His severity in adhering to the morality of the old (pre-Punic

Wars) Republic in administering his office as "Censor" set a standard that virtually defined the office and caused him to be known to the present day as "Cato the Censor." He is also called Cato Maior (Cato the Elder) to distinguish him from his great-grandson, the first-century philosopher Cato Uticensis (95–46 B.C.). Thanks to his political career, more of his life is known than that of many other minor literary figures, largely through Cornelius Nepos, Plutarch, and the fourth-century A.D. *De Viris Illustribus* (On Famous Men), as well as Cicero's *Cato Maior de senectute* (On Cato or On Old Age, 45 or 44 B.C.) and *De re publica* (On the Republic, 54–51 B.C.).

Plutarch says that Cato's name was originally Marcus Valerius Priscus, but that later in life he was given the name "Cato" because of his wisdom and experience (*catus* means shrewd or prudent). He was born to plebeian parents at Tusculum, fifteen miles southeast of Rome, in 234 B.C. Though Cato says that his ancestors distinguished themselves in battle for Rome, there is no record of his family name before him, though it became truly distinguished with him. He was left a smallholding in the Sabine territory, where he spent much of his youth. Near his farm was the residence of Manius Curius Dentatus, "the greatest Roman of his day" (according to Plutarch), who had saved his country by driving King Pyrrhus from Italy in 275 B.C. during the Samnite War (298–290 B.C.). On visits to Curius, Cato was impressed as much by the frugality of this great hero's lifestyle, by his contentment with seven acres of land after conquering a rich and powerful foe, and by his rejection of material things ("It is better to conquer men who own gold than to own it oneself."), as by the efficiency of Curius's management of his estate. Cato's neighbor's life thus became the ideal for which he strove. As Cato developed into maturity, he examined his own farm, his own way of life, and especially his own values in light of what he had learned from Curius. Mornings found Cato in one of the small local towns performing what today is called pro bono legal work, defending clients in need without accepting any fees. In the afternoon he devoted himself to his farm, where he worked in the fields with the servants, bare-chested in the summer, wearing only a sleeveless cloak in the winter. After work he shared the same food as his workers.

Cato made his early successes in the army, as he claimed his grandfather and father had before him. Upon Hannibal's invasion of Italy at the beginning of the Second Punic War (217 B.C.), Cato joined the Roman army at age seventeen under the great general Quintus Fabius Maximus (died 203 B.C.), besieging the town of Capua. By the age of twenty (214 B.C.) Cato was military tribune in Sicily. He was a brave fighter

who was wounded many times and was notable for a piercing war cry that he thought frightened the enemy more than the sword. He marched on foot, carried his own arms and armor, and drank only water during the campaign.

In 209 B.C., when Fabius captured Tarentum, Cato met the Pythagorean philosopher Nearchus. Cato was no fan of Greek philosophy (though Timaeus influenced his *Origines,* and Greek agricultural writings were used in *De agri cultura*). He was, however, drawn to Pythagoras's rejection of physical sensations in the interest of the development of the soul and found many of the lessons inculcated by the hero Curius reinforced by the Greek philosopher. Cato continued his army service under Fabius and was at the decisive victory of the war, Metaurus (207 B.C.).

Impressed by Cato's legal ability, management skills, and integrity, his aristocratic neighbor in Tusculum, Lucius Valerius Flaccus, a man of considerable political influence, brought Cato to Rome and introduced him to the society and politics of the capital. With energy fairly emanating from his red hair and fearsome gray eyes, this *novus homo* (new man—one whose ancestors had not held high office) associated himself with his old general, Fabius Maximus, whose integrity of character and simplicity of living were another model for Cato.

In 204 B.C. Cato was made quaestor, or collector and dispenser of revenue, under Scipio Africanus for the army that would invade Africa. While Cato assisted the army's preparations for the invasion in Sicily, he met the poet Lucius Ennius in Sardinia and brought him to Rome in 203–202 B.C. As controller of finances, Cato perceived that Scipio was spending too lavishly on himself and overpaying his troops. Cato rejected the lack of restraint in the character of Scipio as keenly as he admired the characters of Curius and Fabius. Confronting his commander with his complaints, Cato reminded Scipio that if his soldiers had more money than they absolutely needed, they would indulge themselves in the pleasures of the senses; Scipio replied that the Romans did not care about money spent but battles won. Cato did not follow the army into Africa but resigned his position, returned to Rome, and brought charges of mismanagement against Scipio, though ultimately Cato could not prove his case at trial. Nevertheless, his prosecution of the commander began his practice of prosecuting the criminal and/or the corrupt, at first as a largely self-appointed protector of civic virtue.

Known by now as "the Roman Demosthenes," Cato rose quickly in Roman political life. His example of simplicity and morality was set in high relief by the indulgence and extravagance of the general population.

He continued to dress simply, eat sparingly, and run his farm with a calculated (some such as Plutarch might say ruthless) efficiency. Rather than being castigated by those who could or would not follow his model, he was in fact advanced by them. In 199 B.C. he became plebeian aedile, then praetor in charge of Sardinia (198 B.C.). Following a long line of corrupt praetors who were known for milking the province by extortion and extravagance, Cato set a standard that was welcome and appreciated by his subjects as he strictly but fairly enforced the law and traveled to cities on foot with a single slave, not in a great train with a large and costly retinue.

The reward for establishing his reputation for uncompromising morality was his election as coconsul with his friend Valerius Flaccus in 195 B.C. In Rome Cato continued to press for simplicity of lifestyle (particularly for women) by opposing the repeal of the luxury laws imposed on women's wealth in wartime (*Lex oppia*). Assigned the province called Hither Spain, he again asserted his principles of frugality and efficiency. He conquered more than four hundred Spanish towns and, though Scipio attempted to undermine him, was granted a triumphal parade at Rome by the senate in 194 B.C. Following his triumph, Cato laid aside his consular rank and assumed the lesser role of legate, in which role he accompanied the consul Titus Sempronius to Thrace. As military tribune under Manius Acilius Glabrio in Greece in 192 B.C., Cato spent some time in Athens and showed himself so thoroughly a Roman that he addressed the Athenians in Latin, though most Romans of his station would proudly have shown off their ability to speak Greek. In 191 B.C. he played an important role in defeating the Syrian king Antiochus III (the Great) at Thermopylae by capturing Callidromus, a rocky mount. Characteristically, Cato enhanced his own reputation by quickly returning to Rome to report the news of the battle (with full accounts of his own participation, including Glabrio's statement that Rome could never sufficiently reward him for his service to her).

On his return to Rome, Cato began a series of successful prosecutions of members of the Scipionic faction, beginning with Q. Minucius Thermus, and by 188 B.C. had greatly reduced its influence. He unsuccessfully supported the prosecution of Acilius Glabrio, the general who had embraced him at Thermopylae, now an opponent in the consular election of 189 B.C. The Roman historian Livy believed that Cato trumped up the charge by which Scipio Africanus was expelled from the capital and that he was a force behind the conviction in 187 B.C. of Scipio's brother Lucius, who would have gone to prison without the intervention of Tiberius Gracchus. Cato listed among his enemies not only

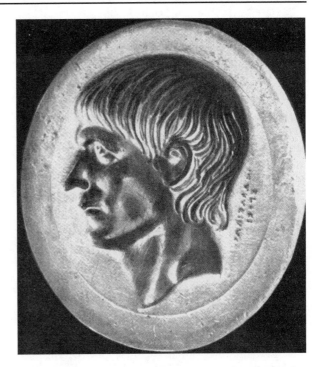

Scipio Africanus, in whose army Cato served as quaestor (portrait by Herakleidas, second or third century B.C.; found at Capua)

Scipio Africanus but also his grandson Scipio the Younger (185–129 B.C.). Many of these prosecutions brought counterprosecutions upon Cato. He himself was brought to trial fifty times but was never convicted. When the last charge was brought against him at the age of eighty-one, he complained that to defend one's conduct before men who grew up in an age different from the one in which he had lived was extremely difficult.

The censorship was a special magistracy that controlled public morals and supervised the leasing of public buildings and areas. It dated from the old days of the Republic (ca. 443 B.C.) and was established to ascertain that citizens had supplied accurate information about their status and property for the list of official citizens (*census*). Those who gave false information or led licentious lives could be expelled from the senate or deprived of their citizenship by the censors (originally two in number, usually one patrician and one plebeian). The office was at the height of its importance and the capstone of a successful *cursus honorum* (sequence of offices held by a Roman leading to the consulate) when Cato was elected censor with his old sponsor Valerius Flaccus in 184 B.C. (Cato had lost in 189 B.C. to two liberal members of the Scipionic Circle), despite the opposition of the Scipios and several other important aristocratic families who feared the loss of the luxury and extravagant lifestyle that the victories over Hannibal had won for them. (The office began its decline in the next generation following severe restrictions by Sulla.) True to their fears, Cato brought strenuous severity to his office, maintaining a conservative, almost reverent interpretation of the *mos maiorum* (old morality), though he may have romanticized it as much as some modern American Southerners idealize the ethos of the antebellum period. He opposed repeal of the *Lex Orchia* (law that limited the number of guests at entertainments) in 181 B.C. and favored the *Lex Voconia* of 169 B.C. that limited the right of inheritance by women. The most famous case is told by Livy and Plutarch (with differences in details) that Lucius Quintius, the brother of the Titus Flamininus who had defeated Philip of Macedon in 198 B.C., had had a prisoner killed at a dinner party to satisfy a personal complaint from a boy to whom Lucius was closely attached. Cato expelled Lucius Quintius from Rome for this act, expelled Lucius Scipio from the equestrian order, and expelled Manilius from the senate for kissing his wife in the presence of his children. Though Cato certainly advanced his own power by these prosecutions, his public position was one of objective adherence to what he perceived as the old frugal morality.

As rigorously as Cato enforced limitations on personal excess, he favored elaborate public building programs suited to Rome's new role as the wealthiest of nations. Though he was continually opposed by powerful factions, he was genuinely admired by the people, and upon his resignation from office a statue and laudatory inscription were set up for him in the Temple of Hygeia; the inscription did not mention his military career but rather his restoration of the strength of the Republic by "wise leadership, sober discipline, and sound principles."

However respected Cato may have been by the masses, his campaign against luxury angered many. Those whose "luxurious" possessions were worth more than a minimum amount (1,500 drachmas) found them assessed at ten times their worth in an effort to assure that those who had the most paid the most taxes. The result was that Cato not only was disliked by those who were able to bear the taxes on their extravagant possessions but also by those who could afford such extravagances but could not afford the taxes on them.

As censor Cato also took guarding the state against outside influence of all kinds as a defense of Roman life. When the Academic philosopher Carneades (214? to 129? B.C.) and the Stoic Diogenes (240–152 B.C.) came as a legation from Athens in 155 B.C. to plead for release from a sentence of five hundred talents, the youth of Rome were attracted to their wisdom and eloquence. Romans in this period were highly enamored of Greek culture, especially those in the cir-

cle of the Scipios, who dressed like Greeks, wrote in Greek, and filled their homes with Greek art. Cato found value in Greek culture but felt that the Scipios would lead the state to surrender what was best about it, its "Romanness." Finding philosophy in general unpractical and at bottom subversive, Cato felt that Greek education was valuable in Greece for the Greeks but that those who pursued Hellenism at Rome (for example, the Scipios) led lives of irresponsibility, extravagance, and licentiousness. Carneades in particular was famed for antilogies (being able to argue two sides of any question), and in his lectures in Rome he spoke one day in favor of individuals "and nations" pursuing moral behavior while on the next day he argued against their seeking it. Cato was duly alarmed that the youth of Rome would be affected by these philosophers (indeed, the third book of Cicero's *Republic* shows the influence of Carneades), would come to reject the old morality, and thus would lose their desire for warfare. He therefore moved the senate to send the philosophers back to Greece.

In the same year that he was prosecuted for the last time, 153 B.C., the eighty-one-year-old Cato was sent as an emissary to Carthage to resolve the conflict between the Carthaginians and the Roman ally, King Masinissa, formerly of Carthage, now of Numidia. The Carthaginians claimed that the tribute exacted from them was cripplingly excessive, but Cato was so struck by the recovery of Carthage from its near destruction in the Second Punic War that he immediately began to press for its total destruction, ending every subsequent speech with the famous words (according to Plutarch) *Praeterea censeo Carthaginem esse delendam* (I am also of the opinion that Carthage must be destroyed).

Cato died a wealthy man, though Plutarch questions the sources of much of his income. As a young man Cato had said that the only ways he knew of making money were by farming and by saving, but once he began his rise in Rome he ceased to view the farm as his sole means of income. He invested in real estate, underwrote maritime operations, and lent money at high interest to anyone, even to his slaves. Inevitably his farm soon became merely a hobby.

He married twice, each union producing a son. He chose his wives on the basis of their families rather than their dowries, thinking high-born women would be more ashamed of any moral transgression than would the merely wealthy. He appears to have exercised the same integrity as husband and father that he demonstrated in his public life. When his sons were babies, he would not miss the child's bath and swaddling for any but the most crucial senate business. He personally undertook the education of his sons, teaching them to read, ride, swim, and fight. It was for his sons that he wrote the history of

Rome from its founding, *Origines* or *De Originibus* (a work since lost), and to his son Salonianus (grandfather of the philosopher Cato Uticensis), he dedicated *De agri cultura.* Concomitant with Cato's distrust of Greek philosophy was his distrust of Greek physicians, based not on the quality of their science but on their untrustworthiness. As a consequence he compiled a book of home remedies, *De medicina,* on which he based the treatment of his household. A wife and son, however, both succumbed to disease without the benefit of Greek medicine. Cato's writing belongs largely to the period of his censorship, and much of it was written as homegrown instruction for his son Marcus Porcius Cato Licianus, born in 192 B.C.

Cicero knew more than 150 speeches by Cato, though today only the titles are known of about eighty. Livy paraphrased Cato's speech against the *Lex Oppia* in 195 B.C. Representative of the fragmentary speeches printed by Enrica Malcovati in 1955 are speeches in which Cato defends his service as consul, avers to Athenians that Latin has become an international language of commerce and diplomacy equal to Greek (both 191 B.C.), argues against the repeal of the sumptuary law *Lex Orchia,* opposes war with Rhodes (167 B.C.–his fullest surviving speech) and in his eighty-sixth year defends the Lusitanians.

De Originibus, or *Origines,* is one of the great losses from antiquity. It was a compendious history of Rome that broke traditions and set standards for histories to come. Previous histories had essentially been self-serving accounts by members of the senatorial class (though not often the leading figures) and concentrated on the role of the individual (usually the author) in the Punic Wars. Cato, on the other hand, was a predominant figure of his age whose history stresses the development of Roman government and culture rather than the glory of the individual. To this end, he names no general of either side in the wars with Carthage, only Hannibal's lead elephant. He does dwell on the heroism of minor figures, whom he names. Cato did, however, refer to his own speeches against the Rhodians and Sulpicius Galba, presumably to offset the many accounts by members of the Scipionic Circle. While senatorial histories concentrate on the virtues of the ruling class, Cato the plebeian is at pains to show that Rome was built by its people, not just its leaders. The glory of Rome is the moral rectitude of its people, particularly those of Cato's native Tusculum.

The account is not chronologically balanced. Only enough fragments remain to indicate that book 1 treated the kings, books 2 and 3 the origins of non-Roman Italian towns and peoples (as interested a Sabine such as Cato), book 4 the First Punic War, book 5 the Second Punic War, and books 6 and 7 the history

First page from a 1515 edition of Cato's writings about rural matters (courtesy of the Lilly Library, Indiana University)

of Cato's time down to the praetorship of Servius Sulpicius Galba in 152 B.C. The fragments show some familiarity with Greek historians. Cato's preface alludes to Xenophon's *Symposium* in saying that historical personages should tell not only of their business but also of how they spend their leisure time.

Cato also wrote a book on military discipline *(De disciplina militari)* along with many short works for his son Licianus. He wrote a storybook by hand for him, a child's book on farming, one on medicine *(De medicina),* and one on rhetoric. The latter, according to Heinrich Jordan, included Cato's famous definition of an orator as a gentleman who can deliver a speech *(orator est, Marce fili, vir bonus dicendi peritus).* Cato probably was not trying to compose an encyclopedic work of compendious reference but rather trying to set down particularly Roman wisdom for the guidance of his son, not so much to advance science as to record Roman traditions. Compendia of his nostrums and mottoes survive.

Not a structured rumination on country life such as Varro's treatise, or the compendious encyclopedia that is Columella's, Cato's *De agri cultura* is a collection of notes advising the investor who already owns a *villa urbana* (city home) on the costs in goods and manpower involved in establishing a plantation of 240 *jugera* (about 150 acres) that concentrates on only a few crops, chiefly olives or grapes, and relies greatly on slave labor, which was abundant after the Punic Wars began. *De agri cultura* is the earliest extended piece of surviving Latin prose and comes from a period when land use was being radically reformed. The goal is not the improvement of the farmer by observation of nature's gifts to man but rather the making of money by maximizing land and slave productivity. To this extent, Cato's fabled spareness of life does not evoke the impoverished farmers who were his early heroes but the canny businessmen-farmers of the late Republic intent on increasing their wealth, even if they must resort to superstition and incantation. As few quotations of the work appear in the texts of other ancient authors, presumably it has survived in tattered form.

The book, which surveys say was addressed to Cato's son, though no such address survives, comprises 162 chapters. Despite its lack of organization, every piece of information in the book was practical and valuable. Chapter 1 describes the selection of the farm. Cato goes on to describe how the absentee owner should get a day-by-day account from the foreman on the productivity and profitability of the farm. He then shifts from short-term to long-term management, describing first the appropriate buildings to be erected, including the owner's *villa rustica* (country home), which should be as comfortable as he can afford so that he will not avoid staying at the farm. Cato describes the duties of the overseer of the slaves (chapter 5) and the planting of the olive orchard and vineyard along with other orchards in the general plan of the property (chapters 6–9). In chapters 10–22 he inventories the equipment necessary to cultivate the olive and vine, describes appropriate construction contracts, and gives examples of the best building materials, including the first known recipe for concrete. Having described the pressing room, the olive press, and the crushing mill, he describes the calendar to be followed by the overseer of the slaves (chapters 23–53), beginning with late-spring harvesting and processing the grapes and olives, interspersed with discussions of tree planting, timber cutting, and the planting of grains. In winter the jobs include building a lime kiln, preparing stakes for the vineyard, and cleaning up the farm. Spring, he says, is devoted to grafting and planting the olive and fruit trees and the vines. There is no mention of grains. Cato concludes the calendar with an account of making hay. Chapters 54–60 list the amount of food needed for the slaves and farm animals for a year, while 61–69 describe contracts for olive pickers and olive pressers. Recipes for daily feed for animals, sumptuous food for people, recycling of olive-oil dregs, winemaking, and preserving are haphazardly listed in chapters 70–130. Cato tries to fill in the gaps of his previous accounts in chapters 131–150 by a hodgepodge of sample contracts for seasonal workers, religious incantations (chiefly the sacrifices before plowing and harvesting), lists of the best towns in which to sell produce, and a description of the proper behavior of the foreman's wife. Finally, chapters 156–160 treat medicinal recipes, with an idiosyncratically extended account of the restorative powers of cabbage. The final chapters treat the growing of asparagus and the curing of hams.

The character of Cato is always present: explanations are minimal and most verbs are in the imperative, rather like the *Praecepta ad filium* (Precepts for His Son) and *Carmen de moribus* (Poem on Morals). There is Cato's way and no other, for his preface makes clear that farming is more noble than lending money or trading; it forms good citizens and soldiers because men are attached to the land and the values necessary to make it pay. The sense of archaic tradition is reinforced by Cato's quotation of homely old proverbs in the presence of his worldly business advice, his use of archaic effects such as liturgically repeated words and phrases, alliteration and word rhyme, and his frequent recurrence to the habits of his ancestors.

References:

Michael von Albrecht, *Masters of Roman Prose from Cato to Apuleius,* translated by Neil Adkin (Leeds, U.K.: F. Cairns, 1989), pp. 1–32;

Alan E. Astin, *Cato the Censor* (Oxford: Clarendon Press, 1978);

Francesco Della Corte, *Catone censore: La vita e la fortuna* (Turin: Rosenberg & Sellier, 1949);

Nels W. Forde, *Cato the Censor* (New York: Twayne, 1975);

Anton Daniel Leeman, *Orationis ratio: The Stylistic Theories and Practice of the Roman Orators, Historians, and Philosophers,* 2 volumes (Amsterdam: A. M. Hakkert, 1963; reprinted, 1986), pp. 43–49;

Enzo V. Marmorale, *Cato maior* (Bari: G. Laterza, 1949);

Howard Hayes Scullard, *Roman Politics 220–150 B.C.* (Oxford: Clarendon Press, 1951;

Rudolf Till, *Die Sprache Catos* (Leipzig: Dieterich, 1936).

Catullus

(ca. 84 – 54 B.C.)

William W. Batstone
Ohio State University

MAJOR WORK–EXTANT: *Carmina* (Poems)–a collection of 113 poems (excluding three poems inserted into the manuscript by P. Muret in 1554 and removed by K. Lachmann in 1829 and not counting those poems that may be conflations of two poems).

Editio princeps: *Valerius Catullus scriptor lyricus Verone nascitur,* edited by Francisci Puteolanus (Venice: Vindelinus de Spira, 1472)–with Propertius, Tibullus, and the *Silvae* of Statius.

Standard editions: *C. Valerii Catulli Carmina,* edited by R. A. B. Mynors (Oxford: Clarendon Press, 1960); T. P. Wiseman, comp. and ed., "Appendix: References to Catullus in Ancient Authors," *Catullus and his World: A Reappraisal* (Cambridge: Cambridge University Press, 1985)–remaining fragments of Catullus's poetry, pp. 246–262.

Translations in English: *The Carmina of Caius Valerius Catullus,* verse translated by Richard F. Burton with prose translation, introduction, and notes by Leonard C. Smithers (London: Privately printed, 1894; reprinted, New York, 1928)–first complete English translation; *Catullus,* translated by F. W. Cornish, with *Tibullus,* translated by J. P. Postgate, and *Pervigilium Veneris,* translated by J. W. Mackail, second edition, revised by G. P. Goold, Loeb Classical Library (Cambridge, Mass.: Harvard University Press, 1988); *The Poems of Catullus,* translated by Peter Wigham (New York: Penguin, 1966), republished as *The Poems of Catullus: A Bilingual Edition* (Berkeley: University of California Press, 1969); *The Poems of Catullus,* translated by James Michie (New York: Vintage, 1971); *Catullus,* edited with introduction, translation, and notes by Goold (London: Duckworth, 1983); *The Poems of Catullus,* translated by Charles Martin (Baltimore: Johns Hopkins University Press, 1990).

Commentaries: C. J. Fordyce, *Catullus: A Commentary* (Oxford: Clarendon Press, 1961); Kenneth Quinn, *Catullus: The Poems* (London: Macmillan, 1970); John Ferguson, *Catullus* (Lawrence, Kans.: Coronado Press, 1985); *Catullus: Edited with a Textual and Interpre-*

Statue of Catullus on the Loggia del Consiglio in Verona

tive Commentary, edited by D. F. S. Thomson (Toronto: University of Toronto Press, 1997).

The poetry of Gaius Valerius Catullus has had two lives. In Rome, Catullus and his generation, the "new poets," played an essential role in the development of Augustan poetry. They helped to create the possibility that one might be a poet by profession. They brought to Rome the learned and self-conscious style of Hellenistic poetry, and they helped to create and explore those interests in erotic pathology that issued in the Roman love elegy. Later, during the empire, Catullus became the model for Martial's epigrams, poems that were witty, often vulgar and satiric observations of life in Rome. Then his poetry was all but lost. With the exception of one marriage poem (ca. 62 B.C.) included in a ninth-century anthology, he was relatively unknown after the time of Aulus Gellius (late second century A.D.) until a stray manuscript was found in Verona early in the fourteenth century. The scattered references to Catullus's poetry can be listed: St. Jerome, Martianus Capella, and Macrobius in the fifth century; Priscian and Boethius in the sixth century; and Isidore in the seventh. Hildemar of Corbie appears to echo Catullus in A.D. 841, and Hiericus of Auxerre quotes a phrase from Catullus in A.D. 873. Bishop Rather, who organized the *scriptorium* of Verona, records in A.D. 965 that he is reading Catullus, whom he had not read before. Two others, William of Malmesbury and Marcus Grabman, appear to echo Catullus's poetry in the twelfth century. In general Catullus remained unknown until a manuscript known as V surfaced in Verona about 1305, only to disappear before the end of the century. Two copies were made from V (O and X). One of these copies is now in the Bodleian Library, Oxford; the other, which was probably owned by Petrarch, was copied twice (G and R in 1375) and then it, too, disappeared.

The fortuitous discovery of V gave Catullus and his poetry a second life, although at first he was quoted, improbably, as a moralist. Soon he became one of the special favorites of European lyric, as his verse responded well to different readers in different ages. For the Renaissance he was the master of wit and brevity. Robert Herrick raised his "immensive cup / of Aromatike wine" to Catullus's "Terce Muse"; John Milton praised Catullus's "satyrical sharpnesse, or naked plainness." For the Romantic poet William Butler Yeats, Catullus was the natural poet, and for Ezra Pound and Robert Frost he was a poet of hardness and clarity, the source of poetic renewal. For most of the twentieth century Catullus has been the lyricist who poured forth his heart in verse addressed to himself or no one and who led the "Catullan revolution" by inventing the deeply felt poetry of personal lyric. In more recent years, classical scholars have emphasized his Alexandrian learning and technical mastery, and most recently critics have begun to talk of him in terms of continuity with the Roman traditions of epigram and comedy.

There is, of course, some truth in all these versions of Catullus, and beyond the irrepressible ability of readers to appropriate texts, his single greatest weakness may be his failure to craft a monumental body of poetry as Horace and Virgil did. Invariably Catullus's corpus fractures along divides between contradictory alternatives or tendencies: learning and passion; seriousness and frivolity; conservative values and revolutionary attitudes; ethical "piety" and vulgar obscenity; accounting and kissing; the great themes of Rome—love and betrayal, war and death; and lesser preoccupations with napkin stealing, urine, buggery, and bad breath. Perhaps for this reason the interpretation of Catullus's poetry has been particularly partial: critics emphasize one characteristic over others or even exclude some poems from the highest "levels of intent" or from serious discussion. Whether they censor his vulgarities or are indifferent to his "occasional verse," readers generally have had both their own "Catullus" and their own collection of poems. He wrote a wide range of poetry, and it has occasioned diverse responses.

Information about Catullus's life, outside of what can be inferred or imagined from his poems, amounts to four pieces of external data. St. Jerome (*Chron. a. Abr.* 150H and 154H) writes that Catullus was born at Verona in 87 B.C. (*An. Abr.* 1930) and that he died in his thirtieth year. Apuleius (*Apol.* 10) writes that the name of Catullus's famous lover Lesbia was really Clodia. Suetonius (*Iul.* 73) tells the reader that, although Caesar knew Catullus's verses had placed an eternal stigma on his name, he nevertheless invited Catullus to dinner on the very day on which Catullus apologized; moreover, Caesar continued to enjoy the hospitality of Catullus's father. None of these bits of information, however, is without difficulty.

Jerome's dates indicate Catullus was dead in 57 B.C., before events that he writes about: Caesar's invasion of Britain (mentioned in poems 11, 29, and 45) took place in 55 B.C., the same year as Pompey's second consulship (poem 113) and the building of his portico (poem 55). Two explanations have been offered. One is that a manuscript error of XXX (30) for XXXX (40) puts Catullus's death in 47 B.C. This theory, however, requires some explanation for the cessation of datable poetic activity by 54 B.C. The other explanation is that if Jerome took the date 87 B.C. from a reference to Cinna's consulship, he may have mistaken Cinna's first consulship in 87 B.C. for his last consulship in 84 B.C. By this calculation, Catullus lived from 84–54 B.C., the dates usually accepted. Although this solution is not universally accepted, it makes the best sense of the information available and provides a reasonable framework into which to place other information.

Apuleius's identification of Catullus's lover as Clodia, a married woman he calls Lesbia, is intriguing and agrees with what is known about the use of pseudonyms in Roman lyric and elegy. But who is Clodia? In a clever epigram, poem 79, against the brother of Lesbia, appropriately called "Lesbius," Catullus puns *Lesbius est pulcher* ("Lesbius is lovely" or "Lesbius is 'Pulcher'") and accuses him of incest. If by analogy with the equation "Lesbia" = "Clodia," "Lesbius" = "Clodius," then the reader is directed to the infamous tribune Publius Clodius Pulcher (*Tr. Pl.* 58). He had three sisters, all called "Clodia" according to the Roman convention, but, according to other information, none of these women was married between 57 and 54 B.C., the time when Catullus wrote his datable poems. This theory leads to another dead end, although most scholars accept Clodia Metellus, whose husband died in 59 B.C., as the most likely candidate. All that can be said with confidence, however, is that Catullus wrote of a love affair with an older woman from a powerful Roman family.

Finally, there is Suetonius's story of the reconciliation between Catullus and Caesar. Caesar with his prodigy, Mammura (vulgarly named "Mentula" or "Dick" by Catullus), is memorably portrayed by Catullus as vicious and obscene. They are both accused of being buggered in poem 57 and in poem 29 of devouring and destroying everything.

> Was it on this account, O singular general,
>
> that you were in the island of the setting sun,
>
> so that fucked-out Dick of yours
>
> could suck down twenty or thirty million?

Caesar might well have felt that these and other verses stigmatized him; however, to establish a date for the alleged reconciliation is difficult. Since these vicious lines refer to Caesar's expedition to Britain, which began in 55 B.C., and since Catullus may have died in late 54 B.C., one must imagine either an undocumented trip to Verona in 54 B.C. by Caesar and Catullus or an unnoted renewal of invective after an earlier reconciliation: "Once more you will be angry at my iambs, singular general, but they don't deserve it" (poem 54.6–7). The details remain intriguing but cannot be reconciled.

Only Catullus's poetry can supplement the above information about his life. Although taking poetic statements as autobiographical fact presents difficulties, the poetry suggests a general and probable outline. Catullus was born in Verona, the son of a man prominent enough to be on social terms with Julius Caesar. The family was apparently wealthy: Catullus speaks of a villa at Sirmio about thirty miles west of Verona (poem 31) and of another villa near Tibur (Tivoli) (poem 44). These references suggest that he did not need either patronage or a large audience; these implications in turn may help to explain his success in creating the kind of elite poetry he wrote. If they are true, his complaints about poverty (poem 13) should probably be taken as exaggerations or as conventional postures. As a young man Catullus says he took up both poetry and sex at about the age of fifteen (poem 68.15–16). At some point (the exact date is uncer-

tain) he came from Verona to Rome. Among his friends were the elegiac poets Cinna and Calvus, and they together, probably under the influence and direction of Parthenius of Nicaea, created a poetic movement (known as the "Neoterics" or "New Poets") that forever changed Roman literature. While in Rome, Catullus fell in love with Lesbia, and made this event central to a set of poems that helped to create the genre of Roman love elegy. If this woman was Clodia Metellius, the affair began before her husband died in 59 B.C.

Catullus (and Cinna) served on the staff of the praetor Memmius in Bithynia-Pontus. When Catullus's brother died he spent some time back in Verona (poem 68), and he wrote of traveling to his brother's grave in Asia Minor near Troy (poem 101), an event that may have taken place while Catullus was in Bithynia. He wrote what appears to be a final poem of dismissal to Lesbia (poem 51) after Caesar invaded Britain, and no poem can be dated later than 54 B.C. Catullus died, still a young man—perhaps, as Jerome says, at the age of twenty-nine.

In the middle of the first century B.C., when Catullus began to write verse, the professional poet in Rome was usually Greek, and the professional poem was the aristocratic epic that served the needs of family pride. Latin epigram and lyric consisted mainly in the kind of literary dilettantism found in men like Q. Lutatius Catullus (consul in 102 B.C.), who translated Hellenistic epigrams into Latin distichs, and in the youthful or amateurish work of Cicero. Poetry was meant to serve the interests and leisure of conservative Romans, men of action and accomplishment.

By the time of Augustus, however, Rome had produced, in addition to the great works of Virgil, an extraordinary and significant body of personal lyric and erotic elegy. The works of Horace, Tibullus, Propertius, and Ovid survive in addition to those of Catullus. In less than sixty years poetry as an art, valuable in itself and not merely the recreation of the powerful or the subsidized extension of family fame, had become established in Rome. This achievement was not simply the result of individual geniuses. A generation of poets, Catullus's generation, melded Roman traditions in epigram, satire, and comedy as well as in epic to the learned and elitist aesthetic standards and values of third-century Alexandria. Together these poets shared an international perspective on literature, a learned and professional tradition of academic poetry, a desperate concern for the future of Rome, and an intense interest in the pathos and pathology of eros. Thus, in an age of civil war and political catastrophe, Roman poets began in a single generation to think and write in new and complex ways of themselves, art, sex, the state, passion, learning, and life.

The ruins of the Palace of Catullus at Sirmio, Italy

Of that generation only Catullus's poetry survives in more than a few fragments. The names of some of the poets are known, those associated with the "New Poetry," as Cicero called it: his intimate friend, the orator and poet Calvus; "the Latin siren, who alone reads and makes poets" (Suet. *Grammat.* 11), Valerius Cato; Furius Bibaculus; Caecilius; Cinna; Ticidas; and the inventor of Roman love elegy, Gallus. Together they made possible the achievement of Horace, Virgil, and Ovid; and while it may be easy to exaggerate the particular role played by Catullus, his work is all that survives of that generation of poets who opened new doors for technique and expression at Rome.

For the modern reader, Catullus's poetry amounts to the 113 or so poems that have come down to the present from the Verona manuscript (X). Modern texts are numbered 1–116, but the poems numbered 18–20 are usually excluded, since they were inserted without authority by Marc-Antoine Muret in his edition of 1554. There is no probability that Catullus wrote these priapic verses. Of the 113 poems in the manuscript, numbers 2, 14, 58, 68, and 95 are thought to be conflations of what were originally two poems. In addition to these

poems, which amount to about 2,310 lines, there are about twenty references in the ancient authors to other poems by Catullus. The manuscript collection is usually divided into three groups. Poems 1–60, generally referred to as the polymetrics, are in a variety of lyric meters with the hendecasyllabic meter (an eleven-syllable line) used in some forty poems. Poems 61–68 form a middle section, the *Opera Maiora* (Longer Works), which share a learned and allusive Alexandrian style and a recurrent interest in marriage. If these poems are taken as a group, then the third section, poems 69–116, form a collection of epigrams (or short poems in the elegiac meter, varying in length from two lines to twenty-six lines). These poems share certain features of style and diction that mark them as a distinctly Roman set of epigrams. Some critics, however, prefer to designate the third group as all poems, long and short, in the elegiac meter, poems 65–116. In poem 65 a programmatic announcement–"I will always sing songs saddened by your death"–is taken to mean, "Hereafter, I will always write in the elegiac meter." Such a programmatic announcement parallels other announcements in the corpus, but few of the epigrams that follow are either sad or concerned with death. The final verdict as to where the second group of poems ends must remain uncertain.

The organization of the whole collection has been a matter of frequent discussion, and although today one commonly sees arguments based upon the assumption that the poems are in the order in which Catullus himself arranged and published them, there is by no means any agreement among scholars that this is the case. The issues are twofold. First, there is the external evidence for a collection; second, there are the internal, aesthetic principles and interpretive consequences of an intentional order.

What, then, is the evidence? The first poem in the collection refers to "this new, pleasant little book" dedicated to Cornelius Nepos. The poet Martial (ca. A.D. 86) also knew of a collection of light poetry called *Passer* (Sparrow), and the second poem begins, *Passer, deliciae meae puellae* (Sparrow, the delight of my girl). According to ancient convention a literary work was commonly designated by its first words. If there was a collection made by Catullus called *Passer,* that collection probably began with the second poem. It would not be the "little book" of the first poem but the poetry that that poem refers to as the "stuff" Nepos had already appreciated. The collection that begins with poem 1, that is, the "little book," would be a second collection. Further, Ausonius (*Eclogues* 1. 1–9) and Pliny the Elder (N.H. 1. *praef.* 1) know of a collection, but one cannot tell whether this collection was the "little book" of polymetric poems, some smaller selection of those poems, or the rather large book (2,310 lines, large for an ancient papyrus roll) of the collected poems. Poem 27 seems to represent a change in Catullus's metrical style; here, he begins to take greater liberty in handling the hendecasyllabic meter. Such changes (when not correlated with subject or mode) usually mark an historical moment; if this is true of Catullus's poems, then the hendecasyllables after poem 27 were probably written after poems 2–26, and the collection preserves some signs of the historical order of composition.

The internal evidence for the poet's hand in organizing the collection(s) may be added to this information. First, there are what critics have identified as "programmatic statements," that is, poems that talk about the collection itself. The dedication poem, for instance, refers to a "little book" and introduces the collection in terms of such aesthetic values as new, polished, small, and playful. Poem 14b has been taken to suggest the emergence of Catullus's new homosexual theme: "If any of you will be readers of this nonsense, and not shrink from touching me with your hands . . . "; poem 27 seems to proclaim a shift to invective: "this is pure Thyonian" (= and now for the bitter stuff). Poem 65 may suggest that hereafter Catullus will write only in elegiacs: "I will always sing songs saddened by your death." Similarly, poems 1, 61, 65, and 116 men-

tion the Muses and allude to the great neoteric inspiration of Callimachus (Greek scholar and Alexandrian librarian). This evidence is often taken by critics to suggest that there was a collection, perhaps several collections, and that the collection(s) was/were organized by Catullus. There is, of course, no agreement about what constitutes the collection(s) or about where the hand of chance or the arrangement of a later editor is seen.

Nevertheless, in addition to the external witnesses and the programmatic poetry there are other signs of an intentional ordering principle in the collection. In the opening sequence of poems, 2–11, poems 2, 3, 5, 7, 8, and 11 suggest the course of the affair with Lesbia from initial desire to final divorce; and another set of closely placed poems (15, 16, 21, 23, 24, 26) focuses on Aurelius, Furius, and Iuventius. Furthermore, throughout the collection related poems are often separated by a contrasting poem (2 and 3, on Lesbia's sparrow, are separated by the mythological fragment of 2B; 5 and 7, on kisses, are separated by a poem to Flavius; 70 and 72, on Lesbia's protestations of love, are separated by a poem on Quintus's armpits). Since either that chance would bring close together so many related poems or that an editor would separate poems related by subject and theme by a single poem seems highly unlikely, many see evidence of the poet's hand in arranging parts of the collection.

This conclusion, however, requires an unruly ordering principle of loose variation and contrast. In the opening sequence, for instance, two poems belong to the beginning of Catullus's affair with Lesbia (2, "Sparrow," and 3, "Mourn for the sparrow"), followed by two poems from the success of the affair (5, "Give me kisses," and 7, "How many kisses"), followed in turn by a failed attempt to end the affair (8, "Poor Catullus") and the bitter rejection of Lesbia (11). Why do these six poems make up the sequence, though, when Catullus wrote eight more polymetrics about Lesbia? And why separate a mock dirge for a dead sparrow from a poem about kisses with a poem about a little boat? Why separate the kiss poems with an amusing and ironic poem about Flavius's "unpleasant and inelegant" mistress? And why does no poem separate the last "kiss poem" from the attempt to end the affair, while two poems (a celebration of Veranius's return and an urbane and ironic record of a conversation in the Forum) separate that failed attempt at separation from the final bitter rejection? Surely, any reader who wants a psychologically effective order can create equally or perhaps more compelling juxtapositions, just as any clever reader can imagine reasons for the present order.

Just this situation, however, distinguishes the Catullan collections: there may not be a rigid architectural order to the poems, but there is a suggestive and meaningful order. There is a structure of relationships that cannot be denied while at the same time it cannot be reduced to a single historical, thematic, or aesthetic principle. The patterns of similarity and difference found in the collection are part of the impression the collection gives of variety and coherence, of dramatic fragments from a life whose themes and concerns recur in old memories and new events. Thus, the collection has a mimetic quality that simultaneously suggests the coherence as well as the interruptions and continuing qualifications of lived experience, and this quality maintains simultaneously maximum variety and maximum resonance. For interpretation, the problem with this principle of order is simply that a varied and resonant text will, even if radically reshuffled, still produce meaningful juxtapositions. Thus, the very looseness that relates the kisses of poem 7 back to the kisses of poem 5 across the voyeuristic poem 6 allows both poem 6 to echo within poem 7 (they are both about the curious spying on love affairs) and poem 7, with its learned geographical rendition of "as many kisses as there are sands in the desert," to resonate with the expansive geographical foil of poem 11 or the travels of the little boat in poem 4. In this way, an otherwise comic version of the foolish lover (poem 8) acquires psychological depth and, for some, tragic implications by being part of the Lesbia narrative and by paralleling another desperately pathological monologue of unrequited love (poem 76). The whole, then, becomes interrelated though a series of metonomies and metaphors, insuring each poem maximum resonance across a maximum number of poems, and in this way the Catullan collection accomplishes the neat trick of gaining a sense of context without losing the autonomy of the moment.

To the extent that this emphasis on the moment and the poet's personal voice and personal experience can be identified with what today is called "lyric," in addition to Catullus's extraordinary gifts as a lyricist in individual poems, he has created a body of poems that enhances the expressive power of individual poems through the resonance of the collection. The order of that collection preserves simultaneously the lyric moment of each poem and the resonance of that moment in the life or the implied life from which it arose. The power of this resonance is evident in the frequency with which critics in the past have attempted to rearrange the poems into a neat narrative. More recently, however, readers have begun to emphasize the ways in which this resonance provokes the desire of readers and contributes to multiple readings as each poem looks forward and backward and across diverse interruptions to multiple variations. The juxtapositions, both continuous and discontinuous, represent a depth of response and not a narrative, a pattern, or a proposition.

Any closure, any collection, however, will always be susceptible to the further resonance created by any additions; even those made by chance or a later editor are necessary corollaries to this principle of maximum variety with maximum resonance. From what can reasonably be inferred, then, about the principles of order and juxtaposition that seem to have guided Catullus, the exact dimensions of the Catullan *libellus* (little book) are unknowable and extraordinarily flexible and permeable. This supposition may not satisfy the desire for historical certitude, but it speaks to the power and attraction of a collection that has continually drawn readers under its spell.

The dedication poem is programmatic. It introduces three major aspects of Catullus's poetic interests and influence and, to some extent, of the generation of poets who brought about the "Catullan revolution." First, it is self-consciously neo-Callimachean, importing the aesthetic values of Hellenistic poetry into Rome; second, it is specifically engaged in the present Roman context, in the Forum and the empire; and third, it engages and performs those elusive self-presentations that characterize the celebratory strength of Roman comedy.

> To whom am I giving my charming, new, little book
> polished just now with the dry pumice stone?
> Cornelius, to you: for you were the one
> who thought this rubbish was something,
> even then, when alone you dared to unfold
> the whole age of the Italians in three papyrus rolls,
> incredibly learned, by Jupiter, industrious sheets.
> Wherefore, take it as yours, whatever it is, this little book,
> however it strikes you; and you, o Muse and patron Virgin,
> let it remain through the years beyond our lifetime.

The terms Catullus uses in this poem allude to the Callimachean program and establish Catullus's position as a Callimachean poet: newness, smallness, polish, intellectual dryness, daring, learning, industry, and immortality. These ideals frequently recur as Roman poets of the next generation work in the shadow of neoteric Alexandrianism and, writing under the daunting aspiration of creating an international tradition, reflect upon their place in that tradition and their contribution to Roman culture. Catullus, with typical lightness and learning, suggests his place in this tradition with a translingual pun. His book is *lepidus*, a term that joins the "urbane charm" (Latin, *lepos*, *lepidus*) of a carefree life in Rome to the aesthetic refinement (Greek, *leptos*) that defined a Callimachean virtue.

In practice, the Callimachean poetic standard meant writing in the smaller poetic forms–short lyrics, epyllions (brief epics), and epigrams; experimenting in new verse forms; playful inversions of genre; an extraordinary ear for phonetic detail; and frequent use of learned and literary allusion. Poem 2 therefore is formally a hymn but is addressed to a sparrow; poem 3 is formally a dirge upon the sparrow's death; both also exploit *passer* as a slang term for the male member. Thus begins the *Passer,* whose consistent metaphor for poetic activity is *ludus* (game), a term with both frivolous and erotic associations. In poem 36, *Annales Volusi, cacata carta* (Annals of Volusius, shitty sheets),

Catullus contrasts the traditional, epic poetry of Volusius with his own refined new poetry. Lesbia has apparently vowed to Venus that she will throw the choicest verses of the worst poet (meaning Catullus's lampoons against her) into the fire if Catullus is restored to her. Catullus imagines returning but repaying the vow with the verses of Volusius and asks Venus to accept the payment:

> Now goddess created from the sky blue sea
> you who honor holy Idalius and windy Urii
> and Ancona and Cnidus with its reeds
> and Amathus and Golgos
> and "Hadria's tavern" in Dyrrachium . . . [.] (11–15)

This catalogue is in part a tour of Catullus's journey home from Bythinia through all the places where Venus was kind to him. More than a biographical tour of Asia Minor, the catalogue is literary and poetic. It recalls Theocritus, the legend of Adonis associated with Golgi, Idalium, and Amathus (a temple of Adonis and Aphrodite at Amathus), and, most likely, the neoteric epyllion, *Zmyrna,* by Catullus's friend Cinna. Thus, as Catullus imagines eluding the fate to which Lesbia had destined his "fierce iambs," he appeals to Venus/Aphrodite in hymnic form with reference to his own journeys and literary affiliations (both traditional and contemporary) and with a poetic range that complements the geographical movement—from Aphrodite's epic or mythological birth to a sailor's slang in a tavern in Dyrrachium. In wit, range, and appreciation for the power of Aphrodite/Venus, Catullus lays claim to his place and the place of his poetry—out of the fire into the tradition. The poem ends:

> But meanwhile come to the fire, you verses,
> full of the farm and infelicities,
> Annals of Volusius, shitty sheets. (12–20)

For Catullus simply to adopt the refined, erudite, and esoteric aesthetic principles of Callimachus, however, was not possible. In the Roman context, both art for art's sake (or art as a replacement for life) and the lyric emphasis on the self and intimacy (giving voice to private feeling) were anathema to conservative manliness. "If I had two lifetimes I still would not have enough time for lyric poetry," said Cicero, and Catullus reflects this voice of antagonism when he calls his own poetry *nugae* (rubbish or stuff) and then claims for himself the aristocrat's traditional desire for immortality. The dedication poem not only recognizes these conflicts but, by adopting his opponents' term of hostility, even makes them themes and thus part of the Catullan newness. A resonant book of short lyric poems that granted privilege to leisure and frivolity was indeed a strange (another sense of the Latin, *novus*) and new production. Catullus's interest in himself, in the private movements of the heart and mind, and in his inti-mate exchanges with others, not as recreation and recuperation for the work of the Forum, but as the essence of his poetry and of a life fully lived was, so far as anyone can tell, new.

These interests, often associated with lyric poetry, and the demands of a learned, academic, Callimachean aesthetic may seen incompatible. For Catullus and his generation, however, the two were inextricably linked, since the Callimachean program made imaginable that kind of poetic professionalism and independence upon which this kind of lyric (as well as other Hellenistic interests) rested. In fact, Parthenius introduced Catullus's generation to learned Alexandrianism as well as to the erotic pathology of Greek myth. Thus, when Callimachus, a learned librarian, refused to write *epic* at the beginning of the second edition of his *Aetia,* he rejected what was for him an outworn and empty genre; this rejection, however, did not prevent him from writing court poetry—for example, "The lock of Berenice." When the neo-Callimacheans at Rome adopted Callimachus's personal and learned voice in opposition to the popular and politically acceptable epic, they took a position that rejected the normal public life and, therefore, could easily stand in judgment of conservative values and practices in Rome. In other words, for Catullus's generation and the poets who followed him, the Callimachean aesthetic was both a political and a poetic position, and Catullus's judgment was sometimes violent.

Catullus was fully aware of the conflicts in which he had become involved by his decision to write learned and refined lyric poetry. He asserted and reflected this antagonism in various moods. In poem 93 he expresses indifference:

> I really do not care whether I please you or not, Caesar;
> or whether you are a pale or swarthy man[.]

He addresses with violent mockery in poem 28 friends who, like him, have served abroad under a difficult governor:

> But as far as I can see, you're in an equal
> state: you've been stuffed by no less
> of a prick: "Seek noble friends!"
> Hell, may the gods and goddesses give them
> much pain, disgraces of Romulus and Remus. (28. 11–15)

In poem 95 he returns to his literary rejection of historical Annals, like those of Volusius:

> But the Annals of Volusius will die in Padua itself,
> and often become loose tunics for mackerel,
> Small monuments are dear to me . . . ,
> But the people rejoice in swollen Antimachus. (95. 7–10)

Finally, the dedication poem introduces elements of the Roman literary tradition that Catullus valued despite

Catullus's villa near Tivoli, Italy

their apparent opposition to the Callimachean aesthetic. That aesthetic, with its emphasis on the erudite and exclusive, had rigorously rejected the outworn, the common, and especially the popular. For Catullus, however, there was a Roman tradition of mime and comedy rich in resources. In contrast to Callimachean exclusivity, it was inclusive and common. Furthermore, this tradition had first undertaken a literary opposition to Roman *gravitas* (seriousness) and its characteristic *senex severus* (severe old man), and it had done so with a keen appreciation for irony, ingenuity, flexibility, and deception. Its favorite event was the staged self. In Catullus, this stage and its resources were more than a literary interest. Raised in the rhetorical tradition of Rome, Catullus felt the rhetorical or performed self as an intimate part of his experience and that of others. The staged self constituted both a resource and an obstacle; in Catullus's writing it became the means by which he explored and revealed the self as well as protected and hid it.

In calling his book a *lepidus libellus* Catullus probably referred to the Callimachean refinement designated by *leptos*. In referring also to the Latin *lepidus,* however, he was using a term much at home in the comedy of Plautus, whose favorite characters (in addition to the clever slave) were the congenial old man *(senex lepidus)* and the sweet

young thing *(lepida puella)* and whose goal was the charming (if deceptive) tale *(lepide fabulari)*. Catullan *lepor* adds to Callimachean refinement a sense of the lightness of life, an urbanity and social refinement that Catullus indulges throughout his poetry. Like the characters in Plautine comedy, it exploits the roles people play and their capacity to change roles; it also delights in that presentation of self that proceeds through an endless disclosure of masks.

The dedication poem is a performance of this ironic and charming elusiveness. When Catullus adopts the term *nugae* (stuff) for his own poetry, he ironically accepts the evaluative terms that the severe old men of Rome would assign to him. When he turns to Cornelius Nepos, he thanks his friend for thinking that this "stuff" is "something." Ostentatiously silent about what exactly his "stuff" is, he continues "whatever it is" and emphasizes the indefiniteness immediately with the adjective *qualecumque* (whatever sort = however it strikes you). Just as *nugae* co-opts and rejects the condemnation of conservative society but remains elusive about its own positive evaluation, so *aliquid* (something) accepts the approval of Nepos without specific evaluation. Together the two evaluative terms are less about Catullus's poetry than about Catullan freedom.

Similarly, Nepos is a peculiarly unlikely dedicatee: not only was his expertise in prose (which Catullus avoided so far as is known), but his history was also the very kind of public prose that was congenial to conservative Romans. He was a friend of Cicero and Atticus and does not seem to have appreciated neoteric poetry. Catullus's praise is suitably ambiguous: he describes Nepos's own writing as *doctis, Iuppiter, et laboriosis* (learned, by Jupiter, and full of labor). One can argue that *labor* is a Callimachean virtue, but that was the virtue enjoined by Apollo, and *laboriosus* (laborious) suggests a little too much work, or work poorly spent. Catullan values, then, elude both his detractors (who call them *nugae*) and his appreciators (who, like Nepos, think they are something, but apparently do not know what). Cornelius Nepos, therefore, is the appropriate dedicatee, not because he represents the best reader or an important patron but because he represents the problem of readers: even when sympathetic, when they share some values, they will interpret shared values differently; they will posture; and they will be merely different.

For the poet the masks assert and protect a subtle and strong claim to originality, but not merely a Callimachean originality–the originality of the forever elusive self, forever different from schools, others, and propositions about self. For the reader, represented by Nepos, the masks both because of and despite their pretensions project the possibility of common ground with many readers. Despite the inevitable problems of difference and separation, Catullus concludes by asking for and projecting a future for his poetry that (to translate the essential meaning of the words precisely) will continue through the years and remain unfailing even beyond the life of anyone now alive. That is, the literary artifact will be prized when all knowledge about the poet himself is hearsay and report, when no one alive will be in direct contact with the world of Catullus.

Catullus's dedication poem, then, introduces key concerns not only for his polymetrics but also for his entire output. He avows an affiliation with Callimachean aesthetics: his poetry will be learned, refined, original, daring, different, and everlasting. He sets this affiliation in a distinctly Roman context, one that he not only refuses to ignore but even celebrates: his poetry will be rubbish, trivial, and antagonistic to some conservative Roman concerns. Finally, he toys with the inadequacy of making statements like these; his poetry uses the resources of language, including the slipperiness of words and names, to perform and present a charming, if elusive, self. When the subtle and rich stylistic means of Callimachean aesthetics joined with both the self-assertiveness necessary in a Roman context and the elusiveness of self endemic to Roman comedy, something new was created–not just the posture of easy, self-confident swaggering play, not just art for art's sake, but a passionate capacity to feel and imagine and give verbal shape to the complex movements of the heart and mind.

One of the polymetrics may quickly illustrate the passion and playfulness of this poetic:

> The other day we spent,
> Calvus, at a loose end
> flexing our poetics.
> Delectable twin poets,
> swapping verses, testing
> form and cadence, fishing
> for images in wine
> & wit. I left you late,
> came home burning with
> your brilliance, your invention.
> Restless, I could not eat,
> nor think of sleep. Under
> my eyelids you appeared
> & talked. I twitched, feverishly,
> looked for morning . . . at last,
> debilitated, limbs
> awry across the bed
> I made this poem of
> my ardour & for our
> gaiety, Calvus. . . . Don't
> look peremptory, or
> contemn my apple. Think.
> The goddess is ill-bred,
> exacts her hubris-meed:
> lure not her venom.
> (poem 50; translated by Jane W. Joyce)

Surely a revolutionary experience of self and feeling and an opposition to the contractual narrowings of the Forum with its *gravitas* (moral and political seriousness) and its *amicitia* (political and practical friendship) preceded these poems, but the essential element that Catullus bequeathed to the next generation of poets was the verbal means of giving form and expression to a varied, exuberant, heterogenous–even trivial and promiscuous–self.

In the polymetrics Catullus not only revived a lyric tradition but in doing so created the conditions that give value to that tradition and allow that tradition to renew itself. Rarely does one sense in Catullus's polymetrics a naive urge for transparent self-expression. The writing of lyric leads him to questions about self and feeling, about the poetic expression of *ego* and the tradition itself, and about the relationship of individual and society, of art and life. To what extent does the poet express himself and to what extent does he fashion himself? His poetic creations attempt to imagine–that is, to give the proper life and meaning to–the rituals of male bonding, the theft of napkins, the creaking of a friend's bed, lust, betrayal, and hatred. In poem 50 an evening of poetic composition is described in the terms of an erotic encounter that leaves Catullus exhausted and hungry for more: art takes its place among the playful displacements that make up life.

In poem 16, though, the intersection of life and art remains an insoluble riddle because one is always implicated in and free from the other. In poem 7, on the other hand, neither the exclusive learning of Alexandria nor the clichés of the comic stage can actually reveal or express common knowledge of the limits of desire. In poem 11 the epic and martial achievements of Caesar contrast with the value of love, and when Lesbia betrays that love, she is imagined in her own epic, but grotesque, *menage-a-trois cents,* while Catullus figures his love as a fallen flower, an image taken from Homer. In this poem, as often, the most intensely felt moments find personal intensity and expression in exaggeration and tradition.

Elsewhere Catullus indulges the power of his art. If a napkin, the *mnemosynum* (memorial) of some dear friends, is stolen, the poetic demand for the napkin to be returned (poem 12) becomes a more eloquent and permanent *mnemosynum* of his dear friends. If Varus will not tell him who makes his bed creak and rattle about the room, then the demand to be told will become a substitute song that is itself a hymn to carnality and that can "sing Varus and his love to the stars." If Catullus fails to make a profit in Bithynia, he will make poetic profit out of the narrative of his embarrassment at being both a failure in the province and a liar in the form about his failures (poem 10).

Catullus also discovered and explored the limits of the lyric voice when faced with the depth and elusiveness of the self, with the betrayals of others (including the political world of his fathers and the intimate world of Lesbia), and with the traditions that shape, distort, and reveal who one is. He cursed Caesar and Pompey for destroying the world and threatened sexual violence upon Furius and Aurelius for misreading his poems. He sent Cicero a letter of thanks in which the ponderous tri-colon crescendo of the grand oratorical style jangles in the hendecasyllabic while honoring the recognizability of that inimitable style. In this regard, it is lyrically fitting that one of the last polymetrics (poem 51), which has often been thought to be one of the first poems Catullus wrote to Lesbia, is a close translation of Sappho that ends with a jarring Roman reflection on the destructiveness of leisure. Both to see the strength and depth of his feeling in a translation and to find that translation inadequate is typically Catullan. In the final analysis, the Catullan revolution was not just the importation or discovery of the lyric self and of the importance of the individual and the range of individual engagement with the world. It was not just the discovery of the resources for lyric expression in Latin, which includes meter, phonetics, the resonance of a book, and the complexity of poetic figures. It was also a self-consciousness about lyricism, language, self-presentation, and figures that was essential to the more ambitious achievements of the next generation of Roman poets.

The long poems are more ambitious, more moving, and at times more terrifying than the polymetrics. They also sometimes lack Catullus's lyric lightness and charm. While they include many of the same concerns, they are in general both greater and less perfect. Some, like poem 64, had an important influence upon later Latin poetry; others, like poem 63, remain relatively unusual.

Poems 61 and 62 are literary versions of marriage hymns. The form was popular in Greek literature and from among Catullus's contemporaries fragments survive from Ticidas and Calvus. Without comparable Latin hymenaeals, to assess with any confidence Catullus's innovations and contributions is difficult. Nevertheless, the poems celebrate the ideals of Roman marriage in a manner perhaps surprising for the urbane young poet of the polymetrics and the affair with Lesbia. Catullus, however, never entirely abandoned the ideals of his youth and his culture: Roman *fides* (faith), *pietas* (piety), and the responsibilities of marriage and family. In fact, those very concepts and the terms associated with them remain central to Catullus's imagination even of the affair with Lesbia.

Poem 63, coming after these two marriage hymns, tells a shockingly different story. Attis, a young Greek devotee of Cybele, the Great Mother goddess, awakes to find that in his frenzied devotion he has castrated himself. Now a woman, she laments her condition, but upon trying to escape is driven back into the wild forests to be the handmaid of Cybele. The poem is probably another hymn; it is written in a strange, frenetic rhythm known as the galliambic, the meter used by the priests of Cybele, the Galli, in their hymns to the Great Mother, and it ends with a prayer:

> Goddess, Great Goddess, Cybele, Dominant Goddess of Dindymus,
> Far from my home, Mistress, may all your fury be:
> Strike others wild, drive others rabid. (91–93)

Catullus has deliberately set in contrast the secure, ritual transitions of traditional sexual roles in an official Roman marriage with this un-Roman tale of fanatic delusion and self-destructive fury; the experience of Lesbia, moreover, who plowed past and killed the flower of Catullus's love (poem 11), is still at work in the background, shaping these poems.

The next poem in the collection is Catullus's longest and most ambitious, a 408-line epyllion that explores in a narrative context many of the issues that have occupied Catullus elsewhere. In this poem Catullus describes the Argonauts' first voyage and the forthcoming marriage of Peleus and Thetis—the arrival of the wedding guests, the palace of Peleus, and the tapestry on the wedding bed. On the tapestry is a picture of Ariadne. This image leads Catullus to tell the story of Ariadne's betrayal by Theseus, her curse, the death of Theseus's father, and the arrival of Dionysus to rescue her. When the story returns to Peleus and Thetis, the mortal guests are leaving, the immortal guests arrive, and the Fates sing a marriage hymn that foretells the Trojan War and the destruction that Achilles, son of Peleus and Thetis, will cause. The poem closes with the poet's comment that this moment was the last time the gods visited mortal men; since then the earth has become drenched in slaughter, impiety, infidelity, and crime.

The major themes are familiar (marriage, fidelity, impiety, love, loss, betrayal, destructive eros, and corruption) and the epyllion form allows the poet to pursue in an essentially lyric and associative mode the narrative that joins these themes. At the center of the poem, on a coverlet in the Palace of Peleus, is illustrated the story of Ariadne's self-destructive passion as it responds to Theseus's betrayal with a curse that destroys Theseus's innocent father as he watches for his son's return from the ramparts of the city. Catullus describes the coverlet and tells the story in a narrative that shifts back and forth in time from the abandoned Ariadne back to the aid she had given Theseus, forward to her lament and curse, and back to Theseus and his father's words when he left Athens. This movement, much like the historical movement of the polymetrics, emphasizes the lyric moments as Catullus gives seventy lines to Ariadne's lament and curse (132–201)–lines that evoke the betrayed, angered, emasculated Catullus of other poems–and fifty lines to Aegeus's farewell to his son. The outer narrative moves chronologically as the mortal guests first arrive and depart, then the immortal gods arrive and the Parcae, or Fates, sing their song.

The poem may be seen in part as an effort to give verbal form to simultaneous but seemingly contradictory feelings: first, that people often are caught in self-destructive patterns that their passions create and to which even Ariadne's desire for marriage contributes; and second, that these patterns are at the same time so interwoven in the fabric of the world that the Ariadne passage, wavering back and forth between past and future, comprehends another truth. The truth is that even before the gods stopped visiting men, even when Peleus and Thetis were married, the future of betrayal and destruction was fixed upon a coverlet, and the future, consisting in Achilles' warfare and the sacrifice of the virgin Polyxena, was intractable. Catullus has attempted to imagine a complex– whether Fate, the Parcae, Nemesis, the Great Mother goddess, or the sickness of passion–that does not operate by the rules of narrative linearity and is not preserved by the total and integrating impact of narrative causality and its power to subjugate. For his imagination, the lyric mode was necessary.

In poem 65 Catullus introduces the reader to his second deeply personal theme–the death of his brother at Troy. Grief, he writes to his friend Hortalus, keeps him from writing original poetry; instead, he will send a translation of Callimachus. Poem 66 follows, a translation of Callimachus's "Lock of Berenice," a poem written for Berenice II (ca. 273–221 B.C.) who vowed a lock of hair for the safe return of her husband, Ptolemy III of Egypt (ca. 280–221 B.C.), from the invasion of Syria. The king returned, the vow was paid, but the lock of hair disappeared. The poet imagines that it has become the new constellation discovered by the royal astronomer. That constellation is still known as *Coma Berenices* (the Lock of Berenice). Catullus's reason for choosing to translate this passage from Callimachus remains unclear.

Poems 67 and 68 are precursors of the Roman love elegy. The first is a dialogue between a questioner and the street door to a house in Verona. The main speaker, the door, tells a clever, sardonic, sometimes obscene tale of the adventures of the door's disreputable former mistress. Propertius, the Roman elegist, also wrote an elegy in which a door tells its story (I. 16). Poem 68 involves some textual difficulties, of which the most important is the status of the poem as one or as two poems. Given the different addressees of the two parts of the poem (68A = 1–40, 68B = 41–160), the repetition of verses 20–24 as 92–96, and the different styles, to treat the poem as two poems seems best. In the first, Catullus writes Mallius to excuse himself from love and love poetry because of his grief for his brother. The second is a complex structure that interweaves Catullus's failed love affair, the death of his brother, and the mythological tale of Laodamia's love for Protesilaus into what most critics think is a strikingly rich if not wholly successful innovation. Like the other longer elegiacs, the style of 68B is refined and Alexandrian. This formal quality in combination with a narrative of personal feeling that is related to a mythological exemplum takes the poem further than any other Catullan composition in the direction that the Roman love elegy was to take. The poem remains, however, Catullan in its combination of issues: loss of a brother, erotic distress, mythological exemplum, and especially the analogy between Laodamia's love as a young bride and Catullus's feelings for his beloved.

The remaining poems in the collection are shorter epigrams that, with only a few exceptions, are written in a style that is more reminiscent of a Roman tradition of epigram than of the Alexandrian traditions that informed both the polymetrics and the longer elegiacs. His topics are often the same as those that had interested him in the polymetrics. Invective takes to task, usually obscenely, Gellius, Caesar, Aemilius, and so on; love and Lesbia are contemplated; social and political ills are pilloried. In the epigrams, Catullus usually emphasizes the couplet structure and addresses his themes in neat, logical terms. Often he aims at contrasts and clarity:

> No one, my woman says she'd rather marry no one
> than me, not if Jupiter himself should ask.
> She says, but what a woman tells an eager lover
> ought to be written in wind and swirling water. (poem 70)

At times it is the failure of clarity that interests him. Thus, in his most famous epigram (85), his contrasts cannot cohere:

> I hate and desire. How can I do it? perhaps you ask.
> I dunno, but it happens, I feel it, it tears me up.
> (poem 85)

Insult is, as usual, a fairly stable enterprise:

> Gallus has brothers, one has the most lovely wife
> the other one has a lovely son;
> Gallus is a fine man: he facilitates sweet love,
> and the pretty boy lies with the pretty girl.
> Gallus is a dolt; he's married but doesn't see
> that the uncle teaches his nephew adultery. (78a)

For most readers the most striking and important innovation of the epigrams is the language used to probe the affair with Lesbia: it is the language of public and political alliance. Despite that the affair was adulterous and that it was probably of short duration, Catullus likens his role to that of a trusted public friend allied to another by good faith *(fides)* and a sacred contract *(sanctum foedus);* he says his love is not like the common passion between men and women but responsible and mature: "I loved you then not as the vulgar love a girlfriend but as father values sons and sons-in-law" (72. 3–4). The metaphor, as remarkable and expressive as it is, was never taken up by the later Roman elegists. Some have speculated that it belonged to the Roman tradition of these epigrams. That may be so, but it was doubtless difficult either to steal the metaphor from Catullus or to develop it beyond the conflicts that it illuminates for Catullus and allows him to explore. The passion was irresponsible; the devotion was as absolute as a contract and as binding as political allegiances; and the betrayal was immoral. The failure of the metaphor revealed the failure of Catullus's underlying requirement that desire and responsibility, choice and bond, intention and reward be commensurate and responsive.

For many, one of the most moving epigrams, and one that is echoed several times in later poets, is the poem written upon his visit to his brother's tomb (101). It shows again the Catullan interest in prior traditions, the limits and powers of poetic voice, the poetic artifact's lack of closure, and the human implication in the larger community. The poem recalls a tradition of epitaphs; it echoes the sentiments of an epigram of Meleager, and its opening line

alludes to Homer's *Odyssey*. Odysseus's heroic homeward journey to wife and family has been displaced in Catullus by loss and distance:

> Many the races and many the waters I have crossed
> Coming, my brother, to these sad funeral rites
> In order to give you the final duties owed the dead
> And speak in vain to your unspeaking ash
> Since fortune has stolen you, you from me,
> O brother, forlorn and wrongly torn from me.
> But, for now, for the meantime, in the ancient manner
> Receive these gifts, sad duty handed down for funeral rites,
> Though they flow with many a brotherly tear,
> And forever and ever, hail, brother, and farewell. (poem 101)

Much is lost in translation, especially phonetic density of the poem, but as the individual phonetic and verbal patterns of the poem interweave ritual and narrative with the clichés of epitaphs and other literary echoes, Catullus succeeds in creating a complex experience. It is one in which words ultimately fail (in vain) and the lament is cut short ("in the meantime"); it is one that requires the supplement of other poems. That the tomb is in Troy gives greater ironic depth to the Homeric echo. As the reader experiences this poem that does not, cannot, say all that needs to be said, the little that the reader carries with himself or herself from the other poems becomes an emblem of the great and personal experience that Catullus carries with him.

The poem, however, does not give form and permanence to this personal experience. Rather, the poem marks the intersection of the personal and the public, the private and the ritualistic. As Catullus moves from spatial extent to temporal extension, the recent and personal past carries with it the tradition of parents and is extended into an endless future of ritual and literary traditions. People share with others—both backwards within the culture and family and forwards into the future—inexpressible loss, echoing sighs, experience unspoken, and temporary steps against the permanent losses of the world. Perhaps nothing looks more in the direction of Virgil than this Catullan mood.

Catullus and his generation opened many doors for the poets that followed. Predictably, those poets did not choose to pass through all those doors. Never again would a poet—certainly not a Roman poet—speak with such frank brutality or in such magnificently obscene exaggerations. In general, after Catullus the small poem was not particularly prized. Horace, after his *Epodes,* turned to the more monumental achievement of the *Odes*. In Martial the Catullan range was reduced to endless epigrams and a courtier's wit. Nevertheless, Catullus's experiments in lyric created new opportunities not only for expression but also for feeling. He and his generation taught Roman poets the use of learning and tradition, the power and limits of poetry, and the uncanny depths of self and society.

Bibliographies and Concordances:

Monroe Nichols Wetmore, *Index verborum Catullianus* (New Haven: Yale University Press, 1912);

Hermann Harrauer, *A Bibliography to Catullus* (Hildesheim: G. Olms, 1977);

James P. Holoka, *Gaius Valerius Catullus: A Systematic Bibliography* (New York: Garland, 1985).

References:

William W. Batstone, "Logic, Rhetoric, and Poesis," *Helios,* 20 (1993): 143–172;

Wendell Clausen, "Callimachus and Latin Poetry," *GRBS,* 5 (1964): 181–196;

Clausen, "The New Direction in Poetry," in *The Cambridge History of Classical Literature,* volume 2, edited by E. J. Kenney (Cambridge: Cambridge University Press, 1981), pp. 178–206;

Steele Commager, "Notes on Some Poems of Catullus," *HSCP,* 70 (1965): 83–110;

John Ferguson, "Catullus," *Greece and Rome: New Surveys in the Classics* no. 20 (Oxford: Oxford University Press, 1988);

William Fitzgerald, *Catullan Provocations: Lyric Poetry and the Drama of Position* (Berkeley: University of California Press, 1995);

E. A. Havelock, *The Lyric Genius of Catullus* (Oxford: Oxford University Press, 1929);

Micaela Janan, *"When the Lamp Is Shattered": Desire and Narrative in Catullus* (Carbondale: Southern Illinois University Press, 1994);

W. R. Johnson, "The Sparrow and Nemesis: Catullus," in *The Idea of Lyric: Lyric Modes in Ancient and Modern Poetry* (Berkeley: University of California Press, 1982), pp. 108–122;

David Konstan, *Catullus' Indictment of Rome: The Meaning of Catullus 64* (Amsterdam: Hakkert, 1977);

Julia W. Loomis, *Studies in Catullan Verse: An Analysis of Word Types and Patterns in the Polymetra* (Leiden: E. J. Brill, 1972);

Kenneth Quinn, *The Catullan Revolution* (Carlton: Melbourne University Press, 1959);

Quinn, ed., *Approaches to Catullus* (Cambridge: Heffer, 1972);

David O. Ross Jr., *Style and Tradition In Catullus* (Cambridge, Mass.: Harvard University Press, 1969);

Daniel Selden, *"Ceveat lector:* Catullus and the Rhetoric of Performance," in *Innovations of Antiquity,* edited by Ralph Hexter and Daniel Selden (London: Routledge, 1992), pp. 461–512;

Arthur Leslie Wheeler, *Catullus and the Traditions of Ancient Poetry* (Berkeley: University of California Press, 1934);

T. P. Wiseman, *Catullan Questions* (Leicester, U.K.: Leicester University Press, 1969);

Wiseman, *Catullus and his World A Reappraisal* (Cambridge: Cambridge University Press, 1985).

Cicero

(3 January 106 B.C. – 7 December 43 B.C.)

James M. May
Saint Olaf College

MAJOR WORKS–EXTANT:

ORATIONS

Pro Quinctio (For Quinctius, 81 B.C.);

Pro Roscio Amerino (For Roscius of Ameria, 80 B.C.);

Pro Roscio comoedo (For Roscius the Actor, 76 or 66 B.C.);

Pro Tullio (For Tullius, 71 B.C.);

Divinatio in Caecilium (Against Caecilius, 70 B.C.);

In Verrem, Actio Prima (Against Verres, First Action, 70 B.C.);

In Verrem, Actio Secunda (Against Verres, Second Action)–five speeches (70 B.C.);

Pro Caecina (For Caecina, 69 B.C.);

Pro Fonteio (For Fonteius, 60s? B.C.);

De imperio Cn. Pompei (On Pompey's Command, 66 B.C.);

Pro Cluentio (For Cluentius, 66 B.C.);

De lege agraria contra Rullum (Against Rullus)–three speeches (63 B.C.);

Pro Rabirio Perduellionis reo (For Rabirius, 63 B.C.);

In Catilinam I–IV (Against Catiline I–IV, 63 B.C.);

Pro Murena (For Murena, 63 B.C.);

Pro Sulla (For Sulla, 62 B.C.);

Pro Archia (For Archias, 62 B.C.);

Pro Flacco (For Flaccus, 59 B.C.);

Post reditum in senatu (Speech of Thanks to the Senate, 57 B.C.);

Post reditum ad quirites (Speech of Thanks to the Citizens, 57 B.C.);

De domo sua (On His House, 57 B.C.);

De haruspicum responso (On the Reply of the Soothsayers, 56 B.C.);

Pro Sestio (For Sestius, 56 B.C.);

In Vatinium (Against Vatinius, 56 B.C.);

Pro Caelio (For Caelius, 56 B.C.);

De provinciis consularibus (On the Consular Provinces, 56 B.C.);

In Pisonem (Against Piso, 56 B.C.);

Pro Balbo (For Balbus, 56 B.C.);

Pro Rabirio Postumo (For Rabirius Postumus, 56 B.C.);

Pro Plancio (For Plancius, 54 B.C.);

Pro Scauro (For Scaurus, 54 B.C.);

Cicero (bust in the Vatican, Rome)

Pro Milone (For Milo, 52 B.C.);

Pro Marcello (For Marcellus, 46 B.C.);

Pro Ligario (For Ligarius, 46 B.C.);

Pro rege Deiotaro (For King Deiotarus, 45 B.C.);

Philippicae (Philippics)–fourteen speeches (44–43 B.C.).

RHETORICAL WORKS

De inventione (On Invention, between 91 and 89 B.C.);

De oratore (On the Ideal Orator, 55 B.C.);

Parititiones oratoriae (Classifications of Oratory, between 54 and 52);

Brutus (46 B.C.);

De optimo genere oratorum (On the Best Kind of Orators, 46 B.C.);

Orator (46 B.C.);

Topica (Topics, 44 B.C.).

PHILOSOPHICAL WORKS

De republica (On the Republic, 54–51 B.C.);

De legibus (On the Laws, between 53/52–51 B.C.);

Paradoxa Stoicorum (Stoic Paradoxes, 46 B.C.);

Academica (Academics, 45 B.C.);

De finibus bonorum et malorum (On the Supreme Good, 45 B.C.);

Tusculanae Disputationes (Tusculan Disputations, 45 B.C.);

De natura deorum (On the Nature of the Gods, 45 B.C.);

De senectute (On Old Age, 45 or 44 B.C.);

De amicitia (On Friendship, 44 B.C.);

De divinatione (On Divination, 44 B.C.);

De fato (On Fate, 44 B.C.);

De officiis (On Moral Duties, 44 B.C.).

LETTERS

Ad familiares, sixteen books (Letters to Friends);

Ad Atticum, sixteen books (Letters to Atticus);

Ad Quintum, twenty-seven letters (Letters to His Brother Quintus);

Ad Brutum, twenty-six letters (Letters to Brutus).

MAJOR WORKS–FRAGMENTARY:

Hortensius (46 B.C.);

Consolatio (46 B.C.).

Editio princeps: *Opera,* edited by Alexander Minutianus (Milan: Guillermus Le Signerre, 1498)–For individual *editiones principes,* see *Companion to Classical Texts,* by Frederick W. Hall (Oxford: Oxford University Press, 1913), pp. 219–228.

Standard editions: Johann Kaspar Orelli (Johann Georg Baiter and Karl Halm), 1845–1863–complete text; Bibliotheca Teubneriana (BT); Oxford Classical Texts (OCT), complete except for philosophical works and fragments–series; Loeb Classical Library, including an English translation–series; Budé, including a French translation–series; A. Mondadori of Milan, *M. Tulli Ciceronis Opera Omnia quae Exstant Critico Apparatu Instructa*–series in progress; *M. Tullius Cicero, The Fragmentary Speeches,* edited by Jane W. Crawford, second edition (Atlanta: Scholars Press, 1994)–oratorical fragments; *[Philosophica] M. Tulli Ciceronis Fragmenta,* edited by Giovanna Garbarino (Milan: A. Mondadori, 1984)–philosophical works; *M. Tulli Ciceronis Consolationis Fragmenta,* edited by C. Vitelli (Milan: A. Mondadori, 1979)–philosophical works; *Hortensius,* edited by Alberto Grilli (Milan: Istituto Editoriale Cisalpino, 1962)–philosophical works; *Poetica fragmenta,* edited by Antonio Traglia (Milan: Mondadori, 1963)–poetry; *Aratea fragments poetiques,* edited and translated by Jean Soubiran (Paris: Les Belles Lettres, 1972)–poetry.

Translations in English: *Opera Philosophica: With English Translations,* Loeb Classical Library (London: Heinemann, 1913–1933).

Commentaries:

SPEECHES: *M. Tulli Ciceronis De Domo Suo Ad Pontifices Oratio,* edited by R. G. M. Nisbet (Oxford: Clarendon Press, 1939); *A Commentary on Cicero's Oration De Haruspicum Responso,* edited by John O. Lenaghan (The Hague: Mouton, 1969); *A Social and Economic Commentary on Cicero's De Lege Agraria Orationes Tres,* edited by Engbert Jan Jonkers (Leiden: Brill, 1963); *In L. Calpurnium Pisonem Oratio,* edited by R. G. M. Nisbet (Oxford: Clarendon Press, 1961); *A Commentary on Cicero In Vatinium,* edited by Lewis Greville Pocock (London: University of London Press, 1926; reprinted, Amsterdam: A. M. Hakkert, 1967); *Cicero, Verrines II.I,* edited by Thomas N. Mitchell (Warminster: Aris & Phillips, 1980); Harold C. Gotoff, *Cicero's Elegant Style: An Analysis of the Pro Archia* (Urbana: University of Illinois Press, 1979); *M. Tulli Ciceronis Pro Caelio Oratio,* edited by R. G. Austin, third edition (Oxford: Clarendon Press, 1960); *Pro Cluentio,* edited by William Yorke Fausset, fourth edition (London, 1901); *A Social and Economic Commentary on Cicero's De Imperio Gnaei Pompei,* edited by Engbert Jan Jonkers (Leiden: Brill, 1959); *Cicero, Pro P. sulla Oratio,* edited by D. H. Berry (Cambridge: Cambridge University Press, 1996); *M. Tulli Ciceronis Pro T. Milone Ad Iudices Oratio,* edited by A. C. Clarke (Oxford: Clarendon Press, 1895; reprinted, Amsterdam: A. M. Hakkert, 1967); *M. Tulli Ciceronis Pro Gnaeo Plancio Oratio Ad Iudices,* edited by Hubert Ashton Holden, third edition (Cambridge: Cambridge University Press, 1891); *Pro P. Quinctio,* edited by Thomas E. Kinsey (Sydney: Sydney University Press, 1971); *M. Tulli Ciceronis Pro C. Rabirio Oratio ad Quirites,* edited by William E. Heitland (Cambridge: Cambridge University Press, 1882); *M. Tulli Ciceronis Pro Publio Sestio Oratio Ad Iudices,* edited by Holden (London: Macmillan, 1883).

PHILOSOPHICAL WORKS: *Academica,* edited by James Smith Reid (London: Macmillan, 1885; reprinted, Hildesheim: Olms, 1966); *M. Tulli Ciceronis De Finibus Bonorum et Malorum Libri I, II,* edited by Reid (Cambridge: Cambridge University Press, 1925; reprinted, Hildesheim: Olms, 1968); *M. Tulli Ciceronis De Finibus Liber I,* edited by Alberto Grilli (Milan: Goliardica, 1966); *De Divinatione,* edited by Arthur Stanley Pease, 2 volumes (Urbana: University of Illinois Press, 1920–1923); *De Natura Deorum,* edited by Pease (Cambridge, Mass.: Harvard University Press, 1925); *De*

Officiis Libri Tres, fourth edition, edited by Holden (Cambridge: Cambridge University Press, 1881); Andrew R. Dyck, *A Commentary on Cicero, De Officiis* (Ann Arbor: University of Michigan Press, 1996); *De Senectute,* edited by J. G. F. Powell (Cambridge: Cambridge University Press, 1988); *On Fate and the Consolation of Philosophy IV.5–7, V,* edited by R. W. Sharples (Warminster: Aris & Phillips, 1991); *M. Tulli Ciceronis Tusculanarum Disputationum Libri Quinque,* 2 volumes, edited by Thomas W. Dougan and Robert M. Henry (Cambridge: Cambridge University Press, 1905–1934).

RHETORICAL WORKS: *Brutus,* edited by Alan E. Douglas (Oxford: Clarendon Press, 1966); *M. Tulli Ciceronis De Oratore ad Quintum Fratrem Libri Tres,* 3 volumes, edited by A. S. Wilkins (Oxford: Clarendon Press, 1881); *M. Tulli Ciceronis ad M. Brutum Orator,* edited by John Edwin Sandys (Cambridge: Cambridge University Press, 1885).

POETRY: *The Poems of Cicero,* edited by W. W. Ewbank (London: University of London Press, 1933).

LETTERS: *Cicero's Letters to Atticus,* 7 volumes, edited by D. R. Shackleton Bailey (Cambridge: Cambridge University Press, 1965–1970); *Epistulae ad Familiares,* 2 volumes, edited by Bailey (Cambridge: Cambridge University Press, 1977); *Epistulae ad Quintum Fratrem et ad M. Brutum,* edited by Bailey (Cambridge: Cambridge University Press, 1980).

Marcus Tullius Cicero, the undisputed master of oratory in ancient Rome, was perhaps more successful and more abidingly influential as a practitioner of his art than any other orator in any other age. The man whose name quickly became synonymous with eloquence itself (*non hominis nomen, sed eloquentiae,* Quintilian 10.1.112) left to his fellow Romans and to posterity a corpus of speeches that are models not only of effective courtroom persuasion but also of brilliantly lucid prose style; yet, to categorize him as merely an orator would do a grave injustice to this consummate man of letters.

As a rhetorical theorist, he was not content to pass on precepts that might result in empty eloquence; Cicero demanded that his ideal orator be equipped with all the noble arts, calling for a marriage between eloquence and wisdom (rhetoric and philosophy), providing a pattern even to this day of the "liberally educated person." As a philosopher, although eclectic in approach and taste and highly dependent on Greek models, Cicero presented his works from a distinctly Roman point of view; he forged for the Latin language a philosophical vocabulary that for centuries was utilized by subsequent writers. He likewise indulged in writing poetry and, despite the rather harsh judgment of posterity, he was, according to Plutarch (*Cicero* 2), the finest poet of his day. Amid such legal and literary activity Cicero maintained an incredibly active correspondence with his closest friend and confidant, Atticus; his brother, Quintus; and many other associates. The nearly one thousand letters that have survived are a veritable treasure trove, providing the greatest single source of information about Roman life and politics of that era. Although a *novus homo* (new man—one who had no ancestors who had attained high political office in Rome before him), Cicero managed to secure election to all the highest magistracies at the earliest possible age. He remained a significant figure in the Roman political scene of the late Republic—along with the likes of Pompey, Marcus Crassus, Julius Caesar, Mark Antony, and Octavius—for most of his life. His dream of a *concordia ordinum* (harmony of social classes) and a *consensus omnium bonorum* (consensus of like-minded patriots), fashioned during his consulship and in subsequent years, was never fully realized. In the final analysis, like so many of his peers of the senatorial class, he was incapable of seeing beyond the social and political constructs of the nobility-dominated state, which he held so dear and of which he became almost a symbol: the death blow struck at Cicero's neck by the sword of Antony's henchman has, for many, appeared emblematic of the impending doom that awaited the Republic soon after. A man of letters as well as a man of action, Cicero's life and work have inspired subsequent generations, not least of whom were the Renaissance humanists, who saw in his intellectual pursuits and loyal commitment to civic duty the traits that still characterize a "Renaissance man."

Marcus Tullius Cicero was born at Arpinum (also the birthplace of C. Marius, the famous Roman general and consul), about seventy miles southeast of Rome, on 3 January 106 B.C. Cicero's family, although technically not members of the Roman nobility, lived comfortably and had important connections (particularly through Cicero's mother, Helvia) in Rome. Cicero's father, a wealthy *eques* (knight), was solicitous of his sons' education and followed the typical Roman custom of entrusting their education, after the rudimentary training received in a Roman grammar school, to an influential and distinguished friend of the family. Marcus and his brother Quintus frequented the house of the famous orator and statesman Lucius Crassus. In that environment Cicero also had the privilege of interacting with the associates of Crassus, including most importantly Antonius, the other great orator of the period, as well as L. Aelius Stilo, the famous Stoic teacher of grammar and rhetoric.

At the age of seventeen Cicero served a brief military stint during the Social War. Returning after his ser-

Cicero's birthplace at Arpinum, seventy miles southeast of Rome (eighteenth-century painting by Richard Wilson; Findlay Galleries, Inc., Chicago)

vice in that year, he studied law, first with Q. Mucius Scaevola Augur and then, after the Augur's death, with his nephew, Q. Mucius Scaevola Pontifex. A year later Cicero was exposed to the teachings of Philo of Larissa, head of the Academy at Athens, who was visiting Rome. Philo's thought was sceptical in nature, holding that nothing could be known entirely for certain, and he advocated debating every issue from all sides. This approach appealed greatly to Cicero and exerted a profound influence upon him. About this time (but perhaps six or seven years later) Apollonius Molon, the renowned orator and rhetorician from Rhodes, visited Rome; Cicero heard his lectures and benefited directly from his criticism. During this period Diodotus, the Stoic philosopher, also took up residence in the house of the young Cicero.

Thus, during his teenage years Cicero had already come in contact with an impressive array of thinkers—philosophers representative of the most important schools, as well as statesmen, orators, and rhetoricians, both Roman and Greek. He was practiced in speaking and writing both Greek and Latin and had spent time composing and translating poetry. Considerable fragments of his translation of Aratus's *Phenomena* are, in fact, still extant. In his early youth Cicero also published his first rhetorical work, *De inventione* (On Invention), most likely written sometime during the years 91–89 B.C. when he was between fifteen and seventeen years of age. Later in life Cicero described the treatise as "the sketchy and unsophisticated work that found its way out of my notebooks when I was a boy, or rather a youth" (*De oratore* 1.5), but clearly the young man had initially intended to write the handbook on a grand scale, covering all parts of oratory. He apparently lost interest in the project and completed only two books. The first includes primarily an account of the four *constitutiones* or *status* (issues or defensive stances) of a speech, along with a discussion of the traditional parts of an oration; the second book deals with the three kinds of oratory—judicial, deliberative, and epideictic. The real significance of *De inventione* (along with the contemporary treatise known as *Rhetorica ad Herennium*, which was mistakenly attributed to Cicero in the manuscript tradition) is that it reveals first-century-B.C. rhetoric as it was studied by Cicero and his peers. In the prologue to the work Cicero already enunciates his strong belief in the importance of combining eloquence (rhetoric) with wisdom (philosophy), a conviction that found its full expression in his mature rhetorical works. The treatise was extremely popular and exerted great influence during the Middle Ages.

Cicero most probably began pleading cases at the age of twenty-four or twenty-five. His first extant oration dates from 81 B.C. and was delivered in a private case on behalf of Quinctius (*Pro Quinctio*), who was in a dispute over property in Gaul with Naevius, his late brother's business associate. Naevius was supported by many influential men, including his own pleader, Hortensius, who was at the time Rome's foremost speaker; the young and inexperienced Cicero makes much of this point in fashioning a clever, and ultimately successful, appeal from his client's (and his own) position of disadvantage. In the following year Cicero entered the public arena in his first criminal case, defending Roscius of Ameria on a charge of parricide (*Pro Roscio Amerino*). In the politically charged atmosphere of the Sullan proscriptions and confiscations, Roscius (Cicero claims) was being framed by the actual murderers, who had killed his father and then placed his name on the proscription list, all in order to get their hands on his property. The mastermind behind the entire scheme was Chrysogonus, a freedman of Sulla. The more experienced and better-known pleaders, according to Cicero, did not dare defend the backward, almost rustic Roscius in the face of Chrysogonus, a fact that the young orator uses to his advantage as he portrays himself as a courageous, outspoken defender of the downtrodden. In fact, the entire speech is a wonderfully rich exposition of the various characters involved and an early example of how Cicero so effectively used ethos (argumentation based on character portrayal), among other tactics, to secure a forensic victory.

For reasons of health and further study, not for fear of Sulla (as Plutarch, *Cicero* 3, states), Cicero sailed for Greece and Asia Minor in 79 B.C., shortly after his early successes. He himself says (*Brutus* 313–314) that he was thin and lacking in strength, with a long neck and weak lungs and voice, which he had strained by speaking continually without modulation and by holding his body tense throughout his delivery. Determined to gain strength and improve his speaking ability, he arrived in Athens and spent six months studying philosophy with Antiochus the Academic and rhetoric with Demetrius the Syrian. He then traveled through all of Asia Minor, where he practiced declamation with the most distinguished orators of the region, including Menippus of Stratonicea, Dionysius of Magnesia, Aeschylus of Cnidus, and Xenocles of Adramyttium. Cicero moved on to Rhodes, where he met again Apollonius Molon, who effectively critiqued Cicero's speaking and worked to repress the youthful, and sometimes excessively exuberant, style evident in his early speeches. Cicero described the results in this way: "I came back after two years' absence not only better trained, but almost transformed. My voice was no longer over-strained, my language had lost its froth, my lungs had gained strength and my body had put on weight" (*Brutus* translated by Hendrickson).

Back in Rome in 77 B.C., Cicero married Terentia and turned his attention once again to pleading court cases and preparing for a political career. His speech on behalf of the comic actor Roscius (*Pro Roscio comoedo*) dates from this period (76 B.C., but perhaps as late as 66 B.C.), as does the fragmentary oration for Tullius (*Pro Tullio*, probably delivered in 71 B.C.). Now thirty years old, Cicero was eligible to run for the quaestorship, the first magistracy in the succession of political offices (*cursus honorum*) that culminated in the consulship. He secured election and served as quaestor in western Sicily in 75 B.C., where he supervised the grain supply. His just and upright dealings in Sicily, in combination with the connections he had made there during his service, made him the Sicilians' first choice as prosecutor when they initiated action in Rome against their former governor Verres before the standing court concerned with extortion.

Verres had been governor in Sicily in 73 B.C. but had served two additional years because of the extraordinary political circumstances involved in the revolt of the slaves and gladiators led by Spartacus. During that time Verres was reputed to have extorted more than forty million sesterces, boasting that the proceeds of one year were enough for him and that those gleaned from the second and third years were sufficient for his defenders and his judges. As a member of the senatorial class, Verres was supported by influential members of the senate and defended by Hortensius, whom Cicero had faced before. Cicero generally preferred the role of advocate for the defense, but it was something of a practice in Rome for a rising politician to undertake the prosecution of a prominent figure in a noble cause. In this case, even while prosecuting, Cicero could again speak for the injured and cast himself in the role of the defender of the downtrodden. In preparing and carrying out the prosecution, Cicero displayed incredible energy. He first had to secure, through the process known as *divinatio,* the right to prosecute, which was challenged by one Q. Caecilius, Verres' former quaestor and certainly his preferred prosecutor for the case (hence the *Divinatio in Caecilium*). Next he had to gather evidence and build a case, all of which Verres,

Hortensius, and their supporters resisted vigorously since they hoped to delay the case until Hortensius (who was a candidate for consul) and other powerful friends might gain more-influential positions in the government. Cicero himself was a candidate for the curuleaedileship (which he won and held in 69 B.C.), and so he had to carry out all these proceedings amid the pressures of running a campaign.

In the speech known as *In Verrem, Actio Prima* (Against Verres, First Action), delivered in 70 B.C., Cicero forgoes the usual heaping up of charges, vivid characterizations, and emotional appeal in favor of a lucid introduction to the case, its political and procedural difficulties, and a straightforward presentation of the evidence. Flabbergasted by this approach, Hortensius failed to respond, and Verres went into voluntary exile. The swift victory did not preclude Cicero from publishing five more speeches against Verres (*In Verrem, Actio Secunda*), cataloguing in great detail and with extraordinary rhetorical flourish the crimes and outrages of the governor. These speeches remain a rich storehouse not only of oratorical models but also of invaluable sources for present-day knowledge of Roman provincial administration. The *Verrines* are an important turning point in Cicero's life and career. The decisive victory garnered for him considerable political support as well as the reputation of having become Rome's premier orator.

In 69 B.C., while serving his term as curuleaedile, Cicero defended Aulus Caecina (*Pro Caecina*) in a complicated case involving ownership of property and the rights of heirs. To argue the case required detailed knowledge of the civil law, of which Cicero was justly proud; he later cited this oration (*Orator* 102) as his own favorite example of a speech in the plain style. Cicero's defense of Marcus Fonteius (*Pro Fonteio,* 60s? B.C.) on a charge of extortion in Gaul may also have taken place at this time. The speech presents an interesting contrast with the *Verrines,* since Cicero employed several arguments on behalf of Fonteius that might well have been used in defending Verres.

Cicero's extant correspondence begins about this time and continues for another quarter century, offering an unusual view of Roman politics and daily life. Once again a candidate for public office in 67 B.C., Cicero again was elected and served as praetor in 66 B.C. During that time he delivered *De imperio Cn. Pompei* (On Pompey's Command, also known as *Pro lege Manilia,* On the Manilian Law), his first oration before the people, supporting the proposal of the tribune Manilius to transfer the command of the war against King Mithridates of Pontus from Lucullus to Pompey. Cicero seems to have been eager to display his allegiance to Pompey, an allegiance that endured, to a greater or lesser degree, throughout the rest of his life.

The speech presents an idealized portrait of the general, praising his virtues of *virtus, auctoritas, et felicitas* (courage, authority, and good fortune) while making every effort not to insult Lucullus and the senatorial party, the majority of whom opposed Manilius's law (which, in the end, was easily ratified). This year also was the occasion of Cicero's longest and perhaps most complicated defense, delivered on behalf of Aulus Cluentius (*Pro Cluentio Habito*), charged with the attempted poisoning of his stepfather as well as earlier having bribed a jury to convict the same stepfather on a false charge of murder. The oration is a masterpiece of persuasion, filled with vivid narrations of familial relationships and feuds, detailed and lifelike portrayals of character, and skillful variations of style. Cicero was particularly proud of his victory in this case and is reported to have boasted later that he "had thrown dust in the eyes of the jury" (Quintilian 2.17.21).

The decade of the 60s B.C. was a particularly eventful time for Cicero. He lost his father and became a father himself with the birth of his son, Marcus. Cicero was also enjoying the hard-earned reputation of being Rome's premier orator. He had secured political prominence with his accession to the praetorship and his support of Pompey, the great general and leading figure among the conservative republican government. Now, as his year of eligibility grew closer, all of Cicero's attention turned to climbing to the top rung of the *cursus honorum,* the consulship. He worked continuously to garner support from every possible corner. When the election results for the year 63 B.C. were announced, and once again Marcus Tullius Cicero's name topped the list–this time the list for the consulship–Cicero realized his dream. He had accomplished (with the help of his oratorical ability, hard work, and the support of the Roman knights, not to mention the threatening presence of Lucius Sergius Catilina (Catiline) on the same ballot, which shifted senatorial support to him) what only a handful of others in several previous generations had managed: a *novus homo,* the son of a Roman knight having no noble ancestors, he had secured, at the youngest possible legal age, Rome's highest political office. This accomplishment was obviously one of the defining moments in Cicero's life. He was justly proud of it and never ceased speaking about it–often to the dismay and irritation of his opponents and critics. It invested his character with a measure of prestige and authority that he would continuously wield in his subsequent oratorical and political career.

Cicero's consular year of 63 B.C. was marked by an extraordinary level of administrative and oratorical activity. In his first official act as consul he opposed in three speeches an agrarian bill brought by the tribune Servilius Rullus (*De lege agraria contra Rullum*), which aimed, among other things, at dividing up the *ager publi-*

The Temple of Concord, where Cicero delivered his oration against Catiline before the Roman Senate (restoration by H. G. Marceau and H. B. Rebert)

cus (public land) in Campania. The first speech, which is fragmentary, is addressed to the senate; the other two are addressed to the people *(contio)* in public meeting. Although Cicero repeatedly claims to be a true leader of popular sentiment (a *popularis*), advocating peace, harmony, and calm, while Rullus and the Board of Ten Commissioners are characterized as hypocrites who feign support of the people in order to further their own agenda, his pro-Pompey, senatorial sentiments are apparent. That year Cicero again displayed strong support of senatorial policy in his defense of Gaius Rabirius *(Pro Rabirio perduellionis reo)*, an aged Roman knight and political scapegoat of sorts who was charged by the democrats with treason for having put to death Saturninus thirty-seven years earlier (in 100 B.C.). The motivation for the charge was to challenge the right of the senate to act on the authority of its general decree of emergency *(senatus consultum ultimum)*. Cicero valued his victory and his speech, which he cited as his finest example of the

grand style *(Orator* 102). In a strange sort of way this challenge presaged the challenge that Cicero himself subsequently faced over the same issue only a few years later.

Toward the end of his year of office Cicero, through careful attention, diligent investigation, and the fortunate confluence of several circumstances, uncovered a revolutionary plot to overthrow the government. Its leader was Catiline, who had been a rival of Cicero in the consular elections—a disenchanted, bankrupt senator of noble descent who, despite Cicero's characterization of him, possessed considerable intellectual and physical abilities and a personal magnetism that was capable of attracting a loyal following. The four speeches that the consul delivered concerning the conspiracy, known as *In Catilinam I-IV* (Catilinarian Orations), are justly famous and familiar to nearly every student who has studied Latin. The first, delivered to the senate on 8 November following an abortive attempt to assassinate Cicero in his home, is a frontal attack aimed at Catiline, who came–probably unexpectedly–to the senate meeting on that day. Cicero, seeing Catiline seated in isolation from the rest of the senators, began his speech with an unorthodox series of rhetorical questions–for example, *Quousque tandem abutere, Catilina, patientia nostra?* (How long, Catiline, will you continue to abuse our patience?), and proceeded to inform the senate of the conspiracy while urging Catiline to go into voluntary exile. The second speech, delivered to the people on the next day, informed them of the plot and the actions taken by Cicero to ensure their safety while presenting vivid portraits of the savage conspirators and the ever-provident consul. The third speech, given to the people on 3 December, was precipitated by the arrest of several conspirators, along with the apprehension of crucially incriminating evidence. Two days later, on the Nones of December, the senate met to debate the fate of the conspirators. Caesar, among others, argued against execution, while Cicero, armed with the *senatus consultum,* argued strenuously in the *Fourth Catilinarian* in favor of it; it was, however, the speech of Cato the Younger that carried the day, and that evening the five conspirators in custody–including a praetor, Cornelius Lentulus Sura–were strangled to death in the Tullianum, Rome's prison. Cicero is said, upon emerging from the scene, to have delivered his shortest speech: *vixerunt* (they have lived).

Rather amazingly, amid the flurry of activity during the conspiracy and sometime between the delivery of the *Second Catilinarsian* and *Third Catilinarian,* Cicero was called upon to defend the consul-elect for 62 B.C., Lucius Murena, on a charge of bribery. The rhetorical challenges facing Cicero were daunting: the case could not have come at a more inconvenient time; the charges were being leveled by two of Cicero's own friends and supporters, Servius Sulpicius (whom Cicero, in fact, had supported for election against Murena) and Marcus Cato the Younger; and finally, the pressing concern that, if Murena were convicted, the new year would begin with only one consul in office while the state was still embroiled in the conspiracy. The speech that results *(Pro Murena)* is one of Cicero's rhetorical masterpieces. In it he neutralizes the powerful authority of the prosecutors with the genial wit for which he was famous, poking fun at Sulpicius as a professional lawyer and Cato as an overly rigid Stoic, all the while maintaining the crucial plea that the new year must open with two consuls at the helm of state. Cicero's victory was overwhelming, and Murena served as consul in 62 B.C.

Following the execution of the conspirators, a public thanksgiving was decreed and Cicero was hailed as *Pater Patriae* (Father of the Fatherland). Yet, only a few weeks later, when Cicero was laying down his office on 31 December, the tribune Q. Metellus Nepos prevented him from addressing the people in customary fashion on the grounds that, by executing the conspirators, he had put to death Roman citizens without a trial. Making the best of the situation, Cicero confined himself to the oath that he had performed the duties of the consulship faithfully, swearing that by his efforts the city and the state had been saved. The people roared their approval, but storm clouds lingered on the horizon. A year later P. Clodius Pulcher, a patrician descended from one of the noblest families of Rome, was caught disgracefully dressed as a woman at the festival in honor of the Bona Dea, which, incidentally, had been held at the house of Julius Caesar. In the subsequent judicial investigation Clodius, on trial for sacrilege, claimed to have been ninety miles away from Rome at the time. Cicero, however, had seen him in Rome within three hours of the time of his alibi and testified to that effect. Despite this testimony and the obvious guilt of Clodius, a bribed jury acquitted the perpetrator. Contributing further to the enmity between them, Cicero, on another occasion, employing his characteristic quick repartee and caustic wit, humiliated Clodius publicly in the senate. Personal hatred would soon turn into public vindictiveness.

At about this same time the senate obstinately (and shortsightedly) snubbed the requests of three of its most powerful members–Pompey, Caesar, and Crassus–actions that led to the formation (in 60 B.C.) of the coalition among these men known to history as the First Triumvirate. Cicero himself was courted by Caesar as a fourth member of the group, certainly on the strength of his legal knowledge and powers of persuasion, but the orator could not bring himself to support in an active way Caesar's manipulation of the constitution. In fact, Cicero spoke out against it. In 59 B.C. Clodius (a noble patrician), still bent on revenge, arranged to have himself adopted into a plebeian family in order to run for the office of tribune (which was open only to plebeians). Cicero surely saw the handwriting on the wall, but he seemingly refused to acknowledge it. As late as November of 59 B.C., he expressed confidence in his future. He even went so far as to refuse a generous offer from Caesar to become one of his *legati* (deputies) in Gaul or a commissioner for supervising the division of public lands. Clodius secured the office of tribune and the support of the consuls for 58 B.C., L. Piso and Aulus Gabinius, in order to avenge himself. Finally, in March of 58 B.C., Clodius secured the adoption of a law that outlawed from Rome anyone who had put Roman citizens to death without a trial. The senate was powerless, and help from the consuls and triumvirs (who were content to have Cicero removed from the scene for a time) was not forthcoming. Cicero decided to leave Rome, retiring into exile in northern Greece. A second law, naming Cicero specifically (and hence unconstitutional), was passed shortly thereafter. Clodius then engineered the razing of Cicero's house on the Palatine, managing to have part of it consecrated to Liberty. Other of Cicero's property suffered damage, and his wife and children were forced to take shelter with relatives.

Only three speeches survive from the years between Cicero's consulship and his exile. In 62 B.C. Cicero defended Publius Sulla *(Pro Sulla)* on a charge of complicity in the Catilinarian conspiracy. The speech illustrates important tactics that became staples of Ciceronian persuasive strategy; namely, the increased use of Cicero's own character, now enhanced by consular prestige, as a source for proof, as well as Cicero's identification with his client in order to lend more authority to the character and case of his client. Cicero's defense of Sulla resides essentially in the argument that he himself, the enemy of the conspiracy, is speaking on behalf of Sulla; Sulla must therefore be innocent.

One of Cicero's most beloved speeches, his defense of Archias the poet *(Pro Archia),* also dates from 62 B.C. Cicero is technically defending Archias's claim to citizenship, but the speech in large part is a stirring and eloquent defense of the study of literature and the noble arts. *Pro Flacco,* delivered in 59 B.C., is Cicero's defense of a friend (who had assisted in the apprehension of the Catilinarian conspirators) and former governor of the province of Asia on a charge of extortion. Cicero employs humor in combination with a kindling of Roman prejudice against the provincials and an effective use of consular authority to secure the acquittal of a client who was probably guilty.

It was psychologically devastating for Cicero to face the fact that his crushing of the Catilinarian conspiracy, the crowning glory of his consulship, was likewise the cause of his forced departure from Rome. The year and a half that he spent in exile was the low point of his life. Letters from that period to his friend and confidant Atticus reveal a feeling of depression that led him to contemplate suicide. Friends and supporters back in Rome, however, were not lacking. The consuls and tribunes of 57 B.C. were favorable to Cicero's cause, and Pompey, who had done nothing to throttle Clodius's previous attacks, was now irritated by his actions and actively supported Cicero's recall. On 4 August 57 B.C. the senate passed a law authorizing his return; a month later he arrived in Rome amid an atmosphere of great triumph. He immediately set about reestablishing his private and public standing.

The speeches delivered during this time are generally known collectively as *post reditum* (after his return). Cicero formally thanked the senate on the day after his return *(Post reditum in senatu);* on the next day he addressed the people from the rostra and expressed his thanks to them *(Post reditum ad quirites)*. *De domo sua* (On His House) was delivered before the college of priests; in it Cicero argued for the recovery of his property on the Palatine and pointed out the illegality of its consecration to Liberty at the instigation of Clodius. *De haruspicum responso* (On the Reply of the Soothsayers) was delivered in the senate in early 56 B.C. and responded to Clodius's assertion that Cicero had offended the gods by restoring his house on a consecrated site. These speeches, as well as the others dating from this period, are marked by certain themes that resonate throughout. They are often characterized by being as much apologies on behalf of Cicero as political deliberations or defenses of clients. Cicero presents himself as the consular orator who now has saved the state twice without recourse to arms, once through his thwarting of Catiline, the second time by his voluntary departure from Rome (to keep the peace, as he claims). At times he identifies himself closely with the state; at other times he presents himself as the sacrificial victim who was offered up on its behalf.

The fine speech delivered in March 56 B.C. in defense of Publius Sestius *(Pro Sestio),* the former tribune who had championed the cause for Cicero's recall and who had been indicted for violence, illustrates all of these points. In addition to offering a defense of Sestius and an apologia on his own behalf, Cicero sets forth a stunning manifesto of his political philosophy wherein, among other things, he effectively characterizes the *optimates* (best men), who support the senatorial and constitutional government of the Republic, as well as the band of thugs and revolutionaries, supporters of men such as Clodius, who call themselves *populares* (friends of the people). The speech was followed by *In Vatinium* (Against Vatinius), a scathing, invective-filled cross-examination of the former tribune and supporter of Caesar, who had testified against Sestius. A month later Cicero was at his oratorical best in his justly famous defense of Marcus Caelius, a young protégé who had been charged with several counts of violence *(Pro Caelio).* Leaving behind the politics of exile and restoration, Cicero presented a successful defense based largely on clever characterizations of Caelius, Clodia (according to Cicero, the real force behind the prosecution), and even Clodius (her brother), along with their noble ancestors.

Elated by his successful recall, the recovery of his building site and damages for the loss of his house and estates, and the recent overwhelming victory in the Sestius case, and further encouraged by what he perceived as a growing rift among the triumvirs, Cicero proposed, the day after his speech for Caelius, that the senate should, the following month, reopen the discussion of Caesar's distribution of the Campanian land. Once again Cicero had miscalculated the strength of the optimate position and their ability to foil the will of the triumvirs. His action precipitated the so-called conference of Luca, a meeting held in order to patch up their differences. Cicero was soon brought to heel following an encounter between Pompey and Cicero's brother Quintus, during which Pompey called in all his markers, so to speak, reminding Quintus of the pledges he had given Pompey (about Cicero's future conduct) previously when Quintus had sued for his brother's recall, making clear that Cicero's silence, if not his cooperation, was expected. As a result Cicero, crestfallen and humiliated, withdrew his motion and for the next several years presented no opposition to the three. In fact, he was forced into delivering (in June or July of 56 B.C.) what he called his "palinode" or "recantation" (*Ad Att.* 4.5), most probably the *De provinciis consularibus* (On the Consular Provinces), in which he argued for an extension of Caesar's Gallic command. He was all too aware of the inconsistency of his actions, and he found it embarrassingly exasperating, as he candidly revealed in private conversations and letters to his closest friends, such as Atticus.

Later that year, after being ridiculed in the senate by his old enemy, the former consul Piso, Cicero replied with a vitriolic invective *(In Pisonem),* but again he was called upon to defend partisans of the triumvirs–Balbus (in *Pro Balbo,* 56 B.C.), Rabirius (in *Pro Rabirio Postumo,* 56 B.C.), and even more embarrassingly, Vatinius (whom he had attacked so fiercely only two years previously) and Gabinius (the consular colleague of Piso who in 58 B.C. had aided and abetted Clodius's measures against him). The fragmentary *Pro Scauro* (54 B.C.), given in defense of Scaurus on a charge of extortion, again stirs up prejudices against the provincials, this time the Sardinians, in an emotionally charged proceeding that brought to bear the authority and influence of six *patroni* (fellow patrons) and the character testimony of nine consulars, including Pompey. *Pro Plancio* (54 B.C.) is Cicero's defense of the man who, four years earlier as quaestor in Macedonia, had given Cicero aid during the dark hours of his exile. As is the case in so many of Cicero's speeches, the actual charge of election bribery retreats into the background, giving way to the presentation of Cicero's own character and deeds, and the authority with which he supports his client.

How does one deal with such trying times of personal inconsistency, not to mention the humiliating realization of having gravely compromised one's principles? For Cicero, his consolation was always the same: he took refuge in literature, returning to his youthful studies of rhetoric and philosophy and writing about them. During the half-decade following Luca, he com-

posed three important treatises–*De oratore* (On the Ideal Orator), *De republica* (On the Republic), and *De legibus* (On the Laws). The three books that comprise the *De oratore,* Cicero's finest and most important rhetorical treatise, were written in 55 B.C. and completed. The dramatic date of the dialogue is 91 B.C., and Cicero set the discussion at the Tusculan estate of his former mentor, the legendary orator Crassus, who is joined by Antonius, the other great orator of the age; Scaevola the augur; and several other prominent speakers and men of state. The treatise is unusual among ancient rhetorical writings in that it abandons entirely the format, the language–that is, the jargon–of typical rhetorical handbooks. In fact, Cicero has his characters openly criticize the handbooks at virtually every opportunity. Still, most of the rhetorical precepts (at least in abbreviated form) are there, woven skillfully into the dialogue and discussed in a vocabulary that avoids the traditional technical terminology. In the course of the discussion a portrait of the ideal orator emerges, a man in possession of both eloquence and wisdom, steeped not only in the knowledge of rhetoric but also more importantly in philosophy, law, human character, and emotion–in short, all of the noble arts–the product of a cultural education that has prepared him to speak on any topic and assume any position of leadership in the state. In many ways, of course, this portrait is made in Cicero's own image and likeness, and it, along with the work as a whole, stands as a monument to his rhetorical and oratorical genius.

By 54 B.C. Cicero was already engaged in another dramatic dialogue, *De republica* (On the Republic), this time set in 129 B.C., with Scipio the Younger and others of his circle serving as interlocutors. Originally disposed in six books, parts of the work are lost. Book 1 outlines the three forms of constitutions–democracy, aristocracy, and monarchy–and judges the Roman Republic, a composite of the three, as the finest constitutional form. Rome's course in developing such a constitution is traced in book 2; book 3 includes an argument over whether justice depends on expediency; and book 4, largely fragmentary, deals with education and culture within the community. The final two books, also fragmentary, present the picture of the ideal statesman and his rewards, culminating with the justly celebrated *Somnium Scipionis* (Dream of Scipio), in which Scipio relates how his adoptive grandfather, the great Africanus, appeared to him in a dream and revealed to him a view of the universe, the immortality of the soul, and a promise of an eternal reward amid the harmony of the spheres for those who have served the community and their fellows well. *De legibus* (On the Laws), begun probably in 53 or 52 B.C. but interrupted by Cicero's subsequent governorship and the civil war, is something of a sequel to *De republica.* Inspired by Plato's *Laws,* this dialogue between Cicero, his brother, and Atticus explores the general nature of law and justice, religious law, and laws affecting magistrates. Only three books survive of the original five or six. In addition to his writing Cicero's only other consolation during this time for the Republic was his election as augur in 53 B.C.

During the same time that Cicero was writing about the ideal state and its laws, the Roman state was in chaos—embroiled in bribery, political maneuvering, disorder, and violence. Elections had been postponed repeatedly because of the unrest, and riots between rival gangs, headed by Clodius and Milo, a candidate for office and friend of Cicero (who had, as tribune, worked for his recall from exile), were frequent. In January 52 B.C. the companies of Clodius and Milo met, probably by accident, on the Appian Way; fighting broke out, and in the scuffle Clodius was killed. To control the further unrest that ensued Pompey was appointed sole consul and enforced strict measures to govern the subsequent proceedings. Cicero delivered his speech on Milo's behalf *(Pro Milone)* in a packed forum under the eye of Pompey and his armed guard. Visibly shaken by the circumstances, Cicero completed his speech, but not with his accustomed effectiveness. Milo was convicted and went into exile. The speech as transmitted to readers is an extraordinary rhetorical composition, employing the three modes of persuasion—logical argumentation, ethos (portrayal of character), and pathos (appeal to the emotions)—to near perfection.

Unlike many Roman magistrates, Cicero never had a desire to leave Rome as a governor of a province. He had refused such duty after his praetorship and consulship. In March of 51 B.C., much to his dismay, he was sent as proconsul to the large province of Cilicia in Asia Minor. Upon his arrival he found matters, both civil and military, in much disarray. He set about restoring order, fixing reasonable interest rates, and fighting extortion. Faced with the threat of a possible invasion by the Parthians, he shored up his military forces and undertook a small campaign against the hill tribes of Mt. Amanus. After a siege of forty-six days, he captured the stronghold and was granted a *supplicatio* (public thanksgiving) by the senate. Although he long cherished hopes for a triumph, these were never realized.

Cicero returned to Rome in early January of 49 B.C. to find political turmoil and the state on the brink of civil war. Crassus had been killed in Parthia in 53 B.C., and the relationship between Pompey and Caesar, so often strained in the past, had now reached the breaking point. Even after Caesar had crossed the Rubicon, Cicero hoped to be able to negotiate some sort of reconciliation that might secure peace. Appointed by the government as district commissioner

at Capua, he spent the next several weeks away from the city, in Campania and at his estate in Formiae debating with himself, in true Academic fashion, his best course of action. He realized that war, no matter who the victor, would precipitate confiscation, bloodshed, and proscription; he could not stomach the unconstitutionality of Caesar's actions but was equally repulsed by many deeds of Pompey's supporters. On 28 March, Caesar himself visited Cicero at Formiae and requested that he come to Rome to work for peace. The orator frankly set forth conditions that Caesar could not accept, so in the end Cicero did not go to Rome. Eventually he joined the republican forces in Greece. After Caesar's victory at Pharsalus on 9 August 48 B.C. (from which Cicero was absent because of illness), and having subsequently refused command of the army proposed to him by Cato, Cicero returned to Italy, and passed an anxious year in Brundisium. In September of 47 B.C. Caesar returned and graciously gave Cicero permission to remain in the country.

Cicero abstained from politics under the dictatorship of Caesar. In 46 B.C., however, he broke a six-year silence by delivering in the senate *Pro Marcello* (For Marcellus), which is actually not a defense of Marcellus (who had been an opponent of Caesar) but a panegyric in praise of Caesar's clemency. This is the first of the so-called Caesarian Speeches. The other two, *Pro Ligario* (a beautifully crafted, cleverly argued speech from 46 B.C. defending Ligarius for waging war in Africa against Caesar) and *Pro rege Deiotaro* (defending, in 45 B.C., King Deiotarus, who was charged with the attempted murder of Caesar some years before), are forensic speeches both delivered before Caesar, who as dictator had assumed extraordinary judicial authority.

The troubles that Cicero faced in his public, political life during this period were compounded seriously by the troubles he experienced in his private life. After thirty years of marriage he divorced his wife Terentia in 46 B.C., the culmination of an estrangement that had begun several years before. He almost immediately married the young Publilia, but then came the greatest blow, the loss of Tullia, his beloved daughter, who died from complications of childbirth. Cicero, in extreme grief at the death of his daughter, was nearly inconsolable, and Publilia's lack of sympathetic support led quickly to divorce. Once again, as he had done a decade earlier, he took refuge in philosophy and literature. Writing day and night because he could not sleep, Cicero's literary output during the next two years was absolutely astounding. Among lost works, *Consolatio* (46 B.C.), a record of the deaths of great figures inspired by the death of Tullia, and the *Hortensius* (46 B.C.), a protreptic to the study of philosophy that would later have a profound impact on St. Augustine, are most noteworthy.

In rhetoric he composed two works that can rightly take their place alongside the *De oratore*. The *Brutus* (46 B.C.) presents an invaluable history of Roman oratory that is detailed by Cicero's critical assessment of orators of the past, along with a few of his own day; the *Orator* (46 B.C.), again dedicated to M. Brutus, presents a portrait of the perfect orator. Both these works essentially corroborate oratorical principles as set forth ten years earlier in the *De oratore*, but the emphasis has shifted to questions of style. During the intervening decade a classicizing movement known as Atticism (or neo-Atticism) had gained prominence; it recommended (largely in reaction to oratory such as Cicero's) employing a simpler style of speaking and models (especially the Attic orator Lysias) that fostered such a style. In these works Cicero answers such critics, claiming that the neo-Atticists have abandoned practical persuasion for stylistic nicety. According to Cicero, the consummate Attic orator was Demosthenes, the master of all three styles (plain, middle, and grand), and it is his kind of oratory that must be emulated. Another minor work, *De optimo genere oratorum* (On the Best Kind of Orators), an introduction to a proposed (but apparently never completed) translation of Aeschines' and Demosthenes' speeches *On the Crown*, also dates from this period.

Even more impressive are the range, scope, and number of philosophical treatises composed during this time. *Paradoxa Stoicorum* (46 B.C.) is a brief treatment of six paradoxes of Stoic philosophy (for example, the wise man alone is rich) exploring Stoic doctrine, which had always been of interest to him. *De finibus bonorum et malorum* (On the Supreme Good, 45 B.C.) examines in five books the question of the highest good. L. Manlius Torquatus expounds the Epicurean doctrine in book 1, which is refuted by Cicero in book 2. M. Porcius Cato explains Stoic doctrine in book 3, which is refuted again by Cicero in book 4, while M. Pupius Piso explains the Academic and peripatetic views in book 5. Such a mode of argumentation and presentation was a standard of operation for students of the Academy, which, sceptical of one's ability to discover absolute truth, advocated arguing every point from every possible angle in order to arrive at a view that was closest to the truth. Of all philosophical approaches, this was the most compatible with Cicero's nature and his preferred method of dealing with most questions, both in his treatises and in making his private decisions. *Tusculanae Disputationes* (Tusculan Disputations, 45 B.C.), named for Cicero's estate where the discussions are set, considers in five books the nature of death, the endurance of pain, how wisdom fortifies a person from sorrow and mental anguish, and why virtue is sufficient to secure happiness. *Academica* (45 B.C.) has come down to the present as a conflation of two editions, changing the interlocutors from Catulus, Lucullus, and

Coin depicting Pompey, a member of the First Triumvirate who recommended Cicero's recall to Rome from exile

Hortensius in the first edition to Varro and Cicero himself in the second. The work explores the epistemology of scepticism and the Old, Middle, and New Academies. *De natura deorum* (On the Nature of the Gods, 45 B.C.) is a dialogue set in 77 B.C. that examines the theological views of the Epicurean, Stoic, and Academic schools. Again the interlocutors (here Velleius the Epicurean, Balbus the Stoic, and Cotta the Academic) present their own views of the subject, which are then debated, discussed, or refuted by one of their peers. Its chief importance lies in its presenting the religious thought of an educated Roman of the late Republic.

Cicero was not present on the Ides of March in 44 B.C. when Caesar was assassinated, but he certainly rejoiced in the deed: "How I wish you had invited me to that splendid banquet on the Ides of March!" he later wrote Trebonius (*Ad familiares* 10.28). On March 17 Cicero delivered a speech in the senate urging a general amnesty for the conspirators, like that declared in Athens after the expulsion of the Thirty Tyrants. The arrival in Rome of the young C. Octavius (Octavian), Caesar's adopted son and heir, further buoyed the hopes of the republicans. Antony, however, who had been Caesar's colleague in the consulship and had, after the assassination, gained possession of Caesar's political papers and private fortune, continued to strengthen his own position. Cicero soon found himself losing hope, fearing that Rome had merely substituted one tyrant for another. Again he turned to philosophy. He completed *De divinatione* (On Divination, 44 B.C.), which he had begun before the Ides of March, presenting arguments in favor of the Roman practice of augury in the first book (in the character of his brother Quintus) and against divination (in his own character) in the second book. The fragmentary *De fato* (On Fate) also dates from this time (the most interesting aspect of which is Cicero's spirited defense of free will), as do two other short treatises that are recognized universally as Cicero's most charming efforts, *De senectute* (On Old Age, 45 or 44 B.C.) and *De amicitia* (On Friendship, 44 B.C.), both of which are dedicated to Atticus. Cicero set his discussion of old age in 150 B.C. at the house of the famous statesman Cato the Elder, who, speaking with Laelius and Scipio, goes on to refute the reasons why people generally consider old age to be an unhappy time. In *De amicitia* Laelius, at his home in 129 B.C., discusses the topic of friendship with Fannius and Scaevola the Augur. Both of these works have been extremely popular throughout the ages and have served as school texts, a fact that is easily understood considering the elegance of their prose, their convenient length, and their enduringly relevant subject matter.

Also during this time Cicero began his last, and perhaps most influential, philosophical treatise, *De officiis* (On Moral Duties), written not in dialogue form but as an expository epistle to his son. The first book discusses the cardinal virtues of wisdom, justice, fortitude, and temperance. According to Cicero, the human race is a community bound together by the ties of speech and reason. Humans should employ speech and reason (or eloquence and wisdom) for the advancement of their community, which is more important than any one individual. Book 2 speaks of duties and discusses the notion of *utile* (the expedient), which cannot be divorced from *honestum* (the honorable). Book 3 explores the question of the apparent conflict between the expedient and the honorable; Cicero maintains that such conflict is only an imagined one, since what is dishonorable or wrong can never really be expedient. *De officiis* is perhaps one of Cicero's most original, and in many ways most "Roman," of his philosophical treatises, setting forth for his son a kind of blueprint for the man of action in private and public life. It exerted a tremendous influence on Western humanistic culture.

Many thoughts about duties, the honorable, and the expedient must have been swirling about in Cicero's mind when, on his way to Greece in July of 44 B.C., he heard news that a reconciliation between Antony and the conspirators was probable and decided to turn back in order to attend the senate meeting scheduled for 1 September. (During part of this truncated trip to Greece, the sea voyage from Velia to Rhegium,

Cicero wrote, from memory and without the aid of books, his *Topica*, dedicated to Trebatius, an Aristotelian-inspired treatise that presents topics for oratorical arguments—for example, more and less; time past, present, and future; contraries; and likenesses.) Back in Rome, Cicero found the situation less promising than he had hoped and decided not to attend the meeting, claiming that he was ill. Antony, angry at his absence, delivered a speech against him and made offerings to the deified Caesar. On the next day, 2 September 44 B.C., Cicero took the first step on a journey from which there would be no turning back when he answered Antony (who was absent) with the first of *Philippicae* (Philippics), a speech critical of Antony though free of harsh personal attack. Cicero's final sentence proved an appropriate valediction for the final year of his life: "For myself, I have lived pretty well long enough, whether in years or in glory. If more is to come, it will come not so much for me as for you and for the Commonwealth" (translated by D. R. Shackleton Bailey).

Antony retired to prepare his reply, which he delivered in the Senate on 19 September 44 B.C. Cicero countered with his celebrated *Second Philippic,* a scathing invective showing no restraint, which he sent to Atticus for approval in late October. The speech was never delivered but published as a pamphlet in late November. Cicero referred to his speeches against Antony as Philippics (*Ad Brut.* 2. 4), purposely drawing a comparison between these attacks on Antony and those that the great Greek orator Demosthenes had made on Philip II of Macedon three hundred years earlier. From this point on, all of Cicero's energies were directed to rousing the senatorial order in hopes of recapturing the spirit and the glory of the languishing Republic. During the next half year Cicero delivered twelve more Philippics, two to the people and ten to the senate, all aimed in one way or another at warding off any sort of reconciliation between the senate and Antony. These orations are marked by great clarity of style and purposefulness, and they rely heavily on presentation of character and emotion for their effectiveness. The ethos of Cicero the patriot is present again, marked now by a reinvigorated sincerity and intensity of purpose; Antony, like Cicero's previous adversaries (Verres, Catiline, Clodius, and others), represents all things not Roman, even inhuman, and personifies the forces of despotism, madness, evil, and darkness.

That this type of eloquence had the power to move hearts is readily confirmed by the subsequent events. In the end, of course, Cicero's hopes were dashed; yet, the effect of his oratory lingered, enough so that its target felt the need to exact vengeance. After the trio of Antony, Lepidus, and Octavian had sealed their compact and were appointed commissioners for the reorganization of the state in November (a compact known to history as the Second Triumvirate), they immediately set about removing their enemies from the scene. Cicero's name appeared prominently on the list of the proscribed (despite, according to Plutarch, the objections of Octavian). At first, Cicero thought of fleeing to the East, but after a half-hearted attempt to escape, he ordered his slaves to stand aside, and with these words, "Let me die in the country that I have so often saved" (Livy 120.50), he offered his neck to Antony's minions (7 December 43 B.C.). His head and hands were carried back to Rome and, to the horror of the people, nailed to the Rostra, where Antony's wife further disfigured them.

Perhaps Caesar Augustus, formerly known as Octavian, an ultimate if not entirely willing collaborator in the destruction of Cicero and the Republic, provided the most succinct and fitting valediction for the great orator. Many years after Cicero's death, the emperor spied his grandson trying to hide a scroll of one of Cicero's works under the folds of his toga. "Seeing it, he took it from the boy and read through a great part as he stood there; then giving it back to the lad, he said, 'This was an eloquent man, my child, an eloquent man and a lover of his country'" (Plutarch, *Cicero* 49).

Bibliographies and Concordances:

Hugo Merguet, *Lexikon zu den Philosophischen Schriften Ciceros*, 3 volumes (Jena: G. Fischer, 1873–1884);

Merguet, *Lexikon zu den Reden des Cicero*, 4 volumes (Jena: H. Dufft, 1877–1884);

William Abbott Oldfather, *Index Verborum Ciceronis Epistularum* (Urbana: University of Illinois Press, 1938);

K. M. Abbott and others, *Index Verborum Ciceronis Rhetorica* (Urbana: University of Illinois Press, 1964).

References:

D. R. Shackleton Bailey, *Cicero* (London: Routledge, 1971);

Christopher P. Craig, *Form as Argument in Cicero's Speeches* (Atlanta: Scholars Press, 1993);

Jane W. Crawford, *M. Tullius Cicero: The Lost and Unpublished Orations* (Göttingen: Vandenhoeck & Ruprecht, 1984);

T. A. Dorey, ed., *Cicero* (London: Routledge & Kegan Paul, 1964);

Alan E. Douglas, *Cicero* (Oxford: Clarendon Press, 1968);

Christian Habicht, *Cicero the Politician* (Baltimore: Johns Hopkins University Press, 1990);

Rudolf Hirzel, *Untersuchungen zu Ciceros philosophischen Schriften,* 3 volumes (Leipzig: S. Hirzel, 1877–1883);

H. A. K. Hunt, *The Humanism of Cicero* (Carlton: Melbourne University Press, 1954);

W. R. Johnson, *Luxuriance and Economy: Cicero and the Alien Style* (Berkeley: University of California Press, 1971);

George A. Kennedy, *The Art of Rhetoric in the Roman World* (Princeton, N.J.: Princeton University Press, 1972);

A. D. Leeman, *Orationis Ratio: The Stylistic Theories and Practice of the Orators, Historians, and Philosophers* (Amsterdam: A. M. Hakkert, 1963);

Paul MacKendrick, *The Philosophical Books of Cicero* (New York: St. Martin's Press, 1989);

MacKendrick, *The Speeches of Cicero* (London: Duckworth, 1995);

James M. May, *Trials of Character: The Eloquence of Ciceronian Ethos* (Chapel Hill: University of North Carolina Press, 1988);

Alain Michel, *Rhétorique et Philosophie chez Cicéron* (Paris: Presses Universitaires de France, 1960);

Thomas N. Mitchell, *Cicero: The Ascending Years* (New Haven: Yale University Press, 1979);

Mitchell, *Cicero the Senior Statesman* (New Haven: Yale University Press, 1991);

J. G. F. Powell, ed., *Cicero the Philosopher* (Oxford: Clarendon Press, 1995);

Elizabeth Rawson, *Cicero: A Portrait* (Ithaca, N.Y.: Cornell University Press, 1983);

Richard E. Smith, *Cicero the Statesman* (London: Cambridge University Press, 1966);

David Stockton, *Cicero: A Political Biography* (Oxford: Oxford University Press, 1971);

Wilfried Stroh, *Taxis und Taktik: Die advokatische Dispositionskunst in Ciceros Gerichtsreden* (Stuttgart: Teubner, 1975);

Ann Vasaly, *Representations: Images in the World of Ciceronian Oratory* (Berkeley: University of California Press, 1993);

Jakob Wisse, *Ethos and Pathos from Aristotle to Cicero* (Amsterdam: A. M. Hakkert, 1989);

Cecil W. Wooten, *Cicero's Philippics and Their Demosthenic Model* (Chapel Hill: University of North Carolina Press, 1983);

Tadeusz Zielinski, *Cicero im Wandel der Jahrhunderte,* fourth edition (Leipzig: Teubner, 1929).

Columella

(fl. first century A.D.)

Ward Briggs
University of South Carolina

WORKS–EXTANT: *Res rustica,* 12 books (Farming); *De arboribus,* 1 book (On Trees).

WORKS–LOST: *Adversus astrologos* (Against Astrologers).

Editio princeps: *Lucii Junii Moderati Columellae rei rusticae liber primus,* edited by Georgius Merula, in *Scriptores rei rusticae* (Venice: Nicolaus Jenson, 1472).

Standard editions: *L. Iuni Moderati Columellae opera quae exstant,* edited by Vilhelm Lundström, Åke Josephson, and Sten Hedberg (Uppsala-Göteborg, Sweden: Lundequist, 1897–1968); *Die handschriftliche Überlieferung des L. Junius Moderatus Columella, mit einer kritisch Ausgabe des X. Buches,* edited by Joseph Häussner (Karlsruhe, Germany: G. Braun, 1889); *Corpus poetarum Latinorum,* edited by J. P. Postgate (London: G. Bell, 1905), pp. 206–209; *Zwölf Bücher über Landwirtschaft,* 3 volumes, edited and translated by Will Richter (Munich: Artemis, 1981–1983).

Translation in English: *On Agriculture,* 3 volumes, translated by Harrison Boyd Ash, E. S. Forster, and Edward H. Heffner, Loeb Classical Library (Cambridge, Mass.: Harvard University Press, 1941–1955).

Commentaries: J. M. Gesner, *Scriptores rei rusticae veteres Latini I* (Leipzig: C. Fritsch, 1735); Johann G. Schneider, in *Scriptores rei rusticae veteres Latini II* (Leipzig: C. Fritsch, 1794).

Lucius Junius Moderatus Columella was the author of the most comprehensive, systematic agricultural manual to survive from antiquity, but his birth and death dates are uncertain. Internal references and some remarks in the works of other writers indicate that he was one of many prominent writers of the Neronian period (including the Senecas and their nephew Lucan) who were of Spanish descent. Columella was born in Gades (modern Cadiz), a *municipium* (self-governing community) in the southern Spanish province of Baetica, probably toward the end of the first century B.C.

His parents are unknown, but he mentions an uncle named Marcus Columella, whom he calls a *doctissimum et diligentissimum agricolam* (very learned and careful farmer, 2.15.4) on whose farm near Gades he spent much of his youth and from whom he may have derived much of the knowledge and inspiration for his work. Plutarch mentions a Pythagorean philosopher named Moderatus who was also from Gades (*Quaest.* 8.7.1). Columella speaks of a grandfather who was in the generation of Varro (*temporibus avorum,* 1 *pref.* 15) and writes that he himself lists as contemporaries Seneca the Younger (3.3.3) and the encyclopedist Aulus Cornelius Celsus, who wrote under Tiberius (A.D. 14–37; 1.1.4). Pliny the Elder quotes Columella as a contemporary author (*N.H.* 14.49–51).

At some point Columella moved from Spain to Italy, establishing farms in the Latium (west-central Italy) towns of Carseoli, Ardea, Albanum, and particularly a farm near Caere in Etruria (the ancient pre-Roman country also in west-central Italy) named "Ceretanum." An inscription in a work by Tarentum lists Columella as legionary tribune (a position by which one could enter military service elsewhere than one's hometown) with the *Legio IV Ferrata* in Syria (*Corpus Inscriptionum Latinorum* 9.235). Columella writes that he witnessed certain plants in Cilicia and Syria (2.10.18), perhaps during this same tour of military duty. The inscription itself may well be Columella's epitaph, indicating that he died and was buried at Tarentum. He may have been elderly at his death, to judge by the conclusion of *Res rustica,* where he claims to be an old man (12.59.5), but the text is problematic.

Scholars do not know when Columella wrote *Res rustica,* nor do they know much of the dedicatee, one Publius Silvinus, whom Columella describes as his farming neighbor, but who is otherwise unknown. Publius Silvinus may have run a school by himself or with Columella (to judge by 4.1.1), and not inconceivably, if that was the case, the *Res rustica* was intended as its textbook. Columella's work provides material for some suppositions about his method of composition. That

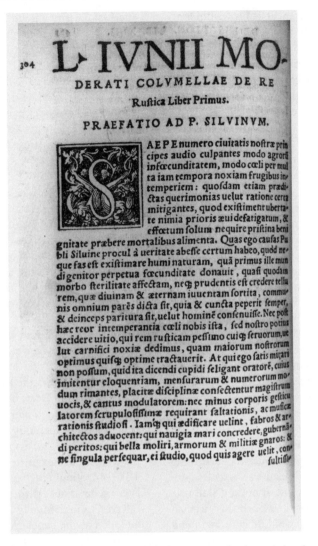

Page from Gymnicus's 1536 edition of Columella's Res rustica, *the most comprehensive agricultural manual to survive antiquity (courtesy of the Lilly Library, Indiana University)*

the beginning lines of each book usually refer to the previous book and the concluding lines announce the topic of the next suggests that each book was written in the order that it has come down to the present. Silvinus apparently read each book critically and to students as he received it from Columella and then returned it with their comments and his.

Throughout the *Res rustica* the tone and attitude is Virgilian, and Virgil is frequently invoked by quotation or allusion (for example, 3.1.1–2). Obviously Columella had studied his many sources carefully. His use of the surviving treatises of Cato and Varro (arrangement of subject matter and careful expansion of subjects they had merely limned or omitted) indicates Columella must have handled his sources with great care, intending to provide a comprehensive account of the

information available and to argue for state-of-the-art practices, refuting his authorities (politely) where necessary. Though he owes clear debts to the surviving agriculturists, he also acknowledges a multitude of sources for his agricultural writing in typical catalogue fashion (1.1); most of them are lost (for example, Triptolemus, Aristaeus, Tremellius, Saserna, and Stolo), and he must have used his nearer models such as Atticus, Celsus, and Graecinus. It is a testimony to the completeness of Columella's work that his sources were no longer needed after *Res rustica* appeared, and so all but the best (Cato and Varro) disappeared. Unfortunately much the same fate befell Columella when his work was epitomized by Palladius in the fourth century. The majority of Columella's sources are Roman and relatively contemporary, but his reverence for the accomplishments

of his distant predecessors is as great as his wistful longing for the era of hard work and agrarian vitality in
which they lived.

Apart from factual material, Columella adopts the
conservative moral and political positions common to
his genre. By maintaining that public and private morality have declined as agriculture has slipped away from
the center of Roman life, Columella associates his position with that of the reactionary father of his genre,
Cato the Elder. Indeed the crime and squalor of Rome
initiated Varro's *De re rustica,* and Virgil had much the
same view as Columella of the moral value of farming.

Columella felt compelled to write his agricultural
encyclopedia because, as he laments, ignorance of farming had befallen his contemporaries. There had been a
general migration to the cities, and the role of agriculture as a force for good in Roman society had declined.
Records of the time indicate that wheat supplies were in
fact diminished and vineyards had ceased to be reliably
profitable. More and more working farmland was being
converted to pasture (on the advice of Cato's *De re rustica* that this use of land was the easiest and most profitable). If farming is in decline and fields are barren,
Columella does not blame *violentia caeli* (the violence of
nature) but rather *nostrum vitium* (man's own fault, 1.
praef. 3). He goes on to say that the Romans have
schools established to train orators, scientists, musi-
cians, contractors, and masters of other trades, "but
only agriculture, which is without doubt the next thing
to wisdom, as if it were a blood-relative, has as few students as it has teachers." The most important skill necessary to life has been the least developed. In Virgilian
fashion he decries those who expend their strength and
intelligence on the empty arts of warfare, trading,
usury, and sycophancy when they could better profit
themselves and the state by engaging in the noble and
honest practice of agriculture, which had been a point
of pride to honest sons of Roman soil such as Cincinna-
tus and others. Instead, men have become effeminate,
gluttonous urbanites who live by night and sleep by
day. Their flabby weakness is in sharp contrast to the
taut strength of the rustic, whose battle with the land
has always kept him in shape when it came time to go
to war. Though Romans of his day, according to Columella, thought farmwork beneath them and sent only
the most ignorant and useless to work in the fields, in
fact, to master agricultural science requires considerable
knowledge and intelligence, and the care and maintenance of a successful plantation should be undertaken
only by the best and brightest, those capable of understanding the multifarious knowledge and multitudinous
tasks required by the farm. Discipline, flexibility, and
awareness of the nature and habits not only of all the
various plants but also of the animals is essential. The
successful farmer is he who has not only knowledge,
but also and the ability and the will (*colere sciet et poterit et
volet,* 1.1.1) to employ it. Thus, Columella aims to
return farmers of the large estates to the personal over-
sight of the efficient cultivation of traditional Roman
crops, both sown and planted, and to animal husbandry. The model ever before him seems to be his
learned and painstaking uncle, the *agricola doctissimus et
diligentissimus.* The uncle's orderly and precise habits are
evident in his nephew's careful arrangement and exposition of subject matter.

Columella arranges his topics *ordine suo* (in their
own order, 1. *praef.* 33). Book 1 treats the situation of
the farm, the selection of the property, the placement of
buildings, and the roles assigned to the workers. Book 2
begins the subject of agriculture with discussions of
plowing and fertilizing and of the multitude of cereals
and vegetables grown in Italy. Books 3, 4, and 5 treat
the growing, grafting, and pruning of trees, chiefly
olives and vines. Book 6 treats large animals—discussing
first the selection and breeding of horses, cattle, and
mules; a section on veterinary medicine then follows.
Book 7 treats smaller animals—sheep, goats, pigs, and
dogs; book 8 treats the care and raising of poultry and
fish; and book 9 treats bees.

Book 10 is a curious and mostly unsuccessful
experiment. Apparently both Gallio and Silvinus had
asked Columella to "complete" the *Georgics* by composing a book in hexameters on a topic Virgil said (*Geo.*
4.147–48) should be treated not by him but by those of
later generations—gardens. Though this book, often
referred to individually as *De cultu hortorum,* was clearly
intended as the conclusion of the work (see the preface
to book 10), Silvinus urged Columella to compose two
more books (in prose): book 11 is a kind of farmer's
almanac ascribing the proper times for the *vilicus* (overseer) to perform his duties according to the motions of
the heavens; book 12 treats gardens in prose, completing what Columella could not include in book 10. This
last book, directed to the overseer's wife, includes an
account of her duties and many recipes for making
wine and for preserving fruits and vegetables.

For all Columella's nostalgia for the old smallholders of the early republic who served the state when
they were not plowing their fields, the book really concerns men of Columella's class: the owners of the *latifundia* (large plantations)—the equivalent of factory
farms today—run by large staffs for profit, not simply
for subsistence. His description of his typical farm in
1.6 depicts a huge site with a manor house, a farmhouse
and a storehouse, slave quarters, stables, a home for the
bailiff, apartments for wranglers and shepherds, and
rooms to process oils and distill wine, among other
uses. Distinctively, though, Columella's admiration for

Ancient mosaics at St-Romain-en-Gal: apple picking (left) and plowing and sowing in intercultivated land (right), techniques used in the time of Columella's Res rustica

the tough morality of his forebears does not extend to their custom of hardscrabble accommodations. He describes elaborate and luxurious accommodations for the planter such as one would find in the city: how else can the wealthy landowners and their families be convinced to leave their plush apartments in the city and return to their country estates (for the owner's presence in the fields with the workers is important) except in part by the promise of similar luxury? Old Cato would rotate in his grave at the thought, but Columella understood the realities of his time.

The arrangement of his topics shows the relative importance of crop and animal management for these large estates, which maintained permanent staffs of slaves managed by an overseer. Columella devotes the largest section to vines (roughly one-fourth of the entire work) and animal husbandry (roughly one-tenth), reflecting the importance of these two areas in the economy of the day. Virtually passed over are the cereals and legumes of book 2, crops of little importance at the time. On a profit-making enterprise that is so labor-intensive, Columella is the first to leave an account factoring the costs of human labor as an operating expenditure. He analyzes the work one man should be able to do in one day on one *iugerum* (a unit of land measure corresponding roughly to two-thirds of an acre).

Clearly Columella was an experienced and learned farmer himself, not a high-minded poet like Virgil nor a dilletante like Varro. He filled his work with useful information, acknowledged his sources, and often tried to refute them. In many ways he took the shorter treatises of Cato and Varro and filled them out with information they either did not have or did not care to include. Not often does one find in Columella's work the spare practicality of Cato, the chatty dialogue of Varro, or the lyrical digressions used to such effect in the didactics of Lucretius and Virgil (see 7.12.1 and 8.8.10). His style is clean and dignified, as one would expect from an author who took his desire to communicate his subject effectively and persuasively almost as seriously as he took the subject itself. Nevertheless, in an age of rhetoric, in which style often counted over substance, some accused him of having a style too refined and deliberate for his subject matter (compare with the light and easy style of Varro, for example). Though unscientific matters such as planting and reaping legumes by the dark of the moon (2.10.11) occasionally creep in, and astronomical matters go awry in book 11, in general the work deserves its longstanding reputation for learning and diligence.

What survives of *De Arboribus* appears to come from the second book of a shorter work on farming that may represent a first edition of *Res rustica*. Perhaps when Cassiodorus (*Inst.* 1.28.6) speaks of Columella's sixteen books on agriculture, he means the twelve of *Res rustica* plus four of *De arboribus*. The work may be addressed to Epirus Marcellus, praetor in A.D. 49 and later an informer under Nero. One manuscript mentions a book addressed to Eprius Marcellus titled *De cultura vinearum* (On the Cultivation of Vines), but this reference may be to *De arboribus* as a whole. In any case, the surviving work treats the cultivation of vineyards, olive trees, and orchard trees, covering much of the same ground as books 3–5 of the *Res rustica*. Because of this overlap, a significant value of *De arboribus* is the aid it gives in deciphering some textual problems in book 5 of the *Res rustica*.

Columella was the master in his field, and he enjoyed a reputation as a supreme authority in antiquity. He was cited by writers as varied as the historian of nature Pliny, the veterinarians Pelagonius and Eumelus, and the agriculturist Palladius in the fourth century, Cassiodorus in the sixth century, and Isidore in the seventh. After Palladius abridged Columella's works, though, they were scarcely read.

Apart from John Milton's directing of students to the agricultural writers for ease in understanding Latin (*Of Education,* 1644), Columella has not been widely read since the Renaissance. His appeal is mainly to the relatively few specialized historians of agriculture, not to those who cherish rich language or read great literature. Yet, he is a window into the mentality of the ancient Roman, whose gift for management, arrangement, punishment and reward, respect for the past and cautious progressivism, reliance on hard science, and belief in a transcendently beneficent deity helped create an empire of a thousand years.

Columella is also of value for his educational views. So many and varied are the tasks of the owner of a plantation in his day that one cannot hope to master all the knowledge necessary. Rather, the farmer should be prepared by the same kind of broadly based education that Cicero, Quintilian, and Virtuvius recommend for orators and architects. A training in the liberal arts and sciences places the farmer in the best position to understand and adapt to the vagaries of the rustic life and the multifarious knowledge that management of any kind requires.

Alas, the combination of modern luxury with old-style diligence, comfort with hard work, the reliance on slave labor with a rational system that projected output in man-days (slaves would never have the incentive to work as hard as the freeholder of a small farm), has made of Columella's vast, exacting, encyclopedic plan more a dream than a reality.

Index:

G. G. Betts and W. D. Ashworth, *Index to the Uppsala Edition of Columella* (Uppsala, Sweden: Uppsala University, 1971).

References:

Karl Ahrens, *Columella über Landwirtschaft,* second edition (Berlin: Akademie-Verlag, 1976);

B. Baldwin, "Columella's Sources and How He Used Them," *Latomus,* 22 (1963): 785–791;

Wilhelm Becher, *De L. Iuni Moderati Columellae vita et scriptis* (Leipzig: Teubner, 1897);

Tore Janson, *Latin Prose Prefaces: Studies in Literary Conventions,* Studia Latina Stockholmiensia no. 13 (Stockholm: Almquist & Wiksell, 1964), p. 83ff;

K. D. White, *Roman Farming* (London: Thames & Hudson, 1970).

Quintus Curtius Rufus

(fl. A.D. 35)

Michele Valerie Ronnick
Wayne State University

MAJOR WORK: *Historiae Alexandri Magni,* 10 books (Histories of Alexander the Great)—books 1 and 2 lost.

Editio princeps: *Historiae Alexandri Magni* (Venice: Vindelinus de Spira, ca. 1471) or (Rome: Georgius Lauer, not after 1472).

Standard editions: *Historiarum Alexandri Magni Macedonis libri qui supersunt,* edited by Theodor Vogel (Leipzig: Teubner, 1904); *Quintus Curtius,* 2 volumes, edited by John C. Rolfe, Loeb Classical Library (Cambridge, Mass.: Harvard University Press, 1946); *Geschichte Alexanders der Grossen,* translated by Herbert Schönfeld, edited by Konrad Müller (Munich: Heimeran, 1954).

Translations in English: *The History of Alexander,* translated by John Yardley, introduction and notes by Waldemar Heckel (Harmondsworth, U.K.: Penguin, 1984).

Little is known about the author of the only full-length biography of Alexander the Great written in Latin. Doubts have been raised not only about his name but also about the title of his work and the era in which he composed it. In regard to the author's name, most of the manuscripts mention a Curtius Rufus in their titles, but the colophons of the same manuscripts provide an additional name and read Quintus Curtius Rufus. The title, when it is not wholly lacking, varies from *Historiae* to *Historiae Alexandri Magni Macedonis* to *Historiae Magni Macedonis Alexandri.* Thus, in an irony of history, this biographer-historian seems to have left few clues as to his own story, and the questions remaining likely will not be answered.

Because so little information about Curtius Rufus has come down to present-day readers, and most of that was interpolated from his own words, his identity has frequently been questioned by scholars. Over the years he has been said to have lived anywhere from the first century A.D. up to the early fourth century A.D. Furthermore, despite his rise to popularity during the Middle Ages, a good part of the mystery surrounding him seems to have begun during his own lifetime, for he is completely absent from the literary records of classical antiquity. In fact, the first solid evidence of his name conjoined with a history of Alexander appears during the ninth century. Both are found in the heading of one of the earliest manuscripts of the *Historiae.* Preceding this record there was for centuries no trace of his work. Such a void in the record has disturbed some scholars. During the sixteenth century, for example, in a work published at Frankfurt in 1594 titled *Animadversiones in Quintum Curtium,* Valens Acidalius (1567–1595) attempted to account for this blank by suggesting that the details concerning Curtius Rufus's life had been blotted out by a conspiracy of silence.

Scholars have therefore made efforts to identify him with figures found in various texts from Greco-Roman times who bore the same name. The first of these men has been dismissed as having lived in a period that is entirely too early. This Quintus Curtius Rufus lived in the middle of the first century B.C. and is remembered for prosecuting Gaius Memmius for political corruption in the late 50s. Extant is a letter written by Marcus Cicero in 55 B.C. to his brother that describes Quintus Curtius Rufus as a *bonus et eruditus adulescens* (noble and learned youth). Two other men, who lived during the early empire, figure more prominently in the problem. The first of these two is a certain Quintus Curtius Rufus listed in the index of Suetonius's *De Grammaticis et Rhetoribus.* From the position of this Quintus Curtius Rufus's name in the list, which is arranged chronologically, scholars believe that he was active during the reigns of the first four Julio-Claudian emperors—that is, Augustus, Tiberius, Caligula, and Claudius. Yet, nothing much can be concluded from this identification, even if it is correct, except that the pronounced rhetorical nature of the *Historiae* would be directly related to its author's occupation as a professional rhetor.

The last possibility is the Curtius Rufus who was mentioned by Tacitus (*Annales* 1.20.3–21.3; 11.21.2) and Pliny the Younger (*Ep.* 7.27.2–3), who lived at the same time as the aforementioned Quintus Curtius Rufus. Sources mention that this Curtius Rufus was a soldier and politician who rose from humble origins to become

Illumination depicting the birth of Alexander the Great, from the manuscript for a 1468 French translation of Quintus Curtius's Historiae Alexandri Magni *(Bodleian Library, Oxford)*

proconsul of Africa around A.D. 50, and he died there in A.D. 53. As a solution to this problem of double identity, G. V. Sumner and others have suggested that these two men were actually the same person. They posit that Curtius Rufus spent the first part of his career at the court of Tiberius during the high tide of the fortunes of Sejanus. After the collapse of Sejanus's regime in A.D. 31, Curtius Rufus retired from politics and took up a career in rhetoric, during which time he also wrote his account of Alexander. If this conclusion is accurate, then two prominent features of the *Historiae* are neatly explained—its highly rhetorical style and its tone of world-weary experience as expressed by one who spent a lifetime in civil and military service. This theory, despite the strong appeal of its apparent "neatness," has not convinced everyone.

Nevertheless, no part of these ideas detracts from recent scholarship that favors the placement of Curtius Rufus in the reign of Claudius. Statements made in several digressions in the text of the narrative support this assign-

ment. One of these digressions, a passage comparing a troubled but unidentified situation in Rome with the tumultuous situation that followed Alexander's unexpected death, is at 10.9.1–6. There Curtius Rufus mentions the restoration of peace to the principate after a time when the *discordia membra* (discordant members) of the empire were thrown into disorder since they were *sine suo capite* (without a head). These details, along with references to a night that was "almost our last," match the uncertain and hazardous period of interregnum that came after the assassination of Gaius and before the Praetorian Guard endorsed Claudius at the start of A.D. 41. Curtius Rufus, for this and other reasons, has been placed by most scholars interested in the chronology of Roman historiography beside Velleius Paterculus (ca. 20 B.C.–ca. A.D. 40) and between Livy (59 B.C.–A.D. 17) and Tacitus (ca. A.D. 56–ca. 118).

Close examinations of the *Historiae* have provided some idea of Curtius Rufus's sources. One source is the work of Cleitarchus (fl. 290 B.C.), son of the Greek historian Dinon, who began to write soon after the death of Alexander in 323 B.C. Curtius Rufus mentions Cleitarchus at two points in the text (9.5.21 and 9.8.15). Only fragments of his work, one written, as Cicero said, *rhetorice et tragice* (in rhetorical and tragic mode), remain today. Another influence comes from Ptolemy the Lagid (305 B.C.–238 B.C.), one of Alexander's most trusted generals, who made himself king of Egypt upon Alexander's death. Ptolemy's account, written in his later years, was a factual one and circulated a few years before that of Cleitarchus. It, like Cleitarchus's history, however, exists only in fragments now.

Among the writers of the Augustan age whose words shaped those of Curtius Rufus are Pompeius Trogus, Virgil, and Livy. Trogus's work, the *Historiae Philippiae*, examined the history of the Macedonian monarchy. Small parts of it remain today in the form of brief transcriptions of various passages selected by Justin (fl. second century A.D.) for his *Historiarum Philippicarum Libri XLIV*. The fragmented state of that evidence, however, precludes fuller understanding of the relationship between Curtius and Trogus. On the other hand, portions of Virgil's *Aeneid* clearly left their mark on Curtius Rufus. One example is Curtius Rufus's description of a pair of Alexander's soldiers who were close friends. One was named Alexander and the other, Charos. Together they led the attack in the spring of 326 B.C. on Aornus, the "eagle's nest," near the Indus River (8.11.10–17). Alexander was soon slain in a heroic struggle to emulate his king and namesake. Charos found his comrade and was slaughtered shortly afterward in a brave, but futile, attempt to save his friend, who had already suffered a fatal wound. That Curtius Rufus's narrative has incorporated elements of Virgil's treatment of Nisus and Euryalus at *Aeneid* 9.176 ff. is not difficult to see. The most important influence of all on Curtius Rufus, however, was Livy's sweeping history that began with the foundation of Rome, *Ab urbe condita*. In 1915 R. B. Steele identified a significant number of parallels between the two histories and determined that Curtius Rufus extracted "material freely" from Livy, reconfigured it, and gave "us an Alexander whose history is permeated with Roman coloring." There are also verbal links between Curtius Rufus's text and those written by Valerius Maximus, Seneca the Elder, Lucan, and Seneca the Younger, but these connections may well result from the use of a common source known to them but since lost.

Of the ten books that Curtius Rufus wrote, the first and second books have been entirely lost. The fifth book has extensive gaps at its end, while the sixth book has gaps at the beginning, as does the tenth book. The work has been preserved in many manuscripts—the earliest dating from the ninth century. All surviving codices descend from a lost archetype (A), and all are of French origin. The earliest, Parisinus 5716, is known as P and comes from the ninth century. After P come three manuscripts from the tenth century: Leidensis 137 (L), Bernensis 451 (B), and Vossianus 20 (Q). Each has been emended by correctors, and all include an assortment of revisions, annotations, corruptions, and erasures. There are, in addition, many later manuscripts that have not been studied. The scrutiny of a few of these *interpolati* (heavily emended manuscripts), according to Michael Winterbottom, has yielded some good results, but further examination is needed.

In a self-perceived and perhaps self-generated need to fill in mutilations and lacunae in the narrative of the text, various writers during the Middle Ages wrote supplements to the *Historiae*. Several examples have come down to the present. One example was an attempt to supply the missing portions at the start of the text. Oxford Corpus Christi College MS 82 is of French origin, dating to the eleventh century. This supplement begins with a short treatment of Alexander's start in life from his birth to his young manhood. After commenting on Alexander's education and the character of his father, the author shifts his narrative to a description of Alexander's preparations for his campaign against Darius. After bringing order to Athens and the divided Greeks, Alexander then crosses over to Asia, where he is met with letters from Darius that attempt without effect to scare him off. The battle at the Granicus River ensues, and the Persian general Memnon and his troops are crushed. At that point the "genuine" text of Curtius Rufus begins.

A synopsis of this supplement along with other passages was recently discovered in the final fifteen leaves of MS London BL Cotton Titus D.XX. held by the British Library. The manuscript dates to the fourteenth or fifteenth century, and a transcription of that text of this epitome was published in 1991. The range of the manuscript's complete contents—that is, a series of excerpts from many authors concerning Western philosophy, rhetoric, and literature—suggests that it was used as a school text. According to Edmé Smits, this "particular Curtius text left traces of its existence in other medieval literary works." The writers of these works include the French poet Alberic de Pisançon (ca. A.D. 1130), whose rendition of the battle at the Granicus River reveals an acquaintance with this text; the Cistercian writer Helinand of Froidmont (ca. 1170–ca. 1229); and a Portuguese writer at the Burgundian court of Charles the Bold, Vasque de Lucène, who put this text into French prose in 1468 as a part of his translation of the entire body of works. In addition Curtius Rufus may well have influenced the "best read man of [his] century," William of Malmesbury (ca. 1090–1143), for his description of the arrival of William the

Conqueror on the coast of England in his *De gestis regum Anglorum* (3.238) bears evidence of such an influence.

The most famous supplement of all is that written by the philologist Johannes Caspar Freinshemius (1608–1660). His Latin panegyric of Gustavus Adophus written in 1632 led to an invitation to Sweden and to a university chair in history that he accepted. His supplement to Curtius Rufus was popular. It went through twenty editions and was printed again in 1964 by P. G. Schmidt.

Curtius Rufus's life of Alexander was frequently studied and imitated during the Middle Ages. Men such as Einhard at the court of Charlemagne (ca. 770–840) and Servatus Lupus of Ferrières (ca. 805–862) were among his readers. The number of manuscripts that survive from this period and the many adaptations and translations of it attest as well to the influence of this biography. The work was a firm part of the school curriculum in Germany and England from around 1600 to around 1800. It is also found excerpted many times in florilegia. Examples include the *Florilegium Angelicum* (ca. 1175), a work dedicated to Pope Alexander III, and one portion, known as the *Speculum Historiale,* of the larger encyclopedia, the *Speculum Quadruplex,* written by Vincent of Beauvais (d. 1264).

Keen interest in the legend of Alexander pervaded the culture of many countries during that time, and Curtius Rufus's account of Alexander was just one among several sources that were read. Thus it had to compete with more popular histories. Two of the most important of these histories are Leo Archipresbyter's *Historia de Preliis* from the tenth century and the *Epitome* of Julius Valerius, who is known also as Pseudo-Callisthenes and is sometimes identified as Aesopus. One serious complication stems from the confusion caused by the entry "Historia Alexandri," commonly used in the medieval library catalogues. Because that entry was a generic one, any or all of these works were catalogued under that heading. As a result, attempts to trace the full extent of Curtius's readership with precision and exactitude are difficult.

The most popular of all medieval Latin epics is indebted to Curtius Rufus. This work is the *Alexandreis,* written by the most distinguished poet of his time, the humanist poet Walter of Châtillon (ca. 1135–ca. 1203). During the years 1178 to 1182 he created his own conscious imitation of the classical Latin epic, a ten-book poem in Latin hexameters. His principal source for the work was Curtius Rufus. Many copies of the poem circulated, and many of those were filled with explanatory notes. Writers such as Henry of Settimello and Alanus de Insulis (d. 1202) borrowed from it or mentioned it. Many Alexander books by several hands were founded on it. These works include the mid-thirteenth-century Spanish *Libro de Alexandre, Alexanders Geesten,* written by Jakob van Maerlant around 1258; *Alexander,* written by Ulrich von Eschenbach between 1270 and 1288; *Alex-*

anders Saga of Brandr Jónsson around 1260; and *Alexandreis,* written in old Czech, from about 1265. In Germany, at about the same time, Rudolf von Ems wanted to write an historical account of Alexander that would depict him as an instrument of God. The result of his ambition was a monumental work, written between 1230 and 1250, that totaled 21,643 lines of Latin hexameters. The poem was based in the main upon the text of Curtius Rufus, but it also drew from other sources. The author's skillful combination of these sources resulted in a unified poem based upon factual evidence that is considered in the words of George Cary "to be the best of the German Alexander-books."

During the Renaissance, the editio princeps of *Historiae* was published in 1471, about twenty-one years after the invention of printing. Historians who study incunabula are uncertain whether credit for the first printing should be given to the edition produced by Georg Lauer in Rome in 1471 or that by Vindelin de Spira published in Venice. Among the other Italians who invested time and energy in the work was Pomponius Lactus (1425–1498), a former student of Lorenzo Valla (1406–1457), who produced an edition of Curtius Rufus toward the of his life. In France in the following century Jacques Davy Du Perron (1556–1618) was said to have preferred a single page of Curtius Rufus to one of Tacitus. Commentary on Curtius Rufus appears one hundred years later in the Faroe Islands, according to Jozef Ijsewijn's *Companion to Neo-Latin Studies* (Leuven, 1990) in the annual dissertations delivered in Latin, which the University of Copenhagen required of its students. Among those given in the fall of 1732 was that by Morten Mortensen titled *Responsum Abdolonymi nihil habenti nihil defuit,* which concerned an anecdote of the *Historiae* 4.1.

After the Renaissance, Curtius Rufus maintained his place in the school curricula of the nineteenth and early twentieth centuries. Textbooks from England around 1900 featured Alexander's episodes in India, and Edmé Smits notes that there were "quite a few school texts which are exclusively made up of parts" of the Indian accounts. In the United States, Professor William Henry Crosby of Rutgers bore witness to this situation. In the introduction to the fourth edition of his fairly popular school edition of the *Historiae* titled *Quintus Curtius Rufus: Life and Exploits of Alexander the Great* (1883) he states that "it is an undoubted, though unaccountable, fact, that Quintus Curtius's *History* . . . is a work almost unheard of in the Academies and Colleges of the United States, while in England, and more especially on the continent, it holds a high place in the estimation of classical instructors" and is "one of the most entertaining as well as instructive of the Classics." "As to the style of Curtius," he says, "nothing can be more pleasing. Heinsius, indeed, with somewhat of a disregard of gender, speaks of him as 'Venus Historicorum.' Bartholomew Merula applies to his narratives the phrase 'elegantissime conscriptas,' and

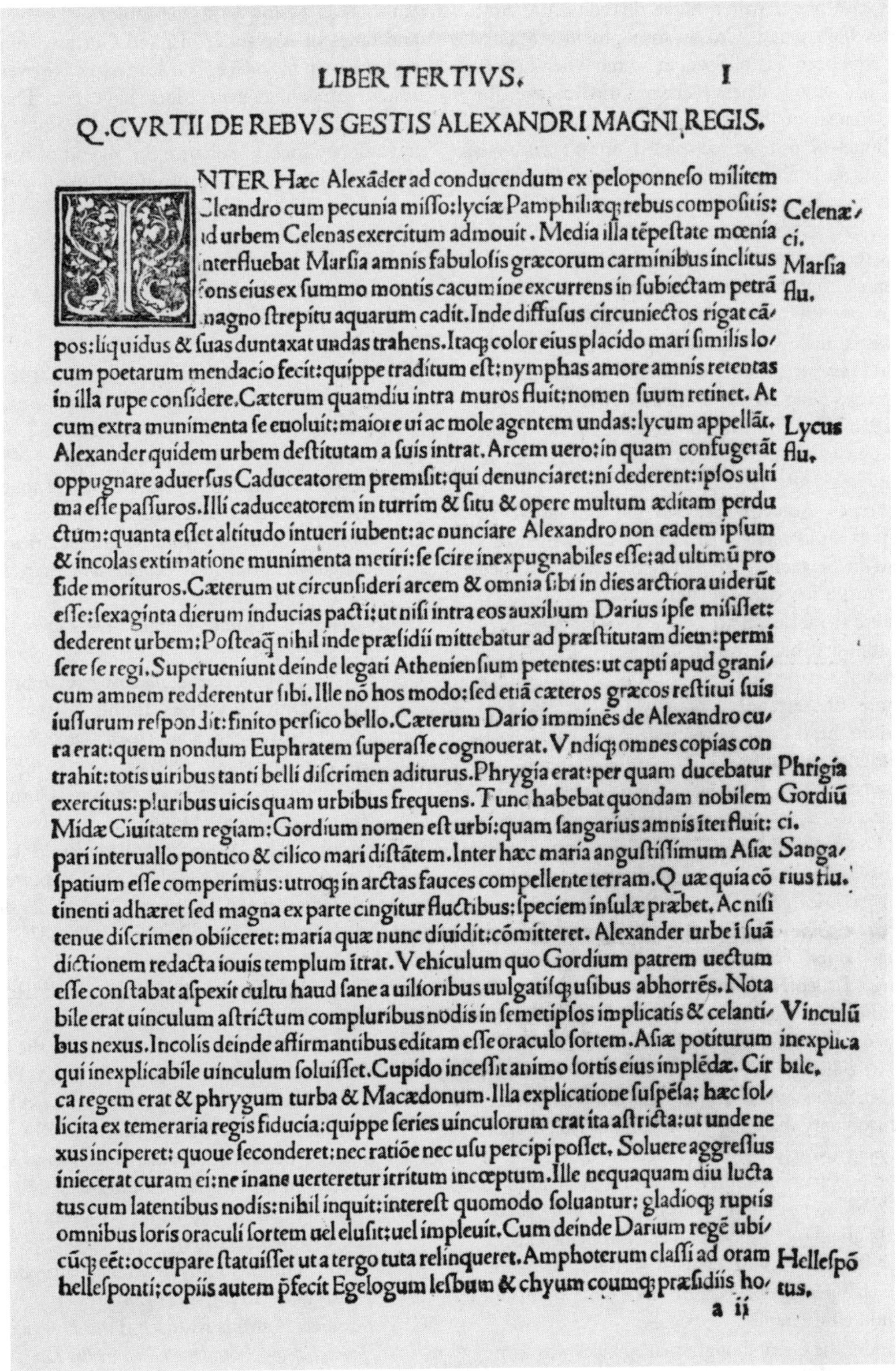

LIBER TERTIVS. I

Q .CVRTII DE REBVS GESTIS ALEXANDRI MAGNI REGIS.

NTER Hæc Alexãder ad conducendum ex peloponnefo militem
Cleandro cum pecunia miffo:lyciæ Pamphiliæꝗ rebus compofitis:
ad urbem Celenas exercitum admouit . Media illa tẽpeſtate mœnia
interfluebat Marfia amnis fabulofis græcorum carminibus inclitus
fons eius ex fummo montis cacumine excurrens in fubiectam petrã
magno ſtrepitu aquarum cadit.Inde diffufus circuniectos rigat cã‐
pos:liquidus & fuas duntaxat undas trahens.Itaꝗ color eius placido mari fimilis lo‐
cum poetarum mendacio fecit:quippe traditum eſt:nymphas amore amnis retentas
in illa rupe confidere.Cæterum quamdiu intra muros fluit:nomen fuum retinet. At
cum extra munimenta fe euoluit:maiore ui ac mole agentem undas:lycum appellãt.
Alexander quidem urbem deſtitutam a fuis intrat.Arcem uero:in quam confugerãt
oppugnare aduerfus Caduceatorem premifit:qui denunciaret:ni dederent:ipfos ulti
ma effe paffuros.Illi caduceatorem in turrim & fitu & opere multum æditam perdu
ctum:quanta effet altitudo intueri iubent:ac nunciare Alexandro non eadem ipfum
& incolas extimatione munimẽta metiri:fe fcire inexpugnabiles effe:ad ultimũ pro
fide morituros.Cæterum ut circunfideri arcem & omnia fibi in dies arctiora uiderũt
effe:fexaginta dierum inducias pacti:ut nifi intra eos auxilium Darius ipfe mififfet:
dederent urbem:Poſteaꝗ nihil inde præfidii mittebatur ad præſtitutam diem:permi
fere fe regi.Superueniunt deinde legati Athenienfium petentes:ut capti apud grani‐
cum amnem redderentur fibi. Ille nõ hos modo:fed etiã cæteros græcos reſtitui fuis
iuffurum refpondit:finito perfico bello.Cæterum Dario imminẽs de Alexandro cu‐
ra erat:quem nondum Euphratem fuperaffe cognouerat.Vndiꝗ omnes copias con
trahit:totis uiribus tanti belli difcrimen aditurus.Phrygia erat:per quam ducebatur
exercitus:pluribus uicis quam urbibus frequens.Tunc habebat quondam nobilem
Midæ Ciuitatem regiam:Gordium nomen eſt urbi:quam fangarius amnis iter fluit:
pari interuallo pontico & cilico mari diſtãtem.Inter hæc maria anguſtiffimum Afiæ
fpatium effe comperimus:utroꝗ in arctas fauces compellente terram.Q uæ quia cõ
tinenti adhæret fed magna ex parte cingitur fluctibus:fpeciem infulæ præbet. Ac nifi
tenue difcrimen obiiceret:maria quæ nunc diuidit:cõmitteret. Alexander urbe i fuã
dictionem redacta iouis templum itrat.Vehiculum quo Gordium patrem uectum
effe conſtabat afpexit cultu haud fane a uilioribus uulgatifꝗ ufibus abhorrẽs. Nota
bile erat uinculum aſtrictum compluribus nodis in femetipfos implicatis & celanti‐
bus nexus.Incolis deinde affirmantibus editam effe oraculo fortem.Afiæ potiturum
qui inexplicabile uinculum foluiffet.Cupido inceffit animo fortis eius implẽdæ. Cir
ca regem erat & phrygum turba & Macædonum.Illa explicatione fufpẽfa: hæc fol‐
licita ex temeraria regis fiducia:quippe feries uinculorum erat ita aſtricta:ut unde ne
xus inciperet:quoue feconderet:nec ratiõe nec ufu percipi poffet. Soluere aggreffus
iniecerat curam ei:ne inane uerteretur itritum incœptum.Ille nequaquam diu lucta
tus cum latentibus nodis:nihil inquit:intereſt quomodo foluantur: gladioꝗ ruptis
omnibus loris oraculi fortem uel elufit:uel impleuit.Cum deinde Darium regẽ ubi‐
cũꝗ eẽt:occupare ſtatuiffet ut a tergo tuta relinqueret.Amphoterum claffi ad oram
helleſponti;copiis autem pfecit Egelogum lefbum & chyum coumꝗ præfidiis ho‐

Marginal notes (right column):
Celenæ,
ci.
Marfia
flu.

Lycus
flu.

Phrigia
Gordiũ
ci.
Sanga‐
rius fiu.

Vinculũ
inexplica
bile.

Helleſpõ
tus.

a ij

Opening page of the third book in the 1496 Venetian edition of Quintus Curtius's Historiae Alexandri Magni *(courtesy of the Lilly Library, Indiana University)*

Decembrius calls him a writer 'mirae dulcedinis.' As testimony to this high praise, Crosby then provides a story about King Alphonso VII of Spain at a time when he was suffering with a serious illness. "Having tried in vain the many prescriptions of his physicians," he "attempted to solace his hours of pain by perusing Curtius's *History of Alexander*"; and such, it is related, was the happy effect of his new remedy that he was soon restored to health. When convalescent, he was heard to exclaim, "Valeant Avicenna, Hippocrates, medici caeteri; vivat Curtius, sospitator meus!" (May Avicenna, Hippocrates, and the rest of the physicians go their own way; let Curtius, my preserver, live!).

Curtius Rufus's work has been put to other uses. In sixteenth- and seventeenth-century France, a prose translation of the *Historiae* into French by Claude Favre de Vaugelas (1585–1650) played an important part in the debate over style, translation theory, and linguistic thought. In 1719, seventy years after its original publication in Paris in 1653, the French Academy selected the translation for study. A report on its merits made by Academy members was finished in September 1720. Favre's style remained noteworthy; just a few decades later Voltaire (1694–1778) declared Favre's translation to be "le premier livre écrit purement" (the first book written faultlessly). In this century an attempt was recently made to make an ex post facto diagnosis of Alexander's bout with blindness after being hit on the head or neck at the siege of Cyropolis in 329 B.C. The ancient sources (Curtius Rufus, Plutarch, and Arrian) were scrutinized in the light of modern discoveries in ophthalmology, and his symptoms were attributed to a syndrome of transient cortical blindness.

Another issue that has engaged scholars of late concerns the question of genre. Curtius Rufus has written a "history," but one that exhibits almost as many aspects of biography as it does of history. Thus the *Historiae*, as E. I. McQueen noted, "represent in some sense a fusion of both genres." Without the introduction to the work no one can be exactly sure what Curtius Rufus himself thought he was trying to achieve. Nevertheless, political, rhetorical, and literary elements appear throughout the work. It can be said with certainty that the author exhibits a keen interest in personality, a tendency to embellish some parts of the narrative and truncate others, a strong inclination to moralize, a positive fascination with the power of *fortuna* (fortune), and an affinity for pointed epigrammatic expressions. Other features include detailed accounts of battles and sieges, elaborate set speeches, and descriptions of geography and ethnography.

Alexander the Great thought that Achilles was fortunate to have had Homer, the consummate artist, to recount his deeds and insure his place in the larger cultural record. In regard to Alexander and the account of his actions written by Curtius Rufus, that sort of connection is neither so linear nor so unilateral. Nevertheless, Curtius

Rufus is in many ways Alexander's "Homer." The life and times of Alexander inspired Curtius Rufus to write, and although his own epoch seems to have overlooked the result, subsequent generations have not. The meanings and methods taken from the *Historiae* by later generations have done much to enhance the legend of Alexander. At the same time, they have also made sure that the name of its author will be remembered.

Index:

Jean Therasse, ed., *Index Verborum: Relevés lexicaux et grammaticaux* (Hildesheim: Olms, 1976).

References:

J. E. Atkinson, *A Commentary on Q. Curtius Rufus' Alexandri Magni, Books 3 and 4* (Amsterdam: J. C. Gieben, 1980);

Wendy Ayres-Bennett, "From Malherbe to the French Academy on Quinte Curce: The Role of Observations, Translations and Commentaries in French Linguistic Thought," *Seventeenth-Century French Studies,* 19 (1997): 1–9;

Henry Bardon, "Quinte Curce," *Les Etudes classiques,* 15 (1947): 3–14;

George Cary, *The Medieval Alexander* (Cambridge: Cambridge University Press, 1956);

Simon Noël Dosson, *Etude sur Quinte Curce: Sa vie et son oeuvre* (Paris: Hachette, 1887);

J. R. Hamilton, "The Date of Quintus Curtius Rufus," *Historia,* 37 (1988): 445–456;

J. Lascarotos, "The Wounding of Alexander the Great in Cyropolis (329 B.C.)–The First Reported Case of the Syndrome of Transient Cortical Blindness," *Survey of Ophthalmology,* 42 (1997): 283–287;

E. I. McQueen, "Quintus Curtius Rufus," *Latin Biography,* edited by T. A. Dorey (London: Routledge & Kegan Paul, 1966), pp. 17–43;

C. Reynolds, "'The History of Alexander the Great'–An Illuminated Manuscript of Vasco-Da-Lucena's French Translation of the Ancient Text by Quintus Curtius Rufus," *Burlington Magazine,* 139 (1997): 707;

Paul Gerhard Schmidt, *Supplemente lateinischer Prosa in der Neuzeit: Rekonstruktionen zu lateinischen Autoren von der Renaissance bis zur Aufklärung* (Göttingen: Vandenhoeck & Ruprecht, 1964);

R. B. Steele, "Quintus Curtius Rufus," *American Journal of Philology,* 36 (1915): 402–423;

G. V. Sumner, "Curtius Rufus and the *Historiae Alexandri,*" *Journal of the Australasian Universities Language and Literature Association,* 15 (1961), 30–39;

Michael Winterbottom, "Curtius Rufus," *Texts and Transmission: A Survey of the Latin Classics,* edited by L. D. Reynolds (Oxford: Clarendon Press, 1983), pp. 148–149.

Ennius
(239 B.C. – 169 B.C.)

Richard L. S. Evans
St. Agnes Academy, Houston, Texas

WORKS–FRAGMENTARY:

EPIC
Annales, 18 books (Annals).

TRAGEDIES (Greek plots)
Achilles;
Aias;
Alcmeno;
Alexander;
Andromacha;
Andromeda;
Athamas;
Cresphontes;
Erectheus;
Eumenides;
Hectoris lytra;
Hecuba;
Iphigenia;
Medea;
Melanippa;
Nemea;
Phoenix;
Telamo;
Telephus;
Thyestes.

TRAGEDIES (Roman plots)
Ambracia;
Sabinae.

COMEDIES
Cupiuncula;
Pancratiastes.

EPIGRAM
Epigrammata.

SATIRE
Saturae (Satires).

PHILOSOPHIC WORKS
Epicharmus;
Euhemerus (sacra historia);
Protrepticus.

PARODIC VERSE
Sota.

CELEBRATORY POEM
Scipio.

DIDACTIC POEM
Hedyphagetica (Delicatessen).

Editiones princepses: *Fragmenta poetarum veterum Latinorum, quorum opera non extant,* Robert and Henri Estienne (Geneva, 1564); *Q. Enni poetae vetustissimi quae supersunt fragmenta,* G. Colonna (Naples, 1590).

Standard edition: *Ennianae poesis reliquae,* Johannes Vahlen (Leipzig: Teubner, 1854; second edition, 1903).

Translation in English: *Remains of Old Latin,* volume 1, edited and translated by E. H. Warmington, Loeb Classical Library (Cambridge, Mass.: Harvard University Press, 1935; third revised edition, 1979).

Musae quae pedibus magnum pulsatis Olympum (Muses who Strike Great Olympus with Your Feet) is the revolutionary introduction to the *Annales* (Annals) of Quintus Ennius, announcing a new program in Roman epic that was followed by writers of Latin epic poetry from Lucretius to Petrarch. Not only does Ennius invoke the Muses by their Greek name, breaking with his predecessors Livius Andronicus (fl. 240 B.C.) and Gnaeus Naevius (fl. 235 B.C.), but he also uses for the first time in Latin epic the Greek epic meter, dactylic hexameter. The significance of these two related poetic innovations for the future of Roman epic cannot be overemphasized, for Ennius, whose various works survive only in paltry fragments, was one of the most important early Roman poets.

Quintus Ennius was born in southern Italy at Rudiae in 239 B.C. near present-day Lecce, in an area where Oscan and Greek, as well as Latin, were spoken; Ennius himself was trilingual, and thus linguistically sophisticated—a factor, no doubt, in his later bold experimentations in modeling Latin epic verse out of Greek

Bronze bust of a poet whom some scholars believe to be Ennius (from the Villa of the Papyri at Herculaneum)

hexametric patterns. He seems to have received an education in Homer and the Greek poets, probably at Tarentum, before coming to Rome in 204 B.C., perhaps after auxiliary service in the Roman army. He may have been helped to Rome by the powerful Marcus Porcius Cato, the Censor (234–149 B.C.). When Ennius arrived in Rome, he made his way by teaching and by writing tragedies and comedies. By 190 B.C. he had built a secure literary reputation that he continued to develop by working in a variety of genres in addition to drama—philosophy, satire, parodic verse forms, and epigram. According to tradition, he lived modestly on the Aventine with only one servant as a helper.

Despite his modest lifestyle, Ennius seems to have had powerful connections as well as literary friends: he followed the consul Marcus Fulvius Nobilior on campaign to Greece as poet-propagandist (189–187 B.C.) and perhaps through his son Ennius received Roman citizenship (184 B.C.). Ennius wrote a poem celebrating the victory of Scipio Africanus in the Second Punic War, a fact which suggests some relationship to the great Scipio. Also, Ennius was friends with the comic writer Caecilius Statius (fl. 179 B.C.) and must have known his sister's son, Marcus Pacuvius, the tragedian and Ennius's successor as a writer of tragedy.

Living in an era of aggressive Roman expansion and literary ferment, the versatile Ennius wrote in several genres in both poetry and prose. Of his formative influences on many genres of Latin literature, his most lasting literary influence was surely the development of Latin epic. Romans loved to read their own history far more than did the Greeks and after 240 B.C. were intoxicated with their victories over Carthage in the Punic Wars, victories that established Rome as the supreme power in the world. Before Ennius's *Annals* most historical epic, which was as popular a genre in Rome as it was unknown in Athens, was written in annalistic form by the commanders who had wrought the victories over Hannibal. Their annals were basically self-serving memoirs in a primitive meter. Ennius had served the appetite for history in his dramatic works and only turned to writing his *Annals* in the last years of his life, starting from 173 B.C. until his death in 169 B.C. The *Annals,* then, was the culmination of a literary career: it was a lengthy historical epic, the topic of which was nothing less than the entire history of Rome, following chronological order from the arrival of Aeneas in Italy to the events of Ennius's own day, in eighteen books—hence the title *Annales,* Latin for *yearly records.* Ennius is credited with the significant departure from his forebears in Latin epic: he brought elements of the Greek epic into the Latin beyond mere subject matter and characters. Ennius took a bold, new direction that had lasting consequences for Roman epic. Both Livius Andronicus in his popular translation of Homer's *Odyssey* into Latin (ca. 240 B.C.) and Naevius in his Roman epic, the *Punic War,* used a native Italic meter, the Saturnian measure, based on word accent (as is English meter) and alliteration. Although the precise nature of Saturnian meter is still debated by metricians, one plausible theory of the meter is to see natural word accent and metrical accent as coincident, with the line falling into two parts, the first part having three accents and the second part having two. Thus, a traditional Saturnian line was read according to the natural prose accent of Latin words as follows:

Dábunt málum Metélli Naévio poétae.
(The Metelli will give the poet Naevius trouble.)

In contrast to the original conjunction of word accent with metrical accent in Saturnian verse, Ennius took the bold step of forging a new meter in Latin verse by adopting the Greek hexameter line in Latin. While the archaic Saturnian meter, like English meter, depended on stress, Greek verse, in contrast, was based on a musical principle of alternating long and short syllables. In the pronunciation of Ancient Greek each long syllable was held twice as long as each short syllable so that verse was intoned as a musical cadence. This metrical innovation by Ennius made Latin epic poetry sound more like Greek epic when read aloud, thus binding Roman epic verse closer to Greek models. A Greek hexametric line, somewhat simplified, with five dactyls (‿◡◡) and a final trochee (‿◡), might be presented visually like this:

‿◡◡|‿◡◡|‿◡◡|‿◡◡|‿◡◡|‿◡

Ennius further Hellenized the new Roman epic in the first line of the *Annals,* where he called the Muses by their Greek name, *Musae,* rather than their old Latin name, *Camenae,* which had been used by Livius Andronicus and Naevius. Thus, Ennius declared his independence from the native Roman meter and its linguistic orientation and instead made himself an heir of the Greek tradition, a path many of the greatest poets of Rome later followed. Moreover, he recounts a dream, much as had Hesiod in his *Theogony* and as had Callimachus in his *Aitia,* in which the poet is given his poetic mission by divine revelation. In Ennius's case, the spirit of Homer declares itself reincarnated in Ennius. In fashioning the *Annals,* of whose eighteen books only about six hundred verses remain, Ennius used not only Homeric verse patterns but also much stock Homeric machinery such as similes, invocations of the Muses, divine councils, battle scenes, heroic speeches, prayers, and prophecy. It was left to Lucretius, Catullus, and, of course, Virgil, to realize fully the program that Ennius had inaugurated. Ennius was more closely tied in his understanding of epic to the Hellenistic tradition of Callimachus and his circle, who favored historical court epic (which celebrated–often banally, with an infelicitous mixture of myth and history–the exploits of Hellenistic monarchs), than Virgil wished or chose to be. Nevertheless, Ennius firmly established the legitimacy of history as a subject within the Roman epic tradition; there would have been no Virgil, who could artfully incorporate Roman history within a mythological scheme by both imitating and rewriting Homer, and certainly no Lucan, without the prior Homerizing of Latin epic by Ennius. In fact, Ennius's conscious representation of himself in the *Annals* as Homer reincarnated is an emblem of a new direction taken self-consciously for Latin epic. By choosing no less a subject than the thousand-year history of the Roman state, Ennius enabled Ovid to paint on an even greater canvas the myth and history of the known world in his *Metamorphoses.* To Ovid and Virgil, Ennius also may have given the triadic structure of his epic.

The *Annals* falls into six triads: books 1–3 begin with the fall of Troy and the escape of Aeneas to Italy. Ennius believed Romulus and Remus were Aeneas's grandsons, thus greatly telescoping the period preceding the regal era, with which the first triad closes. The next three books cover the beginning of the Republic to the invasion of the Gauls (book 4), the Samnite Wars (book 5), and the war against Pyrrhus (book 6). Books 7–9 report the Punic Wars, covering the first Punic War quickly, as it had been treated previously and popularly by Naevius, ending book 7 with the invasion of Hannibal in 218 B.C. Books 8 and 9 tell of the second Punic War (218–201 B.C.), ending just at the beginning of Ennius's own time, when many of his contemporaries could recall events from personal experience. Roman actions in Greece after the Punic Wars are included in books 10–12. Wars in Syria take up books 13, 14, and 15. The last triad, books 16–18, is fragmentary and, according to Pliny, focused on Roman actions contemporary with the poet's last years down to 171 B.C., chiefly the Istrian War.

Throughout the *Annals,* Ennius follows Naevius, his immediate predecessor, in the vision that Roman military exploits (Roman imperialism) were, in fact, a worthy subject for epic celebration. But Ennius moves beyond Naevius by developing a special poetic language for Roman epic, a language transferred from Homer, with archaic and honorific resonance. In the long interaction of Greek texts with Roman adaptive innovation that constitutes the history of Latin literature, Ennius figures as a major player for having created a linguistic medium suitable to Latin epic. Known and imitated by Lucretius, Cicero, and Virgil in their hexameters, Ennius would have had a secure place in Latin literature on the basis of the *Annals* alone. He was the great epic poet until Virgil supplanted him; the *Annals,* a Roman favorite because of its glorification of Roman imperialism, continued to be read through the second century A.D. but then seems to have faded from view. Yet, the *Annals* alone, despite its formative influence on Roman epic, does not fully account for the literary influence of Ennius.

As a writer of tragedy, Ennius contributed twenty-two titles, twenty adapted from Greek plays and two based on Roman situations. As he relied on Homer for much of his epic inspiration, so Ennius turned to the great Athenian tragic poets and their subjects, abandoning (except for two dramas) Roman history in favor of Greek myth. He leaned heavily on Euripides as a source for *Hecuba, Medea, Iphigenia,* and *Phoenix,* although he also used Aeschylus as a model for the *Eumenides* and Sophocles as a model for *Aias.* Ennius's final tragedy, the *Thyestes,* was brought out in 169 B.C., the year of his death, attesting a long and important career as a composer of tragedy, a genre never as important in Rome as it was in Athens, where it reached heights in the fifth century B.C. not to be

Portrait of a man some scholars believe to be Hannibal, whose invasion of Italy in 218 B.C. is described by Ennius in his Annales *(Annals), book 7 (from a silver coin struck in Spain ca. 220 B.C.)*

attained again in European literature until the Renaissance. Nevertheless, Ennius in many respects made possible the artificial and stylized tragedies of Seneca Tragicus nearly two hundred years later in the court of Nero. Seneca likewise wrote a *Thyestes* and a tragedy on (then-recent) Roman history, *Octavia.* Comedy, too, was part of Ennius's repertoire, but he was apparently much less successful in this genre, judging by the mere two surviving titles, than with tragedy. Ennius and many of his contemporary experimenters in Greek genres and subjects such as Accius and Pacuvius learned that despite the best efforts of a talented literary generation, Athenian tragedy and comedy are essentially creations of their time and place and could not be successfully imported into a Roman state that was struggling to make its own history, its own legends.

Furthermore, Ennius was an imitator and experimenter in the mode of the Hellenistic or Alexandrian *doctus poeta* (learned poet) in genres that were especially associated with the Alexandrian literary tradition. He wrote a didactic poem on gastronomy, the *Hedyphagetica,* often translated as the *Delicatessen.* This poem may well have been a parody, as was his poem *Sota,* which was based on the "sotadean" verse of the Alexandrian Sotades of Maronea, a form used for parodic and obscene purposes. In addition, Ennius wrote a philosophic poem, the *Epicharmus,* and two prose pieces on philosophical matters, the *Euhemerus* and the *Protrepticus.* The *Euhemerus* is interesting because it continued the thought of the philosopher Euhemerus of Messina (ca.

300 B.C.), who argued that the gods were simply human kings who had been deified after their deaths by adoring subjects. The Christian author Lactantius (A.D. 240–320) knew and used the text of Ennius's *Euhemerus* for Christian propaganda to trivialize the nature of pagan gods by explaining away their origin as mere human beings. Ennius also wrote a celebratory poem, the *Scipio,* in the manner of Hellenistic court poetry, for Scipio Africanus, victorious Roman commander in the second Punic War. Finally, there survive several epigrams composed in elegiac couplet. It is possible that Ennius introduced this Greek metrical form as well as the hexameter line to Rome. The elegiac line was later to be the line of choice for the love poetry of Propertius, Tibullus, and Ovid. If Ennius was, in fact, responsible for the importation of the elegiac meter, he would again, for this innovation alone, have a place of marked significance in the history of Latin poetry.

A further indication of the foundational position of Ennius's literary productivity in Roman letters, indeed showing that Ennius was not content to work with Greek-derived genres only, is the four to six books of the *Saturae,* of which only some thirty verses survive. Of the genres, satire alone was recognized by the Romans as their own native genre, not arising primarily from imitation of Greek literary elements, as Quintilian (10.1.93) asserts: "Satura quidem est tota nostra . . ." (Satire is completely ours). The Roman word *satura* means a "mixture," and Roman satire was consequently a mixture of elements, prose and poetry, on a variety of topics, later developed to include political, personal, and moral denunciation. The *Saturae* of Ennius was a mixture of separate poems on a variety of topics in different meters. Some of the poems were satiric and moralistic in tone while others were fables, dialogues, or even allegories, such as the *Contest between Life and Death.* The style was free and colloquial, perhaps reminiscent of Plautine comedy. Ennius seems not to have used the *Satura,* as Lucilius did, for personal attacks on enemies but to have kept more to general, public moralizing. Ennius is important as an initiator of this genre that was brought to its full definition by Lucilius (died 102 B.C.), whose lost work links Ennius to the great triad of satirists of the Empire–Horace (65–8 B.C.), Persius (A.D. 34–62), and Juvenal (A.D. 60–130).

Time and history have not been kind to the literary production of Quintus Ennius. Only scraps and fragments of his many works survive. Except for a few scattered papyri, Ennius is known today only by quotation from other writers whose works enjoyed a better fate. The works of Ennius cannot be shown to have survived the breakdown of antiquity in the sixth century A.D., although his name and significance were known and cited in the Renaissance by Petrarch in his

Africa. There he praised Ennius as the founder of authentic Roman epic (*Africa* 2.441 ff.) and as associated with the tradition of crowning the poet (*Africa* 9.398 ff.). Clearly the greatest influence of Ennius is to be understood as arising from those Roman poets who form the foundation of European literature and in whose works he continues to live, fulfilling his own prediction of poetic fame in this epitaph:

> NEMO ME LACRIMIS DECORET NEC FUNERA
> FLETU
> FAXIT. CUR? VOLITO VIVUS PER ORA VIRUM.

(Let no one honor me with tears nor adorn my funeral rites with weeping. Why? I continue to fly, living, through the mouths of men.)

Bibliography:

Michael von Albrecht, *A History of Roman Literature,* volume 1, revised by Albrecht and Gareth Schmeling (Leiden: Brill, 1997), pp. 144–146.

References:

Michael von Albrecht, *A History of Roman Literature from Livius Andronicus to Boethius,* 2 volumes, revised by Gareth Schmeling and von Albrecht (Leiden: Brill, 1997);

Gian Biagio Conte, *Latin Literature, A History,* translated by Joseph Solodow, revised by Don Fowler and Glenn Most (Baltimore: Johns Hopkins University Press, 1994);

A. S. Gratwick, "Ennius' *Annales,*" in *Latin Literature,* volume 2, edited by E. J. Kenney, The Cambridge History of Classical Literature (Cambridge: Cambridge University Press, 1982), pp. 60–76;

Eduard Norden, *Ennius und Vergilius: Kriegsbilder aus Rome grosser Zeit* (Leipzig: Teubner, 1915);

Otto Skutsch, *Annales* (Oxford: Clarendon Press, 1985);

Skutsch, *Ennius,* Entretiens sur l'antiquité classique, 17 (Geneva: Fondation Hardt, 1972).

Frontinus

(ca. A.D. 35 – A.D. 103/104)

Harry B. Evans
Fordham University

MAJOR WORKS: *Stratagemata* (Stratagems, late 80s A.D.);

De aquaeductu urbis Romae (On the Water System of the City Rome, ca. A.D. 98).

Editiones principes: *Stratagemata* in *Scriptores rei militaris sive Scriptores veteres de re militari,* edited by Giovanni Sulpizio da Veroli (Rome: Eucharius Silber, 1487); *Aqueducts,* edited by Pomponio Leto and Giovanni Sulpizio da Veroli (Rome: Eucharius Silber, 1483–1490).

Standard editions: *Les aqueducs de la ville de Rome,* edited and translated by Pierre Grimal (Paris: Budé, 1944)–with French translation, edition to be superseded by that of R. H. Rodgers (Cambridge: Cambridge University Press, forthcoming); *Sex. Iulii Frontini De aquaeductu urbis Romae,* edited by Cezary Kunderewicz (Leipzig: Teubner, 1973).

Translations in English: *Frontinus, The Stratagems and the Aqueducts of Rome,* Loeb Classical Library, edited and translated by Charles E. Bennett and Mary B. McElwain (Cambridge, Mass.: Harvard University Press, 1925); *Water Distribution in Ancient Rome: The Evidence of Frontinus,* translated by Harry B. Evans (Ann Arbor: University of Michigan Press, 1994), pp. 13–52.

Although Frontinus was a successful general and prominent political figure in the late first century A.D., his primary importance rests on his extant writings on a variety of technical subjects. Most interesting, and a crucial source on Roman topography and administration in the early empire, is his treatise on the aqueduct system of ancient Rome, *De aquaeductu urbis Romae,* written when he assumed responsibility for the *cura aquarum* or water commission under the emperor Nerva in A.D. 98. His other major works are four books of *Stratagems* written in the late 80s A.D. and several treatises on land surveying that survive only in fragments (C.O. Thulin,

Title page for a sixteenth-century Venetian edition of Frontius's military writings (courtesy of the Lilly Library, Indiana University)

ed., *Corpus Agrimensorum Romanorum* [Stuttgart: Teubner, 1913]).

Frontinus's early life is obscure; he was probably born in the last years of Tiberius's principate, since Tacitus cites him as urban praetor in A.D. 70 (*Hist.* 4.39.1–2). Little is known about Frontinus's family or birthplace (perhaps southern Gaul, from epigraphical evidence), but the name of his gens and his appoint-

The Porta Maggiore (formerly the Porta Praenestina) in Rome, part of the aqueduct system Frontinus described in De aquaeductu urbis Romae
(On the Water System of the City Rome, ca. A.D. 98)

ment as *curator aquarum* (superintendent of the water supply), a position held by leading senators, indicate a distinguished background. Following his election to the consulship in A.D. 73/74, Frontinus was appointed provincial governor of Britain, where he subdued the Silures in South Wales. He was succeeded in this position by Julius Agricola in A.D. 77/78; Tacitus praises Frontinus's achievements in Britain in his biography of his father-in-law, Agricola (*Agr.* 17.2).

Following this governorship Frontinus appears to have participated directly in Domitian's campaigns in Germany (*Strat.* 1.1.8, 1.3.10, 2.11.7); he was also appointed proconsul of Asia in A.D. 84/85. He seems to have played no major part in public life in the politically dangerous later years of Domitian's principate but rather to have occupied himself safely with literary activities; the *Stratagemata* (Stratagems, late 80s A.D.) and a lost work on military theory were probably writ-

ten at this time, along with the treatises on surveying. Martial describes a sojourn at Anxur in Frontinus's company (*Epist.* 10.58), and Pliny the Younger refers to Frontinus as a prominent figure in Roman society (*Epist.* 5.1.5).

After the accession of Nerva, Frontinus's public career was dramatically resurrected. In A.D. 97 he accepted an appointment as superintendent of Rome's water system (*Ag.* 1.2, 102.17) and also served on a senatorial commission investigating possible economies in imperial administration (Pliny, *Pan.* 62.2). He held a suffect consulship in A.D. 98, with Trajan as his colleague, and received the extraordinary honor of a third consulship, again with Trajan as colleague, in A.D. 100. Frontinus must have died by A.D. 103/104 when Pliny succeeded him in the College of Augurs (*Epist.* 4.8.3).

The four books of *Stratagems* present different examples of effective military strategy to illustrate rules

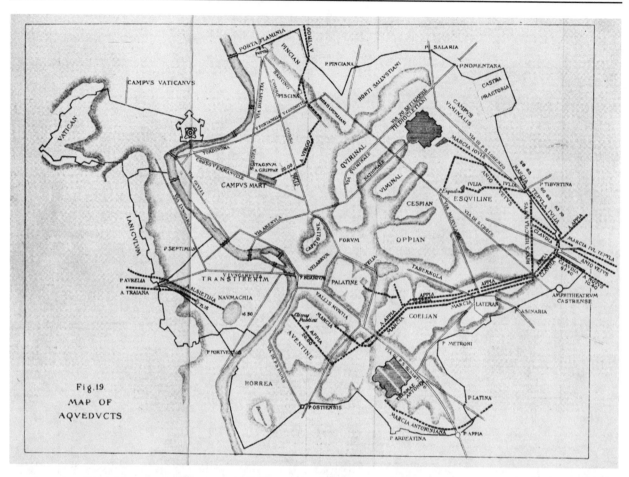

Map of Roman aqueducts from Rodolfo Amedeo Lanciani's 1897 Ruins and Excavations of Ancient Rome
(by permission of Houghton Mifflin Co.)

of military science and to inspire in readers, presumably military officers, the desire to act like their successful predecessors. The first three books give examples of skillful generalship before, during, and after battle, respectively; the fourth book, the authenticity of which has been doubted by some scholars for stylistic reasons, illustrates military leadership through problems of discipline, determination, restraint, and troop morale. Frontinus describes his treatise as an aid to commanders (*Strat.* 1. proem.), and Aelian, a contemporary Greek writer on military matters, states that he consulted Frontinus as an expert source (*Tactica,* proem. 3).

Much more interesting is *De aquaeductu urbis Romae,* which Frontinus states he compiled as a *commentarius* or notebook for himself, or a possible successor, to serve as a *formula administrationis,* a "rule and guide" of office (*Ag.* 2.2–3). Such a statement is immediately suspect: why would the author have published a treatise written primarily for his own edification? Scholars such as Pierre Grimal have described the book as a celebration of Nerva's administrative reforms by a dedicated

public servant and therefore a political document affirming the virtues and benefits of senatorial administration as demonstrated by Frontinus's own sense of responsibility on assuming the office of curator. The problem, however, merits closer attention.

De aquaeductu, despite its claim to be a rule and guide for office, is hardly a comprehensive account of the city water system: Frontinus provides a brief history of the aqueduct system (4–16), discusses the elevations of individual lines (17–22), as well as their capacity (64–76) and distribution figures (77–86), and outlines current improvements and procedures for administration and maintenance (87–130), but he omits many practical details, such as mechanics of repair and costs involved. More than a third of the book is devoted to a listing of capacity for fifteen pipes in use within the water system, as well as ten other pipes not in use (23–63). The reader is left with the conclusion that *De aquaeductu* is prescriptive rather than descriptive, written not to be a personal guide but rather a public document for a general readership.

Throughout the book Frontinus complains that as water commissioner he has inherited a corrupt and inefficient staff of *aquarii* (watermen), who must be carefully supervised (9.6–7, 75.2–3, 113.3–4, 114–115, 117.4). Earlier superintendents, although described as *principes civitatis* (leading citizens) (1), are criticized for carelessness in their record keeping and conduct of office (74.2, 101.2-4, 117.4), in contrast to Frontinus's own sense of responsibility and "hands-on" approach, modeled on the emperor himself (1, 64.1, 130). *De aquaeductu* gives a striking picture (largely contradicted by archaeological evidence, attesting to extensive repair and upgrading under the Flavians) of a water system much deteriorated from that of the Augustan administration under Marcus Agrippa and his immediate successors, demanding the full attention of the new curator. Frontinus, citing both his dedicated approach to his office and specifically the maps he prepared to facilitate maintenance of the system (17.3–4), presents himself as a new Agrippa, assuming the role of public servant determined to restore efficient administration after years of neglect. In this way the treatise becomes a self-promoting document, published to celebrate its author and the emperor who appointed him as curator. Indeed, Frontinus's description of his office is itself an anomaly, for the post of water commissioner had become largely ceremonial after Claudius's introduction of professional procurators in the *cure aquarum* during his principate as part of his expansion of the aqueduct system in the mid first century. While hardly "a simple and truthful narration of facts," as it has been characterized by Charles E. Bennett, Frontinus's treatise remains an essential source for understanding Rome's aqueducts and their administration. As one of the few documents surviving from antiquity that treat the city as an organic whole, it provides a capsule history of Rome's water system and detailed, if partial, statistics from a highly knowledgeable source on aqueduct distribution at the end of the first century.

Index:

Frontini Index, edited by Jenaro Costas Rodriguez (Hildesheim: Olms, 1985).

References:

Anthony R. Birley, *The Fasti of Roman Britain* (Oxford: Clarendon Press, 1981), pp. 69–72;

Christer Bruun, *The Water Supply of Ancient Rome: A Study of Roman Imperial Administration* (Helsinki: Societas Scientiarum Fennica, 1991), pp. 10–62;

Brian Campbell, "Teach Yourself How to be a General," *Journal of Roman Studies,* 77 (1987): 13–29;

Werner Eck, "Die Gestalt Frontins in ihrer politischen und sozialen Umwelt," in *Wasserversorgung im antiken Rom* (Munich: Oldenbourg, 1982), pp. 47–62;

A. Trevor Hodge, "Frontinus: A Study in Military History, Hydraulic Science, and Public Administration," *Aufstieg und Niedergang der römischen Welt* II, 37, no. 6 (Berlin & New York: De Gruyter, 1997).

Horace
(65 B.C. – 8 B.C.)

Jeanne Neumann O'Neill
Davidson College

MAJOR WORKS–EXTANT: *Iambi* (Epodes, 30 B.C.); *Sermones* (Satires: Satires I, 35/34 B.C.; Satires II, 30 B.C.); *Carmina* (Odes: Odes I–III, 23 B.C.; Odes IV, 13 B.C.); *Epistulae* (Epistles: Epistles I, 20–19 B.C.; Epistles II: 2.1, ca. 14 B.C.; Epistles II: 2.2, ca. 19 B.C.); *Ars poetica* (date uncertain, 23–18 B.C. or 13–8 B.C.).

Editio princeps: *Quinti Horati Flacci Opera*, ca. 1470.

Standard editions: *Quintus Horatius Flaccus, Opera*, edited by Richard Bentley, third edition (Berlin: Weidmann, 1869); *Q. Horati Flacci Opera*, edited by E. C. Wickham, second edition edited by H. W. Garrod (Oxford: Clarendon Press, 1912); *Q. Horati Flacci Opera*, edited by Friedrich Klingner, third edition (Leipzig: Teubner, 1959); *Horatius: Opera*, edited by Istvan Borzsák (Leipzig: Teubner, 1984); *Horatius, Opera*, edited by D. R. Shackleton Bailey, third edition (Stuttgart: Teubner, 1995).

Translations in English: *Horace: The Odes and Epodes*, translated by Charles E. Bennett, Loeb Classical Library (Cambridge, Mass.: Harvard University Press, 1914); *Horace: Satires, Epistles and Ars Poetica*, translated by H. Rushton Fairclough, Loeb Classical Library (Cambridge, Mass.: Harvard University Press, 1926); *The Odes and Epodes of Horace*, translated by Joseph P. Clancy (Chicago: University of Chicago Press, 1960); *Ad Pyrrham: A Polyglot Collection of Translations of Horace's Ode to Pyrrha (Book 1, Ode 5)*, compiled by Ronald Storrs (London: Oxford University Press, 1959); *Horace: Odes*, translated by James Michie (New York: Orion Press, 1963); *The Satires of Horace and Persius*, translated by Niall Rudd (New York: Penguin, 1979); *The Complete Works of Horace*, translated by Charles E. Passage (New York: Ungar, 1983); *The Essential Horace*, edited by Burton Raffel (San Francisco: North Point Press, 1983); *The Complete Odes and Epodes with the Centennial Hymn / Horace*, translated by W. G. Shepherd

Portrait of Horace from the first illustrated edition of his works, printed by J. Grüninger in Strasburg, Germany, 1498

(New York: Penguin, 1983); *Horace, Epistles*, translated by Colin W. Macleod (Rome: Edizioni dell'Ateneo, 1986); *Horace's Odes and Epodes*, translated by David Mulroy (Ann Arbor: University of Michigan Press, 1994); *Horace in English*, edited by D. S. Carne-Ross and Kenneth Haynes (New York: Penguin, 1996); *The Odes of Horace*, translated by David K. Ferry (New York: Farrar, Straus & Giroux, 1997); *Horace: Odes and Carmen Saeculae*, translated by Guy Lee (Leeds, U.K.: Francis Cairns, 1998).

Commentaries: *The Works of Horace: 2 Volumes*, edited by E. C. Wickham, second edition (Oxford: Oxford University Press, 1877–1891); *Q. Horatius Flaccus*, edited by Adolf Kiessling and Richard Heinze, part 1: *Odes & Epodes*, fourteenth edition (Berlin: Weidmann, 1984); part 2: *Satires*, eleventh edition (Berlin: Weidmann, 1977); part 3: *Epistles,* eleventh edition (Berlin: Weidmann, 1984; first edition, edited by Kiessling, Berlin: Weidmann, 1884–1889).

ODES AND EPODES: *Horace. Odes and Epodes,* edited by T. E. Page (London: Macmillan, 1895; reprinted, New York: St. Martin's Press, 1969); *Horace, Odes and Epodes,* edited by Charles E. Bennett (Boston: Allyn & Bacon, 1901; reprinted, New York: Caratzas, 1984); *Horace: The Odes,* edited by Paul Shorey and Gordon J. Laing (Boston: Sanborn, 1910; reprinted, Pittsburgh: University of Pittsburgh Press, 1982); *The Third Book of Horace's Odes,* edited by Gordon W. Williams (Oxford: Clarendon Press, 1969); *A Commentary on Horace: Odes Book I,* edited by R. G. M. Nisbet and Margaret Hubbard (Oxford: Oxford University Press, 1989); *A Commentary on Horace: Odes Book II,* edited by Nisbet and Hubbard (Oxford: Oxford University Press, 1991); *Horace: The Odes,* edited by Kenneth Quinn (Newburyport, U.K.: Focus/R. Pullins, 1996); *Horace, Epodes and Odes,* edited by Daniel H. Garrison (Norman & London: University of Oklahoma Press, 1991); *Epodes,* edited by David Mankin (Cambridge: Cambridge University Press, 1995); *Horace, Odes I. Carpe Diem. Text, Translation and Commentary,* edited and translated by David West (Oxford: Oxford University Press, 1995).

SATIRES AND EPISTLES: *Oeuvres d'Horace: Satires,* edited by F. Plessis and P. Lejay (Paris: Hachette, 1911; reprinted, Hildesheim: G. Olms, 1966); *Horace Satires and Epistles,* edited by Edward P. Morris (Norman: University of Oklahoma Press, 1980); *Horace: Epistles Book I,* edited by O. A. W. Dilke, third edition (London: Methuen, 1989); *Horace on Poetry,* edited by C. O. Brink, 3 volumes, second edition (Cambridge: Cambridge University Press, 1982–1985); *Epistles, Book II and Epistle to the Pisones ('Ars Poetica'),* edited by Niall Rudd (Cambridge: Cambridge University Press, 1989); *Horace, Satires I,* edited by M. P. Brown (Warminster, U.K.: Aris & Phillips, 1993); *Horace, Satires II,* edited by Frances Muecke (Warminster, U.K.: Aris & Phillips, 1993); *Horace Epistles Book I,* edited by Roland Mayer (Cambridge: Cambridge University Press, 1994).

Horace wrote poetry ranging from *iambi* (epodes) and *sermones* (satires and epistles) to *carmina* (lyrics). These poems paint a detailed self-portrait—laughing poet of moderation; ironic and gentle moralist; enigmatic observer of the Augustan principate; and self-deprecating lover of the Italian countryside, good wine, his

friends, and, most of all, his art. By offering a poetic persona who speaks to so many human concerns, Horace has encouraged each reader to feel that he or she is one of the poet's circle, a friend in whom he confides. Horace's life, however, is as much masked as revealed by his confessional narratives, which present a literary autobiography—the author as he wishes his audience to view him. The poet's delight in shifting perspectives also serves as a reminder that the poetic *I* gives voice to a persona and mood only of the moment. Perhaps the greatest irony of the poet who so relished irony is that by constantly talking about himself, he has left a portrait of a man varying not only from generation to generation but also from reader to reader.

In addition to the literary portrait offered by his own poetry, readers may learn something of Horace's life from a short biography written by Suetonius (fl. late first, early second century A.D.). Suetonius may have gleaned his material partly from the poetry itself, however, so both sources must be used cautiously.

Quintus Horatius Flaccus, the son, as he claimed, of a freedman, was born 8 December 65 B.C. under the consulship of L. Cotta and L. Torquatus. He was born in Venusia, a town in southeast Italy on the border between Lucania and Apulia (modern Calabria), where the Romans had founded a colony in 291 B.C. after the third Samnite War. Horace's father was not necessarily a slave who was later freed by his master. Venusia, typical of the towns to the south of Rome, provided a barricade between Rome and potentially hostile neighbors. In 91 B.C. the citizens of many towns such as Venusia revolted against their alliance with Rome. Venusia joined the revolt in 90 B.C. When the town was recaptured in 88 B.C., three thousand Venusian citizens were captured and, as was the custom, enslaved. Horace's father could thus have been a freeborn native, enslaved for siding with the revolutionaries in the Social War, who later regained his freedom. The elder Horace's freedman status might have been a fiction, part of the poet's literary persona.

Horace mentions a nurse, Puglia (*Odes,* 3.4.10), but not his mother or any siblings. He calls his father a modest landowner and a *coactor,* that is, a middleman who handles the cash in a sale of goods (*Sat.* 1.6; *Epist.* 1.20). Suetonius adds the rumor that Horace's father was a *salsamentarius* (a seller of salted fish). Neither profession was prestigious, but "fishmonger" is probably a literary rather than a biographical reference. Horace associates "salty wit" with the caustic humor of Bion of Borysthenes, a popular Hellenistic philosopher who also claimed his father was a freedman seller of salted fish (*Epist.* 2.2.60), as well as with his satiric predecessor Lucilius, who, Horace says, "rubbed down the city with a good deal of salt" (*Sat.* 1.10. 3–4).

Horace speaks with loving respect, not embarrassment, of his freedman father and portrays him as ambitious for his son, but not at the cost of personal virtue. The elder Horace is presented as a man of irreproachable character who wanted his son to live modestly and to comply with accepted social decorum. Like Demea, the strict and conservative father in Terence's comedy the *Adelphoe,* Horace's father taught his son appropriate behaviors by examples illustrating traditional viewpoints; he was proud of *not* being a philosopher, of guarding his son's behavior and reputation, and of educating him according to ancestral custom. Horace's biographical narratives turn the taunt "son of a freedman" to his own advantage: a poor man from a simple birth, versed in the straightforward ethics of the Italian countryside, makes a more convincing moral commentator than a rich and sophisticated one.

Instead of having his son educated by the local schoolmaster, Flavius, in the company of *magni . . . pueri magnis e centurionibus orti* (big sons sired by big centurions, *Sat.* 1.6.73–74), Horace's father took his son to Rome for his education (*Sat.* 1.6.76–78; *Epist.* 2.2.41–42). He wanted his son to have the best and to be taught in the city among the children of knights and senators, rather than with the children of small-town former army officials (*Sat.* 1.6.72–78). Horace's schooling suggests that his father's poverty was relative to the standards of the poet's later associations: his father could afford to move to Rome and to have his son educated and equipped with the proper accoutrements to render him indistinguishable from the sons of the elite. Although Horace did not have the education of the truly rich (both Cicero's son and nephew, for example, were privately educated at the home of Crassus), he did have the best of a semiprivate education: his teacher, Orbilius (*Epist.* 2.1.70–71), was eminent enough to be included in Suetonius's biography of distinguished *grammatici et rhetorici* (grammarians and rhetoricians). The Rome of Horace's adolescence was home to ambitious and experimental poets such as Lucretius and Catullus (both of whom probably died before Horace arrived in Rome), Calvus, Cinna, and Cornelius Gallus, and to philosophers who lectured on Hellenistic ethical thought.

During the poet's formative years in the Italian countryside, violent political factions plagued Rome. When Horace was two (63 B.C.), the consul Cicero discovered and suppressed Catiline's conspiracy against the government. When Horace was five (60 B.C.), Pompey, Julius Caesar, and Crassus joined political forces in the so-called first triumvirate, and Caesar was granted a five-year command in Gaul; in 56 B.C. their alliance and Caesar's command in Gaul were extended for an additional five years. Three years later Crassus

died, leaving Caesar and Pompey to vie for power. Horace was fifteen (and surely in Rome) when Caesar's army crossed the Rubicon, the river that separated his province from Italy, thus breaking the law and beginning a civil war (49 B.C.). While Horace studied, Caesar battled Pompey and his supporters throughout the Mediterranean, returning victorious to Rome in 46 B.C.

Perhaps the same year, Horace went to Athens to study philosophy (*Epist.* 2.2.43–45), where he may have tried his hand at writing poetry in Greek (*Sat.* 1.10.31–35). Horace was in Athens when Caesar was assassinated by a group of Romans who feared his autocracy (44 B.C.). When the republican leader Marcus Brutus arrived in Athens about six months after Caesar's death, Horace left school to become a tribune in Brutus's army (43 B.C., *Epist.* 2.2.46–50). The tribunate was a junior military post usually held by either young men of equestrian rank or those whose family finances were large enough (400,000 sesterces) that the post would establish them as equestrians and offer an entrée into public life. Horace might already have been part of the latter group; it is also possible that the exigencies of war superseded the normal requirements for appointment.

Marcus Antonius (Mark Antony) and Octavian, Caesar's great-nephew and heir, defeated Brutus's republican forces at the Battle of Phillipi in November 42 B.C. An ode published nearly twenty years later, celebrating the return to Italy of a comrade-in-arms, Pompeius places Horace at the battle (*Odes,* 2.7). It also shows the difficulties inherent in reading Horace autobiographically. In typical Horatian fashion, the poet mixes a likely occurrence (that he was at Philippi under Brutus) with literary embellishment. Horace presents himself as a young soldier throwing away his shield in a panic to facilitate his escape, an allusion to the Greek lyric poets Archilochus and Alcaeus, who also claimed to have thrown away their shields while beating a hasty retreat. Just as Aphrodite saved her son Aeneas from battle in Homer's *Iliad,* so too Mercury wraps Horace in a cloud and carries him safely off the dangerous battlefield.

When Horace returned to Italy under the general amnesty granted to the defeated troops by the second triumvirate of Octavian, Antony, and Lepidus, he found his family's land confiscated (*Epist.* 2.2.50–51). He procured a post in Rome as *scriba quaestorius* (a scribe in the Treasury). The scribes in general were just below the equestrians as a social group; the *scribae quaestorii* were the highest-ranking scribes, however, and many achieved equestrian status. While little is known about the *scribae,* a candidate probably needed backing by a wealthy and powerful connection as well as the financial resources to purchase the desired post. Even at this early stage of his career, Horace may have had influential friends who recommended him for the appointment. (Some scholars have suggested Asinius Pollio, the consul of 40 B.C.). Whether wealthy supporters also helped Horace financially or despite the loss of his family property, he had sufficient resources to secure the office for himself is not clear.

Horace says almost nothing about his activities as a scribe beyond listing the expectations that accompany the post among the pressures of the city from which his country estate affords pleasant escape (*Sat.* 2.6.36–37). His duties provided him with income and left him time to write, although he later claimed (as part of an argument that he would rather nap than write poetry) that he wrote poetry when he was young because he was poor and needed the money (*Epist.* 2.2.51–54).

At some time between his return to Rome and 38 B.C., Horace became a friend of another young poet five years his senior, Virgil. In 38 B.C. Virgil and the poet Varius introduced Horace to Gaius Maecenas (died 8 B.C.), a wealthy equestrian descended from Etruscan nobility who was patron to the new generation of talented poets such as Virgil and, later, Propertius. As Octavian's longtime friend, Maecenas enjoyed a great deal of unofficial power in Rome, but he is best known for his prominent role in Horace's verse.

Horace gives his version of his first encounter with Maecenas and their subsequent friendship in *Sat.* 1.6, a poem that illustrates Roman social decorum, a prominent theme in Horace's poetry. The social gulf between him and Maecenas at first made Horace tongue-tied. Maecenas spoke with him briefly, asked questions that the young poet answered forthrightly, and then ended the interview. Eight months later Maecenas invited Horace to join his circle of friends. The poem compliments Maecenas for his recognition that nobility is a state of mind rather than of rank and reveals Horace as a worthy man who is comfortable with his role and status relative to Maecenas. As a result of temperament and training, Horace suggests, advancement in public life held little attraction for him. In fact, ambitious for literary prestige, he poured his competitive energies into writing poetry. The poem also suggests that, while Horace and Maecenas developed a friendship in the modern sense of the word during their long association, their relationship began as one of unequals, in which Maecenas was more powerful. The social dynamic that accompanied this unequal status did not wholly disappear with the growth of a companionable easiness between the two men.

By the time of his introduction to Maecenas, Horace was writing in at least two genres: satires that he called both *sermones* (verse conversations) and *saturae* (satires) as well as poems that he referred to as *iambi* (iambics), although that collection is commonly called the *Epodes.* Horace may have begun the iambics as early as 42 B.C., and he may have started working on the satires at the same time or earlier. Not until several years later did he publish a full work, *Satires I* (ca. 35 B.C.).

Greek poets had cultivated a lively satiric spirit, especially in iambic poetry and in comedy, but the genre itself was, as Quintilian claimed, completely new and Roman: "Satura quidem tota nostra est" (*Institutio Oratoria,* 10.1.93). Only scattered fragments remain of Ennius's (ca. 239–169 B.C.) several books of *saturae.* Horace, however, credits Lucilius (second century B.C.) with originating the genre (*Sat.* 2.1.30–34) and setting the precedent for dactylic hexameter as the meter of a satiric verse that claims moral authority against all manner of human failings.

Satire as a genre is something of a hodgepodge with a fitting name. Although the derivation of *satura* has long been the subject of controversy, it most plausibly refers to a *lanx satura,* or plate full of various foodstuffs. Food is a natural focus for satire, and several of Horace's satires center on food and mealtime decorum, but the "mixed plate" metaphor refers more to the variety of topics in this genre that center on human foibles. The humble imagery also suits the low status of the genre in the literary hierarchy, a status reflected in the arrangement of the various genres in complete texts of Horace's works: the epodes, satires, and epistles are printed after the more exalted genre of lyric. Combination and variety furthermore typify satire: Hellenistic philosophical diatribe joins with comic lampoon, iambic invective, and folksy narrative full of animal fables and deftly drawn character sketches. Sexual and scatological humor, although inappropriate in more-elevated genres, are quite at home in satire. The phallic god Priapus indulges in earthy language and jokes in the eighth satire, while the second, the bawdiest of the satires, concerns proper sexual partners.

Like the *Eclogues* (the book of bucolic poetry published by Virgil), each collection of Horace's satires was meant to be read as a poetry book. The ten poems of *Satires I* are presented to their audience both as distinct poems and as a unified work whose individual poems should be considered in relation to their neighbors and to the book as a whole. The careful arrangement of the poetry in the book invites division into parts large and small. Smaller components such as paired poems, sometimes adjacent and sometimes not, complement, contrast with, or comment on each other (as in *Sat.* 1.4 and 1.10, satires about writing satire). Poetry books often present a related series of poems, as in the three satiric diatribes that, part philosophical lesson and part harangue, begin *Satires I.* Scholars have divided *Satires I* into halves (1–5 and 6–10) and into thirds (1–3: diatribes; 4–6: the literary, ethical, political Horace; 7–9:

The foundations of Horace's house near Licenza in the Sabine Hills

short narratives; 10: conclusion). Another pattern balances the diatribes (1–3) followed by the first of the two "satires on satire" in the book (4) with the narrative satires (7–9) followed by the second of the literary satires (10). Between these sets are the two central poems focusing on Horace's friendship with Maecenas, the first a narrative of a shared journey (*Sat.* 1.5), the second an account of Horace's upbringing and introduction to Maecenas, which stresses the poet's lack of political ambition and contentment with his place in Roman society (*Sat.* 1.6). These divisions are complementary rather than definitive and are part of the complexity of the book.

The first poem of a poetry book, often programmatic, sets the tone for the rest of the book and provides information on the matter and style, the dedicatee, and the place of the work in the literary tradition as well as the poet's innovation. The discursive chatter to Maecenas in the opening poem of *Satires I*, which centers on discontent and greed, places Horace in the Lucilian literary tradition. Lucilius's persona was that of a wealthy equestrian confidently publicizing his opinions. The haphazard logic of Horace's narrator mimics the careless authority of those accustomed to voicing any and all of their opinions; his style is that of someone comfortably making judgments in the company of those who share his values and assumptions. The poem cannot be called a philosophical argument: the transitions are awkward, and the logic wanders.

Solid ethical sense, however, shines through: people should be content with what they have, enjoying their resources and advantages instead of hoarding and competing with others.

Two famous characterizations of Horace come from this first satire. The first typifies his facetious manner: "ridentem dicere verum / quid vetat" (What's wrong with someone laughing as they tell the truth? *Sat.* 1.1.24–25). The second signals the balance and moderation that mark his work as a whole: "est modus in rebus, sunt certi denique fines / quos ultra citraque nequit consistere rectum" (there is a middle ground in things; there are, finally, definite boundaries, on either side of which Right is unable to take a stand, *Sat.* 1.1.106–107).

The second and third satires, similarly discursive treatments of sex (*Sat.* 1.2) and friendship (*Sat.* 1.3), illustrate the poet's interest in Hellenistic ethical thought. The second mentions Philodemus, a prominent Epicurean philosopher. Horace ridicules and dismisses followers of the doctrines of Chrysippus, the head of the Stoic school during the third century B.C. (*Sat.* 1.3.127), like Fabius (*Sat.* 1.1.14; 1.2.134) and Crispinus (*Sat.* 1.1.120; 1.3.139; 1.4.14). The third satire criticizes Stoic tenets such as all failings are equal; justice is natural, not normative; and only the wise man is good. The poem advocates a mutual and affectionate acceptance of failings among friends rather than a rigid stoicism.

The book on the whole is a testimony to Horace's friendship with Maecenas. The narrator represents himself as an enthusiastic, loyal, and deserving friend who has access to a close relationship with the powerful Maecenas. Satisfied with his role and having no political ambitions, the poet enjoys the company of a group that–while exclusive, intellectually sophisticated, and powerful–is yet internally free from ambition and competition. Saying he is following Lucilius in composing witty, conversational narratives straight from his life (*Sat.* 1.4.1–8), Horace portrays his life as a poet and friend of Maecenas as he would have his audience see it, often to their frustration. Written against a backdrop of great political turmoil and change, the satires do not willingly yield firm information or political nuances. Consequently, Horace's relationship to and attitude toward the leading figures who play a role in his poetry continue to be subjects of speculation and controversy.

The spectre of civil war had not yet passed, even though the satirist had traded in his armor for a stylus. From 40 B.C. until the battle of Actium in 31 B.C., full-scale civil war was avoided by, in effect, a division of the Roman world, with Antony controlling the East and Octavian the West. The sparring between Octavian and Antony prompted two peacekeeping expeditions to southern Italy. A teasing version of the poet's participation in such a diplomatic expedition is the subject of *Sat.* 1.5, often called the Journey to Brundisium. *Sat.* 1.5 has been read in various ways: as a political portrait aimed to influence Roman opinion, as a reminiscence composed primarily for the pleasure of his fellow travelers, as a realistic depiction of an actual event, as a purely literary creation, and as a programmatic poem reacting to Lucilius, who had also written a satire about a journey.

The goal of the expedition that forms the background for *Sat.* 1.5 was of considerable interest to Horace's ancient audience and is still of interest today, for its goal was the reconciliation of the two leading men of Rome. Horace intensifies and frustrates the reader's curiosity about what he, as a companion to Maecenas, saw and heard on that journey. The reader learns virtually nothing of political significance. Instead, the poem emphasizes that the traveling party is a solid and intimate group. Even mishaps—an overnight stopping place almost catching on fire (71–81) and Horace's anecdote about his sexual frustration after waiting half the night for a woman who does not appear (82–85)—are presented as bonding experiences, memorable if unpleasant events evolving into anecdotes that continued to bind the group even after the experience has ended. When the party finally arrives at Brundisium, Horace ends the narrative, having provided only enough information to assure the reader that he was a part of an elevated inner circle.

Sat. 1.9 also gives the poet the opportunity to reveal much by revealing little about the close—and closed—group around Maecenas. The poet makes clear that his interests and talents lie in writing poetry, not in social maneuvering, by telling a tale at his own expense about the antics of an ambitious pest who confounds Horace's attempts at escape. A stranger to guile, Horace is at the mercy of his pursuer, who seeks an introduction to Maecenas. Horace declares that the group is free from social posturing and competition: each member knows and is happy with his own place (48–52):

> We do not live there
> as you suppose. There is no house more unsullied than
>   this one
> or more free from such mischief. It bothers me not at all, I
>   assure you,
> because someone is more affluent or more learned; each
>   one has
> his own place.

While the reader might agree with his antagonist that Horace's claims are difficult to believe, the idealized representation of the lesser-status friend who is secure in his own place and free from ambitious envy

has a long tradition in Roman culture. The glimpse available to outsiders makes the group more desirable and at the same time more unattainable.

Sat. 1.9 is the last of a series of three fairly short narratives. *Sat.* 1.7 vividly recounts an anecdote from Horace's army days in Asia–a legal altercation (with Brutus presiding) between a proscribed Italian and a Greek businessman. The witch Canidia makes the first of her several appearances in Horace's poetry in *Sat.* 1.8. She and Sagana, another witch, are frightened from the Esquiline by a flatulent statue of Priapus, a fertility god who protected gardens.

The intersection of literature with life, implicit in all Horace's poetry, is the explicit focus of the two literary satires, 1.4 and 1.10. Both these poems explore satire as an amalgam of the aesthetic and the ethical in explicit comparisons with Lucilius. Horace prides himself on following his predecessor's tradition of courageously attacking the failings of people of any rank. While there is a good deal of dismissive raillery at the expense of those outside of his social and literary circles (for example, the pest in *Sat.* 1.9, the fawning praetor in *Sat.* 1.5, and the witch Canidia in *Sat.* 1.8), the satires are in fact neither biting invective nor attacks against powerful living people. Rather, homespun wisdom tinged with Hellenistic philosophy in a conversational style is directed in a manner more mocking than vituperative at the victims the poet can afford to scorn–and at himself.

Horace also criticizes his predecessor's metrical and rhetorical practice: in highly polished, concise, and exact verse, Horace reproves Lucilius as a muddy, verbose, and slipshod writer (*Sat.* 1.4). The charges levied against Lucilius are repeated in the final satire of the book (*Sat.* 1.10). Just to be witty is not enough, insists Horace. A poet's thoughts should run smoothly and at the right pace; there should be a good variety in tone; and the poet should assume different roles suited to the matter at hand. The language itself should be plain and pure Latin, with no Greek neologisms mixed in. Horace evades the question of the literary status of the genre, insisting the satires are merely versified conversations. Despite its informality and mundane subject matter–the antithesis of epic–satire in Horace's hands is more than versifying. Behind the informal veneer of the genre, every word has been chosen and placed with a tightly controlled artistry of which the poet is justifiably proud.

The two satires look at the context of the genre from different perspectives. The fourth satire roots Horace's literary endeavors in the rigorous ethical training of his childhood and credits his father with instilling the lessons that inspire satire. The tenth focuses on the present; Horace compliments by name poets writing in other genres and literary friends whose approval he seeks. The poet's expression of his preference for an elite and refined group of readers over popular acclaim closes the book.

Sometime between the publication of the first book of satires (35/34 B.C.) and 31 B.C. Horace acquired an estate in the Sabine Hills outside of Rome. Although he also had a home in Rome and later at Tibur, a fashionable resort town northeast of Rome, the Sabine estate figured most prominently in Horace's poetry. It afforded the poet not only a peaceful place in which to think and write but also the landed respectability so important to the Romans. Maecenas has usually been credited with helping Horace to acquire the Sabine estate. In recent years, however, some scholars have suggested that Horace, a man of equestrian rank and a scribe, had the financial resources to buy the estate without Maecenas's aid. Assuming that he did so, however, ignores the references to substantial material benefits received from Maecenas (for example, *Epod.* 1.31–32 and possibly *Odes* 2.18.11–14, 3.16.37–38). The extent of Maecenas's financial assistance is uncertain. Further, ancient sources have not provided enough about relative wealth in Rome to demonstrate that even a man of equestrian rank would necessarily have the wherewithal to afford an estate in the Sabine Hills.

Five years later (30 B.C.) Horace published a second book of satires; this book both continues and departs from its predecessor. Food and philosophy—and even food as philosophy—play prominent roles in this book whose individual poems balance and comment on one another. Book 2 is full of advice, but, unlike the advice of book 1, little is offered by the poet's persona. The dialogue of the first satire sets the tone for the rest of the book. Instead of diatribes sprinkled with a few interlocutors (book 1, 1–3) or monologues (*Sat.* 1.4, 1.10, 1.6) or narratives recounted either by the poet's persona (*Sat.* 1.5, 1.7, 1.9) or, in *Sat.* 1.8, by a wooden statue of Priapus, the second book presents various scenes. The poet may take the secondary role as the interlocutor while other characters speak in diatribes (*Sat.* 2.3, 2.7). A chance encounter becomes the stimulus for a lecture on food (*Sat.* 2.4) or a narrative about a fancy dinner gone awry (*Sat.* 2.8).

The reader hears several of the narratives at a far remove. Catius repeats a lecture (4); Fundanius, a story (8); the poet, the precepts of Ofellus (2) and the fable of his neighbor Cervius (6); Damasippus, the lecture of Stertinius (3); and Davus, the precepts of Crispinus as overheard by his doorkeeper (7). Twice, however, the reader eavesdrops on conversations. In keeping with one of the motifs of the book, both concern expert advice. The book opens in the midst of a consultation

between the poet and the legal expert Trebatius. Just as in the literary satires of the first book, the poet takes the stance of having been attacked for writing satire. Trebatius counsels his friend to give up satire, or, if he has to write, to compose epic praises of Octavian. The poem defends the poet's talent as well as his choice of genre; no matter what, Horace promises, he will write (57–60):

> In short: whether a peaceful old age waits for me
> or death circles with black wings,
> rich, poor, at Rome, or if thus chance bids, an exile,
> whatever the complexion of my life, I will write.

The second consultation begins the second half of the book. In this poem the reader is transported to the underworld of Greek mythology to eavesdrop on the famous seer Tiresias advising Odysseus on the best way to ingratiate himself with the elderly rich in hopes of being left a legacy (*Sat.* 2.5).

Ofellus, the focus of the second satire, stands in contrast to other characters in the book. Ofellus lost his farm—but retained his convictions—when his land was transferred to veteran soldiers. Against Ofellus's precepts that hard work, simple food, and plain but unstinting living are best, Horace has set those of Catius (*Sat.* 2.4), who zealously recounts in philosophical style a lecture he has just heard on gourmet delicacies. Balancing Catius's amusing precepts is the story told by Fundanius, Horace's friend and writer of comedies (*Sat.* 1.10.40–42), about the dinner party given by Nasidienus, who tries to impress Maecenas with trendy food and wines (*Sat.* 2.8).

Two diatribes directed at Horace make fun of, among other things, the ripple effect of contemporary interest in Hellenistic ethical thought (*Sat.* 2.3, 2.7). Both take place during the December Saturnalia, when the distinction between slaves and masters is blurred. Damasippus, a convert to philosophy, sees his new learning as yet another in a string of schemes to get ahead in the world (*Sat.* 2.3). A captive Horace is treated to the various proofs that all fools are mad and only the Stoic wise man is sane, arguments that Damasippus has learned from a single encounter with the Stoic Stertinius, whose lecture he reiterates at length (the poem is 326 lines, Horace's longest next to *Ars poetica*). In *Sat.* 2.7 Davus, one of Horace's slaves, also takes advantage of the license allowed during the Saturnalia to accuse his master of the shallowness and pretense of virtue that other characters in the book display. Davus had become a philosopher through the servant grapevine: he learned the rudiments of Stoic argumentation from the Stoic Crispinus's doorkeeper, who had in turn learned them by eavesdropping on his master's lectures.

Davus's harangue comments on Horace's self-portrait in *Sat.* 2.6 and points out the complex presentation of the satires. The praises of simplicity in *Sat.* 2.6 contrast with the extremes of philosophizing (*Sat.* 2.3, 2.7), gourmandizing (*Sat.* 2.4, 2.8), and moneygrubbing (*Sat.* 2.5) portrayed in the book. The poet represents himself as grateful and content, living a simple life far from ambitious Rome, where folk wisdom and animal fables–like the tale of the city mouse and country mouse with which the satire ends–take the place of urban philosophizing. In the next poem, however, Horace offers a different reading of *Sat.* 2.6 and makes the reader wonder if the poet is partly the object of his own satire in both poems. The effusive gratitude and deep contentment expressed in the previous satire, Davus's tirade suggests, reflect the poet's mood, not a stable sentiment: "you can't stand your own company for an hour, you are unable to make good use of your leisure and, a fugitive and a wanderer, you avoid your very self, seeking one minute to drink away, the next to sleep away your troubles" (112–115). Davus uses the argument that all fools are slaves to eradicate the social distinctions between himself and his master. His master suffers from all the same desires and foibles as Davus, but the master's social station allows him to make aesthetic distinctions and masquerade in ways unavailable to (and unnecessary for) his slave.

Satiric spirit finds a more forceful expression in some of the *Epodes,* published around the same time as *Satires II.* All but the final poem (17) are written in couplets in which the two lines are of different lengths and sometimes different metrical patterns–hence the designation epode, which means "after the ode" and technically refers to the second verse of the couplet. Horace, however, referred to the poems as *iambi,* putting himself in the literary tradition of the archaic Greek poet Archilochus of Paros, whose meter and manner he claims to imitate (*Epist.* 1.19. 23–25).

Horace adapted various combinations of Archilochus's meters to his native Latin, but Archilochus is not the only model for the iambs. The prolific works of the third-century-B.C. scholar-poet associated with the Mouseion at Alexandria, Callimachus of Cyrene, include thirteen iambs, followed in the manuscripts by four lyric poems, for a total of seventeen, the same number of poems as Horace included in his iambs. Callimachus associates his iambs with the sixth-century-B.C. poet Hipponax, whose work also influenced Horace.

Unlike Archilochus, however, for whom the iamb was a weapon (*A. p.* 79), Horace's aggressive epodes attack only safe or fictional characters. As part of his warning that his adversary be wary of attacking one well-equipped to retaliate, the narrator of the sixth epode names the well-known enemies of Archilochus, Lycambes and Hipponax (Bupalus), but his own victim remains anonymous. Horace attacks unnamed women in *Epodes* 8 and 12, both poems so scathing and coarse that they are often explained away as "allegories" or "literary exercises." An indignant citizen berates a nameless former slave in the fourth poem, accusing him of rising to the status of military tribune through newly acquired wealth and political connections. This poem has sometimes been thought to repeat inaccurate gossip against Horace's own military past (referred to in *Sat.* 1.6).

Some named characters in the iambs may or may not refer to historical individuals. In a distorted propempticon (*Epod.* 10), a type of poem in which the gods are invoked to give safe voyage to a friend, Horace prays for Maevius's death at sea (identified by the scholia as the same poet Virgil had mentioned disparagingly in *Eclogue* 3.90). The fervent champion of rural life in *Epode* 2, one of Horace's most frequently imitated poems, turns out, in the end, to be Alfius, an urban moneylender. Canidia, a favorite character in the epodes (as in the satires), is a predatory witch who kidnaps a young boy in order to use his entrails in a love potion (*Epod.* 5). She is the automatic suspect when Horace complains Maecenas has poisoned him with a garlic-laden feast (*Epod.* 3); her spells finally overwhelm the poet, who in vain begs release from his torment (*Epod.* 17).

A perverse eroticism is a vehicle for invective against Canidia in *Epodes* 5 and 17 as well as in the eighth and twelfth epodes. Of the three other erotic poems in the collection, only one is aggressive; two touch on the effect of love on writing poetry. A rejected Horace promises his past lover that he will have the last laugh in a poem that comes closest to the *Odes* in tone (*Epod.* 15). In *Epode* 11 the narrator complains that he is love's perpetual victim, suffering a misery not even writing poetry can alleviate; in *Epode* 14 being in love provides an excuse to Maecenas for promised but unfinished poetry.

Iambic poetry is appropriate for political expression as well, and the epodes reflect a poetic reaction to the political upheaval of their time. As the book opens, Horace, despite his unwarlike character, announces he will follow Maecenas anywhere, even off to war. The dedication to Maecenas underscores the poet's gratitude toward and concern for his friend, made vivid by the crisis of civil war. Horace may in fact have accompanied Maecenas, early in their relationship, to the battle at Cape Palinurus, where Octavian suffered a naval

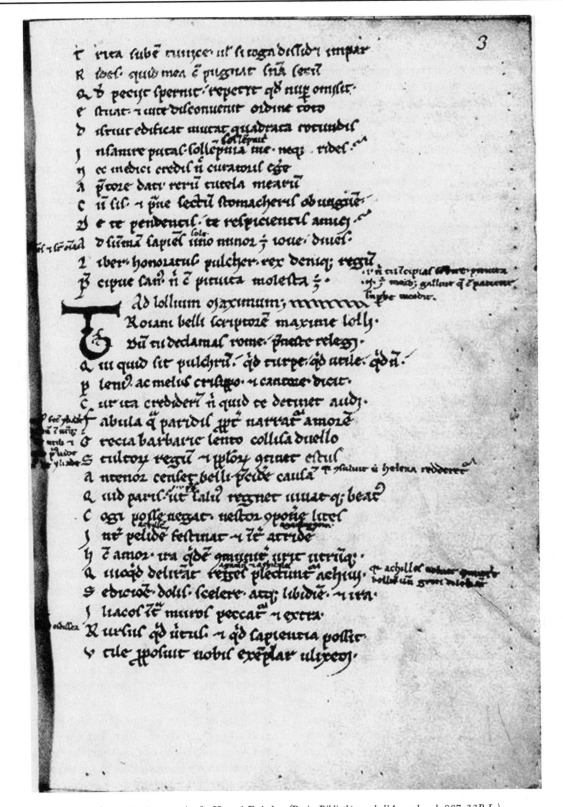

Page from a 1218 manuscript for Horace's Epistles *(Paris, Bibliothèque de l'Arsenal, cod. 887, 33B.L.)*

defeat (*Odes* 3.4.28). Horace may also have been with Maecenas at Actium, the occasion of the ninth epode.

Whether or not he actually witnessed the battle, the war, either directly or in the background, informs much of the book. In *Epode* 7 the poet appeals to his countrymen to stop the destruction and frenzy, a curse he says is rooted in Romulus's fratricide. In a poem that is frequently compared with Virgil's fourth eclogue, Horace proposes that Rome's best citizens abandon the city, which has been ravaged by its own might. Under the guidance of Horace as their *vates* (prophet-poet) Romans can find a new home set in a golden age (*Epod.* 16). The sorrows of war inform a sympotic epode as well (*Epod.* 13). The poet encourages his companions to turn a winter storm to their advantage and to chase away their worries with old wine, scented oils, and song. As an authority for the curative powers of wine, the poet cites the centaur Chiron, Achilles' tutor. After revealing to Achilles his fate in the Trojan War, the centaur encourages his ward to banish trouble and sorrows with wine and song, even in the midst of war.

Between publication of the *Epodes* and *Odes I–III*, Rome underwent momentous changes. Returning triumphant to Rome, Octavian began the refashioning of the state that won him the honorific title Augustus in 27 B.C. Part of his vision included building on the Palatine River a temple to Apollo, which was connected to his home (dedicated in 28 B.C.). The temple complex also housed two libraries—one Latin, one Greek—which held the best of Greek and Latin literature. Horace writes of having one's works shelved in the library as an honor, a symbol of acceptance into the Roman literary canon.

Horace was not alone in striving for inclusion in the Palatine library. These were years of great literary activity. Virgil published the *Georgics* (29 B.C.) and began the *Aeneid*. The next year Propertius published the *Monobiblos* and joined Maecenas's circle. A few years later Tibullus published his first book of elegies; Propertius published his second and third elegiac books. In prose, the historian Livy was working on his sweeping annals of the rise of Rome, and Vitruvius published his *De architectura*. The prestige of native literature was increasing so much that Caecilius Epirota, a schoolmaster, began to teach Virgil's poetry.

During this time Horace was working on what many consider his masterpiece, three books of lyric poetry to rival Greek lyric in Latin *(Odes I–III)*. The earliest datable poem, *Odes* 1.37, concerns the Battle of Actium (31 B.C.) and the subsequent suicide of Cleopatra. Horace worked on the odes for at least seven years and published them in 23 B.C. when he was forty-two. The three books comprise a total of eighty-eight carefully arranged poems. The number of poems in each book varies (book 1 includes thirty-eight poems; book 2,

twenty poems; and book 3, thirty poems), as does the total number of verses (book 1 includes 876 lines; book 2, 572 lines; and book 3, 1,008 lines) and length of individual poems (from the shortest, which consisted of eight lines, to the longest, which consisted of eighty).

Both names for Horace's lyric, odes and *carmina,* are reminders of the roots of the genre in song accompanied by the lyre. The *Odes* display the influence of Greek monodic (for a single performer) and choral poetry from the archaic through the Hellenistic periods. Horace knew and imitated the seventh-century-B.C. monodic poets Alcaeus and Sappho of Lesbos and the sixth-century-B.C. Anacreon of Teos. The special debt owed to the meter and themes of Alcaeus is acknowledged by the reference to the lyre of Lesbos at the close of *Odes* 1.1. Horace also admired the sixth-century-B.C. choral poets Stesichoros and Simonides and the fifth-century-B.C. Bacchylides, who provided a model for the mythological *Odes* 1.15. Among the choral poets, however, the fifth-century-B.C. poet Pindar most influenced Horace (as in *Odes* 1.12, 3.4, and 4.2).

Although he admires—and imitates—Pindar's rushing torrents of verse, Horace prefers his own "slender Muse," whom he likens to a small bee fashioning painstakingly elaborated poems (*Odes* 4.2). Horace's *tenuis Musa* plays several roles. A poetic talent suited only for lighter, personal themes provides Horace an excuse, in a poetic form known as the *recusatio,* for not writing the epic praises of great men. He compliments Agrippa (*Odes* 1.6) and Augustus (*Odes* 2.12, 4.2), for example, by telling them that his talents are not equal to creating the poetic praise they deserve. The poet's ethical as well as literary aesthetics are shaped by the opposition between the grand and the slight. As in the satires, there are many statements of Horace's preference for the small and simple over the grandiose.

The opening poem, dedicated to Maecenas as judge of the worth of the collection, challenges the lyric tradition and offers Horace as a candidate for the ranks of the Greek lyric poets. Horace writes that the rarefied company of the great Greek lyricists will mark him as learned and win him literary acclaim. In an extended priamel (in which a series of foils highlight the poet's own preference), the poet rejects various pursuits that engage human ambition in favor of poetic success. In the middle of the poem, literary ambition is balanced by the equally Horatian image of a man taking a break from the long day, stretched out with some good wine in the cool shade or by a refreshing spring. Meticulous dedication, the soul of Horace's poetry, is offset by a love of the simple pleasures of living in the present, enjoying the gifts of the hour. Serious poetic ambition is tempered by the comic self-deprecation recurrent in

Horace's work: the poem ends with the image of an exalted Horace banging his head on the stars.

The priamel of the first ode hints at other themes familiar through the *Satires* and the *Epodes*–a love of the countryside that dedicates a farmer to his ancestral lands; the ambition that drives one man to Olympic glory, another to political acclaim, and a third to wealth; the greed that compels the merchant to brave dangerous seas again and again rather than live modestly but safely; and even the tensions between the sexes that are at the root of the odes about relationships with women.

While indebted to Greek literary tradition, the *Odes* are a quite Roman production. Horace's declaration of success in bringing Aeolic poetry into Latin meters centers on Rome: his poetry will last as long as the empire, extending from Rome to his beloved native Apulia. His boast of immortality–that he, a man of humble beginnings, will continue to win praise and appear contemporary in succeeding ages–has been more than fulfilled. Not only a "monumentum aere perennius" (monument to outlast bronze, *Odes* 3.30.1), the *Odes* are a challenge no other Latin poet equaled. Although Aeolic verse forms had been used in Latin by the early tragedians, by the comic playwright Plautus, and later by Catullus, who experimented with Sapphics and the fifth Asclepiadian, nothing like the *Odes* had ever before been attempted in Latin poetry. Although Horatian lyric would significantly influence later poetry, in antiquity few Latin poets imitated Horace's lyric precedent.

Greek Aeolic meters all begin with two syllables that may be either long or short; Horace nearly always begins the line with a spondee (__). His lines are also built around a choriambic core–that is, two long syllables enclosing two short syllables (_◡◡_). The chief meters are Asclepiadic (five variations, called first through fifth Asclepiadian), Alcaic, and Sapphic. But the Asclepiad meters, in all their variations, are only the second most common meter in *Odes I–III* (27 of the 88 odes). Most frequent is Alcaic (33/88); third is Sapphic (23/88).

The language that fills these complex metrical units is lucid and plain, often mined from the vocabulary of prose. Horace addressed the critical importance of pure diction and arrangement, obvious in all his works, in the *Ars poetica*: a clever juxtaposition rendering a familiar word new is the mark of superior diction (*A. p.* 46–48). These brilliant juxtapositions have lured and frustrated his translators. Pyrrha's beauty, for example, is "simplex munditiis" (*Odes* 1.5.5), which John Milton's otherwise impressive translation rendered "plain in thy neatness" (lines 1–8):

> Quis multa gracilis te puer in rosa
> perfusus liquidis urget odoribus

> grato, Pyrrha, sub antro?
>   cui flavam religas comam
> simplex munditiis? heu quotiens fidem
> mutatosque deos flebit et aspera
>   nigris aequora ventis
>   emirabitur insolens!

> (What slender youth, bedew'd with liquid odours,
> Courts thee on roses in some pleasant cave,
> Pyrrha? For whom bind'st thou
>   in wreaths thy golden hair,
>   Plain in thy neatness? O how oft shall he
>   On faith and changed gods complain, and seas
>   Rough with black winds, and storms
>   Unwonted shall admire!)

Like Pyrrha, the beauty of the rich economy in the odes has attracted many suitors in many languages, whose attempts at translation were gathered into the volume *Ad Pyrrham* (1959) by Ronald Storrs. Friedrich Wilhelm Nietzsche's frequently quoted appraisal suggests the lapidary appeal of Horace's verse:

> To this day, no other poet has given me the same artistic delight that a Horatian ode gave me from the first. In certain languages that which has been achieved here could not even be attempted. This mosaic of words, in which every word–as sound, as place, as concept–pours out its strength right and left and over the whole, this *minimum* in the extent and number of signs, and the maximum thereby attained in the energy of the signs–all that is Roman and, if one will believe me, *noble* par excellence ("What I owe to the ancients," in *Twilight of the Idols,* 1).

Horace's simple diction and exquisite arrangement give the odes an inevitable quality; the expression makes familiar thoughts new. While the language of the odes may be simple, their structure is complex. The odes can be seen as rhetorical arguments with a kind of logic that leads the reader to sometimes unexpected places. *Odes* 1.9, often called the Soracte Ode, has a setting reminiscent of the wintry symposium in *Epode* 13. The poem begins with a description of Mount Soracte and the countryside laboring under the snow and cold and concludes with a scene in the middle of Rome on a warm evening. It moves from the particular (a snowscape) and its pleasures (a roaring fire and good wine) to a general observation and exhortation (weather changes; people should leave to the gods things beyond their control and not fret about the future). John Dryden's rendering of the advice of the poem adds rhyme (14–17):

> quid sit futurum cras, fuge quaerere, et
> quem Fors dierum cumque dabit, lucro
>   adpone, nec dulcis amores
>   sperne puer neque tu choreas . . . [.]

(To-morrow and her works defy,
    Lay hold upon the present hour,
And snatch the pleasures passing by,
    To put them out of fortune's power:
Nor love, nor love's delights disdain;
Whate'er thou get'st to-day, is gain.)

From its central recommendation the poem moves out again to the particular, but in a different direction–Thaliarchus's youth and its appropriate pleasures–and ends with a scene of lovers flirting on a balmy evening in the Campus Martius; Dryden translates, "The pleasing whisper in the dark, / The half unwilling willing kiss, / The laugh that guides thee to the mark" (37–39).

Even the poet's distribution of meter shows the consummate artistry of the *Odes.* The first nine odes of book 1, for example, are often referred to as the Parade Odes, since each of them displays a different Greek meter made to sing in the Latin language. The meters are distributed among these poems as follows: first Asclepiadian, which appears in only one other poem in *Odes I–III,* closes the collection in *Odes* 3.30; Sapphic appears twenty-two times in I–III; fourth Asclepiadian, ten times in I–III; third Asclepiadian, six times in I–III; second Asclepiadian, eight times in I–III; first Archilochean, also called Alcmanian, two times in I–III; second Sapphic, only here in Horace; and finally, Alcaic, Horace's favorite meter, thirty-three times in I–III.

The meters in other books are also carefully arranged. The first thirteen poems of book 2 alternate between Alcaics (1, 3, 5, 9, 11, 13) and Sapphics (2, 4, 6, 8, 10). Variety plays with pattern in the rest of the book: odd-numbered poems continue to be in Alcaics; Sapphics appear only once in the remaining even-numbered poems (*Odes* 2.16). Similarly, book 3 opens with a six-poem series of Alcaics, called the Roman Odes because of their concern with Rome and its values. The poem that immediately follows this procession of stately Alcaics, however, is neither stately nor Alcaic but a light poem in the erotic tradition and Asclepiadian meter.

The Parade Odes in the first book demonstrate a variety of themes and addressees as well as a variety of meters. Some are addressed to political dignitaries: the *princeps* (emperor) Augustus (2); Agrippa, Augustus's general and advisor (6); Sestius, consul during the year the *Odes* was published (4); and Munatius Plancus, one of the senators who had suggested the title Augustus for the *princeps* (7). After honoring Maecenas and Augustus with the first and second odes, Horace reserves the third for Virgil. Scattered among these luminaries are characters either fictitious or otherwise unknown: Thaliarchus, whose name means "leader of the feast" (9); Pyrrha, the "fire girl" (5); and Lydia (8). Lydia is also the subject of three other erotic odes (*Odes* 1.13, 1.25, 3.9).

Many of the themes of the collection appear in the Parade Odes as well. Public poems look to the state–Augustus and the New Regime. Private poems praise wine and Eros, compare the cycles of the year with the seasons of human life (in which springtime signals thoughts of death, not rebirth), and exhort one to live in the present, as in the famous phrase *carpe diem* (seize the day, *Odes* 1.11). The capricious turns of life, often personified by Necessity or Fortune, and the ever-present specter of death put human aspirations and appetites in larger perspective.

Horace especially loves to explore the literary possibilities offered by the Hellenistic ethical goal of the tranquility that comes through balance, as in two stanzas (*Odes* 2.10,13–20) of an ode advising Licinius to cherish the *aurea mediocritas* (golden mean):

> Hopeful in adversity, cautious in success
> is the heart well prepared for the opposite lot;
> Jupiter brings back the shapeless winters;
> he also
> takes them away; and not, if things go badly now,
> will it always be so: sometimes Apollo wakes
> his silent muse with his cithara; he doesn't always
> stretch his bow.

The collection includes several hymns, such as *Odes* 1.10 to Mercury, *Odes* 1.21 to Diana and Apollo, *Odes* 1.35 to the goddess Fortuna, and even a parody of a hymn addressed to a wine jar (*Odes* 3.21). Other odes issue invitations and celebrate parties, birthdays, and homecomings. The poems resonate more with affection for poetry and the Italian countryside than for the various lovers who appear in Horace's poetry. While the love poems may lack the intensity of personal feeling found in the poems of Catullus, the importance and joys of friendship in a poet who calls both Virgil and Maecenas "half of my soul" ring true (*Odes* 1.3.8, 2.17.5). One of Horace's dearest friends is his Muse, his poetic talent, which is often the subject of a poem and always a part of it (for example, *Odes* 1.26). The world of the *Odes* is bound inextricably with their poetics.

Part of Horace's persona–lack of political ambition, satisfaction with his life, gratitude for his land, and pride in his craft and the recognition it wins him–is an expression of an intricate web of awareness of place. Horace in the country on his own estate becomes quasi-emperor in his own right. His rural retreat is the ideal setting for poetry and the place where the gods especially smile on his poetic talents (as in *Odes* 1.17). But there is also a side of Horace that longs to be in the middle of the action, despite the attendant demands on his time and energy. Rome is the proving ground for poets as well as politicians, and Horace is not without competitive instincts.

QVOD SATIS EST CVI CONTIGIT,
NIHIL AMPLIVS OPTAT.

CURÆ INVEVITABILES.

Illustrations (1607) by Otto van Veen for (left) the lines in Satire 1 *that state "The person who wants just as much as he needs does not draw water stirred up with mud" (1.1) and (right) the lines in* Ode 2 *that state "Corrosive anxiety mounts bronzed ships and does not abandon the ranks of horsemen" (2.16) (from Philip Von Zesen,* Moralia Horatiana, *1656)*

While Horace was composing the *Odes,* Augustus was, in a sense, composing a new Rome, or rather trying to fashion Rome and Romans to reflect the values they more boasted of than practiced. Italy had been torn by strife for as long as anyone alive could remember and for the last quarter century had first teetered on the brink of, then plunged into, civil war. Augustus's vision included peace and renewal of the state on all levels—political, religious, domestic. Through an ambitious architectural program he constructed or refurbished temples and public buildings; through laws and public examples he exhorted Romans to live by the morals valued by their ancestors. Many of Horace's odes reflect and reinforce the call to renewal at the heart of Augustus's program. In the Roman Odes (for example, *Odes* 3.1-6) the poet sets himself apart as a priest of the Muses admonishing Rome. Much of what Horace says, familiar from his earlier work, is presented fresh in lyric, rather than satiric, arguments. The first ode, for example, argues for wanting just what is enough to avoid the anxieties that accompany excess of wealth and ambition.

Beyond praises of the old-fashioned virtues of simplicity, chastity, reverence for the gods, tempered ambition, respectable poverty, and love of Rome, Horace's odes praise the *princeps* himself for bringing peace to an empire torn by war. The odes cannot be divided easily between public and private, however. Often the two spheres blend, as in *Odes* 3.14, where a comparison between the triumphant Augustus and Hercules, and the public joy over the safe return of the *princeps,* leads into the poet's anticipation of a private celebration with Neaera.

What did Rome think of this unprecedented accomplishment? *Epist.* 1.19 complains of chilly public opinion and attributes Horace's lack of popularity to his refusal to curry favor with envious critics who judge him harshly while secretly reading and assiduously–albeit badly–imitating his verse. Ostensible attacks on his poetics, however, are a favorite literary stratagem (for example, *Sat.* 1.4, 1.10, and 2.1); the poet's complaints in *Epist.* 1.19 might be motivated less by the reception of the *Odes* than by the opportunity to assert his literary program and expose the flattery inherent in envious imitation. A lyric hiatus of six years before *Odes IV* and Suetonius's remark that the fourth book was written at Augustus's request might also suggest they were not received as well as Horace might have liked. The ten-year gap separating the verse conversations of *Satires II* and *Epistles I* does not suggest that the satires were badly received, however; nor are Suetonius's remarks conclusive. As often with ancient authors the truth is irretrievable.

Three years later, in 20 or early 19 B.C., the forty-five-year-old poet published his first book of verse letters, *Epistles I*. As with the rest of his works, Horace presents the first book of epistles as a poetry book, introduced by a programmatic poem and closed by a poem addressed to the book itself. The first poem of the collection announces to Maecenas the poet's intention to retire from Rome in general and poetry in particular in order to study philosophy, or, as he puts it, "what is true and fitting." Rather than following any particular philosophical school, the poet takes refuge in whatever philosophy offers a lodging place during the storm of the moment, a stance that allows Horace to explore unhampered (*Epist.* 1.10–15) the literary possibilities of his subject:

Now, therefore, I am putting aside poetry and other play-
    things:
my concerns, my questions, my whole being is in this:
"What is true and fitting?" I am gathering and storing
things I can later fetch out. And in case you should ask
under whose leadership, at whose hearth I am guarding
    myself:
bound to swear allegiance to no master,
wherever the storm snatches me I am carried, as a guest.

The philosophy of the *Epistles* is professedly practical—whatever is useful for the situation or whatever suits the poet's temperament at the moment. Unlike Lucretius in his Epicurean epic *De rerum natura* (which, written a generation earlier, greatly influenced the letters), Horace in the *Epistles* is not concerned with explicating a particular philosophical system and winning over his audience to a new way of thinking. Rather, the letters reflect the intellectual perambulations of someone ceaselessly analytical, yet eminently human and delightfully fallible. The philosophical stance in the letters combines an exploration of Socrates' belief that the unexamined life is not worth living, with Horace's awareness that examining one's weaknesses is not the same as mastering them.

The letters are both a return to satire and a new literary experiment. They are verse conversations in a different voice and a different mode. Like the *Satires*, the *Epistles* are full of exempla from literature and life: the profligate Maenius, who had appeared in *Sat.* 1.1

and 1.3, reappears in *Epist.* 1.15; the historical general Lucullus and the probably fictitious Gargilius are exempla in *Epist.* 1.6; heroes from Homer's epics suggest ethical lessons in *Epist.* 1.2; the conflict between Pentheus and Dionysius (*Epist.* 1.16) and the references to Amphio and Zethus (*Epist.* 1.18) and to the iconoclast philosopher Aristippus (*Epist.* 1.17) are allusions to Greek legends. Animal fables play a role as well: a puppy in *Epist.* 1.2, and a horse and a stag in *Epist.* 1.10.

The narrative stance is sometimes reminiscent of the satires as well. In *Epist.* 1.1, for example, Horace assumes a philosopher's freedom of speech with his benefactor similar to that of Davus, the convert with more enthusiasm than expertise in *Sat.* 2.7. Having listed a cornucopia of faults that philosophy can cure—such as greed, love of glory, envy, anger, laziness, drunkenness, and lust—Horace picks greed and applies it to his addressee, calling Maecenas (quite inappropriately) a merchant. Like Davus, the persona gets so enthusiastic about his project of philosophical reflection that he begins spouting whatever ethical formulae come to mind, forgetting, it seems, that he has just stressed that the object of his search is his own edification and betterment.

The human weaknesses catalogued in the first poem show the *Epistles* are a continuation of, rather than a break from, Horace's earlier poetry; the ethical concerns that had been part of the fabric of his lyric poetry and of his satires have become the explicit focus of the letters. The *Epistles* take place against a background of concerns both contemporary and timeless—independence, friendship, consistency, ambition, public versus private life, getting ahead and getting along with others, social advancement versus contentment, and, as always, literature.

Associations of place are especially marked. Geographical distance often invites reference to a physical place, and the epistolary genre lends itself to the investigation of the relationship between physical place and psychic state. On the most literal level Horace makes much of his surroundings, whether the location is the frenetic capital or his beloved country estate. Such exploration of place encompasses intangible place as well. Simplicity and clarity (ethical, social, and political) distinguish the countryside from its complicated urban counterpart. While physical place can often have an impact on psychological happiness, the poet also stresses the priority of internal peace over external surroundings; he chides his *vilicus* (overseer) and himself as well for supposing a change of scene will bring happiness (*Epist.* 1.14, 1.8). To his traveling friend Bullatius, he writes in *Epist.* 1.11.26: "caelum, non animum, mutant qui trans mare currunt" (those who dash across the sea change their climate, but not their state of mind).

The letters are addressed both to known historical individuals–such as Maecenas (*Epist*. 1, 7, 19), Augustus's stepson Tiberius (7), the advocate Trebatius (5), and Albius (probably the poet Tibullus, 4)–and to others who are otherwise unattested and perhaps friends only of the poet's imagination. Some addressees appear only in the letters while others appear elsewhere–for example, Julius Florus is also the addressee of a second letter (*Epist*. 2.2) and Iccius is the recipient of an ode as well as an epistle (*Odes* 1.29 and *Epist*. 1.11). In addition to being the addressee of *Epist*. 1.10 and *Odes* 1.22, Horace's close friend Aristius Fuscus appears among the readers whose critical approval Horace values (*Sat*. 1.10) and as the friend who refuses to extricate the beleaguered Horace from the unwanted attentions of a social climbing pest (*Sat*. 1.9).

In letters written to a range of addressees about ethical issues, the interplay between the specificity of social expectations and the universality of philosophical ideals comes to the fore. Horace's own interaction with the social dynamics of Rome is also prominent in these letters. At times he seems to stand apart and scrutinize his society (*Epist*. 1.6) or give magisterial advice (*Epist*. 1.2, 12); at other times he combines advice to acquaintances with revelations about his own failings (*Epist*. 1. 8, 11) or seems to concentrate exclusively on himself (*Epist*. 15). Several letters play on what Horace has learned about interacting with those at the top of Rome's social hierarchy. Horace keeps the reader aware of the potential for tension and conflict between human aspirations for the socially advantageous life and the ethically commendable one. Instead of rationalizing the potential for conflict, Horace points to it. He suggests to Quinctius (*Epist*. 1.16) that being deemed a good man by social standards does not entitle him to the corresponding ethical accolade; he warns Scaeva (*Epist*. 1.17) that his social status bars him from an aggressive pursuit of his goals; and he advises Lollius (*Epist*. 1.18) that as he grooms himself for the role of patron, he must play the role of dependent. Horace does not expose Roman social life as a fraud but instead shows a complex ethical awareness in action among people of different social levels in a society that places a high premium on competition and advancement.

Horace's shifting focus keeps the reader from feeling that he has found a smooth solution to keeping the balance he advocates. Thus, for example, Horace's claim that he prefers peaceful Tarentum to regal Rome (*Epist*. 1.7) is followed by an admission that he can find contentment nowhere (*Epist*. 1.8). So too he enthusiastically embraces reflective withdrawal in *Epist*. 1.1 and judges it excessive in *Epist*. 1.4 when he encourages Albius to leave his pensive solitude. Yet, the book as a whole suggests a real balance, perhaps because the reader constantly feels Horace's self-awareness as he portrays his world as a place where ethical considerations are always present, even if ethical ideals are not always realized. Even virtue is not an absolute, but exists in a social context: "Insani sapiens nomen ferat, aequus iniqui, / ultra quam satis est virtutem si petat ipsam" (Let the wise man be dubbed crazy and the fair man unjust if he should pursue virtue herself beyond what is enough, *Epist*. 1.6.15–16).

An epitome of the poet's career in the final poem puts a personal seal on the collection. It also offers a brief physical description matched by a jest in one of Augustus's letters recorded by Suetonius. Horace presents himself as short, prematurely gray, fond of sunning himself, and as quick to be appeased as he was prone to anger. Augustus wrote that Horace composed poems to match his stature–short. Horace should remember that he is also stout and could measure the length of his poems by the circumference of his stomach. Such facetious letters from Augustus show that over the years Horace came to be on friendly terms with the emperor himself. In these letters the emperor encourages Horace to treat him as an intimate, addressing Horace with affectionate bantering. Suetonius also records a letter in which Augustus, overwhelmed by infirm health and the duties of his position, tells Maecenas he would like Horace's help in answering his abundant correspondence. Horace declined the post of secretary, pleading his own ill health. Apparently not slighted by the refusal, Augustus jokingly wrote a letter in which he assured the poet that he still thought highly of him, even if Horace had spurned a closer friendship.

In addition to frequent generous gifts, Augustus honored the forty-eight-year-old poet by engaging him to write the hymn for the secular games (*Carmen saeculare*, 17 B.C.). The *Ludi saeculares* were intended to commemorate the transition from one *saeculum* (or the longest human life span, counted as a period of one hundred years) to another. The previous ceremonies had taken place in 146 B.C., and there may have been plans for secular games in 46 B.C.; none, however, took place. Preparations began in the 20s B.C. for an unparalleled celebration to help herald a new age of peace and prosperity, appropriately coinciding with the arrival of a comet. From May 30 to June 3, the days and nights were full of unprecedented pomp and fanfare–rituals, sacrifices, and purification ceremonies that involved both Roman leaders and the people. Horace's hymn, performed on the final day by twenty-seven girls and twenty-seven boys, reflects the emphasis of the games on peace, prosperity, fertility, and the simple values of trust, honor, and chastity.

While the hymn has not elicited much critical admiration, Horace's justifiable pride in being chosen as Rome's vatic voice for what must have been a spectacular and unforgettable celebration is reflected not only in the solemnity of the *Carmen saeculare* itself but also in the fourth book of *Odes,* published sometime after the emperor's return from Spain to Rome in 13 B.C. According to Suetonius, Augustus asked Horace to compose victory odes for his stepsons Tiberius and Drusus after their successful campaign against the Vindelici in 15 B.C. (*Odes* 4.4 and *Odes* 4.14) and to compose a fourth book of *Odes.* Four of the fifteen poems celebrate the *princeps* and his heirs directly (*Odes* 4, 5, 14, 15), and a fifth, a *recusatio,* praises Augustus while denying the poet's ability to laud the emperor in the Pindaric style he deserves. Horace's final book of odes insured that the memory of Augustus and his stepsons would not lack a sacred poet.

In the opening poem of the fourth book Horace declares himself too old for love even as he is swept away by desire for the boy Ligurinus. It is not the only erotic poem in the collection: *Odes* 4.10 chides Ligurinus for his arrogant cruelty and warns him that one day he too will grow old and undesirable; the thirteenth ode wavers between Eros and revenge as the poet gloats that his former lover Lyce now indeed grows old, despite her efforts to appear young. The poet invites Phyllis to a birthday party for Maecenas in a poem that combines eroticism, a festive occasion with wine and song, and ethical reflection (*Odes* 4.11).

Much of the focus of the book, however, is on the poet's love affair with his art and its power. The poet of book 4 exults in his well-defined and secure place as esteemed poet of Rome. In the style of Pindar he declares himself not a Pindaric swan but a bee of the Italian countryside fashioning tightly worked poems (*Odes* 4.2). The swan soars; Horace stays happily by the Tiber. To the muse Melpomene, Horace expresses his gratitude for the literary prestige he has won (*Odes* 4.3). The sixth ode weaves mythological references to Apollo's supremacy over Niobe, Tityos, and Achilles into a hymn of gratitude for the gifts that Erato has bestowed on Horace and an exhortation to the chorus of young boys and girls who will sing the *Carmen saeculare.*

Horace's promise that the youthful chorus will cherish the memory of their performance at the secular games looks to a conspicuous argument of the book—the power of poetry to immortalize otherwise mortal men, including the poet. *Odes* 4.7, which the poet A. E. Housman considered the most beautiful poem in ancient literature and translated in 1897, moves from the flight of winter and the joyous return of spring to the ageless cycle of seasons and the ephemeral nature of human life:

> frigora mitescunt Zephyris, ver proterit aestas,
>   interitura, simul
> pomifer autumnus fruges effuderit, et mox
>   bruma recurrit iners.
> damna tamen celeres reparant caelestia lunae:
>   nos ubi decidimus
> quo pius Aeneas, quo dives Tullus et Ancus,
>   pulvis et umbra sumus.

> (Thaw follows frost; hard on the heel of spring
>   Treads summer sure to die, for hard on hers
> Comes autumn, with his apples scattering;
>   Then back to wintertide, when nothing stirs.
> But oh, whate'er the sky-led seasons mar,
>   Moon upon moon rebuilds it with her beams;
> Come *we* where Tullus and where Ancus are,
>   And good Aeneas, we are dust and dreams.)

The lament on the brevity of life and the finality of death is immediately followed by two poems on the immortalizing power of poetry. In *Odes* 4.8 Horace lists, only to reject, gifts of great wealth in preference for the gift of a lyric poem. Instead, the poem offers Censorinus the gift of immortality: while all unrecorded merit fades away, poets have rescued the worthy from death forever. The next poem makes a similar point (*Odes* 4.9.25–28) with the highly memorable proclamation: "Many brave men lived before Agamemnon, but all, unwept and unknown, are pressed by the long night because they lack a sacred poet." Poetry alone conquers death.

Whereas throughout *Odes I–III* Horace used his poetic talents to promote a simple lifestyle rooted in the kind of values found in rural Italy, in the final book of *Odes* he celebrates renewed moral strength and peace. In *Odes* 4.5 he says a golden age has returned, not as a world of the imagination created by poetry (as in, for example, *Odes* 1.17) but as a benefit of Augustus's rule. A comparison of *Odes* 4.5 with *Odes* 3.6 shows that homes that know only purity have replaced a lamentable lack of chastity, while a return to simple, stable values and religious traditions replaces the wistful yearning for past glories. The final ode celebrates Augustus's return and glorifies the emperor's accomplishments. Peace reigns at home, abroad, and, it seems, in the heart of Rome's poet laureate. The final two stanzas show Horace not the removed *vates,* but one with the people, mingling his call for wine and song with images of family and religious observance indicative of Rome's renewal.

Maecenas appears only once in the fourth book, in an ode that celebrates his birthday (*Odes* 4.11). The centrality of Maecenas in Horace's poetry evolved toward an increased involvement with and investment in the *princeps*. This shift has often been linked to an event that occurred the same year that *Odes I–III* were published. Terentius Varro Murena, Maecenas's brother-in-law, and celebrated in *Odes* 3.19 and 2.10, was involved in a conspiracy against the *princeps*. Maecenas is said to have told his wife Terentia that her brother had been found out; Maecenas's indiscretion was of no help to Murena and may have harmed Maecenas's own relations with Augustus. Maecenas may have played a less-active role after this time, but the tone of *Odes* 4.11, as well as the several poems addressed to him in the first book of letters (*Epist.* 1, 7, 19), indicates continued strong friendship between Horace and his patron.

Augustus had been the subject of many laudatory odes but not the direct recipient of one of the more informal *sermones*. The closest he came to receiving a letter was *Epistle* 1.13, a barrage of anxious instructions from the poet aimed at the courier who was to deliver scrolls of poetry (probably *Odes I–III*) to the emperor but directed more as a compliment to the emperor himself, expressing the poet's concern for a decorous introduction of his work. Suetonius writes that when Augustus had read some of the *sermones* (probably referring to the epistles), he wrote Horace a witty complaint, accusing him of not wanting to acknowledge their friendship. Horace's response was the first of the two poems that comprise *Epistles II,* the opening lines of which (1–4) praise Augustus's leadership while offering an excuse for the poet's hesitation in addressing one of his verse letters to the emperor:

> Since all by yourself you shoulder so many and such important public affairs, you keep Italy safe by arms, furnish her with good values, correct her faults with laws: I should offend the public good, Caesar, if I should waste your time with lengthy conversation.

The letter is, in fact, a fairly lengthy conversation (270 lines) about literature. The force of tradition is so strong at Rome, Horace complains, that the highly polished works of contemporary poets are dismissed in favor of the "classics," the works of the pioneers of Roman literature, valued more for their antiquity than for their merit. The impulse to diminish contemporary literature has not, he says, discouraged his countrymen from trying their hands at verse. Horace advises Augustus to look on this literary mania as a good thing since poets are harmless folk, dedicated to their art and beneficial in their own way to the public good (124–133). The poet is, in W. Colin Macleod's translation:

> . . . useful to his country
> if you grant that great affairs can be helped by small ones.
> The poet moulds our tender, fumbling lips

in childhood, tweaks our ears away from smut;
later he shapes our hearts with kind advice,
corrects our roughness, envy and bad temper,
records good deeds, supplies the age with models
from the past, consoles the poor and despondent.
How would the choirs of virgin girls and boys
learn to sing prayers, if the Muse had made no bards?

The emperor should especially value the writers whose work is aimed at a small, select audience of readers, rather than those who seek to please the masses by writing for large public performances. Painstaking contemporary poets (such as Horace) may not have large public appeal, Horace argues, but they contribute to the lasting legacy of Roman literature.

The letter has taken on a special irony over the centuries. Horace scoffed at the idea of preferring inferior older literature to more-recent and greater works, and insisted that a writer continually earn his audience. *Odes* 3.30 gives an answer to his own challenge, anticipating his future as a poet who wins fresh acclaim with each generation.

Literature and ethics are the focus of the letter to Julius Florus (*Epist.* 2.2), perhaps published before the letter to Augustus. Since Florus is traveling (Florus accompanied Tiberius to Armenia, *Epist.* 1.3), the letter was probably written around the same time as the first book of epistles. Florus was also a poet, and Horace adopts the stance of a seasoned mentor. The opening sets the tone, which is as informal as the letter to Augustus is ceremonious. Horace protests that his failure to produce the poems he had promised needs no excuse; just like an honest slave dealer who had warned the buyer of a slave's defects, Horace had warned his young friend that he was lazy. To Augustus, Horace had written about literature as it relates to an emperor's interests. To Florus, however, Horace gives a fellow poet's point of view in a list of excuses for his lack of productivity: Rome provides a rich mine for examples and character sketches but not a proper environment for writing; in a city teeming with poets competing for literary prestige, many demands are placed on Horace's time and patience; and incompetent poets can enjoy the luxury of loving their own work while real poets, talented and dedicated, know the torment and frustration involved in writing well. Horace's final justification for not writing–that he is studying ethics instead–moves the argument to a series of ethical reflections and exhortations reminiscent of *Epist.* 1.1.

The *Ars poetica* remains in many ways a mystery. The *Ars* was not grouped in the manuscript tradition as it is now, with the second book of the *Epistles,* but was listed as a separate publication. Its date of composition (variously put between 23–18 B.C. or 13–8 B.C.), the identity of the addressees, and even the title, are dis-

Sandro Botticelli's Primavera; *inspired in part by Horace's* Odes, *1.4 and 30. 4.7 and 12 (Uffizi Gallery, Florence)*

puted. Sometimes called the *Epistula ad Pisones* (Letter to the Pisos), the poem is better known by the title first recorded by Quintilian, *Ars poetica*. The Pisos are identified by the scholiast Porphyrio as the sons of Lucius Calpurnius Piso (Pontifex), the consul of 15 B.C.; Piso's sons have been lost to history, however. Some argue that the poem honors Cn. Calpurnius Piso (consul in 23 B.C.) and his two sons, or perhaps the father of Lucius Calpurnius Piso (Pontifex), Lucius Calpurnius Piso Caesoninus, who was the patron of the Epicurean philosopher and poet Philodemus, whose work both Horace and Virgil knew and admired.

The *Ars* itself is a rambling, difficult poem. Porphyrio says that Horace modeled his precepts of literature after those of Neoptolemus of Parium (third century B.C.), some aspects of whose works are polemically discussed in fragments of Philodemus. Analyzing the structure, arrangement, and meaning of the *Ars*, however, has long kept readers busy. The poem can roughly be divided into two halves: the first half is about *ars* (technical skill, lines 1–294) and can be subdivided into a short introductory section on content (1–

44) and a much longer discourse on style (45–294); the second half is devoted to the *artifex* (poet, 295–476). Using the classifications Philodemus attributes to Neoptolemus, the *Ars* can also be divided into an introduction (lines 1–40); a section on *poiema* (style, 41–118); a section on *poiesis* (content, 119–294); and the longest part, a section on the poet (295–476).

Also puzzling is the prominence of drama (tragedy, comedy, and satyr plays), since scant evidence for Augustan theater exists. The focus of the *Ars* on the large-scale genres is sometimes credited to the importance of drama and epic in Aristotle (and thus in the peripatetic Neoptolemus). The letter to Augustus also focuses on drama and appeals to the emperor to cultivate literature that is read rather than watched (*Epist.* 2.1.214–218), a suggestion that implies that Augustus's literary interests may have affected the emphasis on this genre.

Neoptolemus was surely not the sole source for the *Ars*. Horace's debt to Philodemus and Epicurean poetics may become clearer with further discoveries from his works in the Villa de Papyri in Herculaneum. Some of Horace's precepts correspond to those found in Cicero's *De oratore,* and many of them are familiar from Horace's other writings about literature. Although little is known of the literary debates and theories in Horace's time, contemporary Roman thought certainly had an impact on the *Ars.*

The *Ars* is often linked with Aristotle's *Poetics* and *Rhetoric* (in the Renaissance they were sometimes considered virtually interchangeable). The poet's approach, however, is quite unlike the philosopher's. Instead of analytical classifications that aim at explicating the *whys* and *hows* of human discourse, Horace presents his reader with a view of the poetic art metamorphosed into poetry. Horace's persona in the *Ars poetica* is also distinct from that of the third most famous work on literary criticism in antiquity, Longinus's *On the Sublime* (probably written mid first century A.D.). For Longinus, great literature conveys an intellectual and emotional thrill to the reader. Full of literary enthusiasm, *On the Sublime* looks to the literature of the past as reference points for future writers and proposes to identify and explain what makes great literature great.

The *Ars* is harder to classify, and interpretations range from a serious didactic essay for young poets to a parody of literary treatises. The poem begins with the principle of poetic unity, but its own synthesis is less than harmonious, and its narrator is sometimes reminiscent of Catius spouting culinary precepts in *Sat.* 2.4. A vivid image (*A. p.* 1–5) opens the poem:

> Suppose a painter wanted to join a horse's neck to a human head and to add on various feathers, with the limbs collected from all the species, so that what begins above as a lovely woman winds up horribly in a black fish—could you hold your laughter, friends, if you were admitted for a look?

This whimsical creation illustrates the principle that every poem should be unified and harmonious: "denique sit quidvis, simplex dumtaxat et unum" (23); George Gordon, Lord Byron, translates the line: "In fine, to whatsoever you aspire, / let it at least be simple and entire" ("Hints from Horace," 37–38). Between the opening sketch and the maxim the reader is treated to more vignettes—the epic poet who puts *purpurei panni* (purple patches, 15) in all the wrong places (14–19), a self-indulgent votive painter (19–21), and an inept potter (21–23). Between this quite Horatian beginning and the closing sketch of the mad poet (453–476), the *Ars* is liberally sprinkled with observations, exhortations, literary history, commentary on the contemporary literary scene, and more satiric portraits.

If an ideal craftsman could be constructed from Horace's work, he would be someone whose art is furthered by natural talent (408–411) and who knows

himself and his abilities well (38–40); someone who is willing to work hard (289–294), to be satisfied with excellence alone (372–373), and to accept criticism (385–390, 438–452). He would especially understand the importance of decorum, the principle that harmonizes style and content, a key theme of the *Ars.* He would strive to write poetry that both pleases and teaches (99–100, 333–334, 343–344).

The authority of the *Ars* comes in good part from its well-stated principles of sound composition. As Pope said, "Horace still charms with graceful negligence / and without method talks us into sense" (*Essay on Criticism,* 653–654). Even a meager sampling shows the continued relevance of Horace's eloquently written precepts: "brevis esse laboro, / obscurus fio" (I struggle to be brief—I become obscure, 25–26), "scribendi recte sapere est principium et fons" (Good sense is the first principle and source of writing well, 309), "verbaque provisam rem non invita sequentur" (Once the subject has been thought out, the words willingly follow, 311), "omne tulit punctum qui miscuit utile dulci" (The writer who mixes the useful with the sweet carries the whole vote, 343).

Despite its many difficulties, the *Ars* has enjoyed a considerable literary afterlife. An important text during the Middle Ages and Renaissance, its principles of unity, characterization, arrangement, and diction greatly influenced literary theory then and afterwards. From the sixteenth century there are translations in French, Spanish, and Italian—a partial gauge of its influence. Boileau in his *L'art poétique* (1674), which was translated into English by Sir William Soames and John Dryden, looked to Horace as an authority for French literature. In the eighteenth century Alexander Pope in his *Essay on Criticism* owed a heavy debt to the *Ars* as well. In "After Horace" the poet Michael Longley suggests that the present-day reader might profit from closer attention to the aesthetics of the *Ars:*

> We postmodernists can live with that human head
> Stuck on a horse's neck, or the plastering of multi-
> Coloured feathers over the limbs of assorted animals
> (So that what began on top as a gorgeous woman
> Tapers off cleverly into the tail of a black fish).
>
> Since our fertile imaginations cannot make head
> Or tail of anything, wild things interbreed with tame,
> Snakes with birds, lambs with tigers . . . [.]

Suetonius supplies what little is known of the end of Horace's life. Maecenas, who died in the late summer of 8 B.C., had recorded his affection for Horace in a codicil of his will to the Emperor: "Horati Flacci ut mei esto memor" (Keep Horatius Flaccus in mind as you would me). Horace, who had written many years before that when

Maecenas died, so would he (*Odes* 2.17), died fifty-eight days after Maecenas on 27 November 8 B.C. at age fifty-seven. Augustus was proclaimed his heir in front of witnesses, since the violent decline in Horace's health did not permit him to have his will signed and witnessed. He was buried at the periphery of the Esquiline next to the tomb of Maecenas.

Recognized as the leading lyric poet of Rome during his own lifetime, Horace, soon after his death, became an author studied in schools. In the final poem of *Epistles I,* the poet addresses the book, personified as a slave eager to run off and try his luck in Rome. Putting oneself in the hands of the public entails many risks, warns Horace, including *"Hoc quoque te manet, ut pueros elementa docentem / Occupet extremis in vicis balba senectus"* (this also is in store for you, that a stammering old age will take you by surprise as you teach children their letters in far-off villages, 17–18).

During the centuries immediately following his death, scholars edited the text of Horace's poetry and wrote scholia–collections of notes of varying length (and accuracy) that accompanied the text in the manuscript transmission. At the end of the second century Helenius Acron wrote a scholarly commentary. Acron's commentary partially survives in a much-expanded and reworked version, the scholia of Pseudo-Acron, much of which was written in the fifth century A.D., with many later additions. The scholia of Pomponius Porphyrio, written in the third century, also survive. Modern texts of Horace are based on manuscripts dating from the ninth to the twelfth century, which in turn derived from two or three medieval manuscripts.

Horace's ability to work complex arguments and homely commonplaces into verses masterly in their balance and variety has attracted admirers since antiquity. In the century after Horace's death the satirist Persius praises Horace's ability to make a friend laugh–and to keep him as a friend–while pointing out that friend's every fault (1.116–118). In Petronius's *Satyricon,* the poet Eumolpus judges "Horatii curiosa felicitas" (Horace's painstaking fluency, 118.5) as a touchstone of poetic expression. In his work on the training of orators, Quintilian gives several examples of Horace's eloquence and calls him Rome's chief lyric poet: "At lyricorum idem Horatius fere solus legi dignus: nam et insurgit aliquando et plenus est iucunditatis et gratiae et uarius figuris et uerbis felicissime audax" (Of the lyric poets Horace is nearly the only one who deserves to be read: for at times he soars and he is full of a pleasing delightfulness and varied in his expression and most excellently bold in his choice of words, *Institutio Oratoria,* 10.1.96).

Horace's success as a poet can be measured partly by how difficult he is to imitate and translate and by

Title page for Richard Bentley's edition of Horace, *published by Cambridge University Press in 1711*

how many admirers have sought to do both. Readers in the Middle Ages looked to Horace as a moralist and as a literary critic and appreciated the *Satires* and *Epistles* more than the more difficult *Odes.* The enthusiasm of the Italian Renaissance poets Petrarch (fourteenth century), Landinio, and Politian (late fifteenth century) for the *Odes* encouraged the popularity of Horace's lyric. Horace was one of Montaigne's (sixteenth century) favorite poets. The themes and poetics of both the lyrics and the satires greatly influenced Ben Jonson (late sixteenth, early seventeenth century), Robert Herrick, Andrew Marvell, Milton, and Dryden (seventeenth century). The *Odes* continued to be springboards for much of both public and private seventeenth-century English lyrics. Pope was the leading Horatian poet writing in English during the eighteenth century, the Age of Augustanism, especially imitating Horace's hexameter poetry, while Alfred, Lord Tennyson, Matthew Arnold, Byron, and Rudyard Kipling were among Horace's enthusiasts in the nineteenth century. Horace has continued to inspire modern poets, among them Ezra Pound.

While the different genres of his work have specific qualities, they all share in being Horatian, a quality that many have tried to define. In Nietzsche's view, Horace's peerless artistry separates him from all other poets. Compared to Horace's *Odes,* "All the rest of poetry becomes, in contrast, something too popular–a mere garrulity of feelings" ("What I owe to the ancients," *Twilight of the Idols,* 1). Horace transforms "feelings"–his love for friends, the countryside, the comforts of life, and his art; his keen sense of physical, social and ethical place; and his exhortations to enjoy life in the present–into what Pope in *An Essay on Criticism* (1711) called "true wit" or "nature to advantage dressed; / What oft was thought, but ne'er so well expressed" (297–298). In his informal satires, epistles, and iambics as well as in his lyrics, Horace transformed many of the varieties of human experience and sensibility into unforgettable, immortal poetry.

Concordance:

Dominic Bo, *Lexicon Horatianum* (Hildesheim: Olms, 1965–1966).

References:

David Armstrong, *Horace* (New Haven: Yale University Press, 1989);

D. R. Shackleton Bailey, *Profile of Horace* (Cambridge, Mass.: Harvard University Press, 1982);

Steele Commager, *The Odes of Horace: A Critical Study* (New Haven: Yale University Press, 1962);

Gregson Davis, *Polyhymnia: the Rhetoric of Horatian Lyric Discourse* (Berkeley & Oxford: University of California Press, 1991);

Eduard Fraenkel, *Horace* (Oxford: Oxford University Press, 1966);

Kirk Freudenburg, *The Walking Muse* (Princeton, N.J.: Princeton University Press, 1993);

S. J. Harrison, *Homage to Horace: A Bimillenary Celebration* (Oxford: Clarendon Press / New York: Oxford University Press, 1995);

Ferdinand Hauthal, ed., *Acronis et Porphyrionis Commentarii in Q. Horatium Flaccum,* 2 volumes (Amsterdam: Springer, 1966);

W. R. Johnson, *Horace and the Dialectic of Freedom: Readings in Epistles I* (Ithaca, N.Y.: Cornell University Press, 1993);

Otto Keller, ed., *Pseudacronis scholia in Horatium vetustiora,* 2 volumes (Stuttgart: Teubner, 1967);

Ross S. Kilpatrick, *The Poetry of Friendship: Horace, Epistles I* (Edmonton: University of Alberta Press, 1986);

Kilpatrick, *The Poetry of Criticism: Horace, Epistles II and the Ars Poetica* (Edmonton: University of Alberta Press, 1990);

Michèle Lowrie, *Horace's Narrative Odes* (Oxford: Oxford University Press, 1997);

R. O. A. M. Lyne, *Horace. Behind the Public Poetry* (New Haven & London: Yale University Press, 1995);

M. J. McGann, *Studies in Horace's First Book of Epistles* (Brussels: Latomus, 1969);

Charles Martindale and David Hopkins, *Horace Made New* (Cambridge: Cambridge University Press, 1993);

Jacques Perret, *Horace,* translated by Bertha Humez (New York: New York University Press, 1964);

David H. Porter, *Horace's Poetic Journey* (Princeton, N.J.: Princeton University Press, 1987);

Michael C. J. Putnam, *Artifices of Eternity. Horace's Fourth Book of Odes* (Ithaca & London: Cornell University Press, 1986);

Kenneth Reckford, *Horace* (New York: Twayne, 1969);

Niall Rudd, *The Satires of Horace* (London: Cambridge University Press, 1966; republished, Newburyport: Focus/R. Pullins, 1994);

Rudd, ed., *Horace 2000: A Celebration: Essays for the Bimillennium* (London: Duckworth, 1993);

Matthew S. Santirocco, *Unity and Design in Horace's Odes* (Chapel Hill & London: University of North Carolina Press, 1986);

Richard J. Tarrant, "Horace," in *Texts and Transmission,* edited by L. D. Reynolds (Oxford: Oxford University Press, 1983), 182–186;

L. P. Wilkinson, *Horace and His Lyric Poetry,* second edition, revised (London: Bristol Classical Press, 1994);

G. W. Williams, *Horace,* Greece and Rome, New Surveys in the Classics (Oxford: Clarendon Press, 1972);

Williams, *Tradition and Originality in Roman Poetry* (Oxford: Clarendon Press, 1968).

Julius Caesar
(100 B.C. – 44 B.C.)

Craige B. Champion
Allegheny College

WORKS: *Commentarii de bello Gallico* (Gallic War, 51 B.C.);
Commentarii de bello civili (Civil Wars, ca. 47 B.C.).

Editio princeps: *Commentarii* (Rome: Conradus Sweynheym and Arnoldus Pannartz, 1469).

Standard editions: *C. Iuli Caesaris Commentariorum Libri,* 2 volumes, edited by René Louis Alphonse DuPontet (London: Oxford University Press, 1978); *C. Iulii Caesaris Commentarii Rerum Gestarum,* 2 volumes, edited by Otto Seel and Alfred Klotz (Leipzig: Teubner, 1979); *C. Iulii Caesaris Commentarii rerum gestarum,* 1 volume (*Bellum Gallicum*), edited by Wolfgang Hering (Leipzig: Teubner, 1997).

Translations in English: *Caesar: Alexandrian, African, and Spanish Wars,* edited by A. G. Way, Loeb Classical Library (Cambridge, Mass.: Harvard University Press, 1955); *Caesar: The Civil Wars,* translated by Arthur George Peskett, Loeb Classical Library (London & Cambridge, Mass.: Harvard University Press, 1957); *The Civil War,* translated by Jane F. Gardner (Harmondsworth, U.K. & New York: Penguin Books, 1967); *Caesar: The Gallic Wars,* translated by Henry John Edwards, Loeb Classical Library (London and Cambridge, Mass.: Harvard University Press, 1979); *The Conquest of Gaul,* translated by Stanley Alexander Handford, revised by Jane F. Gardner (Harmondsworth, U.K.: Penguin Books, 1982); *Julius Caesar: The Battle for Gaul,* translated by Anne and Peter Wiseman (Boston: Godine, 1985); *War Commentaries of Caesar,* translated by Rex Warner (New York: New American Library, 1987).

Commentaries: *C. Iulii Caesaris Bellum Alexandrinae,* edited by Rudolf Schneider (Berlin: Weidmann, 1888); *Commentarii rerum in Gallia gestarum VII,* edited by T. Rice Holmes (Oxford: Clarendon Press, 1914); *C. Iulii Caesaris Commentarii de bello Gallico,* 3 volumes, edited by Friedrich Kraner, Wilhelm Dittenberger, Heinrich Meusel, and Hans Oppermann, 20th edition (Zurich & Berlin: Weid-

Bust of Julius Caesar

mann, 1961–1964); *C. Iulii Caesaris de bello civili,* edited by Kraner, Friedrich Hofmann, Meusel, and Oppermann, thirteenth edition (Berlin: Weidmann, 1963); *Caesar's War in Alexandria: Bellum Civile III.102–112, Bellum Alexandrinum 1–33,* edited by Gavin B. Townend (Bristol, U.K.: Bristol Classical Press, 1988).

No history, however bent on emphasizing collective decisions, can manage to get rid of the disturbing presence of individuals, they are simply there.

—Arnaldo Momigliano,
The Development of Greek Biography (1971)

Such was the pronouncement of one of the most important classical scholars of the twentieth century. Gaius Julius Caesar is perhaps history's greatest testimony to the truth of those words. Octavian, Caesar's eventual successor and adopted son, inherited his name and, as the emperor Augustus, ushered in the historical period of the Principate and the autocracy of the Roman emperors. In subsequent western history Caesar became a symbol for the power of both absolute monarchy and imperial conquest—a symbol that manifested itself in the designations of Russian *Czar* and German *Kaiser*. His influence has extended beyond the realms of history and politics. Many high-school students know the tale of Caesar's dramatic final days and assassination as William Shakespeare immortalized them in his play *Julius Caesar* (written 1599, published 1623), and in a bygone day elementary Latin students knew Caesar as their first Latin author; his phrase "Gallia est omnis divisa in partes tres" (Gaul as a whole is divided into three parts, *Gallic War*, 1.1.1) may well have been the only scrap of Latin they remembered in later life. In literary and historical representations Caesar has been romanticized as an enlightened political visionary and condemned as a bloodthirsty Machiavellian whose ambitions knew no bounds. Providing a famous reflection of the former position, Dante ranks Caesar's assassins, Brutus and Cassius, with Judas Iscariot in the lowest depths of Hell (*Inferno*, 34). Regardless of differing assessments of his character, there must be consensus that Caesar was a man who changed the world and continues to be a figure larger than life.

Yet, even in the case of this towering personage, historical context is essential to a proper understanding of the individual's life and achievements. Caesar was in a sense the end product of sweeping historical forces that had been radically transforming Roman society for a century or more before his birth on 13 July 100 B.C. In the course of the second century B.C., Rome enjoyed a remarkable series of military successes. Having passed its severest trials in the previous century with the defeat of its nemesis, Carthage, in the first two Punic Wars, the Roman state now went on to conquer the Hellenistic Greek kingdoms in quick succession. With the Roman destruction of Corinth and Carthage in 146 B.C., Rome emerged as undisputed master of the Mediterranean basin. The Roman governmental apparatus, however, had developed in the context of the more localized struggles for control of Latium and then peninsular Italy. Only twelve annually elected magistrates were available for foreign wars and provincial administration; the system was not well suited for the governance of an extensive empire. The burden fell on the collective body of aristocrats who made up the Roman Senate.

Despite recent scholarly protestations that there was a significant democratic element in Roman Republican political life, the traditional view that the Roman Senate controlled the state in the middle Republican period (264–133 B.C.) is not likely to undergo any widely accepted, substantial revision. The Senate was comprised of an aristocratic oligarchy whose members continually fought for the status and prestige that could only come from elected office and military command. This oligarchy failed to meet the challenges that the acquisition of an empire had thrust upon it. As members of the senatorial aristocracy, Roman provincial commanders committed abuses against native populations or turned a blind eye to the excesses of the non-senatorial Roman knights who bought state contracts as provincial tax farmers, or *publicani*. At home, members of the senatorial order used their increasing wealth and power to occupy large tracts of the public land in Italy, thereby forcing smallholders off the land and into urban areas, particularly Rome itself, where they swelled into an unwieldy proletariat. This impoverished urban mob presented new difficulties for the Roman army, as the proletariat did not possess the requisite property qualification for military recruitment. Moreover, there was the troublesome question of the Italian allies who fought Rome's wars of imperial conquest without partaking of the rights and privileges of Roman citizenship. In the 130s and 120s B.C., the brothers Tiberius and Gaius Gracchus, both of whom held the elected plebeian office of the tribunate, attempted legislation aimed at correcting these unhealthy directions that Roman society was taking, but the obdurate senatorial aristocracy murdered them for their efforts.

To speak of political parties in the modern sense of the term for this period in Roman history is anachronistic, but from the late second century B.C. onward two distinct political orientations developed for the Roman elite: the *boni* or *optimates,* conservative senators who resisted reform and insisted upon the traditional rights and prerogatives of the Roman Senate, and the *populares,* politicians who in the tradition of the Gracchi brothers adopted populist measures aimed at serving the people's interests. Caesar, as the nephew of the *popularis* Marius and son-in-law of the demagogic Cinna, was in this latter camp. In any event, the solutions to Rome's problems were not primarily found in politics and legislation; change was forced through the threat of military intervention or on the field of battle.

The strains of imperial success created a disequilibrium in Roman factional politics that eventually undermined the system. Massive armies on extended campaigns increasingly looked not to the Senate, but rather to their commander in chief in the field, as their benefactor. The enormously successful Roman general who returned to Rome triumphant and laden with the spoils of war potentially had the wherewithal to attract a *clientela* (network of political clients) of unprecedented scale and thereby dominate the game of competitive senatorial politics at Rome. Publius Cornelius Scipio Africanus, the conqueror of Hannibal in the Second Punic War (218–202 B.C.), was the first such threat to the oligarchic club of the Roman Senate, and in the late second and first centuries B.C. a series of warlords arose, men such as Marius and Sulla, who initiated the Roman revolution that brought Republican government and any real power of the Roman Senate to an end. The pernicious combination of charismatic general and loyal army destroyed the Roman Republic, and Julius Caesar, as the general who perhaps first understood both the inevitability and the significance of this historical development, paved the way for the monarchic rule of the Roman emperors. Civil wars ensued upon Caesar's assassination, and new warlords vied for his preeminent position, but Caesar had already set the future course of the Roman world under the direction of a monarch.

Julius Caesar was of an old noble Roman family. Indeed, the patrician Julian clan claimed descent from the goddess Venus and the mythic hero Aeneas. Yet, Caesar's family had not enjoyed spectacular political success in recent times. His father had reached the praetorship and the proconsulate of Asia. On his mother's side he was related to several consuls of the 70s and 60s B.C. He certainly had a respectable pedigree, but it gave little indication of his future greatness. More important for Caesar's subsequent political career was his familial connection to the great military hero Marius, whom his paternal aunt Julia had married. In 84 B.C. Caesar married Cornelia, the daughter of Cinna, the consul of 87 B.C. Marius and Cinna had been political allies, and both had pursued policies that endeared them to the Roman populace. These associations must be viewed as important factors in Caesar's populist political tendencies. Caesar early on showed the independence of spirit and opposition to traditional senatorial politics that were to characterize his later career. Defying the authority of the dictator Sulla, he refused this conservative politician's commands to divorce Cinna's daughter Cornelia and lay down his priesthood as *flamen Dialis* (priest of Jupiter).

At the end of the decade of the 80s B.C. Caesar served in the Roman province of Asia. There the young Caesar enjoyed a victory over a military force of the Pontic king and inveterate enemy of Rome, Mithridates VI, of Pontus. Upon returning to Rome in 77 B.C., Caesar unsuccessfully prosecuted the former supporters of Sulla, Dolabella, and C. Antonius. Although

Bust of Octavian, Caesar's adopted son, called Augustus after he became emperor (bust at the Vatican Museums)

Caesar failed to win these prosecutions, he succeeded in establishing himself as a promising young orator to be reckoned with in the future. Then followed a period of retirement on the island of Rhodes for academic study, since study of rhetoric and philosophy in the Greek east was a fairly regular practice for Roman aristocratic youth in this period. From 75 to 74 B.C. he served against the pirates who plagued the Mediterranean sea as a result of Rome's shortsighted policy of crippling the maritime state of Rhodes in the aftermath of the Third Macedonian War in the mid second century B.C. This menace was finally eradicated in the extraordinary command granted to one of Sulla's veterans and the future political ally and ultimate rival of Caesar, Gn. Pompeius Magnus (Pompey). The young Caesar supported this appointment, as he had earlier supported Pompey's campaign to restore the full powers of the office of the tribunate, which Sulla had stripped earlier.

Caesar was elected quaestor for 69 B.C., and his magistracy was eventful. He conducted elaborate funereal celebrations for his mother, Aurelia, and his wife Cornelia before leaving for service in Further Spain.

Upon his return to Italy, Caesar founded Latin colonies north of the Po River for which he demanded Roman citizenship. Although the proposal for the extension of the Roman franchise in Transpadane Gaul failed, Caesar laid the foundations for a personal patronage of this region that would have considerable consequences in the future. In this year of his quaestorship, Caesar had already demonstrated some of the hallmarks of his subsequent career: regaling the Roman populace, gaining political capital in the process of cultivating a public image, and revealing a progressive and enlightened perspective on the extension of Roman citizenship. Caesar also demonstrated his political adaptability in this period. He married Pompeia, a granddaughter of Sulla, hardly an act to be predicted of a "Marian" *popularis*. And with Pompey away from Rome on foreign command against the pirates and Mithridates VI, Caesar forged an alliance with another former Sullan subordinate and political opponent of Pompey, M. Licinius Crassus.

Crassus was one of the wealthiest Romans of the day, and his financial backing most likely enabled Caesar to spend lavishly as curator of the Appian Way and as aedile in 65 B.C. In 63 B.C. Caesar was elected to the highest Roman priesthood, *Pontifex Maximus,* in the face of stiff competition from men who had held the consulship. This was the year of the infamous Catilinarian conspiracy, an attempted coup engineered by the indebted and disgruntled Roman noble L. Sergius Catilina (Catiline), a man who had been thwarted in his attempts to win the consulship. Caesar was accused of complicity in the plot, but the consul who had uncovered the conspiracy, the famous orator M. Tullius Cicero, dismissed the charges against him. In a speech that the historian Sallust has preserved in his *Bellum Catilinae* (The Catilinarian War), Caesar opposed the death penalty for those conspirators who were detained at Rome, but to no avail. Elected to the praetorship for 62 B.C., Caesar was briefly suspended from the office for his support of Q. Caecilius Metellus Nepos's proposal to recall Pompey and his forces from the east in order to deal with the Catilinarian insurrection. This event illustrates the turbulence of Roman politics in the 60s B.C. Scandal also threatened when Caesar's wife Pompeia was accused of adulterous relations with the tempestuous P. Clodius Pulcher, who, disguised as a woman, had gained admission to the exclusively female rites of the goddess Bona Dea, over which Pompeia presided. Caesar promptly divorced Pompeia.

Upon reinstatement in office, Caesar obtained Further Spain as his propraetorian command. He now was heavily in debt, and his creditors attempted to block his departure for Spain. Again the financier Crassus stepped in and stood surety for a substantial part of Caesar's debt; as propraetor Caesar would have to recoup the remainder in the spoils of war from his command in Spain, for which he departed in June 61 B.C. In Spain he showed some of the strategic brilliance that characterized his later career as general and commander. He more than covered his debts with the booty won by attacking independent Iberian tribes and returned to Rome in mid 60 B.C. Caesar decided to forego his right to triumph for victories won in Spain in order to enter the city and legally seek the highest annual magistracy in the Roman state, the consulship. Again Caesar needed the political and financial support of those who were more powerful than he at this juncture; he found that support in Crassus and Pompey, with each of whom he had previously enjoyed connections.

Crassus and Pompey were able to arrive at a truce through the offices of Caesar. Both were eager to use Caesar as consul in order to further those of their own interests that had met with opposition in the Senate. Crassus's financial schemes included the remission of a portion of the Asiatic tax contracts of the year 61 B.C.; Pompey wanted senatorial ratification of his eastern settlement and land grants for his veteran legionaries. Caesar promised to satisfy both Crassus and Pompey in return for their political support in the consular elections. Caesar, by far the weakest member of this political alliance sometimes referred to as the First Triumvirate, was elected consul for the year 59 B.C., along with a colleague who opposed his agenda, M. Calpurnius Bibulus.

Caesar's consulate was eventful. In addition to securing land grants for Pompey's soldiers, ratification of Pompey's eastern settlement, and a rebate on the Asiatic tax contracts for Crassus, Caesar passed an important law against provincial extortion, forced publication of acts of the popular assemblies and resolutions of the Senate, and strengthened the Latin colony of Comum with some five thousand new settlers, recognizing these colonists as Roman citizens. Caesar's settlement at Comum reveals his enlightened vision of the needs of the Empire. Such colonies could siphon off the excess urban population of Rome to relatively unpopulated regions under Roman sway. Caesar's colonization thereby alleviated the provisioning needs of Rome, whose population was rapidly approaching a million inhabitants, and established enfranchised Roman communities throughout the Roman dominion. Caesar also pursued this policy in the future, and in terms of the historical evolution of ancient Rome, the gradual extension of Roman citizenship must be viewed as a key factor in the longevity of the Empire.

During his year as consul, Caesar was again in enormous debt. His political future depended upon the continued support of Pompey. Caesar strengthened his ties to Pompey by giving him his only daughter, Julia, in marriage in April 59 B.C. He had made many enemies thus far in his political career, and many of his acts as consul had run roughshod over constitutional norms. Caesar desperately needed a significant proconsular command in order to restore his financial independence and to establish a military reputation equal to Pompey's. The Senate was prepared to thwart Caesar's designs with an unimportant assignment, but through Pompey's assent and his own henchman, the tribune P. Vatinius, Caesar obtained the command of Cisalpine Gaul and Illyricum for a period of five years. A cowed Senate soon thereafter added Narbonese Gaul to Caesar's governorship. The strong-arm tactics of the First Triumvirate revealed the weaknesses of the moribund Republic under the direction of the Senate and set the tone of Roman political life for decades to come.

Aggressive actions of the Gallic tribe of the Helvetii provided the opportunity for Caesar to launch the Gallic War, from which over roughly the next decade he acquired untold wealth in spoils and forged a hardened, highly disciplined, and formidable army whose loyalties lay with its commander. Before departing for Gaul in March 58 B.C., the final breach with the senatorial majority came when Caesar refused overtures at constitutional ratification of his consular legislation. His actions in Gaul cannot be whitewashed; they evince crass opportunism and a nearly inhuman severity. Caesar amassed much of his Gallic fortune from the sale of war captives as slaves; in 57 B.C. he enslaved some fifty-three thousand treacherous tribesmen of the Atuatuci.

After the successful siege of the rebellious town of Uxellodunum, Caesar turned to political terrorism by having the hands of all the prisoners who had carried arms against him cut off. Such acts provided fodder for the designs of his political enemies back in Rome, men such as Cato Uticensis and L. Domitius Ahenobarbus, who ceaselessly worked at recalling and prosecuting him. Domitius ran for the consulship of 55 B.C., while the renowned orator Cicero worked behind the scenes to detach Pompey from Caesar. These plans were thwarted after the triumvirs renewed their political alliance at Luca in 56 B.C., and Crassus and Pompey were elected consuls for the following year. Crassus received the command of Syria, while Spain fell to Pompey; most importantly, Caesar's proconsular command was extended for another five years. He was thus enabled to complete the conquest of Gaul.

In these years Caesar's political standing at Rome deteriorated. The attempts of his opponents to destroy him had not abated. The triumvirate, the main prop of his political power in the capital, began to disintegrate when his daughter Julia died in 54 B.C., dissolving the

C. IVLIVS CÆSAR.

Portrait of Julius Caesar used as the frontispiece for the 1677 London edition of The Commentaries of C. Julius Caesar *(courtesy of the Lilly Library, Indiana University)*

matrimonial connection with Pompey. Moreover, Crassus perished on campaign in Syria at Carrhae in 53 B.C. Pompey now began a slow drift into the opposition camp. In 52 B.C. he revealed his shifting allegiances with his marriage to the daughter of one of Caesar's staunchest opponents, Q. Caecilius Metellus Pius Scipio, with whom he served as consular colleague. Pompey did, however, support a law that enabled Caesar to stand for the consulship for 48 B.C. in absentia, thereby retaining his command and remaining immune from political prosecution until the end of 49 B.C.

There was violent protest against the illegality of these arrangements, however, and in the end Pompey sided with Caesar's enemies. Caesar's *Commentarii de bello Gallico* (Gallic War), published in 51 B.C., which is in part a defense of the legality of his actions in Gaul and of his personal dignity, must be placed in the context of these events. On 1 January 49 B.C. the Senate

Cleopatra VII, Caesar's mistress; portrait on a coin struck in Alexandria, ca. 40 B.C. (from Christian Merier, Caesar, 1995)

voted that Caesar lay down his Gallic command and return to Rome, where he would be at the mercy of his political enemies. On 10 January 49 B.C. Caesar crossed the Rubicon River under arms, an act in defense of his personal dignity and the rights of the tribunes, according to him, but in the eyes of his foes, an act of treason. This move was the supreme risk of his career, and in crossing into Italy he is reported to have said, "Let the dice fly high." A devastating civil war had begun.

Caesar and his hardened veterans swept all before them in their descent upon Rome. In book 1 of his *Commentarii de bello civili* (Civil Wars), composed somewhere around 47 B.C., Caesar repeatedly stresses that on the march he continued to make overtures of peace that his opponents rejected. The veracity of these claims is dubious, to say the least. Meanwhile, Pompey had managed to slip away to Greece, and he had good hopes for his own ultimate victory, as Sulla before him had provided an historical precedent in marshaling his power in the east for his return to Italy and victory over the opposing Marian forces. Sulla had also provided Caesar with historical precedent for marching on Rome. Caesar first turned against the Pompeian troops in Spain; the campaign was crowned with the capitulation of Pompey's subordinates Afranius and Petreius near the Iberian town of Ilerda. In his return Caesar also gained control of the strategically important town of Massilia, modern-day Marseilles.

In 48 B.C. Caesar effected a difficult crossing to Greece over waters infested with Pompey's ships and besieged Pompey at Dyrrhachium. Pompey scored a victory in a sortie there, but rather than seize the chance to inflict the death blow, he retreated into Thessaly, where both sides received reinforcements. In August Caesar won complete victory in a battle at Pharsalus. Pompey fled to Egypt; Caesar pursued. Upon arriving in Egypt, Caesar learned that Pompey had been murdered and was offered Pompey's severed head as proof. Caesar then became embroiled in the bitter internal dynastic struggles in Alexandria and spent several months attempting to reestablish order there. In the end he set up his mistress Cleopatra VII as queen, with whom he fathered his only son. Caesar next proceeded to Asia Minor, where he defeated the Bosporan king Pharnaces. In this campaign Caesar is reported to have uttered the famous phrase *veni, vidi, vici* (I came, I saw, I conquered).

In April 46 B.C., after a brief return to Rome, where he restored order, and the celebration of a magnificent quadruple triumph (Gallic, Alexandrian, African, and Pontic), Caesar defeated the remaining Pompeian forces in Africa at the battle of Thapsus, at which time the Stoic Cato Uticensis chose suicide rather than tyranny. Back in Rome, Caesar was named dictator for ten years. He left the capital in late autumn and extinguished the last-gasp effort of the Pompeians in March of the following year in Spain at the battle of Munda. Caesar could claim to have achieved his stated objective in crossing the Rubicon of bringing peace to the Roman world. The civil wars were over.

Upon his triumphant return to Rome in October 45 B.C., Caesar was showered with extravagant honors. He enjoyed his fourth consulship in that year, and an unprecedented perpetual dictatorship followed. Caesar avoided direct acknowledgment of his de facto position as Roman monarch and would not allow himself to be hailed by the hated word *rex* (king). Yet, in addition to the inviolability of the tribunes and the censorial powers over Roman morality that he received at this time, the dictator consented to emblems of royalty such as the purple cloak, a temple to his own clemency, various statues, and a priesthood of his own divinity. Such honors were an affront to Roman Republican sensibilities and bred hatred among a substantial number of senators. In 44 B.C. Caesar became consul for the fifth time, and, perhaps sensing that his presence in the capital only served to exacerbate senatorial resentment at his preeminent position, he planned an extended absence in a massive eastern expedition against the Parthian kingdom; but the prospect of the unrest in Rome that was likely to ensue with the Caesar's departure and his political style, which trampled upon Republican traditions, proved intolerable. A conspiracy led by Brutus and Cassius formed against him. On the Ides of March

Caesar fell beneath a rain of senatorial daggers, dying before the statue of his great opponent and erstwhile friend, ally, and son-in-law, Pompey the Great.

Caesar was a man of great contrasts; in him are both the ruthlessly ambitious Roman politician competing in a zero-sum game with his senatorial colleagues and the political visionary who saw the shape of the future for Rome. In this sense he was a man rooted in the Roman past, but he was also a harbinger of the evolution of the empire. Caesar carried out extensive public works projects in Rome and throughout Italy. He hastened the process of extension of Roman citizenship that was eventually to result in a blanket Roman franchise for all free inhabitants of the Roman world through the *constitutio Antoniniana* (Antonian constitution) of A.D. 212. In this regard Caesar enfranchised Cisalpine Gaul through the Roscian law of 49 B.C., and he founded other important Roman colonies in Spain. He extended Roman citizenship to Greek doctors and teachers of liberal arts residing in Rome. He fostered the integration of the provinces into the Roman system by recruiting non-Italians into the Senate, which swelled to nine hundred under his dictatorship. The number of recipients of state-subsidized grain in Rome itself was reduced, and the *collegia* (associations) that were a source of urban violence in this turbulent period were abolished.

Suetonius, Caesar's biographer, states that Caesar settled eighty thousand Roman citizens in overseas provinces (*Julius,* 42.1), thereby fostering the diffusion of Roman culture. Caesar worked with the Alexandrian scholar Sosigenes in reforming the Roman calendar, which had become hopelessly out of synchronization with actual time by the mid first century B.C. With minor adjustments, this is the calendar in use today. Caesar attempted to regularize the local government of the provinces through issuing municipal charters, and he carried through some sumptuary legislation. The master of the Roman world was sensitive to the glorious past of Greece: Caesar dedicated funds for the "Roman agora" at Athens in addition to building forums at Antioch and Alexandria; he seems to have provided tax relief of some sort for the Greeks in Asia and in Sicily; and he rebuilt the venerable city of Corinth, which the Romans had destroyed in 146 B.C. Carthage was also revived as an important commercial center, an act that the reformer C. Gracchus had unsuccessfully attempted in the previous century.

In addition to his accomplishments as general and statesman, Caesar left an indelible mark upon Roman cultural history as an intellectual and man of letters. His municipal charters reveal a thorough grounding in Roman law, and as dictator he planned comprehensive legal reform (Suetonius, *Julius,* 44.2). As Cicero remarks (*Brutus,* 75; 261–262), Caesar's oratorical skills were formidable. He was concerned with the purity of the Latin language and wrote a work titled *De analogia* on Latin grammar and usage. Highly accomplished in the Greek language as well, Caesar is recorded as having composed Greek poems for the Asian pirates who briefly held him captive as a youth (Plutarch, *Caesar,* 2). He studied with the celebrated Greek rhetoricians Gnipho and Molon, and he later planned Greek and Latin libraries for Rome. Indeed, tradition has it that Caesar spoke in Greek in uttering the famous words on the gamble he was taking in crossing the Rubicon and that in his final words he addressed his assassin Brutus in Greek. Caesar had many Greek intellectuals in his entourage; he may have collaborated with the Alexandrian Sosigenes in composing a work on the calendar titled *De astris* (On the Stars), and he suggested that Tyrannio (a Greek grammarian) compose a work on poetic meter.

Caesar was, then, a genuine polymath. The best evidence for Caesar the intellectual and writer comes from his two extant works, the *Commentarii de bello Gallico* and the *Commentarii de bello civili.* These war commentaries formed a new literary genre and provided the skeletal framework for later historians. Both must be viewed in part as political tracts justifying Caesar's actions in Gaul and his role in the war against the Pompeians. These works are models of the force and concision inherent in the Latin language. No translation can capture their literary artistry. The following excerpt from the *Commentarii de bello Gallico,* recording a military engagement against the Belgians in 57 B.C., demonstrates Caesar's powers as a prose stylist:

> Caesari omnia uno tempore erant agenda: vexillum proponendum, quod erat insigne cum ad arma concurri oporteret, signum tuba dandum, ab opere revocandi milites, qui paulo longius aggeris petendi causa processerant arcessendi, acies instruenda, milites cohortandi, signum dandum. Quarum rerum magnam partem temporis brevitas et successus hostium impediebat.

> Caesar had everything to do at one moment—the flag to raise, as signal of a general call to arms; the trumpet call to sound; the troops to recall from entrenching; the men to bring in who had gone somewhat farther afield in search of building materials for the ramp; the line to form; the troops to harangue; the signal to give. The shortness of the time and the advance of the enemy prevented a great part of these duties.

> (*Gallic Wars,* 2.20, translated by H. J. Edwards, with slight modification)

*Marcus Junius Brutus, friend who participated in
Caesar's assassination; portrait on a coin struck
by Lucius Plaetorius Cestius, ca. 43–42 B.C.
(from Christian Merier,* Caesar, *1995)*

The figure of Caesar dominates this passage, and the report in the third person, maintained throughout the work, creates the impression of both objectivity and omniscience. In this passage a staccato series of future passive participles swiftly depicts the general's situation: Caesar must try to be in all places and do all things at once. The brevity of the time and the advance of the enemy are given in the sequence modifier-noun-noun-modifier, a standard rhetorical device that the Greeks called chiasmus. The shortness of time and the advent of the Belgians are one and the same thing whereby through the rhetorical figure of hendiadys ("one-through-two") the compound subject may take a singular verb form. On the other hand, the grammatical dissonance of subject-verb disagreement also conveys something of the chaos and urgency of the Roman predicament. Caesar reveals himself as a masterful writer at work creating a powerful word picture.

Literary genius, field commander without peer, and enlightened statesman, Gaius Julius Caesar was also a power-hungry opportunist who placed his personal glory and dignity above all else. Not surprisingly, then, the most diverse opinions on his life and career are found in antiquity. The Greek biographer Plutarch wrote that Caesar was like a most gentle physician sent from heaven, while the Sicilian historian Diodorus called him the greatest of the Romans. Conversely, T. Amplius Balbus wrote a violently anti-Caesarian work, no longer extant, while Cicero maintained that Caesar

directed all of his considerable powers to one end, the subjugation of the free state.

Modern scholarship on Caesar exhibits equally diverse assessments, but all historians agree that Caesar has had an enormous impact upon world history. Historical accounts based upon the Great Man in History are no longer fashionable. In *The German Ideology* (published in full, 1932) Karl Marx wrote that "circumstances make men just as much as men make circumstances." In a similar vein, in a letter to Heinz Starkenburg of 25 January 1894, Marx's collaborator Friedrich Engels observed " . . . that, if a Napoleon had been lacking, another would have filled the place, is proved by the fact that the man was always found as soon as he became necessary: Caesar, Augustus, Cromwell, etc." Many present-day historians follow these pronouncements insofar as they focus more upon larger, impersonal historical movements and less upon the force of the individual in history. Yet, if the individual is ever to disappear entirely from history, Julius Caesar may well prove one of the most difficult to extricate from its pages.

References:

Frank Ezra Adcock, *Caesar as Man of Letters* (Hamden, Conn.: Archon Books, 1969);

Adcock, *Julius Caesar: A Political Biography* (New York: Atheneum, 1967);

Adcock, "The Ides of March," *Historia,* 7 (1958): 80–94;

Adcock, "Auctoritas, Dignitas, Otium," *Classical Quarterly,* new series, 10 (1960): 43–50;

J. P. V. D. Balsdon, "Caesar's Gallic Command," *Journal of Roman Studies,* 29 (1939): 57–73, 167–183;

Stanley Frederick Bonner, *Education in Ancient Rome: From the Elder Cato to the Younger Pliny* (Berkeley: University of California Press, 1977);

Peter Astbury Brunt, "The Roman Mob," *Past and Present,* 35 (1966): 3–27;

J. H. Collins, "On the Date and Interpretation of the *bellum civile,*" *American Journal of Philology,* 70 (1959): 125–130;

P. J. Cuff, "The Terminal Date of Caesar's Gallic Command," *Historia,* 7 (1958) 445–472;

Geoffrey Rudolph Elton, "The Terminal Date of Caesar's Gallic Proconsulate," *Journal of Roman Studies,* 36 (1946): 18–42;

Elaine Fantham, *Roman Literary Culture: From Cicero to Apuleius* (Baltimore: Johns Hopkins University Press, 1996);

Matthias Gelzer, *Caesar, Politician and Statesman* (Oxford: Blackwell, 1985);

Erich S. Gruen, *The Last Generation of the Roman Republic* (Berkeley: University of California Press, 1995);

Christian Habicht, *Cicero the Politician* (Baltimore: Johns Hopkins University Press, 1990);

Thure Hastrup, "On the Date of Caesar's *Commentaries of the Gallic War*," *Classica et Mediaevalia,* 18 (1957): 59–74;

T. Rice Holmes, *Caesar's Conquest of Gaul* (Oxford: Oxford University Press, 1911);

Jorma Kaimio, *The Romans and the Greek Language* (Helsinki: Societas Scientiarum Fennica, 1979);

George Alexander Kennedy, *The Art of Rhetoric in the Roman World, 300 B.C.–A.D. 300* (Princeton, N.J.: Princeton University Press, 1972);

Andrew William Lintott, *Violence in Republican Rome* (Oxford: Clarendon Press, 1972);

Lintott, "Electoral Bribery in the Roman Republic," *Journal of Roman Studies,* 80 (1990): 1–16;

Henri Irenee Marrou, *A History of Education in Antiquity* (Madison: University of Wisconsin Press, 1982);

Christian Meier, *Caesar,* translated by David McLintock (New York: Basic Books/HarperCollins, 1995);

Agnes Kirsopp Michels, *The Calendar of the Roman Republic* (Westport, Conn.: Greenwood Press, 1978);

Robert S. Miola, "Julius Caesar and the Tyrannicide Debate," *Renaissance Quarterly,* 38 (1985): 271–289;

Thomas N. Mitchell, *Cicero, The Senior Statesman* (New Haven: Yale University Press, 1991);

Nikolaos K. Petrocheilos, *Roman Attitudes to the Greeks* (Athens: National and Capodistrian University of Athens, 1974);

Elizabeth Rawson, *Intellectual Life in the Late Roman Republic* (London: Duckworth, 1985);

Rawson, "Caesar's Heritage: Hellenistic Kings and Their Roman Equals," *Journal of Roman Studies,* 65 (1975): 148–159;

James P. Sabben-Clare, *Caesar and Roman Politics, 60–50 B.C.* (Oxford: Oxford University Press, 1971);

Robin Seager, *Pompey: A Political Biography* (Berkeley: University of California Press, 1979);

Raphael Sealey, "Habe Meam Rationem," *Classica et Mediaevalia,* 18 (1957): 75–101;

A. N. Sherwin-White, *The Roman Citizenship,* second edition (Oxford: Clarendon Press, 1987);

Courtenay Edward Stevens, "The Terminal Date of Caesar's Command," *American Journal of Philology,* 59 (1938): 169–208;

Stevens, "The *bellum gallicum* as a Work of Propaganda," *Latomus,* 11 (1952): 3–18, 165–179;

Ronald Syme, *The Roman Revolution* (Oxford: Clarendon Press, 1974);

Lily Ross Taylor, *The Divinity of the Roman Emperor* (Middletown, Conn.: American Philological Association, 1931);

Taylor, *Party Politics in the Age of Caesar* (Berkeley: University of California Press, 1975);

Taylor, *Roman Voting Assemblies from the Hannibalic War to the Dictatorship of Caesar* (Ann Arbor: University of Michigan Press, 1966);

Gavin B. Townend, "A Clue to Caesar's Unfulfilled Intentions," *Latomus,* 42 (1983): 601–606;

Allen Mason Ward, *Marcus Crassus and the Late Roman Republic* (Columbia: University of Missouri Press, 1977);

David Wardle, "'The Sainted Julius': Valerius Maximus and the Dictator," *Classical Philology,* 92 (1997): 323–345;

Alan Wardman, *Rome's Debt to Greece* (New York: St. Martin's Press, 1976);

Stefan Weinstock, *Divus Julius* (Oxford: Clarendon Press, 1971);

Chaim Wirszubski, *Libertas as a Political Idea at Rome during the Late Republic and Early Principate* (Cambridge: Cambridge University Press, 1950);

Zvi Yavetz, "*Existimatio, Fama,* and the Ides of March," *Harvard Studies in Classical Philology,* 78 (1974): 35–65;

Yavetz, *Julius Caesar and His Public Image* (London: Thames and Hudson, 1983);

Yavetz, *Plebs and Princeps* (Oxford: Clarendon Press, 1969; New Brunswick, N.J.: Transaction Books, 1988).

Juvenal

(ca. A.D. 60 – ca. A.D. 130)

F. M. A. Jones
University of Liverpool

MAJOR WORK–EXTANT: *Saturae,* 16 satires, in five books, possibly arranged by Juvenal, the sixteenth surviving in an incomplete state (Satires).

Editio princeps: *Decimus Junius Juvenalis Saturae* (Venice: Vindelinus de Spira, 1470).

Standard edition: *A. Persi Flacci et D. Iuni Iuvenalis Saturae,* edited by W. V. Clausen (Oxford: Oxford University Press, 1959; revised, 1992).

Translations in English: *The Sixteen Satires* [by] *Juvenal,* translated by Peter Green (Harmondsworth, U.K.: Penguin, 1967); *The Satires: Juvenal,* translated by Niall Rudd (Oxford & New York: Oxford University Press, 1992).

Commentaries: J. E. B. Mayor, *Thirteen Satires of Juvenal* (London: Macmillan, 1877); J. D. Duff, *D. Iunii Iuvenalis Saturae XIV* (Cambridge: Cambridge University Press, 1898); John Ferguson, *The Satires: Juvenal* (Basingstoke: Macmillan / New York: St. Martin's Press, 1979); E. Courtney, *A Commentary on the Satires of Juvenal* (London: Athlone Press, 1980); Susanna Morton Braund, *Juvenal: Satires Book I* (Cambridge & New York: Cambridge University Press, 1996).

The primary evidence for the life of Juvenal is the small amount of information that can be gleaned from the *Saturae* (Satires) themselves. The first satire relates that Juvenal received the standard Roman school education and performed the rhetorical exercise, the *Suasoria,* a piece of improvised advice to mythical or historical characters (1.15–16). The third satire suggests that he had some connection with Aquinum (3.318–320); most likely he had property there. In the eleventh satire he appears to have a place in Rome (11.193–198) and a Tiburtine farm (11.65–69). A passage in the fifteenth satire (15.44–46) implies some sort of knowledge of Egypt, although its nature remains unclear. There is no reason to suppose that the mention of a place in Rome and a farm at Tibur in the eleventh satire implies that Juvenal did not possess these earlier, nor does mention of these properties suggest the change of tone in the later satires can be explained on the basis of a hypothetical amelioration in his material circumstances. That the poems are not dedicated to any patron may suggest that his social status was relatively high.

Several other sources are in various degrees unproductive. The name Decimus Junius Iuvenalis perhaps suggests an African origin. An inscription found near Aquinum (*CIL* 10.5382), first recorded in 1772 but lost by 1846, attests a dedication to Ceres (cf. *Sat.* 3.320) by a leading municipal official who had been tribune of a military cohort and whose name is restored as Junius Juvenalis. This man may have been a relative of the poet, or the inscription may have been a fabrication produced by local opportunism. A group of several more sources suggests nothing further: the comments of the scholiast who produced a commentary on the poems in the second half of the fourth century (on 1, 4.37, 7.92, and 15.27), an allusion in Sidonius Apollinaris (*Carm.* 271) in the second half of the fifth century, a biography that may be later still (attributed by Valla in his 1486 edition of Juvenal to "Probus"), and the chronicle of John Malalas in *Corpus Scriptorum Historiae Byzantinae* (1831). These references combine to produce a narrative whose core is that Juvenal was exiled to Egypt by Domitian because of an attack he made on an actor, which he subsequently incorporated into the seventh satire (7.90–92). This synopsis glosses over details that are inconsistent, incompatible, and sometimes fantastic. Juvenal lived too late to be included in Suetonius's biographies of poets, and there is little or nothing in this detail or the other details that could not be explained as merely exaggerated inferences from the poems or extrapolations from the life of another satirist, Horace. There are other biographies, late and clearly worthless.

A Juvenal is addressed in three epigrams by the poet's older contemporary, Martial (7.24 and 7.91, of A.D. 92, and 12.18, of A.D. 101–102). The first parallels Martial's feelings for Juvenal with the friendship of Orestes and Pylades and other mythological pairs. The second purports to accompany a Saturnalia present of nuts and addresses Juvenal as "facundus" (eloquent). The third addresses Juvenal and portrays him as a poor client wandering in the less pleasant parts of Rome and wearying himself in frequenting the houses of rich patrons. If the reader assumes that Martial's Juvenal is the same as the satirist, there is still small gain in information. The "eloquence" is unspecified, and the portrait of Juvenal as a client (which could be compared at a general level to Juvenal's portrayal of Umbricius in *Sat.* 3) is based on a heavily conventional contrast of the town (where Juvenal is) and country (where Martial is). Horace and Persius provide models, and Martial's poem is literary posturing between literary people. That Juvenal knew Martial's epigrams well and frequently used their material is certainly true.

The chronology of the *Satires* cannot be worked out in detail, but indications are that the five books succeeded each other. This probability and the fact that books 1, 2, and 3 have, arguably, clear formal structures may suggest that the arrangement of at least the first three books is Juvenal's own. The incomplete state of satire 16 and close similarities between the detail and rhetorical format of satires 12 and 13 (crossing a book boundary) may contribute to a feeling that book 5 was a posthumously edited collection (or perhaps even books 4 and 5). Book 1 includes satires 1–5; the first satire refers to the trial of Marius Priscus in A.D. 100 (1.49–50), or to Pliny's account of his and Tacitus's role in the case (Pliny, *Ep.* 2.11), and satire 2.102 probably alludes to Tacitus's *Histories* (ca. A.D. 107 or later). The one poem of book 2, satire 6, in lines 407ff. mentions a comet that is likely to be the comet of A.D. 115 and the Parthian campaign that began in A.D. 116. In book 3, if the Caesar referred to at the start of the seventh satire is Hadrian (A.D. 76–138), the satire cannot have appeared before Hadrian became emperor in A.D. 117. Book 4 includes satires 10–12, and the passages concerning Sejanus and Silius in satire 10 are likely to draw on Tacitus's *Annals,* but that work cannot be dated firmly. In the fifth book, satire 13 refers to the addressee as sixty years old in Fonteius's consulship (13.17); Fonteius could be the consul of A.D. 58, 59, or 67 and adding sixty years makes the date A.D. 118, 119, or 127, but satire 14 alludes to events in A.D. 123 (14.196) and satire 15 refers to the consulship of L. Aemilius Juncus (A.D. 127) as recent (a rather elastic term), and 14.99 must have been written before A.D. 132. Book 5, then, seems to come from ca. A.D. 130.

According to Quintilian, the tradition of Latin satiric writing is twofold. He refers to an "older" strand (perhaps older than Lucilius, the figurehead of Roman verse satire, perhaps just older than Persius and Horace) written by M. Terentius Varro (116–27 B.C.)

in a mixture of prose and verse and characterized as more learned than eloquent. It may be that this strand, Menippean Satire, died out with Varro; certainly Petronius's *Satyrica* and Seneca's *Apocolocyntosis* do not belong to it, and there are no other classical examples. The main strand, verse satire, has roots that can be traced back to Quintus Ennius (239–169/168 B.C.) and Pacuvius (220 B.C.–ca. 132 B.C.). Ennius wrote four books of satires in various meters (only thirty-one lines survive, the longest fragment a six-line quotation in Donatus), including a debate between Life and Death (Quintilian, 9.2.36) and an Aesopian fable (Aulus Gellius, 2.29.1). No fragments of Pacuvius's satire survive, but it was, apparently, like Ennius's (Diomedes, *GLK* 1.485).

Later writers regarded Gaius Lucilius (ca. 170–ca. 102 B.C.) as the founder of the genre, and the later satirists–Horace, Persius, and Juvenal–treated him as a figurehead (especially Horace, satire 1.10.48, 2.1.62). Lucilius's poetry survives only in fragments, but as they total somewhat more than one thousand lines, and as later satirists provide characterizations of Lucilius (albeit each creates a picture skewed to provide the desired model), to make some assessment of the nature of his output is possible. Five books (numbered 26–30) were, like Ennius's, in various meters, but Lucilius subsequently (books 1–21) settled on the hexameter, which then remained the standard meter for verse satire. The fragments cover a miscellany of subject matter–for example, dinners, parasites, mistresses, social behavior, friends, enemies, and spelling. Abuse is often vigorous, and Lucilius was subsequently regarded, or described, at any rate, as a poet of fierce moral invective who was not afraid of naming the targets of his attacks, and this practice became in some sense a defining characteristic of satire, although one that subsequent satirists rather pretend to follow than actually follow.

Q. Horatius Flaccus (65 B.C.–27 B.C.) refined and limited Lucilius's scope. He wrote two books of *Satires,* and the first book of his *Epistles* is also relevant to the development of the genre, since both Persius and Juvenal sometimes use epistle form. The first book of *Satires* includes a group of sermonizing pieces, entertaining narrative pieces, and program poems discussing the nature of satire and Horace's attitude toward it. Horace's *Satires* actually include comparatively little criticism by name and none of important living characters; instead, they include much material subtly supporting the ruling elite and a consistent interest in ethical issues of the kind raised in the comedies of P. Terentius Afer (ca. 190–159 B.C.). At least one poem had a particular model in Lucilius (satire 1.5). As in Lucilius's *Satires,* there is much autobiographical content, although in Horace it is carefully designed to sub-

Fragment of an eighth-century French manuscript for Juvenal's works, found in the Abbey of St. Guillem-le-Desert, near Montpellier, France (Milan, Bibl. Ambros. Cimelio 2, recto)

stantiate the moral stance. The second book predominantly uses dialogue form, and the attitude taken toward the main speaker is deeply evasive. The interest in ethical issues remains, but the topics—for example, food, the dinner party, will-hunting, and Stoic paradoxes—tend to be more stylized. The first book of *Epistles* is similar in many ways to the first book of *Satires*.

Persius (A.D. 34–62) produced six satires with a short preface in choliambic meter. In subject matter they are closely comparable with Horace's, and the language draws heavily on Horace but is much denser and depends much more on metaphor and image. Despite the literary allegiance to Horace (who is now named along with Lucilius as a generic model), Persius does not follow Horace's rather vacillating version of Epicureanism but maintains a strong Stoic posture. Autobiographical material is present but more limited than in Horace's works, and he replaces Horace's conversational manner with an angry, alienated stance and a style compressed and full of elliptical jumps. Also unlike Horace's poetry, Persius's is distinctly apolitical, and the whole tenor is quite generalized; he employs little criticism by name.

Another figure is important for the background to Juvenal—Turnus, a satirist under Domitian praised by Martial (7.97, 11.10). Two lines of a satire survive, quoted by the scholiast at Juvenal 1.71 because Turnus, like Juvenal, mentions the Neronian poisoner Lucusta. Although this evidence is desperately meager, it is at least possible that Turnus's reference prefigures Juvenal's use of noncontemporary, scandalous material.

Like Horace and Persius, Juvenal expresses allegiance to the Lucilian model (and, like Persius, names Horace as another generic model), but Juvenal's satires are quite different. The style is neither that of reasonable conversation nor Persius's denser version of the Horatian style; the content is not the kind of social-ethical material Horace used or the generalized Stoic material of Persius; neither pro-ruling elite nor apolitical, it lacks all but the tiniest fragments of autobiography. Instead, Juvenal presents a glistering prospect of the vices and crimes of the (mainly) upper classes of past times, in a style drawn from epic and declamation and colored with wit, irony, and literary allusion. Juvenal's earlier satires include a marked posture of anger and disgust (and so the Horatian autobiographical mode would have been rhetorically inappropriate), although as the first book advances, Juvenal increasingly exposes this perspective to irony. In the first satire Juvenal takes the stance of a heroic moral polemicist (and draws his picture of Lucilius to match). At the end of the sixth satire he assumes a tragic posture. Near the beginning of the tenth satire he holds up as models Democritus and Heraclitus, who stand for the comic and the tragic view, respectively; he makes fun of the tragic view of Heraclitus, but he also handles the alternative ironically (and the rest of the satire is a patchwork of different tones). By the thirteenth satire Juvenal explicitly condemns anger and espouses common sense. These are Juvenal's chief programmatic indications.

Part of Juvenal's rhetorical style is the use of *sententiae,* pithy, clinching formulations that sum up a point and were a feature of Roman Declamation. (The *Controversiae* of the Elder Seneca [ca. 54 B.C.–ca. A.D. 40] is largely a collection of such *sententiae.*) Some examples are "probitas laudatur et alget" (honesty is praised—and gets frozen, 1.74); "dat veniam corvis, vexat censura columbis" (judgment pardons the ravens, pursues the doves, 2.63); "nemo repente fuit turpissimus" (No one was at the peak of vice all at once, 2.83); "si verum excutias, facies non uxor amatur" (if you shake out the truth, it's the face that's loved, not the wife, 6.143); "sed quis custodiet ipsos custodes?" (But who will guard the guardians? 6.347–348); "rarus venit in cenacula miles" (Soldiery rarely breaks into a garret, 10.18); "cantabit vacuus coram latrone viator" (The empty-handed traveler will sing amidst the brigands, 10.22); "quis enim virtutem amplectitur ipsam, praemia si tollas?" (Who embraces courage itself, if you should take away the rewards? 10.141–142).

Juvenal's use of examples is also rhetorical in origin (though it fits the Lucilian model of criticism by name, too). His satires are more densely packed with names than either Horace's or Persius's. They are chiefly drawn from Roman history, particularly the early empire, and literature. Often there is just a brief reference; sometimes there is a cluster (as at satire 10.219–226 or the beginning of satire 8, where the density has some relevance to the theme of the worthlessness of aristocratic names) or more extensive treatment (as Sejanus in satire 10.58–107). But Juvenal is not always necessarily straightforward in his purpose. Sometimes the examples are gratuitously inappropriate. Examples are Quintilian, who was not poor, and Palaemon, whose "poverty" was due to his expensive tastes, not to any lack of remuneration (satire 7.188 ff., 7.215 ff.), and Hector's corpse, borne on the shoulders of his brothers (twenty-five on each side? 10.259–260). Occasionally a passage is sparing with names for special effects, as in the programmatic first satire at lines 55–78, where the section follows mention of Horace and reflects his manner (just as the preceding section, lines 22–45, is fairly dense with names and follows the reference to Lucilius), or the first half of the long section on old age in the tenth satire (lines 188–245), where the anonymity of old age is part of its unpleasantness.

Another major characteristic is Juvenal's attention to specific, vivid, and sometimes exaggerated detail. At 1.33 Matho's litter is described as *plena ipso* (full of himself); at 1.65 *cathedra* suggests that Maecenas's litter is a portable armchair; at 1.72 the mention of husbands killed by poison in one neighborhood includes the detail of their "nigros" (blackened) bodies; at 1.104 a freedman comes to a rich patron's morning session and his social provenance is marked by the holes left by heavy earrings, which Juvenal calls *fenestrae* (windows); at 2.33 Julia's abortions are called *offas* (lumps or dumplings); at 3.258 a pile of building materials that collapses on a passerby is called a *montem* (mountain); at 4.21 another litter, roomy and well windowed, is called an *antro* (cave); at 4.107 Montanus is called *Montani venter* (Montanus's stomach); at 10.238–239 the picture of the former prostitute who has latched onto a rich old man singles out her mouth as vividly relevant; and at 11.37–38 poverty is described as having only a *gobio in loculis* (gudgeon in your pocket). This feature overlaps with a more general characteristic, Juvenal's use of unusual or unexpected words, ingeniously placed.

The literary texture is also a conspicuous feature. Most of satire 3 consists of a speech by one Umbricius. The name suggests *umbra* (shadow), and it and a range of words derived from it—*umbraculum, umbratilis, umbraticus, umbrosus*—all connote the unreality of the rhetorical schools. Umbricius's speech is declamatory in theme (compare, for example, Quintilian's 2.4.24, "Is town or country life better?" and Juvenal's 3.197 and the following lines with the passage of Papirius Fabianus's declamation quoted by Seneca the Elder in *Controversiae* 2.1.10 and following lines). Umbricius's manner is also declamatory, and his name is located near his reference to *honestis artibus* (that kind of education), but the speech is also literary. A passage on orientals, prostitution, and music (3.62–66) blends Lucan's epic (*Bellum Civile* 7.404–405) and Propertius's *Elegies* (2.23.21). Later, a second passage on prostitution blends references to Persius (1.17 and following) and Martial (3.30). The passage on burning apartment blocks in Rome (Juvenal's 3.197), already noted as reminiscent of declamatory material, is worked around an allusion to the fall of Troy in Virgil's *Aeneid* (2.311–312) and an epigram of Martial (3.52). Later the accidental death of a pedestrian in the street while his family are unaware at home is based on Hector's death, as yet unknown to Andromache (Homer's *Iliad* 22.437–438), thus complementing the earlier Virgilian allusion. In addition, the treatment of this pedestrian's death blends Epicurean materialist physics (the obliteration of the soul along with the body) and the mythological iconography of the Styx and Charon. The end of Umbricius's speech alludes to the end of Virgil's eclogue 1. Other poems

are equally literary (there are some thematic and ironic allusions to Catullus, Propertius, and Ovid in the sixth satire), but in the case of the third satire the implication that Umbricius is more in touch with literature than reality seems to be intended.

The *Satires* demonstrate a firm grasp of structure at all levels. The first satire, which introduces book 1, is made of four blocks. Lines 1–21 are a general introduction raising the question of why Juvenal wants to follow Lucilius (referred to by a geographical periphrasis) and write satire. The next block, lines 22–80, is a single unit built on one pattern, "when x, y, and z happen, it is hard not to write satire." The block is split into two by a reference to Horace (by geographical periphrasis) and concluded by a reference to an unknown satirist, Cluvienus (unless it is another geographical reference, to an unknown satirist from Cluvium). The third block (lines 81–146) is an analysis of contemporary vice, structured as a set of rings. Lines 94–95 and 135–146 concern the rich, eating extravagantly and unsocially on their own. Lines 95–109 and 117–134 concern the *salutatio* and *sportula,* the social events that embody the patron-client relationship of *amicitia* (friendship) that framed the day, but which are blended into a satiric composite. Both passages include small dramatic illustrative vignettes. At the heart of this block, lines 109–116 depict the deification of money, an explanation of the surrounding context. There are elaborate chiastic word correspondences between the corresponding sections. The final block resumes the programmatic argument (and can be compared with Horace, satire 2.1 and Persius, 1), repeats the appeal to Lucilius's example, and concludes with a mock-cowardly resort to criticizing the dead instead of the dangerous living.

Juvenal presents his first satire as the furious improvised tirade made by a listener at a conventional poetry reading. Satire 2 maintains the angry tone. It is framed by references to the far north at the beginning and the far east at the end and a kind of oscillation from and to Rome. The structure is twofold, the contents concerning hypocrisy and effeminacy, but there is a problem: at first hypocrisy is clearly held to be worse than naked vice (2.15–21), but later (from line 83 onward) shameless vice appears to overtake hypocrisy. Either Juvenal is simply not consistent, or the satire presents a genuine moral question.

One character in satire 2, the prostitute Laronia, is foregrounded as a spokesperson against hypocrisy and makes a speech of some thirty lines (37–63) as angry in tone as the first satire, but including some suspiciously implausible claims, and closed off with agreement by the poet so conclusive that the agreement sounds ironic. Juvenal's use of Laronia prefigures the use of Umbricius in satire 3. This poem, the longest in

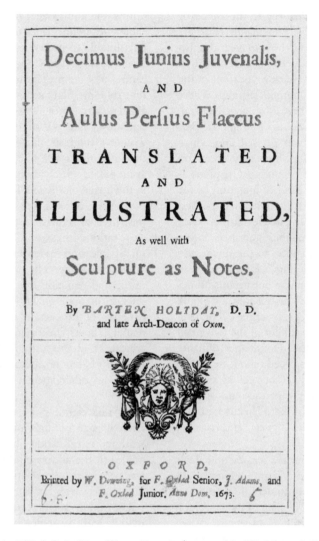

Title page for the 1673 Oxford edition of Juvenal's works (courtesy of the Lilly Library, Indiana University)

book 1, and occupying a central position, has an introduction in the poet's mouth (lines 1–20) and a coda in the interlocutor's mouth (lines 315–322). In between is the bulk of Umbricius's speech explaining why he is leaving Rome: to escape Greeks and vice. Since Juvenal has already said that Umbricius's destination is Cumae and laid emphasis on its proximity to Baiae, readers can only be suspicious when Umbricius's speech gets under way since Cumae was the oldest Greek colony in Italy and still under heavy Greek influence, while Baiae had had a bad moral reputation at least since the late republic. The speech falls into two main parts, each having three sections. The first part deals with Umbricius's gripes about his precarious financial hold in Rome. Lines 21–57, general complaints; lines 58–125 deal with complaints about being dislodged by Greeks; and lines 126–189 deal with complaints about the poor Romans.

The second part concerns the dangers of living in Rome—lines 190–231, fires; lines 232–267, death in the streets; and lines 268–314, other violence and death. The second part conjures up a nightmare vision of Rome as resembling Troy in its collapse, clearly darker in tone than the first part. This part connects with an observation about the beginning of the poem so that the satire has in fact a double introduction. The theme of fires and collapsing buildings is sounded by Juvenal at lines 6–9, while Umbricius introduces the more personal monetary complaints at the beginning of his speech (lines 21–28), as though the one part is meant to be less authorized than the other.

The fourth satire, like the second and third, concerns *amicitia*, this time at the imperial level. The structure is tripartite, dealing with Crispinus and his purchase of a large and expensive fish (lines 1–27), the capture of a vast fish and its delivery to the Emperor Domitian (lines 37–72), and the meeting of courtiers summoned by Domitian to decide how to treat the fish (lines 72–154). The Crispinus section is couched in indignant style and linked by a mock invocation of the Muses at the beginning of the Domitian sections, where the mock-epic tone persists. (There is a particular connection between this part and Statius's lost epic *De Bello Germanico,* in which Domitian was praised and which included a council from which four lines survive and on which Juvenal draws.) At the beginning Crispinus is described as though he were a kind of imitation of the imperial figure: within the court he is neither the best nor the worst of the counselors. The eleven men summoned are catalogued in epic manner, and their corporate characterization draws attention to the terror and hatred inspired by the emperor. There is an element of ring composition overall: Crispinus's outrageous crimes are dealt with first, then a folly, then a folly of Domitian, and then Domitian's outrageous crimes. The contrast in manner between the treatment of the two main characters suggests both that Domitian's villainy dwarfs anger and that anger displaced onto lesser malefactors is misplaced. The poem can be seen as an even more pessimistic, though grimly witty, account of ways of surviving in an imperial court than Tacitus had provided, rather defensively, in the *Agricola, Histories,* and *Annals.*

The fifth satire again concerns *amicitia* and deals with a rich patron, Virro, a poor client, Trebius, and a prospective dinner (food and dinners are frequent motifs in Roman moralizing). The plan of the poem follows the courses of the meal. Consistently Virro receives food with imperial and glamorous mythological connotations, and Trebius receives food with menial and disgusting connotations, except for the main course, when Trebius gets nothing. The most disgusting item on Trebius's menu, a sewer-fed fish, the item that most ought to rouse him from his abjectness, is followed by a calm apostrophe by Juvenal to Virro. The implication appears to be that although Trebius is angry, his anger is an inadequate reaction. This poem is the last in book 1 and serves as a culminating treatment of the theme of *amicitia*–its final word is *amico* (friend, 5.173)–as well as confirming the increasing irony to which anger, programmed in satire 1 (which it almost matches in length), is exposed in this book.

The sixth satire, at nearly seven hundred lines, is a vast piece–apparently unparalleled in Roman satire and occupying the whole of book 2–on women and marriage, a well-worn rhetorical topic (compare with Quintilian, 2.4.25). It is arranged as an introduction mocking the concept of the good old days (lines 1–24), a recurrent theme in Roman literature, and urging Pos-

tumus, the addressee, not to marry (lines 25–59). Four catalogues follow: lines 60–183, examples of women as not suitable to marry (an ironic version of Ovid's *Ars Amatoria*); lines 184–285, trivial but unbearable faults; a central passage presenting as an explanation of the current state of affairs a pastiche of historiographical moralizing; and lines 286–351, an account of female sexuality. The set of catalogues then resumes with women's interests (lines 352–473) and the events in their day (lines 474–633). The poem ends with a program passage disclaiming exaggeration and culminating in the image of a Rome filled with female murderers.

With book 3, the seventh, eighth and ninth satires, Juvenal returns to the theme of *amicitia.* The seventh satire addresses a Telesinus, supposedly at work on an epic, and reviews the state of literary and educational patronage. The surface value of his case is the traditional equation–mean patrons cause literary production of poor quality–but Juvenal is ironical at the expense of the actual abilities of the practitioners–namely, poets, historians, and lawyers–and also the educators–*rhetores* and *grammatici.* (The sequence is the reverse of that in Suetonius's biographical series and similar to other ancient reviews of the state of literature.)

The eighth satire questions the worth of aristocratic lineage and falls into three sections–a general and scathing introduction (lines 1–70), a piece of ironic advice to the addressee (lines 71–145) on how to govern provinces (the relationship of Rome to the provinces was seen as analogous to the patron/client relationship), and a catalogue of bad and good (but mainly bad) examples in reverse chronological order, which end with the origins of Rome as a sanctuary for criminals, a sort of parody of a family tree.

The ninth satire is a dialogue between Juvenal and Naevolus, who makes four speeches in response to Juvenal's questions about the meanness of his rich patron, Virro (the same name and character type as in the fifth satire). This satire presents *amicitia* as a mercenary homosexual arrangement. While Naevolus is angry and embittered (also pompous and maudlin), Juvenal is remote and ironic; thus, the ninth satire increases the distance from the savage posture of the first satire.

In the remaining satires *amicitia* loses its central thematic position. The tenth satire is a sermon on the folly of men in what they pray for. Juvenal arranges the material much as in satire 7: after an introduction, there are five blocks; the first three are in the public sphere–political power (lines 56–113), eloquence (lines 114–132), and military glory (lines 133–187); the last two are domestic–old age (lines 188–288) and beauty (lines 289–345). The conclusion suggests one should pray for a sound mind in a healthy body (lines 346–366). The longest section, that on old age, is remarkable. It falls into two contrasting parts: the first (lines 188–245) is set in Rome and, unusually for Juvenal, sparing with named examples but filled with graphically repellent material; the second (lines 246–288) uses named mythological examples, some comically inappropriate. There is a sort of tragic-comic polarity, but with the roles reversed: the tragic and epic material are somewhat comic.

The eleventh satire begins with fifty-five lines of vigorous satire on gourmandizers; it begins as another sermon like satire 10, but it turns into an epistle at line 56. The addressee, Persicus, is invited to what seems to be a moderate and old-fashioned meal. But Persicus's name has suspicious connotations of luxury, and Juvenal intersperses his treatment of Persicus with increasingly ironic touches. Juvenal is no longer interested in consistent dramatization (as he was in earlier satires) but plays a sophisticated game with the audience in which the addressee is merely a prop whose character depends on the rhetorical needs of the moment.

Like the eleventh satire, the twelfth and (crossing over the boundary into book 5) thirteenth satires are clearly addressed; furthermore, all three poems relate to occasions for which rhetorical precept and models were available—the invitation (satire 11), the thanksgiving for escape from trouble or illness (satire 12), and the consolation (satire 13). In addition, in satire 12 Juvenal experiments further with the opportunistic treatment of the occasion and characterization; the relationship between Juvenal, Corvinus (the addressee), and Catullus (the friend for whose escape from a storm at sea Juvenal expresses gratitude) is impossible to pin down. Rather, Juvenal plays with audience expectations and conventions. The addressee has a name suggesting a *corvus* (raven), a frequent metaphor in Roman descriptions of will-hunting (the topic of the second half of the poem), and the storm Catullus has escaped is a parody of epic storms. Catullus also seems to be assimilated into a standard satiric target, the greedy merchant.

The thirteenth satire consoles Calvinus (a name that strongly suggests considerable wealth) for the loss of an amount of money Juvenal explicitly assesses as moderate. Calvinus's money had been deposited with a friend for safekeeping in his absence, and the friend has denied the deposit (the theme and the amount are paralleled in Declamation). Calvinus is angry, and Juvenal explicitly criticizes this reaction and uses the standard techniques of Roman consolations, at first in the usual way, to mitigate the excesses of the sense of loss, but subsequently to suggest ways in which Calvinus will have his desire for vengeance satisfied. Pandering to the emotion is so counter to the role of consolations that

scholars infer Juvenal is ironically making the point that Calvinus's feeling for his money (consolations were almost always for the loss of humans) is insatiable.

Satires 14, 15, and 16 are all addressed to individuals, but in these cases the addresses are pure formalities, marking the poems as epistolic, whereas in the earlier poems the addressee had some role in the poem itself. Satire 14 blends two themes, greed and parental influence. Satire 15 expands from a tale of cannibalism in Egypt—a startling novelty in the usually urban world of Latin satire—to a disquisition on human nature. Traditional ideas on the growth of civilization and the susceptibility of the human heart to pity are juxtaposed to a picture of utmost barbarity. Only sixty lines of satire 16 are preserved; they deal ironically and unsympathetically with life in the army, another novel topic for the genre (though there are some brief foreshadowings in Persius), but the satire is too incomplete for further comment.

The interpretation of Juvenal's *Satires* is problematic. Older views emphasize Juvenal's rhetoric and wit; scholars in the nineteenth century and much of the twentieth though, have often characterized Juvenal as a serious moralist expressing his anger at a shortsightedly quirky selection of targets. But from around the 1960s a different perspective has appeared, reemphasizing rhetorical display and wit. In recent years awareness of the importance of performance and its concomitant multiplicity of interpretations has been growing; Juvenal is sometimes seen as producing opportunistic pastiches of stereotypical views without giving his own feelings away at all. Satire 3, for example, can be seen as a parody of declamatory commonplaces, though for all its wit the tenth satire seems straightforward. A passage in satire 3 illustrates the complexity of tone. At lines 131–136 Umbricius complains that whereas some rich man's slave (implicitly a Greek) can afford to spend huge amounts merely to have sexual intercourse once or twice with a Calvina or a Catiena (aristocratic Roman names), the poor Roman such as Umbricius cannot even afford to "take down from her lofty seat" (the exact meaning of this line is not clear) the pleasing-faced Chione (a Greek prostitute). Earlier (lines 62–66), Umbricius's views on prostitution appeared to be more moralistic, and now readers might wonder whether they are intended to detect double standards. They might also wonder whether they are meant to feel sympathy for the poor Roman (as in Martial 3.52), who at least notices Chione's face, and contempt for the sheer casualness of the Greek slave, for whom the identity of his one- or two-night stand is immaterial. Are readers meant to feel that the poor Roman's spurious sentimentality is part of the criticism of him?

Juvenal has been taken as a racist and a misogynist, but the grounds for this view are less than they seem. The most obvious claim for racism depends on satire 3, but the attack on the Greeks and orientals is put in Umbricius's mouth, and Juvenal has clearly set him up earlier as an inadequate moral spokesperson. The most obvious evidence for misogynism is in satire 6, but this satire can be taken as ad hominem irony at the expense of the addressee, Postumus (or perhaps Ursidius Postumus), or as an opportunistic pastiche of common stereotypes. If readers look for recurrent features, they are more likely to be struck by the way Juvenal repeatedly parodies the concept of the good old days–especially in satires 6, 11, and 13–or subverts the usual simplistic polarization of traditional oppressors and their victims, as the rich patron and poor client–especially in satires 3, 4, 5, 7, and 9–arguably the husband and wife in satire 6, the will-hunter and his rich victim in satire 12, and the defrauder and his rich victim in satire 13.

Bibliography:

S. H. Braund, *Roman Verse Satire* (Oxford: Oxford University Press, 1992).

Concordance:

Michel Dubrocard, *Juvenal: Satires: index verborum* (Hildesheim & New York: Olms, 1976).

References:

Joachim Adamietz, *Untersuchungen zu Juvenal* (Wiesbaden: F. Steiner, 1972);

Willism Scovil Anderson, *Essays on Roman Satire* (Princeton, N. J.: Princeton University Press, 1982);

S. H. Braund, *Beyond Anger: A Study of Juvenal's Third Book of Satires* (Cambridge & New York: Cambridge University Press, 1988);

Braund, ed., *Satire and Society in Ancient Rome* (Exeter: Exeter University Publications, 1989);

C. J. Classen, "Satire–the Elusive Genre," *Symbolae Osloensis,* 63 (1988): 95–121;

Michael Coffey, *Roman Satire* (London: Methuen / New York: Barnes & Noble, 1976);

Josué de Decker, *Juvenalis Declamans:* ètude sur la rhétorique déclamatoire dans les Satires des Juvenal (Ghent: E. Van Goethem, 1913);

Lowell Edmunds, "Juvenal's Thirteenth Satire," *Rheinisches Museum,* 115 (1972): 59–73;

John Ferguson, *A Prosopography to the Poems of Juvenal* (Brussels: Latomus, 1987);

S. C. Fredericks, "Rhetoric and Morality in Juvenal's 8th Satire," *Transactions and Proceedings of the American Philological Association,* 102 (1971): 111–132;

W. C. Helmbold, "Juvenal's Twelfth Satire," *Classical Philology,* 51 (1956): 14–23;

Gilbert Highet, *Juvenal the Moralist* (Oxford: Oxford University Press, 1954);

Richard Jenkyns, *Three Classical Poets* (London: Duckworth / Cambridge, Mass.: Harvard University Press, 1982), pp. 151–221;

E. J. Kenney, "Juvenal: Satirist or Rhetorician?" *Latomus,* 22 (1963): 704–720;

R. A. La Fleur, "*Amicitia* and the Unity of Juvenal's First Book," *Illinois Classical Studies,* 4 (1979): 158–177;

L. I. Lindo, "The Evolution of Juvenal's Later Satires," *Classical Philology,* 69 (1974): 17–27;

Amy Richlin, "Invective against Women in Roman Satire," *Arethusa,* 17 (1984): 67–80;

G. B. Townend, "The Literary Substrata of Juvenal's Satires," *Journal of Roman Studies,* 63 (1973): 148–160;

Paul Wessner, *Scholia in Iuvenalem vetustiora* (Leipzig: Teubner, 1931);

Martin M. Winkler, *The Persona in Three Satires of Juvenal* (Hildesheim & New York: Olms, 1983).

Livy

(59 B.C. – A.D. 17)

Tracy Keefer
University of South Carolina

MAJOR WORK: *Ab urbe condita libri* (History, 142 books; 1–10 and 21–45 survive; fragments and summaries of the rest survive).

WORKS–LOST: Philosophical dialogues.

Editio princeps: *Historiae Romanae decades,* edited by Joannes Andreae (Rome: Conradus Sweynheym and Arnoldus Pannartz, ca. 1469).

Standard editions: *Titi Livi Ab urbe condita libri,* edited by Wilhelm Weissenborn, Moritz Müller, and W. Heraus, 6 volumes, second edition (Leipzig: Teubner, 1902–1912; reprinted, Dublin: Weidmann, 1962?–1968); *Titi Livi Ab urbe condita libri XXIII–XXV,* edited by T. A. Dorey (Leipzig: Teubner, 1976); *Titi Livi Ab urbe condita libri XXVI–XXVII,* edited by P. G. Walsh, second edition (Leipzig: Teubner, 1989); *Titi livi Ab urbe condita libri XXVIII–XXX,* edited by Walsh (Stuttgart: Teubner, 1986); *Titi Livi Ab urbe condita libri XXXI–XL,* 2 volumes, edited by John Briscoe (Stuttgart: Teubner, 1991); *Titi Livi Ab urbe condita libri XLI–XLV,* edited by Briscoe (Stuttgart: Teubner, 1986); *Titi Livi Ab urbe condita,* 5 volumes, edited by R. S. Conway and C. F. Walters; volume 1 [books 1–5], revised by R. M. Ogilvie; volume 4 [books 26–30], edited by S. K. Johnson; volume 5 [books 31–35], edited by A. H. McDonald (Oxford: Clarendon Press, 1919–1974).

Translations in English: *Livy,* translated by B. O. Foster; volumes 6–8 translated by Frank Gardner Moore; 9–11 translated by Evan T. Sage; 12 translated by Sage and Alfred C. Schlesinger; 13–14 translated by Schlesinger, index by Russell M. Geer, Loeb Classical Library, 15 volumes (Cambridge, Mass.: Harvard University Press, 1919–1967).

Commentaries: *Titi Livi Ab urbe condita libri,* 2 volumes, edited by Wilhelm Weissenborn and H. J. Müller, fourth edition (Berlin: Weidmann, 1910; reprinted, 1962–1965); *A Commentary on Livy: Books 1–5,* edited by R. M. Ogilvie, second edition (Oxford: Clarendon Press, 1969); *Livy Book XXI,* edited by P. G. Walsh (Bristol: Bristol Classical Press, 1985); *Ab urbe condita Book XXXVI,* edited by Walsh (Warminster: Aris & Phillips, 1990); *A Commentary on Livy Books XXXI–XXXIII,* edited by John Briscoe (Oxford: Clarendon Press, 1973); *A Commentary on Livy Books XXXIV–XXXVII,* edited by Briscoe (Oxford: Clarendon Press, 1981); *Livy Book XXXVII,* edited by Walsh (Warminster: Aris & Phillips, 1992); *Livy Book XXXVIII,* edited by Walsh (Warminster: Aris & Phillips, 1993); *Livy Book XXXIX,* edited by Walsh (Warminster: Aris & Phillips, 1994); *Livy Book XL,* edited by Walsh (Warminster: Aris & Phillips, 1996).

Not much is known of the life of Titus Livius, Rome's most ambitious and, arguably, greatest historian. Livy himself offers almost no autobiographical information in his monumental—and only surviving—work, the *Historiae ab urbe condita libri.* Most of the facts on Livy's life come from later sources, and some of this information is surely apocryphal. According to the chronicle of the Christian priest Jerome, Livy was born in Patavium (later, Padua) in 59 B.C. He died there sometime between A.D. 12 and A.D. 17. An inscription on a tomb at Patavium commemorating a Titus Livius, if authentic, supports Jerome as to both the place and time of Livy's death. Livy's family appears to have been of the middle class, possibly merchants. The family was well-to-do, for Livy apparently never wanted for money and was able to devote his life to the writing of history.

Patavium, located in Cisalpine Gaul (northern Italy) on the coast of the Adriatic Sea, only received full Roman citizenship in 49 B.C., ten years after Livy's birth. The inhabitants of the city seemed to have responded to their newfound identity as Romans with a firm alliance to the conservative factions in the Senate and a passion for traditional Roman values. Livy was imbued with the political and moral conservatism characteristic of his homeland. The sympathies of Patavium during the period of the civil wars lay always with the Senate as the embodiment of the Republic. Any attempt to bring the state under the command of a single man was viewed with suspicion; for example, Patavium firmly supported the Senate in its sanctions against Marcus Antonius in 43 B.C. Livy grew up during the civil wars, in which first Julius Caesar and then Octavian obtained sole rule of the Republic, and those events certainly affected his political views. Livy regarded the accession of Caesar as an aberration and admired Brutus and Cassius in their attempts to restore the Republic by murdering the dictator. Livy viewed with wistful regret the simpler days of early Republican Rome.

He probably obtained at least his early education at Patavium. The skilled use of rhetorical devices in his writing suggests that he received advanced schooling in the practice of oratory. At some point he went to Rome, but he may not have done so in order to further his education. There is no evidence that Livy's studies ever encompassed travel outside Italy. Despite his interest in philosophy, he never rounded off his education by studying with the philosophers in Greece, as did many of his compatriots. His references to other areas, such as Greece and the eastern provinces, betray no firsthand knowledge. Livy also seems to have had no military training; his knowledge of things military seems to have been gathered from other sources. His accounts of specific battles, tactics, equipment, and strategy are exceedingly vague, and his description of one engagement reads much like that of another.

As an outsider to Roman politics, a member of the provincial middle class, Livy never entered politics except peripherally, when he came to the attention of the emperor Augustus (27 B.C.–A.D. 14), no doubt through his increasing renown as an historian. As a private citizen apparently supported by family funds, Livy was free to devote himself entirely to literary pursuits. His apparent lack of need for a patron meant that he could write a history untainted by an obvious political agenda. According to Seneca the Elder, Livy made a brief foray into philosophical subjects (*Ep.* 100.9), but he gave up the study of philosophy when he conceived the idea of writing a massive history of Rome, an undertaking that would occupy him for the remainder of his life.

How long Livy resided in Rome is an open question, but there are several indications that he spent a considerable amount of his professional life there. Although he gives no indication why or when he chose to move to Rome, he probably did so following the peace brought about by Octavian's victory at Actium in 31 B.C. Livy may have been seeking better teachers than Patavium had to offer, or he may have been looking for work. What is known is that after he came to the attention of Augustus, Livy served as a tutor to the future emperor

Claudius, who aspired to write history. This occupation implies that Livy was in Rome on a regular basis throughout the reign of Augustus. Livy seems to have associated with the emperor often, and these meetings no doubt took place at Rome. As a professional historian, Livy was connected to Rome in the eyes of his readers. According to Pliny (*Ep.* 2.3.8) it was at Rome, not Patavium, that an admirer who had journeyed from Spain sought out the famous historian. And finally, Livy must have wanted to take advantage of the myriad sources Rome had to offer for the writing of his history. That he ever accessed the Roman archives cannot be proven, but Livy certainly needed to consult the works of the early annalists, which were probably not available at Patavium.

Livy's family life remains obscure. The identity of his wife is unknown, as are the names of his children. His family was a literary one. The grammarian Quintilian relates only that Livy had two sons and one daughter (10.1.39). One son wrote on geography; the other was a rhetorician. Livy's daughter married the rhetorician Lucius Magius (Seneca, *Contr.* x, proem. 2).

Livy's magnum opus was the *Historiae ab urbe condita libri,* a history of Rome intended to span the period between the founding of the city and Livy's own day (as had the now-lost *Origines* of Cato the Elder, the first great history of Rome). When he completed the work, Livy had produced 142 books in all. Of these, only books 1–10 and 21–45 survive intact. Some fragments also exist, including one preserved by Seneca the Elder on the death of Cicero and *Periochae* (Summaries) of the lost books.

Livy's organization of his *History,* particularly in the earlier books, was based on the annalistic tradition of historical writing. In marked contrast to writers such as Sallust, who tended to focus on single men and events in the form of monographs, Livy covered all the events that occurred in one year before moving on to the events of the next. Often this practice forced him to abandon his narrative of events that spanned several years in medias res to enable him to discuss the other important occurrences of that year. However, the disjunction this chosen method of organization may have caused was more than counteracted by Livy's ordering of the work into a series of pentads (five books) and decades, which were generally meant to be perceived in concrete units with clearly defined themes. The history seems to have been published originally in pentads, and it continued to be copied, bound, and stored in these discrete units throughout late antiquity and the early Middle Ages, a practice that may explain the survival of those books that are still extant. They form multiples of five: the decades 1–10 and 21–40, and the pentad 41–45.

There is some indication, however, that Livy did not have an overall plan for executing his history. He seems to have limited himself to mapping out a decade at a time. But even these smaller units required more time and space than he had anticipated, for in his introductions to some of the decades, particularly the fourth, he expressed some alarm at undertaking a project that constantly threatened to grow beyond his capacity. As it was, if (as most scholars believe) Livy began his task in about 27 B.C., then he averaged about three books a year for the remainder of his life.

In his preface to the history, Livy began by expressing his trepidation at the thought of writing the history of Rome when there was *tanta scriptorum turba* (such a crowd of writers) who were likewise ambitious to do so. But he quickly distinguished his own attempt by the immense amount of labor he planned to devote to it, for, unlike his competitors, who had apparently preferred to confine themselves to more-recent events, Livy desired to start with the foundation of the city and work his way to the present day. His professed humility, his fear lest his *fama in obscuro sit* (fame be obscure), scarcely masks his pride in the monumentality of his work.

Livy further explained why, when his audience clearly preferred histories of more-recent events, he insisted upon spending so much time and space on the early history of Rome. No other Latin author had focused upon the events he wished to relate. Furthermore, despite Livy's protestations to the contrary, there was clearly a newfound interest in antiquarian subjects in Augustan Rome, an intense desire to unearth and set down the ancient traditions of the city. Livy's reluctance to deal with more-recent history was also rooted in his strong sense of political conservatism, which made him wary of criticizing the protagonists of the recent bouts of civil war, particularly Augustus's great-uncle Julius Caesar.

Finally, Livy gave in the preface his reason for giving preferential treatment to the earlier history of Rome: only in that period could he find sufficient examples of what he considered moral behavior exhibited by men of strong character. For Livy bad examples were as profitable as good, but good examples were much more difficult to find among the men of his own day. "It is this especially that makes the reflection on history most salubrious and profitable," said Livy, "that you have before you the records of every sort of example; from them you can take what you wish to imitate both for yourself and for the state, from them you can also avoid what is evil in conception and in result."

Livy was firmly convinced that Rome was the greatest state in the world and its people the most virtuous, but he also believed that in recent times a dangerous dissolution had begun to set in. "These are the things which I believe everyone should examine most carefully," he said, "what life and morals were like, by which men and by which means, in both peace and war, our dominion was established and increased; and then with the incremental loss of discipline, at first morals were relaxed, and then more and more rapidly they sank and began a headlong decline, until we came to these current times in which we can endure neither our vices nor their remedies." Livy was referring undoubtedly to the period of civil war, which he attributed to the greed for power; the remedies were almost certainly a reference to Augustus's attempts to bring an end to the strife and to impose new guidelines for the moral behavior of the Romans.

The first decade of the history covers the period from the founding of the city, in 753 B.C., to the third Samnite War, in 293 B.C. In book 1 Livy recounted many of the legends of the founding of Rome and the establishment of the distinctive Roman character. This interest in antiquarian issues—the origin of the Roman people, their character, and their social, political, and religious institutions—coincided with Augustus's attempts to repair the damage caused by civil war by reviving, at least nominally, the traditions and values of early Rome. Virgil, for example, wrote the *Aeneid* (ca. 29 B.C.) during Augustus's reign in an attempt to give the Romans the sense that the antiquity of their own origins at Troy rivaled that of the Greeks.

While Livy devoted only a few lines to the voyage of Aeneas, Virgil devoted an entire poem to the story. The two men have often been compared because they both wrote in the time of Augustus, and both demonstrated an interest in the founding of Rome. The similarity must stop there, however. Virgil wrote his *Aeneid* at a time when Augustus was still attempting to blacken the reputation of his recent opponent in the civil war, Mark Antony. Virgil had Aeneas leave Dido at Carthage because he considered his duty to seek his destiny more important than an affair with a foreign queen; this episode has been seen as an ill-concealed reference to Antony's failure to put the interests of the state above his obsession with Cleopatra. Livy wrote considerably later, when Augustus was secure in his rule; there was less need for such propaganda, and in any case Augustus never directly patronized Livy.

Livy next focused upon the legends surrounding the creation of Rome and its expansion. He intended simply to present the various accounts he consulted, as he states in his preface, refusing *ea nec adfirmare nec refellere* (either to affirm or refute them). Some of these legends were certainly fables. Livy related several stories that have become famous, most particularly that of the foundation of the city of Rome. He wrote that

Page from an early manuscript for Livy's Ab urbe condita libri (Biblioteca Laurenziana, Florence, manuscript 63, 5, Livy, Decade III, folio)

Aeneas's descendants, the brothers Numitor and Amulius, feuded over the right to rule Alba Longa, the city founded by Aeneas's son Ascanius. Amulius destroyed Numitor's male children and had his daughter, Rhea Silvia, appointed as a Vestal Virgin so that she could not have any male offspring who might claim the throne. She was raped by Mars, however, and gave birth to twin sons, whom Amulius then ordered killed. The agent of the king, loathe to drown the infants in the Tiber, left them on the banks instead, whence they were rescued by a she-wolf and brought up in the house of a royal shepherd. Eventually, the twins Romulus and Remus were discovered to be of royal blood. Having decided to found a new city of their own, they argued over who should rule it; Romulus killed Remus in a fit of anger and gave his name to Rome.

Another story that became justly important to later ages was that of the death of Tarquinius Superbus. If Romulus had ushered in the Regal Period (753–509 B.C.), Tarquinius the Etruscan is credited with making urgent the need to found the Republic, for his tyranny led the Roman people to overthrow the monarchy. Livy told the story in a terse but dramatic style. Tarquinius Superbus and several of his Roman companions sat about drinking one night, and each bragged about the virtue of his own wife. One Roman, Tarquinius Collatinus, boasted that his wife Lucretia was the most virtuous of all. Deciding to put their wives to the test, the men rode first to Rome and then to Collatina, intending to surprise the women and find out the true nature of their pursuits. All but Lucretia were taking advantage of their husbands' absence to engage in revelry. Lucretia, the only virtuous woman, hard at work in her spinning, inspired in Tarquinius Superbus the "evil desire to debauch her by force." He followed this evil impulse, but Lucretia revealed the rape to her husband and her father, saying, "'Even as I absolve myself of any wrongdoing, I do not liberate myself from the penalty: never in future shall any immodest woman live through the example of Lucretia.' Plunging into her heart the knife which she was hiding beneath her dress, she slipped forward and fell dying over the wound" (1.58). Tarquinius Collatinus and Junius Brutus led the overthrow of Tarquinius Superbus and were themselves elected the first consuls of the Roman Republic. Ever afterward the notion of a king was repugnant to the Roman people. Lucretia became the symbol of the sacrifice made for the new Republic, and she continued to be depicted in art through the time of the Renaissance.

Book 1 ends with the institution of the Republic. In books 2–6 Livy turned to two themes: the development of the institutions of the Republic and Rome's expansion at the expense of the other Italian city-states—the Aequi, the Volsci, the Sabines, and the Etruscans. Much of Livy's attention on the domestic front was focused on the so-called Conflict of the Orders, the struggle between the patricians (nobility) and the plebeians (commons). His account of this internal strife, as well as his list of magistrates for this period, seems to be reliable. The plebeians, who resented that the patricians denied them a political voice but still expected them to fight for the state, gradually wrung concessions from the patricians by refusing to take up arms. On the eve of an invasion by the Volsci, who desired to take advantage of Roman disunity, "the plebeians were overcome with delight at the prospect of invasion. . . . Let the patricians, they contended, take up arms and fight, let those bring upon themselves the dangers of war who reaped the rewards of it" (2.24). The plebeians' determination gained them the right to appoint their own officers, called tribunes (ca. 471 B.C.), the right of access to the law (452 B.C.), the right to hold the consulship, and the right to intermarry with the patrician class (*lex Canuleia,* 445 B.C.).

Book 5 ends with the famous sack of Rome by the Gauls in 390 B.C. Almost completely unprepared for the assault, the Romans met the Gauls with a weak defense that caved in almost immediately, and Livy paints an affecting picture of the chaos of the city, with women and children desperately seeking protection while their men fought in vain against the Gauls. The patricians, resigned to their inevitable defeat, desired to set a noble example for the panicked citizens: "the grey-haired senators had gone home to await, unflinching, the approach of the enemy. Those who had held the most honored offices of the Republic wished to meet death dressed in the clothes in which they had conducted their duties . . . " (5.41). Sitting before their great houses, they met the Gauls with stoic calm as the barbarians stormed the city.

In book 6 Livy begins his account of the wars between the Romans and the Samnites. This pentad, books 6–10, is of questionable veracity. None of the available sources, such as Diodorus, corroborate Livy's account, and those facts that can be verified, most particularly geographical ones, do not support Livy's version of the events. Livy seems to have been concerned to paint the Romans as far more heroic in their resistance to the Samnites than was warranted.

The next decade, books 11–20, is lost. It addressed the war with Pyrrhus and Tarentum and the first war with Carthage. The extant books, 21–45, cover the period from 219 B.C., the beginning of the Second Punic War, to 167 B.C., the end of the wars with Macedonia. This portion of the *History* is vastly different from the preceding books for two reasons. First, Livy devotes far more space to far fewer events: an entire decade is given over to the War with Hannibal, a period of just seventeen years. Second, Livy's sources are both more reliable and fewer. Livy cited the historian Coelius Antipater (ca. 121 B.C.), who wrote seven books on the Second Punic War, for domestic events and Hannibal's rampage through Italy. Coelius's influence is especially apparent in the first two books of the third decade. Because Coelius's focus was on Carthage rather than Rome, Livy was forced to amend his facts in order to place more emphasis on Rome. For domestic developments, Livy used the late-Roman annalists Valerius Antias (ca. 75 B.C.) and Claudius Quadrigarius (ca. 82 B.C.). From book 24 on, Livy became increasingly dependent upon the account of the historian Polybius (ca. 200–ca. 118 B.C.), a Greek from Achaea brought to Rome as a political prisoner, who wrote about the rise of Rome to imperial power. The value of Polybius cannot be overestimated. His account of the wars with Carthage and Macedonia was detailed and accurate, if stylistically uncouth. In addition, Coelius and Polybius seem to have used the same sources for their histories, lending a marked similarity to their versions of the events.

Livy frequently chose to expand upon his sources; unfortunately his attempted emendations, which were factual as well as stylistic, often resulted in distortions of varying magnitude. In some cases Livy was completely incorrect. Often such a lapse in accuracy was due to his intense patriotism and his strong bias against the Carthaginians, as when, for example, he sought to embellish Polybius's rather staid depiction of the motivations and character of Hannibal. In Livy's account of the inception of the Second Punic War, he paints a virulent picture of Hannibal and his insane desire to seek any excuse for going to war with Rome. According to Livy, Hannibal was indoctrinated at an early age by his father, Hamilcar, to hate the Romans: "It has been reported that when Hannibal was scarcely nine years old and was teasing his father Hamilcar to take him to Spain, his father, who was sacrificing after the African war was over and was about to take his army across, made him touch the sacred altar and take an oath that as soon as he could he would be the enemy of the Roman people." Livy thus intimates that Hannibal's invasion of Roman territory was an unjustified act of aggression. His deft portrait of Hannibal confirms this impression:

> Neither his body nor his spirit could be overcome by labor or exhaustion; he bore heat and cold equally well; his consumption of food and drink was occasioned by natural appetite rather than pleasure; his schedule for waking and sleeping was not marked by the time of day or night. . . . He was often seen sleeping upon the ground amongst those on watch, wrapped in

his military cloak; he was the first to enter battle and the last to leave it. . . . But such great virtues had equal vices to balance them: inhuman cruelty, and perfidy worse than Punic; truth was nothing to him, and nothing was sacred; he feared no god, respected no oath, and knew no religion.

Any account of the Hannibalic War must concern itself with battles and their strategy, and with these Livy was often at a loss, even with Coelius and Polybius as his guides. He clearly had no taste for describing military engagements, and even the most important of them are lacking in detail and factual precision. But Livy made up in drama what he lost in veracity. His account of the psychological effect of war on the protagonists is always compelling. In describing, for example, Hannibal's passage over the Alps into Italy, Livy emphasized in excruciating detail the toll on men and beasts as they toiled through the virtually impassable drifts of snow and steep terrain. He sometimes left off his narrative of a battle to describe the reactions of the Roman people to each advance made by Hannibal. Livy knew the dramatic effect on the reader of the knowledge that Rome was perilously close to annihilation by the Carthaginian general. He relates the situation after the disastrous battle at Cannae: "Never, except when the city was captured [by the Gauls in 390 B.C.], was there such terror and confusion within the walls of Rome. . . . Now it was not one wounding after another, but a calamity of enormous proportions, when it was announced that two consuls and two consular armies were lost, and no longer was there a Roman camp, Roman general, Roman soldier; Apulia, Samnium, already almost all Italy was under the domination of Hannibal" (22.54).

The remaining extant decades (including books 31–45) treat the war with Philip V of Macedon, the triumph over Antiochus, and the Third Macedonian War. The last extant book brings the history to the year 167 B.C. Livy was so reliant upon Polybius for the portions of his *History* dealing with events in the East that his own account is virtually a glorified and augmented translation. Unfortunately, Polybius's version of these events has survived only in fragments, making Livy's adaptation the only record of much of his history. Some scholars have argued that the most valuable sections of Livy's *History* are those that he altered the least in transferring them from Polybius's Greek to his own Latin. For those events that occurred in the West during this period, Livy seems to have depended upon other sources, including Antias, Claudius, and M. Porcius Cato (consul, 195 B.C.).

The contents of the remaining lost books can only be hinted at by the *Periochae,* but even the contents are lacking for books 136–137. Polybius, Antias, and Claudius seem to have remained Livy's primary sources for his *History* to 146 B.C. For the later books Livy used a variety of sources, some of which are still extant. For the Sullan period he seems to have followed Sulla's own memoirs, Lucullus (consul, 74 B.C.), and Sisenna (ca. 67 B.C.). Asinius Pollio's *Historiae* (History of the Civil Wars) brought Livy to 60 B.C., after which he made use of Caesar's writings for the period of civil war. The *Periochae,* written in the third or fourth centuries A.D., were themselves probably compiled from earlier epitomes of the *History.* From them scholars know that by Book 142 Livy had reached the death of Drusus, Augustus's stepson, in A.D. 9.

Livy's use of sources leaves something to be desired. His aim was to produce a literary history that was widely accessible to the reading public, presenting all the history of Rome in a single source. He cared more for readability than for accuracy. Language was more important to him than factual precision, and he was content to amplify the accounts he gleaned from other historians. He seems often to have based his choice of sources on ease of access rather than reliability, avoiding entirely the exhaustive research that the collection of primary data would have entailed. To consult inscriptions and documents, to visit personally the settings he wished to describe, and to walk the battlefields and tour the cities—all the practices recommended by Polybius to the potential historian—Livy was unwilling or unable to do. He preferred simply to make use of the data compiled by Polybius instead. A substantial number of the documents used by Livy's predecessors were still available in Rome's archives in Livy's time, but to save time he apparently refrained from consulting them.

Livy seldom named the historians who provided him with facts, unless he disagreed with a particular interpretation or there was the possibility of several different interpretations. But many of the sources that Livy used have been identified by careful comparisons between his accounts and those of other sources. By his own admission, Livy relied heavily upon the information of several late-Roman annalists for the first decades of his *History.* He cites the works of Antias, Aelius Tubero (ca. 46 B.C.), Licinius Macer (d. 66 B.C.), Claudius Quadrigarius, and Fabius Pictor, who lived at the time of the Second Punic War. Of these works, some exist in fragmentary form, and some are known only through Livy's quotes of their works or, in some cases, his mention of their names. But the precise nature of Livy's debt to these and other historians is often difficult to assess, primarily because so many of them have been lost, possibly because Livy's *History* superseded them and rendered them, in the eyes of subsequent generations, obsolete.

Page from Decades, *a 1506 edition of Livy's history (courtesy of the Lilly Library, Indiana University)*

Some of Livy's other drawbacks include his uncertain command of geography, a fault that makes him unreliable for many events that were situated outside—and even some of those inside—Italy. One of the most glaring examples is his account of Hannibal's passage over the Alps, which displays not only Livy's own ignorance of the geography of Gaul and northern Italy but also his inability to reconcile his conflicting sources for Hannibal's route, including that of Polybius. Livy rejected Polybius's tracing of the route, choosing to have Hannibal begin his march over the mountains from Allobroges rather than Grenoble and the Little St. Bernard Pass, but he confused matters after the crossing of the Rhone River; he seems to have added another historian's account to that of Polybius and thus had Hannibal covering the same territory twice. The problem, according to one scholar, is that Livy seems to have been attempting to supplement the information he found in Polybius's work, which on occasion was too vague or used terms unfamiliar to Livy.

Even more unfortunate was Livy's lack of experience in military matters. Since many of the surviving books concern Rome's wars with Carthage and in the East, the modern reader often sees Livy out of his element. His battle descriptions follow set patterns from the early books of the *History* on through the Macedonian Wars, relieved only by the specialized and exact information gained from Polybius. Livy often oversimplified even Polybius's information to the point of inaccuracy. His accounts of battles read much like the accounts in Caesar's Gallic Wars, with which Livy was no doubt familiar: the Romans face an enemy that vastly outnumbers them but rise through adversity to victory, often by means of the valiant actions of their commanders.

Finally, while Livy's status as an outsider to Roman politics often allowed him to deliver a remarkably unbiased account, there is no denying that he was politically naive. His knowledge of the workings of Rome's government was basically sound, but he was insufficiently informed on the factional disputes of the great families of Rome, largely because he avoided consultation of their extensive records. Livy was often completely unaware of the underlying causes and ramifications of many of Rome's important policies. Livy's sometimes uncritical use of his sources, such as the senatorial annalists, also meant that he unwittingly incorporated their biases into his own account.

Do his methods make Livy a bad historian? Admittedly the factual accuracy of many of Livy's accounts is suspect, and often his narrative is frustratingly vague. Much of this inaccuracy is the result of his chosen method of using accounts already written by others, for if his source was vague, Livy was forced to be vague as well, and often the task of reconciling the facts in several conflicting sources led to the perpetuation of error. Despite these deficiencies, Livy was more often in line with the practice of history writing in antiquity than in violation of it. The disinclination to name sources was standard, and in Livy's day to do so would have been seen as nothing more than a waste of time and space. For most of his readers, Livy's disclaimers that much of the information on early Rome was tradition (*ut ferunt*) rather than solid fact was sufficient. Many in Livy's audience, indeed, read him to learn and emulate his literary style rather than to gather information. Finally, Livy recognized a lack, and he filled it: up to his time there was no single comprehensive history of Rome in Latin. Polybius's account was undoubtedly superior to Livy's—and was indeed Livy's source—for the events it covered, but unfortunately for Latin-reading audiences of the Augustan age its drawbacks may have outweighed its advantages. It was written in Greek; it did not address the early history of Rome; and it ended with the Macedonian Wars.

For Livy, the literary style of his *History* was one of his more-important considerations. A point in Livy's favor is his desire to tell an interesting story. If he shortchanged the battle scenes, he invariably spent the time on the psychological and emotional motivations of his protagonists. Like most ancient historians, Livy used the technique of invented dialogue to communicate the individualism of his historical characters to the reader, and in these speeches he displayed all his rhetorical acumen. His tendency was always to dramatize events. His language, which bordered on the florid, was alternately criticized and praised for its complexity. Quintilian approved Livy's *lactea ubertas* (milky richness; 10.1.32), even as he related Asinius Pollio's disparaging remark on Livy's *Patavinitas* (Patavinian or Paduan origins).

The remark "on Livy's *Patavintias*" is an obscure one. Clearly Pollio did not approve of Livy's style, but what constitutes the misfortune of being Paduan is not clear. Pollio seems to have been referring to a certain provincialism in Livy's style as exemplified by the use of the dialectal oddities of Padua. Pollio was a stringent critic and advocate of a spare style, and Livy's elaborate grammatical constructions, his flair for the dramatic, seems to have deeply offended Pollio's sense of decorum. In any case, Livy consciously adopted his style in marked contrast to the terseness of Sallust, whom he criticized for his *brevitas* (brevity [Seneca, *Contr.*, 9.1.13]). Despite the criticism Livy was capable of great variety; he modified his style to suit the material. His elaboration, reserved primarily for speeches, gave way to archaic, terse language used to recite early Roman religious rites and a spare, dry listing of facts when explaining, for example, the development of the *comitia centuriata* (assembly of centuria—divisions of the Roman people) under the king Servius Tullius.

The subject of patronage for Livy's *History* is perhaps one of the most difficult questions to answer regarding this already obscure historian. There is little evidence to suggest that Augustus patronized Livy as he did Virgil or Horace; yet, many of Livy's aims were the same as the emperor's. Can Livy's *History* be considered propaganda for Augustus's political program? Modern scholars seem to be divided on this question. Earlier historians were more willing to make the claim that Livy was indeed promoting the Augustan program; one even went so far as to call Livy Augustus's "improving publicist," according to Ronald Syme. Later scholars, in the absence of any real evidence to support this sort of statement, have been more tentative. Some, such as Andrew Feldherr, have sidestepped Livy's relationship to Augustus entirely, saying that Livy never intended his *History* to be a political document at all but a work of literature. Others, such as Mark Toher, have been less cautious, but in concentrating on the nature of Roman historiography, they have managed to avoid a definitive statement on the propaganda issue either way. They have pointed out that Livy's position as an outsider—that is, a Paduan of recent Roman citizenship—and a bourgeois allowed him to divorce politics from his writings. He was a professional historian, not a senator, and as a result his *History* was relatively devoid of party politics. Other scholars have attempted to demonstrate that Livy's aims for his *History* happened to coincide with those of Augustus but were not necessarily directly influenced by the emperor's political program, much less deliberate propaganda for it. Indeed, based on the evidence, this last claim seems to be the strongest that can be made on this question.

What is the nature of the evidence? First, Livy's non-Roman origin, which made him an outsider to Roman politics, was sufficient cause for some of his rivals to criticize him. Pollio made his famous and disparaging remark about Livy's "Patavinitas," and Quintilian repeated it. But his relatively obscure beginnings meant that Livy had no interest in promoting his family or his politics in his *History*. There is also the indication that his foreign status as an alien to Rome and his recent acquisition of Roman citizenship, still coveted by outsiders, made him more desirous of glorifying Roman history. The excessive zeal of recent converts often makes them more tendentious and vehement in support of their newfound faith than those who were born into it. A comparison with Polybius's work illustrates this truth. Although Polybius was a Greek prisoner of war, he was one of Rome's most ardent panegyrists.

None of the books on Augustus survive, except in the *Periochae*. Therefore, it is virtually impossible to assess Livy's opinion of the emperor. There are a few hints, however. First, the epitomizer says in the introduction to book 121, *qui editus post excessum Augusti dicitur* (It is said that [Livy] produced this book after the death of Augustus). From this passage scholars have hypothesized that Livy deliberately delayed publication of the books dealing with the reign of Augustus. If his sympathies were not with Augustus, perhaps Livy waited until Augustus was safely dead before publishing an account of the events following the Battle of Actium in 31 B.C.

Second, according to the account preserved by the abridger of his works, Livy concentrated his last nine books—that is, those dealing with the events following the Battle of Actium, Augustus's early reign and the beginning of the Principate—on foreign rather than domestic topics. Livy may have returned to his earlier emphasis on the foreign wars that dominated Rome's history from its beginnings. The delay also may have

been an attempt to avoid discussion or possible criticism of Augustus's domestic policies for fear of angering the emperor.

Was Livy afraid of repression by Augustus? He was either extremely careful or remarkably unbiased. Where his sympathies lay is difficult to say. Unlike Tacitus, who was quite obviously a staunch Republican and highly critical of usurpation of Rome by quasi-kings, Livy makes no statement that can be unequivocally construed as anti-imperial. According to Velleius Paterculus, Livy was one of the few historians of his day who attempted to write on the reign of Augustus, but clearly he concentrated on earlier events as long as he could. Whether or not Livy refrained from partisanship out of fear is questionable. Augustus went out of his way to avoid any indication of tyranny. He adopted a policy of tolerance for views that opposed his own, and he was not generally known for destroying works that criticized his policies or his person. Although he did exile Ovid, he never tried to have Ovid's works destroyed.

Livy himself got away with some interesting speculation, in Augustus's presence no less, if Tacitus and Seneca can be believed. Seneca states that Livy wondered aloud to Augustus whether it would have been better had Julius Caesar never been born (*N.Q.* 5.18.4). The implications for Augustus had Caesar not been born are obvious, and Augustus could not possibly have missed them. Such a comment would not have been taken well by Tiberius or Caligula, but whatever Augustus may have felt about Livy's politics, the two retained their friendship. That Livy tutored Claudius implies at least tolerance of the historian on the part of Augustus.

Tacitus makes this point plain when he puts this speech in the mouth of a senator about to be executed by Tiberius for extolling the virtues of Brutus and Cassius: "Livy, outstanding for objectivity as well as eloquence, praised Pompey so warmly that Augustus called him 'the Pompeian,' but their friendship did not suffer" (*Ann.* 4.34). In this period such a reference to Pompey, who was on the senatorial and therefore Republican side in the civil war with Caesar, was one way of stating Republican sympathies. Caesar was the flawed king, Pompey the vanquished Republican. But these indications of Livy's political leanings are confined to hearsay reported in later sources. Significantly, whatever Livy may have said to Augustus in their friendly exchanges, none of this sort of partisanship appeared in the *History*. Livy's objectivity is the characteristic that comes through strongest in his *History*.

Apocryphal accounts aside, what can be gleaned from Livy's own words? Livy's view of his own time can hardly be called wholehearted admiration. In his

Statue of the Emperor Augustus, who engaged Livy as a tutor for his son Claudius (Vatican Museums, Vatican City)

preface to his *History,* he says that he preferred to spend his time on the early history of Rome so "that I might avert my gaze from the troubles which our age has been witnessing for so many years." He contrasts the morals of the early Republic with those of the present age:

> Here are the questions I would have every reader give his close attention: what life and morals were like, through what men and by what policies, in peace and in war, the empire was established and enlarged. Then let him note how, with the gradual relaxation of discipline, morals first gave way, as it were, then sank lower and lower, and finally began the downward plunge that brought us to the present time, when we can endure neither our vices nor their cure.

He contrasts the morals of the early Republic with those of his own age, emphasizing what he perceived to be a severe decline throughout the period of civil war until it reached the low point of his own day, when "we can endure neither our vices nor their cure."

This passage has led some scholars to think that Livy is referring to the policies of Augustus as the "remedies." Livy does not emphasize Augustus per se anywhere in his *History.* His few comments on the emperor are remarkably benign. Livy may be hinting at the moral reforms by which Augustus attempted to restore some semblance of order after the years of civil war, specifically the emperor's legislation on marriage in 28 B.C. However, Livy could have approved of Augustus's moral program without the emperor's having patronized him to extol such aims in his *History.* Livy's own moral sense as expressed in the *History* seems to be the result of a zeitgeist, a spirit of reform that the recent restoration of peace after years of civil war made possible, rather than the result of any specific patronage. Augustus seems to have reserved his patronage for the poets. Horace and Virgil extolled the party line in a way that Livy did not.

An even more telling sign that Augustus did not officially patronize Livy's *History* is that he did not seem particularly to make use of it in his own policies. For example, Augustus did not even use the interpretations of the great men of Rome that Livy labored so hard to provide. Those men whom the emperor preferred appeared in the inscriptions in the forum at Rome, and they do not correspond in many cases to Livy's portraits.

Livy's agenda for his *History* did, however, coincide to a certain degree with Augustus's political program. In his preface Livy said that he wanted to trace the inverse relationship between Rome's increasing *imperium* on the one hand and declining *mores* on the other. With regard to book 1, Livy's account of the regnal period and the transition to a republican form of government can be taken as the historian's attempt to present a series of cautionary exempla to the emperor. Tarquinius Superbus was on every Roman's mind during Caesar's dictatorship; Tarquinius represented the worst sort of tyranny to the Romans. Livy was careful to point out that Tarquinius ruled by force, not "by popular decree or senatorial sanction," a passage that might have made Augustus somewhat uncomfortable. Livy went on to describe Tarquinius's proscriptions of the senatorial order, saying that he "tried capital cases without advisers and . . . inflicted death, exile, and forfeiture of property, not only upon persons he suspected or disliked, but also in cases where he could have nothing to gain but plunder." This portrait probably called into the reader's mind parallels with other men who had recently seized power unlawfully–Marius, Sulla, Caesar, and Antony. Augustus could not have failed to understand the implications for his own reign.

If Tarquinius was presented as a warning to the emperor, however, there were positive examples for him as well. Augustus could congratulate himself that, like Servius Tullius, he had combined the religious devotion and domestic concerns of the kings Numa and Ancus Marcius with the successful foreign campaigns of Romulus and Tullius. More likely, though, Augustus never identified his own rule with any of the early kings, at least publicly. His official persona was that of the *princeps,* first man of the Senate, who carried more authority and had more power than anyone else in Rome but was no king. He could cite his willingness to relinquish power in 27 B.C. as proof enough of that.

Livy's legacy in later ages was a varied one. He was well known and respected in his own time. Later historians continued to use his *History* as a model for their own. Even Tacitus, who was notoriously critical, approved of Livy and praised both his style and his moral character. Livy's Republicanism appealed to senators of Tacitus's time, who felt keenly the repression of the less-than-enlightened emperors who followed Augustus. Later emperors, indeed, did not exhibit Augustus's tolerant attitude toward diversity of opinion: Gaius Caligula banished the works of Livy and Virgil from the public libraries at Rome.

Livy's *History* began to be collected almost immediately. Its enormity posed problems of space for admirers such as Martial, who complained that his library could not hold it all: "Pellibus exiguis artatur Livius ingens, quem mea non totum bibliotheca capit" (Enormous Livy is compressed into tiny pages, but my library still cannot completely hold him, 14.190). The late Roman senator Q. Symmachus collected all of Livy's works, and it is through his efforts that the first decade survives at all. Medieval readers seldom ventured to read works as large as Livy's, often preferring epitomes. Some exceptions exist, such as Einhard, John of Salisbury, Lambert of Hersfeld, and Dante. During the medieval period, however, the pentads of the *History* were separated and dispersed, and the integrity of the *History* was forever lost. Individual monastic libraries housed single groups of pentads, and Renaissance scholars searched them in their attempts to reconstruct Livy's work. The efforts of these humanists are largely responsible for the survival of the thirty-five books still extant. Petrarch located the most significant find, unearthing the first, third, and fourth decades at Chartres. The first printed edition of 1469, therefore, included most of the modern corpus, books 1–10, 21–32, 34–39, and part of book 40. In 1527 Simon Grynaeus added books 41–45, which he discovered at the monastery of Lorsch. Finally, Horrio found the first part of book 33 in 1615 at Bamberg, completing the modern collection.

The passion of the Renaissance humanists for Livy did not end with the attempt to recover lost material. Once these books were found, several scholars devoted themselves to the work of editing and correct-

ing the texts, including Petrarch, Giannantonio Campano, and Lorenzo Valla. Livy influenced many men of the Renaissance in their own work. His Republicanism and apparent antimonarchial sentiments appealed to political scientists who hoped to establish or preserve a Republican form of government in their city-states. Machiavelli took a particular interest in Livy that is manifested in *The Prince* and in his *Discourses* on the first decade of Livy's *History*. Petrarch modeled his epic *Africa* on Livy's account of Scipio Africanus and the Punic Wars. A renewed interest in their ancient countryman induced the Paduans to claim several obscure tombs as belonging to Livy, including two at the church of Santa Giustina. The first was a slab on the wall inscribed with the name "Livius," and the second was a casket that the Paduans assumed contained the bones of Livy. Neither identification is likely.

References:

T. A. Dorey, *Livy* (London: Routledge & Kegan Paul, 1971);

Andrew Feldherr, "Livy's Revolution: Civic Identity and the Creation of the Res Publica," in *The Roman Cultural Revolution,* edited by Thomas Habinek and Alessandro Schiesaro (Cambridge: Cambridge University Press, 1997), pp. 136–157;

Karl Galinsky, *Augustan Culture: An Interpretive Introduction* (Princeton, N.J.: Princeton University Press, 1996), pp. 280–287;

Mary Jaeger, *Livy's Written Rome* (Ann Arbor: University of Michigan Press, 1997);

M. L. W. Laistner, *The Greater Roman Historians* (Berkeley: University of California Press, 1966);

D. S. Levene, *Religion in Livy* (Leiden & New York: E. J. Brill, 1993);

James Lipovsky, *A Historiographical Study of Livy, Books VI–X* (New York: Arno Press, 1981);

T. J. Luce, "Livy, Augustus, and the Forum Augustum," in *Between Republic and Empire: Interpretations of Augustus and His Principate,* edited by Kurt A. Raaflaub and Mark Toher (Berkeley: University of California Press, 1990), pp. 123–138;

Luce, *Livy: The Composition of His History* (Princeton, N.J.: Princeton University Press, 1977);

Gary B. Miles, *Livy: Reconstructing Early Rome* (Ithaca, N.Y.: Cornell University Press, 1995);

Ronald Syme, "Livy and Augustus," *Harvard Studies in Classical Philology,* 64 (1959): 27–87;

Mark Toher, "Augustus and Roman Historiography," in *Between Republic and Empire,* pp. 139–154;

P. G. Walsh, *Livy: His Historical Aims and Methods* (Cambridge: Cambridge University Press, 1961);

Walsh, *Livy. Greece and Rome. New Surveys in the Classics* (Oxford: Clarendon Press, 1974).

Lucan

(A.D. 39 – A.D. 65)

Botham Stone

WORK–EXTANT: *De bello civili* (The Civil War), alternatively *Pharsalia*, 10 books, unfinished.

WORKS–FRAGMENTARY: *Catachthonion* (Trip to the Underworld);

Iliacon (Song of Troy);

Orpheus;

Epigrammata (Epigrams).

WORKS–LOST: *De incendio urbis* (On the Burning of the City, A.D. 64);

Epistulae ex Campania (Letters from Campania);

Laudes Neronis (In Praise of Nero);

Medea;

Salticae Fabulae (Pantomimes);

Prosa oratio in Octavium Sagittam (Speeches in Favor of and against Octavius Sagitta);

Silvae (Occasional Verse);

Saltice fabulae (Libretti for Mimes);

Saturnalia.

Editio princeps: *Lucan Pharsalia,* edited by Joannes Andreae (Rome: C. Sweynheym & A. Pannartz, 1469).

Standard editions: *M. Annaei Lucani Belli Civilis, libri decem,* edited by Carl Hosius, third edition (Leipzig: Teubner, 1913); *La Guerre civile (La Pharsale),* edited by Abel Bourgery and Max Ponchot (Paris: Les Belles Lettres, 1926–1929); *M. Annaei Lucani Belli civilis libri decem,* edited by A. E. Housman, second edition (Oxford: Blackwell, 1950); *Der Bürgerkrieg,* edited and translated by Georg Luck (Berlin: Akademie, 1985); *M. Annaei Lucani de Bello Civili Libri X,* edited by D. R. Shackleton Bailey (Stuttgart: Teubner, 1988).

Translations in English: *Lucan. The Civil War,* translated by J. D. Duff, Loeb Classical Library (Cambridge, Mass.: Harvard University Press, 1928); *Pharsalia: Dramatic Episodes of the Civil Wars,* translated by Robert Graves (Baltimore: Penguin, 1957); *Lucan's Civil War,* translated by P. F. Widdows (Bloomington: Indiana University Press, 1988); *Civil War,* translated by S. H. Braund (Oxford: Clarendon Press, 1992); *Pharsalia,* translated by Jane Wilson Joyce (Ithaca, N.Y.: Cornell University Press, 1993).

Commentaries: *M. Annaei Lucani Pharsalia,* edited by C. E. Haskins (London: G. Bell, 1887); *M. Annaei Lucani De bello civili liber primus,* edited by Paul LeJay (Paris: C. Klincksieck, 1894); *M. Annaei Lucani De bello civili liber I,* edited by R. J. Getty (Cambridge: Cambridge University Press, 1955); *Bellum civile liber primus,* edited by Pierre Wuilleumier and Henri Le Bonniec (Paris: Presses Universitaires de France, 1962); *M. Annaei Lucani De bello civili liber II,* edited by F. H. M. van Campen (Amsterdam: J. C. Gieben, 1991); *De bello civili Book II,* edited by Elaine Fantham (Cambridge: Cambridge University Press, 1992); *M. Annaei Lucani Bellum civile Book III,* edited by Vincent Hunink (Amsterdam: J. C. Gieben, 1992); *M. Annaei Lucani Belli civilis liber V,* edited by Pamela Barratt (Amsterdam: A. M. Hakkert, 1979); G. B. Conte, *Saggio di Commento a Lucano: Pharsalia VI, 118–260, L'Aristia di Sceva* (Pisa: Libreria Goliardica, 1974); *De bello civili liber VII,* edited by J. P. Postgate, revised by O. A. W. Dilke (Cambridge: Cambridge University Press, 1960); *Lucan Civil War VIII,* edited by Roland Mayer (Warminster, U.K.: Aris & Phillips, 1981); Manfred G. Schmidt, *Caesar und Cleopatra: Philologischer und historischer Kommentar zu Lucan 10.1–171* (Frankfurt am Main: Lang, 1986).

What is known of the short life of Marcus Annaeus Lucanus comes primarily from four sources: Tacitus's *Annals,* Statius's *Silvae* 2.7 (called *Genethliacon Lucani*), Suetonius's life of Lucan in his *De viris illustribus,* and a life *(Vita Lucani)* by the sixth-century grammarian Vacca. Lucan was born in the Spanish city of Corduba (modern Córdoba) in A.D. 39. The history of his birthplace gives evidence of the young Lucan's formative interests. M. Claudius Marcellus had established a Roman colony there in 169 (or 152) B.C. as a means of opening Roman colonization of the province. The high birth of many of its inhabitants gave the town its first colonial name, *Colonia Patricia* (Patrician Colony), and there are reports of locals writing poetry as early as 62 B.C. During the Civil War, which was the subject of Lucan's great poem, Julius Caesar established Corduba as his headquarters in 49 B.C., but Pompey seized it in 45 B.C. Caesar retook the town and sacked it later that year, killing more than twenty-two thousand men. After the ascendancy of Augustus, the city was settled by veterans and became as well known for the refinement and high birth of its citizens as it was for maintaining the richest intellectual and artistic life in Spain.

The Annaei were one of the distinguished families of Corduba. Lucius Annaeus Seneca (Seneca the Elder) had three sons: Marcus Annaeus Novatus, known as Gallio, the proconsul in Achaea who refused to judge Paul in Acts 18.12–17; Lucius Annaeus Seneca (Seneca the Younger), the philosopher and tragedian; and Marcus Annaeus Mela, a financier who married Acilia, the daughter of Acilius Lucanus, a distinguished orator of the city. Their son was given the cognomen of his maternal grandfather.

Both the elder and younger Senecas had moved to Rome to make their ways in the world, and in A.D. 40, shortly after Lucan's birth, Mela took his family there as well. Lucan was supposed to be put under the tutelage of his uncle, Seneca the Younger, but Seneca was in exile for most of the next decade, and by the time he returned in A.D. 49 Lucan had already become the student of another grammarian, possibly Quintus Rhemnius Fannius Palaemon. Beginning at about the age of twelve, Lucan was schooled for five years by a rhetorician, following the normal procedure, and then probably by the Stoic Lucius Annaeus Cornutus, perhaps a freedman of one of the Annaei, who was also the tutor of Persius, five years older than Lucan and, like Lucan, later to become a Stoic. Cornutus had written a monograph on Virgil's works and may well have enhanced Lucan's appreciation of the master. Lucan would have been assigned the composition of speeches either for a *controversia* (hypothetical trial) or speeches giving advice to a *suasoria* (an historical personage about to make a decisive step)—for example, Caesar about to cross the Rubicon. These speeches relied on grand rhetorical effects and *sententiae* (impressive summarizing statements) that Quintilian cites as a particular characteristic of Lucan's poetry. After a few years with Cornutus, Lucan studied for one year in Athens. He completed his education at approximately the age of twenty-one.

In his youth Lucan showed a remarkable productivity. He was no doubt encouraged by the active liter-

ary circle around Nero emulating the masters of the traditional genres: the great Stoic satirist Persius, who drew heavily upon the works of Horace; his uncle Seneca, whose tragedies imitated the Greek; and Calpurnius Siculus, who wrote his *Eclogues* in pale imitation of Virgil's. Lucan wrote poems on Orpheus, the underworld, and the fall of Troy; he also wrote epigrams, tragedies, declamations, and letters. He apparently began to write his poem on the civil war early in his career. All the while he pursued the career in the law that he had been trained for and studied the rules of rhetoric that could be used as efficaciously in the salons as in the courtrooms. Poetry at Rome was meant to be performed, not read, and the appreciation of rhetorical skill was high. Indeed, Lucan did not displease his audience. As Quintilian says (10.1.90), Lucan was "fiery and passionate and notable for his *sententiae* (opinions) and, to be honest, was more suited for imitating by orators than by poets."

Before long Lucan's literary abilities attracted the eye of the young (less than a year older than Lucan), popular emperor Nero, who was himself a student of Seneca the Younger. Seneca was part of the emperor's court and was soon called back from Athens by Nero in A.D. 59 to be present at court as one of the emperor's *cohors amicorum* (circle of friends). Nero fancied himself a complete artist and especially a literary man who sought the company of gifted poets and added them to his entourage, as he had Petronius, Seneca, and others. At the poetry competition for the new festival of the arts called the Neronia in A.D. 60, Lucan made a brilliant public debut by reciting his panegyric on Nero *(Laudes Neronis)*. Shortly thereafter Nero preferred upon Lucan the quaestorship and augural priesthood (with concomitant membership in the Senate) at least a year in advance of the legal age (twenty-five) for holding Senate membership. These appointments may well have had as much to do with Seneca as with Lucan, for the uncle was trying to distance himself from the increasingly erratic young emperor.

The poet and emperor likely enjoyed a cordial relationship for the next few years, but in A.D. 62 Seneca was forced out of politics, and Lucan may have left government at the same time. An alternative tradition holds that they entered a public poetry competition that Lucan won. Suetonius says that during one of Lucan's public readings Nero suddenly called a meeting of the Senate, depriving the poet of an audience and "freezing him out" *(nulla nisi refrigerandi sui causa)*. Angry and embittered, Lucan retired to what Juvenal (7.79–80) called Lucan's "marble gardens," where he may have realized that the only hope for advancement of his career as a poet was the death of the emperor.

Gaius Calpurnius Piso had been exiled by Caligula, who then forced Piso's wife to leave her husband and become the emperor's mistress in A.D. 40. The emperor then charged her with adultery. Under Caligula's successor Claudius, Piso became *consul suffectus* (substitute consul) and one of Rome's most popular men. Piso's pleadings on behalf of rich and poor made his political future bright, but his popularity made him suspect to Nero. As early as A.D. 62 Nero's agents suspected Piso as the emperor's behavior became more outrageous and embarrassing. In this same year Lucan may have begun work on *De bello civili* (The Civil War). On 19 June A.D. 64 a fire broke out near the Circus Maximus and raged for nine days, sparing only four of the eighteen regions of Rome. Nero was thought to have instigated the fire and to have paid more attention to reciting his poems than to curbing the fire; his supposed purpose was to confiscate nearly one hundred and twenty-five acres of previously private land in the center of Rome for an elaborate palace called the *Domus Aurea,* or Golden House. He publicly blamed Christians for the fire and burned many of them alive as punishment. This occasion may have been when Lucan wrote what Suetonius calls "an intemperate poem," perhaps *De incendio urbis* (On the Burning of the City, A.D. 64). Tacitus and others say that the vindictive Nero forbade the publication or recitation of Lucan's poetry (and also forbade Lucan from pursuing his legal practice). Nero's continued prosecution of real and supposed enemies, his erratic behavior, and particularly his confiscations so disturbed the upper classes (he remained popular with the masses) that some of them formed a conspiracy designed to murder Nero and establish Piso as emperor. The conspiracy was betrayed in A.D. 65, and most of the participants either committed suicide (just as did Piso and Lucan, whom Suetonius called the "standard bearer" of the insurgency) or were executed. Nero's paranoia only increased, and Seneca and Petronius soon came to the same end as Lucan.

Lucan's state of mind at this time seems clear from the concluding books of *The Civil War.* His dream of a doomed and weakened ideal republic of free and noble men (one may compare romanticized notions of the American antebellum South) became more and more an obsession with him. He was young and politically inexperienced, but authorities differ on his role in the conspiracy: Suetonius says that Lucan played a significant role in managing the conspiracy and that his own rashness led to the betrayal of the plot, while Vacca says Lucan was deceived by Piso. When Lucan and the others were betrayed, he pleaded for his life. Tacitus (*Annals* 15.57) compares the bravery of a freed slave-girl named Epicharis, who refused under terrible torture to tell what she knew, with Lucan, who, having

at first declined to inform on his coconspirators, once having been promised impunity, named all, including his mother, Acilia (she was not prosecuted). Nero nevertheless ordered Lucan to die. He wrote his father about some corrections to be made to his poem and then had his veins opened by a surgeon on 30 April A.D. 65. As he lay bleeding to death, Lucan recited his own lines about a soldier dying in the same manner, though for a nobler cause. When Mela tried to recover his son's property, he was also forced to commit suicide.

In part, the short meteoric life and hapless death of the young poet assured the survival of his poem. The poem has historical value, represents the longing for the old Republic so common among the patriotic intelligentsia of the period, and includes passages of rhetorical brilliance and poetic splendor. But from its first appearance *De bello civili* has been the subject of dispute and has had adherents every bit as virulent as its detractors.

There has been some dispute over the title. The poem was long known as the *Pharsalia* because Lucan refers to *Pharsalia nostra* at 9.985, and Statius at *Silvae* 2.7.66 calls the poem *Pharsalia bella.* But Petronius calls it a *belli civilis ingens opus* (huge work on the civil war, 118) and Vacca, along with the best manuscripts, refers to it as *De bello civili,* its common name today.

Lucan chose as his subject the decisive battle in the long series of wars that led to the establishment of the Roman Empire and the demise of the Roman Republic. That result is the reason this war was "worse than civil." (The battle that finally ended the century of civil strife at Rome was Octavian's defeat of Marcus Antonius and Cleopatra at Actium in 31 B.C.) The Republic, not a single man of legendary or heroic stature like Achilles or Odysseus, is the tragically doomed hero of this epic.

The poem begins with Caesar's crossing of the Rubicon in 49 B.C. and climaxes a year later with the Battle of Pharsalus in August of 48 B.C. and Pompey's death on 29 September. Lucan relied on the historical accounts of Livy, Asinius Pollio, and of course Caesar, whose *Civil War* breaks off at the point where Lucan's poem ends.

The Romans' taste for historical epic can be traced to their earliest literature. The Greek Choerilus of Samos (ca. 450 B.C.) is thought to have written the first historical epic, on the Persian Wars. Rhianos (third century B.C.) wrote epics on regional history. The best of the early Roman epics were Naevius's *Bellum Punicum,* on the Punic Wars, and Ennius's *Annales,* on the entire history of Rome from its founding to Ennius's own time. These poems were in dactylic hexameter and included epic similes and conventional scenes, such as councils of the gods discussing the mortals' fate. The bulk of this type of

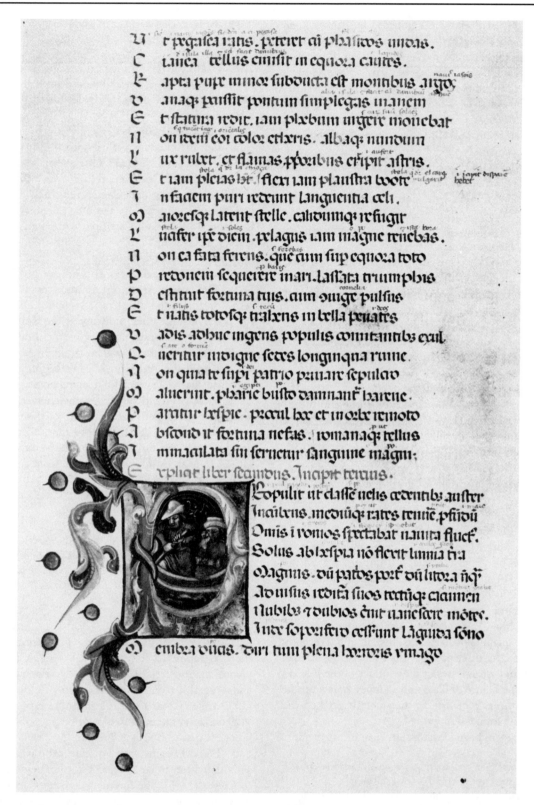

Illuminated page from a 1378 Italian manuscript for Lucan's De bello civili *(The Civil War), which begins with Caesar crossing the Rubicon in 49 B.C. and ends with Octavian's defeat of Marcus Antonius and Cleopatra in 31 B.C. (British Library)*

poetry written at Rome was composed by hacks, often hired by victorious generals to record their exploits in verse. In the generation of Catullus, Furius Bibaculus (*Bellum Gallicum*) and Cornelius Severus (*Carmen Regale*) continued the tradition. Even Cicero wrote two autobiographical epics, *De consulatu suo* (On His Own Consulship) and *De temporibus suis* (On His Own Times), notable even in his own times for self-serving bombast. Enough is known of some obscure later contemporaries of Virgil who wrote historical epics (now lost) on the Roman Civil War–Severus, Rabirius, Albinovanus Pedo, Sextilius Ena, and the author of the *Bellum Actiacum* (The War of Actium) among them–to see that Lucan was working in an active tradition when he chose recent history as his subject.

This tradition allowed writers of historical epic not to feel themselves bound to historical fact nor prohibited from the fantastic. Epic convention allowed Cicero to portray himself addressing a council of the Olympian gods called to deal with the threat of Catiline's insurrection. Lucan himself creates a totally fictitious meeting between Pompey and Cicero on the eve of the battle of Pharsalus, a battle that, Plutarch says (*Cicero* 29), Cicero was too ill to attend.

After Virgil, no one could (or successfully did) write national mythological epic like the *Aeneid*. While Ovid's prodigious gifts allowed him to write a grand mythological history of the universe up to the apotheosis of Augustus, most writers worked in the practical fields of history in order to glorify Augustus and his family or to feed the national hunger for historical narrative. Nor could the audience of Lucan's day take the traditional Olympian gods of epic with any measure of credibility. Virgil had single-handedly made the gods palatable in his Augustan epic, but Lucan assigned the governance of men's lives and the guidance of the destinies of nations not to divinities but to two Stoic conceptions, Fate and Fortune.

Nor could Lucan rely on a single hero to encompass all the qualities of an Aeneas. Instead, it has recently been argued, his three protagonists combine the various strengths and weaknesses of the founder of the Roman race, and the failure of Cato and Pompey points up the greed and cruelty of Caesar that have overtaken the Roman state founded in virtue by Aeneas.

The poem begins with a statement of the theme:

> Wars worse than civil we sing, waged on Emathia's plains;
> Justice given over to crime; a powerful people,
> its conquering sword-hand turned to strike its own vitals;
>
> kindred front lines; and, after tyranny's pact had shattered,
> all the stricken world's forces locked in a struggle,
> rivals in evil; standards charging belligerent fellow-

standards; dueling eagles, and javelin menacing javelin.

(1–7, Joyce)

Virgil's theme *arma virumque* (arms and the man) is replaced by *cognatas acies* (kindred front lines). Virgil had sung the furor of the gods; Lucan sings about the furor of citizens.

He castigates the citizens of Rome for their fratricidal fury in initiating such a war (8–32), then gives elaborate praise to Nero (33–66). The causes of the war are the deaths of Crassus and Julia, which inflamed the rivalry of Pompey and Caesar (98–157). The period was full of corruption by the time Caesar crossed the Rubicon (158–227) and captured Arminium (228–260). Caesar meets with allies, addresses his troops, and calls forth his troops from Gaul (261–465). The Senate, terrified at his approach, flees as prodigies bode ill (466–583). The priest Arruns performs rites that begin a series of portended disasters (584–695). The action of the book begins rather suddenly at the Rubicon in 83 B.C. after a rambling analysis of the causes–not in medias res as had the *Aeneid*, but at the beginning of the war itself, at the Rubicon. Lucan's beginning has not been considered a successful opening book.

Book 2 is divided between the characters of Cato and Caesar. The gods are chastised for permitting man to know the future (1–15). All of Rome is terrified (16–66), just as it was during the wars of Marius and Sulla (16–233). Marcus Junius Brutus and Cato confer (234–325) while Marcia, Cato's former wife, returns to him and they are remarried (326–379). Cato's character is memorably described at 380–391:

> This was the manner, this the unshakeable creed
> of stern Cato–to seek the mean and fix a limit,
> to respect Natural Order and repay his land with his life,
> to believe he was born not to serve himself, but the whole world.

(2.380–383, Joyce)

Following Pompey's withdrawal to Capua, Lucan describes the geography of Italy (392–438), and Caesar campaigns in northern Italy (439–525). Pompey tries to encourage his troops but retreats to Brundisium (526–627), while Caesar's son is sent to the East (628–649). When Caesar attempts to block Pompey (650–679), the latter escapes to Epirus (680–736).

Book 3 begins with Pompey's late wife and Caesar's daughter, Julia, appearing to Pompey on his way to Epirus (1–45). She forecasts disaster. Caesar returns to Rome while sending some of his troops to Sicily and Sardinia (45–98). Caesar seizes the public treasury (99–168), and Pompey's allies (169–297), largely from the East, move to meet Caesar's, who are besieging Massilia (Marseilles) (298–398). Caesar cuts down the Druids' grove (399–452) and moves to Spain, while his troops unsuccessfully attack Massilia (453–508). Decimus Brutus wages a successful naval battle against Caesar's ships (509–762).

Book 4 describes the contest in Spain. Caesar's troops face floods and famine but eventually put Pompey's forces to flight (1–156). Soldiers of both sides converse in a friendly manner (157–204) until Marcus Petreius, governor of Hither Spain, massacres those of Caesar's soldiers who have harmlessly entered the camp (205–253). Caesar prevents the Pompeians from reaching water, and Afranius surrenders (254–401). Antonius, in Illyria, makes his escape while a military tribune, Gaius Vulteius Capito, holds off the Pompeians with signal bravery, then commits suicide with his men rather than be captured (402–580). In Africa, Gaius Scribonius Curio defeats Varus (581–714) but is then surprised by Juba (715–792) and is killed (793–824). Lucan's encomium of Curio points out the theme of his poem:

> Never did Rome produce
>   a citizen of such promise,
> nor one to whom her laws owed more,
>   while he steered right.
> but his was the ruinous age
>   that worked the city's downfall,
> when Ambition and Luxury
>   and Wealth with its power to corrupt
> had swept his wavering purpose away
>   On a treacherous tide.
>
> (4.812–821, Joyce)

Book 5 turns to the Senate, meeting in exile in Epirus (1–14) on the first of January 48 B.C. Lentulus moves that command be given to Pompey, and the allies are rewarded (15–64). One senator, Appius, goes to Delphi to consult the oracle of Apollo, but after coaxing the old Sibyl, he receives an ambiguous answer (65–236). Caesar's troops briefly mutiny but are put down (237–373). Caesar gathers a fleet, returns to Rome, becomes dictator, sails to Epirus, and sets up his camp near Pompey's (374–475). Crossing to Epirus from Brundisium in a small boat on a treacherously stormy night, Caesar runs afoul of a storm as menacing as that faced by Aeneas in the *Aeneid* (476–677). The soldiers berate Caesar for his recklessness, and Antonius follows in the clear day with the remaining troops (678–721). Pompey meanwhile sends his wife to the safety of Lesbos, and the book closes with a touching description of Cornelia's first night without her husband (722–815).

Book 6 opens with a description of Pompey's siege of Dyrrachium in northern Greece (1–332). Scaeva is Caesar's brave but foolhardy centurion, who blocks Pompey's attacks on the outskirts of the encampment. Pompey wins the battle despite Scaeva's efforts, but Pompey allows Caesar to escape to Thessaly. Thessaly, a region known for its witches, whom Pompey consults (413–506), is described at length (333–412). The most awful of the witches is Erictho, whom Pompey's son Sextus consults, as Appius had consulted Apollo in book 5 (507–623). Erictho revives a dead soldier, who responds to her questions and dies again (624–830). The ending of this book bears many parallels with the ending of book 6 of the *Aeneid,* including a "parade of heroes" at lines 777–792.

Book 7 is the most significant of the poem, for it includes the decisive battle itself. Like book 3, this one opens with Pompey dreaming, this time of a day in the theater he built in Rome in 55 B.C. (1–44). At daybreak the troops, eager for battle (45–67), are represented by Cicero, who charges that Pompey is delaying the attack (68–85). Pompey reluctantly agrees to join battle (85–150). This scene is historical fiction: Cicero was not actually present at the battle. Lucan may well have intended Cicero to stand for the frenzied Republican whose better judgment was clouded by his eagerness to restore the old government. Pompey's troops arm themselves, arrange their battle lines, and observe the prodigies (150–234). On the other side, Caesar addresses his troops in eager anticipation of victory (235–336). Pompey addresses his troops (337–384), and the battle is begun.

The central section of the book is not the battle itself but Lucan's reflections on the outcome of the battle (385–459). Lucan then describes, almost reluctantly (at 552 ff. he declares himself unwilling to complete the story), the battle itself and Pompey's defeat (460–585). He eulogizes the Republican heroes, Marcus Brutus (585–596) and Domitius (597–616), and then mourns the outcome of the battle (617–646).

The final section of the book includes another contrast of Pompey and Caesar (647–728). Pompey flees the field, thinking it will save lives, while Caesar takes his morning meal on the field of battle, in Pompey's camp, delighting in the bodies being eaten by scavenging birds and animals. Then follows a short address on the guilt of Thessaly for being chosen by the gods to host such a slaughter. The book concludes with a reminiscence of Virgil's *Georgics* 1.493–497, in which a farmer turns up rusted implements of war with his plough. In Lucan's version, the poet invokes the ability of the land to absorb the blood and carnage and thus absolve the combatants of their personal and national guilt (847–872).

Book 8 describes the flight and death of Pompey. Having left the field in a deliberate fashion, Pompey speaks to his wife in a frenzy, and she responds (1–

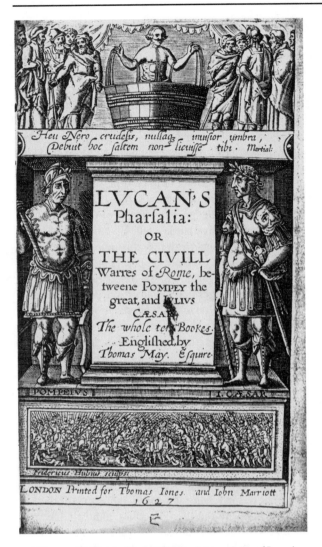

Title page for Thomas May's 1627 English translation of Lucan's
Pharsalia (courtesy of Special Collections, Thomas
Cooper Library, University of South Carolina)

by the quaestor Cordus, a historical scene referred to by Virgil at *Aeneid* 2.506–558 (712–823). The book concludes with an address to Egypt (823–872).

With the end of book 8, the central action of the poem concludes. Book 9, the longest book, is clearly the beginning of a third (and unfinished) phase of the poem. The central figure is Marcus Porcius Cato Uticensis (95 B.C.–A.D. 46), though his activity had little impact on the war. The book begins with a description of Pompey's soul flying to the kingdom of Pure Light and then returning to earth to inhabit the souls of Brutus and Cato, who must now assume leadership of the Republicans (1–18). Cato then flees to Africa, joined by Pompey's widow, Cornelia (19–119). Pompey's sons mourn him at a memorial service (120–185), and Cato eulogizes him in restrained Stoic manner (186–217). After calming a mutiny (217–293) comparable to the mutiny of Caesar's troops in 5.237–373, Cato sails to Africa (294–410) and encounters a storm in the Gulf of Sidra, the description of which is a rhetorical tour de force of paradox. In Libya (411–497) all are overcome by thirst on the march to Numidia, as a land storm the equal of the sea storm engulfs the men (445–492). Cato refuses to drink (498–510). At the Temple of Jupiter Ammon in an oasis, Cato refuses to consult the oracle (511–586), and they continue to cross the desert (587–618), though many are killed by serpents (619–838), which are fully described in a lengthy catalogue. Though the troops are unhappy (839–941), they finally arrive in Leptis on the African coast, guided by the helpful tribe of Psylli, comparable to Homer's Phaeacians (942–949).

The scene now shifts to the Troas in Asia Minor, where Caesar examines the site in a clearly satirical passage, echoing the *Aeneid* (Aeneas's arrival in Carthage in book 1 and his tour of Italy in book 8), in which Caesar ironically promises to rebuild Troy even as he is, in Lucan's mind, destroying Rome. Caesar proceeds to Egypt in pursuit of Pompey, is shown Pompey's head on his arrival, and castigates the Egyptians for murdering him (950–1108).

In book 10 Caesar visits the grave of Alexander (1–52), a figure he sees as his predecessor in conquest as at the end of book 9 he saw the Trojans as his familial ancestors. Ptolemy's sister, Cleopatra, fearing prosecution for complicity, puts herself under Caesar's protection and entertains him at an elaborate banquet reminiscent of the banquet Dido gave Aeneas (53–171). Caesar is told of the origins of the Nile by Acoreus, Ptolemy's good adviser (172–331). Pothinus and Ptolemy's palace prefect Achillas now attack Caesar, who, having been at Cleopatra's court, is now as weak and indecisive as Aeneas had been at Dido's court. The troops are assembled, and Caesar is left on a narrow

108). He decides against going to Mitylene and instead leaves Lesbos with her for Phaselis, where he will ask the Parthians for help (202–325). Lentulus and the Republicans oppose Pompey's plan and instead sail the fleet to Egypt (325–471).

The second section is set in Egypt in King Ptolemy's council. Pothinus, one of Ptolemy's advisers, suggests that Ptolemy be assassinated (472–540). Lucan addresses Egypt and Ptolemy (541–560) and then begins the slow account of Pompey's death. Having been led to a small boat, Pompey is killed by Lucius Septimius, formerly a tribune under Pompey, now a mercenary (560–636). Cornelia grieves (637–662); Pompey's head is cut off and preserved (663–691); and Lucan laments Pompey's death (692–711). Pompey's headless corpse is unceremoniously buried on the shore

bridge between the island of Pharos and the mainland (332–503). Here the poem suddenly ends.

In his *Satyricon,* Petronius gives a mock version of Lucan's poem, saying in his preface that history is not the stuff of poetry (*non enim res gestae versibus comprehendendae sunt,* 118), for it is the paradox of historical epic that while the poet must create fictional characters and contexts, historians must record accurate fact. Since most of his contemporary readers would have known most of the events already, Lucan tends to subordinate the narrative accounts to rhetorical grandiloquence and moral sermonizing. When he wants to, he feels free to invent situations (Cicero at Pharsalus) and to conflate characters (Cordus is an amalgam; Pompey was in fact buried by two men, one of his freedman and a passing soldier) to highlight his theme of the world turned upside down and against itself. This invention is quite apart from his considerable number of geographical errors, such as his confusion of Phillipi and Pharsalus, the two Mount Idas in Phrygia and Crete (4.322), and Indians and Ethiopians (9.517–518, 10.291–293), errors that nevertheless do not detract from the force of the descriptions. The geography of Africa is hopelessly confused, but the mistakes do not damage the description of the long march and Cato's leadership.

Vacca relates that Lucan published only books 1–3 in his lifetime. It is arguable that Lucan was aiming at a twelve-book poem centered on three chief figures—Caesar (books 1–4), Pompey (5–8), and Cato (9–12). He may have intended to continue the poem to the assassination of Caesar, or, to judge by the scope and pace of the poem, he may have intended two more books to carry out the events through the suicide of Cato. That he would have carried the poem to the death of Caesar, however, is doubtful.

No one familiar with classical literature can miss the references to Virgil in the poem. Virgil had first crystallized the agony of the civil wars in the *Georgics,* 1.466–514. Since this passage did not occur in Virgil's epic, it was easier for Lucan to use it in his epic. Lucan alludes to many other famous passages. For example, the description of Pompey as an oak tree felled by Caesar as lightning (2.29–57) recalls the description of the stout oak of the vineyard in the *Georgics* (2.288–297) and the spark that sets trees afire in 2.303–311, or the simile of Aeneas as a stout oak buffeted by the tirades of Dido in the *Aeneid* 4.437–449. The sick horse in 4.754–758 recalls the beasts dying of plague at the end of *Georgics* 3. In most cases Lucan reverses Virgil's dark optimism with his own pessimism: the Fate and Fortune that had been instrumental in establishing the Roman Empire were now causing its destruction; Pompey's retreat from Italy to Africa is the opposite of Aeneas's journey; that which was virtue in Virgil's day is now a

crime (1.2. 167–168; 6.147–148). Both Virgil and Lucan employ digressions, geographical set pieces, and addresses to the reader, but Lucan employs all these to a far greater extent than his predecessor. Virgil's line was part of a symphony of metrical effects and rhythms; Lucan's line is monotonous and free of Virgil's musical variety, the better to imitate prose oratorical delivery in his rhetorical passages and to express his themes in the prose language of philosophy. His poem employs descriptions Virgil would shudder at—the necrophiliac Erictho, for one (6.564–569), in a grotesque scene drawn from the consultation of the Sibyl in *Aeneid* 6. Over and over Lucan employs a prose word such as *cadaver* for the more normal *corpus,* or *mors* for *letum.* Virgil's epic is a continuous narrative, but Lucan's is episodic; Virgil treats one human hero, Lucan, three, though the real hero, as mentioned above, may be seen as the Republic. In his Underworld, Virgil depicts the heroes of future Rome, while Lucan mentions only the scoundrels. But the chief differences come from what was not available to Lucan: living gods and authentic heroes.

The machinery of Olympus Virgil used to embody the contrary forces of nature and fortune at work in his poem was transformed by Lucan. The absence of any popular belief or state religion in Lucan's age was a major literary and ethical problem. The gods were not only colorful but also highly useful parts of the epic apparatus. Virgil could have his Bronze Age characters take the gods and their advice seriously even though his audience could only take the gods as personifications of aspects of human behavior or as mere literary conventions. But by Lucan's day the situation was even worse. So diminished was the stature of the old gods by the Julio-Claudian emperors' becoming gods themselves (1.33–66) that reasonable men could not take the Olympians seriously (as Cato disregards Jupiter Ammon in book 9). Instead, the gods that are trusted are not Roman (Apollo's shrine at Delphi is shut down in book 5; Jupiter Ammon is ignored as mere superstition in book 9) but eastern gods, or a witch (especially Erictho in 6). Lesser characters such as Appius, Sextus, and Labienus may look to the useful oracles (for example, 5.64–236; 9.511–586), but only as one would consult a fortune-teller at a fair, not as a true believer at a shrine. Even the grotesque necromancy of 6.413–830 is a means of revealing information that another poet would have had revealed by gods. In addition, the noticeable absence or deafening silence of the gods implies that Olympus, if it exists, has already decided the destiny of the Republic.

The absence of belief in the gods means that a source of revelation of the future or the meaning of the past is absent as well. The typical revelations that gods

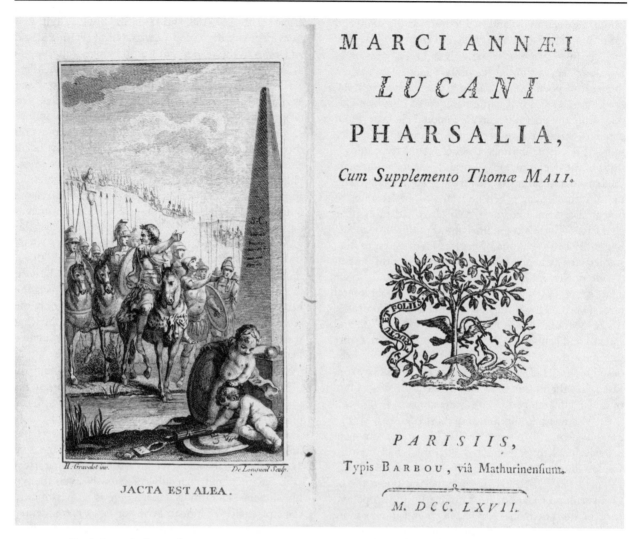

MARCI ANNÆI

LUCANI

PHARSALIA,

Cum Supplemento Thomæ MAII.

PARISIIS,

Typis BARBOU, viâ Mathurinenſium.

M. DCC. LXVII.

JACTA EST ALEA.

Frontispiece and title page for the 1767 Paris edition of Lucan's Pharsalia *(courtesy of the Lilly Library, Indiana University)*

make to humans in previous epics (Athena to Odysseus, Venus to Aeneas) are in Lucan's epic accomplished to a greater extent than in previous epics—not only by the prophecies and oracles mentioned previously but also by dreams and portents. Before he crosses the Rubicon, Caesar envisions Rome as a woman in mourning (1.185–203). Julia, Pompey's first wife, appears on the funeral pyre to denounce Pompey's marriage to Cornelia (3.8–35). At 7.7–19 Pompey dreams of his past successes, an indication that he is no longer capable of success. At 7.760–786 Caesar and his troops dream of the battle to come and the fellow citizens they will kill.

The presence of the gods normally raises the tone of an epic; without them Lucan relied on allusion to other epics, geographical digression, and oratorical bombast to lift the historical narrative to epic propor-

tions. One technique is to treat remote lands as characters in themselves and to address them at length as such. Epics always involved remote lands, and by characterizing and addressing Thessaly in book 6 and Libya in book 9, Lucan adds a perspective and weight to his poem. The revolt in the underworld as Elysians fight Tartareans at 6.777–802 gives the epic scope. Scientific digression is used to impressive effect, particularly in the catalogue of Libyan snakes at 9.619–937, which employs anthropology, mythology, and natural history. Caesar's tour of Troy at 9.950–979 employs broad topographical and historical knowledge leavened by political satire.

But Lucan needed something to take the deterministic roles of the gods in his poem, and in the place of the outworn religion, which offered no spiritual fulfillment for man, Lucan offers Stoicism as the means to a richer life. The poem explores the meanings of courage, patriotism, and leadership. In line with Stoic doctrine, Lucan proclaims one presiding beneficent deity (9.578)–a universal soul that rules the world by means of fate (1.33–34), a universe that was created from fire, the source of all existence (2.7), and will end (1.72–80). Lucan calls *fatum* (Fate) the force that destroyed the Republic and established the Empire. The same force had vouchsafed the escape of the Aeneadae from Troy and overseen the founding of Rome in the first place. The force that brings victory, *fortuna* (Fortune), is entirely on the side of Caesar. It had once been with Pompey but had since abandoned him (2.699). Fate is inexorable; Fortune is fickle; but regardless of one's fate, man himself is responsible for his actions and for maintaining his *fortuna*. The best Stoic, Cato, is to Lucan a god (*factura deum es,* 9.604). A sense of duty and participation in civic affairs marks the Roman Stoic, and the ethos of the poet leads to the conclusion that Lucan joined the forces of the conspirator Piso just as Cato joined Pompey.

Lucan did not have Virgil's gods available to him, and he did not have Virgil's great hero either. Instead, some scholars have recently argued that Lucan crafted his three protagonists–Caesar, Pompey, and Cato–to represent separate aspects of the Trojan prince Aeneas. Caesar represents Aeneas's warrior ambition; Pompey, his self-doubt; and Cato, his suppression of self for the good of the state. A combination of these qualities could yield a singular hero, but no one in Lucan's poem is of heroic stature because, as S. H. Braund points out, "in civil war there can be no heroes."

Caesar seems the character most suited to epic. He is a pure warrior–intelligent as Odysseus, competent as Hector, fearsome as Achilles. Like Aeneas, he is intent on founding a new Rome after the destruction of the old Republic just as Aeneas founded a new Troy after the destruction of the old Troy.

Pompey is the aging warrior who no longer has the qualities of body or mind to save the Republic. Lucan glorifies Pompey for what he had been rather than for what he was at Pharsalus. At this point he cannot make decisions; he doubts himself; and he is covered by the aura of doom throughout. Notable, however, is Pompey's warm and happy marriage to Cornelia, set in contrast to Caesar's loveless unions made for political advantage.

Cato is a preeminent Stoic wise man who subsumes his personal ambition for the good of the state. He seems not to be a fully fleshed-out human being but more of a philosophical construct. Even his remarriage to his wife Marcia in book 2 is dispassionate and austere.

If the goodness of the model citizen and philosopher Cato is set off by the grasping, immoral aristocrat

Caesar, then the bad emperor Nero has no positive counterpart except, perhaps, his younger self. Nevertheless, in the prologue he appears as almost a god on earth; he assumes Apollo's role as the overlord of poetry. Lucan says, "if the Fates have found no other way for Nero's advent . . . until after / the wars of the savage Earth-born Giants– / then, O Gods above, / we make no further complaint" (1.33–39). So lavish is Lucan in his praise of the emperor-as-Muse that the subsequent references can only be explained by two causes: an assumption that books 1–3 were published while its author was still on good terms with Nero (in 62 B.C.), or the literary convention of apotheosizing leaders that is observable from Virgil and Horace on. If the prohibition on publication of Lucan's poem also prevented revision of the already-published books, then that is a possible reason for the different approach to Nero in books 4–10. Nero's great-great-grandfather Lucius Domitius Ahenobarbus is portrayed at Corfinum (2.478–525) as a noble opponent of Caesar, who had traitorously betrayed his own men. Ahenobarbus led a wing of Pompey's troops at Pharsalus and cursed Caesar with his dying breath. Caesar's tour of Troy in book 9 may reflect Nero's patronage of the Ilians (Trojans) before he became emperor. The young Ptolemy is obviously a parallel to the young Nero, with his good adviser (Acoreus to Nero's Seneca) and his bad adviser (Pothinus to Nero's Tigellinus). Lucan's description of Cleopatra's banquet hall at 10.104–171 may recall the Domus Aurea, begun in A.D. 64.

Writers other than Virgil also influenced Lucan. Chief among them are Manilius, from whom he seems to have acquired many stylistic traits (for example, the use of participles such as *auctus, mixtura,* or *ductus*) as well as his recurrent belief in the role of the planets in determining fate. Seneca's *Naturales Quaestiones* may have sparked Lucan's love of description, as for instance, in the digression on Libyan snakes.

Lucan's style, in contrast to Virgil's, was as innovative and astounding as his subject matter and theme. Petronius, a friend at court and admirer of Lucan, nevertheless thought the poem excessively innovative and stylistically tortuous. Petronius's character Eumolpus recites his own 295-line treatment of the topic in a simpler, more traditional tone (*Satyricon* 119–124). In a famous statement in his handbook on rhetoric Quintilian declared that Lucan was *magis oratoribus quam poetis imitandus* (of more use to orators than poets). Tacitus's *Annals* is a main source for the Pisonian conspiracy, but in another work, the *Dialogus de oratoribus,* Tacitus arranges a debate on Lucan's merits that the opposition wins. Martial says that Lucan cannot be considered a poet because he so violated the conventions of poetry. Statius (and perhaps Martial) seems to have observed

Lucan's birthday and been friends with his widow, Polla Argentaria. Statius even composed a poem to Polla, detailing many facts of Lucan's life, and his *Thebaid*, like the *Punica* of Silius Italicus and the *Argonautica* of Valerius Flaccus, owes much to the rhetorical skill at the core of the poem but does not share Lucan's dangerous political views.

Lucan was esteemed long after the Silver Age concluded. Claudian and Prudentius wrote of him admiringly. In the next century Vacca wrote Lucan's biography. Dante lists Lucan along with Homer, Virgil, and Ovid among the sublime pagan poets of the First Circle of the *Inferno*. Among the many European translations of the post-Renaissance, Christopher Marlowe's version of book 1 (1600) is supreme. Nicholas Rowe's translation (1718), called by Samuel Johnson "one of the greatest productions of English poetry," was for a long time the only complete one. The Romantics, with their love of personal freedom and iconoclastic style, warmed to Lucan. Percy Bysshe Shelley professed to prefer *The Civil War* to the *Aeneid*. He lists Lucan with Chatterton and Sidney as poets who died young (*Adonais* 45). When Shelley's wife, Mary Wollstonecraft, was writing *Frankenstein,* she may have thought of the scene of Erictho reviving the dead soldier in book 6.

Politics and literature may never have been so closely united in one ancient author as they are in Lucan. The great gifts of rhetorical ease, verbal dexterity, and generic innovation combined with themes of Stoic patriotism, virtue, and leadership give an endlessly romantic appeal to Lucan's unfinished poem just as Lucan's unfinished life appeals romantically. The promise of what might have been, for Rome and its literature, had Lucan and his kind survived is almost as entrancing as what was.

Bibliography and Concordance:

Roy J. Deferrari, Sister Maria Walburg Fanning, and Sister Anne Stanislaus Sullivan, eds., *A Concordance of Lucan* (Washington: Catholic University of America Press, 1940);

Werner Rutz, "Lucan 1964–1983," *Lustrum,* 26 (1984): 103–203.

References:

Frederick Ahl, *Lucan: An Introduction* (Ithaca, N.Y.: Cornell University Press, 1976);

R. T. Bruère, "The Scope of Lucan's Historical Epic," *Classical Philology,* 45 (1950): 217–235;

Erich Burck and Werner Rutz, "Die *Pharsalia* Lucans," in *Das römische Epos,* edited by Burck (Darmstadt: Wissenschaftsliche Buchgesellschaft, 1979);

B. Dick, "*Fatum* and *Fortuna* in Lucan's *Bellum Civile,*" *Classical Philology,* 62 (1967): 235–242;

O. A. W. Dilke, "Lucan and English Literature," in *Neronians and Flavians: Silver Latin,* edited by D. R. Dudley (London: Routledge & Kegan Paul, 1972), pp. 83–112;

Dilke, "Lucan and Virgil," *Proceedings of the Virgil Society,* 8 (1968–1969): 1–12;

O. S. Due, "An Essay on Lucan," *Classica et Mediaevalia,* 23 (1962): 68–132;

Marcel Durry, ed., *Lucain* (Geneva: Fondation Hardt, 1968);

Miriam T. Griffin, *Nero: The End of a Dynasty* (London: Batsford, 1984);

J. G. W. Henderson, "Lucan: The Word at War," in *The Imperial Muse: Ramus Essays on Roman Literature of the Empire,* 2 volumes, edited by A. J. Boyle (Berwick, Australia: Aureal Publications, 1988), pp. 122–164;

Vivian L. Holliday, *Pompey in Caesar's Correspondence and Lucan's Civil War* (The Hague: Mouton, 1969);

W. R. Johnson, *Momentary Monsters: Lucan and His Heroes* (Ithaca, N.Y.: Cornell University Press, 1987);

Michael Lapidge, "Lucan's Imagery of Cosmic Dissolution," *Hermes,* 107 (1979): 344–370;

B. M. Marti, "Lucan's Narrative Techniques," *Latomus,* 30 (1975): 74–90;

C. A. Martindale, "Paradox, Hyperbole, and Literary Novelty in Lucan's *De bello civili,*" *Bulletin of the Institute for Classical Studies,* 23 (1976): 45–72;

Martindale, "The Politician Lucan," *Greece and Rome,* 31 (1984): 64–79;

Jamie Masters, *Poetry and Civil War in Lucan's De Bello Civili* (Cambridge: Cambridge University Press, 1992);

M. P. O. Morford, *The Poet Lucan* (Oxford: Blackwell, 1967);

Rutz, ed., *Lucan* (Darmstadt: Wissenschaftsliche Buchgesellschaft, 1970);

Lynette Thompson and Bruère, "Lucan's Use of Vergilian Reminiscence," *Classical Philology,* 63 (1968): 1–21.

Lucilius

(ca. 180 B.C. – 102/101 B.C.)

W. Jeffrey Tatum
Florida State University

WORK–FRAGMENTARY: *Saturarum Libri* (Satires).

Editio princeps: *C. Lucili . . . Satyrarum quae supersunt reliquiae,* edited by Johan van der Does (Leiden: Plantiniana F. Raphelengij, 1597).

Standard editions and commentaries: *C. Lucilii Carminum Reliquae,* 2 volumes, edited by Friedrich Marx (Leipzig: Teubner, 1904–1905); *Lucilio e i suoi frammenti,* edited by Ettore Bolisani (Padua: Del Messaggero, 1932); *C. Lucilii Saturarum reliquiae,* edited by Nicola Terzaghi, third edition, revised by Italo Mariotti (Florence: Le Monnier, 1966); *C. Lucilius Satiren,* 2 volumes, edited by Werner Krenkel (Leiden: Brill, 1970); *Satires,* 3 volumes, edited and translated by François Charpin (Paris: Les Belles Lettres, 1978–1979).

Translation in English: *Remains of Old Latin,* volume 3, edited and translated by R. H. Warmington, Loeb Classical Library (Cambridge, Mass.: Harvard University Press, 1938).

Gaius Lucilius was, if not the inventor of Roman satire, certainly its founder as an important literary genre. Later satirical writers, Horace, most significantly, looked back specifically to Lucilius as an inspiration and as an object of emulation. All subsequent poets, moreover, were influenced by Lucilius's success in composing ostensibly autobiographical poetry and in his capacity for developing a literary personality that could serve as the locus for an examination, sometimes serious and sometimes playful, of aesthetic, literary, intellectual, and social issues.

Lucilius descended from a rich Italian family whose seat was at Suessa Aurunca, which lay on the edge of Campania. He was probably born in 180 B.C., though 169/168 B.C. remains a possibility. His brother, Manius Lucilius, was a Roman senator, and his father may also have held senatorial rank. The family prospered well enough to retain its station: a niece of Lucilius was married to the flamboyant Pompeius Strabo and was the mother of Pompey the Great. Lucilius himself eschewed political office and thus remained a member of the equestrian order. He held estates in Campania and Sicily, and he possessed a splendid house in Rome. The extant fragments of his poems do not state explicitly that he was a Roman citizen or that he married, but he probably was the former. Lucilius's status is important: he was by no means a noble or grandee, but he was nevertheless a privileged aristocrat to whom complete *libertas* (freedom of speech and action) was nothing short of an entitlement. Typical of his class, he did not extend such liberties to lesser men: he brought an unsuccessful lawsuit against an actor (or playwright) who had attacked him on the stage.

Lucilius served as an officer in the Numantine War (134–133 B.C.) under the command of Scipio Aemilianus, with whom he established a profound and lasting friendship. As a friend of Scipio, Lucilius was familiar with such men as Gaius Laelius, Terence, the Greek polymath Panaetius, and the historian Polybius—all members of what has come to be known, rather misleadingly, as the Scipionic Circle. Whatever the value of that designation, Scipio, Laelius, and Lucilius were certainly men conspicuous for their carefully measured philhellenism. If Lucilius did not actually travel to Athens, his name was nonetheless known in philosophical circles there, since the skeptic Clitomachus, who was the head of the Academy in Athens, dedicated one of his works to Lucilius.

The date of Lucilius's birth is a subject of controversy. According to Jerome, Lucilius died in Naples in 102/101 B.C. at the age of forty-six and was honored with a public funeral. These data, however, render Lucilius improbably (though not impossibly) young to have participated in the Numantine War. (Another common objection is that these data make Horace's reference to Lucilius at *Satires* 2.1.34 as a *senex,* an old man, seem strange, but since in Latin a man in his forties could quite naturally be so described, this point is best brushed aside.) One solution has been to emend Jerome's XLVI to LXVI, thereby dating Lucilius's birth to 169/168 B.C. Another possibility, however, and the more commonly accepted one, is that Jerome has simply confused the consuls of 180 B.C. with the consuls of 148 B.C. (whose names were similar), making this mistake the source of the problem in his account.

"Satire," insisted Quintilian, "is an exclusively Roman genre" (*Inst.* 10.1.93). The claim is generally allowed, though the origins of *satura* were already obscure in antiquity. The late grammarian Diomedes (fourth century A.D.), no doubt relying on much earlier sources, derived *satura* (which he, like others, gives as *satyra*) from the Greek word *satyr,* "because ridiculous and shameful things are said in this brand of poetry, just as ridiculous and shameful things are said and done by satyrs" (H. Keil, *Grammatici Latini* 1.485). In other words, Diomedes sought to connect satire with the Greek satyr play. Serious difficulties hamper this proposition, but Livy in *Ab urbe condita libri* (7.2.4–10) makes another attempt to link the original satire to drama, in that instance a subliterary dramatic form that exhibited music and lyrics but no plot. Diomedes' second explanation for the term remains the commonly accepted one: the expression *satura* is an adjective meaning "mixed," understood in this literary usage to be applied to some unexpressed (feminine) noun; its sense can be inferred from such phrases as *lanx satura,* a dish filled with many different firstfruits that was offered to the gods, or *lex satura,* an omnibus act of legislation that included separate and unrelated provisions (the examples are Diomedes'). Thus, a *satura* is a medley, a poetic hodgepodge. Roman satire is certainly characterized by its mixture of meters, topics, and tones, but this explanation of the significance of the term hardly helps in determining the origins of the genre.

Naevius may have written satire, if the attribution recorded in Festus (late second century A.D.) of a single quotation is accurate (it reads: *Naevius in Satyra*). Ennius certainly composed four or six books called *Saturae.* They included miscellaneous poems in a variety of meters, mostly in iambic-trochaic meters and in diction suggesting comedy (hence, perhaps, the habit of mind, established early on, of connecting satire to drama) and dealing with a diverse range of topics. Autobiographical moments emerge from the fragments, as do moralizing and comic passages. Ennius's nephew Pacuvius also composed *saturae,* but nothing is known of them. It has reasonably been proposed that one should seek the impetus to Ennius's creation, though not his actual models, in Hellenistic collections such as the *Chreiai* (Anecdotes) of Machon (third century B.C.), the *Silloi* (Lampoons) of Timon of Phlius (third century B.C.), or the *Iamboi* of Callimachus. When Varro turned to the writing of satire, he looked through Lucilius and Ennius to Menippus of Gadara (third century B.C.), whose compositions were a mixture of poetry and prose. (Quintilian, who distinguished the Menippean satire of Varro from that of Lucilius and Horace, identified Ennius and not Menippus as Varro's model.) How Roman one should ultimately deem satire, then, is a matter of semantics. The Roman quality of Lucilian satire, however, despite the obvious Greek influences (and the presence of actual Greek) and despite its highly fragmentary state of preservation, is undeniable. And it was to Lucilius, not to Ennius or Pacuvius, that Horace looked as his chief predecessor.

Of the totality of Lucilius's writings, only approximately thirteen hundred verses survive. They are ordinarily cited in reference to an edition of Lucilius's works in thirty books, said to have been assembled by the grammarian Valerius Cato in the first century B.C. This edition arranged the books by meter. Books 1–21 were in dactylic hexameter, books 22–25 were (probably) in elegiac couplets, and books 26–30 were mostly in iambic-trochaic meters. But this sequence did not reflect the original order either of composition or of publication. Lucilius first published five books of satires (corresponding to books 26–30 in the later collection), apparently arranged in chronological order, to which he added as a preface an important programmatic poem, which became the model for Horace's *Satires* 2.1. (Because this programmatic poem refers to the activities of tax farmers in Asia, the publication of this first collection was once dated to sometime after 123 B.C. It is now known that tax farmers were active in Asia before that time, a fact that means the collection could have been published as early 129 B.C. This point is perhaps minor, but it is one that is nearly always overlooked in literary surveys.) In his programmatic opening, Lucilius described his ideal reader (one who should be neither too much nor too little learned) and put forward a strong assertion of his own poetic identity, in which he rejected, in favor of remaining the Lucilius of the poems that followed, the highly profitable and distinguished career of a *publicanus* (an executive in a corporation established in order to collect taxes in Roman provinces; the *publicani* were enormously influential equestrians). Already one discerns the significance of the discrepancy in status between Lucilius and his literary predecessors in Rome, who were foreigners or men of humble status who established themselves solely on the basis of what they wrote. For Lucilius, poetic composition is a choice, an assertion of the freedom and the leisure that is the peculiar property of the aristocrat. Although his poems ranged widely in their topics, the constant subject was the literary persona of their author—a complex, informed, Roman personality capable of criticism, of condescension, of ridicule, and of comic self-examination. Little wonder that Horace could write that "Lucilius used to entrust his secrets to

C. LVCILII

RELIQVIÆ,

quæ supersunt ex incerto

SATYRARVM LIBRO.

I. VIRTVS (*Albine*) *est, pretium persoluere verum,*
Queis in versamur, queis viuimu' rebus, potesse:
Virtus est homini, scire id, quod quæque habeat res.
Virtus, scire homini rectum, vtile, quid sit honestum;
Quæ bona, quæ mala item, quid inutile, turpe, inhonestum:
Virtus, quærendæ rei finem scire modumq́,:
Virtus, dinitiis pretium persoluere posse:
Virtus, id dare, quod re ipſâ debetur honori;
Hostem esse atque inimicum hominum morumq́, malorum,
Contrà defensorem hominum morúmque bonorum,
Magnificare hos, his bene velle, his viuere amicum:
Commoda præterea patriæ sibi prima putare,
Deinde parentum, tertia iam postremáque nostra.

VIRTVTIS definitio.

Lactantius Dininarum Instit.lib.VI. cap. V. Quæcunque in definitionem virtutis solent dicere, paucis versibus colligit & enarrat Lucilius, quos malo equidem ponere, ne dum multorum sententias refello, sim longior, quam necesse est: Virtus, Albine, est, pretium &c. Ab iis definitionibus , quas poëta breuiter côprehendit, M. Tullius traxit Officia viuendi, Panætium Stoicum secutus : eáque tribus voluminibus inclusit. Hæc autem quam falsa sint, mox videbimus, vt appareat , quantum in nos dignatio diuina contulerit, quæ nobis aperuit veritatem. Virtutem esse dixit, scire, quid sit bonum, & malum, quid turpe, quid honestum, quid vtile, quid minus: breuius facere potuit, si tantum bonum ac malum diceret , quia nihil potest esse vtile vel honestum, quod non idem bonum sit: nihil inutile ac turpe, quod non idem malum. Quod & Philosophis videtur, & idem Cicero in tertio supradicti operis libro ostendit. Verum scientia non potest esse virtus, quia non est intus in nobis, sed ad nos extrinsecus venit. Quod autem transire ab altero ad alterum potest, virtus non est; quia virtus sua cuique est. Scientia igitur alieni beneficij est , quia posita est in audiendo. Virtus tota nostra est, quia posita est in voluntate faciendi bona. Sicut ergo in itinere celerâdo, nihil prodest, viam nosse, nisi conatus ac vires suppetant ambulandi: ita verò scientia nihil prodest, si virtus propria deficiat. Nam ferè etiam ij qui peccant, etsi non perfectè, tamen quid sit bonum & malum sentiunt: &, quoties aliquid improbè faciunt , peccare se sciunt, & ideò celare nituntur. Sed cum eos boni & mali natura non fallat, cupiditate mala vincuntur, vt peccent: quia deest illis virtus, id est, cupiditas recta & honesta faciendi. Ex hoc igitur apparet, aliud esse scientiam boni malíque, aliud virtutem: quia potest esse scientia sine virtute, sicut in plurimis philosophorum fuit. In quo quoniam rectè ad culpam pertinet, non recisse, quæ scieris, rectè; voluntas praua & vitiosus animus , quem excusare ignoratio non potest, punietur. Ergo sicut virtus non est, bonum ac ma-
ium

A

The first page of the 1597 Leiden edition of Lucilius's Satyrae *(Satires), edited by Johan van der Does*

his books, as if to a faithful friend, nor did he change the subject if he had come out of something badly, and the result is that every aspect of his life lies exposed as if written down on a votive tablet" (*Sat.* 2.1.30 ff.). Whether or not Lucilius used the word *satire* to describe his poems is uncertain. He certainly called them *ludus ac sermones* (playful conversations) and *schedia* (improvisations), modest expressions recalling Catullus and Horace. Indeed, it is safe to say that the genius of Catullan and Horatian verse finds its genesis in Lucilius.

The surviving fragments of Lucilius's works are neither representative nor random. Many are preserved by the fourth-century-A.D. grammarian Nonius Marcellus, who cited Lucilius for the sole purpose of culling rare and difficult words. Consequently, it is difficult for the modern reader to characterize the nature and style of Lucilian satire, the totality of which may have varied to a degree that cannot be recovered. There has long been a tendency to specify invective as the hallmark of Lucilian satire. Some, perhaps many, of Lucilius's attacks rose to the level of full-blooded vituperation. Frankness and candor were aristocratic prerogatives that Lucilius never denied himself, and it is possible, even out of the meager remains of his poems, to assemble a lengthy and distinguished list of Lucilius's literary victims—men such as L. Lentulus Lupus (consul 156 B.C.), Metellus Macedonicus (cos. 143 B.C.), L. Opimius (cos. 121 B.C.), and Q. Mucius Scaevola (cos. 117 B.C.). The poetic license to criticize such figures was a vital element in the construction of his public and literary identity, one that marked him off from other writers—and one that attracted the envy of Horace, who, though himself an equestrian and well-connected, lacked Lucilius's secure social autonomy (*Sat.* 2.1). Lucilius also dealt with literary and intellectual rivals: he mocked the styles and the ideas of Accius and Pacuvius; he ridiculed elite philosophical pretensions; he deflated "Asianic" rhetoric; and he made fun of indiscriminate hellenizing. The elder Pliny went so far as to claim that it was Lucilius who invented "the nose for style" (*N.H.* praef. 7). Censure and captiousness were without doubt important ingredients in Lucilian satire. Nevertheless, invective is an aspect of Lucilian style that has been too much exaggerated by modern critics, largely on the basis of Horace's efforts to distinguish his own, allegedly gentler, brand of satire from his predecessor's harsher abuse (for example, *Sat.* 1.4; 1.10; 2.1). In antiquity the most common stylistic judgment was that Lucilius was the paradigm of *gracilitas,* the "plain" or "Attic" style (Varro with Gellius 6.14; Fronto 113).

The plain style, while certainly capable of leveling criticisms, was not the natural mode, from the perspective of a rhetorically trained critic (such as Varro or Fronto), for shrill invective. In his iambic-trochaic verse, Lucilius could frequently accommodate everyday vocabulary, and throughout his satires he employed more technical terms and more actual Greek than would suit the literary tastes of a later age (the style of Cicero's letters, as critics have noticed, is an apt comparison). A degree of both elegance and ease, in combination with urban vernacular, must have pervaded Lucilius's verses. Cicero (*De Orat.* 1.72; 2.25; *Fin.* 1.7; 1.9) characterizes Lucilius as *doctus* (learned), *venustus* (charming), *facetus* (witty), and *perurbanus* (supremely cultivated). Even Horace refers to *urbanitas Luciliana* (Lucilian cultivation, *Sat.* 1.3.40). Lucilius's stabs, then, were often personal ("I write my poetry from the heart," he claims in one fragment), but he ordinarily endeavored to make his point with the stiletto, or, in coarser moments, with the shiv, rarely (despite Juvenal's characterization at *Sat.* 1.165–167) with a heavier or blunter blade.

The first book of Lucilius's satires incorporates a parody of a typical epic scene, the council of the gods (familiar in Homer and in Ennius), in order to ridicule the pretensions and the immorality of L. Cornelius Lentulus Lupus, the consul of 156 B.C. who, though he had been convicted of extortion, was nevertheless elected censor for 147 B.C. and, in the census of 131 B.C., was named *princeps senatus* (foremost position in the senate). In Lucilius's satire, the election of such a man to offices of lofty moral authority signified the corruption of the whole state, as a consequence of which the gods met in council to deliberate the fate of Rome and of Lentulus Lupus. Lupus emerges as a perversion of Romulus, whose deification the gods had debated in Ennius's *Annales.* The gods themselves observe the procedures of the Roman senate, with comic results, and one of them compares his own wits—unfavorably—with those possessed by the deceased philosopher Carneades. The divine Romulus, in an ugly mixture of Greek and Latin, complains of the Romans' oriental luxuriousness and of their tendency toward an ugly mixture of Greek and Latin. Lupus was defended, but in the end the gods decreed that he should fall prey to his own appetites for exotic fish sauces and that the decadent Romans should be visited by a punishing storm. This witty moralizing, a burlesque of epic, was itself assimilated to the later epic tradition when Virgil appropriated parts of it for his own council of the gods in book 10 of the *Aeneid.*

Incompetent orators and indiscriminate philhellenes are the targets of a famous episode in book 2, Lucilius's account of the extortion trial of Q. Mucius Scaevola Augur (cos. 117 B.C.), who was prosecuted by T. Albucius in 119 B.C. for provincial maladministration during his governorship of Asia. Scaevola was the son-in-law of the Stoic Laelius and known for his strict Stoicism. Yet, Albucius was allowed a lengthy speech condemning the morals of the defendant—and of his friends—and, in his examination of witnesses, he "gouged out" even more scandalous allegations. Albucius's oratory is represented as excessively, perhaps ineptly, mannered, but the imputations resonate nevertheless. In his response, Scaevola denounced Albucius's resort to Greek terminology and went so far as to claim that his prosecutor's hatred of himself found its origin in Scaevola's earlier ridicule of Albucius's unrestrained Hellenism. In historical fact, Scaevola was acquitted and went on to be elected consul, and Lucilius's account must have stressed Albucius's failure (he himself was condemned, on the same charge, around 103 B.C.; he retired to philosophical study); yet, one has the sense that, in this satire, neither party escapes unscathed.

Themes less grandiose, but no less interesting, suffuse Lucilius's satires. In book 3 there was a lively account of the poet's journey to Sicily, which became the model for Horace's description of his own journey to Brundisium (*Sat.* 1.5). In the sixth book came an account of Scipio's difficulties in extricating himself from the attentions of an unwelcome client, again an inspiration to Horace, who cleverly cast himself in the patrician's role in *Satires* 1.9. A disquisition in book 9 on (Hellenistic) principles of literary criticism, in this instance the distinction between *poesis* (a long and unified poem) and *poema* (a short poem or a passage from a longer one), gives an indication of Lucilius's range. Book 16 was devoted to elegiac love, and book 29 to sex and prostitutes. In book 30 the disgusting dinner party of Granius sets the precedent for similarly tasteless occasions hosted by Nasidienus (Horace, *Sat.* 2.8) and Trimalchio. Juvenal may owe something to the same book, the remains of which suggest that, in one satire, Lucilius denounced the contemporary practices of Roman society by cataloguing the varieties of its women.

The influence of Lucilius on later writers of the Golden and Silver Ages of Latin poetry can hardly be overestimated. After his death, his poems were the objects of literary lectures and of commentaries. By the first century it was deemed necessary to edit his works into a comprehensive collection. Horace, Persius, and Juvenal looked to Lucilius as the source for the sort of satire they preferred to compose. The prevalence of dactylic hexameter as the meter characteristic of later Roman satire results from Lucilius's personal predilection for this particular meter. Lucilian satire was still read into the time of Quintilian and of Tacitus. Thereafter, however, his poems increasingly became known only at second hand, and soon they became curiosities better known to lexicographers and grammarians than to general readers. Today they are known mainly from these less-than-entirely satisfactory sources. Lucilius's satires are a sore loss: he was a poet of merit and an intelligent, if highly opinionated, observer of his own society. Even if one remains unable to develop an appreciation for Lucilius's artistry, one must nevertheless lament what the loss of his work means to the social historian, for whom the second century B.C. remains so difficult to view through Roman eyes. Lucilius desired to be read neither by those who were extremely ignorant nor by those who were extremely learned. Now he is read only by those who, by circumstance and by training, must be both simultaneously.

Index:

Index Lucilianus, edited by L. Berkowitz and T. Brunner (Hildesheim: Olms, 1968).

References:

Michael Coffey, *Roman Satire,* second edition (Bristol: Bristol Classical Press, 1989), 24–32;

George C. Fiske, *Lucilius and Horace: A Study in the Classical Art of Imitation* (Madison: University of Wisconsin Press, 1920);

Ulrich Knoche, *Roman Satire,* translated by Edwin S. Ramage (Bloomington: Indiana University Press, 1975), pp. 17–30;

Werner Krenkel, "Zur biographie des Lucilius," *Aufstieg und Niedergang der Römischen Welt,* 2, no. 1 (Berlin: de Gruyter, 1972), pp. 1240–1259;

Italo Mariotti, *Studi Luciliani* (Florence: La Nuova Italia, 1960);

Mario Puelma Piwonka, *Lucilius und Kallimachos: Zur Geschichte einer Gattung der hellenistische römischen Poesie* (Frankfurt am Main: V. Klosterman, 1949);

Wendy J. Raschke, "Arma pro amico—Lucilian Satire at the Crisis of the Roman Republic," *Hermes,* 115 (1987): 299–318;

J. Svarlien, "Lucilianus Character," *American Journal of Philology,* 115 (1994): 253–267.

Lucretius

(ca. 94 B.C. – ca. 49 B.C.)

David Wray
University of Chicago

WORK: *De rerum natura,* didactic poem on Epicurean philosophy in six books (On the Nature of Things).

Editio princeps: Brescia, ca. 1473.

Standard edition: *Titi Lucreti Cari De Rerum Natura Libri Sex,* 3 volumes, edited, with translation and commentary, by C. Bailey (Oxford: Clarendon Press, 1947, 1950).

Translations in English: *Lucretius: On the Nature of Things,* translated by Cyril Bailey (Oxford: Clarendon Press, 1910); *Of the Nature of Things: A Metrical Translation,* translated by William Ellery Leonard (London: Dent / New York: Dutton, 1916); *The Way Things Are: The De Rerum Natura of Titus Lucretius Carus,* translated by Rolfe Humphries (Bloomington: Indiana University Press, 1968); *On the Nature of Things,* translated, with an introduction, by Martin Ferguson Smith (London: Sphere, 1969); *Lucretius: About Reality,* translated by Phillip F. Wooby (New York: Philosophical Library, 1973); *On the Nature of Things: De Rerum Natura,* translated by Palmer Bovie (New York: New American Library, 1974); *De Rerum Natura,* edited and translated by W. H. D. Rouse, revision and new text, introduction, notes, and index by Martin Ferguson Smith, Loeb Classical Library (Cambridge, Mass.: Harvard University Press, 1975); *The Nature of Things,* translated by Frank O. Copley (New York: Norton, 1977); *On the Nature of the Universe,* translated by R. E. Latham, revised, with an introduction and notes, by John Godwin (London and New York: Penguin, 1994); *On the Nature of Things,* edited and translated by Anthony M. Esolen (Baltimore: Johns Hopkins University Press, 1995); *Lucy Hutchinson's Translation of Lucretius, De Rerum Natura,* edited by Hugh de Quehen (Ann Arbor: University of Michigan Press, 1996); *On the Nature of Things,* translated by John Selby Watson (Amherst, N.Y.: Prometheus Books, 1997); *On the*
Nature of the Universe, translated by Sir Ronald Melville, with an introduction and explanatory notes by Don P. and Peta G. Fowler (New York: Oxford University Press, 1997).

Commentaries: H. A. J. Munro, *T. Lucreti Cari De Rerum Natura Libri Sex,* 3 volumes, fourth revised edition (Cambridge: Deighton, Bell / London: Bell, 1886); William Augustus Merrill, *T. Lucreti Cari De Rerum Natura Libri Sex* (New York: American Book, 1907); William Ellery Leonard and Stanley Barney Smith, *T. Lucreti Cari De Rerum Natura Libri Sex* (Madison: University of Wisconsin Press, 1942); Cyril Bailey, *Titi Lucreti Cari De Rerum Natura Libri Sex,* 3 volumes (Oxford: Clarendon Press, 1947, 1950); E. J. Kenney, *Lucretius: De Rerum Natura, Book III* (Cambridge: Cambridge University Press, 1971); C. D. N. Costa, *Lucretius: De Rerum Natura V* (Oxford: Clarendon Press; New York: Oxford University Press, 1984); John Godwin, *Lucretius: De Rerum Natura IV* (Warminster, U.K.: Aris & Phillips, 1986); Robert D. Brown, *Lucretius On Love and Sex: A Commentary on De Rerum Natura IV. 1030-1287* (Leiden: Brill, 1987).

"When a single day brings the world to destruction, only then will the poetry of the sublime Lucretius pass away." This judgment by the Roman poet Ovid, written in the generation after Lucretius's death, has been echoed by such writers as Voltaire and George Santayana; the author of *De rerum natura* (On the Nature of Things) holds a place in world literature as one of the great philosopher-poets. Of the life of Titus Lucretius Carus scholars know less, perhaps, than in the case of any other Roman poet. The dates assigned to his birth and death are based primarily on a brief notice in a chronicle compiled by St. Jerome in the fourth century A.D., placing Lucretius's birth in 94/93 B.C. and his death in his forty-fourth year. Jerome makes two other claims about Lucretius's life, both of which have plagued scholars: first, that after he had

Diſtate a ſpeculo tátum ſemota uidetur
Quare etiam atq; etiam minime mitari par eſt
Illis quæ reddunt ſpeculog ex æquore uiſum
Aciebus binis quoniam res conſit utraq;
Nunc ea quæ nobis membrog dextera pars eſt
Inſpeculis fit ut in leua uideatur eo quod
Planitiem a ſ ſpeculi ueniés cú offendit imago
Non cóuertitur incolumis ſed recta retrorſum
Sic eliditur ut ſi qs prius arida q̃ ſic
Cærea pſona ad ludum pilæ ue trabi ue
Atq; ea cótinuo rectá ſi fronte figuram
Splendida porro oculi fugitant uitamq; tueri
Sol etiam cæcat contra ſi tendere pergas
Propterea qa uis magna eſt ipſius & alte
Aera per pug grauiter ſimulacra ſeruntur
Et feriu it oculos turbantia cópoſituras
Præterea ſplendor q cúq; eſt acer adurit
Sæpe oculos ideo quod ſemina poſſid& ignis
Multa dolorem oculis quæ gignút inſinuando
Lurida præterea fiunt quæcunq; tuentur
Arquati quia luroris de corpore eorum
Semina mauult fluunt ſimulacris obuia rerum
Multaq; ſunt oculis in eorum deniq; mixta
Quæ cótage ſua palloribus omnia pingunt
Ex Tenebris Quæ Sint In Luce Videri Et Rurſú
Ex Luce Quæ Súit In Tenebris Videri Nó I eſſe
E TENEbris auté quæ ſút in luce tuemur
Propterea quia cú propior caliginis aer
Ater inſt oculos prior: & poſſedit apertos
Inſequitur candens confeſtim lucidus aer
Qui quaſi purgat eos ac nigras diſcutit umbras
Aeris illius: nam multis partibus hic eſt
Mobilior multisq; minutior & mage pollens
Qui ſimul atq; uias oculorum luce repleuit
Atq; pateſecit quas ante obſederat ater
Continuo rerum ſimulacra ſequuntur

Page from the editio princeps of Lucretius's De rerum natura *(Brescia, ca. 1473)*

been driven to madness by a love potion, he worked at his poem during his lucid intervals until he finally committed suicide; and second—less luridly but still intriguingly—that Cicero later "corrected" or revised the poem after Lucretius's death.

The latter claim has a bit of circumstantial (and inconclusive) evidence in the only certain contemporary mention of the poet. In a letter dated February of 54 B.C., Cicero wrote to his brother that "the poetry of Lucretius is, just as you say in your letter, filled with many flashes of native talent, but also with much literary art" (the exact meaning of Cicero's words is disputed). Some have argued that Cicero's remark proves that Lucretius was already dead by the beginning of 54 B.C.; this inference is

far from certain. Interestingly, Cicero's philosophical works, written over the next decade, make no direct mention of Lucretius's poem. Jerome's other claim, that of Lucretius's madness, is in one sense easy to dismiss: no other surviving ancient author mentions it, including the earlier Christian apologist Lactantius, who wrote scathingly against Lucretius's philosophical arguments and who presumably would not have missed the opportunity to impute actual insanity to an author who denied the soul's immortality and the divine creation of the universe. In another sense, however, the taint of the suspicion of madness still troubles the contemporary reception of the *De rerum natura*. English-speaking readers, especially, often still come to this author already prejudiced by the vivid depiction of the poet's derangement and suicide in Alfred Tennyson's *Lucretius* (1869). Material for the justification of such a predisposition can be found in the passionate intensity and almost missionary zeal of Lucretius's philosophical argumentation in the cause of Epicurean doctrine. Certain descriptions of disease and decay in Lucretius's poem, too, have at times been interpreted as signs of a morbid pessimism on the part of its author.

The date of Lucretius's death is highly uncertain. Another fourth-century-A.D. source, a life of Virgil attributed to the grammarian Donatus, states that Lucretius's death coincided with Virgil's assumption of the "toga of manhood" on his seventeenth birthday (15 October 53 B.C.). The account, however, includes at least one chronological error, quite apart from the fact that age seventeen seems a bit late for a Roman youth's rite of passage. This statement is best viewed as a fanciful image of one poet passing the torch to another—a token of the esteem in which Lucretius was held (at least among pagan readers) at the time and perhaps also an acknowledgment of the great debt of influence owed by Virgil to his immediate predecessor among Roman poets. The year 55 B.C. was for some time a "traditional" date of death among modern scholars, based partly on Cicero's letter to his brother and partly on an adjustment of the dates in the account attributed to Donatus. Jerome's account gives a date of 50 or 49 B.C., and Jerome almost certainly had access to a life of Lucretius written by Suetonius (late first or early second century A.D.). Finally, another of Cicero's letters, this one written to Atticus in early 49 B.C., makes mention of a friend of Cassius named Lucretius. At least one scholar has argued for the identification of this Lucretius with the poet. Still, 49 B.C. is at best a provisional date of death and rather later than the common opinion.

The great fact of Lucretius's life, at least of what is known of it, is his poem, a didactic epic in six books (7,415 verses, not counting lines lost in transmission) bearing the title *De Rerum Natura* (On the Nature of Things); evidence that Lucretius gave his work this title is that he plays upon it in the proem to book 1. While the ancients did not recognize didactic poetry (or other poetry written in hexameters) as a genre separate from epic, *De Rerum Natura* can usefully be regarded as belonging to a tradition of instructional poetry stretching back to Hesiod and including such works as the fifth-century-B.C. *On Nature* by the pre-Socratic philosopher Empedocles (whom Lucretius admired and seems to have imitated), the third-century-B.C. *Phaenomena* by the Hellenistic poet Aratus (which Cicero translated into Latin and which enjoyed a perennial interest in antiquity), and the *Georgics* by Virgil. The last two examples represent, arguably, a kind of didactic poetry

in which poetic and artistic aims take the upper hand over the content of the poem. By contrast, Lucretius can be said to represent the more archaic type of instructional poetry: there can be little doubt as to the singleminded sincerity of purpose that informs every verse of his didactic epic. This purpose does not mean that Lucretius is unconcerned with poetry or that the poetic form of his writing is either inessential to his work or separable from it. It simply means that in the case of the *De Rerum Natura,* unlike that of the *Phaenomena* or the *Georgics,* the poet has set out to convey through his poetry an explicit and relatively unambiguous "message"; the content of that message is the teaching of Epicurean philosophy.

Epicurus of Samos (341–270 B.C.) was an important Hellenistic philosopher whose teachings were circulating widely in the Roman world during Lucretius's time. Only a small fraction of Epicurus's substantial output has survived, but other ancient accounts of Epicurean teachings (most of them hostile), together with Lucretius's poem, are sufficient to reconstruct the broad outlines of Epicurus's teachings. The purpose of philosophy, according to Epicurus, was the practical aim of securing a happy life. Epicureans sought pleasure as the supreme good, though not by the hedonistic overindulgence attributed to them by critics both pagan and Christian. The Epicurean ideal of living was *ataraxia* (freedom from disturbance), which was to be attained by avoiding public life and all attachments to things for which the pains might outweigh the pleasures, and the study and contemplation of philosophy. One was to undertake the study of nature, of humankind, and of the cosmos, not out of a disinterested desire for objective knowledge but rather as a means to the end of achieving freedom from disturbance. Epicurus taught that all things were made of atoms, including the human soul, which was consequently as mortal as the body. He taught that though the gods exist, in a blissful state to be imitated by mortals, they neither created the physical world nor intervened in it. The clear aim of these teachings, together with the injunctions to avoid public life and cultivate moderate pleasure, was the elimination of all anxiety regarding human life and all fear of death and the supernatural. Little wonder that both the Roman political establishment and later the Christian church regarded Epicureanism as a dangerous threat.

Lucretius's *De Rerum Natura* is the only surviving full-length exposition of Epicurean philosophy. In all likelihood Lucretius conveyed his master's teachings with faithful orthodoxy; the major propositions included in the poem all have extant parallels in other Epicurean sources. The tone of argumentation is often forceful, with frequent direct addresses, made sometimes simply in the second person but often by name, to a certain

Memmius, for whom Lucretius claims to have written the poem. The name almost certainly refers to Gaius Memmius, a prominent Roman aristocrat whose political career went aground after a bid for the consulate in 53 B.C. and who went into exile in Athens the following year. In 51 B.C. Cicero wrote Gaius Memmius at Athens, asking Memmius to spare from destruction a certain house that Epicurus's followers venerated as having belonged to their master; the tone is ironical, almost amused, and includes a suggestion that Memmius was not kindly disposed toward Epicureanism. One of several suggestions put forward by scholars is that Memmius may have taken offense at Lucretius's dedication. Memmius also appears in the poetry of Catullus, raising the possibility that the two poets may have known each other. One speculation, if correct, indicates some degree of enmity between them. Catullus addresses one of his milder invectives (poem 47) to two men whom he calls by the nicknames *Porcius* (Piggy) and *Socration* (Little Socrates). "Little Socrates" may possibly refer to Philodemus of Gadara, another Epicurean philosopher-poet, writing in Greek, who lived in Italy during Lucretius's lifetime; by the same token, "Piggy"–Epicureans were already called pigs by their enemies–may represent Catullus's jab at Lucretius, as R. F. Thomas suggests.

The six books of the poem are bound together structurally as three pairs: books 1 and 2 treat the workings of the atoms; books 3 and 4 deal with the human soul and spirit and with human life, desires, and death; and books 5 and 6 describe the workings of the universe and the causes of various celestial phenomena. This global structure based on pairs and threes is in a sense replicated throughout the poem: in the crafting of his verse, Lucretius takes special delight in parallel pairs of verses or portions of verses and in the rhetorical device known as *tricolon,* in which three clauses or members of a list are strung together. Each book opens with a proem and closes with a finale, both marked off by elevation of tone and subject matter. The diction is archaic in places and in many instances must represent conscious archaizing on Lucretius's part. Scholarship on Latin poetry of the late Republic has for some time focused upon the influence of Callimachus on Roman poets and on the birth of a new poetic sensibility based on Hellenistic canons of taste that favored short, elegant, and highly learned poetry. Lucretius, though he was certainly not unaware of Hellenistic poetry, stands mostly outside this current. The attempts of some scholars to "rehabilitate" Lucretius aesthetically by showing him to have been secretly a Callimachean poet arguably do more harm than good to his poetic reputation. The beauties of Lucretius's verse are best appreciated on their own terms and within the context of his philosophical program.

Colophon for the Juntine edition of Lucretius's De rerum natura, *edited by Pietro Candido and printed in Florence, 1512–1513*

The work opens with one of its best-known passages, a hymnic invocation to Venus as source of all pleasure and beauty and as generative principle of all life (1.1–49). Edmund Spenser imitated these lines closely (*The Faerie Queene* 4.10.44–47, 1596); Geoffrey Chaucer, in the proem to the *Canterbury Tales* (ca. 1387), recalled Lucretius's vivid description of the springtime awakening of nature. The entire poem is simultaneously given its title and placed under Venus's patronage in a stroke of characteristic Lucretian wordplay: since Venus alone governs the nature of things, the poet seeks her alliance as he opens his poem *On the Nature of Things* (1.21–28), written for the benefit of Memmius. Lucretius pictures the goddess with Mars reclining on her lap, throwing back his sinewy neck to kiss her lips. Lucretius begs her to take the opportunity to intercede with the war god on behalf of a troubled Rome in which both Lucretius's philosophical program and Memmius's political career are beset with difficulties. The proem closes with a description of the nature of the gods in Epicurean philosophy: "for all divine nature must, of itself, enjoy immortal life with deepest peace, distant and far removed from our own lives . . . neither touched by our services nor moved to anger" (1.44–49). Epicurus taught that the gods existed but took no part in human life or nature. By invoking Venus at the beginning of a poem expounding Epicurean teaching, some might have seen Lucretius as falling into a contradiction. The lines on the nature of the gods (if Lucretius in fact placed them there in the poem) convey a kind of assurance to the reader that the figure of Venus is intended allegorically or symbolically. Tennyson in his *Lucretius* has the poet say of Venus: "Ay, but I meant not thee; I meant not her." This statement is not the only instance in the poem of a foray into mythology brought up short by the reassertion of Epicurean doctrine; in book 2 Lucretius's description of Earth as mother of all things leads into a depiction of the worship of the *Magna Mater,* or Mother of the Gods, which in turn concludes with a reminder that Earth in fact is not a divine being and possesses no sensation whatsoever (2.644–660). The verses from the proem on the nature of the gods in book 1 appearagain in this later passage.

From the proem Lucretius passes to a warning, addressed directly to Memmius, against judging the poem's Epicurean teaching to be impiety. Epicurus liberated humanity from the oppressive weight of religion by showing the true nature of things; impious crimes, Lucretius continues, have often been committed in the name of religion. The scene of Iphigenia's sacrifice follows in an unforgettable passage. On the day she was to wed Achilles, she came forward to the altar; when she saw her father's grief and attendants hiding a knife, she fell to her knees and began to beg for her life, in vain. She was offered as a sacrificial victim for the passage of the Greek fleet. The scene closes on a line that Voltaire cherished: "so many evils has Religion persuaded men to do" (1.101). Religion and its hold upon the mind is the target of Lucretius's entire poem, as the subsequent argument makes clear. The fear of death, a fear based upon ignorance, gives "the threats of priests" (1.109) their power and keeps people in darkness. Only the study of the true nature of things, as discovered and set forth by Epicurus, can dispel this terror of the mind, the ultimate source of which is the fear of death. Lucretius urges that people must study the laws and nature of the universe, not primarily as a pure intellectual pursuit but rather as a means of overcoming the crushing terror of what lies beyond death.

Lucretius passes directly to the exposition of Epicurean physics, opening with the proposition that "nothing

can ever be generated out of nothing by divine power" (1.151). He offers six proofs of this assertion, all in the mode of negative proof or reductio ad absurdum. If something could come from nothing, then anything could arise from anything: humans could come from the sea, fish from the earth, and all manner of fruit from the same tree. No particular season and no length of time would be required for living beings to come to maturation. Crops and animals would need neither rain nor food; men could grow to the size of mountains; land unsown and untilled would bear rich crops. A similar series of proofs is advanced for the proposition that nothing in nature is ever reduced to nothing. If things could be reduced to nothing, they would disappear. Furthermore, everything would long since have died from lack of nourishment or else have disappeared. A touch would be sufficient to reduce things to annihilation. Finally, nature shows that the death of one thing gives life to another: when the father, the sky, showers rain into the lap of mother earth, the drops of water pass away; but soon sparkling crops arise, the branches are heavy with fruits, the countryside teems with crops and the cities with children, and newborn calves, drunk on their mother's milk, disport themselves over tender grass on tremulous young limbs. This first pair of propositions already brings to the fore certain recognizable features of Lucretian argumentation–a passionate, almost missionary, intensity and insistence; a sense of wild and woolly absurdity lurking beneath the surface of the rational; and a keen observation and lyrical expression of the beauties of nature.

Lucretius had already used the terminology of Epicurean atomism in the first two sets of proofs, and even earlier in the book he had warned the reader of his use of many different terms to represent the almost "untranslatable" Greek *atomon* (first beginnings, first bodies, or seeds of things). He then undertakes to prove the fundamental proposition of atomistic materialism: everything is composed of particles too small to be seen. Here the argument proceeds not by reductio ad absurdum but rather by analogy or similarity; there are invisible things other than atoms whose existence is beyond doubt. Ironically enough, Lucretius begins to preach invisible atoms with the same image used by Jesus to preach of invisible spirit: "the wind bloweth where it listeth, and thou hearest the sound thereof, but canst not tell whence it cometh, and whither it goeth" (John 3:8). Lucretius's wind is a disastrous twister, strewing fields with entire forests and giving Virgil a benchmark of the fever-pitch capabilities of Latin hexameter verse for his own storm in the first book of the *Aeneid*. Lucretius's windstorm ends on another, almost evangelical, note: "wherefore, again and again, there are invisible bodies of wind, since in deeds and manner they are found to rival great torrents, whose bodies are visible" (1.295–297). A series of similar arguments follows: one does not see scent, heat, cold, or sound; one does not see water flowing out of clothes as they dry; one does not see the wearing down of finger rings, plow teeth, pavements, or statues; nor does one see the growth of the young or the wasting away of the old. The indisputable reality of such occurrences, though, suggests that Nature works through invisible bodies.

The next series of proofs deals with the existence of void in addition to matter and with the proposition that no third thing exists that is neither matter nor void. Time, for example, has no existence of itself but is instead a property or accident of matter and void. At this point Lucretius engages in what might at first seem mere wordplay based upon a particularity of the morphology of the Latin verb: when one says that "Helen of Troy, daughter of Tyndareus, *was* abducted" *(Tyndaridem raptam . . . esse),* one is not thereby constrained to admit that Helen of Troy still *is (Tyndaridem . . . esse).* Latin uses the present tense of the verb "to be" with a past participle to make the perfect tense in the passive voice; an overliteral construing leads to the conclusion that that which "has been" still "is". After a series of proofs that atoms are indestructible comes an Epicurean critique of the physical doctrines of three pre-Socratic philosophers. Heraclitus, who taught that fire was the original substance, is attacked first and most severely; Lucretius makes at least one unfavorable etymological play upon Heraclitus's name, and the *stolidi* (fools) who admire Heraclitus's obscure but impressive language are perhaps the similar-sounding Stoics. Empedocles of Agrigentum in Sicily, second of the three, presents a special and interesting case; while Lucretius disagrees with Empedocles' doctrine of the four elements (as he must, for it contradicts Epicurus), Lucretius shows a reverential admiration for Empedocles' power of expression as a philosopher-poet. Anaxagoras's doctrine of *homoeomeria*–bones made not of atoms but of small bones, flesh of flesh-particles, and so on throughout nature–is refuted with thoroughgoing care.

Lucretius then sets forth a kind of statement of his poetic and philosophical program: he claims for his poetry the status of first of its kind in the Latin language, and he explains why he has chosen to write philosophy in the form of a poem (a fair question for an Epicurean philosopher, since Epicurus seems not to have approved of poetry). Lucretius intends to use the deceptive charm of poetic art in the service of his reader's enlightenment:

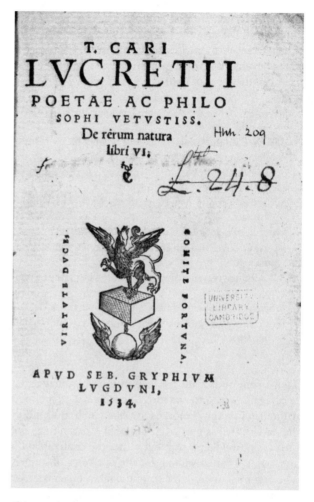

Title page for the 1534 Lyons edition of Lucretius's De rerum natura

Just as doctors, when they try to give children foul-tasting
    wormwood, first touch the rim around the cup
with the sweet, golden liquor of honey,
    to trick the children's naive youth
just as far as the lips, so that meanwhile they drink down
        the bitter
wormwood's juice: the intent is deceptive, but not destruc-
        tive:
it is restoration of the patients' health that they seek.
                                                        (1.936–943)

One of the most avid readers of Lucretius and a fellow "dangerous author," the Marquis de Sade, placed these lines as an epigraph to his epistolary novel *Aline et Valcour* (1795). The first book closes with proofs that the universe is infinite in extent. Lucretius suggests that one walk to its edge and throw a spear. If the spear flies forward, it must have encountered space; if it stops in its path, then it must have encountered matter. Too, if the world were destructible, it would long since have been destroyed.

The proem to the second book, another well-known and often quoted passage, takes the form of a *priamel;* a series of analogical examples leads up to the statement that Epicurean philosophy is a temple of refuge from the cares of human life:

> Sweet it is, when the winds are troubling the waters over the deep sea,
>
> to look, from the vantage-point of dry land, on the distress of another;
>
> not that the sight of another's vexation is itself a delightful pleasure,
>
> but rather because it is sweet to see what evils you are without.
>
> Sweet, too, to look upon the massive struggles of a war
>
> all arrayed over the battlefield, when you have no stake in the risk.
>
> But nothing gives more joy than to dwell in a fortified temple,
>
> unshakable, built high on the teachings of the wise.
>
> From there you can look down and see everyone wandering astray. . . .
>
> (2.1–9)

The proem ends with another memorable image that once again brings to the fore Lucretius's ultimate aim: without philosophy, mortals are like children afraid of the dark. What is needed to dispel that darkness is not the rays of the literal sun, but rather the contemplation and rational understanding of the workings of nature. The argumentation of the second book is taken up with the properties of the atoms, beginning with their motions. All atoms, Lucretius says, are falling faster than the speed of light through space, with the heavier particles moving no faster than the lighter ones (Epicureanism here anticipated Galileo). Two difficulties arise from this proposition: first and more obviously, if all atoms are moving downward at the same rate of speed, they can never hit against each other, lock their "hooks" (in French one still speaks of two compatible personalities as having *atomes crochus*), and form combinations of perceptible material objects and beings. The second difficulty is more subtle and points to an implicit analogical relation between physics and moral philosophy: if all motion is the result of the fall through space of atoms, then all action is determined by that fall (the Latin *casus* means both "fall" and "chance"), and consequently there is no place for free will. Fate, as an unbroken chain of causality was in fact part of the teaching of the Stoics, and of Democritus and Leucippus before them; clearly Epicureanism, a philosophical system for which pleasure is the highest criterion of good and the aim of which is to remove all fear and anxiety from human life, must necessarily militate against the notion of a stern determinism.

Epicurus's solution to these difficulties was to posit a *clinamen* (swerve) in the motion of the falling atoms; the degree of the swerve was literally minimal, the smallest movement possible by which the atoms' motion could be differentiated from a straight downward fall. Lucretius's account of the *clinamen* is the most extensive one surviving. Although the *clinamen* is not described in Epicurus's extant works, other authors, including Cicero, attest that Epicurus was the author of the doctrine. Lucretius emphasizes that the *clinamen* "breaks the chains of Fate" and allows for the possibility of motion born of will rather than of external causality; however, neither Lucretius's nor any other account makes clear the precise manner in which such motion comes about. The *clinamen* has passed into the terminology of contemporary literary criticism through Harold Bloom's *The Anxiety of Influence* (1973).

A description of the various properties of atoms leads to the propositions that they are limited in shape and kind, that nothing consists of only one kind of element, and that the earth is made up of all kinds of elements. Lucretius interrupts the philosophical exposition with a vivid description of the earth-goddess under her cultic title *Magna Mater*. Lucretius describes her iconographic image with a crown representing the walls of a city, and he alludes to her ritual worship by *Galli* (eunuch-priests) and by *Curetes* (armed dancers) representing the youths who clashed their armor to drown out the cries of the infant Jupiter, who was being nursed on Crete, hidden from his father Saturn. Lucretius brings the mythographic excursus up short with a reminder of the falsity of myth, together with an affirmation of its beauty and appropriateness for poetic discourse: "though these things are set forth well and excellently, still they are far removed from true reasoning" (2.644–645). The passage immediately following includes the verses that the manuscripts also show at the end of the invocation to Venus in book 1: all divine nature must enjoy immortal life in profound peace and is neither touched nor moved to anger by human service. The passage seems to enter abruptly in book 1; here it is prepared and motivated by what came before. Whether this "doublet," one of several in the poem, is the result of corruption in the textual tradition or represents what the poet actually wrote is difficult to say. If the manuscripts are correct, then whether or not the doublet represents a lack of final revision in the poem is also difficult to say. The section ends with an even more explicit statement of the nature of mythopoetic language: "if anyone prefers to call the sea Neptune and crops Ceres, and to use the name of Bacchus rather than to utter the name proper to that liquor, then let us allow also that he refer to the earth as the Mother of the

Illustrations by R. de Hooge for the 1701 Dutch translation of Lucretius's works: the Universe, holding the world and a horn of plenty, while kneeling before Venus in her chariot; and Pygmalion (left) looking on as the figure he has brought to life receives a heart from Prometheus

Gods, provided that he forbear in reality to infect his mind with foul religion" (2.655–660).

The argument for a limited number of types of atom continues with an analogy that links Lucretius's text to its subject in an important way: just as the *elementa* (letters of the alphabet), limited in number, are common to many different words and combine in many different orders to produce the different words included in the verses of the poem, so likewise the different kinds of atom, though limited in number, combine in different ways to produce humans, animals, plants, and all that exists. This analogy, of course, survives in the contemporary use of the term *element* (originally a letter of the alphabet) in the chemical sense. Its use is not far from a kind of alphabetic mysticism that one finds in traditions such as Kabbalah. To set up an analogy between letters and atoms is implicitly to call attention to the signifying power of language; hence,

scholars have studied this passage in the light of both ancient and modern theories of language and signification.

Lucretius puts forward a series of arguments to prove that atoms are lacking in both perceptible qualities and sense-perception: they have no color; they are without heat, sound, moisture, or smell; they have no feelings and no emotions, for if they did they would be mortal, and if they could feel emotions, then they would also laugh, weep, deliver philosophical discourses on nature, and argue with each other. After a developed poetic image of earth and sky as mother and father of the universe comes a fanfare announcing the revelation of a new and strange truth: there is a multiplicity of worlds. Since the universe is limitless in every direction and since this world was formed not by divine agency but naturally by a chance combination of atoms, humankind must admit that not only other worlds but also identical replicas of the one they know exist elsewhere in the cosmos. Atoms are eternal, but everything born of their combination passes away. Earth has already begun the downward motion toward decline and decay. The second book ends with the image of an old farmer complaining that in an earlier, more godfearing time, a small plot of land easily produced what a larger one now ekes out with difficulty. He does not understand, Lucretius explains, that everything decays little by little and, wearied by long passage of time, makes its way toward annihilation.

As he turns from the study of atoms to that of the human soul, Lucretius opens his third book with an invocation addressed directly to Epicurus as bringer of enlightenment to humankind and as the model that Lucretius follows at a respectful distance, like a swallow imitating a swan. The language recalls the invocation of Venus in book 1 in several particulars: as the clouds receded before Venus's springtime appearance, so the light of the teachings issuing from the divine mind of Epicurus dissipates the terrors of the mind. Book 3 also includes another play upon the title of the poem: Epicurus's power of reason gives utterance to the nature of things. His hearers' minds are filled with images of blissful divinity, without a trace–and this peaceful state is Lucretius's target throughout the book–of the fear of Acheron, the place of punishment in the afterlife. That fear, Lucretius proceeds to relate, is the cause not only of terrors and anxieties to mortals but also of ambitious greed and murderous cruelty; indeed, many humans are driven by the fear of death, paradoxically, to take their own lives. The only cure for this fear, again, is not the rays and light of the literal sun, but rather the contemplation and rational understanding of nature.

Another abrupt break between proem and exposition is followed by definitions and distinctions among parts of the human faculties. *Animus* for Lucretius is essentially synonymous with "mind"; it resides in the chest and rules over the *anima* (spirit or, perhaps better, life force), which is dispersed through the limbs of the body, the two faculties forming a cohesive unit. Both mind and spirit are parts of the body, no less than feet or hands–the Greek doctrine of soul as a *harmonia,* Lucretius opines, is an unfortunate misapplication of a word better left as a technical musical term–and both mind and spirit are mortal, dissipating when the body dies. Both are corporeal (that is, material), since they act upon the body, and only body can act upon body. The lightest and swiftest of atoms compose both; proof rests in the mind's velocity, together with the fact that bodies weigh the same before and after the moment of death. The soul, in Epicurus's system, is composed of four component parts acting together to form a whole: breath (or wind), air, heat, and a nameless fourth substance, a kind of "soul of the soul." The first three components are described in terms of a characterological typology similar to the Hindu Sankhya system of three *gunas* as described in the *Bhagavad-Gita:* "heat," like the Sanskrit *rajas,* is the active force, prominent in lions (the animal examples are Lucretius's) and in men quick to anger; "wind," a passive force like the Hindu *tamas,* is to the fore in the nature of deer and other timid creatures; and "air," prominent in cows (and sages), is a neutral and peaceful nature like *sattva.* An excess of any of these components produces a flawed or sick soul. It is the goal of Epicurean doctrine to rid the soul of all but the merest traces of such defects. (Precisely how this cure is to happen remains unclear.) The whole formed by mind and spirit cannot be removed from the body without producing death; still, the body itself, while alive, possesses the power of sensation. The eyes, for instance, are not "windows of the soul," but rather organs of sense perception. If the eyes are merely portals through which the soul sees, then tearing out the eyes ought to allow the soul to see more clearly.

The remainder of the book is devoted to Lucretius's central and most passionate argument, set forth in "verses long sought out and found with loving labor" (3.419): the soul is in every part mortal, dying utterly with the death of the body. Lucretius then includes a series of no fewer than thirty separate arguments for this key proposition; a few examples suffice to give their exalted tone. The mind is born with the body; a mind as it passes through life grows and ages; likewise, and naturally, the mind born with the body dies with it. The mind suffers disease and delirium; it is affected by wine. Are these the marks of an immortal being? The mind and spirit are thrown into dire confusion when the body is shaken by epilepsy; how might a disembodied spirit, then, continue its life at the mercy of the powerful winds that shake the world? The life force can be divided into parts–a severed limb or a snake cut into segments will twitch–and what can be divided is not immortal. If immortal souls are introduced into mortal bodies, why do souls have no memory of an earlier existence? Hereditary resemblance of character, too, proves that mind and spirit are not introduced from without into the body but rather are born with it and destined to die with it. "Trees cannot exist in the air"– the rhetorical figure is known as *adynaton,* from the Greek for "impossible"–"nor clouds in the deep sea; fish cannot live in the fields; there can be no blood in branches nor resin in rock . . . so the soul by nature cannot exist alone without body and apart from muscles and blood" (3.784–789). The conclusion and climax of this line of argumentation raises the tone still higher, opening out into a sweeping passage informed

with the vividly colorful rhetoric of philosophical diatribe that brings the book to its end:

> Death, therefore, is nothing to us, and matters to us not a
> whit,
> since the nature of the soul is held to be mortal.
> Just as in times past we had no sensation, were not trou-
> bled,
> when the Carthaginians were coming from all sides to
> fight in battle,
> and all the war-struck world shook hard with tumult,
> trembled and quivered beneath high heaven's breezes,
> and no one knew which people would win empire
> and rule over all humans on land and sea;
> just so, when we no longer are, when body from soul is
> split
> asunder—those parts whose whole is our being—
> nothing can happen, be sure of it, nothing can happen to
> us then,
> for then we shall not be, and nothing can make us feel,
> not if the earth dissolve into the sea, and the sea into the
> sky.
>
> (3.830–842)

Even if the atoms that form organisms were to return
again to their present configuration, which in time they
will, again and again (and to that extent Epicureanism
can be said to include a doctrine of eternal return), still
those configurations of atoms will not be the organisms,
since the continuity of life and memory is broken at
death. To feel distaste at the thought of rotting in the
tomb or becoming food for dogs is to imagine, wrongly,
that one shall survive himself in death, as if one were
standing by his own corpse mourning the loss of himself. An unannounced interlocutor, representing a
mourner addressing a dead man, takes the floor (in a
manner comparable to the interlocutor in Roman satire): "now nevermore will your happy home welcome
you, nor your excellent wife, nor your sweet children
run up to snatch kisses from you." The poet breaks in:
"and they neglect to add that you will no longer have
the slightest desire for these things, nor feel their loss."
By the device of *prosopopoeia* (personification—used, for
example, by Plato in the *Crito,* where the laws of Athens
address him directly), Lucretius makes Nature herself
address the old man who fears to die, upbraiding his
shameless, boorish greed for a life longer than his share.
If life has been pleasant, then why not retire from the
table like a well-fed guest, praising the host's generosity? If wretched, then why this unseemly urge to pro-
long what gives pain and repeat what is tiresome?

A final series of images attacks directly the fear of
afterlife punishment by means of an astonishingly mod-
ern-sounding argument: the great sinners tormented in
Hades described in mythology are in fact allegorical
images for the sufferings mortals foolishly inflict upon

themselves in this life. There is no Tantalus in the
underworld fearing an overhanging rock; but there are
those who make their lives miserable through morbid
fear of the gods. Sisyphus pushing the rock uphill again
and again is not to be found in the underworld; he is an
ambitious politician who runs unsuccessfully for office
year after year (Memmius, if he ever read the poem
dedicated to him, was not likely to have been flattered
by this image). The daughters of Danaus, who murdered their husbands and were condemned in the
underworld to fill vessels full of holes, are an image of
those who, in this life, glut themselves with pleasures
but are never satiated. Those hellish monsters Cerberus, the Furies, and Tartarus exist, but only in the
mind: they are representations of the torment produced
by the anxiety of a guilty conscience.

Book 4 opens with a proem composed almost
entirely of verses that appeared earlier in the poem.
The announcement of Lucretius's poetic program is in
a sense more appropriate here at the midpoint of the
poem (a traditional place to insert a second proem at
least since Apollonius Rhodius); however, the image of
the cup of wormwood sweetened with honey perhaps
fits less well in this spot than in its earlier place in book
1. The burden of book 4 is the existence and nature of
simulacra, membrane-like images that all bodies constantly throw off from themselves like a snake or
cricket shedding its skin. These images account for both
waking senses and visions in dreams. Reflection of
objects in mirrors is one of the strongest proofs of the
existence of simulacra; the reversal of the reflection
shows that the image flies straight off the object and so
impacts the organs of sight. The simulacra move with
extraordinary swiftness, and their properties account
for all phenomena coming under the category of "opti-
cal illusions," of which Lucretius gives a dizzying catalogue. These so-called illusions, he explains, do not
deceive the senses but rather the mind interpreting the
sense impressions. The senses are in fact the sole criterion of truth and foundation of reason. Certain types of
simulacra are blunted or blocked by different bodies.
Glass allows light to pass through it, but wood does
not. Sound passes through the walls of a house, but the
walls muffle it. Sound is no less corporeal and material,
though; a man who has just given a long oration can
attest that he has lost a part of his body. Taste and
smell are somewhat different in operation but no less
explicable: taste results from particles squeezed out of
food that land upon the palate; smell is the result of
larger, heavier particles than those that produce sight or
sound.

Just as the senses constantly receive impressions,
so too simulacra of things impact the mind. The simulacra that affect the mind are subtler and far thinner

than the sense-producing images; because they are like a spider's web or leaves of gold, these images easily cling together in the air and produce strange images in the mind. Thus, the mind perceives mixed or distorted images of things that never existed in reality–for example, mental visions of Centaurs, monsters, and ghosts. The images seen in dreams, too, are the result of these flitting simulacra perceived by the mind. That one can perceive motion in objects, both those seen in reality and those seen in dreams, must be the result of an unbroken succession of simulacra striking the perceiving organ. A difficulty arises: how is the mind able to call up any image at will? The easiest explanation is probably that although many images are available to the mind, perceives only the ones focused on; once the mind calls up one image, other associated images follow in rapid succession. The working of the senses, of course, is an argument often put forward in favor of creation by a providential deity; Lucretius is quick to anticipate this argument and warn against it. The uses of the senses did not in any way precede their existence–the "teleological" argument, common apparently to pagan and Judeo-Christian religions, that a divinity gave mortals eyes in order that they might see. Senses, Lucretius argues, came first, and the use of the senses came afterward. The senses are not like the labor-saving tools and devices that humans have invented with a specific and preexisting purpose in mind, nor is the natural urge that makes living creatures seek their food something to be marveled at. Since all things cast off bodily particles, and living things, through constant motion, expend themselves more quickly than other inanimate objects, for them to seek to restore what they have lost from themselves is natural and proper.

Through a description of the operation of sleep and dreams, including pubescent wet dreams, Lucretius passes to the closing section of the fourth book on sexual desire and love, another well-known passage and one that has often been misunderstood. What Lucretius counsels against is not sexual enjoyment but rather what the Roman elegists called *servitium amoris* (love's servitude). The danger, Lucretius explains, comes not so much from the object of desire as from the simulacra of the beloved acting upon the mind while the actual beloved is absent. The preventive cure that Lucretius puts forward against the mad sickness of love is not abstinence but rather variation of sexual partners, *volgivaga Venus* (promiscuous Venus): "it is proper to flee from simulacra, to frighten away the fuel of love, to turn the mind toward another object and to cast the collected fluid into any body, not to retain it, being fixed once for all upon the love of a single one, and so hold on to care and certain pain" (4.1063–1067). A satirical passage gives an inventory of the doting terms, mostly

in Greek, by which a lovesick man glosses over a woman's various shortcomings: if she stutters and cannot speak, *traulizi* (she lisps divinely); if her lips are too thick, *philema* (she's all kiss). This unforgettable Lucretian moment takes its place in a long tradition that includes Semonides' *Females of the Species* (as Hugh Lloyd-Jones titled his 1975 translation) and the scene in Lorenzo da Ponte's libretto for Wolfgang Amadeus Mozart's *Don Giovanni* in which Leporello reviews his master's catalogue of conquests. Molière used parts of the passage almost unchanged in his *Misanthrope* (1666). Recent critics have pointed out that the misogyny, both implicit and explicit, of this passage and of the entire section on love and sex is less an instance of Epicurean (or Lucretian) cranky originality, and far closer to a conventional ancient view, than had formerly been believed. The book closes with some homely advice for promoting fertility–this passage is the context of Lucretius's infamous prescription that wives (unlike prostitutes) during coitus should lie perfectly still with their legs up–and with the observation that love in fact results not from the divine agency of Venus's arrows but rather from habit and passage of time, just as a rock is slowly worn down by drops of water.

Books 5 and 6 are occupied largely with the study of the cosmos. Rather like Dante's *Paradiso,* this final third of the work has tended to captivate less than a proportionate share of attention over the history of Lucretius's reception. The book 5 proem, addressed again to Memmius, is an encomium of Epicurus and says his equal will not be found among mortals: he deserves truly to be called a god. Epicurus's benefits to humankind are more precious than those associated with Ceres and Bacchus (crops and wine), and his deeds are more impressive than those of Hercules: Epicurus has purged the human mind of error and delusion. Lucretius would follow in his master's footsteps and teach the great truth that all things that exist in the universe are mortal and must eventually pass away with time; only the false simulacra of what is dead continue to deceive the mind in sleep. The world with its treble nature–land, sea, and sky–must one day be reduced to destruction (and this passage is the one that Ovid had in mind when he wrote the verses at the head of this article). Lucretius invokes the authority of reason, an authority greater than that of the Delphic oracle of Apollo, to proclaim a great truth: the world is not divine in origin, nor does it possess sensation of any kind. The gods, further, have no dwelling in this world; their bodies are subtle and removed completely from the realm of human senses. To say that the gods created the world for humans is plain foolishness: what would the gods have stood to gain from it? What good have humans gained? The world is too faulty to be of

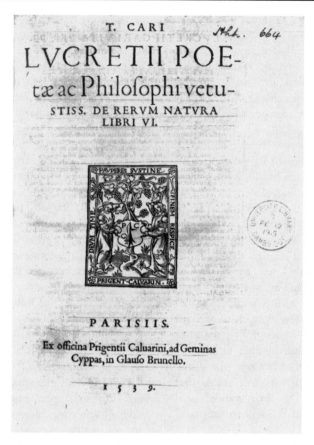

Title page for the 1539 Paris edition of Lucretius's De rerum natura

divine origin: two-thirds of it are uninhabitable, and the rest would be covered with nothing but brambles if not for humans' hard work. There is disease, there are predatory beasts, and the human child is the most helpless of all animal young, cast like a sailor onto savage waves, lying naked on the ground, without speech and utterly dependent on others for every support of life. Every part of earth waxes and wanes. That which is mortal in its every part must be mortal in its entirety. Only the solid matter of atoms and the void of space will last forever; the world is neither of these two things and must therefore be mortal. The end may come through the victory of one element over the others: conflagration, or perhaps universal flood. The world came about through the chance meeting of atoms; slowly the different constituent elements differentiated themselves to produce the world the senses now perceive.

Lucretius next takes on celestial motion. His arguments present a series of alternate explanations among which he refuses to choose; the essential point is that, while the precise natural explanation is not known, the correct explanation must be a natural and not a divine one. A great wind may be sweeping the entire sky;

again, heaven may feed the stars, and what drives them forward is desire for food. The sun, moon, and stars are all about the size that they appear in the sky; their outlines can be seen clearly, and bright flames often look about the same size from a greater distance as from a shorter one. Lucretius then gives possible explanations for dawn and sunset, for the light of the moon, and for eclipses.

Throughout the rest of the book Lucretius comes down from the heavens to present a kind of universal history of the earth and of humankind. The earth, the great mother of all, first brought forth trees, then birds, then larger animals. Her childbearing days are over; there will be no new species. Just as many beings, such as hermaphrodites, are born but cannot survive, so likewise many species have come into being but since passed away. The monsters of mixed species described in mythology, such as centaurs, never existed. Humankind in its earliest days was hardier than now (a commonplace of ancient literature) and was able to live, like the animals, on what nature provided. Lucretius works into the narrative certain *topoi* of Golden Age mythology: though men lived in fear of wild beasts, for instance, they did not have to fear death in battle or by shipwreck. They died of hunger at times, but no one destroyed his health through overindulgence. Civilization came about gradually and naturally. With the development of the bonds of friendship (valued in Epicurean teaching) came alliances and eventually communication through language, which also developed naturally rather than arbitrarily: even animals make different sounds in different circumstances and to express different emotions. The discovery of metals under the earth, particularly gold, brought lust for power, kings, wars, and crimes. Religion, which has long since filled the earth with its altars, began with visions in dreams (again, the dire operation of simulacra) and even in waking. Men attributed to these visions all that religion now teaches about the gods, including the creation and governance of the world, eternal life, and the desire for sacrifice. True piety, if they only knew, consists not in covering the head and worshiping at every altar but in "being able to view all things with a mind at peace" (5.1202). An account of the development of various human arts brings the book to what is by far the most optimistic close in the poem: "little by little, time draws forth each thing into the midst and reason lifts it into the regions of light; for [men] saw one thing after another brighten into clarity in their minds, until through their arts they attained the highest pinnacle" (5.1454–1457).

The sixth and final book opens with a proem close to the length of the proem in book 1. As in the previous book, the sixth book begins with the praises of Epicurus, this time celebrated as the fairest gift to the world from Athens (Lucretius may have believed his master was a native Athenian). Epicurus, in the narrative of the proem, looked about and saw that the human race had made as much external progress as was possible (Lucretius seems to continue the idea from the end of the previous book of humankind at the peak of its progress in arts) but was still "vexing life without ceasing in ungrateful hearts, and being driven to rage furiously with racking distress" (6.15–16). The problem, Epicurus realized, lay in the human mind itself– "the pot was making its own flaw" (6.17).

The opening reference to the gifts of Athens to "suffering mortals" seems to presage the dire and abrupt ending of the book–and the poem–with a description, adapted from Thucydides, of the famous plague that broke out in Athens near the beginning of the conflict between Athens and Sparta. Read in this light, this proem and its Epicurean teaching that one's troubles lie within the mind has seemed to several recent scholars almost inevitably to invite an ironic reading. Indeed, for some time scholars supposed that Lucretius had left the poem unfinished and that the final version would have somehow incorporated the

plague into a more philosophical and seemingly less tragic view of human life. Study of endings and closure in classical poetry (in particular of the abrupt and unsettling end of the *Aeneid,* with its image of Aeneas killing Turnus after Turnus's surrender. which also was once widely attributed to the poem's unfinished state) has made clearer that the abrupt ending of the *De rerum natura* is far less an anomaly than earlier readers suggested. The opening reference to Athens and suffering mortals is likely a structuring device linking the beginning and end of the book. At any rate, the sixth book clearly constitutes the end of the poem in Lucretius's overall plan, not only because he has created the neat structure of three pairs of books but also because he announces this book as the final one near the end of the proem, with a punning invocation of the Muse Calliope and a reminiscence of the prayer to Venus in book 1: "Precede me and mark out my course, as I run my stint to the white line of my final goal, *callida Musa Calliope* (clever Muse Calliope), repose of men and delight of gods, that with you as leader I may win the crown with signal glory" (6.92–95).

In the middle of the book Lucretius presents a description and explanation of precisely those celestial and terrestrial phenomena most often attributed to divine agency by religious fear: thunder, lightning, rainstorms, earthquakes, and volcanic eruptions. As in the previous book, he often presents a series of possible alternate explanations; the essential point is that all phenomena in nature come from natural rather than divine causes. Some scholars have asserted (and perhaps not entirely with justification) that Lucretius misrepresented or exaggerated the level of religious fear with which Romans of his time regarded such phenomena, with the enlightened (and elite) skepticism of a Cicero or, a bit later, of a Horace put forward as an example. After a description of other natural phenomena, such as magnetism, Lucretius turns to the description of disease, passing quickly to the plague at Athens. A final scene depicts the Athenian temples full of unburied corpses and survivors fighting each other for access to funeral pyres.

The literary "fortunes" of Lucretius's poem have been, to say the least, varied. One of his closest readers was Virgil, the poet of the next generation who was to write the *Aeneid,* the central poetic text of the Latin language. Virgil knew Lucretius's work and had absorbed the rhythm and contours of Lucretian verse so thoroughly and so well that direct allusion is difficult to distinguish from conscious or unconscious imitation. A single but representative example is a phrase spoken by Virgil's Dido in a tirade delivered to Aeneas as he is leaving her: *moribundam deseris, hospes* (you desert me in my dying, my guest; *Aeneid* 4.323). Lucretius's description of the soul's vital heat departing from a dying body was ringing in Virgil's ears: *moribundos deserit artus* (it deserts our limbs in their death; *DRN* 3.129). Lucretian echoes of this type are not rare in Virgil, though they are less well known than Virgil's explicit reference to Lucretius in the *Georgics:* "happy he who was able to learn the causes of things, and cast down at our feet all fears, inexorable fate, and the roar of greedy Acheron" (*Georgics* 2.490–492). Ovid's praise of Lucretius comes from the youthful *Amores,* in a list of "immortal" Greek and Roman authors (of whose works some survive only in fragments). Statius, writing in the first century A.D., mentioned the "lofty furor of learned Lucretius." As stated at the outset, the *Life of Virgil* attributed to Donatus attests to Lucretius's reputation in late antiquity, and Lactantius and Jerome show that Lucretius was already regarded as a dangerous enemy of religion by the fourth century A.D.

Those two currents–admiration for Lucretius's poetic achievement and hostility toward the philosophical content of his poem–were both renewed with the rediscovery of *De rerum natura* early in the fifteenth century. Lucretius as ethical teacher has not been without his champions since that time, beginning with certain early modern humanists. The anti-Lucretian strain passed from Christian polemics–with Cardinal Polignac's 1747 *Anti-Lucretius*–to a kind of early version of deconstruction, viewing Lucretius as a poet hopelessly divided against himself. Lucretius's reputation among classical scholars and students of literature is still not entirely out of these shadows, though recent years have seen a new and growing literary appreciation for the philosophical poetry of this universal poet.

References:

Luciano Canfora, *Vita di Lucrezio* (Palermo: Sellerio, 1993);

Diskin Clay, *Lucretius and Epicurus* (Ithaca, N.Y.: Cornell University Press, 1983);

Gian Biago Conte, "Lucretius," in *Latin Literature: A History,* translated by J. B. Solodow, revised by Don P. Fowler and G. W. Most (Baltimore: Johns Hopkins University Press, 1994), pp. 155–174;

Peta G. Fowler and Don P. Fowler, "Lucretius," in *The Oxford Classical Dictionary* (Oxford: Oxford University Press, 1996);

George Depue Hadzits, *Lucretius and His Influence* (New York: Cooper Square Publishers, 1963);

E. J. Kenney, *Lucretius,* Greece and Rome: New Surveys in the Classics, no. 11 (Oxford: Oxford University Press, 1977);

D. N. Sedley, *Lucretius and the Transformation of Greek Wisdom* (Cambridge & New York: Cambridge University Press, 1998);

Charles Segal, *Lucretius on Death and Anxiety* (Princeton, N.J.: Princeton University Press, 1990);

Richard F. Thomas, "This Little Piggy Had Roast Beef (Catullus 47)," *Prudentia,* 26 (1994): 147–152;

David West, *The Imagery and Poetry of Lucretius* (Edinburgh: Edinburgh University Press, 1969).

Manilius

(fl. first century A.D.)

Ward Briggs
University of South Carolina

WORK: *Astronomica,* 5 books, probably unfinished (Astronomy).

Editio princeps: *M. Manilius Astronomicon primus[-quintus]* (Nuremberg: Johann Müller of Königsberg, 1472).

Standard editions: *M. Manilii Astronomicon,* edited by A. E. Housman, editio minor (Cambridge: Cambridge University Press, 1932); *M. Manilii Astronomica,* edited by George P. Goold (Leipzig: Teubner, 1985).

Translation in English: *Manilius Astronomica,* translated by George P. Goold, Loeb Classical Library (Cambridge, Mass.: Harvard University Press, 1977).

Commentaries: *M. Manilii Astronomicon,* 5 volumes, edited by A. E. Housman (London: Grant Richards, 1903–1930; second edition, 1937; reprinted in 2 volumes, Hildesheim: Olms, 1972); *Manili Astronomicon liber II,* edited and translated by H. W. Garrod (Oxford: Oxford University Press, 1911); *M. Manilius Astronomicon,* edited by Dora Liuzzi, with Italian translation (Galatina: Congedo, 1991–1992, 1994–1995, 1997)–comprises book 1 (1995), book 2 (1991), book 3 (1992), book 4 (1994), and book 5 (1997).

My dear Bridges,

I adjure you not to waste your time on Manilius. He writes on astronomy and astrology without knowing either. My interest in him is purely technical. His best poetry you will find in I 483–531, where he appeals to the regularity of the heavenly motions as evidence of the divinity and eternity of the universe. He has nothing else so good, and little that is nearly so good.

Yours sincerely

A. E. HOUSMAN

(*The Letters of A. E. Housman,* edited by H. Maas [Cambridge, Mass.: Harvard University Press, 1971], 22.)

Who was this Manilius, so lackluster and technical a poet, who nevertheless was edited by three of Europe's greatest classical scholars–Joseph C. Scaliger (1579), Richard Bentley (1739), and Housman (1903–1932)? No facts about Manilius's life have survived antiquity. There is even doubt about his name. Manuscripts give the name Marcus Manilius, but Pliny (*Nat. Hist.* 35.199) refers to an astrological writer named Manilius of Antioch, a slave brought to Rome in the early first century B.C. As practically the only information given by the poem concerning its author is its address to "Caesar," presumably Augustus, it is highly unlikely that Pliny's Manilius is the one under discussion. Though Manilius can safely be dated to Augustus's reign, whether he lived into the reign of Tiberius is nevertheless uncertain. The usual sources are altogether lacking: the poet says nothing of himself in his poem, and there are no *testimonia* (mentions of him by other writers).

Astronomica (Astronomy), which is unfinished and probably was not published in its author's lifetime, yields some evidence about the time of its writing. Book 1.899 gives a definite *terminus post quem* by referring to the *modo* (recent) defeat of Varus by the German Arminius at the Saltus Teutoburgiensis in A.D. 9, during the reign of Augustus. Augustus is clearly alive in books 1 and 2 (1.7, 385, 925–926; 2.508–509), but two related passages may indicate that both the composition of the poem and therefore the life of its poet extended into the reign of Tiberius. At 2.508–509 Manilius says of the constellation Capricorn, the birth sign of Augustus, "what sign can be more wondrous to that man since it shone favorably upon Augustus's birth?" The emperor may still be alive at 4.552, which seems to refer to Augustus's coming transformation, at his death, into a star, but clearly the constellation Libra, birth sign of Augustus's successor, Tiberius, is now *felix* (blessed). A similar problem occurs at 4.764, which calls Rhodes *hospitium recturi principis orbem* (the home of the chief ruler of the world), a reference to the residence of Tiberius from 6 B.C. to A.D. 2, during Augustus's reign. The problem is that *recturi* is in the future tense and can be given two interpretations. The word may indicate the absolute future (Tiberius either currently lives in Rhodes or has lived there, but will someday be emperor) or, as Housman thought, historical future (when Tiberius lived at Rhodes he had yet to become ruler, but it was clear he would, as he now is). No evidence of dating occurs in either book 3 or book 5.

Based on matters of style, the poet may be either Roman, as he seemed to Scaliger, or Asiatic, as he seemed to Bentley. He is probably middle-aged during the composition of *Astronomy* judging by his wish for an *annosa* (extended) life and a *molli vita senecta* (calm old age) so that he may finish the poem (1.115). But that is all that is known, and both the author and the genesis of his work remain so mysterious that his editor and translator George P. Goold declared, "Had the archetype of the *Astronomica* not survived long enough to provide us with copies of the poem, we should have had no reason to suspect its existence, or that of its author."

The Greeks considered didactic poetry to be another form of epic, as it tended to treat great subjects and was written in hexameters. By choosing to write on astronomical subjects, Manilius placed himself in a long tradition of didactic poetry that began in the eighth century B.C. with the *Works and Days* of Hesiod and continued through the philosopher-poets Empedocles (ca. 493–433 B.C.) and Parmenides (ca. 515–after 450 B.C.). Though interest in didactic poetry waned in the fifth and fourth centuries B.C., it was revived by members of the circle around Callimachus (ca. 305–240 B.C.) in Alexandria. Poets such as Nicander, Aratus, and Callimachus himself found a certain appeal in the expense of considerable poetic skill on lowly or prosaic subjects. Poems treated many topics, from farming to mythography and even cures for snakebites. The genre continued in the Greek world into the age of Hadrian (second century A.D.) with Marcellus of Side (medicine) and Dionysius Periegetes (geography), into the next century with Oppian (fishing and hunting), and into the next with Menecrates of Ephesus (farming).

In antiquity, astronomy and astrology were closely allied, with the latter being taken more seriously as a science than it had been in classical Greece or than it is today. The former sought to discover and explicate order in the courses of the heavenly bodies while the latter sought to discover the influence of the celestial phenomena on man's fate. It was assumed that the regularity of the stars in their particular orbits was discernible by man and that knowledge of the terrestrial as well as celestial universe (for example, the coming of storms, navigation by land or sea, and the opportune times for planting and harvesting) was made available to man by the forces that rule the universe. Moreover,

how closely man observed and followed the rules of heaven determined his understanding of not only the world but also the sympathetic forces in charge of it. To observe the heavens was, in a real sense, to practice one's religion. As Virgil advises:

> Blessed is he who could know the causes of things,
> . . . .
> Happy is he who knows the country gods. . . .
>
> (*Georgics* 2.490, 493)

The ability of astronomers to predict unusual phenomena such as eclipses and comets, matched by astrologers who predicted the outcome of human events based on the same star charts, can be traced to early Babylon. Though Hesiod mentions the rising and setting of various star signs as markers of seasons (*Works and Days* 619ff.), and scientific investigation of the heavens was a significant part of the pre-Socratic and Platonic programs (Parmenides thought that the earth was round and that the Moon reflected the light of the Sun), the companion study astrology was not taken seriously until after the death of Alexander the Great in 323 B.C. even though scientists had adapted the Babylonian zodiac to achieve some understanding of the regularity of the seasons through the movement of constellations and the cycles of the Sun and Moon. Following the death of Alexander, the cosmopolitan Egyptian city that bore his name, Alexandria, became the world's center for science, scholarship, and the arts–attracting men of talent from all over the world. Some of those who came from the Middle East brought scientific sophistication to Greek study of the planets, but they also brought the mystical arts of astrology. Men such as Eudoxus, Callippus, and Heraclides of Pontus were formulating a planetary system, and Aristarchus of Samos put the Sun at the center of the universe in his *On the Sizes and Distances of the Sun and Moon*. The third century B.C. produced Archimedes and Hipparchus, who produced the first useful theory of the motion of the Sun and Moon, while Ptolemy (ca. A.D. 140) did the same for the five known planets.

While the science of astronomy was at its height in Alexandria, the lure of astrology began to grow, appealing as it did to the Stoic sense of unity and sympathy throughout the natural world. Serious minds engaged the topic, and scientists such as Hipparchus and Ptolemy employed it in their treatises. Hippocrates advised surgery according to the phases of the moon. The most significant of the Alexandrian astronomic poets is Aratus (ca. 315–ca. 239 B.C.), whose *Phaenomena* in 1,174 hexameter lines exercised influence on several generations of Roman poets, including Lucretius, Virgil, and Ovid.

M. MANILI
ASTRONOMI-
CΩN LIBRI
QVINQVE.

IOSEPHVS SCALIGER
IVL. CAES. F. RECENSVIT,
ac priſtino ordini ſuo reſtituit.

Eiuſdem IOS. SCALIGERI *Commentarius*
in eoſdem libros, ⁊ Caſtigationum
explicationes.

LVTETIÆ,
Apud Mamertum Patiſſonium Typographum
Regium, in officina Roberti Stephani.
M. D. LXXIX.
CVM·PRIV·ILEGIO REGIS.

Title page for a 1579 Paris edition of Manilius's book on astronomy,
edited by Joseph Scaliger (courtesy of the Lilly Library,
Indiana University)

One indicator of the importance of astrology at Rome is that Aratus's poem was translated by no less than Varro of Atax (born 82 B.C.); Cicero; Germanicus Caesar (15 B.C.–A.D. 19), the adoptive son of Tiberius; and Avienus (ca. A.D. 400). Romans such as Varro and Nigidius Figulus (praetor in 58 B.C.) wrote important prose studies, and though leaders tried to banish astrologers or curtail their prognosticating (nine expulsions of astrologers occurred between 139 B.C. and A.D. 93), emperors such as Augustus and Tiberius relied on astrologers consistently.

That in this climate Manilius should treat the topic of the stars and their effect not only on history but also on current events then should be no surprise. Manilius's primary sources for his poem were Greek, and there is a kind of forced Greek economy to his expression that reflects not simply the didactic poets of Alexandria such as Nicander and Aratus but also the tragedians, lyric poets, and Homer. Indeed, Goold said in 1961 that Manilius appears to have been part of a Greek professorial circle at Rome. Among the Romans, Manilius seems most influenced by Lucretius, whom he

imitates in style but whose Epicureanism he is continually at pains to reject, and by Virgil, whose didactic poem *Georgica* (Agriculture) Manilius imitates in several places and also in his title *Astronomy*.

Like most proems, Manilius's opens with a statement of the topic—in this case, astrology—but unlike most, there is no invocation of the gods or Muses:

> I intend to discern from the skies by means of my poetry
> the skills we learn from the gods and the stars, privy to our
>   fate,
> which vary the differing lots of man by the use of divine
>   reason.
>
> (1.1–4)

Like Virgil and poets before and after him, Manilius is more interested in the effects of the motions of the heavens than in the mathematics or physics of the movements themselves. The god Mercury instigated his interest in the subject and led him to be the first poet to treat astrology (25–37). First kings, then priests, learned the mysteries of heaven, and by patient observation and unremitting toil, the priests developed the science of astrology (38–65). Before Mercury showed man that fate could be discerned in the stars, man was blissfully without a clue as to why days were long or short or seasons were fruitful or barren. But then men observed the skies, and their lives improved as they came to understand the basis of thunder and lightning, snow and hail, volcanoes, and other phenomena (66–112). The close of the proem restates that Manilius is the first to essay this theme in poetry, and he begs of fortune that he may have a life long and serene enough to complete his poem.

Before he can discuss astrology, however, he must establish the geography, so to speak, of the heavenly bodies. He thus begins in Aratean order (first the stars, then the planets) his description of the spherical heaven that surrounds the earth. He begins with an analysis of the cosmological theories of such men as Xenophanes, Hesiod, Leucippus, Heraclitus, Thales, and Empedocles (118–254), then the stars in their zones (255–531), the planets (532–538), and the fixed celestial orbs—arctic circle, summer tropic, equator, winter tropic, and antarctic circle (539–804; Housman transposed 805–808 to follow 538). The book closes with an account of comets, leading to a peroration on the portentous comets that accompany political or military disasters, a clear imitation of the close of Virgil's first book of the *Georgics,* where Augustus is also the hero of Rome's salvation.

With his celestial geography established, Manilius turns to astrology in book 2. Another lengthy proem treats Greek hexameter poetry from Homer on in an effort to establish Manilius's claim to originality of subject (1–149). Curiously, he does not mention Latin poets. Indeed, the only Roman work referred to in the whole poem is Ennius's *Annales* (3.23–26). Book 2 elaborates the signs of the zodiac (150–269), their conjunctions (270–432), their tutelary divinities (433–452), body parts influenced by the signs (453–465), interrelationships between the signs (466–692), and dodecatemories (693–970).

The proem to book 3 is much shorter than the first two and takes the form of a *recusatio,* a listing of the themes he will not treat in order to specify the subject he has in fact chosen (1–42). He then treats the circle of the *athla* (twelve lots, 43–159), especially the Lot of Fortune (160–202), the horoscope (203–509), two theories of chronocrators (signs that govern the ages of man, 510–617), and the signs Cancer, Capricorn, Aries, and Libra (tropic signs, 618–682).

Book 4 opens with a most Lucretian prologue by a most anti-Lucretian poet:

> Why do we waste our lives with years of anxiety
> And why do we torture by fear and the empty desire of things
> old men with endless worries; while we seek old age, we in fact
> lose it and with no limit on our wishes for things, we live
> as men waiting to live, but who never, in fact, live.
> Each man is poorer because of his wealth because he always wants more
> and he does not count what he has, but only wants what he does not have. . . .
> Release your souls, mortal men, lighten your cares,
> and free your life of so many empty complaints.
>
> (4.1–13)

Man may be able to read his destiny in the stars, but he cannot control it; nevertheless, he must live life in virtue and avoid vice.

The book then treats the particular characteristics of those people born under each sign (122–293), the divisions of each sign or its *decans* (294–407), and the degrees of the zodiac (408–584). Manilius describes the seas and lands of the earth (585–817) and concludes with a discourse on eclipses (818–865). The book ends with a closing statement on the Stoic notion that the man who already participates in the divine by virtue of his existence moves closer to the divine state as he understands the origin and operation of the universe as it can be discerned from the heavenly signs. The close thus links with the proem.

The poem might well have concluded with book 4, but Manilius says that he will go on to describe the kinds of people affected by *paranatellonta,* constellations outside the zodiac (32–709). The book ends abruptly, largely due to losses in the manuscript, but the peroration following a description of the magnitude of the stars (710–733) may have been Manilius's intended close of the poem, a description of a commonwealth of the heavens:

> Just as the populace in great cities is arranged in groups,
> and the senators hold the chief positions and the equestrian rank
> the next place, the knights are followed by the common people,
> the common people by the lazy crowd and then the nameless mob,
> so a certain commonwealth may be seen even in great heaven,
> which nature, who has founded a city in the sky, has made.
>
> (5.733–739)

Manilius concludes with a statement that the commonwealth structure insures the survival of the heavens against the chaos of the undifferentiated Milky Way.

Readers are left disappointed. The poem ends as suddenly and inconclusively as Virgil's *Aeneid*. Whether the manuscripts were robbed by later generations or whether the poet simply forgot to add his promised sections or whether he died before he could write them, he did not write of the effects of the planets (promised at 2.965), or of Perseus, Hydra and Flumina, and Deltoton and Corvus. The loss of portions of book 5 is particularly grievous as this book shows more of Manilius's skill at observation of human rather than celestial activity and behavior. Such and worse are the fates of much of ancient literature.

Stylistically and thematically Manilius placed himself squarely in the didactic tradition of Hesiod, Callimachus, Lucretius, Virgil, and Ovid. He employed the rhetorical devices of didactics, addressing the reader as a teacher with phrases such as *nunc age* (now look here) and *perspice nunc* (observe this); he stresses that what he delivers is knowledge as opposed to superstition (as poets have done since Hesiod), and he claims on the basis of his originality a place in the poetic pantheon. His sources show a kind of progression also. Book 1 is owed largely to Aratus, with a conclusion heavily Virgilian. Books 2 and 3 are based on the Greek astrologers, book 4 relies on Lucretius and Egyptian sources, while book 5 shows the influence of Virgil (the republic of stars is like the republic of bees at the end of *Georgics* 4) and Ovid, in his diverting story of Perseus and Andromeda (538–618).

The Ovidian charm of the Andromeda story is singular in this poem. The conclusion reinforces Manilius's firm Stoicism, as strongly as had the passage cited by Housman, a refutation of Epicurean "chance" as the determining factor in creation:

If chance gave such a world as this to us, then that very
    chance would rule it.
But then why do we see the constellations rise in arrayed
    courses
And follow these scheduled courses as if on command,
with none jumping ahead and none left behind?
Why do the same stars adorn the summer evenings,
The same always the winter? Why does each day return
To the sky a set pattern and take a set pattern with it?

                                (1.494–500)

In the same way kingdoms on earth rise and fall, and
men's lives can oscillate between slavery and rule.
Against all the vagaries of man's fortune, heaven
remains eternally the same, for the stars bear the
imprint of the divine.

All things created by mortal rule change
And the earth does not notice that it bears
a varied look as the years pass.
But the heavens remain unchanged and preserve all of its
    aspects,
which neither the long day increases nor old age dimin-
    ishes;
Its motion does not divert it slightly nor does it tire in its
    course;
It will be the same always because it has been the same
    always.
Our fathers saw no different sky; nor will our children.
It is God, who is not changed over time.

                                (515–523)

Housman's interest, like that of Scaliger and Bentley, was chiefly "technical"–that is, the challenges the
difficult manuscript problems presented to their supreme
gifts for textual criticism. Housman declared that his
text was prepared only for "the next Scaliger or Bentley," and he cared little to make the poem more accessible to the average reader. That he devoted his
appreciable poetic skill with the Ovidian line to a didactic poem on the heavens may seem a waste to many.
But Manilius is significant for advancing the astronomical didactic beyond the merely descriptive (for example,
Aratus) to the philosophical; he also reduced the number of Lucretian and Virgilian poetic digressions (the
honey that eased the dose of instruction) while maintaining Lucretius's principles of argument and arrangement of information. He markedly increased the sheer
volume of information included because he felt that the
information itself was holy; he described in Ovidian
ease these highly technical matters and rendered them
into a flowing hexameter. His chief claim on the readers' interest–whether they care at all for astronomy,
astrology, or Stoicism–may be that he is chronologically the first Latin poet of the Silver Age.

References:

Franz Cumont, *Astrology and Religion among the Greeks and
    Romans* (New York: Putnam, 1912);

Robinson Ellis, *Noctes Manilianae* (Oxford: Clarendon
    Press, 1891);

George P. Goold, "A Greek Professorial Circle at
    Rome," *Transactions and Proceedings of the American
    Philological Association,* 91 (1961): 168–192;

August Kraemer, *De Manilii qui fertur astronomicis* (Mar-
    burg: N.p., 1890);

Gustave Lanson, *De Manilio poeta eiusque ingenio* (Paris:
    Hachette, 1887);

Carmelo Salemme, *Introduzione agli "Astronomica" di Manilio*
    (Naples: Società editrice napoletana, 1983);

Ferdinand Schwemmler, *De Lucano Manilii imitatore*
    (Giessen: Robert Noske, 1916);

R. B. Steele, "The *Astronomica* of Manilius," *American
    Journal of Philology,* 53 (1932): 320–343;

A. M. Wilson, "The Prologue to Manilius I," *Papers of
    the Liverpool Latin Seminar,* no. 5 (Liverpool: F.
    Cairns, 1986), pp. 293–298.

Martial

(ca. A.D. 40 – ca. A.D. 103)

William J. Dominik
University of Natal

WORKS–EXTANT: *Epigrammaton Liber* or *Liber de Spectaculis,* short poems on the opening of the games for the Flavian amphitheater (Book of Epigrams, Book on the Games, A.D. 80);

Xenia and *Apophoreta,* mainly couplets in elegiac meter designed to accompany gifts at the Saturnalia festival (Gifts, Dinner Gifts, A.D. 84 or 85);

Epigrammaton Libri, miscellaneous poems in twelve books (Books of Epigrams, A.D. 86–102).

Editiones principes: *Marci Valerii Martialis Epigrammatum Libri XV* (Rome: Sweynheym and Pannartz, ca. 1470); *Martialis Epigrammatum Libri XIV* (Ferrara: Andreas Belfort, 1471); *Marci Valerii Martialis Epigrammatum Libri XV,* edited by Georgio Merula (Venice: Vindelin de Spira, ca. 1471).

Standard editions: *M. Valerii Martialis Epigrammaton Libri,* edited by W. Heraeus (Leipzig: Teubner, 1925; republished by I. Borovskij with a few corrections and additions, 1976); *M. Val. Martialis Epigrammata,* second edition, edited by W. M. Lindsay (Oxford: Oxford University Press, 1929); *Martial: Épigrammes,* 2 volumes, edited and translated by H. J. Izaac (Paris: Budé, 1930–1933); *M. Valerii Martialis Epigrammaton Libri post W. Heraeum,* edited by D. R. Shackleton Bailey (Stuttgart: Teubner, 1990).

Translations in English: *Martial: The Twelve Books of Epigrams,* translated by J. A. Pott and F. A. Wright (London: Routledge / New York: Dutton, 1924); *Martial: Epigrams,* edited and translated by Walter C. A. Ker, 2 volumes, second edition, Loeb Classical Library (London & Cambridge, Mass.: Harvard University Press, 1968); *Martial: Epigrams,* edited and translated by D. R. Shackleton Bailey, 3 volumes (London & Cambridge, Mass.: Harvard University Press, 1993).

Commentaries: F. A. Paley and W. H. Stone, *M. Val. Martialis Epigrammata Selecta* (London: Whittaker / George Bell, 1868); H. M. Stephenson, *Selected Epigrams of Martial* (London: Macmillan, 1880); R. T.

Bridge and E. D. C. Lake, *Select Epigrams of Martial,* 2 volumes (Oxford: Clarendon Press, 1908); Edwin Post, *Selected Epigrams of Martial* (Boston: Ginn, 1908); Peter Howell, *A Commentary on Book One of the Epigrams of Martial* (London: Athlone Press, 1980); Howell, *Martial, Epigrams V* (Warminster, U.K.: Aris & Phillips, 1995); Neil M. Kay, *Martial, Book XI* (London: Duckworth, 1985); T. J. Leary, *Martial, Book XIV* (London: Duckworth, 1996).

On learning of the recent death of Marcus Valerius Martialis in about A.D. 103, the younger Pliny wrote (*Epistles* 3.21),

I hear that Valerius Martial is dead and I am very distressed. He was a man of remarkable talent; he had a perceptive and sharp mind; and his writings are no less exceptional for their charm as for their wit and sarcasm. . . . He gave me as much as he could and would have given me more if he had been able to do so. Surely, however, nothing greater can be conferred upon a man than a tribute that will bring him fame, praise, and immortality? But the poems he wrote will not be immortal. Perhaps they will not be, but he wrote them with the intention that they would be read by future generations.

Pliny confirms that Martial, no less than other ancient poets, aspired to achieve immortality through the favorable reception of his verses. However, Pliny was wrong in his prediction of Martial's poetic oblivion, for the epistolographer's desire to confer immortality upon his friend with this tribute proved unnecessary.

Martial's entire corpus consists of around 1,560 epigrams, not including some verses expurgated from book 10 and lost from the shortened book 12. There was a long and thriving tradition of epigrammatic composition preceding Martial. Following in the tradition of the original genre that had been popular in Greece for many centuries, many of his epigrams are single couplets, have only one subject, and conclude with a witty

Martial being crowned by the Emperor Domitian; illustration from the 1501 edition of Martial's epigrams, published by Aldus Manutius of Venice (from the copy in the British Library)

most polished exponent. Despite the formal consistency of the epigrammatic model he established, Martial developed the genre to its greatest versatility, making it a weapon that highlighted human idiosyncrasies and weaknesses through the clever use of wit, humor, ambiguity, paradox, irony, invective, ridicule, sarcasm, and obscenity. He aimed to elevate the epigram to a level of literary respectability and by adopting a stance of mock playfulness to subvert indirectly the more traditional and prestigious genres of epic and tragedy. In this respect he represents a culminating point in the development of the vers de société as exemplified in the genres of elegy, lyric, satire, and, of course, the epigram. Martial was largely successful in achieving his aims, as he firmly established the place of the epigram in the European literary tradition, despite the objections of later commentators to some aspects of his revolutionary program.

Martial was born ca. A.D. 40 in Bilbilis, a town in the Roman province of Tarraconensian Spain; he was given the name Martialis because he was born on March 1. His parents, Valerius Fronto and Flacilla, ensured that he was educated in the usual manner of the age by instructing him in grammar and rhetoric. In or shortly before A.D. 64 he settled in Rome, following in the footsteps of other Spanish men of letters such as Lucan and the younger Seneca, who had preceded him in moving to the city and establishing for themselves a considerable reputation and influence among its prominent literary circles. Rome was to be Martial's home for thirty-four years, although his epigrams on traveling and sightseeing reveal that he was familiar with the towns and countryside of Italy. His desire for a standing at the imperial court similar to that of his Spanish colleagues was dashed when Lucan and Seneca, who had probably become his benefactors and friends, were implicated in the Pisonian conspiracy in A.D. 65 and took their own lives.

During the reigns of Nero, Vespasian, Titus, and Domitian, Martial sustained himself in a humble apartment in Rome by composing occasional verses for a succession of apparently parsimonious patrons. Under Nero, or more likely the Flavian emperors, probably Titus (reigned A.D. 79–81) and Domitian (reigned A.D. 81–96), Martial was granted the military tribunate, a rank that gave him the rights of a member of the equestrian class, and was awarded the *ius trium liberorum* (the right of three children), a privilege usually granted to political aspirants of at least three legitimate children, despite possibly never having been married. His poetry reveals that he either was given or inherited a farm at Nomentum, fifteen miles northeast of Rome, in about A.D. 83, and was eventually able to purchase a small

or clever turn of thought; some are translations of Greek epigrams. They were written to be put on tombstones, to accompany gifts and other special purposes, and to celebrate occasions. The popularity of the epigram in the Latin literary tradition is well attested, since poets such as Catullus, Virgil, Ovid, Lucan, and Petronius wrote them. At the time Martial began composing epigrams, the topical and metrical scope of the genre had already widened considerably, embracing virtually every imaginable subject in a variety of meters, but there were still certain conventions and requirements that an epigrammatist was expected to follow.

While Martial incorporated traditional elements of the genre as he inherited it, he felt compelled to justify his development of new techniques and subject matter. His contributions to the genre are so important, moreover, that he is widely regarded as its greatest and

house sometime before A.D. 94 in the Quirinal, a sought-after section of Rome.

Martial may not have been received as favorably during Nerva's reign (A.D. 96–98), given his flattery of Domitian in his epigrams, and that fact may have provided the impetus for him to leave Rome for his native Bilbilis in A.D. 98, but he also had become tired of the urban distractions that impinged upon his writing. With the assistance of his friend Pliny, who paid his traveling expenses, Martial retired to the rural estate given to him by his wealthy patroness Marcella. While Martial praises the Epicurean ideal of the quiet life that he must have enjoyed at first in his change to a country environment, eventually he did not find Bilbilis as agreeable as he had hoped. There was a lack of stimulating material for epigrammatic composition; he was besieged by the local townspeople requesting his help; he had little patience for the gossip-mongering of a small provincial town; and he probably missed the recognition, respect, and incentives of patronage that only Rome could accord him. Nevertheless, he managed to complete his last book of epigrams there before dying ca. A.D. 103.

Martial's literary fame, social standing, and economic fortunes improved after his publication in A.D. 80 of the *Liber de Spectaculis* (Book on the Games), originally known under the title *Epigrammaton Liber* (Book of Epigrams), a series of epigrams composed to commemorate the emperor Titus's grand opening of the games for the Flavian Amphitheater (the Colosseum). D. R. Shackleton Bailey's Teubner edition (1990) includes only a few dozen poems, but the surviving collection is incomplete. The initial epigrams celebrate the greatness of the Flavian Amphitheater and the beneficence and benevolence of Titus: the Flavian Amphitheater surpasses the wonders of the ancient world (*On the Games* 1); the house and grounds of the cruel Nero have been reclaimed by Rome for the entertainment of her people under the rule of Titus (2); the games, attended by spectators from every corner of the empire, are presided over by its true father (3); and informers whose possessions formerly lined the imperial coffers of Titus's predecessors now are flogged in the arena and exiled (4–5).

The bulk of the pieces in this collection celebrate some of the spectacles of the games. Many of the events described had been reenacted according to well-known incidents in myth but are represented as being more spectacular than their mythical versions. The spectacles include a performance of the bull mating with Pasiphae (*On the Games* 6); Mars and Venus serving Caesar (7); wild animals being slain by gladiators (8, 11–18, 32) or other animals (21–22, 26); gladiators and criminals, some taking on the roles of mythical characters, being torn apart by beasts (9–10, 19, 24–25); an elephant kneeling to pay homage to Titus (20); Titus calling for gladiators to enter the arena (23); mock sea battles, some featuring mythical characters, held in the flooded arena (27–28, 34); a water spectacle featuring groups of Nereids (30); a gladiatorial contest in which both combatants are declared victors (31); and a hind who prayed to Titus and was spared by hounds (33). Some of these spectacles seem especially cruel according to modern sensibilities, but they served to illustrate to his people through the public punishment of criminals the importance of adhering to the legal and social codes of the state and the potential consequences of violating them. In addition, the spectacles provided a means for the emperor to display publicly his generosity and affection for his subjects.

So well-received was the *Liber de Spectaculis* that Martial actually sent a copy to Titus. Despite the success of this commemorative collection, which made the public eager to read more of his epigrams, not until four or five years later in A.D. 84 or 85 did Martial meet this public demand by publishing two books known as *Xenia* (Gifts) and *Apophoreta* (Dinner Gifts), which now appear in Martial's extant corpus as books 13 and 14, respectively, of the *Epigrammaton Libri* (Books of Epigrams). These collections are mainly of historical rather than literary interest. With its emphasis upon food, drink, and clothes, *Xenia* reveals much about the culinary and fashion trends of the late first century, while *Apophoreta,* with its descriptions of various objets d'art, conveys a sense of the aesthetic taste of the Romans and something of the spirit of the Saturnalia, a festive celebration held in December in which the barriers between classes were temporarily removed. Mainly single couplets in elegiac meter, the poems in these books were written to accompany presents given during festivals, particularly the Saturnalia, and other occasions of gift-giving such as birthdays, weddings, and anniversaries.

Xenia includes 127 epigrams that were used to accompany gifts, mainly of food and drink, sent to friends. The collection is structured around the various components of a lavish Roman dinner: the central four sections, which feature the possible dishes for each of the four main courses, are ringed by two sections of side dishes and drink available during the dinner; these sections in turn are framed by prefatory epigrams and epigrams on non-food gifts. Martial mentions a large variety of vegetables, grains, fruits, dairy products, meat, seafood, wine, sauces, and honey. Two examples from the collection illustrate the way that he cleverly plays on the meaning and sense of key words. In a couplet that was to accompany the gift of a rooster, he writes (*Epigrams* 13.63), "So that the *gallus* (rooster) not

Site of Bibilis, Martial's birthplace in the Roman province of Tarraconensian Spain

become skinny by exhausting his groin, / he has lost his testicles. Now to me he will be a–*Gallus* (Gaul)"; he plays on the two meanings of *gallus/Gallus,* "rooster" and "Gaul," that is, a priest of Cybele, a eunuch. In another epigram that was to accompany a gift of vinegar, Martial writes (13.122), "Don't despise a jar of Nile vinegar. / When it was of wine, it was *vilior* (more despicable)"; in this epigram he plays on two senses of the word *vilior,* "cheaper" and "more despicable."

Apophoreta includes 223 poems that were to be taken away with gifts given at dinner parties. Some of the gifts are valuable, others inexpensive. Most of the gift categories are subdivided and arranged so that they are juxtaposed with other groups. The gifts include a wide range of writing materials, tablets, and cases; games and balls; objects of personal hygiene, comfort, and beautification; weapons and sharp instruments; furniture and lighting; athletic paraphernalia; toys; medicine and medicine chests; musical instruments and accessories; food; pets and cages; whips and rods; cloths, bags, and wool; domestic and kitchen utensils; jewelry; clothes, hats, and footwear; bedding and mattress stuffing; statuettes, paintings, and other domestic adornments; editions of ancient writers; and slaves of various occupations. As in his earlier collections, Martial reveals a wry sense of humor and a penchant for the unexpected twist. In a poem that was to accompany the work of the epic poet Lucan, Martial says (*Epigrams* 14.194), "There are some who say that I am no poet; / but the bookseller who sells me thinks I am." In

another poem that was to go with a gift of a slave-stenographer, he writes (14.208), "Although the words run along, the hand is swifter than they. / The tongue has not yet finished and the right hand has finished its work."

Not until after Martial published book 1 of the collection known as *Epigrammaton Libri* (Books of Epigrams), probably in A.D. 86, was his literary standing assured. He counted among his associates and friends some of the main literary figures of the century, including his Spanish compatriot Quintilian, the distinguished teacher of rhetoric; the satirist Juvenal; the epicist Silius Italicus; Frontinus, who wrote on military and municipal affairs; and, of course, the younger Pliny. Martial addressed some of the epigrams in this collection to his friends and benefactors; the epigrams were circulated among them or presented at private and public recitals prior to formal publication. The dedications help to provide some idea of the original arrangement of these epigrams in their published form. Martial wrote on average one book every year and a half until the publication of the twelfth and final book in or just after A.D. 102.

The surviving collection of approximately 1,175 poems ranges widely across the spectrum of literary and human experience. Although its themes and subjects recur many times, this collection manages to avoid becoming tedious to the reader not only through the immense variety of subject matter but also through the careful arrangement of individual poems within each of its books. Martial portrays throughout the collection scenes and figures from everyday life in Rome, but he does not necessarily strive to give them a realistic treatment. Instead he takes stereotypical situations and characters and hyperbolizes, distorts, and ridicules them. The result is an astonishing kaleidoscope of pictures, images, cameos, vignettes, and caricatures. These epigrams include not only physical descriptions of Rome itself, especially its religious buildings, places of public entertainment, lavish residences, and works of art, but also satirical depictions of various characters and scenes.

While Martial gives the names of real friends and patrons, he uses disguised names and concealed personalities for the victims of his satirical epigrams. This practice is understandable, given the circumstances of the early empire, since a writer could incur punishment for an attack upon a powerful or wealthy person. Although Martial maintains that his attacks are innocuous and that his real aim is to expose vice, his epigrams probably offended some individuals. Martial directs verbal fusillades at his targets with unrelenting force—fusillades intensified by the bullets of obscenity, personal invective, double entendre, and caustic wit. He satirizes a host of professionals and tradespeople such as doctors, lawyers, teachers, architects, auctioneers, moneylenders, prostitutes, innkeepers, wine sellers, fishmongers, barbers, cobblers, tanners, undertakers, gladiators, charioteers, and lyre players.

Martial also lampoons many character types, including parasites, bores, coxcombs, charlatans, drunkards, freaks, skinflints, reprobates, adventurers, impostors, and vulgarians. He presents these figures in a panorama of settings, such as the forum, the amphitheater, the baths, the circus, the theater, the market, the street, and the private house. Few character types and social practices escape being at some point the target of his indignation and mordant wit. There is the dinner seeker, who leaves nothing unventured in his efforts to gain an invitation so that he does not have to eat at home (*Epigrams* 2.14); the poor client who dines on meager fare while his host satiates himself on the finest delicacies (3.60); the ladies' man who whispers in a woman's ear and hums tunes from the Nile (3.63); the legacy hunter who sends expensive gifts to old men and widows to ingratiate himself with his prospects (4.56); the man in the theater who claims an equestrian seat to which he has no right and is evicted by the usher (5.8); and the shopper who examines precious objets d'art, inquires as to their prices, but finally buys cheap wine cups (9.59).

While the expression of indignation in a satirical fashion is a distinctive feature of these epigrams, the use of obscenity had long been part of the Latin epigram-

matic tradition and was consistent with contemporary practice. In keeping with this tradition and practice, Martial maintains that an epigram requires a drop of gall to avoid insipidity and that obscenity is suitable, even necessary, for the genre. The epigrams that include obscenity and pornography in his extant body of works amount to fewer than ten percent. Some of these epigrams reflect religious, ritual, festive, hymeneal, procreative, or apotropaic contexts. *Epigrams* 11.72 combines aspects of religion and fertility: "Natta devours the *pipinnam* (little willy) of his young athlete, / compared to whom Priapus is a *gallus/Gallus* (eunuch)." The Latin for "little willy" in the epigram is *pipinnam,* but this word can also be rendered literally as "teeny peeper," as R. E. A. Palmer (1982) does, since it is related to *pipio,* "baby bird." Martial cleverly contrasts *pipinnam* with *gallus/Gallus,* which, as in *Epigrams* 13.63, means "rooster" and "Gaul," a priest of Cybele, a eunuch. Priapus, a god of procreation, was often represented with a large male organ, so the graphic image of Natta performing fellatio on his exceptionally well-endowed boyfriend is mind boggling. Other epigrams seem designed solely to titillate or to shock the senses through their sexual explicitness. The ostensibly gratuitous pornography and vulgarisms of *Epigrams* 11.85 are blatant: "Zoilus, your tongue was struck with an abrupt paralysis / while you were licking. Surely, Zoilus, you screw now."

Martial is a slippery character himself and maddeningly difficult to pin down, as is evident in his ambivalent treatment of the female sex. He praises extravagantly certain upper-class Roman ladies such as Arria, who took her own life out of devotion to her condemned husband Paetus (*Epigrams* 1.13); Porcia, who killed herself after hearing news of her husband Brutus's death (1.42); Nigrina, who handed over her wealth to her husband (4.75); Polla, who commemorated her dead husband Lucan's memory (7.23); Aretulla, who expressed the hope for her brother's imminent return from exile (8.32); and his patroness Marcella, who gave him an estate near Bilbilis (12.21). Martial's praise of specific aristocratic women, though, is juxtaposed with seemingly contradictory attitudes toward women generally. These attitudes can be deduced from the epigrams that deal with female sexuality. The social role of Roman matrons requires them to obey the social code and not to engage in erotic activity other than with their husbands, and certainly not with the lower classes—that is, slaves and freedmen. There are many epigrams on this subject, including one in which Marulla, wife of Cinna, is said to have made her husband a father seven times, but the children were illegitimate, since neither her husband, friends, nor neighbors impregnated her (6.39). On the other hand, Martial suggests, aristocratic males

Emperor Titus, for whom Martial wrote a series of epigrams to commemorate the opening of games at the Colosseum in A.D. 80 (portrait on a brass coin; from Michael Grant,
The Twelve Caesars, *1975)*

(including the poet himself) may engage in sexual relationships with slaves and prostitutes of both sexes, who may be praised if they play their roles as expected. Martial's attitudes toward women and male sexual privilege seem to the modern reader to constitute a blatant double standard, but they are based upon traditional class and gender structures.

Martial's view of Roman society, which seems to be based on a qualified acceptance of the ideological substructures that underpin it, is essentially conservative and moralizing. J. P. Sullivan (1988, 1991) outlines the poet's hierarchical vision of this society: members of the ruling class, especially the emperor himself, are at the top of the social and political hierarchy; beneath these emperors are other figures of the aristocratic classes, who count among their duties to serve the imperial elite and to dispense patronage, especially to a literary client such as Martial, who addresses many of his epigrams to his patrons; finally, at the bottom of this social hierarchy are vast hordes of freedmen and slaves. While Martial glorifies the good emperors (whom he names as Augustus, Titus, Domitian, Nerva, and Trajan) and praises their exploits, he condemns bad emperors, notably Nero. When Domitian is alive, Martial praises him for his military victories and commends him for his moral reforms, but after Domitian dies, Martial stresses the emperor's hypocrisy and the failure of his moral edicts. This ambivalence has encouraged some critics, including Frederick M. Ahl and J. Garth-

waite, to argue that Martial's superficial flattery of Domitian conceals a subtext critical of the emperor.

The Rome that Sullivan neatly outlines, however, was undergoing immense social, cultural, and physical transformation. The factors responsible for this change defy ready definition and explanation on account of their sociological complexity. Martial's Rome can reasonably be described as a society turned upside down by the prosperity achieved through the attainment of its imperialist objectives and the resultant expansion of its economy. A massive program of public building—including temples, theaters, baths, and porticoes—attest to the immense wealth that poured into the city from the provinces. On a private scale the erection of opulent residences and the flowering of the visual and literary arts bear witness to the cultural renewal made possible by this economic prosperity. The senatorial and equestrian orders are served by freedmen and slaves, many of whom have come to Rome from the various regions of its vast empire, creating a cosmopolitan environment unparalleled in its history. What emerges through the eyes of Martial is a picture of a society in which the established traditions and codes buttressing the aristocratic classes have disintegrated. Social and economic barriers are in a state of near collapse. Against this background Martial satirizes unsophisticated parvenu freedmen for daring to equal the wealth, if not the social standing, of the upper classes, and impudent slaves who aspire to follow in the footsteps of their masters.

In spite of his lack of enthusiasm for the social and economic changes that gave rise to a new class of wealthy, powerful freedmen, Martial does not argue specifically against the upward social mobility of the lower classes; nor does he strive particularly to promote the ideals of the aristocracy. Perhaps this ambivalence toward social evolution is reflected in the harsh treatment of his own slaves for disobedience, despite his criticism of other slave owners for their abuse of power. Martial is concerned primarily with exposing the facade of pretense and hypocrisy beneath which both classes attempt to conceal their many transgressions, including sexual perversion, profligacy, avarice, and stinginess. The satirical and mocking tone of many of his epigrams reflects his shock, disgust, and outrage at these people and the institutions and professions they represent.

While Martial's verses are conspicuous for the aforementioned qualities, there are many other facets of his poetry. Memorial poems to deceased friends, patrons, acquaintances, and other figures, expressions of condolence, wishes for and expressions of gratitude for recuperation from illness, as well as poems concerning marriage and anniversaries, friendship, and the simple pleasures of rural life reveal a sensitive and compassionate side to his nature. Many of the memorial poems appear in the form of epitaphs, but even in these poems the poet often does not resist the urge to display his mordant wit. Characteristic of his clever use of wordplay and ambiguity is this fictitious epitaph (*Epigrams* 9.15): "The murderess carved on the tombs of her seven husbands that / 'she,' Chloe, 'did it.' What could be plainer?" Roman matrons often had carved on their tombstones an inscription celebrating their chastity and devotion to their husbands. In this epigram Martial plays on these traditional virtues and epitaphic conventions. The words "she did it" ostensibly refer to Chloe's erection of these tombs with the accompanying inscriptions attesting to her wifely devotion, but the phrase also cleverly suggests that she actually murdered her husbands.

In *Epigrams* 10.47, one of the most frequently cited of Martial's epigrams, the poet itemizes the elements that constitute the ideal life, including inherited wealth, social position, productive land, an informal lifestyle, a robust constitution, comfortable friendship, and a compatible concubine (female or male). This epigram, although it praises the values of human friendship and the pleasures of the simple life, actually draws attention to the social, political, and economic structures that made such a life a possibility for only a tiny minority of Romans. In the case of Martial, this ideal mode of life would have been possible only with the largesse of a wealthy patron, but this level of support eluded him.

Martial's bold reshaping of the traditional epigram into a tool of double-edged wit and humor, however, is what exposed the foibles and hypocrisy of Roman society and ensured his literary fame. From a variety of authorial stances, he depicts a society in which there is apparently no shortage of material to illustrate corruption and absurdity at all levels from slave to emperor. By adopting the stance of an outraged observer of societal perversity, Martial realizes the effective technique of apparently answering offense with offense, audacity with audacity, outrage with outrage. Even his epigrammatic self-portrait, alternately modest and arrogant, and gnomic reflections on human life are important features of his literary program. Almost no other Roman poet attempted to the extent that Martial did to connect with his audience. By apologizing deferentially for his satirical, sometimes obscene, presentations from the adopted stance of a popular poet of modest financial means and social status, Martial is able to play effectively on the contradictions and incongruities of the society he portrays even as he confides in and disarms his implied reader.

A poet's work need not, however, serve to reflect his manner of life, and Martial himself stresses this point in one of his better-known poems addressed to Domitian (*Epigrams* 1.4):

If by chance, Caesar, you should touch upon my little books,
Set aside the censoriousness that is world's lord.
Your triumphs also were accustomed to bear jokes;
Nor does it shame a leader to be material for words of jest.
With the outlook you display when you watch Thymele [a stage actress or character] and the joker Latinus [a comic actor],
With that outlook, I pray, may you read my poems.
A censor can allow harmless amusements:
My page is licentious, my life upright.

Ultimately readers are left with a vivid impression of a brash yet engaging poet (or poetic persona) whose experience of life, insight into humanity, and ambivalence toward society are reflected in a host of seriohumorous observations. Martial plays with his readers, pokes fun at his characters, and mocks his world. Above all, he makes his readers think.

Martial reveals one of the most striking paradoxes of his poetic personality in his highly self-conscious remarks on his reputation and epigrams. His self-estimation as a poet reveals a seemingly contradictory attitude toward his achievement and the nature of his art. In many places Martial dismisses his epigrams as mere trifles or rubbish. Elsewhere he makes strong claims to present and future fame, notably in the first poem of the *Epigrams,* where he states his name and observes that his readers have given him more fame throughout the world while he is alive than many poets have after their deaths. Yet, this inconsistency in self-appraisal is not quite what it seems. The Latin word for "trifles" (*nugae*) that Martial uses to refer to his epigrams was commonly employed by poets such as Horace (65–8 B.C.) and Catullus (87–54 B.C.) to refer to their poetry, especially, as in the case of the latter, in reference to short, witty poems in contrast to the long, elevated poems of epic and tragedy.

There is enough in the epigrams of Martial, though, for him to assert that they constitute more than mere trifles. For Martial mythological epic and tragedy are genres of fantasy and irrelevance, whereas epigram in his hands is the genre of daily life, social relevance, and individual self-awareness. Even when Martial suggests that he deserves to be taken seriously as a poet, he reveals his apprehension about his achievement from a mock-modest stance of humor and self-depreciation. In the preface to *Epigrams* 9 he writes,

I am he whose trifles are second in praise to no one,
whom, reader, you do not marvel at but, I think, you love.
Let greater men orchestrate greater poems. Even though I speak of little things
I am content to return often to your hands.

M·V·MARTIALIS EPIGRAMMATA·

IN AMPHITHEATRVM CAESARIS.

ARBARA PYRAMIDVM
ſileat miracula Memphis,
Aſſiduus iactet nec Babylona
labor,
Nec Triuiæ templo molles lauden
tur honores,
Diſſimuletʠ; Deum cornibus ara frequens·
Aere nec uacuo pendentia mauſolea
Laudibus immodicis cares in aſtra ferant·
Omnis cæſareo cedat labor amphitheatro·
Vnum pro cunctis fama loquatur opus·
Ad eundem Cæſarem·
Hic ubi ſydereus propius uidet aſtra coloſſus,
Et creſcunt media pægmata celſa uia,
Inuidioſa feri radiabant atria Regis,
Vnaʠ; iam tota ſtabat in urbe domus·
Hic ubi conſpicui uenerabilis amphitheatri
Erigitur moles, ſtagna Neronis erant·
Hic ubi miramur uelocia munera thermas,
Abſtulerat miſeris tecta ſuperbus ager·
Claudia diffuſas ubi porticus explicat umbras,
Vltima pars aulæ deficientis erat·
Reddita Roma ſibi eſt, & ſunt te præſide Cæſar
Deliciæ populi, quæ fuerant domini·
Ad eundem·
Quæ tam ſepoſita eſt, quæ gens tam barbara Cæſar,
Ex qua ſpectator non ſit in urbe tua?

A ii

Title page for the edition of Martial's epigrams published in 1501 by Aldus Manutius of Venice (courtesy of the Lilly Library, Indiana University)

What matters to Martial is that his readers find his epigrams interesting and pleasurable so that they read them again and again.

Martial's style is not easy to describe because of its extraordinary richness and variety, but verbal dexterity is its hallmark. His epigrams are remarkable for their use of concise language, onomatopoeic words, sententious reflections, witty conceits, hyperbolic situations, comic surprises, theatrical images, vivid metaphors, and biting comparisons. In order to achieve these effects, Martial employs an impressive variety of stylistic devices such as alliteration, assonance, and anaphora. The rhythmic and acoustic effects produced by these devices can be difficult to render in English, but this adaptation of six lines from Shackleton Bailey's (1993) translation of *Epigrams* 5.24 illustrates Martial's technique:

Hermes, favorite fighter of the age;
Hermes, tempest and tremor of his school;
Hermes, who alone makes Helius afraid;
Hermes, taught to win without wounding;
Hermes, darling and distress of gladiators' women;
Hermes, menacing with marine trident.

This translation mirrors the poet's use of anaphora and alliteration in the original text.

Chief among Martial's poetic techniques is syntactical manipulation. He is fond of balance and parallelism, especially at the beginning and end of lines. He places words of opposing meaning at opposite ends of the same line as if to demonstrate visually the difference between them. In *Epigrams* 12.30, Martial writes: "Aper is dry and sober. What is that to me? / A slave I so praise, not a friend." The second line of this couplet draws a contrast between the slave, who is expected to be sober, and a friend, who is not. Sometimes a word or phrase appears to be withheld intentionally until the end of an epigram to produce an unexpected and dramatic turn of thought, as in *Epigrams* 10.8: "Paula wants to marry me. I don't want to marry Paula: / she is an old woman. I would be willing if she were an older woman." Logically the reader expects Martial to say that he would be willing to marry Paula if she were younger—not older. The suggestion is that Martial (or the persona through whom the poet speaks) would be willing to marry Paula if she didn't have too many years left before he could inherit her wealth.

The above-mentioned stylistic and dramatic effects come packaged in a wide variety of formal metrical structures. More than three-quarters of the epigrams are elegiacs, a couplet form that consists of a single line composed in dactylic hexameter (six measures) followed by one in dactylic pentameter (five measures). Most of the rest are written in hendecasyllables (lines of eleven syllables) and scazons (lines of three measures), with the balance in hexameters and iambics (lines consisting of measures of one short followed by one long syllable). Most epigrams prior to Martial's were brief couplets. Martial appears to be innovative in the frequency with which he employs the hexameter and in the length of his epigrams, which range up to forty lines.

Martial's technical and metrical virtuosity attest to his mastery of the epigrammatic form. The obituary that Pliny wrote affords some additional clues as to the reasons for Martial's standing as one of the important figures in the history of European poetry. The ambiguous qualities of wit, sarcasm, and charm that Pliny identifies in Martial's work help to explain its enormous appeal to contemporary Romans and to subsequent generations of poets, translators, and readers. During his own time, for instance, the satirical epigrams of

Martial influenced Juvenal in the composition of his satires. Therefore, the recurrent popularity of Martial in the various literary traditions that followed him is not surprising. Virtually every great European literary movement records littérateurs who have either attempted to emulate Martial in the composition of their own poetry, who have translated his epigrams, or who have merely admired his wit and ingenuity. In ages when the less traditional literary forms were especially popular, his reputation grew and he assumed a major role in the shaping of the western literary sensibility.

Although Martial has not always been widely read or cited, at no time has he completely disappeared from the literary scene after the imperial period. In late antiquity poets such as Ausonius (ca. A.D. 310–395), Claudian (died ca. A.D. 404), Sidonius Apollinaris (ca. A.D. 430–ca. 479), Fortunatus (ca. A.D. 540–ca. 600), Luxorius (parts of the fifth and the sixth centuries), and Isidorus (ca. A.D. 600–636) imitated and quoted from Martial's body of epigrams, while various grammarians often used his work for illustrations. Citations and imitations of his poetry appear among the manuscripts of various scholars and poets from late antiquity to the Middle Ages, especially during the Carolingian period of the ninth century. In the early Middle Ages Martial was imitated and quoted by many English littérateurs, notably Godfrey of Winchester (ca. A.D. 1050–1107), John of Salisbury (ca. 1115–1180), and Vincent of Beauvais (died 1264). The North Italian prehumanists of the thirteenth century were familiar with Martial, as were the famous Italian Renaissance humanists Francesco Petrarch (1304–1374) and Giovanni Boccaccio (1313–1375). In the fifteenth century Martial's popularity and influence throughout Italy is apparent in the many imitations of and commentaries on his epigrams, including those of Poggio Bracciolini (1380–1459) and Antonio Beccadelli (1394–1471).

The importance of Martial as a literary figure becomes especially evident in the sixteenth and seventeenth centuries, when Renaissance poets in Britain, Spain, France, and Germany translated and imitated his poetry in the vernacular. In England his satiric epigrams inspired many English emulators and devotees, including Henry Howard (ca. 1517–1547), John Harington (1560–1612), Robert Herrick (1591–1674), Ben Jonson (1573–1637), and Abraham Cowley (1618–1667), while in Wales John Owen (1564–ca. 1628) composed 1,500 epigrams (almost the same number as Martial), which received virtually as much attention as those of his Roman model. On the European continent Martial influenced Spanish poets such as Baltasar Gracián (1601–1658) and Francisco Quevedo (1580–1645) in the *siglo de oro;* French poets of the *Pléiade* such as Clément Marot (1497–1544) and Joachim du Bellay (ca. 1525–1560); and the German epigrammatist Johann Scheffler (1624–1677), who composed 3,560 epigrams. During the latter part of the twentieth century, Martial once again has found favor among critics and readers, whose own aesthetic sensibilities, irreverent tastes, and appreciation of the complex range of meanings and associations generated by language are arguably more in tune with those of the Romans of Martial's time.

Martial's reputation, though, has varied enormously throughout the ages, and his poetic productions have sometimes been disparaged on moralistic and aesthetic grounds, most recently during the late eighteenth, nineteenth, and early twentieth centuries. Critics have condemned the amount of obscenity and pornography in his verses, while they have also objected to the many poems of flattery addressed to Domitian and to his patrons. Even Martial's wit and humor, the most salient features of his polyphonous body of works, which are manifested in amusing wordplay and absurd situations, are not readily transferable to other cultures and generations, whose aesthetic codes may be quite different from those of Romans in the early empire. Martial is a product of his age: his style is an index of the complex attitudes produced by the prevailing social conditions and literary tastes. In accordance with literary conventions and the expectations of the institution of patronage, he honors his emperor and benefactors by praising them exuberantly in his poems, but he juxtaposes this praise with ridicule of the institution itself. Even the obscene and pornographic elements, at least in part, are his way of reflecting upon the social and moral realities of the sociocultural environment within which he moved and functioned. The controversy that sometimes has surrounded these and other aspects of his poetry over the ages serves to highlight rather than to obscure his influential role in the European literary tradition.

Bibliographies and Concordances:

G. W. M. Harrison III, "Martialis 1901–1970," *Lustrum,* 18 (1975): 300–337;

Edgar Siedschlag, *Martial Konkordanz* (Hildesheim, Germany: G. Olms, 1979).

References:

Frederick M. Ahl, "The Rider and the Horse: Politics and Power in Roman Poetry from Horace to Statius," *Aufstieg und Niedergang der Römischen Welt II,* 32, no. 1 (1984): 40–110;

Walter Allen Jr. and others, "Martial: Knight, Publisher and Poet," *Classical Journal,* 65 (1970): 345–357;

William S. Anderson, "*Lascivia* vs. *Ira:* Martial and Juvenal," *California Studies in Classical Antiquity,* 3 (1970): 1–34;

A. J. Boyle, "Martialis Redivivus: Evaluating the Unexpected Classic," *Ramus,* 24, no. 1 (1995): 82–101;

J. C. Bramble, "Martial and Juvenal," in *The Cambridge History of Classical Literature,* Volume 2: *Latin Literature,* edited by E. J. Kenney (Cambridge: Cambridge University Press, 1982), pp. 597–623;

A. G. Carrington, "Martial," in *Neronians and Flavians: Silver Latin I,* edited by Donald Reynolds Dudley (London and Boston: Routledge & Kegan Paul, 1972), pp. 236–270;

J. Wight Duff and A. M. Duff, *A Literary History of Rome in the Silver Age,* third edition (London: Benn, 1964), pp. 397–421;

D. P. Fowler, "Martial and the Book," *Ramus,* 24, no. 1 (1995): 31–58;

R. W. Garson, "Martial on his Craft," *Prudentia,* 11 (1979): 7–13;

John Garthwaite, "Martial, Book 6, on Domitian's Moral Censorship," *Prudentia,* 22, no. 1 (1990): 13–22;

Garthwaite, "The Panegyrics of Domitian in Martial Book 9," *Ramus,* 22, no. 1 (1993): 78–102;

Garthwaite, "Putting a Price on Praise: Martial's Debate with Domitian in Book 5," in Toto Notus in Orbe: *Perspektiven der Martial-Interpretation,* edited by Favouk Grewing (Stuttgart: Franz Steiner, 1998), pp. 157–172;

H. A. Mason, "Is Martial a Classic?" *The Cambridge Quarterly,* 17 (1988): 297–368;

R. E. A. Palmer, "Martial," in *Ancient Writers: Greece and Rome,* Volume 2: *Lucretius to Ammianus Marcellinus,* edited by T. James Luce (New York: Scribners, 1982), pp. 887–913;

Michael D. Reeve, "Martial," in *Texts and Transmission: A Survey of the Latin Classics,* edited by L. D. Reynolds (Oxford: Oxford University Press, 1983): pp. 239–244;

W. H. Semple, "The Poet Martial," *Bulletin of the John Rylands Library,* 42 (1969–1970): 432– 452;

J. P. Sullivan, *Martial: The Unexpected Classic. A Literary and Historical Study* (Cambridge: Cambridge University Press, 1991);

Sullivan, "Martial," in *The Imperial Muse,* edited by A. J. Boyle (Berwick, Scotland: Ariel Publications, 1988), pp. 177–191;

Sullivan, *Martial,* The Classical Heritage (New York & London: Garland, 1993);

Bruce W. Swann, *Martial's Catullus: The Reception of an Epigrammatic Rival* (Hildesheim, Germany: G. Olms, 1994);

R. G. Tanner, "Levels of Intent in Martial," *Aufstieg und Niedergang der Römischen Welt,* 32, no. 4 (1986): 2624–2677.

Naevius

(ca. 265 B.C. – 201 B.C.)

Sander M. Goldberg
University of California, Los Angeles

WORKS–FRAGMENTARY: *Bellum Punicum* (The Punic War), an epic;
Comedies and tragedies in Greek dress, historical plays on Roman themes.

Standard editions: *Scaenicae romanorum poesis fragmenta,* 2 volumes, edited by Otto Ribbeck (Leipzig: Teubner, 1871–1873; reprinted, Hildesheim: Olms, 1962); *Cn. Naevii Belli Punici carmen,* edited by Wladyslaw Strzelecki (Leipzig: Teubner, 1964); *Fragmenta poetarum latinorum epicorum et lyricorum praeter Ennium et Lucilium,* edited by Willy Morel and Karl Büchner; third edition, edited by Jürgen Blänsdorf (Stuttgart & Leipzig: Teubner, 1995).

Translation in English: *Remains of Old Latin,* volume 2, edited by E. H. Warmington, Loeb Classical Library (Cambridge, Mass.: Harvard University Press, 1967).

A Campanian by birth, and therefore probably not a Roman with the full rights of a citizen, Gnaeus Naevius nevertheless stands as one of the most interesting, talented, and allusive figures in the early history of Roman literature. He was a pioneer both on the stage and in the study. None of his works survives complete: there remain only fragments of tragedies and comedies based on Greek models, of a new kind of historical play on Roman themes called the *fabula praetexta,* and of the first original Latin epic. He was also the subject of much biographical speculation, and colorful stories about him circulated in antiquity.

Naevius was said to be a free spirit, a man quick to voice even political opinions from the stage and prepared to pay the price of that license. "Libera lingua loquemur ludis Liberalibus" (We will speak with free tongue at Freedom's games, 1 13R), says one character with an alliterative gift. One verse with an ambigious meaning, "fato Metelli Romae fiunt consules" (by fate the Metelli become consuls at Rome), was said to have earned him the enmity of the powerful family of the Caecilii Metelli, who replied with a verse of their own:

"dabunt malum Metelli Naevio poetae" (The Metelli will make trouble for the poet Naevius). And so they did. Some say that Naevius was jailed (and entertained his jailors by writing two witty comedies while confined) or was put in the stocks (and so earned the sympathy of the comic writer Plautus) and/or was eventually banished from Rome, dying in exile in Utica. As so often occurs with matters of ancient biography, however, the most colorful details are the least likely to be true. Naevius probably began his career ca. 235 B.C. and may even have had dealings with the Metelli, but he almost certainly did not speak from the stage in his own voice, and what his characters say cannot be given political meaning out of context.

A good example of the problem caused by doing so comes from a play called *Tarentilla* (The Girl from Tarentum):

uae ego in theatro hic meis probavi plausibus,
ea non audere quemquam regem rumpere:
quanto libertatem hanc hic superat servitus!

(I don't think that any big shot would dare to wreck
what I have tested with my applause in the theater here:
that's how much this servitude beats this freedom!)

The fragment is preserved without dramatic context: Charisius, a grammarian of the fourth century A.D., cites it simply to illustrate the adverb *quanto* (by how much). Some scholars have nevertheless placed the lines in the prologue to the play and hear in them Naevius's assertion of his right to free speech. According to this reading, the "big shot" Naevius defies is Q. Caecilius Metellus, consul in 206 B.C. and the putative target of the "fato Metelli" barb. This interpretation, however, is fanciful. The lines are unlikely to have come from a prologue. Only Terence, two generations later, expressed personal opinions in dramatic prologues, and these were literary opinions expressed in the third person. Naevius's speaker was almost certainly speaking in character. He was probably a clever slave boasting of his ability to overcome the opposition of a rich opponent: the *servitus* is real, and *rex,* literally "king," is a stock term in Roman comedy for a rich, self-important man. The lines are not topical but traditional. The situation, characters, vocabulary, tone, and even the play with dramatic illusion they suggest are all familiar from the comedies of Plautus, and these shared features say something more important about Naevius's art than about his biography.

Latin stage comedy based upon Greek originals and performed in Greek dress, the so-called *comoedia palliata,* was introduced at the *ludi Romani* (Roman Games) of 240 B.C., and Naevius was therefore part of Rome's first generation of dramatists. It is thus particularly striking that the fragments of his comedies, though scant (fewer than 140 lines survive), nevertheless show such strong affinities of style, character, and subject with the works of Plautus, written a generation later when the genre was in its prime. Naevius's titles (thirty-two are attested) include names known from Plautus to be the names of clever slaves (for example, *Lampadio, Stalagmus*) and words denoting trickery, a mainstay of Plautine plots (for example, *Dolus, Technicus*). Others—such as *Colax* (The Flatterer), *Pellex* (The Concubine), *Dementes* (The Madmen), and *Quadrigemini* (The Quadruplets)—suggest characters and dramatic situations with long histories on the ancient stage. Indeed, the voices of slaves, fathers, courtesans, and young men in love can all be heard among their fragments. Naevius probably also wrote songs of the kind found in Plautus: one fragment is in cretics ($\_ \cup \_$) and another almost certainly in bacchiacs ($\cup \_ \_$), two of Plautus's favorite lyric meters. Only one play, though, the *Tarentilla,* is sufficiently well attested to suggest something of its plot: two young men carouse with a courtesan, probably the Tarentine girl of the title, and are caught by their two fathers. There is no doubt that his plays helped establish the norms of this popular (and traditional) genre. Terence refers to Naevius as an honored predecessor (*Andria* 18–20), and Volcacius Sedigitus, who wrote about the ancient dramatists in the early first century B.C., ranked Naevius's talents just below those of Plautus.

Naevius also wrote tragedies, though barely sixty lines and only six titles survive. All are drawn from Greek myth (for example, *Danae, Iphigenia*). Again the meters include spoken and lyric verse. Naevius, however, does not appear to have been as successful with his tragedies as he was with his comedies. Unlike the tragedies of Ennius, Pacuvius, and Accius, Naevius's tragedies did not become classics of the Roman stage. Perhaps only one, *Equus Troianus* (The Trojan Horse), outlived him: it was apparently reproduced for the

inauguration of Pompey's great theater in the Campus Martius at Rome in 55 B.C.

More interesting, though even less well attested, is Naevius's experiment with plays on Roman themes, the *fabula praetexta.* The genre may even have been his invention. Only three titles survive and scarcely six lines. Two titles, *Romulus* and *Lupus* (The Wolf), suggest, if they are not alternative titles for the same work, plays on the founding of Rome. The third, *Clastidium,* takes its title from the town where the consul M. Claudius Marcellus won a major victory over the Gauls in 222 B.C., killing the Gallic chief Viridomarus in single combat. Since the Romans did not tolerate the representation of living men on the stage, the production of *Clastidium* is usually dated either to Marcellus's funeral games in 208 B.C. or to his son's dedication in 205 B.C. of a temple to Honor and Courage that Marcellus had vowed before the battle. Though to infer from this commission that Naevius was in some sense a client of the Claudii Marcelli would be wrong, Naevius's choice of subjects for this new genre of the *praetexta* does suggest an ongoing interest in glorifying Roman achievements and fostering an emerging Roman sense of self. Such interests are certainly at work in Naevius's last great creation, *Bellum Punicum* (The Punic War).

The first Punic War (264–241 B.C.) not only gave Rome control of Sicily but also elevated Rome to the status of world power, a development with both material and cultural ramifications. Its newly won trade routes to the western Mediterranean fostered Rome's imperial ambitions even as, on the cultural front, the city celebrated its great victory by commissioning Latin plays for the Roman Games of 240 B.C. in order to bring this native celebration up to the sophistication of a Greek international festival. Small wonder, then, that in the last quarter of the century, as Hannibal's string of military victories in the second war with Carthage shook Roman confidence to its foundations, an aged Naevius would look back to the triumphs of that first struggle, in which he himself had participated, and make them the subject of the first true Roman epic. Though the motive seems clear, the style of the poem is curious. Naevius drew not on the dactylic meter of Homer (which he certainly knew) or on the iambic rhythms of drama that he had perfected in his plays but on what may have been a native Italian meter that later Roman scholars called the Saturnian. Unfortunately, the metrical principles behind the Saturnian are unknown. The verse was used in epitaphs, inscriptions, and liturgies, and Naevius's predecessor Livius Andronicus had composed a Saturnian translation of the *Odyssey,* but too few verses survive to permit a convincing analysis of the meter's origin and form. The only certain feature of authentic Saturnian verses seems to be that they

Relief carving of a Roman ship carrying legionaries, similar to the ships in the fleet that took Roman troops to Carthage for the second Punic War,
described by Naevius in his history (Biblioteca Apostolica Vaticana)

are formed of two metrical units or cola, the second of which is generally one to three syllables shorter than the first. Thus, for example, Naevius records the invasion of Sicily by Manius Valerius Maximus in 263 B.C. (Fr. 3):

> Manius Valerius
> consul partem exerciti in expeditionem
> ducit

> (Manius Valerius
> the consul led part of his army
> on a foray)

At first glance, the Saturnian may not seem to be a particularly promising kind of poetry, but the testimony about and fragments of the *Bellum Punicum* reveal some interesting features. The poem had a complex structure. Embedded in the early part of the historical narrative—quite possibly presented as a flashback dur-

ing Valerius's expedition to Sicily—was the story of Aeneas's flight from Troy, his sojourn in Carthage, and the eventual founding of Rome. Some of the most moving fragments from the poem come from this mythological section, such as this one describing the wives of Aeneas and Anchises (Fr. 5):

> amborum uxores
> noctu Troiad exibant capitibus opertis
> flentes ambae, abeuntes, lacrimis cum multis

> (Their wives
> escaped Troy by night with covered heads,
> both weeping, going out, with many tears)

The fragment also illustrates a tendency in Saturnians to put main ideas in the first colon and ornamental or summarizing expressions in the second, sometimes bridging the colon boundary with assonance and alliteration. Historical fragments show the same pattern, as in this one describing the invasion of Malta in 257 B.C. (Fr. 32):

> transit Melitam
> exercitus Romanus. insulam integram
> urit vastat populatur, rem hostium concinnat.

> (The Roman army
> crossed to Malta. The untouched island
> it burned, wasted, destroyed. It finished the enemy's
> affairs.)

The alliterative bridge between cola is especially marked in fragment 37: "superbiter contemtim conterit legiones" (arrogantly and contemptuously he exhausted the legions). Naevius's epic was clearly a poem of complexity and art, and it was not without influence over the poets to come.

The *Bellum Punicum* kept a readership until well into Augustan times. It was edited and divided into seven books by the scholar C. Octavius Lampadio in the late second century B.C., and Horace still saw it in bookcases late in the first century B.C. Poets, however, had by then moved Latin epic in a rather different direction. Within a generation of Naevius's death, Q. Ennius (239–169 B.C.) found the Saturnian verse hopelessly archaic and wrote his own *Annales* (Annals), the first truly great narrative poem in Latin, in the dactylic hexameter familiar from the Greek epic tradition. Horace eventually likened this vanishing of the Saturnian to the draining of a marsh. Yet, even Ennius did not repeat the story of the first Punic War in his *Annals* of Roman history: Naevius's achievement endured and made that repetition unnecessary. Even more striking is that famous moments in Virgil's *Aeneid*—such as the storm in book 1 and Venus's appeal to Jupiter, as well as Aeneas's dalliance in Carthage—were apparently taken complete from the *Bellum Punicum*. Such borrowing is striking testimony to the continued influence of the old poem.

Later generations knew what purported to be Naevius's own epitaph for himself. It was written in Saturnians:

> immortales mortales si fores fas flere,
> flerent divae Camenae Naevium poetam.
> itaque postquam est Orchi traditus thesauro
> obliti sunt Romae loquier lingua Latina.

> (If immortals could mourn for mortals.
> the divine Muses would mourn the poet Naevius.
> After he was passed to Orcus's treasury,
> they forgot at Rome how to speak Latin.)

The verses are preserved by the antiquarian Aulus Gellius, who found them "full of Campanian arrogance." That claim is hard to judge, but they certainly preserve a color and a confidence appropriate to Rome's first literary personality. Whether or not the sudden return of Naevius's work from Orcus's treasury would actually restore great poetry to the Latin canon, major chapters in the history of Roman literature would no doubt have to be rewritten if Naevius's influence upon it could be judged at first hand.

References:

Harriet I. Flower, "*Fabulae Praetextae* in Context: When Were Plays on Contemporary Subjects Performed in Republican Rome?" *Classical Quarterly,* 45 (1995): 170–190;

Sander M. Goldberg, *Epic in Republican Rome* (New York: Oxford University Press, 1995), pp. 32–37, 73–82;

Erich S. Gruen, *Studies in Greek Culture and Roman Policy* (Berkeley: University of California Press, 1996), pp. 92–106;

H. T. Rowell, "The Original Form of Naevius' *Bellum Punicum,*" *American Journal of Philology,* 68 (1947): 21–46;

Michael Wigodsky, *Vergil and Early Latin Poetry* (Wiesbaden: Steiner, 1972);

John Wright, *Dancing in Chains: The Stylistic Unity of the comoedia palliata* (Rome: American Academy, 1974), pp. 33–59.

Nepos

(ca. 100 B.C. – post 27 B.C.)

Jane Che
University of Pennsylvania

MAJOR WORK: *De viris illustribus,* 16 books or more (On Famous Men, 35–34 B.C.; second edition before 27 B.C.)–comprising the section *De excellentibus ducibus exterarum gentium* (On Outstanding Leaders of Foreign Nations) and *Cato* and *Atticus* from *De historicis Latinis* (On Latin Historians).

WORKS–ATTRIBUTED:
De Romanorum imperatoribus (On Generals of the Romans); *De historicis Graecis* (On Greek Historians); *De regibus* (On Kings); *De poetis* (On Poets); *De oratoribus* (On Orators); *De grammaticis* (On Scholars).

WORKS–LOST:
Chronica, 3 books; *Exempla,* 5 or more books; *Life of Cato; Life of Cicerorotic Poems; Letters to Cicero.*

Editio princeps: *Vitae imperatorum, sive De vita illustrium virorum* (Venice: Nicolaus Jenson, 1471).

Standard editions: *Corneli Nepotis vitae,* edited by E. O. Winstedt (Oxford: Clarendon Press, 1904); *Cornelii Nepotis quae exstant,* edited by Henrica Malcovati (Turin: Paravia, 1945); *Oeuvres,* edited and translated by A. M. Guillemin (Paris: Les Belles Lettres, 1961); *Cornelii Nepotis vitae cum fragmentis,* edited by Peter K. Marshall (Leipzig: Teubner, 1977).

Translations in English: *Cornelius Nepotis vitae,* translated by John C. Rolfe, Loeb Classical Library (Cambridge, Mass.: Harvard University Press, 1894); *Cornelius Nepos: A Selection, including the Lives of Cato and Atticus,* edited by N. M. Horsfall (Oxford: Clarendon Press, 1989).

Commentaries: *Cornelius Nepos,* edited by Karl Nipperdey and K. Witte, twelfth edition (Berlin: Weidmann, 1912); *Vies d'Hannibal, de Caton et d'Atticus,* edited by Michel Ruch (Paris: Presses universitaires de France, 1968).

Cornelius Nepos is known mainly as the founder of the technique of parallel biography whose innovative *De viris illustribus* (On Famous Men, 35–34 B.C.) launched the literary genre of political biography at Rome and paved the way for the great biographical work of Plutarch, *Parallel Lives.* Not much is known of Nepos except what can be extrapolated from the work of others. His birth date is given by St. Jerome's *Chronicles* as 100 B.C. Pliny the Elder claims that Nepos died after 31 B.C., or perhaps nearer to 27 B.C., when the reign of Augustus was known as the "principate." Nepos's praenomen is unknown. He was born and reared in the Po Valley of Cisalpine Gaul, but the exact place of birth is unclear, though Ostiglia and Pavia are mentioned. Obviously he left his home at some point and immigrated to Rome, but the date is unknown. Cicero's speech *Pro Cornelio* (For Cornelius) in 65 B.C. makes clear that Nepos had been in Rome for some time. Within the year he befriended his patron Titus Pomponius Atticus (110–32 B.C.), Cicero's close friend, who introduced him to the Roman literary circle of such esteemed writers as Cicero, Catullus, and perhaps Varro and Sallust, though Nepos was never the artistic equal of any of them.

Writers of the Late Republican period were greatly influenced by the different philosophical schools of the Greeks, especially the Academy, the Peripatos, and the Stoa. Rhetoric, dialectic, and *grammatica* (literally the study of language and philosophy) derived from the Greeks and were prevalent in the young Roman's education. Rhetoric greatly influenced historiography because it eased the difficulty of writing a coherent narrative of complex events. For any writer of artistic prose, rhetoric was the means by which the record of events was organized and delivered. Although teachers of rhetoric were held in fairly low esteem by society at large, and the art they taught was suspect for its ability to empower the evil person as well as the good with the strength to persuade, rhetorical skill was nevertheless indispensable for the historian as well as for the politician.

The Romans' fabled love of history was nurtured early in Nepos's education. Students of rhetoric were encouraged to read history for its useful examples of virtuous and wicked behavior by their forbears, and

Nepos even collected a volume of such stories, his *Exempla,* of which a few fragments remain. This collection of anecdotes from Roman history, illustrating by example the virtues and iniquities of the past, was a useful resource for orators. The historian Valerius Maximus's *Dicta et facta memorabilia* clearly was written on the model of the *Exempla.* Rhetoricians also read history for an understanding of the arrangement of complex sequences of events. The history that Romans of the Early Republic read was often written by men of senatorial rank (and usually patrician status), who were eager to establish their own role in Roman history. Cato's lost *Origines* is a prime example, though Cato was a plebeian. Cicero's "epics" *De consulato suo* and *De meis temporibus* show this tradition taken to what seems to moderns an extreme.

Unlike many of his literary counterparts and like Atticus, Nepos (who was likely an *eques,* or a man of equestrian rank) did not pursue a political career. His interest was in the life of literature at Rome. His friendship with (or perhaps patronage by) Atticus may have developed from a shared interest in historiography. In 59 B.C. Atticus tried unsuccessfully to persuade Cicero to write a geography, which at that time had never been done. Nepos took on his friend's project, though the work does not survive.

Nepos's friendship with Atticus, along with his own talents, kept him in the thick of the literary world. His correspondence with Cicero comprises two books largely centered on philosophy and other intellectual, rather than worldly, topics, much as Atticus's letters tended toward the linguistic, literary, and historical. Nepos may have used Atticus as a source in his histories and dedicated his book on foreign generals to him. The biography of Cato the Elder was written at Atticus's request. Catullus, another young man from Cisalpine Gaul, addressed a poem to his older countryman clearly following the publication of the *Chronica* and, perhaps, influenced by it.

> To whom shall I give this charming little book
> polished with dry pumice-stone?
> To you Cornelius, since you thought my trifling poems
> Of value, even when you, alone of all Italians,
> Dared to write the history of the entire world
> In three books, very learned and, by God, carefully worked.
> So take this little book for yourself and, such as it is,
> May it last, o patron Muse, more than one lifetime.

Nepos had clearly encouraged the younger poet, though it is not clear that he valued Catullus as highly as he is esteemed today. Nor can it be assumed that Catullus found the *Chronica* a model of his admired style: in poetry he esteemed works that were *docta* (learned) and *laboriosa* (carefully worked), as he calls Nepos's work, but these compliments may be fulsome. Indeed, in his *Atticus,*

Nepos maintains that the greatest poet after the death of Lucretius and Catullus was not one of the poets Catullus most esteemed from his own circle, such as Calvus or Cinna, nor the elegist Cornelius Gallus, so admired by Virgil, but the unknown Lucius Julius Calidius (*Atticus* 12.4). On this basis Wendell V. Clausen concluded that Nepos was not a particular devotee of neoteric verse but was kind to his fellow countryman and had a taste for the scurrilous kind of hendecasyllables that were in the early poems of Catullus's first book.

Nepos wrote a biography, unfortunately lost, of his correspondent Cicero. The life of Atticus also gives Nepos's evaluation of his friend. Nepos helped prepare eleven volumes of Cicero's letters for publication in 34 B.C. and recognized that they gave a virtually continuous history of the era (*Atticus,* 16). He also credited Cicero not only with unusual sensibility to current events but with a canny foresight *quae nunc usu veniunt cecinit ut vates* (that sang like a prophet the events that we are now undergoing).

Jerome calls Nepos, Varro, and Santra (first century B.C.), Rome's first biographers, though biography was not considered a literary genre comparable to historiography. Joseph Geiger has argued that Nepos was the first to write political biography, a genre distinct from regular historiography. While Nepos was writing his biographies in the late 30s B.C., Varro was writing his *Imagines* (39 B.C.), a work of seven hundred portraits of famous men from political and literary backgrounds, the first comprehensive biography, consisting of epigrams accompanying each portrait; it also may have been the first record of the reconstruction of the history of art in Italy. According to Pliny, Nepos included three artists in *De viris illustribus* and with Varro earned a reputation for treating both Roman and non-Roman subjects in biographies.

The *Chronica,* in three volumes, was a departure from the old straightforward presentation of events in annalistic sequence: it focused on the synchronization of Greek and Roman events spanning the period from the earliest times to his own day. The technique of synchronization was not new, for such compilations had existed in Greece. In addition, previous Roman historiography tended not to include Greek events; it had most often treated Greek and Roman history as separate and distinct. Nepos's innovation was twofold: to bring this form of historiography to Rome and to treat the events of Greek and Roman history together in one compilation. His attempt to compare the two histories systematically may have been a failure, but it at least inspired Atticus to accomplish a more successful rendition, his convenient and limited one-volume *Liber Annalis* (Book of Years), which became a standard. Atticus wisely addressed solely Roman events, paying much attention to the lin-

*The Leiden codex, the basis for the Boeclerus (Johann Heinrich Boekler) edition of Cornelius Nepos's works, published in Strasbourg in 1640 (Leiden,
Bibliotheek der Rijksuniversiteit, Cod. Leid. B.P.L. 2011)*

eage of the patrician Roman magistrates, thereby gaining him favor with the aristocracy. Nepos, on the other hand, perhaps because he had no political ambitions, showed no such exclusive interest in the ruling class. Thus, Nepos is remembered as an innovator rather than as a master of his genre. This spirit of innovation is best exampled in his biographies, which likewise bind Greek and Roman history. Nepos strove for a balance of Greek and Roman material as much in *De viris illustribus* as he had in *Chronica.*

As in the *Exempla,* where Nepos had combined Greek and Roman history, so in *De viris illustribus* he developed a series of biographical sketches and objective comparisons of both Roman and non-Roman (mainly Greek) political and literary figures. Rome's strong interest in rhetoric and philosophy overshadowed the genre of biography. Political biography, which most likely developed from the largely unrhetorical traditional funeral oration, took on the peripatetic style in which a man's character was measured by his actions. *De viris illustribus* did not simply give a biographical account of each figure but also displayed the achievements of Romans and Greeks side by side in the style of the peripatetic school. Not only is this comparison of Roman and non-Roman elements an original concept, but by using this parallel construction within the structure of the less-serious genre of biography, Nepos established a work that exhibited characteristics hitherto unseen in Roman literature. By first separating biography from traditional historiography, Nepos's work helped establish two distinct literary genres.

Similar in style to Varro's *Imagines,* Nepos's *De viris illustribus* does not confine the biographical sketches to political figures but treats literary ones also. Of the sixteen books that comprised *De viris illustribus,* only the second edition of the book on foreign generals is extant. Nepos grouped the lives into professional categories: kings, generals, historians, grammarians, orators, and others. Supposedly a pair of books were designated to each category; one book dealt with the Roman representative while the other dealt with the Greek counterpart. The conclusion of the book on foreign generals indicates evidence of this construction of two comparative books for each category.

Despite his innovative approach and subject matter, Nepos is to be faulted on account of both his writing style and the many conspicuous errors he makes in *De viris illustribus.* One may consider his omission of the foreign general Brasidas in the book of foreign generals a serious mistake for a political biographer like Nepos, but plenty of other obvious errors in his writings are prevalent, particularly in his descriptions of famous battles. For instance, Nepos confuses the battles of the Mycale and the Eurymedon, and his account of the Battle of Mara-

thon is erroneous. Inaccuracies bedevil even his description of Hannibal's crossing of the Alps. He is also prone to errors of geography (Lemnos, an island in the northern Aegean, is set in the southern Aegean) and prosopography; in his *Life of Miltiades,* he misleads his readers for two chapters by confusing the Athenian aristocrat and general Miltiades, the victor of Marathon, with his less-famous uncle of the same name. In the chronology of his *Life of Themistocles* Nepos's faulty calculation of the Persian king's journey leads him to claim that Themistocles made his journey to Asia in six months and his return in only thirty days. Nepos's aim may have been to entertain his readers by applying his anecdotal style to these historical accounts, but it has prevented his having made a significant contribution to historiography in the strictest sense.

De viris illustribus may have been Nepos's last ambitious project. The dedication to Atticus reveals that the original form must have been published during Atticus's lifetime. Nepos published a second, revised edition of the book on foreign generals that appeared after the death of Atticus in 32 B.C. The revised edition is longer than the original, which left out the lives of Datames, Hamilcar, and Hannibal. According to Geiger, the size of *De viris illustribus* is relevant in establishing it as a work in the genre of political biography, since a true political biography meant a detailed and lengthy account of a life, not the mere bare sketches of the life and death of a figure taken from historical sources like a funeral oration. The size of a political biography became a precedent in the genre, and the voluminous size of Nepos's *De viris illustribus* helped establish it in that category. Plutarch's *Parallel Lives,* based on Nepos's model, is a work of relatively great length. Due to its popularity, Plutarch extended his biographical series to include more lives, thereby proving it to be a biographical work, not an historical one.

The influence of Nepos's *De viris illustribus* on Plutarch's *Parallel Lives* was not limited to size; the two works are also similar in composition and subject matter. Nepos wrote an introduction that included the main themes before each biography. This style, significant to Nepos, is also evident in *Parallel Lives,* in which Plutarch begins his biography with a brief preface. Plutarch apparently was familiar with Nepos's work and adopted the construction of parallel comparison with a stronger, more developed peripatetic trait in his biographies. Even in his selection of subjects, Plutarch models his book on Nepos's by treating some of the same figures, namely Cato the Elder, Cicero, and the Gracchi. Plutarch's category of Athenian generals is said to be exactly like Nepos's, and the category of Roman generals begins with the same person as Nepos's *De viris illustribus.*

A point of departure in the similarity between Nepos and Plutarch can be seen in Plutarch's political

CORNELII
NEPOTIS
Vitæ
Excellentium
Imperatorum
cum
quorumdam
Iconibus

LUGD. BATAV.
Apud SAMUELEM LUCHTMANS 1734.
ACADEMIÆ TYPOGRAPHUM

Title page for an eighteenth-century edition of Nepos's lives of the Roman emperors (courtesy of the Lilly Library, Indiana University)

slant in his selection of Romans of primarily Republican times. Nepos did not stress the magnificence of Rome even as Augustan influence became more prevalent. Instead, he forewarned his readers about foreign customs so that the Roman reader would not be so quick to stigmatize foreigners. He intended the reference of non-Roman material as a point of comparison for the reader. Since Nepos was not politically motivated in his writings, he neither supported foreign policies nor disparaged traditional Roman values. His goal was to render an objective comparison through parallel arrangement as a means of fair evaluation.

Another point worth mentioning is the significance of Nepos's biographies of Cato the Elder and his patron Atticus. Nepos wrote the *Life of Cato* at Atticus's proposal, which came before the period of 35–32 B.C. It was Atticus's intimate friendship with Cato the Elder that warranted such a request. Up until that time there was no true biography in Roman literature. Nepos may have

written his *Life of Cato* before *De viris illustribus* and perhaps after the suicide of Cato the Younger in 46 B.C. *Life of Cato* appeared before the time when biography burgeoned as a genre (mid to late 40s B.C.), thereby ensuring Nepos's place as an innovator in Roman literature.

Like *Life of Cato,* Nepos's other extant biography, *Life of Atticus,* is also innovative; indeed, it is the first of its kind in the late Republic, a biography written about a living person, Nepos's friend, and one written contemporaneously with the events described. The events themselves can thus be given in greater accuracy and detail than, for example, the chronological details of his book on long-ago foreign generals; the dates of events are precise in *Life of Atticus* because of Nepos's personal involvement in the life of his friend. The biography provides a revealing source of Late Republican affairs and of the attitudes of Roman society. The *Life of Atticus* exposes a rare glimpse into the social changes and subtleties of Roman nobility and of other contemporaries, partly by dealing mainly with present-day issues and emphasizing the personal and ethical growth of its subject rather than by dealing with the development of his political career. This biography is reflective of its time, when society was undergoing ethical changes of such subtlety that they might easily have been overlooked or unknown had the biography not been a contemporary one.

Nepos has received much criticism because of his simplistic style of writing, especially when compared to his contemporaries Cicero and Varro, but he was addressing an audience less familiar with Greek and less knowledgeable culturally. On a literary scale Nepos does not rival his contemporaries, and his historical accuracy (for example, on Hannibal's crossing of the Alps) is often lacking. But his lackluster style is made up for by his innovative contributions to Roman literature. His synchronization of Roman and Greek events in the *Chronica* and his introduction of Greek influences gave Roman historiography a new sophistication. His parallel biographies deeply influenced Plutarch, who borrowed heavily from Nepos in composition, style, and structure in his *Parallel Lives.* As he was the first to write a biography of a living person, Nepos's influence may also be felt in the work of many other later historians and biographers such as Suetonius and Tacitus, not only for his extending the importance of biography in historical work but also, for his attention to the cultural and ethical milieu that produced the subjects of his studies. When Velleius Paterculus came to write his idiosyncratic and personal outline of history, he found models in Nepos and Atticus. From Nepos he learned the value of examining a great man's personal life and background as keys to understanding the events of the day. Along with Varro, he provided much source material for Pomponius Mela's *De Chorographia.*

Nepos's innovations have influenced the basic tenets of biographical writing from antiquity on, and he would likely have subscribed to the view of Aby Warburg, that one will have far more success in understanding an era if one approaches it through the life of one of its great men, rather than if one approaches the men through a study of the era. This concept was surely the innovation Nepos bestowed upon Roman history, and this innovation and others, rather than the quality of his writing, give Nepos his importance to Roman and later to Western literature.

References:
Wendell V. Clausen, "Catulli Veronensis Liber," *Classical Philology,* 71 (1976): 37–43;

C. Dionisotti, "Nepos and the Generals," *Journal of Roman Studies,* 68 (1968): 35–49;

Joseph Geiger, *Cornelius Nepos and Ancient Political Biography* (Wiesbaden, Germany: Steiner, 1985);

E. Jenkinson, "Cornelius Nepos and the Early History of Biography at Rome," in *Aufstieg und Niedergang der Römischen Welt,* part 1, volume 3 (Berlin & New York: W. de Gruyter, 1973), pp. 703–719;

Jenkinson, "Nepos: An Introduction to Latin Biography," in *Latin Biography,* edited by T. A. Dorey (London: Routledge & Kegan Paul, 1967), pp. 1–15;

Fergus Millar, "Cornelius Nepos 'Atticus' and the Roman Revolution," *Greece and Rome,* 35 (1988): 40–55;

Arnaldo Momigliano, *The Development of Greek Biography* (Cambridge, Mass.: Harvard University Press, 1971), pp. 96–99;

Elizabeth Rawson, *Intellectual Life in the Late Roman Republic* (London: Duckworth / Baltimore: Johns Hopkins University Press, 1985), pp. 227–232.

Ovid

(20 March 43 B.C. – A.D. 17)

Peter E. Knox
University of Colorado, Boulder

MAJOR WORKS–EXTANT: *Heroides* (Heroines, single letters 1–14, before 16 B.C.; double epistles 16–21, ca. A.D. 8);

Amores, second version in three books (Loves, after 16 B.C.);

Ars Amatoria (Art of Love: books 1–2, ca. 1 B.C.; book 3, added later);

Remedia Amoris (The Cures for Love, between 1 B.C. and A.D. 2);

Metamorphoses (A.D. 8);

Fasti (Calendar, A.D. 8, with later revisions);

Tristia (Sorrows, A.D. 9–12);

Ibis (ca. A.D. 11);

Epistulae ex Ponto, 4 books (Letters from the Black Sea, books 1–3, A.D. 13; book 4, probably posthumous).

MAJOR WORK–FRAGMENTARY: *Medicamina Faciei Femineae,* the first one hundred lines survive (Cosmetics for a Woman's Face, before book 3 of *Ars Amatoria*).

WORKS–LOST: *Amores,* first version in five books (Loves, ca. 16 B.C.);

Medea;

Phaenomena.

WORKS–SPURIOUS: *Heroides* (Hermione, 8), (Deianira, 9), (Medea, 12), (Laudamia, 13), (Hypermestra, 14), (Sappho, 15);

Priapea, 3;

Somnium (*Am.* 3.5);

Halieutica;

Nux;

Consolatio ad Liviam.

Editiones principes: *P. Ovidius Naso: Opera* (Rome: Conrad Sweynheym and Arnold Pannartz, 1471); *P. Ovidius Naso: Opera* (Bologna: Baldassare Azzoguidi, 1471).

Standard editions: Heinrich Sedlmayer, *P. Ovidi Nasonis Heroides* (Vienna: Konegen, 1886); Heinrich Dörrie, *P. Ovidi Nasonis Epistulae Heroidum* (Berlin: Walter de Gruyter, 1971); E. J. Kenney, *P. Ovidi Nasonis Amores, Medicamina Faciei Femineae, Ars Ama-*

Ovid (bust in the Uffizi Gallery, Florence)

toria, Remedia Amoris, second edition (Oxford: Clarendon Press, 1994); Hugo Magnus, *P. Ovidi Nasonis Metamorphoseon Libri XV* (Berlin: Weidmann, 1914); William S. Anderson, *Ovidius: Metamorphoses,* fifth edition (Stuttgart & Leipzig: Teubner, 1991); E. H. Alton, D. E. W. Wormell, and E. Courtney, *P. Ovidi Nasonis Fastorum libri sex* (Leipzig: Teubner, 1978); S. G. Owen, *P. Ovidi Nasonis Tristium Libri Quinque, Ibis, Ex Ponto Libri Quattuor, Halieutica, Fragmenta* (Oxford: Clarendon Press, 1915); J. A. Richmond, *Ovidius: Ex Ponto Libri Quattuor* (Leipzig: Teubner, 1990); Friedrich Walther W. Lenz, *P. Ovidi Nasonis Halieutica, Fragmenta, Nux. Incerti Consolatio ad Liviam,* second edition (Turin: Paravia, 1952); Lenz, *P. Ovidi Nasonis Ibis,* second edition (Turin: Paravia, 1952).

Translations in English: Arthur Golding, *The XV Bookes of P. Ouidius Naso, entytuled Metamorphosis, translated oute of Latin into English meeter* (London: Willyam Seres, 1567); George Turberville, *The Heroycall Epistles of the Learned Poet P. Ovidius Naso Translated into English Verse* (London, 1567); Christopher Marlowe, *Ovid's Elegies* (ca. 1596); George Sandys, *Ovid's Metamorphosis Englished* (London: W. Stansby, 1632): John Dryden, and others, *Ovid's Epistles Translated by Several Hands* (London: Jacob Tonson, 1680); J. G. Frazer, *Ovid: Fasti* (Cambridge, Mass.: Harvard University Press, 1931); Guy Lee, *Amores* (New York: Viking, 1968); G. Showerman, *Ovid: Heroides and Amores,* second edition, revised by G. P. Goold, Loeb Classical Library (Cambridge, Mass.: Harvard University Press, 1977); F. J. Miller, *Metamorphoses,* 2 volumes, second edition, revised by Goold, Loeb Classical Library (Cambridge, Mass.: Harvard University Press, 1977); J. H. Mozley, *Ovid: The Art of Love and Other Poems,* second edition, revised by Goold, Loeb Classical Library (Cambridge, Mass.: Harvard University Press, 1979); A. D. Melville, *Ovid: Metamorphoses* (Oxford: Oxford University Press, 1986); A. L. Wheeler, *Ovid: Tristia, Ex Ponto,* second edition, revised by Goold (Cambridge, Mass.: Harvard University Press, 1988); *Ovid: The Love Poems* (Oxford: Oxford University Press, 1990); *Sorrows of an Exile (Tristia)* (Oxford: Clarendon Press, 1992); Peter Green, *The Poems of Exile* (London: Penguin, 1994); Betty Rose Nagle, *Ovid's Fasti: Roman Holidays* (Bloomington: Indiana University Press, 1995).

Commentaries: J. C. McKeown, *Ovid: Amores,* 4 volumes (Leeds: Francis Cairns, 1989–); Peter E. Knox, *Heroides. Select Epistles* (Cambridge: Cambridge University Press, 1995); E. J. Kenney, *Heroides XVI–XXI* (Cambridge: Cambridge University Press, 1996); A. S. Hollis, *Ars Amatoria I* (Oxford: Clarendon Press, 1977); A. A. R. Henderson, *P. Ovidi Nasonis Remedia Amoris* (Edinburgh: Scottish Academic Press, 1979); Guy Lee, *Metamorphoses I* (Cambridge: Cambridge University Press, 1953); Hollis, *Metamorphoses VIII* (Oxford: Clarendon Press, 1970); Franz Bömer, *P. Ovidus Naso: Metamorphosen* (Heidelberg: C. Winter, 1969–1986); James George Frazer, *P. Ovidii Nasonis Fastorum Libri Sex* (London: Macmillan, 1929); Elaine A. Fantham, *Fasti. Book IV* (Cambridge: Cambridge University Press, 1998); Bömer, *Die Fasten* (Heidelberg: C. Winter, 1957–

1958); Georg Luck, *Tristia* (Heidelberg, C. Winter, 1967–1977); S. G. Owen, *P. Ovidi Nasonis Tristium Liber Secundus* (Oxford: Clarendon Press, 1924); R. Ellis, *P. Ovidi Nasonis Ibis* (Oxford: Clarendon Press, 1881); J. A. Richmond, *The Halieutica Ascribed to Ovid* (London: Athlone Press, 1962); R. M. Pulbrook, *P. Ovidii Nasonis Nux Elegia* (Maynooth, Ireland: Maynooth University Press, 1985).

Ovid, first poet of the new age of Imperial Rome, died in A.D. 17 at the Greek settlement of Tomi on the western shore of the Black Sea. Most of what is known of his life derives from his poem *Tristia* (Sorrows, 4.10) written during the grim final years of his exile. Ovid was born in 43 B.C., the year in which the ancient Republican system of government finally came to an end when both consuls fell in battle against the would-be usurper Antony. The bloody series of civil wars that culminated in Octavian's victory at Actium in 31 B.C. coincide with the years of Ovid's childhood and adolescence: the chilling events that accompanied the emergence of the princeps cannot have failed to leave their mark, but they do not haunt Ovid's early imagination as they do Virgil's or Propertius's. In his hometown of Sulmo—the ancient seat of the Paeligni, some ninety miles and a world apart from Rome—Ovid could draw on the resources of an old and well-to-do equestrian family. As the second son, his family expected that he would pursue a career in public service and the law as his elder brother did. But Ovid's talents inclined him in a different direction:

> But I, while still a boy, loved Heaven's service;
>   The Muse enticed me to her task by stealth.
> My father often said, "Why try a useless
>   Vocation? Even Homer left no wealth."
> So I obeyed, all Helicon abandoned,
>   And tried to write in prose that did not scan.
> But poetry in metre came unbidden,
>   And what I tried to write in verses ran.
>   (*Trist.* 4.10.19–26, translated by A. D. Melville)

Little is known of the details of Ovid's life as a poet. He studied rhetoric with some of the leading professors of the day. The elder Seneca recalls Ovid's studies with Arellius Fuscus and Porcius Latro, whom Seneca regarded as two of the four best declaimers of his time. Of Ovid's performance as an orator, Seneca remarks (*Contr.* 2.8.8), "He had a neat, seemly and attractive talent. Even in those days his speech could be regarded as simply poetry put into prose." Ovid apparently tried his hand at the civil service, holding two minor posts on the boards of *tresuiri capitales* (criminal) and *decemuiri stlitibus iudicandis* (civil judges). His inclination to verse, however, must have found an early outlet in amatory elegy:

> When I first read my youthful verse in public,
>   My beard had only once or twice been trimmed.
> My talent had been kindled by Corinna
>   (Not her real name), throughout the city hymned.
>   (*Trist.* 4.10.57–60, trans. Melville)

Taken literally, these lines mean that Ovid first began composing love-elegies when he was about eighteen years old or in 25 B.C., but he may also be referring to a literary trope about youthful inspiration. The mention of Corinna identifies the early works in question as the *Amores* (Loves), in which she appears as the object of his affections, or at least attention.

The collection of *Amores* today consists of three books of elegies, mostly concerned with the theme of love treated autobiographically. The collection is headed with a short preface indicating that the present version is a slimmed-down version of an earlier five-book edition. This earlier edition vanished without a trace after Ovid reduced it by two volumes, probably because he was dissatisfied with its juvenile tone. As he says when writing about this period of his career:

> Much did I write, but what I felt was faulty
>   I gave the flames myself for emendation.
>   (*Trist.* 4.10.61–62, trans. Melville)

In antiquity, when each copy of a work was a handwritten production, that a reader would go to the trouble of replacing a first edition with a second was unlikely, especially if the newer edition were simply reduced in scale. Probably Ovid's new *Amores,* which cannot have appeared before 16 B.C. and probably substantially later, was a reaction to favorable public response to later works—for example, his widely admired tragedy *Medea.* Inspired by this success, Ovid may have determined to give his readers a taste of his early work, pruned now of its less successful poems. This theory accounts also for the thematic unity of the *Amores,* which stands in stark contrast to the work of his surviving predecessors in the genre of elegy at Rome, Propertius, and Tibullus. In their elegies love is a recurrent preoccupation of the poet, but other themes come into play as well—for example, religious festivals, contemporary politics, and mythological narrative. With few exceptions (3.6, 3.9) the *Amores* deal exclusively with the poet's preoccupation with his love and his art. In this respect Ovid may look back to the earliest practitioner of the genre, Cornelius Gallus, whose four books of elegies probably also carried the title of *Amores.* Ovid's wry and often ironic treatment of his love affairs marked the

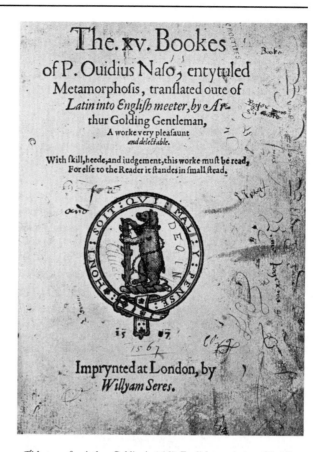

Title page for Arthur Golding's 1567 English translation of Ovid's
Metamorphosis

final development of this minor genre in Augustan poetry. Ovid's wit attracted imitation and translation, most notably that of the young Christopher Marlowe, who published the first English translation in 1596.

The chronological sequence of Ovid's early works is far from certain, but to judge from his own declaration at the end of the *Amores,* after his first venture in elegy he turned to the more prestigious genre of tragedy. The great age of Roman tragedy was the third to second centuries B.C., when poets such as Ennius, Pacuvius, and Accius adapted the classic works of the Greek tragic canon to the Latin language and the Roman stage. The genre did not flourish at Rome, however, despite periodic revivals. In 29 B.C. Octavian celebrated his triumph at Actium with a spectacular festival that included a staging of *Thyestes* by Virgil's friend L. Varius Rufus. The princeps rewarded Varius lavishly for this play, a circumstance that may have affected Ovid. After the weak reception of his first edition of the *Amores,* the young poet may have been tempted to seek fame and perhaps patronage in the officially sanctioned genre of tragedy. His *Medea,* however, like Varius's *Thyestes,* is lost; only two lines survive to provide any hint of why Ovid's contemporaries admired this play (Quint. *Inst.* 8.5.6 and Sen. *Suas.* 3.7). The treatment of Medea in the seventh book of the *Metamorphoses* gives some idea of Ovid's fascination with Euripides' heroine. For his tragedy on the same theme, Seneca is probably also indebted to Ovid.

While he was at work on the *Amores,* Ovid also experimented with a new kind of elegy. In the fourth book of Propertius's elegies is a poem (4.3) that takes the form of an imaginary letter from a woman named Arethusa to her lover Lycotas, a soldier who is away on campaign. This poem likely influenced Ovid when he formulated the idea of a series of imaginary epistles by figures from mythology. This collection, known conventionally as the *Heroides* (Heroines), consists of twenty-one poems. It is a diverse group, including fourteen epistles (1–14) addressed by women from Greek and Roman mythology to their male love interests, one further such poem (15) by the Greek lyric poet Sappho, and three pairs of letters (16–21) by famous couples from Greek mythology. The authenticity of some poems in the collection has long been in dispute. That at least some of the *Heroides* belong to Ovid's early career is demonstrated by the reference to the collection by the poet himself in one of the *Amores* (2.18), but there Ovid cites only a part of the corpus of *Heroides* now extant, and there is no reference at all to the three pairs of epistles that come at the end of the sequence. Some scholars maintain on stylistic grounds that Ovid composed the paired epistles later in his career and that they were subsequently appended to the first group of poems.

In the so-called single epistles, Ovid takes his starting point from literature. The collection opens with a letter addressed by Penelope to Odysseus. From specific references in the poem to Homer's *Odyssey* the reader is able to identify the setting of this epistle in book 19 after Penelope has had a private interview with the stranger who is really her husband in disguise. Ovid exploits the reader's familiarity with the earlier texts to bring out important critical issues. In Dido's epistle to Aeneas, for example, the seventh poem in the series, Ovid focuses upon crucial moments in Virgil's *Aeneid* in which the character of its hero might be open to question: his abandonment of Dido, his false promises to her, his claims of a higher mission. This poem may be viewed as an elegiac commentary on the *Aeneid,* in which Ovid exploits the characteristic themes of love elegy to offer a critical reading of the epic. This same process can be traced in other poems in the collection— for example, the epistle of Briseis to Achilles drawn from Homer's *Iliad* or the epistle of Phaedra to Hippolytus based on Euripides' tragedy. Scholars surmise

that the same pattern is true of other poems in the collection, the sources of which no longer survive.

In many respects the paired epistles represent a logical extension of this conceit. Ovid draws Paris and Helen, the first pair in Ovid's mythological exchange of letters, from early epic, but not from Homer. Ovid's sources for their story include a lost play by Euripides and the early Greek epic *Cypria,* also lost. His characters do retain their Homeric accents, however, and Ovid plays off the reader's familiarity with the sequel to their courtship as it played out in the *Iliad.* As with the other two pairs of letters, the man's comes first, with Paris urging that Helen has no choice but to return to Troy with him. Paris's justification through his life's story gives Ovid the opportunity to incorporate a lengthy narrative of the events that set the story in motion. The purpose of Ovid's narrative is only to provide a backdrop for Helen's reply. In the paired epistles the women are most fully characterized. Ovid's Helen has evidently already made up her mind to go with Paris before she sets pen to papyrus: she is not fooled by Paris's plea; she is the willing accomplice to his scheme. Consistent with his technique in the single epistles, Ovid transforms the heroic lovers into recognizable human beings. Ovid takes the second pair of correspondents, Leander and Hero, from a lost Greek poem, the date and authorship of which can only be guessed. A mutilated papyrus perhaps includes a portion of the poem, but the broader outlines can only be surmised from what Ovid and the late Greek poet Musaeus made of it. Ovid draws the final pair of epistles from the story of Acontius and Cydippe that became famous in antiquity in the version narrated by the Hellenistic poet Callimachus in his elegiac narrative poem *Aetia* (Causes). The epistolary fiction employed by Ovid in the *Heroides* proved extraordinarily popular in the Renaissance and after, spawning countless imitations on the Continent and in England, where they were domesticated in Michael Drayton's *England's Heroical Epistles* (1597).

Ovid's most notorious and perhaps least-understood poem, the *Ars Amatoria* (Art of Love), set a seal upon the early phase of his career. Because of its association with some unspecified error as the cause of Ovid's exile by the emperor Augustus, the *Ars* has always had an undeservedly salacious reputation. Yet, by the standards prevailing in antiquity–not to mention at other times–the treatment of love in the poem is fairly tame. As Dryden remarks of Ovid's erotic poems, "'Tis true they are not to be excused in the severity of manners, as being able to corrupt a larger empire, if there were any, than that of Rome; yet this may be said in behalf of Ovid, that no man has ever treated the passion of love with so much delicacy of thought, and of expression, or searched into the nature of it more philosophically than he." The poem consists of three books, the first two of which address men with advice about how to win a woman's love (book 1) and how to retain it (book 2). The third book was a later addition, composed at the command of Venus herself to level the field in the battle of the sexes:

> "Poor sex," she said, "why treat them in such sort?
> An unarmed mob to be an army's sport!
> Two books to make men expert have been writ,
> It's now our turn to profit by your wit."
>
> (*Ars* 3.45–48, trans. Melville)

Books 1–2 are datable on internal grounds to ca. 1 B.C., and while there is no indication of when the third book was added, it was probably added not much later and almost surely not later than the composition of the *Remedia Amoris* (The Cures for Love) in A.D. 2. There is no indication that Ovid made any changes in books 1–2 beyond adding a transitional couplet after what had been the epilogue to the poem.

The title of the poem advertises its characteristics as a technical treatise: *ars* is the regular Latin word for a textbook dealing with the rules or principles of an art. Such treatises were common in both Greek and Latin prose; Greek poets of the Hellenistic period merged the tradition of early didactic verse represented by Hesiod with the burgeoning field of technical prose to treat a variety of specialized topics. In the third century B.C., for example, Aratus composed the *Phaenomena,* a poem on astronomy that was much admired and imitated by Roman poets such as Cicero, Virgil, Germanicus, and Avienus. Ovid, too, likely wrote in imitation of Aratus in his own poem of the same title, now lost. From references by ancient authors, scholars know of the existence of treatises on sexual technique, although none survives to exemplify the genre. Ovid's parody deals more with courtship than with intercourse, which is discussed only twice and briefly at the end of his advice to men (2.703–732) and women (3.769–808). The rest of the poem is a light and irreverent series of loosely connected instructions on how to find and win one's love in contemporary Rome. Thus, when Ovid digresses to imagine the triumphal procession that the emperor's nephew Gaius will celebrate after his eastern campaigns, he represents the scene as an opportunity for a young man to make a pass at the young woman next to him:

> O glorious object, O surprising sight,
> O day of public joy, too good to end in night!
> On such a day, if thou, and next to thee,
> Some beauty sits, the spectacle to see;
> If she inquire the names of conquered kings
> Of mountains, rivers, and their hidden springs,
> Answer to all thou knowest; and if need be,
> Of things unknown seem to speak knowingly.
> This is Euphrates crowned with reeds, and there
> Flows the swift Tigris with his sea-green hair.
> Invent new names of things unknown before,
> Call this Armenia, that the Caspian shore;
> Call this a Mede, and that a Parthian youth;
> Talk probably, no matter for the truth.
>
> (*Ars* 1.217–228, trans. John Dryden)

Passages such as this one, which represents an official celebration in a frivolous context, seem to substantiate the role of the poem in Ovid's banishment by the emperor several years later. The shorter *Remedia Amoris* (The Cures for Love) is often treated as an afterthought by critics, but it likely formed an integral part of Ovid's parodic plan for the *Ars.* In the *Remedia* Ovid reverses the precepts described in the *Ars* and in the same witty vein suggests strategems for escaping an unwanted love affair. Among the surviving exemplars of the Hellenistic genre of didactic poetry are two works by an obscure poet named Nicander of Colophon, who probably lived in the second century B.C. His hexameter poem, *Theriaca* (Poisonous Creatures), takes as its subject matter snakes, scorpions, spiders, and poisonous insects and is complemented by his *Alexipharmaca* (Antidotes), which describes remedies for their bites and stings. In following the *Ars Amatoria* with the *Remedia Amoris* Ovid is likely mimicking this style of esoteric didacticism. Some inkling of Ovid's fascination with the technical aspect of the genre may be garnered from the hundred lines that survive from one other foray into didactic verse, the *Medicamina Faciei Femineae* (Cosmetics for a Woman's Face). The poem celebrates the advantages of cosmetics, reversing the conventional rejection of such artificiality. The last fifty lines of the surviving fragment include a catalogue of recipes for cosmetics, in which Ovid demonstrates considerable ingenuity in fitting this technical material to the elegiac couplet.

When Ovid began to work on the masterpiece that defines his place in the canon of world literature is not known. He did not necessarily begin to formulate his plans for this work only after he wrote the last lines of his amatory elegies. However, the *Metamorphoses* likely occupied him for much of the approximately six years left to him in Rome. In his later references to the *Metamorphoses* from exile, Ovid suggests that its composition was interrupted by his departure, but the poem shows no signs of incompleteness or lack of polish. In all likelihood this suggestion of an interruption is a pose, an ironic attempt by Ovid to align his hexameter poem with Virgil's *Aeneid,* a poem from which it is altogether distinguished in content, style, and theme. A brief proem announces the topic:

Engraved title page for George Sandys's 1632 translation of Ovid's Metamorphosis

Of bodies changed to various forms I sing:
Ye gods, from whom these miracles did spring,
Inspire my numbers with celestial heat,
Till I my long laborious work complete
And add perpetual tenor to my rhymes,
Deduced from nature's birth to Caesar's times.

(*Met.* 1.1–4, trans. Dryden)

Every translation of the poem is based upon a faulty Latin text that obscures the import of the metaphors Ovid employs to characterize his new work. At the end of the second line the restored text refers to the gods as the agents of change in his poetic enterprise. Ovid thus links the theme of his new poem to the development of his literary craft. Hitherto, he had been known as Rome's greatest elegist, composing with wit and irony on love in its many forms. His new work is in dactylic hexameters, the meter of epic and narrative, a point that Ovid drives home to the reader in the second line, where the rhythm first deviates from the elegiac.

Ovid's metaphors in the last two lines of his proem to indicate the nature of the work are impossible to render in English verse. John Dryden renders the Latin verb *deducere* with its English cognate, "deduce," which conveys none of the other associations of the

original. In Latin the range of associations of the word includes the act of drawing down the thread in spinning. In its various forms, then, this word is used by poets after Virgil to suggest "fine-spun" verse composed in the style of their Hellenistic predecessor Callimachus. Another key term in the final line of the proem also points to this literary background. Where Dryden writes "perpetual tenor," he is grappling with the associations of Ovid's reference to his work as a *perpetuum carmen,* literally a "continuous poem." This phrase is a direct quotation of a disputed passage in the work of his model Callimachus. In the third century B.C. Callimachus produced a narrative elegy in four books called the *Aetia* (Causes). This work survives only in fragments and quotations, the most controversial of which is the polemical prologue in which Callimachus responds to critics who charge that "I did not accomplish one continuous poem of many thousands of lines on . . . kings or . . . heroes. . . ." The *Aetia,* originally a poem of some seven thousand lines with dozens of separate narratives linked into a continuous format, appears to have been his unconventional response to those critics. The *Metamorphoses,* at nearly twice the length, show Ovid outdoing the master while at the same time acknowledging his debt to Callimachus in the critical terminology of the proem.

Other poets had written about the myths of supernatural changes of shape that proliferated in the Greek world and the ancient Near East. The same Nicander whose didactic verse is parodied in the *Ars Amatoria* wrote a hexameter poem called *Heteroeumena* (Metamorphoses). Little of this work survives, although references in a later prose work by the Greek mythographer Antoninus Liberalis reveal something of the stories included in Nicander's *Heteroeumena.* That Ovid made use of Nicander's poem as a source for his own narratives is reasonable to assume, but that he followed this model any more closely than he did in his didactic poems is unlikely. Other poems that might have supplied material for Ovid include the work of an obscure Greek poet of the third century B.C. known as Boios. Ovid's older contemporary Aemilius Macer (*Trist.* 4.10.43) translated or adapted into Latin Boios's *Ornithogonia* (Origins of Birds), and Ovid probably imitated some parts of it in the *Metamorphoses.* Another important source for Ovid may have been the *Metamorphoses* of Parthenius of Nicaea. Parthenius was an influential figure in Latin letters during the first century B.C. who had contact with several Roman poets of the generation preceding Ovid's, such as Helvius Cinna, Cornelius Gallus, and Virgil. Ancient sources refer to Parthenius's treatment of the myth of Scylla and Nisus in his *Metamorphoses,* but they do not say whether this work was a poem or a prose treatise like his surviving mythographical work. The answer to that question is perhaps unimportant for the assessment of Ovid's use of these and other sources in his poem, for in the *Metamorphoses* Ovid is at most only glancing at these earlier treatments of the theme, which he casts in an entirely new mold inspired by Callimachus.

The narrative is arranged as a chronological sequence beginning with the creation of the world when chaos was transformed into order. Ovid proceeds to chronicle the passions of gods and mortals from primordial time to Augustan Rome. The organizing principle of chronology is on more than one occasion strained to the limit to introduce related narratives. Ovid's ingenious transitions were criticized as early as Quintilian (*Inst.* 4.1.77), who refers to a "feeble and childish affectation found in the schools of having the transition itself score some rhetorical point and trying to win applause for this sleight of hand, so to speak, as Ovid usually does without restraint in his *Metamorphoses*." The first extended mythological narrative of the poem after the opening cosmogony is the story of the god Apollo's pursuit of the nymph Daphne, daughter of the river-god Peneus, marked as significant by an abrupt break with the preceding narrative of Apollo's victory over the primordial serpent Python:

Peneian Daphne was the first where Phebus set his love,
Which not blind chaunce but Cupids fierce and cruel
    wrath did move.

(*Met.* 1.452–453, trans. Arthur Golding)

Ovid then reverses course to make the link: Apollo, flushed with his success over Python, had spotted Cupid with his arrows and made fun of him. In revenge Cupid selects one arrow to kindle in Apollo an uncontrollable passion for Daphne, while Cupid targets Daphne with a blunter arrow that turns her cold. The interplay between Apollo, patron of poetry, and Cupid, the god of love, is replete with allusions to the background of elegiac love poetry. So, too, is the portrayal of Apollo's futile courtship. She runs away from him, and as he pursues, Apollo delivers a speech of courtship on the run. In desperation Daphne appeals to the gods to rescue her from her pursuer, calling upon her father and then the earth to change her out of human form:

"Oh, help," she cried, "in this extremest need,
If water-gods are deities indeed!
Gape, earth, and this unhappy wretch entomb,
Or change my form, whence all my sorrows come."
Scarce had she finished, when her feet she found
Benumbed with cold, and fastened to the ground;
A filmy rind about her body grows,
Her hair to leaves, her arms extend to boughs;
The nymph is all into a laurel gone,

The smoothness of her skin remains alone.
Yet Phoebus loves her still, and, casting round
Her bole his arms, some little warmth he found.
The tree still panted in the unfinished part,
Not wholly vegetive, and heaved her heart.
He fixed his lips upon the trembling rind;
It swerved aside, and his embrace declined.

(*Met.* 1.544–556, trans. Dryden)

Ovid achieves some of his finest visual effects in his descriptions of the moment of transformation; they have often served as an inspiration to artists. Illustrations of Daphne's transformation that clearly derive from Ovid's account survive among the wall paintings of Pompeii, but no one has succeeded in capturing the physical moment as effectively as Gian Lorenzo Bernini (1598–1680) in his famous sculpture of Apollo and Daphne. Yet, powerful though such moments are, the significance of metamorphosis in the poem should not be exaggerated. In the search for a single unifying theme for the poem, metamorphosis figures importantly, but it is often of little more than passing importance in the narrative itself. Ovid's sympathetic portrayal of human character, even when represented in the form of the gods, is central to an understanding of the work. Now transformed into a tree, Daphne still declines the god's embrace, a potent representation of the human emotions that brought her to this pass.

Out of the wreck of classical literature Ovid's *Metamorphoses* survived as a sourcebook for artists, writers, and readers seeking access to the world of Greek and Roman mythology. Many of the most familiar-seeming myths of antiquity owe their main outlines, and often their survival, to the form Ovid gives them in his poem: Deucalion and Pyrrha, Phaethon, Europa, Pyramus and Thisbe, and Arachne. Perhaps in no part of the poem, however, are Ovid's resources as an artist as prominently displayed as in the tenth book. This book opens with the story of Orpheus and the death of Eurydice, but most of it, lines 143–739, is occupied by the song that Orpheus sings to console himself upon the loss of Eurydice. This song might best be characterized as the *Metamorphoses* in miniature. Orpheus announces his theme in a brief proem:

                              . . . prettie boyes
That were the derlings of the Gods: and of unlawfull joyes
That burned in the brests of Girles, who for theyr wicke
    lust
According as they did deserve, receyved penance just.

(*Met.* 10.152–154, trans. Golding)

The stories that Ovid tells are accompanied by transformations: Hyacinthus becomes the flower that bears his name; the Cerastae become bulls; the Propoetides are

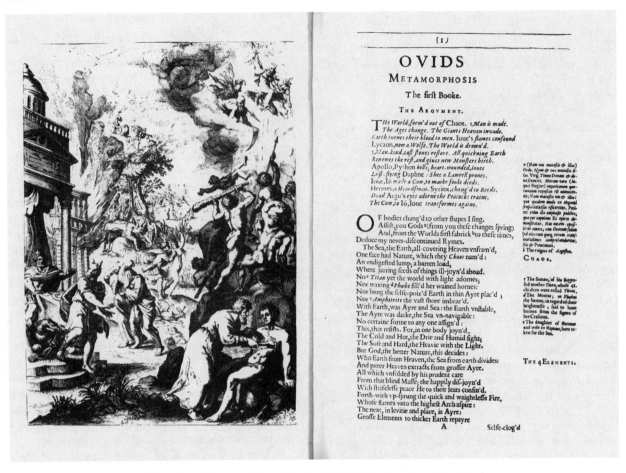

Illustration and first page of text in Sandys's Ovid's Metamorphosis Englished

turned to stone; and Myrrha, the young princess who forms an incestuous passion for her father, becomes the tree from which myrrh is obtained. For modern readers, Ovid is the sole source for these and many other tales in the poem, but Ovid's contemporaries had access to a wealth of literature, both Latin and Greek, in which they might have found other narratives of these same stories as a background against which to read Ovid. The story of Myrrha, for example, surely figured in some Greek poem now lost, and it formed the subject of a narrative poem by Helvius Cinna, friend and contemporary of Catullus, who celebrated Cinna's work in one of his own poems (A.D. 95).

How those earlier treatments differed from Ovid's can only be guessed, but some indications may be teased out of the evidence available. The consensus of the non-Ovidian tradition about Myrrha is that her misfortune is the consequence of Aphrodite's anger over an insult by the girl. In revenge the goddess sent her son to provoke Myrrha's incestuous love. Ovid, however, specifically rejects this explanation when he introduces the story (*Met.* 10.311–312): "The God of love denyes / his weapons to have hurted thee, O Myrrha, and he tryes / himself ungiltie by the fault." The elimination of Aphrodite's revenge as the cause of her feelings is almost surely Ovid's innovation on the traditional account. He portrays Myrrha as an independent agent, and her character becomes the focus of his exploration of the pathology of passion. The monologue in which Myrrha wrestles with her conflicting feelings of acceptance and denial represents Ovid's interpretation:

I ought too love him I confesse: but so as dooth behove
His daughter: were not Cinyras my father then, Iwis
I myght obtaine too lye with him. But now bycause he is
Myne owne, he cannot bee myne owne. The neerenesse of
   our kin
Dooth hurt me. Were I further of perchaunce I more
   myght win.
And if I wist that I therby this wickednesse myght shunne,
I would forsake my native soyle and farre from Cyprus
   runne.
This evill heate dooth hold mee backe, that beeing present
   still
I may but talke with Cinyras and looke on him my fill,

And touch, and kisse him, if no more may further
　　graunted bee.
Why wicked wench? and canst thou hope for further?
　　doost not see
How by thy fault thou doost confound the ryghts of name
　　and kin?
And wilt thou make thy mother bee a Cucqueane by the
　　sin?
Wilt thou thy fathers leman bee? wilt thou bee both the
　　moother
And suster of thy chyld? shall he bee both thy sonne and
　　brother?

　　　　　　　　　　　　(*Met.* 10.336–348, trans. Golding)

In Ovid's creations such conflicts are not necessarily resolved. He highlights such moral ambivalence in the conclusion Myrrha reaches, one common among Ovidian heroines: she knows the right but follows a different course.

What though thy will were fully bent? yit even the very thing
Is such as will not suffer thee the same too end too bring.
For why he beeing well disposde and godly, myndeth ay
So much his dewtye, that from ryght and truth he will not
　　stray.
Would God lyke furie were in him as is in mee this day.

　　　　　　　　　　　　(*Met.* 10.354–355, trans. Golding)

After a failed attempt at suicide, Myrrha contrives with the assistance of her nurse to have intercourse with her unwitting father secretly at night. Myrrha's transformation into a tree comes as something of an anticlimax after the events that follow: discovery by her father, exile, and flight. Her physical transformation into a tree only reflects the mental state into which she has already been changed, a condition "between fear of death and weariness of life." Adonis, the child produced by her incestuous union, forms the link to a final series of tales, with Venus telling him the cautionary tale of Atalanta and Hippomenes. This use of the tale further removes the audience from Ovid as narrator (by the end of Orpheus's song the thread had almost been lost).

In the final book Ovid reaches his stated goal of bringing his narrative down to his own times. The last episode in the poem is the transformation of Julius Caesar into a god and the appearance of the comet that heralded the event. In this respect the architecture of the *Metamorphoses* resembles that of Ovid's model in Callimachus's *Aetia*. Even in its fragmentary state one can reconstruct the end of that poem, which included an astronomical tribute to the ruling house of Ptolemy. Callimachus ended his poem with a personal tribute to the king. Ovid, too, turns the story of Julius's deification into an encomium of the present ruler Augustus, but Ovid follows the story with a bold, direct assertion of his artistic triumph:

Now have I brought a woork too end which neither
　　Joves feerce wrath,
Nor swoord, nor fyre, nor freating age with all the force it
　　hath
Are able too abolish quyght. Let comme that fatall howre
Which (saving of this brittle flesh) hath over mee no
　　powre,
And at his pleasure make an end of myne uncerteyne
　　tyme.
Yit shall the better part of mee assured bee too clyme
Aloft above the starry skye. And all the world shall never
Be able for too quench my name. For looke how farre so
　　ever
The Romane Empyre by the ryght of conquest shall
　　extend,
So farre shall all folke reade this woork. And tyme without
　　all end
(If Poets as by prophesie about the truth may ame)
My lyfe shall everlastingly bee lengthened still by fame.

　　　　　　　　　　　　(*Met.* 15.871–879, trans. Golding)

Callimachus was an important poet at the court of Ptolemy, on terms that Ovid never attempted in his relations with the emperor. What those relations were can never be known; nor would the knowledge affect the reading of Ovid's masterpiece, for the poet says that poetry is his greater care.

Ovid's associations with Augustus and his transformation of the Roman world are more directly a concern of his other great narrative work, the *Fasti* (Calendar). In this poem, too, Ovid adopted a chronological framework, with one book devoted to each month of the year. The Roman calendar was primarily a record of the days when specific legal or political processes might or might not take place. The first official publication of the calendar took place in 304 B.C. By the time of Augustus the *Fasti* might include many other occasions, such as imperial anniversaries or triumphs. The great scholar Verrius Flaccus, an older contemporary of Ovid who tutored Augustus's grandsons, compiled a grand calendar that was inscribed at Praeneste. Some fragments of it still survive. Ovid's decision to employ the calendar as a peg upon which to hang a series of narratives in elegiac verse illustrates his creative engagement with the changing landscape of contemporary culture; but the wellspring of his imagination was still the literary tradition of Hellenistic Greece. In its form as elegy and in its focus on etiological narratives, the *Fasti,* even more than the *Metamorphoses,* is deliberately located in the tradition of Callimachus's *Aetia.* But the *Fasti* is more than a simple nod in the direction of Callimachus, employing the Hellenistic background to investigate the ideology of Augustan Rome; it is a complex intertextual play on the *Aetia,* and as cultural commentary it has more to offer on the fusion of Greek and Roman than on contemporary politics.

The first episode of the poem, for example, is an epiphany. Ovid represents himself beginning the composition of the *Fasti,* with the month of January of course, and musing over the nature of the god Janus. The moment is replete with echoes of the Prologue to the *Aetia,* especially in the image of the poet with his writing tablets about to begin his work when interrupted by an epiphany:

> "And yet, what sort of god should I call you, two-faced Janus?
>   For Greece has no deity the likes of you.
> Tell the reason why alone of the gods you see both
>   what is behind you and what lies ahead."
> With notebook in hand I was pondering these topics,
>   when my house seemed brighter than a moment before.
> Then holy Janus, an amazing sight with those two heads,
>   suddenly met me faces to face.
> Frightened out of my wits, I felt my hair stand on end
>   and suddenly an icy chill gripped my heart.
>   (*Fast.* 1.89–98, trans. Betty Rose Nagle)

But while imitating Callimachus, Ovid also rather pointedly calls attention to the differences. The parenthetical pentameter–"For Greece has no deity the likes of you"–is a striking statement of his independence: Greece has no god like Janus; hence Ovid has no Greek source for his account, which is, paradoxically enough, modeled closely on Callimachus. Janus proceeds to provide Ovid with many different, and not always consistent, explanations of his form. No one fails to note the parallel with Callimachus's *Aetia,* in which the first two books were structured as a question and answer session with the Muses. But critics are now all too eager to write off this similarity as mere Callimachean coloring. Ovid's intertextual play with the *Aetia* is far more pervasive and significant than that.

He repeats the encounter with a divinity at the beginning of book 5, again playing off the opening sequence of the *Aetia.* Unfortunately no surviving portion of Callimachus's first two books is extensive enough to allow a direct judgment of how the dialogue was managed in Ovid's model; but a precious piece of evidence in an ancient commentary summarizes the first episode of the poem: Callimachus apparently began by relating to the Muses three different explanations of the origins of the Graces. When he finished, one of the Muses tells the correct one. Evidence strongly suggests that in the *Aetia* Callimachus addressed the Muses collectively but that just one replied on behalf of all. This scenario suits the persona of the narrator in the *Aetia*–learned, inquisitive, and controlling the discourse. Ovid underlines in book 1 the absence of Greek literary sources for his information.

How does he deal with this difficulty in book 5? He does not merely mimic the Callimachean pose; he clearly subverts it. At issue is the origin of the name for the month of May. Like Callimachus, Ovid addresses his inquiry to the Muses collectively. Unlike Callimachus, however, he ventures no speculations of his own before receiving a reply, and the Muses, not the poet, offer contradictions:

> The Muses gave differing opinions. Polyhymnia was first
>   to begin
>   (the rest were silent and mentally marked her
>   words):
>   (*Fast.* 5.9–10, trans. Nagle)

The other Muses are silent–no surprise for readers familiar with Callimachus, but Ovid introduces a twist at the end of Polyhmnia's recitation:

> Polyhymnia had finished her speech. Clio endorsed her
>   words
>   and so did Thalia, expert on the curved lyre.
> Urania took over. The others maintained silence
>   and not a voice but hers could be heard.
>   (*Fast.* 5.53–56, trans. Nagle)

Two of the Muses indicate their approval of Polyhymnia's account while a fourth begins a different version. Calliope follows her in turn, and when Calliope finishes, her account, too, has its supporters:

> This Muse too had stopped. Her adherents praised her.
>   What to do?
>   Each faction has the same number of votes.
> May the favor of all the Muses alike be with me,
>   and may I praise none of them more than the others.
>   (*Fast.* 5.107–110, trans. Nagle)

The Muses are divided equally into three camps, and Ovid professes he is unwilling to choose one over the others, thus leaving all options open. Ovid's myths are less stable than those in Callimachus's work, and the narrator is less determining; the play with the model text in the *Aetia* highlights this difference.

The incomplete state of the *Fasti* is connected to the relegation of Ovid by Augustus in A.D. 8. No ancient source provides an explanation, and Ovid's reference to the grounds for his exile–"a poem and a mistake"–leaves much to conjecture. The mystery has provided a lively topic for scholarly conjecture since the fifteenth century. While Ovid himself makes clear that the poem in question is *Ars Amatoria,* many theories have been proposed to explain the mysterious "error." Most theories connect Ovid's exile with the exile of Augustus's granddaughter Julia in the same year, on the assumption that Ovid was somehow involved in her adultery and political conspiracy. If that was the case, however, the emperor's punishment seems extraordinarily mild, and Ovid's continuing pleas from exile look dangerous rather than pathetic. Another explanation might be found in the environment of other repressive activity of A.D. 8, which might concern Tiberius, Augustus's designated heir, rather than the emperor himself. At about this time the orator Titus Labienus offended the imperial house. When, in an unprecedented act of censorship, his books were ordered burned, Labienus committed suicide in despair. Another orator and man of letters, Cassius Severus, was relegated to the island of Crete in the same year for unspecified charges of slandering prominent men and women. Other events of that year may have affected Ovid's situation. In that year, Augustus's longtime associate Messalla Corvinus died at a reasonable old age. Not only had Messalla tutored Tiberius in oratory, but he had also been a patron of poets, and Ovid was connected to his circle.

Although Messalla's influence with Augustus waned as the years went on, it might well have been enough to shelter Ovid from action, especially as long as he did nothing else to offend. But he did, and Tiberius may have impelled Augustus to act against the poet of the *Ars Amatoria* at about the same time the books of Labienus were being burned and Cassius Severus was shipped off to Crete. What was it that Tiberius objected to in the *Ars*? In all likelihood, he did not object to the naughty parts or to the fact that the *Ars* could be read as an exhortation to adultery. After all, in the year A.D. 20 Tiberius allowed the return from exile of his wife Julia's lover, asserting that he had never really been exiled in the first place. Tiberius may have objected to the *Ars* because Ovid inserted into it a panegyric of young Gaius Caesar, whom Augustus had preferred to Tiberius in the succession. What was the blunder? It may have been something as trivial as a recitation of the *Ars* at an inopportune time. Clutorius Priscus, another poet, as Tacitus reports, was ruined by a poem, a dirge on Tiberius's son, and an error, his performance of the offensive work before a group of noblewomen.

Exile came as a great shock to Ovid; his reaction to the blow provides some of the most remarkable poetry of personal expression from antiquity. He responded to his changed circumstances by investing his emotions in elegy, the genre in which he had masqueraded as a poet-lover in his youth. The first collection of poems from exile, *Tristia* (Sorrows), consists of five books composed between A.D. 9 and 12. The first book chronicles Ovid's departure from Rome and the long voyage to his place of exile in Tomi at the furthest border of the empire. He structured the second book differently; it consists entirely of a single poem couched in the form of an epistle to the emperor Augustus. It takes the form of an appeal for a recall from exile, in the course of which Ovid addresses only one count in the indictment against him, his poetry. The poem then takes shape as a sustained defense of Ovid's literary career and the integrity of his art. The final three books consist of open letters and appeals, mostly to unnamed friends and associates who might intervene on his behalf. Ovid frequently complains in the works from exile about his failing powers as a poet, and many critics have taken him at his word. But the *Tristia* includes poetry of vividness and power, nowhere more vivid or powerful than when Ovid reflects on the place of art in his life, not only because it was the cause of his personal disaster, but also because it was the source of his salvation in his most desperate hour:

> So then, that I still live and face my travails,
>   Not jaded by my life's anxiety,
> Is thanks, my Muse, to you. You give me comfort;
>   With peace and healing balm you come to me.
> You, guide and comrade, lead me from the Danube,
>   Grant me a place on Helicon divine.
> You've given me (a rare thing) in my lifetime
>   Renown that from the grave's more wont to shine.
>   (*Trist.* 4.10.115–122, trans. Melville)

Ovid's exile poetry is not in the confessional style a modern reader might expect. While Ovid frequently describes the misery of his surroundings, he focuses his defense upon his art. In the *Tristia,* as in the *Heroides* and the *Ars Amatoria,* he is breaking new ground as he tunes the elegy to an unconventional strain.

Every poet needs his library, Ovid no less than others, and an audience. At Tomi he had neither:

> Here's no supply of books to allure and nourish,
>   Only the sounds of bows and weaponry.
> There's no one in this land, if I recited,
>   Whose understanding ear might profit me.
>   (*Trist.* 3.14.37–40, trans. Melville)

In this barren environment Ovid produced during the early years of his exile a minor triumph of learning and obscurity in the *Ibis,* an elaborate curse-poem in 316 couplets. The *Ibis* includes an elaborate catalogue of exquisite curses drawn from mythology. By its title the *Ibis* acknowledges a link with a poem by Callimachus, who cursed an enemy under the pseudonym "Ibis," a bird notorious for its uncleanliness. This poem's existence is known only from later references, and knowledge of other exemplars of the genre consists of little more than a few fragments and a list of titles: for example, Moero's *Arai* (Curses) and Euphorion's *Poteriokleptes* (Cup-stealer) and *Thrax* (Thracian). Ovid's frustration finds an outlet in the same literary tradition that

Statue of Ovid at Sulmona, Italy

Brutus thus framing the whole. Similar patterns may be traced in the arrangement of the interior sections of the three books. Ovid's themes in these epistles reprise the topics of the *Tristia:* bleak descriptions of his sufferings in exile alternate with appeals for a recall and complaints about the decline of his literary powers. The most interesting poems in the collection are those that touch on personal themes. In one of the only two poems in the collection addressed to his wife, he recycles the motifs of elegiac love poetry to paint a picture of a woman worn by cares for her husband:

> You too, who were young when I left the City, doubtless
>   have been aged by my troubles: may the gods
> let me see you as now you are, bestow fond kisses
>   on your brindling hair, fold my arms
> round your far-from-plump body, assure you that "It's worry
>   on my account that's thinned you down so much . . . ."
> *(Epist. ex Ponto* 1.4.47–52, trans. Peter Green)

Conjugal love does not loom large in the literature of antiquity; Ovid's exile poetry is a rare instance that provides a glimpse of life behind the topoi.

Other poems are addressed to influential persons with no direct connection to the poet. Germanicus, the emperor's nephew and adopted son of Tiberius, receives the opening poem of book 2, and Cotys, the client king of Thrace, also receives an epistle. The note of despair that characterizes the seventh epistle of book 3, addressed to his friends in general, is increasingly dominant. The tone makes increasingly clear that Ovid harbored no realistic hopes of a reprieve:

> Now I am out of words, I've asked the same thing so often;
>   now I feel shame for my endless, hopeless prayers.
> You must all be bored stiff by these monotonous poems—
>   certainly you've learned by heart what I want,
> and know the contents of each fresh letter already
>   before you break its seal. . . .
> *(Epist. ex Ponto* 3.7.1–6, trans. Green)

The last lines of this poem are bitterly sarcastic as Ovid declares his intention to face death with courage, since the emperor cannot deny him that.

The fourth and final book in the *Epistulae ex Ponto* may have appeared posthumously; the ninth epistle in this book was written in A.D. 16, and the poet died in the following year. Apparently he wrote until the end. In a despairing epistle addressed to another poet, Ovid writes grimly of his commitment to literature:

> That divine impulse, inspiration's sustenance,
>   once always innate in me, now is gone.
> Today my reluctant Muse works only under compulsion,

inspired his mythological narratives in the *Metamorphoses* and the *Fasti*.

Ovid's last collection of poems resumes the themes addressed in the first collection from exile. The *Epistulae ex Ponto* (Letters from the Black Sea) are addressed to recipients in Rome, now openly named. The first three books were published as a single collection in A.D. 13. The unity of the first three books is reflected in the symmetrical distribution of poems to four patrons. The opening poem of the first book is addressed to Brutus, who may have been Ovid's publisher, and it is followed by a letter to Fabius Maximus, the best known of Ovid's addressees, who had influence and connections at the court. This pattern is reversed in the last two poems of book 3, with letters to

laying a bored hand on the tablets I take up;
writing affords me little–if any–pleasure,
   I find no joy in forcing words to scan.
This may be because I've derived no benefit from it,
   because, indeed, it's the chief source of my woes,
or that writing a poem you can read to no one
   is like dancing in the dark.
         (*Epist. ex Ponto* 4.2.25–33, trans. Green)

Ovid, the last poet of the Augustan Age, was also the first poet of the new Tiberian era. The time was not otherwise distinguished by great literature. Ovid addresses the final poem of the collection, which may be the last poem he wrote, to an unnamed enemy who stands in for the traditional bête noire of Roman poets, Envy. The poem is Ovid's final assertion of his artistic integrity and his claim to fame. In his earliest collection of poems (*Amores* 1.15) Ovid had laid claim to a place among the immortal poets–among them Homer, Hesiod, Callimachus, Ennius, and Virgil. Now he lists thirty contemporaries of his later years, and they are not a distinguished crew; among these poets are Domitius Marsus, Albinovanus Pedo, Julius Montanus, and Cornelius Severus. . . . There is surely a note of disingenuous irony in Ovid's summary remark:

If it's seemly to say so, *my* talent was distinguished,
and among all that competition, I was *fit to be read.*
         (*Epist. ex Ponto* 4.16.45–46, trans. Green)

Ovid's work dominated the literary landscape at Rome after the deaths of Horace and Virgil, and it did not suffer from a lack of awareness. Ovid's personal commitment to the life of letters is documented in the record of his exile poetry with an intensity that is still astonishing. Artists such as Eugène Delacroix in his painting "Ovid among the Scythians" (London, National Gallery) have been fascinated with him as a metaphor for the isolation of the artist from society. The mystery of Ovid's exile, moreover, continues to provide the raw material for serious novels such as David Malouf's *An Imaginary Life* (1978) and Christoph Ransmayr's *Die letzte Welt* (1988), as well as lighter fare such as David Wishart's comic suspense novel, *Ovid* (1995).

Ovid's influence on subsequent generations of Roman poets was vast. One reflection of his impact is the extent to which the tradition tended to assign to Ovid authorship of works composed in imitation of him. *Halieutica,* a fragment of a poem on fishing preserved in a ninth-century manuscript that ascribes it to Ovid, has sometimes been defended as genuine on the grounds that the elder Pliny appears to refer to it in the first century A.D. Scholars are now unanimous in judging it as spurious on metrical and stylistic grounds. *Nux* (Walnut Tree), an elegiac poem in 182 lines that takes

the form of a lament by a walnut tree over the way passersby treat it, appears in manuscripts from the eleventh century onwards as a work by Ovid, but the majority of critics exclude it from the canon. *Consolatio ad Liviam* (Consolation for Livia), a poem of consolation addressed to the wife of Augustus on the death of her son Drusus in 9 B.C., survives in many fifteenth-century manuscripts that identify the author as Ovid. But the ascription to Ovid is clearly false on stylistic grounds; it is probably a literary exercise composed at a later date. Recent attempts at dating have assigned it to the Flavian period when the poem of consolation was a particularly popular genre. In a different category from these three works is the poem known as the *Somnium* (Dream), an elegy of twenty-three couplets that is betrayed as spurious by many stylistic and grammatical anomalies. What is curious is that while the poem was transmitted independently in the medieval tradition, it is also found in manuscripts of the *Amores* in the fifth position of book 3. Some scholars believe that other poems not by Ovid have been insinuated into the manuscript tradition of the *Heroides,* and arguments have been made against Ovidian authorship of five poems in the collection–8 (Hermione to Orestes), 9 (Deianira to Hercules), 12 (Medea to Jason), 13 (Laodamia to Protesilaus), and 14 (Hypermnestra to Lynceus). The *Epistula Sapphus* (Sappho to Phaon) is in a somewhat different category, since it owes its position as the fifteenth epistle in modern editions to a sixteenth-century scholar. Opinions divide over its ascription to Ovid. The so-called paired epistles (16–21) are now generally thought to be genuine, although doubts remain.

Ovid has always appealed more to artists than to scholars. His works never formed part of the school curriculum in antiquity, and in the schoolrooms of the Middle Ages his less risqué works tended to predominate. The *Metamorphoses* were sanitized in an enormous early-fourteenth-century French poem of some seventy thousand verses, the *Ovide Moralisé.* At various points Ovid's poetry was the object of outright suppression. In 1599 a volume including some of Christopher Marlowe's translations of the *Amores* was banned and burned by episcopal order. Nineteenth-and twentieth-century school editions of the *Heroides, Fasti,* and *Ars Amatoria* omitted "objectionable" passages. However, Ovid's works continued to be read. His influence upon English literature began with Geoffrey Chaucer and John Gower, who might be the most "Ovidian" of English poets. William Shakespeare, who perhaps knew Ovid best from Golding's much admired translation, drew heavily on Ovid in his earliest tragedy, *Titus Andronicus,* and Ovid's influence can be traced throughout Shakespeare's career. The poets of the Enlightenment found in the intellectual play that is the hallmark of Ovid's style a deep similarity to their own approach to poetry. Dryden and Alexander Pope not only translated much of Ovid's verse, but they also manifest his influence in all their works. In the twentieth century, readers of Ezra Pound's *Cantos* (published intermittently from 1917 to 1970) and Ted Hughes's *Tales from Ovid* (1997) encounter the poet of the *Metamorphoses* in revivified form. In the visual arts, Ovid's myths have always provided a rich source of inspiration. Depictions of Ovidian myths by Titian and Nicolas Poussin constitute an important component in the body of their work, but the list of painters and sculptors who have treated Ovidian themes is long—such artists as Bernini, Pieter Brueghel, Peter Paul Rubens, Sir Anthony Van Dyck, Eugène Delacroix, and Marc Chagall.

Ovid is surely the most versatile writer of Greek and Roman antiquity whose works have come down to the present. His brilliant innovations on the inherited themes and genres of ancient poetry—love elegy, didactic poetry, epic, narrative elegy, and invective—are the first invitation to a reading. What holds the reader's attention is the dazzling virtuosity of Ovid's technical skills. The difficulties of Ovid's poetry are not linguistic; his verse is distinguished by clarity of expression and syntactical exactness. In this sense Ovid differs starkly from his great predecessor Virgil, who exploits the ambiguities of language to reflect the inherent conflicts of the human condition; Ovid clarifies these uncertainties with unswerving precision. Wit is the defining characteristic of Ovid's style, not as it is understood today, but as in the words of Dryden, "a propriety of Thoughts and Words; or in other terms, Thought and Words elegantly adapted to the Subject." But Ovid, unlike the English Augustans for the most part, never entirely sacrificed the qualities of enchantment; consequently, *Metamorphoses,* in particular, has always been an integral part of the collective literary imagination in the West.

Concordance:

R. J. Deferrari, M. Inviolata Barry, and M. R. P. McGuire, eds., *A Concordance to Ovid* (Washington, D.C.: Catholic University Press, 1939).

References:

Jonathan Bate, *Shakespeare and Ovid* (Oxford: Clarendon Press, 1993);

Barbara Weiden Boyd, *Ovid's Literary Loves: Influence and Innovation in the Amores* (Ann Arbor: University of Michigan Press, 1997);

O. S. Due, *Changing Forms: Studies in the Metamorphoses of Ovid* (Copenhagen: Gyldendal, 1974);

Harry B. Evans, *Publica Carmina: Ovid's Books from Exile* (Lincoln: University of Nebraska Press, 1983);

Hermann Fränkel, *Ovid: A Poet Between Two Worlds* (Berkeley: University of California Press, 1945);

G. Karl Galinsky, *Ovid's Metamorphoses: An Introduction to the Basic Aspects* (Berkeley: University of California Press, 1975);

Geraldine Herbert-Brown, *Ovid and the Fasti: A Historical Study* (Oxford: Clarendon Press, 1994);

H. Jacobson, *Ovid's Heroides* (Princeton, N.J.: Princeton University Press, 1974);

E. J. Kenney, "The Style of the *Metamorphoses,*" in *Ovid,* edited by J. W. Binns (London: Routledge & Kegan Paul, 1973), pp. 116–153;

Peter E. Knox, *Ovid's Metamorphoses and the Traditions of Augustan Poetry* (Cambridge: Cambridge Philological Society, 1986);

Sara Mack, *Ovid* (New Haven: Yale University Press, 1988);

Charles Martindale, ed., *Ovid Renewed: Ovidian Influences on Literature and Art from the Middle Ages to the Twentieth Century* (Cambridge: Cambridge University Press, 1988);

J. F. Miller, *Ovid's Elegiac Festivals: Studies in the Fasti* (Frankfurt am Main: Peter Lang, 1991);

K. Sara Myers, *Ovid's Causes: Cosmology and Aetiology in the Metamorphoses* (Ann Arbor: University of Michigan Press, 1994);

Betty Rose Nagle, *The Poetics of Exile: Programme and Polemic in the Tristia and Epistulae ex Ponto of Ovid* (Brussels: Collection Latomus, 1980);

Brooks Otis, *Ovid as an Epic Poet,* second edition (Cambridge: Cambridge University Press, 1970);

Joseph B. Solodow, *The World of Ovid's Metamorphoses* (Chapel Hill: University of North Carolina Press, 1988);

Ronald Syme, *History in Ovid* (Oxford: Clarendon Press, 1977);

John C. Thibault, *The Mystery of Ovid's Exile* (Berkeley: University of California Press, 1964);

L. P. Wilkinson, *Ovid Recalled* (Cambridge: Cambridge University Press, 1955);

G. D. Williams, *Banished Voices: Readings in Ovid's Exile Poetry* (Cambridge: Cambridwge University Press, 1994).

Persius

(4 December A.D. 34 – 24 November A.D. 62)

Kenneth J. Reckford
University of North Carolina at Chapel Hill

WORK: *Saturae,* a small book of six verse satires (Satires).

Editio princeps: *Satyrae* (Rome: Ulrich Han, 1469 or 1470).

Standard editions: *A. Persi Flacci Saturarum Liber; Accedit Vita,* edited by Wendell V. Clausen (Oxford: Clarendon Press, 1956); *A. Persi Flacci et D. Iuni Iuvenalis Saturae,* edited by Clausen (Oxford: Oxford University Press, 1959); *A. Persi Flacci Saturarum Liber,* edited by Dominicus Bo (Turin: Paravia, 1969).

Translations in English: *Juvenal and Persius,* Loeb Classical Library, translated by G. G. Ramsay (Cambridge, Mass. & London: Harvard University Press, 1918); *Satires,* translated by W. S. Merwin, with an introduction and notes by William S. Anderson (Bloomington: Indiana University Press, 1961); *Horace: Satires and Epistles. Persius: Satires,* second edition, revised, translated by Niall Rudd (Harmondsworth: Penguin, 1979); *Persius, the Satires. Text with Translation and Notes,* edited by J. R. Jenkinson (Warminster: Aris & Phillips, 1980); *Satires,* translated, with an introduction and notes, by Richard Emil Braun (Lawrence, Kans.: Coronado Press, 1984); *The Satires of Persius,* translated by Guy Lee, with an introduction and commentary by William Barr (Liverpool: Francis Cairns, 1987).

Commentaries: *The Satires of A. Persius Flaccus,* edited by Basil L. Gildersleeve (New York: Harper, 1875); *The Satires of A. Persius Flaccus,* third edition, revised, translated, with a commentary, by John Conington, edited by Henry Nettleship (Oxford: Clarendon Press, 1893); R. A. Harvey, *A Commentary on Persius* (Leiden: Brill, 1981); Walter Kissel, *Aules Persius Flaccus Satiren* (Heidelberg: Carl Winter, 1990)—in German.

In the famous trio of Roman verse satirists—Horace, Persius, and Juvenal—Persius is now, but has not always been, the neglected middle child. His *libellus* (little book) of six satires in hexameter verse, published after his death, only amounts to 650 lines, plus a brief fourteen-line preface in choliambics, or "limping iambics"; yet, it may be said to have revolutionized Roman satire, pointing it away from Horace's geniality, tolerance, and moderation and toward Juvenal's grand rhetorical denunciations of folly and vice. Persius's fierce independence, high moral seriousness, and forceful expression of Stoic values were admired and emulated from late antiquity and the Middle Ages, through the high Renaissance, and well into the eighteenth century. What have been less appreciated are his wild Aristophanic humor, his dramatic verve, and the sheer audacity of his poetic style, which has often been criticized for its seemingly willful obscurity, but which, for lovers of poetry, still remains exciting indeed.

Information about Persius's life comes from an apparently reliable *Vita* attributed to the first-century scholar M. Valerius Probus. Persius was born in Volaterra (modern Volterrae) in northwest Etruria on 4 December A.D. 34. He died of a stomach ailment on 24 November A.D. 62, shortly before his twenty-eighth birthday. A Roman knight with blood ties to senatorial families, he came from a rich old Etruscan family and received a first-class education in literature and rhetoric at Rome from two distinguished teachers, Remmius Palaemon and Verginius Flavus. Persius's father died when he was around six; his stepfather died not long afterward. Persius was, says the *Vita,* "a person of most gentle ways, of virginal modesty, handsome repute, and exemplary devotion to his mother, his sister, and his aunt." Scholars have sometimes belittled Persius as a bookish young man surrounded by adoring female relatives; yet, family and friends involved him, at least vicariously, in public life. He was related to the younger Arria, whose parents were forced to commit suicide under the emperor Claudius after a failed conspiracy; he enjoyed some ten years of close friendship with her husband, Thrasea Paetus, the best-known Stoic dissident under Nero. Persius's friends also included the poet Caesius Bassus and some older men who served

Page from an Italian manuscript for Persius's Satyrae *(Satires) dated 29 May 1468–3 February, 1469 and transcribed by Franciscus Phylaretus (from Maggs Bros. catalogue,* The Art of Writing 2800 B.C. to 1930 A.D., *1930)*

as foster fathers and mentors: Servilius Nonianus, a man of affairs; two philosopher-doctors from Greece and Asia; and most important, the learned Annaeus Cornutus, a freedman and scholar who not only wrote Greek treatises on theology and literature but also was a dramatist and, as Persius describes him in *Satire* 5, a Stoic role model par excellence.

In A.D. 54, when Persius was nineteen, Claudius died, and Nero became emperor. Tacitus tells the story in his *Annals:* the "five good years" (A.D. 49–54) when Seneca and Burrus kept Nero under reasonable control; then the escalating brutality, license, and artistic extravagance of A.D. 59–65, culminating in Piso's failed conspiracy in A.D. 65 and the subsequent reign of terror until Nero's assassination in A.D. 68. Decent people faced hard choices. They could "dissimulate" and go along–flattering Nero and doing what little good they could in the senate, the law courts, the provinces, and the army–or they could withdraw into more or less tacit opposition and be exiled or killed. Verginius Flavus, Persius's old teacher of rhetoric, was exiled in A.D. 65; Cornutus was exiled not much later. Thrasea Paetus, after many dodges, was driven finally to open opposition and to forced suicide. Three of the four leading Neronian writers perished in A.D. 65: Lucan, the greatest epic poet after Virgil; Seneca, the wealthy Stoic essayist, playwright, and would-be philosopher-statesman; and Petronius, the novelist, Nero's "Arbiter of Elegance." Persius, the fourth, might well have joined them had he lived three more years, for his satires include at least oblique references to Nero's bad taste in poetry (*Satire* 1), his emotional immaturity (*Satire* 4), and his fake triumphs (*Satire* 6). After Persius's death it was said that he originally wrote, "King Midas has asses' ears" in *Satire* 1, but that Cornutus persuaded him to change the words to the less offensive "Who does *not* have asses' ears?" This story is sheer fiction, yet the fabrication, once introduced into the *Vita,* remained influential well into the eighteenth century.

Persius presents himself as a professed Stoic, a grateful and serious student of the learned Cornutus. He looks to philosophy, not religion, to show him the meaning and purpose of life, how to live well, and how to save his soul from the ordinary confusions and foul corruptions of the world. "Come learn, unhappy people," says his spokesman in *Satire* 3 (in words that the Christian fathers later admired and quoted):

what we're made of; what life we're born to lead;
where we are placed; how to make the most graceful
turn around life's racecourse; what limit's set
for money-making; what is the point of prayer,
or of hard cash; how much it is right to spend
on your country's needs, or your dear relatives;
and who the god has ordered you to be;
and where, in the human world, you have been stationed.

Persius allegedly owned seven hundred books (the number is doubtful) by the early Stoic philosopher Chrysippus, which he left to Cornutus in his will. Surviving fragments of Chrysippus's works, written in hard scholarly Greek, remind readers that studying philosophy, what Persius calls "growing pale over philosophy," was never easy. Like Seneca, Persius evidently considered himself not the complete *sapiens* (wise man or sage), the Stoic ideal, but a *proficiens* (an advancing one), a work in progress. What mattered most was the serious and constant intention to achieve right-mindedness, Seneca's *bona mens.*

Contrary to Nero's fears, Stoics were not republicans or revolutionaries. Many believed in monarchy, but they wanted a just ruler, not a tyrant. A few honorable people such as Thrasea Paetus protested against Nero's crimes, or at least supported the protesters behind closed doors. In a world increasingly marked, according to the historian Tacitus, by slanders, lies, flattery, and dissimulation, private honesty was precious–and Persius's satires are, if anything, a cry for honesty. In the end, perhaps, Stoicism's most useful effect under Nero was to bolster courage and resolution in the face of threats, trials, exile, and death. Under the late Republic, in the time of Cicero and Horace, the old Stoic paradoxes–"Only the Wise Man is Free," "Only the Wise Man is Sane"–seemed pretentious and inhumane. In Persius's *Satires* and Seneca's *Moral Epistles* they make new and surprising sense.

In his brief choliambic preface to the *Satires,* Persius introduces himself as a *semipaganus* (half-civilized outsider; literally, a half-rustic). He rejects the conventional picture of the poet's initiation by the Muses on Mount Helicon and describes instead how crows and magpies are induced by hunger to imitate human speech. The preface leads easily into *Satire* 1, with its thematic complexity, its programmatic importance, and its enduring influence on the conception and writing of satire.

Satire 2 anticipates Juvenal's famous *Tenth Satire,* which Samuel Johnson reworked as "The Vanity of Human Wishes." It begins by contrasting a friend's modest birthday prayers with the foolish, even vicious requests that most people make of the gods. Their behavior ranges from self-defeating superstition to criminal impiety as they try to bribe the gods with gilded statues:

O earth-bent souls, devoid of heavenly traces,
what good is this, to bring our human habits
into the temples, find out the gods' likings
from this accursed flesh? (61–63)

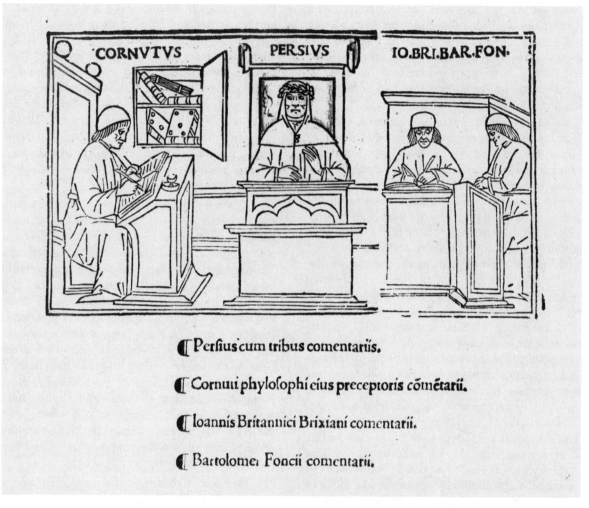

CORNVTVS   PERSIVS   IO.BRI.BAR.FON.

¶ Perſius cum tribus comentariis.

¶ Cornuti phyloſophi eius preceptoris cômétarii.

¶ Ioannis Britannici Brixiani comentarii.

¶ Bartolomei Foncii comentarii.

Persius (center) with three early Italian commentators on his works, Lucius Annaeus Cornutus, Bartolomeo Fonte and Johannes Britannicus of Brescia; illustration from the 1499 Venetian edition of Persius's Satyrae *(courtesy of the Lilly Library, Indiana University)*

These lines are remarkable for their religious feeling and conviction. They show why Persius was read and admired by the Christian fathers, quoted in their letters, and used often in their teaching; indeed, the lines show how his self-characterization as *semipaganus* could take on a new, unexpected meaning: half-pagan implies half-Christian.

Satire 3 exploits an old but still powerful Stoic analogy to show the necessity of moral education. The soul's faults or passions resemble bodily illnesses; they grow steadily, breaking out even in physical symptoms; and they urgently require the attention, care, and advice of the philosopher, the soul's physician. Persius begins with a complex three-way dialogue involving a narrator, a companion or tutor, and a spoiled, reluctant youth with a hangover who must apply himself to study before it is too late:

You're leaking mindlessly, you'll be despised.
No good response comes from the unbaked jar
with its green clay: strike it, you hear the fault.
You are soft wet clay that needs to be taken now,
right now, and shaped unceasingly on the wheel.

The satire gets its remarkable power first from what the scholar-poet A. E. Housman recognized in 1913 as an intense inner dialogue within Persius himself, and second from its grotesque mixed metaphors of fragmented, diseased, and decomposing bodies (and lives), culminating in the description of a fool's sudden, ugly death after ignoring his doctor's advice and his friend's warning.

Satire 4 presents the public consequences of ignorance. In a prelude taken from one of Plato's dialogues, Socrates rebukes Alcibiades, the spoiled and arrogant young aristocrat, for aspiring to political leadership without the right foundation of moral and self-knowledge. The scene opens up to reveal a general wasteland of hypocrisy, prejudice, backbiting, and sexual gossip. "Live in your own house" is the moral; "Know your own deficiencies." That is where "Alcibiades"–or Nero, or the reader–must begin.

Satire 5, Persius's longest poem (191 lines), begins by renouncing fashionable epic bombast in favor of plain satiric truth-telling. He pays a warm tribute to Cornutus, who shaped his impressionable adolescent mind with sound Stoic teachings. A general diatribe follows, illustrating the Stoic paradox, "Only the wise man is free." One's legal status is meaningless unless one knows the right use of possessions, which only philosophy can teach. There is one true standard; all else is subject to error and confusion. The merchant, for example, is driven by the personified figure of Avarice: "Get up, now! Trade something or other! Swear an oath into the bargain!"–but even as he prepares to sail, Luxury mocks his greed for ever-greater profits and challenges him, in a parody of Horace's *carpe diem*, to live and enjoy himself while yet he may. He is "torn by the double hook," pulled in two directions like a slave in comedy. The Lover too, delaying about his mistress's door, unable to break free, comes straight from the comic stage. Ambition is caricatured as throwing candy to the holiday crowd. Superstition (which evidently includes the Jews, the followers of Isis, and other un-Roman types) means strange eating habits and taboos, and such weird practices as chewing garlic to keep away ghosts and goblins. Most everyone, in short, is subject to one addiction or another. Only the wise Stoic is exempt.

Satire 6, the epilogue, explores issues of life and death. It moves back and forth symbolically between the sea, calm and inviting, but also the cause of shipwreck, and the land from which the readers' unknown forefathers were born, and that they must harvest rightly and well before they die. The speaker is content with his life, moderate in his demands, and generous with himself or others as need requires; but his indignation flashes out at the imagined reproaches of a greedy, selfish heir. This reaction is protest, not resignation. The poem ends on a sarcastic note: "Sell your soul for gain. . . " The poet, unlike the miser, knows when to stop.

Although Persius's book was edited (by Bassus and Cornutus) and published after his death, he presumably arranged the satires to be read in their present order. *Satire* 1, which Persius probably wrote last, conveys his satiric intentions or nonintentions; it influenced the later theory and practice of satire more than the other five satires combined; and it serves, in some details, to illustrate both Persius's stylistic daring and,

inseparable from it, his famous "obscurity." The poem begins,

> O endless vanity of human cares!
> "Who'll read this?" "*You're* asking *me?* Lord, no one."
> "No one?"–"Say two, or none. . . ."

If line 1 provides a title of sorts–like the Preacher's "Vanity of vanities, all is vanity" in *Ecclesiastes*–line 2 plunges into intense inner dialogue. "Who will read this?" asks a practical interlocutor or inner voice. Readers expect the usual literary answer, "Good, sensible types like my friends X and Y," but they are deceived: no reliable audience exists this time, for "Everyone at Rome–" the explosive secret breaks off, for now, but the point has been made: "Don't look outside yourself." Persius's satire, like his self-knowledge, must come from within.

The comic vignettes that follow justify his resolve by disclosing an altogether corrupt world where poetry reading and writing are vitiated by pretension, flattery, falsehood, and general bad taste and incompetence. First comes a *recitatio* (grand poetry reading), a kind of literary/erotic fashion show. A second reading, of a dead poet this time, challenges unconsidered assumptions of poetic achievement and "immortality":

> They're all agreed. Are not the poet's ashes
> successful now? Does not the tombstone press
> more lightly on his bones? The dinner guests
> join in the praise: now will not, out of those shades,
> out of that mound and blessed ash, will not
> violets spring? (36–40)

Persius does not reject reasonable praise for his art, but Rome is full of empty flattery, which can be bought. Fat-cat patrons read to their poor clients after dinner, "Tell me the truth about myself." But they would not want to hear the truth.

After further passages in which Persius parodies the all-too-smooth inanities of fashionable Neronian verse, he is warned against satiric roughness: "But why scrape tender little ears with the biting truth?" The words imply both the offensiveness of satire to its victims and, more positively, the surgical operation that it can and should perform on the diseased perceptions of society. Persius pretends to yield to warnings. Everything is fine, he says, just fine; he will not "commit a public nuisance." But then he protests, by citing the examples of his two great predecessors in satire, Lucilius and Horace:

> Lucilius lashed the city;
> hit you, Lupus and Mucius [by name],
> and bit people, and broke his molars on them.
> Clever Flaccus made his friends laugh and felt out

Engraved portrait of Isaac Casaubon, a Renaissance scholar whose praise of Persius's moral seriousness and stylistic brilliance shaped later scholarship on Persius

their every fault, as he fooled around their heartstrings,
hanging the public from his sagacious nose:
and *I'm* not to mutter a word? (114–119)

Persius writes because he must, and in so doing he follows in the great tradition of Lucilius and Horace, even though his circumstances, concerns, and style are so different from theirs. Only now, after rejecting any desire for popular appeal or court favor, can he speak of possible readers—people who pore over the Athenian Old Comedy of Eupolis, Cratinus, and Aristophanes and are moved by it—and of a satiric intention, too, that goes beyond mere self-expression:

Look at my writings too, if you can listen
to pungent, boiled-down stuff, that might steam open
a hot receptive ear. . . . (125–126)

The right readers will find Persius out, after all. In a world of oversensitive, diseased ears and false perceptions, they might find healing in the "distilled strong spirits" of his satire. Similarly, in *Satire* 5, Cornutus speaks approvingly (and directingly) of Persius's style and purpose:

You look for everyday words, joining them keenly,
speak in due measure, know how to scrape the flesh
of pale-sick habits, and how to nail down sin
in free-spirited play. (14–16)

In a typically "keen joining" of metaphors, the satirist is represented both as a skilled craftsman of words and as an honest surgeon cleansing the sick body of a corrupt society. Style and sense, art and truth, aesthetic and moral purpose have become inseparable.

Satire 1 constitutes a brilliant performance, even as it unmasks and ridicules bad literary and social performances. It needs to be read aloud in different voices, and with spirit. The dramatic clash of voices and ideas; the lesser buildup to rhetorical questions and exclamations, and the greater thematic buildup to a long-delayed revelation, an explosion of indignant laughter; the careful juxtaposition and arrangement of words from different linguistic registers; the play with accumulated interlocking metaphors of food, sex, and perception; the vignettes of bad poetry readings that range from the absurd to the pornographic; the uses of turnabout, parody, self-irony, self-sabotaging poetic allusion, and surprise—all these stylistic features and many more give *Satire* 1 its unusual power and excitement.

Persius's famous "obscurity" is the reverse of his brilliance. Gifted poets have always been difficult, and worth the difficulty, from Pindar and Aeschylus to Propertius, John Donne, T. S. Eliot, or Wallace Stevens, and, too, the everydayness of Roman satire and its many topical references have made later readers unusually dependent on commentaries and translations. But Persius is worth the effort. In time, if readers become acquainted with the satires and read them aloud, the difficulties become less troublesome and can even be appreciated as necessary aspects of Persius's highly original modernistic style. Notable among these characteristics are the uncertainty of speakers—and of their relation to one another and to the writer, as in the opening lines of *Satire* 1—and the audacious compression and conflation of metaphors, as in lines 22–23:

Do you, old man, collect scraps for other people's
tender little ears, to which, with your ruined old
joints and hide, you must finally say, " Enough"?

Many critics have struggled with the mix of culinary, sexual, and poetic images in this passage, but the lines have never yet been explicated to everyone's satisfaction. There are also rapid shifts of style, scene, and (ostensibly) subject matter, and the uses of parody and allusion are frequent and confusing. Does Persius, as has been alleged, quote Nero's own verses in *Satire* 1? Does he parody them, or parody contemporary fashions in poetry? The question remains open.

More important than Persius's jabs at unknown poetasters are his pervasive allusions to Lucilius and Horace, his precursors in Latin verse satire. Lucilius, who founded the genre and who is probably quoted in the first line of *Satire* 1, survives only in fragments, so no one can say to what extent Persius reverts from Horace's moderation, tact, and good-humored irony to the older roughness, aggressiveness, and fierce independence of Lucilian satire. Yet, Horace's *Satires* and *Epistles* are complete, and because Horace is everywhere present in Persius, similarities and differences can be detected at every point. Phrase after phrase, line after line recall Horace's situation and attitudes before and under Augustus as a foil to Persius's different ones in the Age of Nero. He knows Horace through and through, as Lucan, his fellow Silver Age poet, knows Virgil; but he cannot be Horace, any more than Lucan could or would be Virgil. Persius rebels against Horace creatively, in style and thought, as a son rebels against his father. His originality within the satiric tradition is thoroughly classical and is the best place to begin to understand, and to appreciate, his achievement—just as Juvenal in turn must be seen and judged against the combined background of Horace and Persius, on whom he builds.

"Once it was published," says the *Vita*, Persius's book of satire was "admired and attacked." As Quintilian, the distinguished professor of rhetoric, said later: "Persius too earned his share of genuine fame, albeit with one book." It quickly became a classic, to be taught in the schools and copied in widely proliferating manuscripts throughout late Antiquity and the Middle Ages. The Christian Fathers knew Persius well and quoted him: sometimes for his witty phrasing and satirical bite and sometimes for passages on virtue, piety, and the control of passion that lent themselves all too easily to Christian writing and preaching. Examples are many, from Lactantius, Jerome, and St. Augustine in the third and fourth centuries to Peter Abelard and John of Salisbury in the twelfth century.

The first printed editions of Persius's *Satires,* in Rome (A.D. 1469/1470) and Venice (1470), were followed by hundreds of others, and until the late seventeenth century, Persius held his own in the satiric triumvirate. Satire viewed as rude, explosive, satyr-like comment, or as a last-ditch surgical effort performed on the sick body of society, was recognizably his offspring. In England, John Donne knew Persius well and imitated him, as did Nicolas Boileau in France. Isaac Casaubon, the great Renaissance scholar, lectured and wrote on Persius, defending him (in 1605) against charges of willful obscurity and praising his moral seriousness and passion and his stylistic brilliance in a fine, thoughtful preface to a commentary that has shaped scholarship on Persius ever since. Only with John Dryden's 1693 "Discourse concerning Satire" was Persius marked down as decidedly inferior to Juvenal and Horace (usually in that order). His last important appearance came in Alexander Pope's 1735 "Epistle to Dr. Arbuthnot," where the ass's ears are now explicitly pinned on King Midas—on George II, that is, assisted by Queen Caroline and Prime Minister Robert Walpole. As Pope, like Persius, adapts Horatian forms, with their superficial humor and politeness, to express a free man's indignation at, and contempt for, a society aesthetically and morally corrupt from the top down, Pope's satire recapitulates the movement of Persius away from Horace and toward his successor Juvenal, with whom he was literally bound up in so many editions and commentaries and by whose stronger and more memorable rhetoric, which builds on that of Persius, he was destined in the end to be eclipsed.

References:

J. C. Bramble, *Persius and the Programmatic Satire* (Cambridge: Cambridge University Press, 1974);

Michael Coffey, *Roman Satire* (London: Methuen / New York: Barnes & Noble, 1976);

Cynthia S. Dessen, *The Satires of Persius: Iunctura Callidus Acri,* second edition (London: Bristol Classical Press, 1996);

Daniel M. Hooley, *The Knotted Thong: Structures of Mimesis in Persius* (Ann Arbor: University of Michigan Press, 1997);

Mark Morford, *Persius* (Boston: Twayne, 1984);

Vasily Rudich, *Political Dissidence Under Nero* (London & New York: Routledge, 1992).

Petronius

(ca. A.D. 20 – A.D. 66)

Gareth Schmeling
University of Florida

WORK–FRAGMENTARY: *Satyrica,* at least twenty books, of which fragments of books 14, 15, and 16 survive (Satyricon, before A.D. 66);

Verse, possibly culled from the above for *Latin Anthology* and other compilations.

Editio princeps: Verse in *Panegyrici veteres,* edited by F. Puteolanus (Milan: Antonius Zarotus, ca. 1482); *Cena Trimalchionis* (Padua: P. Frambottus, 1664).

Standard editions: *Le Satiricon,* edited by Alfred Ernout (with French translation), fourth edition (Paris: Les Belles Lettres, 1958); *Satyrica,* edited by Müller and Wilhelm Ehlers, third edition (Munich: Artemis, 1983); *Petronii Arbitri Satyricon,* edited by Konrad Müller, fourth edition (Stuttgart: Teubner, 1995).

Translations in English: *Petronius,* translated by Michael Heseltine, revised by E. H. Warmington (with Seneca, *Apocolocyntosis*), Loeb Classical Library (London: Heinemann / Cambridge, Mass.: Harvard University Press, 1969); *The Satyricon and the Fragments,* translated by John P. Sullivan (Harmondsworth, U.K.: Penguin, 1965; revised, 1986); *Satyrica,* translated by R. Bracht Branham and Daniel Kinney (Berkeley: University of California Press, 1996); *The Satyricon,* translated by P. G. Walsh (Oxford: Clarendon Press, 1996).

Commentaries: Peter Burman, *T. Petronii Arbitri Satyricon,* 2 volumes (Utrecht: Guilielmus Vande Water, 1709); *Petronii Cena Trimalchionis,* edited by Ludwig Friedländer, second edition (Leipzig: S. Hirzel, 1906)–with German translation; *La cena di Trimalchione,* edited by Amadeo Maiuri (Naples: R. Pironti, 1945); *The Cena Trimalchionis of Petronius . . . ,* edited by W. B. Sedgwick, second edition (Oxford: Clarendon Press, 1959); *Petronius. Cena Trimalchionis,* edited by Thomas Cutt (Detroit: Wayne State University Press, 1970); *Petroni Arbitri Cena Trimalchionis,* edited by Martin S. Smith (Oxford: Clarendon Press, 1975); *The Bellum Civile of Petronius,* edited by Florence Theodora Baldwin (New York: Columbia University Press, 1911)–

with translation; *Dal Satyricon, il Bellum Civile,* edited by Giorgio Guido (Bologna: Patron, 1976); *The Poems of Petronius,* edited by Edward Courtney (Atlanta: Scholars Press, 1991)–verse.

"One of the most licentious and repulsive works in Roman literature" is the way W. E. H. Lecky describes the *Satyrica* (Satyricon, before A.D. 66) in his *History of European Morals* (1911). The English critic and novelist Cyril Connolly in *Enemies of Promise* (1938) recalls his college days fondly because he remembers Petronius: "I had four editions of the *Satyrica.* The best I had bound in black crushed levant and kept on my pew in chapel where it looked like some solemn book of devotion and was never disturbed. To sit reading it during the sermon, looking reverently towards the headmaster scintillating from the pulpit and then returning to my racy Latin." Such is the reputation of Petronius and his *Satyrica,* repulsive and racy, bound in black crushed levant.

The Petronian family apparently had its origins in the Equestrian Order and remained at that level until the late Roman Republic, when it moved to the Senatorial Order. Shortly after the death of Augustus (A.D. 14) Titus Petronius Niger was born, ca. A.D. 20, possibly in Rome. A reasonable assumption is that the family owned an estate at Cumae just north of Naples. The Roman historian Tacitus (ca. A.D. 55–117) provides the only substantial body of information about Petronius the man (*Annals* 16.17–20). Petronius served as proconsul (ca. A.D. 60–61) in the Roman province of Bithynia (the area on the southwest coast of the Black Sea in Turkey) and later (ca. A.D. 62) as consul suffect in Rome.

Before and after his government service Petronius was considered a bon vivant, not a textbook voluptuary, but rather an artist who dealt in luxury. He charmed people because his manner and lifestyle, though unconventional, were clearly natural and engaging. He was, moreover, a capable government administrator. When in service, he did his duty; out of service he enjoyed life uninhibited by restraints of convention.

After successfully and soberly holding two important government posts, Petronius returned once again to days of sleep and nights of work and enjoyment.

As early as A.D. 60 Petronius had probably attracted the attention of the youthful Nero (born in A.D. 37, emperor A.D. 54–68). In the early years of his reign Nero was restrained by his mother Agrippina and two tutors, the Stoic philosopher Seneca the Younger and Sextus Afranius Burrus, Prefect of the Praetorian Guard. In A.D. 59 Nero began to show independence and had Agrippina murdered; in A.D. 62 Burrus died, and Seneca, ever the opportunist, retired into private life. While these restraints on Nero were receding, Petronius grew in influence at court and was named arbiter of elegance by Nero. In succeeding eras Petronius was usually referred to as Petronius Arbiter. Though Petronius had not moved into the innermost circle of Nero's confidants, he was surely in the next closest ring. Judging by what is known of Petronius, he probably did not act in any way to suppress the flamboyant excesses of certain of Nero's unpleasant proclivities. Petronius could not be guilty of preaching; he was surely consulted about manners and style and, if the *Satyrica* is any guide, he made pronouncements laced heavily with irony. Nero and Petronius, perhaps not friends, got along well enough. There are some scholars who believe that the *Satyrica* was written for Nero and his literary coterie, to be read aloud, one chapter per evening, a format that might help to explain the episodic nature of the novel.

In A.D. 65 a feeble conspiracy to assassinate Nero and to make C. Calpurnius Piso emperor was detected before Nero was harmed. Piso, Seneca, Lucan, Scaevinus, and others were executed. Though unhurt, Nero became suspicious of all those around him. C. Ofonius Tigellinus, the new Prefect of the Praetorian Guard, had grown jealous of Petronius's influence over Nero and saw in Nero's distrustful nature a chance to rid himself of a court rival. By bribing a slave, Tigellinus secured evidence that Petronius had been a friend of Scaevinus and thus was probably involved in the Pisonian conspiracy. Petronius reacted by appealing directly to Nero, who happened at the time to be in Campania. Upon reaching his estate at Cumae in Campania, Petronius learned that he could not see Nero. The handwriting was clear. Tacitus says that Petronius refused to live a life of suspense, waiting until Nero pointed thumbs up or down. In Petronius's will he omitted the usual flatteries of Nero and added nothing in an attempt to induce Nero to change his mind. To show his disinterest in imperial matters, Petronius wrote out a list of the emperor's sexual perversions, citing what was new, what was old, and the names of his male and female partners.

In what is probably the most famous suicide in the Roman world Petronius opened his veins and then after light conversation bound his veins; he then reopened them, had a good meal, and rebound them. Even though death was forced on him, Petronius made it appear his choice. Tacitus's description of Petronius's quiet and dignified death is unexpected and jolts the reader. The hedonistic and Epicurean Petronius, the man who loved living, died without a whimper like a Stoic in tune with the universe. He knew not only how to live but how to die.

The noble death of Petronius (A.D. 66), innocent and courageous, stands in marked contrast to the earlier deaths of the real conspirators–the Stoics Piso, Lucan, and Seneca. Piso flattered Nero in his will; Lucan implicated his own mother; and Seneca made a mess of his suicide. One would have expected the three Stoics, who were, after all, guilty of conspiracy to assassinate, to die well and the innocent hedonistic Petronius to shout out his innocence, to cling to life, and to die kicking and screaming. Tacitus relishes the contrast and lets the epigram from history fit neatly into his epigrammatic style.

The *Satyrica* is not a satire; the similarity of *satire* to *satyr* has led some to read the *Satyrica* as a satire. The *Satyrica* is not a romance; it is a novel. In his influential *The Rise of the Novel* (1957) Ian Watt contends that the novel was born in eighteenth-century England and that the works of prose fiction from the ancient world could not be novels because they are "an imitation of another literary work . . . (and) since the novelist's primary task is to convey the impression of fidelity to human experience, attention to any pre-established formal conventions can only endanger his success." Watt goes on to say that

> the previous (Greek and Roman) stylistic tradition for fiction was not primarily concerned with correspondence of words to things, but rather with the extrinsic beauties which could be bestowed upon description and action by the use of rhetoric. . . . So even if the new writers of fiction had ignored the old tradition of mixing poetry with their prose . . . as did Petronius. . . . There would still have remained a strong literary expectation that they would use language as a source of interest in its own right, rather than as a purely referential medium.

Is Watt really interested in the novel, or is his interest in the realistic-commercial novel only? "Realistic" for Watt is no longer a descriptive term but rather an evaluative one. What of the present of realism? Many of the finest novelists of the twentieth century–such as James Joyce, Anaïs Nin, and William Faulkner–broke away from the recent tradition of realism and began to experiment with language and tradition. Watt's definition of a novel is surely too restrictive and excludes many modern English novels.

The *Satyrica* should be labeled a novel because, among other things, it can meet four general criteria of the genre of the novel: the story is quasi-historical rather than traditional, drawn more from life than from literature, and it is new; it is a narrative of private, subjective experiences of individuals; the action of the story unfolds in a context of particularized time and place; and realistic particularity appears both in the narrative and in the characterization.

The *Satyrica* is not only a novel; it is a fragmentary novel. Some scholars argue that what survives is either the only portions of the whole that pious monks thought were respectable enough to be copied or a concentration of the few salacious parts ever to exist in the *Satyrica*, which were copied by "pious" monks for late-night meditation. J. P. Sullivan in *The Satyrica of Petronius: A Literary Study* (1968) speculates on the manuscript evidence that the extant *Satyrica* is part of books 14, 15, and 16 and that the whole was twenty-four books long (or ten times larger than the present novel).

So much of what survives of Greek and Latin literature is serious and often didactic. Even Old Comedy has a message. The Christian world preserved the writings of pagans because much of what they wrote was instructive, useful, and reasonable and provided guidelines for a sober life: Columella on agriculture, Manilius on astronomy, Cicero on friendship, Seneca on anger, Juvenal on the evils of women and city life, and Virgil on duty. Petronius is different in that he wrote to entertain only; he might also have written to prove he could do it. At Nero's court was a coterie of serious writers—Lucan writing epic, Seneca writing bloody plays, and Nero competing in "fixed" contests—and one observer of the political and literary scene, Petronius, who like Horace *nil admiratur* (marvels at nothing). With his eye ever on the incongruities of life—rhetoric versus action, appearance versus reality, and promises versus results—Petronius presents a series of slices of life that reflect his jaundiced view of first-century manners. Alexander Pope struck at the heart of Petronian criticism: "Fancy and Art in gay Petronius please: / The Scholar's Learning, with the Courtier's Ease."

The exterior form of the *Satyrica* is probably in part a parody of the so-called Menippean Satire, a mélange of prose and poetry and a potpourri of literary motifs. In the fragmentary *Satyrica* many poems are scattered, including one of 65 lines and another of 295. In addition, Petronius includes frequent discussions about poetry, deploring in general its sad state. Leading characters in the *Satyrica* likewise deplore the ruined condition of education, religion, local government, and personal morality. The sad state of these institutions and customs was a subject of discussion by many writers before and around the time of Petronius so that by A.D. 66 both the subjects and the discussions had become hackneyed. Petronius's characters discuss overworked and trite subjects because the subjects discussed at banquets and after university lectures are always hackneyed. The high cost of food (to the consumer), the low price of agricultural commodities (to the farmer), the unfair and unethical rise of one's competitors, the dishonest administration and waste by public officials, and the unwarranted vanity of one's neighbor's wife were the topics of conversation in Petronius's *Satyrica* and still are the regular grist of talk at modern cocktail parties. The need of some modern scholars to find a hidden or deep meaning in Petronian pronouncements on luxury and death, to find disintegration in a terribly fragmented piece of prose, and to find a pagan morality in the loose talk of petty tradesmen is to impose on the humor and irony of Petronius a scholastic model that creates order, unifying themes, and a text suitable for a paratext.

All the details of the *Satyrica* come to the reader through the first-person narrator Encolpius, who, having offended Priapus, the god of gardens and vineyards, is hounded like Odysseus around the Mediterranean world. Evidence from the fragments of the *Satyrica* indicates that the novel may have begun in Massilia (Marseille), where Encolpius commits some act of sacrilege against Priapus, who then drives Encolpius from France, south through Italy, and finally perhaps to Lampsacus, a city on the Hellespont and birthplace of Priapus. Yet Priapus to the Romans is an unimportant god, and Petronius sets up the comparison with Poseidon in the *Odyssey* to mock the Asianic import, who is usually portrayed as an erect phallus attached to a stump of wood, used in gardens as a fertility charm or scarecrow and generally is the object of much ridicule and naughty verse. Priapus or a priestess of Priapus has made Encolpius impotent and forced him to seek redemption at the hands of or in the bed of a priestess of Priapus. Petronius uses this format to spoof religion and to blame Priapus for the dominant role that sex plays in life. The object of the burlesque is humor at the expense of no one.

The extant *Satyrica* opens with a scene at a lecture by a rhetorician named Agamemnon; later he and the three leading characters—Encolpius, Ascyltus, and Giton—make up part of a dinner party at Trimalchio's house. After the lecture Quartilla, a priestess of Priapus, tries unsuccessfully in an all-night orgy to cure Encolpius of impotency. About one-third of the extant *Satyrica* is taken up with the "Banquet of Trimalchio," a hilarious comedy of manners. After the trio of Encolpius, Ascyl-

PETRONV.ARBITER.LI
BER.INCIPITFELICITER

...VM. Alio genere furiarum declamatores inquietantur: qui clamant hec uulnera pro libertate publica excepi. hunc oculum pro uobis impendi. date mihi ducem: qui me ducat ad liberos meos. nam succisi poplites membra non substinent. hec ipsa tollerabilia essent. si ad eloquentiam ituris uia facerent. Nunc ae rerum tumore: ae sententiarum uanissimo strepitu. hoc tantum proficiunt: ut cum in forum uenerint. putent se. in alium terrarum orbem delatos: ae ideo ego adulescentulos existimo in scolis stultissimos fieri: qui nihil ex iis que in usu habemus. aut audiunt aut uident. Sed piratas cum cathenis in littore stantes: ae tyrannos edicta scribentes: quibus imperent filiis ut patrum suorum capita precidant. sed responsa in pestilentiam data: ut uirgines tres aut plures immolentur. Sed mellitos uerbor̄

Page from an early-fifteenth-century manuscript for Petronius's works (Vatican Library, Codex Vaticanus Latinus 119, Urb. 670)

tus, and Giton escape the party, the poet Eumolpus replaces Ascyltus. The new trio feels constrained to leave town quickly and finds passage on a boat that only later they discover is owned by Lichas, whose wife Encolpius had earlier seduced. The boat is wrecked near Croton on the south coast of Italy, but the trio escapes. Eumolpus pretends to be a rich man near death and is immediately pursued by legacy hunters. Encolpius has another disastrous love affair and suffers more attempts to cure him by priestesses of Priapus. The *Satyrica* breaks off just where Eumolpus informs the beneficiaries of his will that they must eat his body to inherit his wealth.

Petronius doles out the life of Encolpius in episodes (twenty-four, each corresponding to one book) of about one hour apiece in recitation time. Each episode appears to be a fixed or set piece, whole in itself but loosely attached to what precedes and follows. The sum of episodes can be seen as a loose parody or a comic rewriting of Homer's *Odyssey,* in which the anger of Poseidon has become the anger of Priapus. This structure provides the supertexture of the *Satyrica,* which could be classified as a comic epic told by a bard named Petronius at the court of the Greek king, Nero. The court literati, not the general public, are the intended audience.

Petronius thickens the literary texture by borrowing from the rich ancient past: what appears new is novel only to the uninitiated. The literati appreciate the long tradition and recognize the *Satyrica* as traditional material. The package might be slightly different, the tone more irreverent, the feeling more pessimistic, and the intent less serious, but the stuff of the story is traditional. The extended imaginative narrative package called the novel, into which the *Satyrica* fits, had by the middle of the first century A.D. become popular, particularly in the eastern part of the Roman Empire. Drawing on tragic history (the popular but uncritical historiography of the day), sentimental epic, prose paraphrases of love elegies, idealized and fanciful biography, mime, New Comedy, rhetorical exercises, and travel stories, ancient Greek novelists were producing historical and sentimental novels. Petronius was surely aware of the existence of these Greek novels, and his parody of scenes from them helps to thicken the literary texture of the *Satyrica.*

Petronius produces several examples to illustrate this thick texture. Trimalchio invites Encolpius and his two boyfriends to a banquet at which Encolpius provides a running commentary on the events of the evening. Petronius uses Encolpius as narrator, and the reader learns everything through his eyes. Encolpius supposedly reports the conversations of all the other guests verbatim and without editorial comment. The reader hears the characters speaking directly to him. Because a whole book of the *Satyrica* is taken up with the banquet, Petron-

ius is signaling to the reader that the *Satyrica* at this point is a subspecies of literature known as symposium literature, and he borrows enough from Plato's *Symposium* so that the reader cannot fail to identify the source. Petronius builds Habinnas's drunken entry into Trimalchio's hall upon Alcibiades' entrance in the *Symposium.* The character of the boorish host, Trimalchio, who pretentiously serves his guests many kinds of food, much of it grown on his estates, was inspired at least in part by the host in Horace's *Cena Nasidieni* (*Satire* 2.8). Banquets and boorish hosts were probably not in short supply in Italy, and works of fiction about them can be considered, if applied delicately, as social commentary. Petronius, however, is a literary animal, and Trimalchio, the self-made millionaire host, is the vehicle for Petronius's verbal gymnastics, not primarily for social commentary. Though his Latin grammar is often terrible and his mythological exegesis downright unintelligible, Trimalchio remains a literary creation who for a few brief moments holds center stage along with a collection of freedmen and slaves gathered to tell ghost stories, castigate local officials, and complain about everything. The guests at the banquet represent examples of almost every type of interesting person Petronius could imagine at an Italian table. His imagination leaves no room for a dull guest. That these guests belonged to types satirized by other Roman writers does not mean that Petronius was satirizing them.

Outside the *Cena Trimalchionis* Petronius liberally sprinkles his narrative with naughty interpolated tales (for example, the "Pergamene Boy" and the "Widow of Ephesus"), which continue a tradition begun in the first century B.C. in Miletus in Asia Minor and are still found at the end of the second century in Apuleius's *Metamorphoses.* By inserting a short epic of 295 lines on the Civil War (in praise of Julius Caesar) as a kind of rebuttal to Lucan's epic *Pharsalia* (written in praise of Pompey, Caesar's archenemy), Petronius continues a literary feud he had begun with Seneca, Lucan's uncle. Seneca and Lucan longed for the former days of Republican Rome when the aristocracy ruled, the time before Caesar crossed the Rubicon. Petronius apparently disliked these *laudatores temporis acti* (praisers of past times), these "Catos" who romanticized the politics of the past but tried to alter the course of traditional literature. Not only in politics but also in literary matters Seneca and Lucan sided against Nero (a descendant of Caesar), whom in a roundabout way Petronius defended. Petronius was a literary, rather than political, conservative in love with tradition. He loved Horace and Virgil and despised the new epic of Lucan; he loved the Latin prose of the past and backed away from Senecan sentiment. On the other hand, Petronius was a realist who knew just how dead the Republic was.

Title page for a 1654 edition of Petronius's Satyrica *(courtesy of the Lilly Library, Indiana University)*

The *Satyrica* is easily understood on the level of sense; the action is clear. The Latin of Petronius, beautifully structured in units shorter than Cicero's but longer than Tacitus's, moves briskly and vividly relates a story that strikes even a present-day audience as modern. The Latin is clear but conservative, for Petronius observes literary decorum: Encolpius employs an elegant and studied Latin style in the opening chapters where he is speaking of the decline of rhetoric; where he sets a scene or presents a straightforward narrative or summarized action, he uses an unaffected and informal style (deceptively plain because Petronius pays careful attention to the rhythm of the Latin); and finally the former slave Trimalchio uses the vulgar and even grammatically incorrect Latin of the nouveaux riches of the brave new Empire. These distinctions in language help to keep the reader close to the subject. The reader sympathizes with Trimalchio, an immigrant to Italy

who struggles (and often loses) with the Latin language and so endears himself.

Trimalchio is boorish on a grand scale, so comical that his guests actually need to bury their faces to keep from laughing out loud at him. He is uneducated, clumsy, and boastful, but in the final analysis his character is almost warm; there is no evil or harm in the man. The reader, however, would not invite Trimalchio to a party of polite society. He belongs in a bowling alley decorated with pink flamingos, or in a drinking fraternity at a correspondence school, or in a union hall for untalented actors. The details selected by Petronius to portray Trimalchio have made him memorable without being likable, fascinating without being bearable, and entertaining at a party (as long as the party is not at one's own house).

Encolpius, the narrator of the *Satyrica,* is a sympathetic character, but Petronius's description of him is not warm. Where Trimalchio has a childlike innocence and abiding affection for old friends, Encolpius is a juvenile delinquent who changes friends, enemies, and bed partners as he changes moods. Trimalchio is a simple character, Encolpius complex; Trimalchio is romantic, Encolpius modern; Trimalchio is optimistic, Encolpius pessimistic; Trimalchio wants desperately to live, Encolpius often toys with self-destruction; Trimalchio is emotionally stable, Encolpius unstable. Because Encolpius revels in self-pity and is in need of a psychiatrist, he is also modern, a modern man set in a modern literary form.

An accepted thesis about the survival of works from antiquity is that what is hidden becomes lost. Imperial disfavor and Petronius's suicide surely encouraged the Arbiter's friends to conceal copies of the *Satyrica*, which because of its great length was probably epitomized in the centuries that followed until it became a short collection of witty sayings and strange words. In 1650 in Trogir, Yugoslavia, book 15, the *Cena Trimalchionis*, was unearthed, and the world suddenly had 50 percent more of the *Satyrica* than it had had the year before. Petronius the man, as opposed to his work the *Satyrica*, had never been forgotten because of Tacitus's brilliant biography of him in his *Annals* (16.17–20). What especially caught the imagination of later writers was the manner of Petronius's death. Robert Burton in his *The Anatomy of Melancholy* (1621) and Jeremy Taylor in *The Rule and Exercises of Holy Dying* (1651) refer frequently to the style Petronius chose for his own death. These two works plus the first English translation of the *Satyrica* by William Burnaby (1694) meant that Petronius began to enjoy a real vogue in England. With the disappearance of the dour reign of the Cromwells and with the Stuart Restoration in 1660, a sympathic background set the stage for a Petronian revival.

Petronius has remained a darling of the literary avant-garde. At times he has been forced underground and his *Satyrica* officially banned–but never successfully repressed; at times Petronius was actually popular. Tobias Smollett in *Adventures of Roderick Random* (1748); George Gordon, Lord Byron; Samuel Taylor Coleridge; Thomas Love Peacock (frequently); Jorris-Karl Huysmans in *Á Rebours* (1891); Oscar Wilde in *The Picture of Dorian Gray* (1891); John Millington Synge; James Joyce in *Ulysses* (1922); F. Scott Fitzgerald in *The Great Gatsby* (1925); Aldous Huxley in *Crome Yellow* (1921); Henry Miller; Lawrence Durrell in *The Alexandria Quartet* (1957–1960); and Ezra Pound borrow, cite, or in some way use Petronius and his *Satyrica*. In the 1920s when Petronius was especially popular among English men of letters, T. S. Eliot was Petronius's great champion, defending him in 1922 against the New York Society for the Suppression of Vice and using a quota-tion from the *Satyrica* as the epigraph for *The Waste Land*.

At least three, often completely separate, views of Petronius have come down to the present: he is the *arbiter elegantiae* and Roman consul to Nero, a character from Tacitus who knew how to die; a talented man of letters who wrote the *Satyrica;* a degenerate courtier to the most degenerate emperor; and a man who lived in and wrote filth. The *Satyrica* has been viewed in two radically different ways. To writers such as Peacock, Durrell, and Eliot the *Satyrica* is a masterpiece of Latin prose, a literary landmark to those who appreciate a fine stylist telling an absorbing story. To the vast majority, however, who know the name only, the *Satyrica* is a banned and proscribed book including within its covers a description of all the vices, perversions, un-Christian sex acts, and abominable debauches perpetrated in the dimly lighted recesses of the pleasure palaces of Nero. These people have never read the *Satyrica*, are not under its influence, but have heard about it and know its reputation. It is the reputation, not the reality, of the *Satyrica* that most know.

The *Fellini-Satyricon* is an art movie made by the Italian maestro Federico Fellini in 1969 (not titled simply the *Satyricon* because that title had been put under copyright by the Italian director Gian Luigi Polidoro, who in 1968 used it as an excuse for color pornography). There is some of the ancient *Satyrica* in Fellini's movie, but none of its humor and charm. For the most part the movie is vintage Fellini–his colorings, his Rome. It is a Fellini dream or nightmare about what ancient Rome was like. He attached the name *Satyrica* to it because the *Satyrica* had a reputation.

In 1969 at the Stratford Festival (Canada) the *Satyrica* was performed as a musical. According to the official program, "It was quite a party at Trimalchio's. You know the sort of party–we've all been to them–where the big difference between the wives and the call-girls present is that the latter are better dressed, better mannered and less obnoxious than the former." What some in the present day have for sexual fantasies (and musicals) Petronius supposedly enjoyed as reality.

The reputation of Petronius was secured at a new low point with the publication in 1966 of a book titled *New York Unexpurgated. An Amoral Guide for the Jaded, Tired, Evil, Non-Conforming, Corrupt, Condemned and the Curious–Humans and Otherwise–to the Underground Manhattan* by Petronius. To credit such a book to Petronius shows the power of the name alone.

These three examples demonstrate the current status of Petronius and the *Satyrica* in the popular imagination. It is amusing to observe the disparity between the historical Petronius and his reputation. The reputation seems to have a life of its own. But everything is not lost. The classically educated English novelist Anthony Burgess in *The Kingdom of the Wicked* (1985) provides a sobering corrective: "Latin itself is too cold and legalistic: even the pornography of Petronius reads like a series of court depositions."

Bibliography and Concordance:

Gareth L. Schmeling, *A Bibliography of Petronius* (Leiden: Brill, 1977);

Matthias Korn and Stefan Reitzer, eds., *Concordantia Petroniana* (Hildesheim: Olms-Weidmann, 1986).

References:

William Arrowsmith, "Luxury and Death in the *Satyrica*," *Arion*, 5 (1966): 304–331;

Gilbert Bagnani, *Arbiter of Elegance: A Study of the Life and Works of C. Petronius Arbiter* (Toronto: University of Toronto Press, 1954);

R. Beck, "Emolpus *poeta*, Eumolpus *fabulator:* A Study of Characterization in the *Satyrica*," *Phoenix*, 33 (1979): 239–253;

Beck, "Encolpius at the *Cena*," *Phoenix*, 29 (1975): 271–283;

Beck, "Some Observations on the Narrative Technique of Petronius," *Phoenix*, 27 (1973): 43–61;

J. Bodel, "Trimalchio's Underworld," in *The Search for the Ancient Novel* (Baltimore: Johns Hopkins University Press, 1994), pp. 237–259;

Peter E. Bondanella, *The Cinema of Federico Fellini* (Princeton, N.J.: Princeton University Press, 1992);

Bret Boyce, *The Language of the Freedmen in Petronius' Cena Trimalchionis* (Leiden: Brill, 1991);

A. Cameron, "Myth and Meaning in Petronius," *Latomus*, 29 (1970): 397–425;

Michael Coffey, *Roman Satire* (London: Methuen, 1976);

Gian Biagio Conte, *The Hidden Author: An Interpretation of Petronius's Satyrica* (Berkeley: University of California Press, 1996);

Philip B. Corbett, *Petronius* (New York: Twayne, 1970);

P. George, "Style and Character in the *Satyrica*," *Arion*, 5 (1966): 336–358;

Thomas Hägg, *The Novel in Antiquity* (Oxford: Blackwell, 1983);

Gilbert Highet, "Petronius the Moralist," *Transactions of the American Philological Association*, 72 (1941): 176–194;

Niklas Holzberg, *The Ancient Novel: An Introduction* (London: Routledge, 1995);

David Konstan, *Sexual Symmetry: Love in the Ancient Novel and Related Genres* (Princeton, N.J.: Princeton University Press, 1994);

Costas Panayotakis, *Theatrum Arbitri. Theatrical Elements in the Satyrica of Petronius* (Leiden: Brill, 1995);

H. D. Rankin, *Petronius the Artist. Essays on the Satyrica and its Author* (The Hague: Nijhoff, 1971);

Wade Richardson, *Reading and Variant in Petronius* (Toronto: University of Toronto Press, 1993);

K. F. C. Rose, *The Date and Author of the Satyrica* (Leiden: Brill, 1971);

Gerald Sandy, "Satire in the *Satyrica*," *American Journal of Philology*, 90 (1969): 293–303;

Gareth L. Schmeling, "The *Exclusus Amator* Motif in Petronius," in *Fons Perennis* (Turin: Baccola & Gili, 1971), pp. 333–357;

Schmeling, "T. S. Eliot and Petronius," *Comparative Literature Studies*, 12 (1975): 393–410;

Schmeling, "The *Satyrica:* The Sense of an Ending," *Rheinisches Museum*, 134 (1991): 352–377;

Schmeling, ed., *The Novel in the Ancient World* (Leiden: Brill, 1996);

William J. Slater, ed., *Dining in a Classical Context* (Ann Arbor: University of Michigan Press, 1991);

J. P. Sullivan, *Literature and Politics in the Age of Nero* (Ithaca, N.Y.: Cornell University Press, 1985);

Sullivan, *The Satyrica of Petronius: A Literary Study* (London: Faber & Faber, 1968);

P. G. Walsh, *The Roman Novel* (Cambridge: Cambridge University Press, 1970);

Froma I. Zeitlin, "Petronius as Paradox: Anarchy and Artistic Integrity," *Transactions of the American Philological Association*, 102 (1971): 631–684.

Phaedrus

(ca. 18 B.C. – ca. A.D. 50)

Michele Valerie Ronnick
Wayne State University

WORK: *Fabellae Aesopiae,* 5 books (Aesopian Fables, A.D. 20–50).

Editio princeps: P. Pithou, ed., *Phaedri Aug. Liberti . . . Fabularum Aesopiarum libri V . . .* (Troyes, 1596).

Standard editions: *Phaedri Augusti Liberti Fabulae Aesopiae,* edited by Lucian Müller (Leipzig: Teubner, 1876); *Phaedri Fabulae Aesopiae,* edited by J. P. Postgate (Oxford: Clarendon Press, 1919).

Translations in English: *Babrius and Phaedrus,* translated by Ben Edwin Perry, Loeb Classical Library (Cambridge, Mass.: Harvard University Press, 1965); *Phaedrus,* translated by Christopher Smart (London: J. Dodsley, 1765); *The Fables of Phaedrus,* translated by Paul F. Widdows (Austin: University of Texas, 1992).

Little is known about the life of the fabulist Phaedrus. The title of the principal manuscript of his work, the *Codex Pithoeanus [P],* identifies him as a freedman of the emperor Augustus. All other biographical evidence has been deduced from what Phaedrus himself says or does not say in his writings. His contemporaries, foremost among them Seneca the Younger and Quintilian, make no mention of him, although they both discuss the writing of fables in parts of their works (*Ad Poly.* 2.8.3, *IO* 1.9.2–3). The orthography of Phaedrus's name has come into question as well. The Greek form, Phaedros, is the form used in *Codex P.* About a century ago the French scholars Leopold Hervieux and Louis Havet pointed out that Phaeder, patterned on the formation of the names Alexander and Menander, deserved consideration.

Nevertheless, while a full-scale biography of Phaedrus will probably remain forever beyond anyone to write, the facts known at present are as follows: Phaedrus was born of uncertain parentage around 18 B.C. in Pieria, a mountainous area sacred to the Muses in northern Greece, then part of the Roman province of Macedonia (*Prof.* 3.17–23). His strong desire for recognition and the talent about which he was boastfully con-

fident are made clear at several places in his fables. He declares with pride, for example, in the prologue to the third book, that he "has made a road in place of [Aesop's] footpath, and has invented more topics than he [Aesop] left behind" (*Prol.* 3.38–39). Clear, too, is that he seemed to have been a virtual outcast in Rome, but where he was educated and how he came to Italy is not known. It is possible, as F. Della Corte posits, that the consul L. Calpurnius Piso Frugi brought Phaedrus back from his assignment in Thrace in 11 B.C. to serve as a slave in the household of Augustus. There, as de Lorenzo conjectures, Phaedrus may have attended Lucius Caesar, Augustus's grandson, and studied with him in the school of Verrius Flaccus on the Palatine Hill.

According to Phaedrus himself, at some point before A.D. 31 he was prosecuted by Sejanus, the notorious commander of the praetorian guard under the emperor Tiberius, for something he wrote. Whatever punishment resulted from this mysterious offense Phaedrus deeply resented. The date and place of his death are also uncertain, although the tone of portions of the fifth and final book of his fables suggests that he lived into old age. After his death in the middle of the first century A.D., his name drops out of the written record and is not mentioned again until the fabulist Avianus made note of Phaedrus and his five books of fables in a letter written to Theodosius around A.D. 400 Avianus's work, however, was strongly influenced by the fables of the Greek Babrius and not by Phaedrus.

The five books of *Fabellae Aesopiae* (Aesopian Fables) that remain extant seem to have been written at different stages of Phaedrus's life and to have been published at intervals between A.D. 20 and A.D. 50 under the emperors Tiberius, Gaius, and Claudius. They vary in length from under 200 lines to a maximum of 425 and include respectively thirty-one, eight, nineteen, twenty-five, and ten poems. Their meter is iambic senarius (six iambic feet), one that was used by ancient writers of comedy and was seen in the works of D. Laberius, the first-century-B.C. playwright, and his con-

Page from a ninth-century manuscript for Phaedrus's adaptation of Aesop's fables, Fabellae Aesopiae *(MS 906, f.64v, Pierpont Morgan Library, New York)*

temporary, Publilius Syrus, the actor and moralizer. Thus, it is possible that Phaedrus's style was shaped in part by the mime tradition. In addition, although the three names of his addressees were not Roman (Euty-chus, Particulo, and Philetes or Philetus), his Latin nowhere suggests the diction of a foreigner.

The oldest manuscript, the ninth-century *Codex P,* was found in the late sixteenth century by Pierre Pithou (1539–1596). Its discovery and subsequent publication in 1596 produced great excitement and many editions in Britain and across Europe. The codex was then for many years the private property of the family of the Marquis de Rosanbo and unavailable for study. However, since the acquisition of the codex by the Pierpont Morgan Library in the 1960s, the ninety-four fables and seven other pieces included in it have been open to scholars. The missing fables, which are estimated to be fifty-six, have been reconstructed in part by the *Appendix Perottina* (MS Naples iv. F. 58), a fifteenth-century epitome made by Nicolas Perotti, Archbishop of Siponto (1430–1480). It includes thirty-two fables from books 2 to 5, three addresses, and thirty-two fables not in the earlier manuscripts. Perotti's transcription, which is in the main literal, has some modifications made by omission and by rearrangement. His mention of Phaedrus by name, nearly one thousand years after Avianus's notice, stands as only the second indisputable reference to him.

A body of medieval prose paraphrases derived in large part from a missing common source also survives. There are three manuscripts: the eleventh-century *Leidensis Vossianus* Lat. 0.15, known as *Adem.,* written by Ademar of Chabannes (ca. A.D. 988–1034), a monk at Saint-Martial-de-Limoges, which includes sixty-seven fables; the tenth-century Wolfenbuttel, MS *Gudianus Latinus* 148, known as *Wissenbургensis* or *Wiss.,* which included sixty-two fables; and the *Romulus,* known as *Rom.,* the oldest and best copy of which is the eleventh-century Burney 59, which includes eighty-three fables. From *Romulus* comes the twelfth-century text *Anonymous Neveleti* and its sixty fables in Latin elegiacs.

Scholars believe that Phaedrus used the prose *Aesopica* of Demetrius of Phalerum (ca. 345–283 B.C.), the Athenian statesman, as his main source. That text is thought to have been lost with the great library at Alexandria. Most of Phaedrus's poems are in the form of animal or beast fables. Of the 94 items in *Codex P,* 59 are animal fables, and if the *Appendix Perottina* is included, the proportion is 75 of 126. The fables are a collage of various elements colored by small details from Graeco-Roman life. They present lessons with a moral point, historical anecdotes such as those concerning Simonides, Menander, and Tibe-

rius; short stories; comical incidents; and bits of folk wisdom. Their attitude is that of a wry, yet reserved, conservative who has both chronic and acute interest in writing about the abuse of power, the misapplication of justice, and the oppression of the humble and the weak. Phaedrus hopes that his fables may correct the mistakes of his fellow human beings and sharpen their wits. A prominent theme throughout is the overwhelming importance of freedom, a state more precious than power and riches.

The moral point of many of the fables is underscored by the use of *promythia,* which are brief index-like statements concerning the overarching themes that precede the narratives, and *epimythia,* short explanations that follow the fables when the *promythia* have been forgotten, or lost. The moral point of a fable, at times purely ethical, but often with social implications, is what distinguishes the fable from mere storytelling; for length of sentence and the animal disguises are what permit the author to make subversive attacks upon the status quo, or simply to express frustrations or fantasies.

Phaedrus is fully aware of this dynamic (*Prol.* 3.33–371). In a brief statement concerning the origin of the fable, Phaedrus explains that slaves who were subject to punishment for any offense, since they could not say what they would like, transferred their feelings into fables and avoided censure with jests about things that never happened. Thus, fables such as those of Phaedrus are overtly educational and often covertly propagandistic at the same time. They also include elements of political satire and of class struggle.

In Phaedrus's work there are no radical shifts in power. The strong defeat the weak in almost every instance. The innocent lamb is unjustly devoured by the wolf; the barnyard animals foolishly trust the lion to be fair-minded. Protest avails naught for them, although the strong are on occasion undone. All, however, are shown the fate of the presumptuous and the conceited, for those with such characteristics are often punished in Phaedrus's world.

Phaedrus is considered by historians of literature to be a "minor poet." Nonetheless, his achievement and his subsequent influence deserve full attention, for Phaedrus was a pioneer. He was the first author in Rome to transfer an entire Greek genre (the fable) into Latin literature—and he knew it. At 2.9.1, he says that if his "efforts find favor in Rome, then Rome will have another weapon to carry on the contest with Greece." This accomplishment is not small. Only in verse satire and the novel was Latin literature ever so original and free from Greek influences.

His works were popular for centuries as school texts, and in fact in modern times a journal of children's literature bore his name. The seventeenth and eighteenth centuries were truly his as many scholars labored over his text and published their results. Among them was Jean de La Fontaine (1621–1695), who acknowledged his debt to Phaedrus in form and content in his best-selling *Fables* (1688–1694), a work that remained popular in France during the mid-nineteenth century. La Fontaine said that he relied on his own style (which is charming and light) to make up for his inability to capture fully in French Phaedrus's elegant concision, and he said that he much admired Phaedrus's dramatic and philosophical content. In contrast to such contemporaries as Nevelet, Patru, and Audin of Termes, who championed Aesop, La Fontaine drew the overwhelming majority of his fables from Phaedrus. In England a few decades later the classical scholar Richard Bentley (1662–1742), in a race to beat other scholars into print, published texts of Phaedrus in 1726 and 1727.

In colonial America, Peter Thacher (1752–1802), congregational clergyman and a founder of the Massachusetts Historical Society, responded to Phaedrus's theme of freedom. On the title page of his *Oration Delivered at Watertown, March 5, 1776: To Commemorate the Bloody Massacre at Boston Perpetrated March 5, 1770* (1776) are seven lines from Phaedrus's fable "The Donkey to the Old Shepherd" (1.15.4–10). There the donkey tells his master, who wants to ride away on his back at the approach of some thieves, that he does not care which owner he serves, provided that he carries only one burden at a time. The epigraph clearly foreshadows a major point made in the actual speech. "The legislature of Great Britain is totally corrupt . . . the people have lost their spirit of resentment; and like the most contemptible of animals, bow their shoulders to bear and become servants unto tribute." A sixteen-page pamphlet attributed to his father, Oxenbridge Thacher Jr. (1719–1765), titled *The Sentiments of a British American* (1764), bears the same seven lines.

A different statement concerning the same theme formed the basis of one of the most powerful products of the imagination of the English writer Thomas De Quincey (1785–1859), namely the idea that the "pariah-slave" could triumph over the highborn. This statement was inspired, De Quincey wrote in his autobiography, by lines 1 and 2 of the epilogue to book 2 in which Phaedrus says that the "Athenians had raised a statue to Aesop, and placed a slave on an everlasting pedestal." To this untenable dichotomy between noble manhood and debased servitude De Quincey strongly reacted. "This passage," he wrote, "which might be briefly designated 'The

Title page for the 1667 Amsterdam edition of Phaedrus's adaptation of Aesop's fables

Apotheosis of the Slave,' gave to me my first grand and jubilant sense of the sublime."

Until recent times, the influence of Phaedrus has been long-lived and wide. But today the names Aesop and La Fontaine are more readily recognized than Phaedrus. Nevertheless, a change may be under way. After a two-hundred-year hiatus the English verse translation of P. F. Widdows published in 1992 has superseded that of Christopher Smart from 1765. The irony of this reversal of fortune would not be lost on Phaedrus. At 2.9.18–19 he says that if his work is unappreciated by jealous types, he will suffer the fated banishment with a toughened heart until Fortune grows ashamed of her verdict. Despite the whimsy of animal costume and the amusing touches of humor, Phaedrus's fables are tinged with tragic undertones. In them are lessons for life in an unforgiving and dangerous world.

Lexicon and Bibliography:

L. Tortora, "Recenti studi su fedro (1967–1974)," *Bollettino di studi latini,* 5 (1975): 266–273;

Carlo Angelo Cremona, *Lexicon Phaedrianum* (Hildesheim: Olms, 1980).

References:

A. G. Becher, "Ancients and Moderns: Background to Christopher Smart's *Phaedrus,*" *Studies on Voltaire and the Eighteenth Century,* 305 (1992): 1439–1442;

Becher, "Un de 'ces grands Hommes'–Phaedrus, a Precursor of La Fontaine," *Papers on French Seventeenth Century Literature,* 23, no. 44 (1996): 115–122;

H. M. Currie, "Phaedrus the Fabulist," *Aufstieg und Niedergang der romanischen Welt* II, 32, no. 1 (1984): 497–513;

F. Della Corte, "Phaedriana," *Rivista di Filologia d'Instuzione Classica,* 17 (1939): 136–144;

C. E. Finch, "The Morgan Manuscript of Phaedrus," *American Journal of Philology,* 92(1971): 301–307;

L. Hervieux, *Les fabulistes latins depuis le siécle d'Auguste jusqu'à la fin du moyen âge,* 5 volumes, volume 1: *Phèdre et ses anciens imitateurs* (Paris: Firmin-Didot, 1893–1899);

Samuel Howitt, *A New Work of Animals* (London: E. Orme, 1811);

Attilio de Lorenzi, *Fedro* (Florence: La Nuova Italia, 1955);

P. K. Marshall, "Phaedrus," in *Texts and Transmission,* edited by L. D. Reynolds (Oxford: Clarendon Press / New York: Oxford University Press, 1983), pp. 300–302;

R. P. Oliver, "Perotti's Cornucopiae," *Transactions of the American Philological Association,* 78 (1947): 376–390;

B. E. Perry, *Aesopica* (Urbana: University of Illinois Press, 1952);

Perry, "Demetrius of Phalerum and the Aesopic Fables," *Transactions of the American Philological Association,* 93 (1962): 287–346;

Perry, "The Origin of the *Epimythium,*" *Transactions of the American Philological Association,* 71 (1940): 391–419;

T. C. W. Stinton, "Phaedrus and Folklore, an Old Problem Restated," *Classical Quarterly,* 29 (1979): 432–435;

Carl M. Zander, "Phaedrus solutus vel Phaedri fabulae novae XXX," *Acta regiae societatis humaniorum litterarum Lundensis,* 3 (Lund, Sweden: C. W. K. Gleerup, 1921);

Jan M. Ziolkowski, *Talking Animals: Medieval Latin Beast Poetry, 750–1150* (Philadelphia: University of Pennsylvania Press, 1993).

Plautus

(ca. 254 B.C. – 184 B.C.)

Timothy J. Moore
University of Texas at Austin

MAJOR WORKS–EXTANT: *Stichus,* produced at the Plebeian Games (200 B.C.);

Pseudolus, produced at the Megalensian Games (192/191 B.C.);

Amphitruo;

Asinaria (The Donkey Play);

Aulularia (The Pot of Gold);

Bacchides (The Bacchis Sisters);

Captivi (The Captives);

Casina;

Cistellaria (The Basket);

Curculio;

Epidicus;

Menaechmi (The Menaechmus Brothers);

Mercator (The Merchant);

Miles Gloriosus (The Braggart Soldier);

Mostellaria (The Haunted House);

Persa (The Persian);

Poenulus (The Little Carthaginian);

Rudens (The Rope);

Trinummus (The Three-Penny Day);

Truculentus;

Vidularia (The Traveling Bag).

Editio princeps: *Comoediae,* edited by Georgius Merula (Venice: Vindelinus de Spira, 1472).

Standard editions: *Plauti Comoediae,* 2 volumes, edited by F. Leo (Berlin: Weidmann, 1895–1896); *T. Macci Plauti Comoediae,* 2 volumes, edited by W. M. Lindsay (Oxford: Clarendon Press, 1904–1905); *Tutte le commedie,* edited by Ettore Paratore (Rome: Newton Compton, 1976); *Titi Macci Plauti Cantica,* edited by Cesare Questa (Urbino: Quattro Venti, 1995).

Translations in English: *Plautus,* 5 volumes, translated by Paul Nixon, Loeb Classical Library (Cambridge, Mass.: Harvard University Press, 1916–1938); *Plautus: The Rope, Amphitruo, The Ghost, A Three-Dollar Day,* translated by E. F. Watling (London: Penguin, 1964); *Plautus: The Pot of Gold, The Prisoners, The Brothers Menaechmus, The Swagger-*ing Soldier, Pseudolus, translated by Watling (London: Penguin, 1965); *Plautus: Rudens, Curculio, Casina,* translated by Christopher Stace (Cambridge: Cambridge University Press, 1981); *Plautus: The Darker Comedies: Bacchides, Casina, and Truculentus,* translated by James Tatum (Baltimore: Johns Hopkins University Press, 1983); *Plautus: The Comedies,* 4 volumes, edited by David R. Slavitt and Palmer Bovie (Baltimore: Johns Hopkins University Press, 1995); *Plautus: Four Comedies: The Braggart Soldier, The Brothers Menaechmus, The Haunted House, The Pot of Gold,* translated by Erich Segal (Oxford: Oxford University Press, 1996).

Commentaries: *Commentarius in Plauti Comoedias,* edited by Johan Louis Ussing (5 volumes, Copenhagen, 1876–1892; 2 volumes, Hildesheim: Olms, 1972); Individual Plays: *T. Macci Plauti Amphitruo,* edited by Arthur Palmer (London: Macmillan, 1890); *Amphitruo,* edited by W. B. Sedgwick (Manchester: Manchester University Press, 1960); *Asinaria cum commentario exegetico,* 2 volumes, edited by Ferruccio Bertini (Genoa: Università di Genova Istituto di Filologia Classica e Medioevale, 1968); *T. Macci Plauti Asinaria,* edited by J. H. Gray (Cambridge: Cambridge University Press, 1894); *Aulularia,* edited by Giuseppe Augello (Turin: Paravia, 1972); *T. Macci Plauti Aulularia,* edited by Wilhelm Wagner (Cambridge: Cambridge University Press, 1892); *T. Maccius Plautus: Aulularia,* edited by Walter Stockert (Stuttgart: Trübner, 1983); *Plautus Bacchides,* edited by John Barsby (Oak Park, Ill.: Bolchazy-Carducci, 1986); *The Captivi of Plautus,* edited by W. M. Lindsay, second edition (Oxford: Clarendon Press, 1930); *Casina,* edited by W. Thomas MacCary and M. M. Willcock (Cambridge: Cambridge University Press, 1976); *Plautus' Curculio,* edited by John W. Wright, revised edition (Norman: University of Oklahoma Press, 1993); *T. Macci Plauti Epidicus,* edited by George E. Duckworth (Princeton, N.J.: Princeton University Press, 1940); *Plautus: Menaechmi,* edited by A. S. Gratwick (Cambridge: Cambridge University Press, 1993); *Plauti Mercator,* 2 volumes, edited by Petrus Joannes Enk, second edition (Leiden: A. W. Sijthoff, 1966); *T. Macci Plauti Miles Gloriosus,* edited by Mason Hammond, Arthur M. Mack, and Walter Moskalew, second revised edition (Cambridge, Mass.: Harvard University Press, 1970); *T. Macci Plauti Mostellaria,* edited by Edwin W. Fay (Boston: Allyn & Bacon, 1902); *Mostellaria—Plaute, La farce du fantôme,* edited by Jean Collart (Paris: Presses Universitaires de France, 1970); *T. Maccius Plautus Persa,* edited by Erich Woytek (Vienna: Verlag der Osterreichischen Akademie der Wissenschaften, 1982); Gregor Maurach, *Der Poenulus des Plautus* (Heidelberg: C. Winter, 1988); *Pseudolus,* edited by Malcolm M. Willcock (Bristol, U.K.: Bristol Classical Press / Oak Park, Ill.: Bolchazy-Carducci, 1987); *Rudens,* edited by Andreas Thierfelder (Heidelberg: Kerle, 1962); *Rudens,* edited by H. C. Fay (London: University Tutorial Press, 1969); *T. Maccius Plautus: Stichus,* edited by Hubert Petersmann (Heidelberg: C. Winter, 1973); *The Trinummus of Plautus,* edited by H. Rushton Fairclough (New York: Macmillan, 1909); *Trinummus,* edited by Julius Brix and M. Niemeyer, fifth edition (Leipzig-Berlin: Teubner, 1907); Enk, *Plauti Truculentus,* 2 volumes (Leiden: Sijthoff, 1953).

Titus Maccius Plautus is the earliest Roman author whose works have survived. His plays, valued especially for their lively stock characters, their exuberant language and meter, and the information they provide on many aspects of Roman culture, have had a profound and wide-ranging influence on modern comedy. Ancient tradition held that Plautus was born in Sarsina, not far from modern San Marino. After making money acting or doing some other business involved with the stage, he allegedly lost his fortune in mercantile misadventures and wrote some plays while working in a mill. He then became quite successful and died an old man in 184 B.C. (hence, the guess of 254 B.C., seventy years earlier, for the year of his birth). Most of the tradition is almost certainly apocryphal. Given Plautus's acute sensitivity to what worked in performance, however, the ancient scholars were probably correct in attributing to him much experience in the theater.

Plautus's contribution can be appreciated best by comparing his plays with those of the genre he adapted for the Roman stage—Greek New Comedy. Inspired by the Italian tradition of popular theater, Plautus transformed the generally subdued plays of his Greek prede-

cessors into rollicking farce, adding comic dialogue and monologues, increasing the musical element of the plays, and exaggerating the stock features of the characters. He elevated the individual scene over the play as a whole, often ignoring the demands of consistent characterization and plot development in the interest of immediate comic effect. Most plays of Greek New Comedy revolved around the union of two lovers; Plautus frequently refocused attention away from that union to the deception that made it possible. Thus, for example, the clever slave who acquires a woman for his young master through trickery is often the most important character. Plautus also made his plays more self-consciously theatrical than their Greek originals: at every turn his characters remind the audience that they are actors, doing their best to bring pleasure to the spectators. Finally, while Plautus kept the Greek settings of his originals, he played with the settings to produce various effects. He exaggerated the "Greekness" of his plays: many characters' names, for example, sound even more Greek than real Greek names and have humorous meanings in Greek (for example, Pseudolus, "the tricky fellow," and Philocomasium, "party lover"). Yet, Plautus also included many allusions to Roman realities in his plays, often joking on the resulting incongruity. His audience could thus escape into an exotic world where everyday taboos were flaunted; yet, at the same time they would recognize that the antics onstage were not without relevance to their own surroundings.

Titles of some 130 plays were attributed to Plautus in antiquity. Of the twenty-one surviving plays, only two can be dated securely. The plays are best approached alphabetically rather than chronologically. *Amphitruo* is the only surviving ancient comedy with a plot drawn from mythology. Jupiter, disguised as Amphitruo, has impregnated Amphitruo's wife, Alcumena. Assisted by Mercury, who is disguised as Amphitruo's slave, Jupiter inflicts a series of ruthless and hilarious deceptions on the mortal characters. After the misunderstandings nearly lead Amphitruo and Alcumena to disaster, Alcumena gives birth to Hercules, and Jupiter appears in his own person and explains all. In the prologue Mercury calls *Amphitruo* a *tragicomoedia* (tragicomedy), the first known use of that term. While the play includes features typical of tragedy, such as messenger speeches, hubristic threats, and praise of military virtue, it remains a comedy throughout. Plautus burlesques each of the tragic elements, and Mercury and Jupiter lead the audience through a comic romp at the expense of the mortal characters. *Amphitruo* has inspired many modern imitations, most notably those by Molière, Heinrich von Kleist, and Jean Giraudoux.

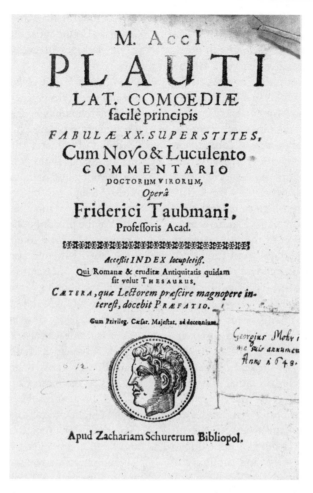

Title page for a collection of Plautus's plays published in Wittenberg in 1605 (courtesy of the Lilly Library, Indiana University)

Asinaria includes one of Plautus's favorite stock characters–the *senex amator* (old man in love). Demaenetus helps his son Argyrippus buy access to the prostitute he loves, but he then demands that the youth share her with him. The old man's scheme is foiled when his shrewish wife finds out about it. The most effective scenes in the play are those involving the two clever slaves, Leonida and Libanus. They epitomize the inversion of social roles that pervades Plautine comedy. After procuring through trickery the money required by Argyrippus, they mock their young master, demand kisses from his beloved, and force him to let one of them ride on his back before they give it to him.

Aulularia, more than any other Roman comedy, is centered on one character–the miser Euclio. Euclio has found a pot of gold, and he guards it with hilarious paranoia, running into his house to check on it at the slightest impulse and assuming that everyone he meets is out to steal it. These precautions lead to the theft of the gold, and the most humorous scenes of the play fol-low. Euclio enters in hysteria and accuses the audience of being thieves. Then Lyconides, the young man who has gotten Euclio's daughter pregnant, tries to confess, but Euclio thinks he is confessing to the theft of the gold, and comic confusion results. The last scenes of the play are lost, but an ancient summary and some remaining fragments suggest that Euclio experienced a conversion and gave some or all of the gold to Lyconides as a dowry. Surrounding Euclio are other well-drawn characters: Megadorus, the rich old bachelor who delivers a long monologue against dowries; Lyconides' mischievous slave, who steals the gold; and several wise-cracking cooks. *Aulularia* is the primary source for Molière's *L'Avare* (1668).

Bacchides is framed by two seductions. In the first extant scene (the same accident that destroyed the end of *Aulularia* also deprived readers of the beginning of *Bacchides*), two prostitutes, the Bacchis sisters, succeed in seducing the young man Pistoclerus. One of the sisters has already won the heart of Pistoclerus's friend, Mnesilochus. At the end of the play, the sisters also seduce the fathers of Pistoclerus and Mnesilochus. In an epilogue the actors explain the surprise ending with mock moralizing: they have, they claim, often seen fathers compete with their sons for prostitutes. In between the seductions, the clever slave Chrysalus manages to carry out three separate deceptions on Mnesilochus's gullible father. His three extensive soliloquies of triumph, including one in which he makes a long comparison between himself and the conquerors of Troy, are among the high points of the play. The survival of a scene from Menander's *Dis Exapaton,* the Greek play upon which Plautus based *Bacchides,* gives readers their only opportunity to view at first hand Plautus's techniques of adaptation. Comparison of the two passages reveals that Plautus eliminated scenes from the Greek play and added jokes to a serious soliloquy.

The captives of *Captivi* are Tyndarus and his master, Philocrates, both captured in battle. Hegio has purchased them, unaware that Tyndarus is his own son, stolen from him as a toddler. When Hegio discovers that Tyndarus has helped Philocrates escape, he has the slave sent to the quarries. Only at the end of the play does Hegio learn that he is Tyndarus's father. The play is the closest Plautus comes to tragedy, and the experiences of Tyndarus raise serious questions about the distinctions between free persons and slaves. Tyndarus defends his actions to the angry Hegio in a scene unparalleled in Plautus for the earnestness and sublimity of its sentiments. The serious aspects of the play have won respect for *Captivi* from many moderns, including Gotthold Lessing, who thought that *Captivi* was the best play ever put on the stage. Nevertheless, the comic element remains dominant through most of the play. Philocrates and Tyndarus's deception of Hegio is in many ways typical trickery of clever slaves, and the parasite Ergasilus offers several stock comic scenes and monologues.

Casina provides a prototype for Beaumarchais's *The Marriage of Figaro* and other plays in which wronged wives turn the tables on their adulterous husbands. Lysidamus conspires to have his bailiff, Olympio, marry Casina, the handmaid of his wife, Cleostrata, so that Lysidamus can enjoy Casina himself. Cleostrata, assisted by her neighbor Myrrhina and her slaves Pardalisca and Chalinus, foils her husband's plans. The final scenes of the play are Plautus's most obscene, and arguably his funniest. Cleostrata disguises Chalinus as the bride Casina, and after a mock wedding scene, Chalinus beats both Olympio and Lysidamus. The old man repents, and Cleostrata forgives him, "so that we don't make this long comedy any longer." The play is remarkable for its portrayal of both the roguish *senex amator,* Lysidamus, and Cleostrata, who transcends the

expectations of the stock *matrona* (wife). The meter in *Casina* is also the most interesting in Plautus's plays, featuring passages of great metrical complexity throughout.

Cistellaria, like *Aulularia* and *Bacchides,* has survived incomplete. When the play begins, the young man Alcesimarchus has broken off his affair with the prostitute Selenium because his father is forcing him to marry a woman of higher status. After some lively comic and melodramatic scenes, it is discovered that Selenium is in fact the long-lost daughter of a respectable family, and Alcesimarchus can marry her. In this play Plautus presents his most sympathetic and complete portrait of the world of the prostitute, one of his most important character types. The most interesting characters in the play are the women who surround Selenium: her good-hearted foster mother, Melaenis; her friend Gymnasium; Gymnasium's bibulous mother; and Melaenis's maid, Halisca, who takes the spectators to task for their laughter at the expense of women.

The title character of *Curculio* is another of Plautus's favorite stock characters—the parasite. The young man Phaedromus is in love with Planesium, who belongs to the pimp Cappadox and has been promised to the braggart soldier Therapontigonus. Curculio steals Therapontigonus's seal ring; with it he acquires Planesium for Phaedromus by deceiving Cappadox and Lyco, the banker who holds on deposit the money Therapontigonus will pay for Planesium. When Therapontigonus tries to reclaim Planesium, he discovers that she is his long-lost sister, and he willingly gives her to Phaedromus. Though *Curculio* is Plautus's shortest play, it includes excellent examples of many of his stock characters—the hungry parasite, the greedy pimp, the love-struck young man, the drunken old woman, and the braggart soldier—as well as a character not found elsewhere, the deceitful banker. It also includes Plautus's longest allusion to Rome: halfway through the play the *choragus* (costume manager) offers a satirical tour of the Roman forum, in which he suggests that shady characters such as the pimp and banker of this play can be found among the audience.

Epidicus is also an extremely short play, but it includes one of Plautus's most complex plots and one of his most successful clever slaves. When the play begins, Epidicus has persuaded his old master, Periphanes, that the lyre player his young master, Stratippocles, is in love with is the old man's long-lost daughter. The young master, however, has fallen in love with another woman, and Epidicus must devise another scheme to get his young master access to her. Both deceptions are uncovered during the course of the play, but Epidicus wins not only immunity from punishment but his freedom when he discovers that the second woman loved by Stratippocles is in fact Periphanes' daughter.

Menaechmi, the primary source of William Shakespeare's *Comedy of Errors,* is the quintessential comedy of mistaken identities. Two identical twins, separated as toddlers, reunite after they and their fellow characters have experienced a long series of hilarious misunderstandings. The play is constructed as a set of variations on a theme, as each new entrance by one of the twins brings a new set of misunderstandings. Music helps to distinguish the two brothers, as most of the entrances of one twin are unaccompanied, while the other spends most of his time onstage in the company of others. Besides its tightly constructed farce, the play offers a diatribe by one of the Menaechmus brothers against abuses of the Roman system of patrons and clients, an amusing discourse on the pains of old age by the father-in-law of one of the brothers, and Plautus's most thorough portrayal of another stock character, the "good slave," Messenio.

Mercator, like *Asinaria* and *Casina,* presents a young man and his father competing for the same woman. Demipho and his son Charinus both fall in love with the prostitute Pasicompsa. Demipho's friend and neighbor Lysimachus agrees to let Demipho use his home for a tryst with Pasicompsa. When Lysimachus's wife, Dorippa, returns home unexpectedly, she assumes that Lysimachus is the one having a fling and responds with predictable fury. Charinus, of course, wins Pasicompsa in the end, with the help of his friend Eutychus. The play includes many comical, overblown soliloquies by the melodramatic Charinus and an unusual speech against the sexual double standard, spoken by Dorippa's octogenarian maid.

Miles Gloriosus offers Plautus's best example of the braggart soldier, a stock character who has since been featured in countless comedies. When the play begins, Pyrgopolynices, the braggart soldier, has kidnapped Philocomasium and also has purchased Palaestrio, the slave of Philocomasium's lover, Pleusicles. Pleusicles, upon learning where his lover and slave are, has become the guest of Periplectomenus, Pyrgopolynices's next-door neighbor, and Philocomasium visits him through a hole dug in the wall between the two houses. Sceledrus, another of Pyrgopolynices' slaves, has spied Philocomasium embracing Pleusicles in Periplectomenus's house. Two deceptions make up the bulk of the play. First, Philocomasium, by running back and forth between houses, convinces Sceledrus that Pleusicles embraced not herself but her twin sister. Then the conspirators add to their number the prostitute Acroteleutium, who, assisted by her handmaid, Milphidippa, persuades Pyrgopolynices that she is Periplectomenus's wife and loves the soldier madly. Pyrgopolynices sends Philo-

comasium and Palaestrio away and rushes into Periplectomenus's house for a tryst with Acroteleutium, only to be beaten and threatened with castration. The play is Plautus's longest, and it is notable for its large cast of characters, including not only the remarkably obtuse soldier but also a most resourceful clever slave, three assertive and competent women, and the old man Periplectomenus, who delivers a long discourse on his unusual personality.

Like *Miles Gloriosus, Mostellaria* can easily be divided into two parts. The first part is a series of delightful vignettes from the life of the corrupted youth Philolaches. In a long and humorous soliloquy, the remorseful Philolaches compares himself to a decaying house. Philolaches then eavesdrops on a conversation between the prostitute he has purchased and her cynical maid and begins a party with his drunken friend, Callidamates. If the first part of the play is static, the second is all motion. It begins with the frantic entrance of Philolaches' clever slave Tranio. In a variation of the stock "running slave" scene, Tranio reports that Philolaches' father, Theopropides, has returned from abroad. Responding to the crisis, Tranio renews the theme of houses begun by Philolaches: with an elaborate ghost story, he persuades Theopropides that he must not enter his own home, for it is haunted. Throughout the rest of the play, more and more unforeseen events complicate Tranio's deception, until he is finally caught and rescued from punishment by a plea from the now-sober Callidamates.

Persa is unusual in Roman comedy, for its clever slave, Toxilus, is also the lover in the play. Toxilus persuades the parasite Saturio to allow his daughter, disguised as a Persian captive, to be sold to the pimp Dordalus, who owns Toxilus's beloved, Lemniselenis. When Dordalus is caught for having purchased a free citizen as if she were a slave, he is subject to severe financial punishment, and the play ends with Toxilus and his friends mocking the hapless pimp. The most interesting character in the play is Saturio's daughter, who virtuously resists being put up for sale but performs convincingly as she and her colleagues deceive the pimp.

Poenulus is another play made up of two distinct parts. During the first part, the clever slave Milphio fashions a deception with which his master, Agorastocles, gains his beloved Adelphasium from the pimp Lycus. The second part features the Carthaginian Hanno, who finds that Adelphasium and her sister Anterastilis are his long-lost daughters and Agorastocles is his long-lost relative. The most surprising feature of the play is its generally sympathetic portrayal of the Carthaginians, a people who, under the leadership of Hannibal, had nearly destroyed Rome during Plautus's

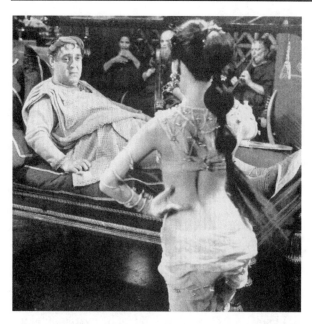

Zero Mostel in a scene from the 1966 movie version of A Funny Thing Happened on the Way to the Forum, *a play based on Plautus's* Pseudolus *and other works (Bettmann/Springer Film Archive)*

lifetime. It also includes an unusual prologue offering much insight into the logistics of performance, two long discourses by Anterastilis and Adelphasium on the life of a prostitute, and a comic chorus of *advocati* (witnesses) who help in the deception of the pimp.

Pseudolus is Plautus's tour de force. In it, the clever slave Pseudolus acquires a prostitute for his young master Calidorus by deceiving his old master Simo and the pimp Ballio. Within this rather ordinary plot Plautus included an unparalleled number of both expected stock elements and novel variations. Not only is Pseudolus exceptionally audacious and successful, but he also delivers stellar examples of all of the monologues that might be expected of a clever slave: two "I don't know what to do" monologues, two "I do know what to do" monologues, a philosophizing monologue, a monologue of anxiety, and a song of triumph. He excels in teasing his lovesick master and insulting the greedy pimp, and he even treats the audience to some drunken dancing at the end of the play. In this play, however, one clever slave, even such an outstanding one as Pseudolus, is not enough. Pseudolus uses a helper, Simia, who outdoes even his instructor in wiliness and braggadocio. Pseudolus's principal antagonist, Ballio, steals the show as he fulfills and exceeds every expectation of a stock comic pimp. His first entrance, as he threatens his slaves and prostitutes with hyperbolic punishments, is a verbal masterpiece. It must also have been one of Plautus's most impressive scenes visually, for it includes an unusually large number of mute

extras, all subservient to the bigger-than-life pimp. The play also includes the longest cook scene in extant ancient comedy, an elaborate "good slave" speech, and excellent examples of several other stock characters: the pining lover and his helpful friend and the *senex durus* (harsh old man) and his friend the *senex lenis* (mild old man). Throughout the play, characters remind the audience in monologues and asides that they are both fulfilling and exceeding all the audience's expectations. Clearly Plautus did everything he could to make *Pseudolus* appropriate for the important festival at which it was produced—the dedication of the temple of the Magna Mater, a goddess who was credited with helping the Romans defeat Hannibal. Considering this play's extraordinary features, when Burt Shevelove, Larry Gelbart, and Stephen Sondheim created *A Funny Thing Happened on the Way to the Forum,* their Broadway musical based on the works of Plautus, they named their lead character Pseudolus.

Rudens takes place on the seacoast of Cyrene, a Greek colony in North Africa, rather than in the urban setting typical of Roman comedy. The central plot of the play is one of virtue rewarded and evil punished. Daemones is reunited with his long-lost daughter, Palaestra, after he helps her escape from the pimp, Labrax, who has been shipwrecked while trying to steal Palaestra from her beloved, Plesidippus. Explicit and heavy moralizing reinforces the moral message throughout the play. After Daemones has found his daughter, however, one of the characters questions the value of moralizing theater like *Rudens.* Gripus, the slave who found the trunk that led to the recognition, complains because Daemones refuses to keep the treasure in the trunk. When Daemones admonishes him with a moralizing speech, Gripus responds that he has often heard actors applauded when they talked like Daemones on stage, but no spectators changed their actions in response to what they had heard. Even a play as moralistic as *Rudens,* Gripus seems to suggest, is not likely to improve its audience's morals.

Stichus has almost no plot but is a series of vignettes. It begins with two sisters, Panegyris and Pamphila, lamenting their husbands' three-year absence but determined to remain loyal to them in spite of the misgivings of their father, Antipho. After a monologue by the parasite Gelasimus, the slave Pinacium, in an elaborate scene, reports that the sisters' husbands have returned. The rest of the play shows three different reactions to the homecoming: the returning brothers reject the hapless Gelasimus; Antipho receives a slave girl; and the slave Stichus and his friends end the play with a joyful party. More a celebration than a play, *Stichus* may have been written in response to the return of so many Roman soldiers at the end of the Second Punic

War, which Rome won a year before the first production of the play.

Trinummus features even more moralizing than *Rudens.* When the play begins, Charmides has been traveling on business for some time. Only his friend Callicles knows that before he left, Charmides had hidden treasure in his house. Charmides' profligate son, Lesbonicus, has since been forced to put the house up for sale, and Callicles has bought the house in order to save the treasure. In the early scenes, Lesbonicus's friend Lysiteles offers to marry Lesbonicus's sister without a dowry. Unwilling that Charmides' daughter be dowryless or that Lesbonicus sell his land, his last remaining possession, for the dowry, or that the spendthrift Lesbonicus find out about the treasure, Callicles plots with his friend Megaronides to hire a shyster (the Sycophant), who will claim to bring a dowry from the absent Charmides. Charmides himself, however, arrives home and intercepts the Sycophant, and comic confusion ensues until Callicles reveals what he has done, and the play ends happily for all. Several characters supplement the moral plot with seemingly endless discourses on morality. Some think Plautus made a great exception in *Trinummus,* abandoning his usual rejection of theatrical didacticism and presenting a morally edifying play. Others find the moral diatribes ironic and comical and see the play as a mockery of smug moralizing.

Truculentus, like *Cistellaria,* offers a close view of the world of prostitutes; but in this play the view is satirical and cynical rather than sympathetic. Phronesium, Plautus's most outrageous femme fatale, has three lovers. The first, Diniarchus, has spent all his money on her and has been relegated to the position of confidant. The second is the soldier Stratophanes; Phronesium pretends that she has just had his baby in order to get more money from him, using for the purpose someone else's unwanted infant. Most of the plot consists of Phronesium's manipulation of these two and a third lover, Strabax, a young rustic. Her handmaid, Astaphium, who also manages during the play to seduce Truculentus, Strabax's grim and severe slave, assists her. Meanwhile, it becomes known that the baby Phronesium is using for her charade is actually the product of Diniarchus's rape of his former fiancée. Diniarchus agrees to marry the girl he raped, but Phronesium persuades him to let her keep the baby until she has received more money from the soldier. Diniarchus seems destined to continue desperate attempts to win Phronesium more securely for himself. As the play ends, Strabax and Stratophanes compete for Phronesium with gifts while the prostitute and her handmaid look on in delight. While *Truculentus* has often been viewed as misogynistic, it is in fact Phronesium's lovers more than Phronesium herself who are satirized most vehemently.

Little remains of *Vidularia.* Like *Rudens,* it has a rural setting. It involves a recognition between an old man and his long-lost son, brought about through the discovery of a traveling bag.

Plautus was an immensely popular playwright in his day. His characters and scenes have continued to delight readers and audiences, both through his own plays and through the many later plays he has inspired.

Bibliographies:

J. David Hughes, *A Bibliography of Scholarship on Plautus* (Amsterdam: Hakkert, 1975);

Erich Segal, "Scholarship on Plautus 1965–1976," *Classical World,* 74 (1981): 353–433;

Frank Bubel, *Bibliographie zu Plautus 1976–1989* (Bonn: Habelt, 1992).

References:

William S. Anderson, *Barbarian Play: Plautus' Roman Comedy* (Toronto: University of Toronto Press, 1993);

W. Geoffrey Arnott, *Menander, Plautus, Terence,* Greece and Rome, New Surveys in the Classics, no. 9 (Oxford: Clarendon Press, 1975);

David Bain, "*Plautus vortit barbare:* Plautus, *Bacchides* 526–561 and Menander, *Dis Exapaton* 102–112," in *Creative Imitation and Latin Literature,* edited by David West and Tony Woodman (Cambridge: Cambridge University Press, 1979), pp. 17–34;

William Beare, *The Roman Stage,* third edition (London: Methuen, 1964);

Lore Benz, Ekkehard Stärk, and Gregor Vogt-Spira, eds., *Plautus und die Tradition des Stegreifspiels,* ScriptOralia, no. 75 (Tübingen: Gunter Narr, 1995);

Gioachino Chiarini, *La recita: Plauto, la farsa, la festa* (Bologna: Pàtron Editore, 1979);

T. A. Dorey and Donald R. Dudley, eds., *Roman Drama* (London: Routledge & Kegan Paul, 1965);

George E. Duckworth, *The Nature of Roman Comedy* (Princeton, N.J.: Princeton University Press, 1952);

Eduard Fraenkel, *Elementi plautini in Plauto,* translated by Franco Munari (Florence: La Nuova Italia, 1960);

Konrad Gaiser, "Zur Eigenart der römischen Komödie: Plautus und Terenz gegenüber ihren griechischen Vorbildern," *Aufstieg und Niedergang der römischen Welt,* 1, no. 2 (1972): 1027–1113;

Erich S. Gruen, "Plautus and the Public Stage," in *Studies in Greek Culture and Roman Policy* (Leiden: Brill, 1990), pp. 124–157;

Eric Walter Handley, *Menander and Plautus: A Study in Comparison* (London: Lewis, 1968);

David Konstan, *Roman Comedy* (Ithaca, N.Y.: Cornell University Press, 1983);

Eleanor Winsor Leach, "De exemplo meo ipse aedificato: An Organizing Idea in the *Mostellaria*," *Hermes,* 97 (1969): 318–332;

Leach, "Ergasilus and the Ironies of the *Captivi*," *Classica et Mediaevalia,* 30 (1969): 263–296;

Eckard Lefèvre, Ekkehard Stärk, and Gregor Vogt-Spira, *Plautus barbarus: Sechs Kapitel zur Originalität des Plautus,* ScriptOralia, no. 25 (Tübingen: Günter Narr, 1991);

Friedrich Leo, *Plautinische Forschungen zur Kritik und Geschichte der Komödie,* second edition (Berlin: Weidmann, 1912);

J. C. B. Lowe, "Aspects of Plautus' Originality in the *Asinaria*," *Classical Quarterly,* 42 (1992): 152–175;

Timothy J. Moore, "*Palliata Togata:* Plautus, *Curculio* 462–486," *American Journal of Philology,* 112 (1991): 343–362;

Moore, *The Theater of Plautus: Playing to the Audience* (Austin: University of Texas Press, 1998);

Frances Muecke, "Plautus and the Theatre of Disguise," *Classical Antiquity,* 5 (1986): 216–229;

Holt Parker, "Crucially Funny or Tranio on the Couch: The *Servus Callidus* and Jokes About Torture," *Transactions of the American Philological Association,* 119 (1989): 233–246;

Gianna Petrone, *Morale e antimorale nelle commedie di Plauto: Ricerche sullo Stichus* (Palermo: G. B. Palumbo, 1977);

Petrone, *Teatro antico e inganno: Finzioni plautine* (Palermo: G. B. Palumbo, 1983);

Cesare Questa, *Introduzione alla metrica di Plauto* (Bologna: Pàtron Editore, 1967);

K. H. E. Schutter, *Quibus annis comoediae Plautinae primum actae sint quaeritur* (Groningen: De waal, 1952);

Erich Segal, *Roman Laughter: The Comedy of Plautus,* second edition (New York: Oxford University Press, 1987);

Niall W. Slater, *Plautus in Performance: The Theatre of the Mind* (Princeton, N.J.: Princeton University Press, 1985);

Ekkehard Stärk, *Die Menaechmi des Plautus und kein griechisches Original,* ScriptOralia, no. 11 (Tübingen: Gunter Narr, 1989);

Dana F. Sutton, *Ancient Comedy: The War of the Generations* (New York: Twayne, 1993);

Barthélémy-A. Taladoire, *Essai sur le comique de Plaute* (Monte Carlo: Imprimerie nationale, 1956);

John Wright, *Dancing in Chains: The Stylistic Unity of the Comoedia Palliata,* Papers and Monographs of the American Academy in Rome, no. 25 (Rome: American Academy in Rome, 1974);

Wright, "The Transformations of Pseudolus," in *Transactions of the American Philological Association,* 105 (1975): 403–416;

Netta Zagagi, *Tradition and Originality in Plautus: Studies of the Amatory Motifs in Plautine Comedy* (Göttingen: Vandenhoeck & Ruprecht, 1980);

Otto Zwierlein, *Zur Kritik und Exegese des Plautus I: Poenulus und Curculio,* Akademie der Wissenschaften und der Literatur, Mainz, Abhandlungen der geistes- und sozialwissenschaftlichen Klasse, Nr. 4 (Stuttgart: Franz Steiner, 1990);

Zwierlein, *Zur Kritik und Exegese des Plautus II: Miles gloriosus* (Akademie der Wissenschaften und der Literatur, Mainz, Abhandlungen der geistes- und sozialwissenschaftlichen Klasse, Nr. 3 (Stuttgart: Franz Steiner, 1991);

Zwierlein, *Zur Kritik und Exegese des Plautus III: Pseudolus* (Akademie der Wissenschaften und der Literatur, Mainz, Abhandlungen der geistes- und sozialwissenschaftlichen Klasse, Nr. 14 (Stuttgart: Franz Steiner, 1991);

Zwierlein, *Zur Kritik und Exegese des Plautus IV: Bacchides,* Akademie der Wissenschaften und der Literatur, Mainz, Abhandlungen der geistes- und sozialwissenschaftlichen Klasse, Nr. 4 (Stuttgart: Franz Steiner, 1992).

Pliny the Elder

(A.D. 23/24 – 25 August A.D. 79)

Paul T. Keyser

University of Alabama

WORK–EXTANT: *Historia naturalis,* 37 books (Natural History).

WORKS–LOST: *De iaculatione equestri* (On Equestrian Javelin-Throwing);

De vita Pomponi Secundi, 2 books (The Life of Pomponius Secundus);

Bella Germaniae, 20 books (German Wars);

Studiosus, 3 books (The Studious Orator);

Dubius sermo, 8 books (Grammatical Problems, A.D. 67);

A fine Aufidi Bassi, 31 books (Continuation of the History of Aufidius Bassus).

Editio princeps: *Historia Naturalis* (Venice: Johannes de Spira, 1469).

Standard editions: *Pline. Histoire naturelle,* translated by J. Beaujeu and others (Paris: Les Belles Lettres, 1947–); *C. Plini Secundi Naturalis historiae libri XXXVII,* 6 volumes, edited by C. Mayhoff (Leipzig: Teubner, 1892–1906; reprinted, 1967–1970); *Il dubius sermo di Plinio,* edited by A. Della Casa (Genoa: Istituto di filologia classica e medioevale, 1969); *Storia naturale Gaio Plinio Secondo,* edited by G. B. Conte and others (Turin: Einaudi, 1982–).

Translations in English: *Pliny: Natural History,* 10 volumes, Loeb Classical Library; volumes 1–6 and 9 translated by H. Rackham, volumes 6–8 translated by W. H. S. Jones, volume 10 translated by D. E. Eichholz (Cambridge, Mass.: Harvard University Press / London: Heinemann, 1938–1962); John F. Healy, *Natural History: A Selection* (Harmondsworth, U.K.: Penguin, 1991).

Commentaries: K. Jex-Blake and E. Sellers, *The Elder Pliny's Chapters on the History of Art* (London, 1896); K. C. Bailey, *The Elder Pliny's Chapters on Chemical Subjects,* 2 volumes (London: Arnold, 1929–1932); Donald J. Campbell, *C. Plinii Secundi Naturalis Historiae* (Aberdeen, U.K.: Aberdeen University Press, 1936).

Life is *uigilia,* wrote C. Plinius Secundus in *Historia naturalis* (Natural History, *pref.* 18), by which the old soldier meant that life is being on watch and on duty. The highest duty and the path of divinity was to help one's fellow mortals (*HN* 2.18, 25.2–3), and Pliny's life, writings, and death were devoted to that end. Although most of his works were lost in the collapse of the western Roman Empire, his surviving work, the *Historia naturalis,* is one of the largest works to survive from antiquity and was the standard encyclopedia of the Latin West until the sixteenth century. The subject of Pliny's work is Nature–that is, life itself (*pref.* 13)–as seen by eyes thoroughly Roman and Stoic. Divine Nature herself provides all that humans need, and they ought to make proper use of Nature's providence–Pliny constantly condemns *luxuria* (luxury) as an abuse of Nature. Romans once read Pliny's opus as a compendium of knowledge, as rich in variety as Nature herself (as his nephew Pliny the Younger says in *Epist.* 3.5.6); now scholars extract from it the history of technology, science, and art in the early Roman Empire.

Pliny was born in A.D. 23 or 24 in the north Italian town of Comum (modern Como) and educated at Rome from the end of Tiberius's reign through the whole of Caligula's reign. He had a sister, whose son he adopted (the writer known as "Pliny the Younger"), though he himself never married and disdained coitus (*HN* 28.58). The family called Plinius belonged to the second tier of Roman society, the equestrian order, the members of which were often bankers, lawyers, merchants, or officers. Pliny, at the end of Claudius's reign, and in the early years of Nero's, was posted to the legions on the Rhine. Tacitus, in books 11–13 of his *Annals,* gives some important biographical information about Pliny. His first post was *praefectus* (captain) of a cohort in *Germania Inferior* (the south bank of the lower Rhine, roughly equivalent to modern Belgium), with the *Legio V Alaudae* at Vetera (?), under Domitius Corbulo, who campaigned against the Chauci. Pliny was then promoted to *tribunus* (junior staff officer) in *Germania Superior* (the Upper Rhine Valley), where he saw successful action (perhaps with the *Legio XXI Rapax* at Vindonissa or else at Moguntiacum with the *Legio IV*

Illumination from a twelfth-century Danish manuscript depicting Pliny the Elder handing his work to the Emperor Titus for Pliny's Natural History *(Florence, Biblioteca Laurenziana, MS. Plut. 82, 1, fol. 2v.)*

Macedonica or the *Legio XXII Primigenia*) against another German tribe. Pliny returned to *Germania Inferior* for his third tour of duty as *praefectus alae* (captain of the cavalry wing of the legion), completing the Rhine levee and repelling immigrants from across the river. While on his last tour in Germany, he opened his literary career with the publication of two short works, both now lost. He composed a handbook on mounted combat and a biography of Pomponius Secundus, his patron and his superior officer at the time (the subject was also a writer, of tragedies now lost). On the frontier Pliny also began his *Bella Germaniae* (German Wars), in honor of Drusus (the long-dead father of the emperor Claudius), who had campaigned in Germany more than sixty years prior, dying at Moguntiacum, and who had appeared to Pliny in a dream imploring him to rescue his deeds from oblivion.

Pliny successfully completed his military career in A.D. 58 and returned to Italy; early in A.D. 59 Nero had his own mother, Agrippina, murdered. (Pliny's nephew was born a few years later.) For the remaining decade of Nero's reign, Pliny kept a low profile, practicing law and writing two lost works: *Studiosus* (The Studious

Orator), on the training of the successful advocate, and *Dubius sermo* (Grammatical Problems, A.D. 67). Upon the accession of the emperor Vespasian, Pliny was able to resume the public service he loved, because the emperor's elder son and assistant, Titus, was a friend of Pliny's from his army days (*HN pref.* 1 and 3; compare with Suetonius, *Titus* 4). Titus, born at the end of A.D. 41, must have served with Pliny on the latter's third tour, as *praefectus alae*. Pliny was first appointed *procurator* (manager) of a province in A.D. 70 and managed various provinces, especially the wealthy *Hispania Tarraconensis* (equivalent to most of modern Spain) and the prestigious *Gallia Belgica* (adjacent to *Germania Inferior* and *Germania Superior,* and comprising roughly Picardy, Champagne, and Bourgogne). In A.D. 76 he was recalled to service at Rome in Vespasian's *consilium* (cabinet); he was also made admiral of the western Mediterranean fleet, stationed at Misenum on the Bay of Naples.

For the rest of Vespasian's reign, Pliny pursued his writing, composing an influential but lost history of his own times and his one extant work, the *Historia naturalis*. On 24 August A.D. 79, while on duty at Misenum, he saw the mushroom cloud of Vesuvius erupting and set out across the bay to investigate and render aid. He died early the next day, either overcome by the sulfurous fumes, or of a heart attack brought on by his exertions (described by his nephew in *Epist.* 6.16, a letter to the historian Tacitus). Pliny's death came only two months after the death of his imperial patron, Vespasian, and just two days after the festival of Vulcan.

Pliny the Younger has left a precise account of his uncle's literary works (Pliny the Younger, *Epist.* 3.5) as well as his uncle's ferociously energetic daily routine of nonstop scholarship and official duties. Pliny the Elder always claimed that "no book was so bad as to be useless" (*Epist.* 3.5.9), and his own books have been useful indeed. Scholars usually attribute to Pliny's histories much of the material reworked by Tacitus (who made it the basis of his narrative in *Annals* 1–6), Plutarch, and Dio Cassius, covering the middle of the first century A.D. Tacitus probably employed Pliny's lost work on Germany throughout his *Annals* (for example, in books 11–13 about the German wars to which Pliny was an eyewitness) and consulted it for his *Germania*. Through this work of Tacitus on the wild German tribes, Pliny influenced the postmedieval view of the "noble savage" (as recounted in *HN* 16.2–6). Grammarians for almost five centuries, down to Priscian, made heavy use of Pliny's work on reconciling analogy and anomaly in the Latin language, which through them became one of the foundations of medieval Latin grammar.

Pliny's greatest work survives intact as a witness to his encompassing spirit, ecumenical world, and baroque imagination. His description of Rome serves as an abstract of his book: "grandeur towers up as if some alien world were concentrated in one spot" (*HN* 36.101). In his preface, Pliny explains that he wrote his nationalistic compendium for the novel purpose of benefiting Rome, as no mere poet could; in the heart of Nature lay Italy, and at the center of Italy sat Rome, the ruler of all the world that mattered. To Rome and her world Pliny offered knowledge, the sole reliable guide to moral action, and the true desire of every virtuous soul (Aristotle, *Metaphys.* A [980a22]).

The preface (11–13) declares that Pliny's Jeffersonian ideal for himself and his reader was the "rustic" citizen-farmer-soldier, in the tradition of Varro, Cato, and especially Marcus Vipsanius Agrippa. That ideal, and his wish to benefit Rome, called forth a serious austerity and utilitarian brevity of style; yet, his imagery is as extravagant and varied as Nature herself. For example, mining commits rapacious surgery on Mother Earth (2.158; see 33.1–3); the river Peneus glitters with pebbles and is melodious with birdsong (4.31); the Taurus mountain range recoils from impeding seas as it wanders westward (5.97–98); and the Black Sea was eroded from the unwilling Earth by the voracious ocean (6.1–2). Pliny lavishes arresting images on people: the sleepy mind wonders where it is (7.90); when one kisses the eyes, he touches the soul (11.145–146); breath, the means of life, stinks and takes away the joy of life (11.277–278; for the remedy, see 25.175); and intemperate wine bibbing destroys memory, breath, and tomorrow (14.137–142). Natural beings tremble with anthropomorphic energy: the Nile rushes down cataracts until exhausted (5.54); the ibex whirls itself on its swordlike horns as if on a catapult (8.214); and the lascivious palm tree is aroused for sexual congress (13.34–35). The productivity of the sea is rich and strange (9.2); upon it the nautilus sails like a pirate ship (9.88); out of it has walked a predatory three-hundred-kilogram octopus (9.92–93); and in it testaceans grow shells of every nameable shape (9.102–103). For his technical vocabulary, Pliny solves Lucretius's problem—the poverty of Latin (Lucretius 1.139–145)—through Horace's device of transliteration (*Ars Poetica* 52–53), not only of Greek words but even of barbarous and lower-class speech (*HN pref.* 13). He frequently indulges his capacity for coining novelties of diction (a practice that he validates, in *HN pref.* 32, by citing an example from Cato), inventing especially abstracts, adjectives, and diminutives.

Pliny's outlook is comprehensively Stoic, imputing moral weight to every fact and object in the universe, pervaded as it is by *pneuma* (the spirit of god). Indulging in *luxuria* abuses Nature because Romans ought to live according to Nature—that is, in a simple way and according to old Roman mores. Nonetheless, culture—by which Pliny naturally means Roman culture—is a positive benefit, instilling order and harmony to the relation with Nature (*HN* 27.1–3). Pliny collects *mirabilia* (marvels) in the Stoic tradition of writing upon the incomprehensible marvels of Nature to show the superhuman power and wisdom of the cosmos (*HN* 2.207–208, 7.7, 11.6, 22.1). His belief that everywhere and in every book is something worth learning is a testimonial to the disseminate rationality of the cosmos. In the end, however, Pliny is neither a technical philosopher nor an uncritical admirer of Greek wise men (*HN* 2.85, 2.95, 2.248, 7.79, 8.81–82, 10.136–167, 29.6, 29.14, and 35.71) but an informed layman and a devout believer.

The same Stoical sensibility is apparent in the skeleton of his work. An index, pioneered perhaps by the physician Scribonius Largus (A.D. 1–A.D. 50; compare with his *Compositiones pref.* 15) or even Cato, serves as a kind of map in the style of Augustus's friend Agrippa, whose *Geographical Commentaries* included a map of the entire Empire. Thus, the *Natural History* represents the natural world digested by Pliny, manifesting its capacious utility for humankind and Pliny's indefatigable labor (*HN pref.* 21–23 and 33). The three dozen books themselves display structure, which for a Stoic was the essence of any living or existing being, maintained by the immanent *pneuma* of Stoic cosmology. There are one-plus-four books (2–6) on the cosmos and earth, balanced by the last five books on useful things obtained from Earth (33–37). Enclosed by those are one-plus-four books on humans and animals (7–11), balanced by five books on useful things made from people and animals (28–32). At the center of the work is a symmetric set of books—eight on plants (12–19) plus eight on useful things from plants (20–27). Humankind's use of the world (8 + 5 + 5 in books 20–37) is thus a mirror of the world itself (5 + 5 + 8 in books 2–19). Pliny's work is deeply, even relentlessly, anthropocentric.

In the thirty-six compartments of his treasury of facts, Pliny records much that he did not understand or that is now known to be confused or false; it is not that he is credulous but that he dutifully reports what has been recorded. He is well-armed with good sources, old and new, which he often uncritically fuses. He displays a genuine and unremitting loyalty for Vespasian and Titus, and a journalist's fascination with marvels and novelties. His task is to present facts, and he does not stop to offer systematic principles or analyses (*pref.* 17; compare with 2.85). His facts are stored and marshaled in quartermasterly divisions (*pref.* 17; compare with 18.19), organized logically by categories of human utility (in most categories, the best or greatest comes first). Nonetheless, his presentation and selection are informed

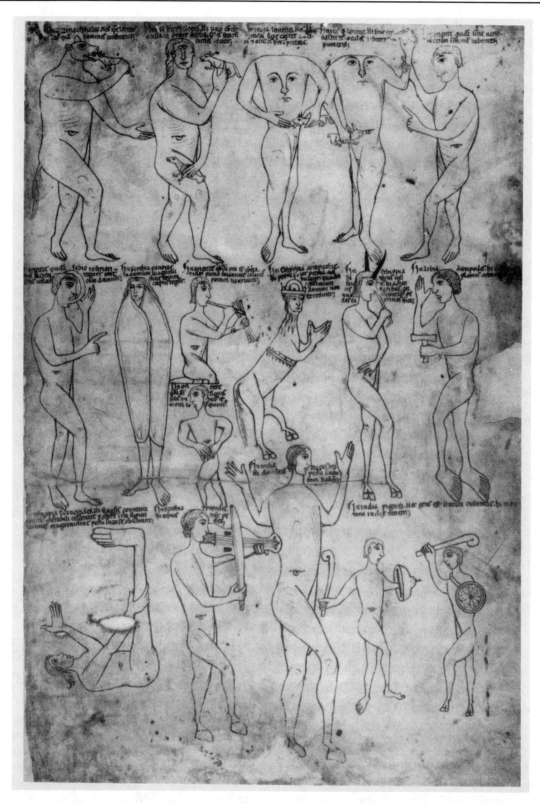

Pliny's monstrous races; drawings from a twelfth-century manuscript for Natural History *(British Library, MS. Harley 2799, fol. 243r)*

by Stoic notions, especially that of sympathy-antipathy (*HN* 20.1–2, 24.1–2, 37.59). His inexorable strategy is to display the anthropocentric plan of Nature so that humankind will use her properly.

Pliny's god, if there is one (*HN* 2.14), is almost identified with Nature (2.27), which acts with benevolent providence, for earth is the Mother of all (2.154–159, 2.208; cp. *pref.* 2). His account of astronomy is up-to-date; he prefers practical (that is, calendrical) astronomy to theoretical (18.200–325); and he rejects astrology on the basis of a "statistical" study of birth dates and life paths (7.160–165). His subdivisions of the cosmos are patronally Roman: on top is Fire (2.1–101), then Air (2.102–153), then Earth (2.154–211), and lowest of all, Water (2.212–234). When he turns to geography (3–6), he mainly follows Agrippa's century-old map (3.17) to form a catalogue of trophy sites paraded like placarded captives in a triumph and organized on the basis of Roman political divisions (3.46). He provides valuable nuggets of primarily political, urban, historical, mythological, and ethnographic data. Pliny is the best source for reconstructing late Republican provincial administration in North Africa (5.1–30), for the voyages of Polybios (5.9–10) and Suetonius Paulinus (5.14–15) to tropical Africa, and for the discovery of the Canary Islands by Iuba of Mauretania (6.198–205).

In his books on humans and animals (7–11), and on medicines derived from them (28–32), Pliny's presentation revolves on his anthropocentric axis (7.1). Poor humans are helpless (7.2); the world is running down (7.73); and happiness is uncertain—but death is secure (7.130–152, 165–173). Nonetheless, humankind possesses astonishing powers (7.81–90), and amazing people exist (7.91–120, 153–164). He presents animals in a "humanocentric" and not biological taxonomy—terrestrial (8), aerial (9), aquatic (10), and insect (11)—and often draws his facts from Aristotle, though Pliny never uses Aristotle's system (8.44, 11.8). Pliny selects for description animals that are of human interest and begins each book with the largest creature: elephant (8.1–34); whale (9.4–7); ostrich (10.1–2); or the one most important to humans, bees (11.11–70). Appreciating the lower animals as marvelous works of Nature's artistry enhances humankind's topmost status and allows humans to use them properly. Pliny's examples of animal "reason" (always qualified) serve to edify his human readers: the elephant's wisdom (8.1–34), the lion mollified by a thorn (8.56, compare with 8.59–60), the loyal dog (8.142–147), the friendly dolphin (9.24–33), the profuse melodies of nightingales (10.81–83), and the architecture of swallows' nests (10.92–94). In the end, despite many similarities in body (11.44–87), humans surpass the beasts through reason, as manifested in speech (11.271).

Remedies derived from people Pliny quickly dismisses, mainly recording charms and rites (28.10–86), because eating human body parts is horribly revolting (28.4–9, 87). Medicines are extracted from foreign animals, one by one, commencing with the elephant as the first of animals (28.88, compare with 8.1–34), the lion (28.89–90, compare with 8.41–60), the camel (28.91, compare with 8.67–68), and the keen-eyed lynx (28.122). He inserts a list of remedies common to all animals—milk, fat, marrow, gall, and blood (28.123–148)—and a section on remedies for snakebites, rabies, and poisons (28.149–162). After this pharmaceutical bestiary, Pliny lists remedies organized by location of ailment from head to foot (28.163–223) and remedies for the whole body (28.224–262). (Such top-down disease-lists had already appeared in Egyptian medical papyri two millennia before Pliny and are common in ancient medicine.) The next two books include remedies from native Roman animals, first by animal (29.1–97), then by disorder from head to foot (29.98–143, 30.28–81), and again ending with whole-body cures (30.82–146). Books 31–32 proffer remedies from the watery element—first, water itself (31.1–71), next, salt (31.73–122), and then living beings, organized as before: by creature (32.1–66), by malady from head to foot (32.67–111), and by remedies for the entire body (32.112–140).

Pliny devotes almost half his encyclopedia to plants: books 12–19 treat plants themselves, and books 20–27 cover plants as remedies. For botanical data, Pliny relies on Theophrastus, while his agricultural and medical information derives primarily from early imperial sources. He emphasizes the importance of plants to an agrarian society (20.1), the need for autopsy in botany (25.8–9), and the utility of the *pax Romana* in bringing far-flung plants to Rome (27.1). For Pliny the field, the garden, and the orchard are the arena of fruitful partnership between Nature and humankind. Again he arrays his facts like soldiers on file: each block of eight books is divided five-plus-three—the first five books focused on plants, their habits, and their properties; the last three focused on human employment of plants.

Pliny begins his history of plants with foreign trees and large plants (12–13), then turns to widely distributed trees and plants that bear fruit or nuts (14–15), and completes the picture with forest trees (16). The books on human employment of Nature's bounty include orchard science (17), the growth of grains and other field crops (18), and facts about the gardening of esculents (19). He provides unusual data on the history of papyrus (13.68–89), the development of cherry-growing in Italy (15.102–104), the Druids' use of mistletoe (16.249–251), and a mechanical harvester in Gaul (18.296). He is the first to record the use of esparto

First page of Christoforo Landino's preface to his 1476 Italian translation of Pliny's Historia naturalis

grass for bast–that is, as a fiber for ropes or cloth (19.26–30).

In his herbal pharmacy, Pliny covers the medical properties of plants in stockroom order: plants, garden (20); plants, flowering (21); plants, spinous and cereal (22); trees, cultivated (23); and plants, wild (24). Food is the greatest work of Nature (20.1), but the belly is a base organ as importunate as a creditor (26.43); apiculture is one of Nature's marvels (21.70–85), and she protects many medicinal plants with thorns (22.14–17). Flowers are humans' oldest and best adornment (21.4–13), and the mere grass crown exceeds in honor those of gold (22.6–13). Nature bestowed on wine many healthful powers, especially for the care of the heart (23.2–51), and this and all native remedies are preferable to foreign imports (24.4–5). The three books on human employment of plants consider native medicinal plants (25), remedies by disease (26), and remedies from imported medicinal plants (27). Those who have discovered new medicines from plants ought to be honored, and first among them are divine figures such as Herakles and Chiron (25.32–37); Mercury (25.38–41); and Melampus, who found hellebore (5.47–61). Historical figures who have risen to this godlike level include Mithridates (25.62–63), Lysimachos (25.72), Iuba (25.77–79), and Themison (25.80). Pliny eschews "unnatural" drugs–that is, those that would interrupt the "natural" processes of life: to promote excess drinking (14.138), abortion (25.24–25), poisons (27.9), and love potions (27.125).

In his final five books (33–37) Pliny examines the civic utility of works of earth stuff (metal, stone, clay, and gems). He concludes that art is what creates fame (through artistic skill and collective memory) so that for Romans the only proper art is what is publicly accessible. Here he explicitly follows Agrippa (35.26) and indeed the old Roman custom of displaying wax masks of ancestors in the entryway of the house (35.6–7). The state of Rome has collected and displays Greek art as triumphal plunder, while the amassing of private collections smacks of uncivil *luxuria*. Pliny treats human use of terrene material in a hierarchical order–first gold and silver (33), then copper, iron, and lead (34). He first narrates the uses and abuses of gold, then its mode of production (33.66–81); for each of the other four of these five metals, Pliny first relates its mode of production from the Earth–silver (33.95–101), copper (34.2–4), iron (34.142–150), and lead (34.156–165)–then its uses and abuses. Gold and silver are the most abused bits of Nature (33.4–65, 33.132–153), since the love of wealth is the fount of all sin, but even gold has its medicinal uses (33.84–85, 92), as do silver and similar substances (33.102–110). The noblest use of bronze (that is, copper) is statuary, of which Pliny gives a long

historical sketch (34.15–93), but this metal is also medicinal (34.100–137). Iron becomes warlike through people's evil artifice (34.138–141) but also confers benefit in medical hands (34.151–155); even lead has curative powers (34.166–176). Pliny's last three books concern "earths" (35)–that is, clay and pigments, mainly employed in the ancient but dying art of painting; next stones, mainly marble (36), used in the living arts of stoneworking–that is, building and sculpting; and finally gems (37). Statues of mere clay were sufficient for early Romans (35.157), and the potter's art is as noble as the smith's (35.151–165). Pliny's sketches of the history of bronze sculpture (34.15–93), of painting (35.50–149), and of marble statuary (36.9–44) are drawn from Varro, who reworked Greek sources of the third century B.C.; they are the only connected ancient histories of art that survive. Pliny discourses on the many wonders of the world (36.64–100), the pyramids at Giza being the largest and most useless (36.76). But Rome is more full of wonders than all the world, and her aqueducts and sewers must especially be admired (36.101–125). Gems provide a compact example of Nature's art (37.1), like the insects (11.2) or miniature sculpture (34.83, 36.43). In the end Pliny claims that he has hymned Nature best of all Romans (37.205).

Rome crumbled–but Pliny endured. The *Natural History* was much used in the remaining centuries of the Roman era, especially by third-century-A.D. authors such as Gargilius, Serenus, and Solinus, as well as by the founders of Western Medieval learning such as Martianus Capella and Isidorus of Seville. Modern scholars have treated him as an unusual repository of cultural data; and indeed he gives more than a dozen "capsule" histories–for example, 13.1–18 (perfume), 26.1–20 (new diseases and new quacks), 30.1–20 (magic), and 33.42–47 (coinage)–which are often the only account to survive. As he desired, he was helpful to his countrymen and to their heirs for centuries thereafter; today he is indispensable to scholars.

Concordance:

P. Rosumek and D. Najock, eds., *Concordantia in C. Plinii Secundi Naturalem historiam*, 7 volumes (Hildesheim: Olms, 1996).

References:

Mary Beagon, *Roman Nature: The Thought of Pliny the Elder* (Oxford: Clarendon Press, 1992);

Jacob Bigelow, "On the Death of the Elder Pliny," *Memoirs of the American Academy of Arts and Sciences* new series, 6, no. 2 (1858): 223–227;

Mary-Ann T. Burns, "Pliny's Ideal Roman," *Classical Journal,* 59 (1963–1964): 253–258;

Roger French and Frank Greenaway, *Science in the Early Roman Empire: Pliny the Elder, his Sources and Influence* (London & Sydney: Croom Helm, 1986);

F. R. D. Goodyear, "Pliny the Elder," in *Cambridge History of Classical Literature,* volume 2: *Latin Literature,* edited by E. J. Kenney and Wendell V. Clausen (Cambridge: Cambridge University Press, 1982);

Mirko D. Grmek, "Les circonstances de la mort de Pline: Commentaire médical d'une lettre destinée aux historiens," *Helmantica,* 37 (1986): 25–43;

John F. Healy, "The Language and Style of Pliny the Elder," in *Filologia e Forme Letterarie: Studi offerti a Francesco della Corte,* volume 4 (Urbino: Università degli studi di Urbino, 1987), pp. 3–24;

Louis Holtz, "Pline et les grammairiens: Le *Dubius Sermo* dans le haut moyen âge," *Helmantica,* 38 (1987): 233–254;

N. P. Howe, "In Defense of the Encyclopedic Mode: On Pliny's *Preface* to the *Natural History,*" *Latomus,* 44 (1985): 561–576;

Jacob Isager, *Pliny on Art and Society: The Elder Pliny's Chapters on the History of Art* (London & New York: Routledge, 1991);

Alexander Jones, "Pliny on the Planetary Cycles," *Phoenix,* 45 (1991): 148–461;

Zoltán Kádár and Maria Bérényi-Révész, "Die Anthropologie des Plinius Maior," *Aufstieg und Niedergang der Römischen Welt* II, 32, no. 4 (1986): 2201–2224;

Heinz Knoll, *Plinius der Altere über Blei und Zinn* (Tübingen: A Hempo, 1989);

S. Citroni Marchetti, *Plinio il Vecchio e la tradizione del moralismo romana* (Pisa: Giardini, 1991);

Pline l'Ancien, témoin de son temps (Salamance & Nantes, 1987)–articles published in *Helmantica,* 37–38 (1986–1987);

Plinio e la natura: atti del ciclo di conferenze sugli aspetti naturalistici dell'opera pliniana: Atti della giornata di studi su

Plinio e l'erboristeria (Como: Camera di commercie, industria, artigiannto e agricoltura, 1982);

Plinio il Vecchio sotto il profilo storico e letterario: atti del Convegno di Como, 5–7 ottobre 1979 (Como: Litotipografia G. Malinverno, 1980);

Franz Römer, "Die plinianische, Anthropologie' und der Aufbau der Naturalis Historia," *Wiener Studien,* 17 (1983): 104–108;

M. Schanz and C. Hosius, "Der Enzyklopaedist C. Plinius Secundus," in *Geschichte der römischen Literatur,* volume 2, fourth edition (Munich: Beck, 1935) § 490–494 (pp. 768–783);

Sergio Sconocchia, "La structure de la *Historia Naturalis* dans la tradition scientifique et encyclopédique romaine," *Helmantica,* 38 (1987): 307–316;

Guy Serbat, "Pline l'Ancien: Etat présent des études sur sa vie, son oeuvre et son influence," *Aufstieg und Niedergang der Römischen Welt* II, 32, no. 4 (1986): 2069–2200;

Brent D. Shaw, "The Elder Pliny's African Geography," *Historia,* 30 (1981): 424–471;

Jerry Stannard, "Herbal Medecine [*sic*] and Herbal Magic in Pliny's Time," *Helmantica,* 37 (1986): 95–106;

Ronald Syme, "Consular Friends of the Elder Pliny," *Roman Papers,* volume 7, edited by A. R. Birley (Oxford: Clarendon Press, 1991), pp. 496–511;

Syme, "Pliny the Procurator," *Harvard Studies in Classical Philology,* 73 (1969): 201–236;

Tecnologia, economia e società nel mondo Romano: Atti del Convegno di Como 27–29 settembre 1979 (Como: Banca popolare commercio e industria, 1980);

Andrew Wallace-Hadrill, "Pliny the Elder and Man's Unnatural History," *Greece and Rome,* 37 (1990): 80–96.

Pliny the Younger

(ca. A.D. 61 – ca. A.D. 112)

W. Jeffrey Tatum
Florida State University

WORKS: *Panegyricus* (A.D. 100); *Epistulae,* 9 books (Epistles, A.D. 103–A.D. 109); book 10, letters to and from Trajan, assembled and published after Pliny's death (ca. A.D. 112).

Editiones principes: *Epistolae,* edited by Ludovicus Carbo (Venice: Christophorus Valdarfer, 1471)–books 1–7, 9; *Epistolae,* edited by Johannes Schurener (Rome: Johannes Schurener, ca. 1474)–comprises books 1–9.

Standard editions: COMPLETE WORKS: *Epistularum libri novem, epistularum ad Traianum liber, panegyricus,* edited by Mauriz Schuster, third edition revised by R. Hanslik (Leipzig: Teubner, 1958); EPISTLES: *Epistularum libri decem,* edited by R. A. B. Mynors (Oxford: Clarendon Press, 1963); *XII Panegyrici Latini,* edited by Mynors (Oxford: Clarendon Press, 1964).

Translations in English: Betty Radice, *The Letters of the Younger Pliny* (Harmondsworth, U.K.: Penguin, 1963); Radice, *Pliny: Letters and Panegyricus,* 2 volumes, Loeb Classical Library (Cambridge, Mass.: Harvard University Press, 1969).

Commentaries: *C. Plinii Secundi Epistulae ad Traianum imperatorem cum eiusdem responsis,* edited by E. G. Hardy (London: Macmillan, 1889); *Panegyrique de Trajan,* edited by Marcel Durry (Paris: Les Belles Lettres, 1938); A. N. Sherwin-White, *The Letters of Pliny: A Historical and Social Commentary* (Oxford: Clarendon Press, 1966); *Fifty Letters of Pliny,* edited by Sherwin-White (Oxford: Oxford University Press, 1967).

The younger Pliny was seventeen when Vesuvius erupted in A.D. 79, according to his *Epistulae* (Epistles, A.D. 103–A.D. 109, 6. 20), a fact that situates his birth in late A.D. 61 or early A.D. 62. He was born in Comum (modern Como), the son of Lucius Caecilius. His father's family, like that of his mother (the Plinii), were wealthy and apparently well-connected municipal landowners. His parents had already divorced by the time of his father's death. His guardian was Verginius Rufus, the general who crushed the revolt of Vindex in A.D. 68, was twice consul, and twice refused to be hailed as emperor. Pliny was brought up by his uncle, Pliny the Elder, who bequeathed his nephew his property and his name: young Caecilius became Gaius Plinius Caecilius Secundus, Pliny the Younger.

Pliny was at once docile and ambitious: at age fourteen he composed a Greek tragedy. In Rome he studied rhetoric under Nicetes Sacerdos of Smyrna and under Quintilian, who left a greater, or at least a more obvious, impression. Having determined upon a forensic career (despite the despair of Tacitus's *Dialogus,* oratory remained a vital profession during the Flavian period and beyond), he began to plead cases at age eighteen. His first important trial came early on: a certain Junius Pastor was prosecuted in the Centumviral Court by "men of great influence, some of them also friends of the Emperor" (*Ep.* 1.18). Familiarity with the Centumviral Court for people today centers mostly on cases of inheritance law, but the competence of the court was considerably wider, and in Pliny's day the Centumviral Court was the venue of many sensational trials. The clout of his adversaries notwithstanding, Pliny won his case, a victory that brought his talents welcome attention and set his brilliant career on its course. Pliny, of course, is the sole source for this episode, in a letter designed both to scold and to encourage the young Suetonius in his own forensic career.

There is no reason to doubt the story or the odds that stood against Pliny. The whole of his career indicates that this successful careerist always understood how to calculate his risks, and in this instance Pliny could also relish the parallel with Cicero's defense of Roscius of Ameria that his letter was doubtless intended to suggest. He began his senatorial career by holding a minor magistracy, then served as a military tribune in Syria, where he audited the accounts of auxiliary forces. He also studied with the philosophers Euphrates and Artemidorus. Back in Rome, he held another minor post, after which, the year is uncertain but sometime in the late A.D. 80s, he became one of the two quaestors attached to the emperor. His merits had attracted the attentions of Domitian. There is no reason to suspect that Pliny was displeased. He advanced to the tribunate of the plebs, an office that had decayed to a mere relic of its republican past but one that Pliny exercised with extraordinary reverence for its traditions and with a spectacular flourish. In order to preserve the dignity of the tribunate and out of a concern that one of his clients might make an anachronistic appeal for a tribune's aid, Pliny refused to practice in the courts for as long as he held the office. The gesture had its desired effect: the emperor accelerated Pliny's rise.

Pliny was praetor in A.D. 93. Baebius Massa, the proconsul of Baetica, was charged at the complaint of his province, and the senate appointed Pliny and Herennius Senecio to prosecute the case. Massa was condemned, but he retaliated by accusing Senecio of treason. Pliny did not flinch: if Massa were creditable, he insisted, he would have attacked both prosecutors and not only Senecio; "Most noble consuls," Pliny cried out, "I am afraid that by not including me in his accusation Massa's very silence has charged me with collusion with himself" (*Ep.* 7.33). Pliny's stand won praise—and congratulations from the future emperor Nerva. As for Senecio, he was tried and found guilty. Indeed, there was a purge. In his panegyric to Trajan, Pliny recollected how thunderbolts were falling all around him. During the event, however, they struck only his friends. Pliny himself flourished. In fact, he went straight on to become one of the prefects in charge of the military treasury, a signal distinction that rarely followed the praetorship so immediately. The evidence of this success is only found in surviving inscriptions: Pliny never mentions it in his letters, and in the *Panegyricus* (A.D. 100) he actually suggests that his career slowed at this point (*Pan.* 95.3). The reason is clear enough: in A.D. 96 Domitian was assassinated, and the official policy of the new dispensation was to revile the memory of that bad emperor.

It was important that Pliny now display his good senatorial credentials. He considered prosecuting Aquilius Regulus (whom he genuinely hated), an elderly, disreputable, formidable, yet now vulnerable orator. He was not vulnerable enough, however, and Pliny turned to a different target: Publicius Certus, the man who had prosecuted Helvidius Priscus, a darling of the senate who had been executed in A.D. 93. Pliny railed against Certus in the senate and praised the memory of Helvidius, thereby inciting a fierce debate. The new emperor did not approve of Pliny's menacing tactic, however, and the ever perceptive Pliny acknowledged the limits of his actions: Certus was not indicted, but Pliny's actions had been enough to eliminate his enemy's prospects of holding the consulship. The membership of the senate, moreover, congratulated Pliny for restoring to that body its ancient vitality and rectitude. Pliny's performance had been deft enough to display his soundness to all parties. He was appointed prefect of the Treasury of Saturn, an office that regularly marked one out as a future consul. Pliny published his speeches from this period and thereafter regarded them as his best.

Then came a sensational opportunity. Marius Priscus, the proconsul of Africa under Nerva, was tried for maladministration early in Trajan's reign. The case was important, not in itself but on account of its implications in defining what would be the future relationship between the senate and the new emperor: each side was keen both to maintain its dignity and to observe the requirements of administrative integrity. Pliny actively sought a role in the prosecution, and, in the end, he and his friend, the historian Tacitus, carried off the case with such effectiveness and decorum that it brought them both much credit. Pliny accepted another prosecution, on the senate's behalf, of yet another corrupt governor. Then, late in A.D. 100, Pliny himself held the consulship.

His rise had been fast and brilliant and smooth, though one could not fairly call it easy. As consul, he was not yet forty. The only hint of a delay came when he sought a priesthood, which the dignity of a man of consular rank demanded. His influential friends, Verginius Rufus and Julius Frontinus, pushed his claim. Pliny had to wait three years, though, until the death of Frontinus, whose place in the college of augurs he took. The postponement, which was hardly protracted, was by no means a slight.

Pliny did not desert the courts. In his defense of Julius Bassus, indicted for illegalities while governor of Bithynia, Pliny displayed the extent of his discrimination and forensic skills. Bassus was an old man who had suffered under Domitian but had been restored to the senate by Nerva. Now his status was at risk once more, not least because the man was in fact guilty as charged. Pliny could not deny his client's actions, but he labored to put them in the least culpable light. More effectively, he called upon the senators to be compassionate and merciful to one of their own who had suffered enough. In the end, Bassus was required to make reparation for his peculations, but he held on to his senatorial rank. Pliny's was a masterly—and realistic—defense.

In A.D. 104 Pliny was elected head of the Curators of the Tiber River. The office was a responsibility more distinguished than it sounds, and its requirements suited Pliny's organizational and financial skills. The term was three years. Thereafter Pliny for once had to

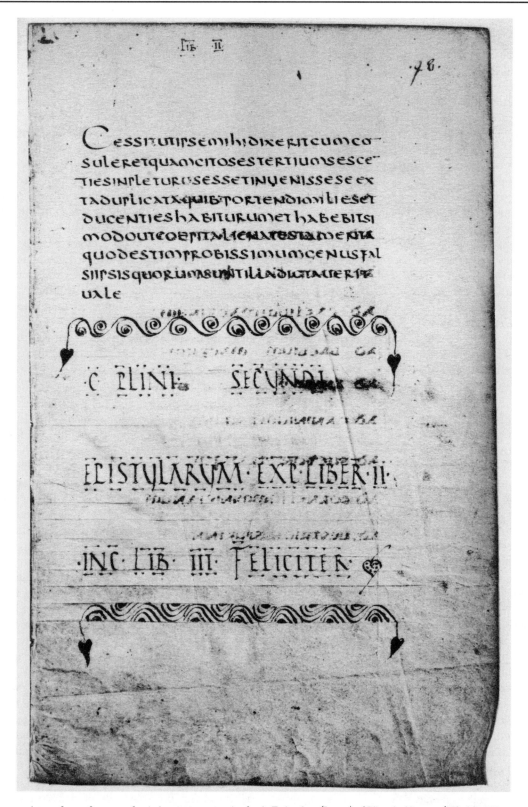

A page from a fragment of a sixth-century manuscript for the Epistulae *(Letters) of Pliny the Younger (MS. M. 462, Pierpont Morgan Library, New York)*

wait for his next assignment, which came sometime between A.D. 109 and A.D. 111: he was sent to the province of Bithynia-Pontus as the emperor's legate. Bithynia had for several years been plagued by problematic administration, and many of its various cities, recent events had revealed, were in difficulties. In his correspondence with Trajan, Pliny documents his activities in Bithynia: he worked with care and industry to restore the stability of the province, in political and in financial terms. The cities of Prusa, Nicomedia, Nicaea, and Claudiopolis were, owing to their own incompetence, economic disasters. There were irregularities in the government as well. Pliny threw himself into municipal finance, urban administration, public safety, and the problems posed by foreign religions–in this instance, by accusations leveled against Christians. In a famous and much-studied letter (*Ep.* 10.96), Pliny provides the earliest pagan account of the conduct, reputation, and teachings of the Christians. This letter also provides the first glimpse of the repression of Christianity by the Roman government. Pliny's correspondence terminates during his governorship in Bythinia. Presumably he died there.

Pliny's was a splendid and shimmering career in public service. He established himself as one of the leading orators of his day, an expert in finance and in management, and a sound and reliable member of the senatorial class. He outstripped men of better birth, and he stayed equal with men whose accomplishments were more glorious–that is, with the military men. It is all too easy for classicists to sneer at Pliny's steady and comfortable conformity to the political demands of his career or to ridicule his excessive courtesies when he communicated with Trajan over unimportant matters, as if deference and flexibility were unnatural elements in any brilliant and sustained rise. Perhaps disapproval is not entirely unjustified, but in reality most people have kowtowed at least once to a superior. Pliny was beyond any question an opportunist of the first order, but that is not the same thing as saying that he acted without integrity. On more than one occasion, as he himself admits, he struggled to steer a course between danger and disgrace. Pliny, as the totality of his published letters makes obvious, believed in Rome, in the duties and privileges of public life, and in the traditions of the senate.

Pliny was rich, and he prudently (and conventionally) kept his wealth in land. He was known by his friends and family to be as capable with private investments as with public monies. Yet, he was generous, both in the style of the traditional aristocracy (for instance, he subsidized friends, freedmen and clients, and he endowed his native city with a library and, through his will, with baths) and in the manner of the new humanitarianism characteristic of Trajan's reign (for example, he established trust funds in Comum to support poor children and provided money to help the town pay for a teacher). He believed that the younger generation should be encouraged, and he often reprimanded men such as Suetonius, who showed too little ambition. If his correspondence is any guide, Pliny delighted in the cultivation, and in the duties, of friendship. He was equally responsible toward his relations. Pliny married three times. His first two wives predeceased him; characteristically, he remained on good terms with their families. His third wife, Calpurnia, was much younger than he, but he was thoroughly devoted to her. The couple were shattered by her miscarriage and their later inability to produce a family, a circumstance that the emperor sought to ameliorate at least to a moderate degree when he conferred upon them the "rights of parents with three children." Calpurnia accompanied Pliny to Bithynia. Later, however, he arranged with the emperor for her to return to Rome by the imperial postal service so that she could attend to her aunt after her grandfather's death. Since Pliny never returned from his province, it was his final courtesy to her.

Pliny was, first and foremost, an orator. Along with Tacitus, he was regarded by his contemporaries as the best speaker of his day. As was the case for Cicero–whom Pliny, well-schooled by Quintilian, much admired–success in the courts promoted Pliny's political aspirations. Eloquence continued in the empire to be a practical resource for helping friends and harming enemies, but it was also a literary pursuit the appropriateness of which was unimpeachable for a Roman senator. Pliny was as capable in prosecution as he was in making a defense; yet, he considered his speeches in the senate on behalf of Helvidius Priscus's reputation to be his finest orations. Throughout his mature career, Pliny kept himself occupied in lovingly revising his speeches for publication, and his references to the study of these publications by others indicates that he was satisfied with their reception. Pliny introduced the practice of reciting his speeches to an audience, as was done with history, drama, and lyric. Some criticized the practice, but Pliny brushed off their disparagement. Martial won Pliny's affection by comparing his speeches with Cicero's (Mart. 10.20). The hated Aquilius Regulus once hoped to wound Pliny by obliquely attacking his pretensions when he addressed Satirius Rufus in court as a man "who makes no attempt to copy Cicero and is satisfied with the standards of oratory today." Pliny later pretended not to see the sting: "Personally, I do try to copy Cicero," he said to Regulus, "and I am not satisfied with today's standards. It seems to me foolish not to aim at the highest" (*Ep.* 1.5).

Title page for the 1518 Milan edition of Pliny the Younger's letters (courtesy of the Lilly Library, Indiana University)

Pliny eschewed most other forms of prose composition: so far as is known, he composed no treatises on rhetoric, on philosophy, or on any subject in which he had demonstrated proficiency, such as finance. In contradistinction to his friends Tacitus and Suetonius, he refused to write history or biography. In a letter to Titinius Capito, an influential equestrian and an active patron of literature who had apparently urged Pliny to historical composition, Pliny insists that oratory is his own natural genre. He extols the significance of history by referring to his uncle's writings and by citing Thucydides' distinction between "a lasting possession" and "a prize essay": "the former is history, the latter oratory." Yet, one should not conclude from this statement that Pliny ranked his own craft below the historian's: "oratory and poetry win small favor unless they reach the highest standard of eloquence, but history cannot fail to give pleasure however it is presented" (*Ep.* 5.8). Pliny chose the more exacting art.

Although he published many of his speeches, the only one that survives is the *Panegyricus*. Public expressions of thanks and praise, to the people or to the senate or to an individual, went back to republican times. A speech of this type was called an *actio gratiarum*. It could also be called a panegyric. Under Augustus it was first a convention and then a requirement that new consuls express their gratitude to the gods and to the emperor, and during the empire these formal gestures of thanksgiving became frequent, though important, occasions. Naturally, there were other events that demanded a speech in the emperor's honor. Speeches for these occasions, too, were designated as panegyrics. Pliny's speech, which was delivered in A.D. 100 in praise of Trajan, was preserved in a collection of twelve Latin panegyrics that was discovered in the fifteenth century. Pliny's speech, by far the longest, heads the list and was clearly the model for the others, which include orations in honor of Maximian, Maxentius, Constantine, and Theodosius.

Pliny's actual *actio gratiarum* was relatively brief, in conformity with normal practice; however, he elected to revise his speech and to expand it substantially. The

Model of Pliny the Younger's Laurentine villa, based on the detailed description in one of his letters

published *Panegyricus* takes about three hours to read, and Pliny enjoyed reading to his friends, who, he claimed, begged for more. The sheer bulk of Pliny's speech offends modern tastes, but to be concerned with present-day reaction is to miss the point. Pliny believed that the bigger the speech the better (*Ep.* 1.20). Size mattered to Romans of all eras, but if one considers only the architecture of the Trajanic period, one is likely to concede that, on the question of scale, Pliny's tastes were fairly typical for his time. So, too, were his tastes in matters of content. The rhetorical challenge of the *actio gratiarum* is to render clichés interesting, which puts heavy demands on an orator's invention and style (hence the virtue in amplification: bigger is harder). Any summary of the speech must be predictable: Pliny enumerates Trajan's virtues in contrast with Domitian's faults. Trajan is the best of emperors, and it is his duty to be a model to the future emperors, lest the dark days of Domitian ever return. A good emperor defers to his senatorial peers, and so Pliny includes didactic passages in which he instructs Trajan on the best exercise of imperial excellence. All Pliny's suggestions had been said before, as he well knew (*Ep.* 3.13), but this hardly

mattered. Pliny expected his readers and listeners to relish his style and to appreciate how he situated himself and his craft in a tradition that harked back to Cicero's *Pro Marcello*.

The reigns of Domitian, Nerva, and Trajan teemed with poets, and Pliny took a keen interest in poetry as his letters indicate. He describes the last days of the epic poet Silius Italicus (*Ep.* 3.7). In Vibius Maximus, Pliny had a friend in common with Statius, though that versatile poet is never mentioned in Pliny's extant writings. Rome was alive with readings and recitations, which Pliny frequented and at which he performed. Pliny versified, and he defended the practice by appealing for precedents to statesmen of the past and by observing the various utilities and benefits (and the sheer pleasure) associated with poetic composition. He perhaps regretted that his reputation as a poet could not compare with his fame as an orator, but, if the surviving specimens of his poetry are a reliable guide (cited in *Ep.* 7.4 and *Ep.* 7.9) to the whole of his output, the judgment of his contemporaries can hardly be regarded as unjust.

The *Epistulae,* nine books of letters that Pliny selected, edited, arranged, and published, represent the greatest of his literary achievements. There is also a tenth book of Pliny's letters, which includes his correspondence with Trajan. These letters, too, are carefully composed, but for different purposes, and, in any case, they seem to have been collected and published after their author's death. So, while they are of considerable historical consequence, they do not form part of Pliny's literary enterprise. The *Epistles,* however, were intended to be an important literary contribution.

The publication of letters was nothing new by Pliny's day. Cicero's correspondence, with which Pliny inevitably contrasts his own, was in circulation. Cicero's letters, with few exceptions, were actual records of private communication, not a literary ensemble composed with posterity in mind. Horace's poetic epistles constitute a more apt precedent. In these poems, the particular combines with the universal for a general effect, and the relationship between the addressee and the content of the piece always requires pondering. More recently, Seneca had put forward his wisdom and advice in the form of his *Moral Epistles,* all directed toward the edification of a single friend. Are they fiction or genuine correspondence? Pliny's collection flirts with both categories. In his first letter, which serves as a preface to the whole, Pliny indicates that he is publishing those letters that he has written "with some care." He goes on to say that the letters do not appear in chronological sequence; in fact, he alleges, they are sorted randomly, "as they came to my hand." None of his explanations is clarifying. In *Ep.* 7.9 Pliny makes plain his view that all letters should be carefully composed. Still, one can hardly overlook that, in his collection, nearly every letter is devoted to a single topic. There is little in the way of clutter or of technical (or even of what one might deem necessary) detail. As to the arrangement, historical analysis indicates that they do in fact tend to come in chronological order, even the least sensitive of readers can discern in the sequence of the letters Pliny's careful variety of themes.

The topics of the letters range widely and give a remarkably full portrait of upper-class life. Pliny discusses public affairs, literature, business, family matters, and personalities. He writes recommendations and exhortations. He describes what pleases him, such as the duties of a landowner, the beauty of a villa, and the prized episodes in his own distinguished career. He rarely turns to unsympathetic matters. It is all the more revealing that he does not introduce philosophical topics, nor technical points of law or philology, nor recondite learning of any sort. There are 247 letters addressed to 105 individu-

als: the letters themselves are not long, but their ensemble is huge, capacious. Once again, bigger is better, but the bite-sized quality of individual epistles, as well as their variety and charm, have given Pliny's collection an appeal that transcends mere antiquarianism or curiosity.

The style of Pliny's letters is graceful and neat. He is careful, even conventional, in his diction, and he shows restraint in resorting to the devices of rhetoric. He delights in wordplay, in antithesis, and in epigram. He does employ them so frequently, however, that they become predictable. He strives for the Ciceronianism of the treatises, and he often achieves it. He does not wear his learning heavily. There are many literary echoes, but mostly to familiar Latin poets and the most accessible of the Greek ones. In *Ep.* 6.31, for instance, Pliny describes the harbor at Centum Cellae, now Civita Vecchia, to which he had been summoned by the emperor. It was a proud moment in his life, and the letter recalling it is one of the longer in the *Epistles.* In composing his description of the beautiful harbor of the town, Pliny appropriates Virgil's account of the African harbor in which Aeneas found refuge after the great storm of book 1 of the *Aeneid.* The intertextuality is obvious but not forced. Its strategy, however, leaves space for pondering: how did so evident an allusion affect Pliny's readers? What was its purpose?

In his letters Pliny does not sound as if he were a contemporary of Juvenal or of Tacitus. In the historian's vision of Rome, every action is pregnant with hypocrisy and menace; the empire totters on the brink of ruin and its leading men on the brink of despair. By contrast, Pliny emerges as contented and happy, and he believes that others are contented and happy as well. He recognizes that terrible things do happen, but he enjoys his friends, his family, his pastimes, and his duties. There is no whiff of fear or dread. The modern academic would rather read, and would rather believe in, Tacitus's cynicism than in Pliny's complacency. That is simply a matter of temperament or taste. On the other hand, for a student of the period to take Tacitus's point of view as the dominant attitude of the age would be a serious error. Pliny's *Epistles* preserve a precious supplement and, in some measure, a corrective.

Why did Pliny publish his letters? It has been suggested that he hoped thereby to establish his own memorial—an attractive and lasting alternative to an autobiography. His letters certainly permitted him to construct for posterity the finest possible account of his own career. There is also something to be said for the idea that Pliny, like Horace and Seneca before him, hoped to present to the world a guide to right conduct, an ethical treatise. For Pliny right living is concentrated in specific, everyday activities. Philosophical pretensions are unnecessary when a reader can see for himself the good life of a good man–in this instance, of Pliny himself. Hence, Pliny employs an emphasis, never heavy but never absent, on suitable manners, on the cheerful observance of one's obligations, and on the industrious undertaking of the work that suits one. Pliny was not, by Roman standards, an immodest man. Whatever else one takes from a reading of his correspondence, though, there is no avoiding the obvious fact that Pliny always remains his own, his truest topic.

Pliny's writings were much admired and studied. Just as his *Panegyricus* became a model for such performances in late antiquity, Pliny's *Epistulae* also found their imitators. Symmachus published a collection of nine books of personal letters, to which he attached one book of public ones. Sidonius Apollinaris also published his letters in nine books. During the Middle Ages, Pliny the Younger's reputation was eclipsed by that of his uncle, Pliny the Elder. However, with the Renaissance the younger Pliny's fortunes rose once more. Like Cicero, Pliny became an important model for prose and for speech. It was a role to which he had aspired throughout his life. His posthumous success would have pleased him.

Index:

Index de Pline le Jeune, edited by Xavier Jacques and Jules van Ooteghem (Brussels: Palais des Academies, 1965).

References:

R. T. Bruère, "Tacitus and Pliny's *Panegyricus,*" *Classical Philology,* 49 (1954): 161–179;

A. D. E. Cameron, "The Fate of Pliny's Letters in the Late Empire," *Classical Quarterly,* n.s., 15 (1965): 289–298;

Federico Gamberini, *Stylistic Theory and Practice in the Younger Pliny* (Hildesheim: Olms, 1983);

Sabine MacCormack, "Latin Prose Panegyrics," in *Empire and Aftermath: Silver Latin II,* edited by T. A. Dorey (London: Routledge & Kegan Paul, 1975), pp. 143–205;

Betty Radice, "Pliny and the *Panegyricus,*" *Greece & Rome,* 15 (1968): 166–172;

A. N. Sherwin-White, "Pliny, the Man and His Letters," *Greece & Rome,* 16 (1969): 76–90;

Selatie Edgar Stout, *Scribe and Critic at Work in Pliny's Letters: Notes on the History and Present Status of the Text* (Bloomington: Indiana University Press, 1954);

H. W. Traub, "Pliny's Treatment of History in Epistolary Form," *Transactions of the American Philological Association,* 86 (1955): 213–232.

Propertius

(ca. 50 B.C. – post 16 B.C.)

J. K. Newman
University of Illinois Urbana-Champaign

MAJOR WORK: *Elegies,* 4 books.

Editio princeps: *Propertii Elegiae* (Venice: Federicus de Comitibus, Veronensis, 1472).

Standard editions: *Carmina Sexti Propertii,* edited by E. A. Barber, second edition (Oxford: Clarendon Press, 1960); *Sexti Propertii Elegiarum libri IV,* edited by Paolo Fedeli (Stuttgart: Teubner, 1984).

Translations in English: *Propertius. Elegies,* edited and translated by G. P. Goold, Loeb Classical Library (Cambridge, Mass.: Harvard University Press, 1990); *Propertius, the Poems Translated,* translated by Guy Lee, with an introduction by Oliver Lyne (Oxford: Clarendon Press, 1994).

Commentaries: *The Elegies of Propertius,* edited by H. E. Butler and E. A. Barber (Oxford: Clarendon Press, 1933); *Elegies,* 4 volumes, edited by W. A. Camps (Cambridge: Cambridge University Press, 1961–1967); *Elegiarum liber I* (Monobiblos), 2 volumes, edited by P. J. Enk (Leiden: E. J. Brill, 1946); *Elegiarum liber secundus,* edited by Enk (Leiden: Sijthoff, 1962); *Il primo libro delle Elegie,* edited by Paolo Fedeli (Florence: L. S. Olschki, 1980); *Il libro terzo delle Elegie,* edited by Fedeli (Bari: Adriatica, 1985); *Elegie: libro IV,* edited by Fedeli (Bari: Adriatica, 1965); *Elegies I-IV,* edited, with introduction and commentary, by Lawrence Richardson (Norman: University of Oklahoma Press, 1977).

Little is known about the life of Sextus Propertius except what may be gleaned from his four books of elegies published at intervals, probably between 30 and 13 B.C. There, he calls himself only Propertius. Donatus's *Life of Virgil* adds the praenomen Sextus (section 30). Propertius's date of birth, though disputed, is often set about 50 B.C., on the assumption that he published his first book of elegies around the age of twenty. The second book, describing the dedication of the Temple of the Palatine Apollo in 28 B.C., hailing Octavian as Augustus (a title adopted in 27 B.C.), and referring to the death of Gallus (ca. 26 B.C.), perhaps followed in 26 or 25 B.C.; and the third book, adapting programmatic themes from Horace's *Odes* I–III, and seemingly commemorating in poem 18 the death of Marcellus (late in 23 B.C.), was published after 23 B.C. Since Propertius's final book alludes to events of 16 and perhaps even 14 B.C., his death occurred after the first of these dates, but scholarly opinion about the exact year varies from soon after 16 B.C. to some time before A.D. 2, when Ovid lists him with the dead Tibullus and Gallus (*Rem. Am.* 764). If this last book of elegies was in fact published in 13 B.C., at the same time as Horace's fourth and last book of odes, their individual brevity may have been mutually supplementary.

Fragments attributed to Propertius by the late grammarian Fulgentius in his *Expositio sermonum antiquorum* (22 and 34), if genuine, imply that Propertius also wrote both elegiac poems not preserved and other poetry in quite different meters. Such a conclusion offers a parallel with Ovid, whose poetic corpus certainly once included material not now surviving, including poems in nonelegiac meters, and would round out the picture of Propertius as a professional poet, both pruning his elegies on formal grounds and writing beyond the confines of a single genre.

His place of birth was the region of Umbria (IV. 1. 63), and perhaps was Assisi (IV. 1. 125, a disputed reading), where the visitor with permission may see what is said to have been Propertius's house under the present church of Sta. Maria Maggiore. In the opening elegy of book IV Propertius writes that his family was once wealthy but lost land to confiscation even before he received the *toga virilis* (usually assumed at the age of about fifteen). His father was probably dead by this time, since Propertius mentions only his mother at the ceremonies (*matris,* IV. 1. 132). Certainly some member of his family seems to have been killed (I. 31 and 32) escaping from Perusia when it was under siege by Octavian (ca. 41–40 B.C.). Such turbulent experiences evidently made a deep impression on the youthful poet.

Pompeiian painting (ca. A.D. 62–79) of Achilles surrendering Briseis in Homer's Iliad, *the model for Propertius's elegy on the loss of Cynthia*

The Perusine War has been described as the last desperate stand of the Etruscans against the Romans. Scholars do not know why Propertius's relation took sides against Octavian in it, but the poet's family name was borne also by a king of the Etruscan city of Veii, as noted by Cato the Elder (fr. 48, p. 64, Peter), a fact which would give added poignancy to the lament for Veii's lost greatness in book 4 (10. 25–30). The poet's direct descendant Paulus Passennus, mentioned by the Younger Pliny (*Epp.* VI. 15. 1; cf. IX. 22. 1), has a typically Etruscan *-nnus* at the end of his name (for example, Lacus Trasimennus). If Propertius was Etruscan (like the Neronian satirist Aulus Persius), that may explain why in some manuscripts he receives the second gentile name of Aurelius. To bear two gentile names (one taken from the mother; compare with *matris*) was an Etruscan custom and is found, for example, in the two gentile names of the undoubtedly Etruscan C. Cilnius Maecenas. Maecenas's own poetry echoes some of the hedonism of the Etruscan way of life (compare with

Seneca, *Epist.* 101. 10), and perhaps Propertius's poetry owes something to that inheritance too. His youthful calamities and inherited flippancy would have combined to lend his elegies their characteristic mixture of seriousness and comedy.

Maecenas, though descended from Etruscan kings, is called by Propertius an *eques* (knight, III. 9. 1), and Propertius himself, even if he too had royal antecedents, was certainly not blue-blooded in any way that could have impressed the Roman aristocracy (II. 24. 37). Yet, whatever losses the poet's family had sustained, he had clearly enjoyed an excellent education (hardly in Assisi) when he came to Rome to seek his fortune, probably in the years leading up to the battle of Actium in 31 B.C. He found immediate access to the highest circles in the new regime. His first book of elegies was dedicated to Tullus, in all likelihood the nephew of L. Volcacius Tullus (compare with I. 6. 19, *patrui*), co-consul with Octavian in 33 B.C. and attested by inscriptional evidence as later (ca. 30–29) proconsul of Asia Minor. The province had been sympathetic to Brutus and before that to Pompey, and evidently only the most trusted lieutenant would be sent out by Octavian to secure its loyalty, or indeed earlier selected as his co-consul in the tense years leading up to Actium.

When the younger Tullus went out to Asia to join his uncle's staff (ca. 30 B.C.), Propertius might have been expected to accompany his patron. This half-formed plan may color, for example, the flourish in the finale of his first elegy (29, 31): "carry me to the ends of the earth, and over the waters / . . . you others must stay behind"). In fact, however, the poet stayed behind in Rome, where he dedicated his second book to Maecenas, Octavian's minister of culture and patron of Virgil and Horace. This dedication was an advance in social status for Propertius, since Horace affirms (*Satires* I. 9. 55–56) that Maecenas was choosy about his literary associates. Propertius apparently eventually kept even more exalted company. In the third and fourth volumes there are more references to "Caesar" (that is, Octavian) than there are to Maecenas. Already in book 2 (10. 15) Propertius addresses Octavian by his new title of Augustus, the first extant Augustan writer to do so.

Such references look like evidence of a poet almost as close to the new regime as was Maecenas. Like Lucilius, the confidant of the Younger Scipio, Propertius would have used his talents partly to satirize the morals of the age (including those of his girlfriend "Cynthia," perhaps comparable with Lucilius's Collyra and others); partly to exalt his patrons; partly, with the aid of some ostensible autobiography, to pose (by way of foil) as the man on the margin unable to get his act together; and partly to reflect on problems of his craft. This program, also owing a debt to Callimachus's *Iamboi*, would provide a poetic umbrella large enough to accommodate, for example, the poet's awareness of his shortcomings (*nullo vivere consilio*, living without a plan, I. 1. 6; *desidia*, idleness, I. 12. 1; and subjection to a woman, III. 11. 1–compare with the conclusions of III. 4 and 5) and elegies such as I. 2 and II. 18b (satire of Cynthia); II. 10 (vatic eulogy of Augustus); and I. 7 (how to write effective poetry). In III. 7 (*Ergo sollicitae tu causa, Pecunia, vitae*), generalizing from Paetus's death at sea, Propertius actually uses terms occurring in moralizing Horace's poems (*sollicitae . . . vitae, Sat.* II. 6. 62; *regina Pecunia, Epp.* I. 6. 37). Like Horace, though, he would not have wanted to wound too deeply. Always his aim would have been to entertain.

However, a different line of interpretation has appealed to some readers. Propertius's first volume of elegies, the "Cynthia," named in antiquity, by a common custom, after its opening, celebrated (though not exclusively) his passionate love affair with the beautiful girl of that name. The book was a sensational success and has tempted modern romantic critics to reconstruct the poet's life from his work (seen as "life transmuted into art"). According to this view, the poet fell in love with a real Cynthia and used her as the inspiration for his first two books (II. 1. 4, for example, where she is said to act in place of his Muse). His third book, dealing with literary problems as much as with her, is said to show a cooling of the relationship caused by her many infidelities and ends with two poems of bitter, self-reproachful farewell. His short fourth book, more objective in style, was allegedly patched together by an unwilling poet, perhaps using some older work, to answer the pressures of his patrons for poems honoring the regime, whose warlike bombast, as is argued, he detested anyway. After this last reluctant effort, he is thought to have died of a broken heart ("as soon after 16 as possible," in the words of a recent literary history).

This stereotypical scenario (boy meets girl; boy loves girl; girl turns out to be a tramp; boy steels himself to dismiss girl and dies of despair) betrays its loose inappropriateness by its equal adaptability to the poetry of Catullus, to some aspects of Horace's iambic epodes (14 and 15), and even to Archilochus (Columbia Papyri 7511). The genre is being interpreted too narrowly. Right from the start, there is far more in the poetry than the story of a love affair. Already in book 1, for example, Propertius clarifies his attitude toward questions of epic versus love poetry (poem 7). His first elegy is not a spontaneous outburst confessing his infatuation but, in its genesis at least, a reworking of an epigram of Meleager, and its *furor* (madness) is a claim to genius. Cynthia is not spared some criticisms even in these early pieces (I. 2). Her quick temper is evidenced in the beautiful third elegy. The sixteenth elegy, introducing a gossipy door too much aware of family scandals, is decidedly in the satirical vein (compare with Catullus's poem 67). It certainly has nothing to do with Cynthia.

Conversely, in book 4, even after the bitter (iambic, Catullan) farewells of 3.24 and 3.25, two long, juxtaposed poems are concerned with Cynthia. The first poem (7) shows her returning from the dead to rebuke the poet for his inattentiveness to her obsequies and, not without some macabre touches, evokes pathetic and affectionate memories of her snobbishness and sharp tongue. The second (8) describes a delicious adventure when Propertius tries to take advantage of her absence from Rome to amuse himself with a couple of party girls only to be rudely interrupted by her unexpected return. Cynthia storms in like a conquering general. Her lover's abject surrender to the terms she imposes ends with a reconciliation in bed. Both poems pay wonderful and tender tribute to the girl, who lives again in the vatic poet's resurrecting verse. They hardly support the suggestion that the poet of book 4 is no longer a poet of love. Such a conclusion seems even less true if one considers the fond Arethusa of the third elegy, a wife writing to her soldier-husband at the front; or the lovelorn Tarpeia of the fourth elegy, who questions the whole basis of the military ethos.

The Romans were not modern romantics. The selectivity of such an approach entails that, as in the case of Catullus, poems that do not support the thesis must be ignored or dismissed. A distinction must be made between the persona projected by the poet in his work, often intended to show off his patrons' contrasting competence, and the writer-craftsman who composed to such effect. If Propertius's life had been ruined by his love, where would he have found the time and energy to write about that love with such attention? Scholars have noted, for example, that the technique of Propertius's pentameters moves more and more toward the Ovidian model of the disyllabic last word as the books advance. More than half the elegies are carefully organized around a central climactic couplet. The poems are often cunningly paired, and there are well-organized cycles. Is this artfulness compatible with spontaneous sincerity? It may be salutary to think of William Shakespeare and the "Dark Lady" of the sonnets. The poetry may hint at a profound passion. The legal documents surviving from Shakespeare's time show an author carefully investing the proceeds of his work, returning to a fine house in his hometown for his retirement, and being concerned about his family. So too Propertius may have returned to a fine house in his hometown. Perhaps he too was concerned about a family. If he had direct descendants, he must have married someone other than Cynthia (II. 7), who in any case was ineligible under the legislation forbidding unions between citizens and prostitutes/actresses traditionally known to Roman jurists as the *Lex Julia.*

A different interpretation then suggests that in the first place Propertius was a conscious artist, manipulating his varied experience in the service of effect and in the service of a genre. "Cynthia" is a book of poems (*Cynthia, facundi carmen iuvenale Properti,* Martial, XVI. 189. 1); Propertius did not meet a girl called Cynthia, though no doubt he met many girls at Roman parties. Cynthia was an imposed name. The original name may have been Hostia (Apuleius, *Apol.* 10), though the attractive suggestion has been made that she was Roscia, a granddaughter perhaps of Roscius, the famous comic actor defended by Cicero, and possibly herself an actress (like Gallus's Lycoris); such an identity might account for her many accomplishments in poetry and dancing, and, since Roscius's family was from near Lanuvium, her visit there (IV. 8. 3 and 48; also perhaps

II. 32. 6). This identity also easily explains why she and Propertius could not marry. The emperor Justinian still found the legal problem irksome when he proposed to marry the mime-actress Theodora.

However, even if Hostia/Roscia supplied the main ingredients for Cynthia, the character immortalized by Propertius is probably a composite, subsumed into a larger whole. "Cynthia" is a divine name (Artemis/Isis; the still visible temple of Isis at the foot of Mt. Cynthus on Delos was rebuilt by the Athenians in 135 B.C.), not found in use for a mortal before he used it (and rarely afterwards). The first use of "Cynthia" after Propertius I and II occurs when Horace suggests a theme for partying Lyde (*Odes* III. 28. 12), and there the name refers to the goddess. The talented and well-educated poet–fatherless, impoverished by his family's loss of its land–came to Rome to improve his fortunes. He quickly found patronage. If the gens Volcacia, to which Tullus belonged, was Etruscan, perhaps an Etruscan background helped. By the same token, the tense atmosphere of the time would have prevented Tullus, so eager to serve on his distinguished uncle's staff, from patronizing a writer whose loyalty to the new government was in any way suspect; and why would such a dissident be taken up later by Maecenas?

Even the choice of the name Cynthia served the new ideology. Plans for the dedication of a temple to Apollo on the Palatine were already afoot when Propertius arrived, and this god became the cultural and ceremonial patron of the sun-king Octavian, eventually Augustus. Already in his programmatic sixth eclogue Virgil uses for Apollo the cult title, found in Callimachus (*Hymn* 4. 10), "Cynthius." He repeats the name in his fantasy at the start of *Georgics* III (36), where "Caesar will be in the midst" (16). "Cynthius" there is "Troy's begetter." Propertius echoes the title in a programmatic elegy at the end of his second book, where he is both eulogizing–and associating himself with–Virgil (II. 34. 80, *Cynthius;* 93, *Cynthia*). "Cynthia" then, the feminine form of "Cynthius," was a loaded name. She was properly Apollo's sister, Diana, goddess of the moon. She was also goddess of the sublunary sphere of folly and madness (*iracunda Diana,* Horace, *A.P.* 454; *furit,* 472). A poet honoring a mistress under this title might be forgiven for uttering a great deal of lunatic nonsense, especially if it was delivered in performance at the symposium among guests looking for light amusement at the end of the official day. Though he may sometimes have claimed there the frankness of the nightclub comedian, Propertius posed no threat to the regime. Indeed, his choice of that unusual sobriquet for his mistress was a proof of his loyalty to the new ideology.

Consistently with this reading, Propertius both speaks of his *furor* in his first elegy (7) and describes

Cynthia in the moonlight in his third. However, he is not quite to be taken at his own valuation. Not only was poetic *furor* an old concept, but Plato and Democritus, according to Cicero (*de Orat.* II. 194; *Div.* I. 80; compare with Seneca, *De Tranq. Animi* 17. 10), had both said that every great poet had to be inspired by it. In the act of disclaiming the power of self-control, Propertius is slyly ranging himself with the great.

He was helped by the revival under Augustus of the term *vates* (seer) as a name for a new type of poet, not just the clever craftsman of the Alexandrians (although he would need to acquire that technical elegance), but the public spokesman of the new ideology (compare with Cassandra's *furor patriae . . . utilis* at III. 13. 65; *utilis Urbi* of the *vates*, Hor. *Epp.* II. 1. 124). The *vates* in his milder moments is akin to the native Roman (self-) satirist, and this (Lucilian) stance is the one normally assumed by Propertius. Yet, there are occasions when he rises to full public stature. In I. 10 and IV. 6, he calls himself a *vates* (both elegies use the name Augustus, the latter quite anachronistically in reference to events of 31 B.C.). His reflections on dead Marcellus (III. 18), or dead Pompey (III. 11), and in the last elegy of all on Cornelia (IV. 11), take this same stance.

Propertius's literary ambition is seen in his rivalry with the Alexandrian master Callimachus (ca. 305–240 B.C.), still regarded by Quintilian (X. 1. 58), for example, as *princeps* (leading figure) in Greek elegy. Roman poets customarily declared themselves the authorized Roman representatives of great Greek predecessors. Among the Augustans, Horace was Archilochus or Alcaeus, and in book 2 Propertius hailed Virgil as the poet of something greater than Homer's *Iliad*. In book 4 Propertius states flatly that he himself is *Romanus Callimachus* (1. 64). Yet, programmatic elegies as early as book 1 make clear that Propertius intended right from the start to rival and even surpass Callimachus, not only as an elegist but also as an epic writer.

This ambition is clear, for example, in the appeal to Mimnermus at I. 9. 11. Mimnermus offered broader scope than Callimachus, who in his preface to the *Aetia* (11) had been critical of some aspects of the older poet's work. Yet, already in book 1 Propertius, impatient with Callimachean caution, is appropriating that larger model. The *Smyrneis* of Mimnermus (seventh century B.C.) in fact included the possibility of elegiac epic (Diehl, fr. 12A) in a rather more obvious sense than the narratives of Callimachus's *Aetia*.

The *Cynthius/Cynthia* pairing of II. 34 illustrates the same ambitious strategy. The first was Virgil's patron, the second Propertius's. A recurring feature of the poems is that so often, in the act of repudiating hackneyed epic, they exemplify by their sonorities and grandeur of imagination what real epic might be like; this maturing inclination explains the ultimate flowering of epic elegies in book 4. More generally, the poet's panoply of proper names, like that of the fashionable Euphorion, imitated by Gallus, rises beyond any merely elegiac need. Already in the second elegy of book 1 are gorgeous lines describing *Leucippis Phoebe* and *Hilaira,* her sister (15–16). (The loading of the pentameter to breaking point heard here is characteristic.)

The same must be said of Propertius's use of myth. Scholars, learned themselves, have naturally been tempted to find in Propertius's myths a display of learning. Why, though, would a poet of romantic love (as those same scholars have interpreted Propertius) wish to offer proof of bookish erudition? At times indeed he uses myth loosely and imprecisely, setting a Castalian tree, for example, on Mount Helicon (III. 3. 13). In his work, myth is an evocation of the suprahuman, transrational heroic world where the divine and stylized Cynthia may be at home. He uses myth to universalize, and that, rather than history (which in his case would have been to keep a diary of an affair), is what Aristotle said was the task of the poet (*Poetics* c. 9).

Consonant with all this evidence of rich poetic genius and of Propertius's sympathy with Varro's derivation of *vates* as *a vi mentis* (from the force of the mind), Propertius repeatedly asserts his *ingenium*. He uses the noun thirteen times. An old literary formula contrasted nature with nurture, talent with training or art (Horace, *Ars Poetica.* 408). In this dichotomy, Callimachus was usually thought to have emphasized art (*Aetia*–pref. 17). Yet, there is no passage in which Propertius lays programmatic claim to art, though he of all poets, identifying himself as the Roman Callimachus, might be thought to have need and justification for so doing. By contrast, in demanding immortality for his verses, he emphasizes his *ingenium* twice in one couplet (III. 2. 25–26). He has in this same elegy compared himself by implication with Homer (33–36).

Donatus notes Virgil's *vox et os et hypocrisis* (voice, delivery, and acting ability, *Vita Verg.* 29), all qualities of the actor. Propertius too must have shone in performance. A somewhat malicious skit by Horace of a contemporary who aims first to rival Callimachus and then Mimnermus (*Epp.* II. 2. 90–105) gives an impression of Propertius's affected and haughty demeanor on these occasions, which a more sympathetic eye might have viewed simply as the nervous mannerisms of a great virtuoso summoning all his powers. To judge by Propertius's own verses, his favorite audience was women. At III. 2. 10, with *turba puellarum* (crowd of girls), the despised Callimachean "crowd," because it is made up of girls, becomes acceptable. The deliberate ambiguity attending Cynthia's exact social status and identity may have been a ploy, enabling any girl in the audience to

SEX. AVRELII VMBRI ELEGIARVM
LIBER PRIMVS.

AD TVLLVM·

Ynthia prima suis miserum me ce
pit ocellis
c   Contactum nullis ante cupidini
bus,
Tum mihi constantis deiecit lumi
na fastus,
Et caput impositis pressit amor pedibus,
D onec me docuit castas odisse puellas
Improbus, & nullo uiuere consilio,
E t mihi iam toto furor hic non deficit anno,
Cum tamen aduersos cogor habere deos.
M imalion nullos fugiendo Tulle labores
Sæuitiam duræ contudit Iasidos.
N am modo partheniis amens errabat in antris,
Ibat & hirsutas ille uidere feras.
I lle etiam psillet percussus uulnere rami
Saucius arcadiis rupibus ingemuit,
E rgo uelocem potuit domuisse puellam,
Tantum in amore preces, & benefacta ualent,
I n me tardus amor nonullas cogitat artes,
Nec meminit notas (ut prius) ire uias.
A t uos deductæ quibus est fallacia lunæ,
Et labor in magicis sacra piare focis,
E n agedum dominæ mentem conuertite nostræ,
Et facite illa meo palleat ore magis,

a

Page from the 1502 edition of Propertius's Elegies *printed by Aldus Manutius of Venice (courtesy of the Lilly Library, Indiana University)*

hope that she was really the center of attention. Too much precision would have been counterproductive.

The poet, aiming to please this audience, claimed to be the hopeless slave of love. Yet, this language was far from novel. The Greeks knew of love as a slavery (Plato, Isocrates, Menander), and Gallus had spoken of Lycoris, for example, as his *domina* (mistress). However, (as with foppish Maecenas, with whom the poet explicitly compares himself in III. 9), behind the mask there was ambition, in this case the ambition of a writer who perhaps knew that his ancestors had lost a kingdom and was determined to use his genius to recover it. He defines his aim quite clearly (II. 34. 55–58): "Look at me! Only a small inheritance left in my house, and no triumph of any ancestor of mine in old campaigns, yet I am king at the party among a throng of girls, thanks to this talent of mine you so disparage." *Conviva* here suggests that Propertius's genius was displayed preeminently at the *convivium* (dinner party).

Yet, this sympathy with women in the poet must not obscure his feeling for the comedy of the relationship between the sexes. He is alert to Cynthia's foibles. He proposes to study Menander on a therapeutic trip to Athens (III. 21. 28), and his sense of human self-delusion often brings his elegies close to the spirit of the mime. The young lover of III. 6, eager for news of his mistress' reaction after a quarrel though more in love with love than her, will not allow his returning messenger, Lygdamus, to interrupt his own reconstruction of the scene he hopes Lygdamus found. In an elegy (I. 8) that has often been wrongly divided, the poet at first reports that Cynthia has decided to leave and steels himself for that parting. Then suddenly the reader discovers that after all Cynthia is to stay. She has yielded to poetry's charms. This ending reverses the usual topos by which the girl preferred hard cash (IV. 5. 53). However, well acted by a performer sensitive to his script's mercurial change of mood, the piece must have brought tears of sentimental mirth to the eyes of its sympotic audience.

Propertius's satire is part of the humor. Assaults on women were a long-standing resource of the iambic/satiric genre. Propertius, writing within these bounds, for the most part tones down the traditional sharpness. Toward the end of book 3 (poem 23) he signals his intention of changing his approach to love poetry by announcing that he has lost his writing tablets. The dismissal of Cynthia in the two subsequent elegies as a mere flibbertigibbet follows inevitably as part of the generic compulsion. In the next book, however, celebrating her death and resurrection, he exercises the sympotic freedom still alive whenever the party guest raises his glass to toast absent friends. Cynthia may be recalled from the dead at will by the simple act of reading Propertius's poems. The solemn commemoration of Cornelia, who from the grave delivers her own *apologia pro vita sua* (defense of her life) in the last elegy of all, is a variant of this gambit. Virgil had memorialized the inability of Orpheus to recover his dead Eurydice. Perhaps here Propertius solves the dilemma.

Yet, Propertius's poetic imagination ranges far more widely than the party and the boudoir. There are great campaigns stirring, notably against the Parthians (II. 10, III. 4). The new Caesar is also the new Pompey (III. 11). Rome is being rebuilt (IV. 1). Antony and his queen have lost to an inspired Roman leader, a new Romulus (IV. 6). Propertius's sense of epic is shown as early as the first elegy of all, with its abruptly intruded tale of Milanion, the hero who won Atalante by sharing her love of the hunt and its hardships, suffering a wound when she was attacked by centaurs. Epic and erotic worlds blend in the figure of the hero of love. This union anticipates the *heros/eros* topos familiar in medieval poetry such as Geoffrey Chaucer's "Knight's Tale" and shared with Ovid's *Metamorphoses* (*Cythereius heros*, xiii, 625; xiv. 584).

If at times for him love is a dangerously inviting ocean on whose shore he stands trembling, Propertius is also a painter of evocative seascapes. The Paetus elegy (III. 7) combines this feeling for the elemental sea with the poet's typical eye for the macabre, akin to the sensibility readers enjoy in Baudelaire's work and later (IV. 7) noticeable in the details of dead Cynthia's appearance. The shore easily blends into the threshold (*limen/litus:* compare with II. 14. 29–32). A recurrent fear surfaces. In a disturbingly powerful fantasy, the poet dreams that Cynthia has drowned (II. 26. 1–6). Marcellus's death is curiously described as a drowning (III. 18. 9).

There is also some metaphysical awareness. The four traditional Empedoclean elements rarely unite in Propertius's world for good. In II. 28, when his *puella* is ill, air (3), earth (4), and fire (5) occur first, but water (8) is destructive. Unexpectedly, the most dazzling and fruitful coition of air, water, earth, and fire occurs in the vatic celebration of Augustus's victory at Actium (IV. 6; notice air, 23; water, 26; earth, 27; fire, 29).

In general, the poet's vocabulary moves at a higher, "nobler" level than that of the Neoterics. He restricts the use of diminutives. Though he names Catullus among his predecessors (II. 34. 87), he has too good an opinion of himself fully to take over Catullus's self-deprecatory terms. He never uses *facetus, ineptie, lepidus/lepos, urbanus,* and certainly not *nugae. Diserta* occurs once (III. 23. 6).

Among his contemporaries, the poet is too easily associated (in the train of Quintilian) with Tibullus and Ovid, neither of whom was anything like as close to the regime of Augustus. He rather forms part of the great trio around Maecenas that included Virgil, whom he profoundly admired, and Horace, with whom he may have had a more difficult relationship, perhaps because of his too-bold imagination. Yet, whatever this personal animosity may or may not have been, Propertius is to be classed with Horace and Virgil. To invent a genre of Augustan elegy to accommodate the three elegiac poets of the day is to make interpretation doubly difficult. Elegy is not Augustan, and neither the themes found in Propertius's works, nor his techniques, nor his allegiance are ultimately those of the other two.

For all his talk about love, Propertius was chiefly interested in himself and his genius. His musical, resonant explorations of his inner world, including its phobias (particularly what has been noted as his "fear of drowning"), leave little room for another. Homer knew that the essence of any relationship between the sexes is dialogue (*Il.* XXII. 127), but Propertius never allows Cynthia to speak at length, least of all in answer to his hectoring. Her longest outburst is reserved for a poem when she is dead (IV. 7), and there the poet himself says nothing. Still less does Propertius describe Cynthia and her social ambience in any detail, though he is interested in painting a sympathetic picture of her character: her temper, her snobbery, her greed, and her vanity. His comic sense, of which these characteristics are evidence, is often that of *comédie noire*. Yet, he certainly had genius and, within the bounds he developed for the elegiac genre, Propertius wrote some of the most memorable poetry to survive from Roman antiquity.

Concordance:

Brigitte Schmeisser, *A Concordance to the Elegies of Propertius* (Hildesheim: Gerstenberg, 1972).

References:

Michael von Albrecht, *A History of Roman Literature,* 2 volumes (Leiden & New York: E. J. Brill, 1997), pp. 769–786;

Gian Biagio Conte, *Latin Literature: A History,* translated by Joseph B. Solodow, revised by Don Fowler and Glenn W. Most (Baltimore: Johns Hopkins University Press, 1994), pp. 331–339;

Rudolphus Helm, ed., *Fulgentius, Fabius Planciades, Opera* (Stuttgart: Teubner, 1898);

Margaret Hubbard, *Propertius* (London: Duckworth, 1974);

Saara Lilja, *The Roman Elegists' Attitude to Women* (Helsinki: Suomalainen Tiedeakatemia, 1965);

Georg Luck, *The Latin Love Elegy,* second edition (London: Methuen, 1969);

John Kevin Newman, *Augustan Propertius* (Hildesheim & New York: Olms, 1997);

H. Peter, *Historicorum Romanorum Reliquiae,* volume 1 (Leipzig: Teubner, 1914);

J. P. Sullivan, *Propertius: A Critical Introduction* (Cambridge: Cambridge University Press, 1976).

Quintilian

(ca. A.D. 40 – ca. A.D. 96)

Christopher P. Craig
University of Tennessee

MAJOR WORK: *Institutio Oratoria,* 12 books (The Education of the Orator, ca. A.D. 92–A.D. 94).

WORKS–LOST: *De causis corruptae eloquentiae* (On the Causes of Corrupted Eloquence, A.D. 89);

Pro Naevio Arpiniano, speech (For Naevius of Arpinum);

"Duo libri artis rhetoricae," notes on Quintilian's lectures.

WORKS–ATTRIBUTED: *Declamationes Maiores* and *Declamationes Minores,* ascribed to Quintilian.

Editiones principes: . . . *M. Fabi Quintiliani Institutionum oratoriarum ad Victorium Marcellum liber xxii [sic] et ultimus explicit,* edited by J. A. Campanus (Rome: Joannes Philippus de Lignamine, 1470); *Dialogus de Oratoribus seu De Causis corruptae eloquentiae,* edited by C. A. Heumann (Göttingen, 1719).

Standard editions: *M. Fabi Quintiliani Institutionis oratoriae libri duodecim,* edited by C. Halm (Leipzig: Teubner, 1868–1869; revised by Ferdinand Otto Meister, 1886–1887); *M. Fabi Quintiliani Institutionis Oratoriae Libri XII,* 2 volumes, edited by Ludwig Radermacher (Leipzig: Teubner, 1907, 1935; revised by Vinzenz Buchheit, 1959); *M. Fabi Quintiliani Institutionis Oratoriae Libri Duodecim,* 2 volumes, edited by Michael Winterbottom (Oxford: Clarendon Press, 1970); *Declamationes XIX Maiores Quintiliano falso ascriptae,* edited by Lennart Håkanson (Stuttgart: Teubner, 1982); *The Minor Declamations Ascribed to Quintilian,* edited, with commentary, by Winterbottom (Berlin: de Gruyter, 1984); *M. Fabii Quintiliani Declamationes minores,* edited by D. R. Shackleton Bailey (Stuttgart: Teubner, 1989).

Translations in English: *The Institutio Oratoria of Quintilian,* 4 volumes, edited and translated by H. E. Butler, Loeb Classical Library, (Cambridge, Mass.: Harvard University Press, 1920–1922); *The Major Declamations Ascribed to Quintilian,* translated by Lewis A. Sussman (Frankfurt am Main & New York: Peter Lang, 1987).

Commentaries: *De Institutione oratoria libri duodecim,* 4 volumes, edited by G. L. Spalding (Leipzig: Siegfried Lebrecht Crusius, 1798-1816); volume 5 added by C. T. Zumpt, 1829; volume 6 (lexicon) added by E. Bonnell, 1834; *Quintilien. Institution oratoire,* 7 volumes, edited and translated by Jean Cousin (Paris: Les Belles Lettres, 1975-1980); *De Institutione oratoria liber primus,* edited by Charles Fierville (Paris: Firmin-Didot, 1890); *M. Fabii Quintiliani Institutiones Oratoriae: Liber I,* edited, with commentary, by F. H. Colson (Cambridge: University Press, 1924); *Institutionis oratoriae liber III,* edited by Joachim Adamietz (Munich: W. Fink, 1966); *The Tenth and Twelfth Books of the Institutions of Quintilian,* edited by H. S. Frieze (New York: Appleton, 1865); *M. Fabi Quintiliani Institutionis Oratoriae Liber Decimus,* edited by W. Peterson (Oxford: Clarendon Press, 1891); *M. Fabi Quintiliani institutionis oratoriae liber duodecimus,* edited by A. Beltrami (Rome & Milan: Società editrice Dante Alighieri di Alibrighi, 1910); *Quintiliani Institutionis oratoriae liber XII,* edited by R. G. Austin (Oxford: Clarendon Press, 1948).

Quintilian (Marcus Fabius Quintilianus) was a teacher of rhetoric and an orator at Rome in the late first century A.D. His only surviving work, *Institutio Oratoria* (The Education of the Orator, ca. A.D. 92–A.D. 94), asserts the educational ideal of the perfect orator, which he sums up in Cato the Censor's phrase *"vir bonus dicendi peritus"* (a good man skilled in speaking, 12.1.1). In a treatment of unprecedented scope, Quintilian sets out to describe both the characteristics and the development of this ideal orator from cradle through retirement. In doing so he presents a rare and influential discussion of primary education, provides the most coherent single treatment of the course of formal education in Rome, offers an indispensable compendium of theoretical and practical information about classical rhetoric and oratory, and, through the readings he suggests as models of style, proffers brief but long-enduring

Portrait-bust of the emperor Galba, who brought Quintilian to Rome in A.D. 68

judgments about standard Greek and Roman authors who preceded him.

Although today Quintilian is not a household word except among classicists, historians of education, and scholars of speech communication, he enjoyed enormous popularity in the Renaissance and beyond. The recovery of a complete text of his work by the distinguished Italian scholar Poggio Bracciolini (1380–1459) in 1416 was celebrated, and his manuscripts bear the comments of such humanists as Lorenzo Valla. After the invention of printing, *The Education of the Orator* went through approximately six hundred editions, winning praise from temperaments as diverse as Erasmus, Martin Luther, and Alexander Pope.

Of Quintilian's life, little is known with certainty. He was born in perhaps A.D. 40 in Calagurris in Hispania Tarraconensis, the modern Spanish town of Cahorres, on the Tagus River near Barcelona. His father practiced declamation (9.3.73) and so may have been a teacher of rhetoric. Of Quintilian's mother noth-

ing is known. The family must have been affluent, for at some point Quintilian went to Rome to pursue his education. That education, as for any young man of aristocratic background or ambition in this period, was focused upon public speaking. His teachers may have included the learned but personally dissolute grammarian Remmius Palaemon. They certainly included the famous orator Domitius Afer (5.7.7). Probably in A.D. 59, and thus at perhaps the age of nineteen, Quintilian returned to his home in Spain, where he probably took an active role in the local courts. In A.D. 68 the Roman governor of Quintilian's province, Galba, brought Quintilian back to Rome with him when he entered the city as Emperor. Galba's reign lasted only until the middle of January in A.D. 69, the "year of the four emperors" that ended with the ascendency of Vespasian and the Flavian dynasty. Quintilian remained in Rome, where he opened a school of rhetoric and was active as a pleader in the courts. He became wealthy and famous and is hailed by his fellow Spaniard Martial (*Epigrams* 2.90) as the "greatest guide of errant youth and glory of the Roman toga." As a pleader, Quintilian was esteemed enough to be invited by Queen Berenice of Judaea to plead for her in a proceeding in which she also presided (4.1.19). He numbered the younger Pliny among his students (Pliny, *Epistles*, 2.14.10). Probably in the A.D. 70s under Vespasian (compare with Suetonius, *Life of Vespasian,* 18; Jerome's date of A.D. 88 must be incorrect), Quintilian became the first professor to receive a salary from the state treasury. After twenty years of teaching (1. pref. 1) he retired from his school in A.D. 88. Soon, however, he was asked to undertake the burden of educating Flavius Clemens's two young sons, whom the emperor Domitian was grooming to succeed him (4. pref.). At this time Quintilian was given another mark of favor, the right to wear the *ornamenta consularia* (insignia of one who had served as consul).

Quintilian's public success was balanced by deep personal loss. In his early forties he had married a much younger woman of good family. She gave him two sons before she died in her nineteenth year. The younger of these boys then died at the age of five, probably in A.D. 89. The older son died four years later. Quintilian's expression of bereavement and grief (6. pref.) is the most poignant passage in his work. The date of Quintilian's own death is uncertain, but there is no evidence that he was alive after A.D. 95.

Several works, now lost, preceded *The Education of the Orator* and are reflected in it. In A.D. 89 Quintilian published a treatise, *De Causis Corruptae Eloquentiae* (On the Causes of Corrupted Eloquence, 6.pref.3; 8.6.76). The theme of the degeneration of eloquence was a common one in first-century-A.D. Rome and is reflected as well in the works of Seneca Rhetor, Petronius, and Tacitus. Quintilian also says that students, without his permission, had published error-laden versions of notes from two sets of lectures that he had given (1.pref.7). Since much of the basis for his book is in his lecture notes, Quintilian's publication served to correct these pirated versions. He also published one of his courtroom speeches, *Pro Naevio Arpiniano* (For Naevius of Arpinum), impelled, he says, by a youthful desire for glory. Other speeches were published without his permission (7.2.24). Finally, in antiquity there were attached to Quintilian's name two sets of declamations; the nineteen *Declamationes Maiores* are far more fanciful than the themes that Quintilian recommends. On the other hand, of the 388 *Declamationes Minores,* the 145 that survive are not inconsistent with his teachings; they might be Quintilian's own, but there is no evidence that they are.

Quintilian undertook his sole surviving work, *The Education of the Orator,* after he had retired from teaching in A.D. 88. In an accompanying letter to his bookseller Trypho, Quintilian says that he had taken more than two years in the research and writing and had wanted to take more time still if his friends had not pressured him to publish. *The Education of the Orator* was probably written during the time A.D. 92–94 and was probably published before the assassination of the emperor Domitian in A.D. 96, since Quintilian takes some pains to flatter the despot (especially in 10.1.91–92). The work is dedicated to Quintilian's friend Marcellus Vitorius, who found a special use for it in educating his son Geta (1.pref.6). In fact, Quintilian regularly addresses his remarks to teachers rather than students. His stated purpose is to describe completely the education of the perfect orator, who can only attain perfection if he is a good man (1.pref.9). Quintilian undertakes this program in twelve book-rolls, which some later editor divided into the chapters used in citing the work today. Quintilian gives the structure of his work (1.pref.21–22) as follows: book 1 treats the part of education before the work of the rhetoric teacher; book 2 covers the basics and nature of rhetoric; books 3–7 are concerned with invention and arrangement; books 8–11 are concerned with style, including memory and delivery (book 10, including his list of authors for the trained orator to read, is oddly inserted in the treatment of style); finally, book 12 describes the complete orator–his character, his rationale for becoming involved with cases, the nature of his eloquence, when he ought to retire, and what he should do after retirement.

To understand Quintilian's project, readers must appreciate the educational traditions of his time. Publicly funded education was foreign to Rome. Children were either educated at home or sent off, between the ages of five and seven, to a primary school where an underpaid teacher drilled by rote (and beat the unpromising) until they mastered the rudiments of reading, writing, and simple sums. After this process, which took perhaps two years, children might attend the grammar school, where they studied the poets with an eye to understanding grammar (including correct use of language and correct reading) and composition. Since the social and economic elite were bilingual, a young student might attend the grammar school in Greek or Latin or both.

Finally, children of the wealthiest classes might study under a teacher of rhetoric, again in Greek or Latin or both. With him they might read prose authors, do further exercises in composition, study rhetorical theory, and perform practice speeches, called declamations. This higher education, which provided a badge of status and culture, had the avowed purpose of training the student as a public speaker, ready to take a leading role in public affairs.

As a teacher of rhetoric, Quintilian's greatest source of annoyance is the way in which declamation, as practiced in most contemporary schools, has hobbled the ability of students to deal with real-life situations (2.10.5ff.; 8pref.26ff.; 8.2.17–21, and elsewhere). Instead, it has developed in would-be orators a propensity for grand speeches on completely fanciful topics, with which students learn to showcase their talents in a style heavy with tortured expressions and pithy maxims. This training encourages speeches that may evoke applause but will hardly coax a verdict from a sensible jury. Quintilian compares some contemporary teachers of declamation to slave dealers who procure soft, effeminate boys to satisfy the perverse tastes of their customers, then castrate their chattels to bring a further accentuation of their softness (5.12.17ff.).

The one historical personage who is at once Quintilian's greatest example of the qualities that these cloistered declaimers lack, the most copious single source of examples for points of both argument and style, and the most nearly perfect orator, is Cicero (106–43 B.C.): "Let one who will especially enjoy Cicero know that he has made progress" (10.1.112). Cicero has several attractions for Quintilian. Although dead for more than a hundred years by Quintilian's time, Cicero still stands in Quintilian's view as Rome's most gifted and proficient orator, "the name not of a man, but of eloquence" (10.1.112). Further, Cicero was also a practicing orator who wrote rhetorical treatises, including his masterpiece *On the Orator* and his later essay *The Orator,* an exploration of the perfect orator focused almost exclusively on style. These works are the sources of the most extensive single quotations in Quintilian's work (9.1.26–36, 37–45). More important, Cicero's work *On the Orator* was specifically concerned

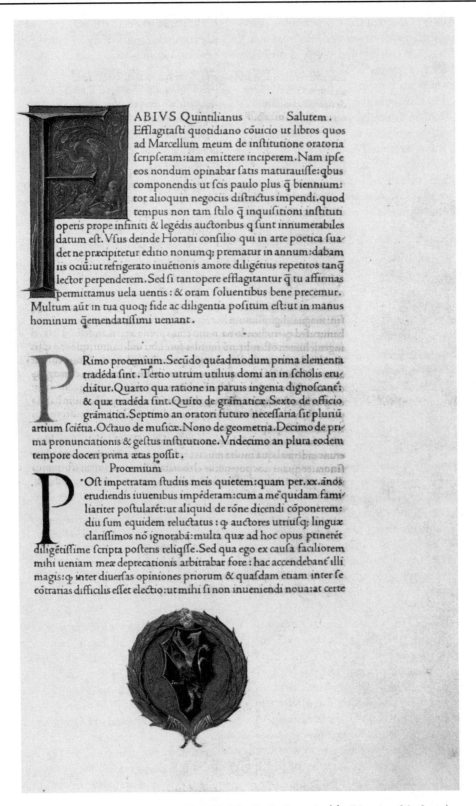

ABIVS Quintilianus   Salutem.
Efflagitafti quotidiano cõuicio ut libros quos
ad Marcellum meum de inftitutione oratoria
fcripferam:iam emittere inciperem.Nam ipfe
eos nondum opinabar fatis maturauiffe:qbus
componendis ut fcis paulo plus q̃ biennium:
tot alioquin negociis diftrictus impendi.quod
tempus non tam ftilo q̃ inquifitioni inftituti
operis prope infiniti & legédis auctoribus q funt innumerabiles
datum eft.Vfus deinde Horatii confilio qui in arte poetica fua
det ne præcipitetur editio nonumq; prematur in annum:dabam
iis ociũ:ut refrigerato inuétionis amore diligétius repetitos tanq̃
lector perpenderem.Sed fi tantopere efflagitantur q̃ tu affirmas
permittamus uela uentis:& oram foluentibus bene precemur.
Multum aũt in tua quoq; fide ac diligentia pofitum eft:ut in manus
hominum q̃emendatiffimi ueniant.

Rimo prooemium.Secũdo quéadmodum prima elementa
tradéda fint.Tertio utrũm utilius domi an in fcholis eru
diátur.Quarto qua ratione in paruis ingenia dignofcant:
& quæ tradéda fint.Quĩto de grãmaticæ.Sexto de officio
grãmatici.Septimo an oratori futuro neceffaria fit pluriũ
artium fciétia.Octauo de muficæ.Nono de geometria.Decimo de pri
ma pronunciationis & geftus inftitutione.Vndecimo an plura eodem
tempore doceri prima ætas poffit.
          Prooemium

Oft impetratam ftudiis meis quietem:quam per.xx.ãnós
erudiendis iuuenibus impéderam:cum a mé quidam fami
liariter poftularét:ut aliquid de rõne dicendi cõponerem:
diu fum equidem reluctatus : q̃ auctores utriufq; linguæ
clariffimos nõ ignorabã:multa quæ ad hoc opus ptinerét
diligétiffime fcripta pofteris reliqffe.Sed qua ego ex caufa faciliorem
mihi ueniam meæ deprecationis arbitrabar fore : hac accendebant illi
magis:q̃ inter diuerfas opiniones priorum & quafdam etiam inter fe
cõtrarias difficilis effet electio:ut mihi fi non inueniendi noua:at certe

Page from a 1471 Venetian edition of Quintilian's Institutio Oratoria *(The Education of the Orator)*

to describe the ideal orator and to argue that broad learning was essential for that ideal. Cicero had both expounded and realized so much of what was to become Quintilian's educational goal that the rhetorician views Cicero with obvious reverence. This reverence, however, is neither blind devotion nor quixotic antiquarianism; Quintilian does occasionally disagree with the earlier orator (for example at 3.2.4; 4.2.64; 7.3.8; 9.1.25; 9.4.79). Further, Quintilian's own style, while it certainly avoids the faults that he imputes to the unrealistic declaimers, is not simply an attempt to ape Cicero. Quintilian wants to set a standard that will render the student an effective speaker in his own time, as Cicero had been in his.

In book 1 Quintilian literally starts molding his ideal orator in the cradle. Quintilian's great guiding principle is nature, and his ideal orator must have natural talent, or training will not bring him to success. Still, more generally, mental activity is as natural to humans as flight is to birds (1.1.1), and education will benefit any child. If a child stops wanting to learn, such reluctance must be due to the neglect of his education (1.1.2). As for the future orator, no detail of upbringing is trivial. The wet nurse must have a proper accent (1.1.4). The pedagogue, who attends to the child's education until he has learned his letters, must be similarly appropriate in his accent and in his character. The parents, even if less educated themselves, must be committed to helping their child excel. Quintilian then goes on to describe how the child's education will progress. He will start Greek, followed quickly enough by Latin, on through the learning of the alphabet, then on to the experiences (described by Quintilian) that he should have in grammar school. Throughout, Quintilian's good sense and rare attention to child psychology are apparent. There is no reason for a child to delay learning until the usual age for primary studies. Young children can learn an enormous amount, as long as the work is presented as play, and the memory of youngsters is especially retentive (1.1.16–20). Quintilian is neither revolutionary nor doctrinaire. He is fundamentally humane, and he insists that educational methods should work. Most famously, he breaks with tradition by expressing absolute opposition to corporal punishment on the grounds that it is ineffectual, can permanently damage a student's character and (as is suggested today) mental health, and gives adults a power that is too easily abused (1.3.13–17).

While Quintilian's ideal orator had learned his letters at home, at the grammar-school level and beyond, home schooling is no longer a proper option; any of the negative influences of the school may just as easily occur at home, and children need to be comfortable in the group and to be stimulated by the competition that the group provides (1.2.1–15). Quintilian's ideal young student (1.3.6–7) is much like the young Quintilian himself, one who is stimulated by praise, wants to succeed, weeps when he fails, thrives on ambition, smarts under criticism, and is driven by honor. He applies himself to grammar, and under a classroom regimen that Quintilian carefully describes, reads Homer, Virgil, and other poets, although he certainly will not read love poetry (1.8.5ff.). The student will also begin oral exercises, such as the retelling of fables, and written compositions, such as paraphrasing passages of poetry. All of these steps are broadly traditional. Finally, whether driven by the broad learning of Cicero's ideal orator or by the general education of the Greeks, Quintilian argues at some length that his future orator should broaden his education with the study of geometry, music, and perhaps even physical exercises that develop grace (1.10).

In book 2, the teacher of grammar yields to the rhetorician. Rhetoric had been Quintilian's calling for twenty years, and his famous description of an effective teacher reveals the man:

> Above all, the teacher should assume toward his students the attitude of a parent and he should regard himself as having stepped into the place of those from whom the children came to him. He should have no vices himself nor tolerate them in others. His strictness ought not to be grim, nor his fellowship unrestrained: the former produces dislike, the latter contempt. He should have much to say about what is honorable and good, for the more often he admonishes, the rarer will he censure. He should not be easily provoked, but neither should he wear a fair face toward what ought to be corrected. He should be straightforward in teaching, hardworking, persistent rather than excessive. He should willingly answer those who question him and himself question those who do not. In praising the work of his pupils he ought to be neither stingy nor effusive, because the one begets discouragement and the other overconfidence. In criticizing what needs correction, he should not be sarcastic nor at all abusive, for many are frightened off from their course of study by the fact that someone finds fault with them as though he hates them. The teacher himself should have something to say, should even have much to say, which his hearers will remember. Although there are enough examples for imitation to be found in reading, still, the living voice, as it is called, gives fuller nourishment and especially the voice of a teacher whom pupils both love and respect if they have been rightly educated. One can hardly exaggerate how enthusiastically we imitate those whom we favor. (2.2.4–8; translated by George A. Kennedy)

From the beginning, when he discusses the definition of rhetoric (2.15), Quintilian takes pains to cite earlier authorities and to indicate where he agrees or

Engraved portrait of Poggio Bracciolini, an Italian scholar who recovered a complete text of Quintilian's work in 1416

parts: invention or the discovery of arguments (books 3–6), arrangement (book 7), style (books 8, 9, and 11), memory, and delivery (book 11). The account of rhetorical instruction is compendious and balanced, intended to be effective rather than original. It includes several important points. The treatment of invention and arrangement provides the most complete Latin source for the theory of stasis (books 3 and 7) and gives detailed instruction on the proper functions of all the parts of speech, including a full discussion of the rhetorical traditions of deductive and inductive argument (book 5). Quintilian gives the first extant treatment of the handling of witnesses (5.7.3–32) and, in his treatment of the peroration, a wonderfully detailed discussion of the rousing of emotions, a task that Quintilian, like Cicero, considers the most important part of persuasion (6.1–2). After a concise summary of all that he has undertaken in books 3–7, Quintilian announces that style is more important than what he has already said (8. pref.). His discussion, initially organized around the four virtues of style–Latinity, clarity, ornament, and appropriateness–includes under "ornament" examples of more than one hundred figures (books 8–9) and a lengthy substantive discussion of appropriateness (11.1), a characteristic that previous rhetoricians tended to avoid because it could not be generalized. After his discussion of memory techniques (11.2), Quintilian offers the best ancient treatment of delivery–with remarks on voice, meticulous instructions about gesture, and even prescriptions about the arrangement of the orator's clothing (11.3).

The most famous part of *The Education of the Orator* is Quintilian's discussion of Greek and then of Latin literature in book 10. It takes its position after his discussion of the first three virtues of style–Latinity, clarity, and ornament–and before his treatment of the final stylistic virtue, appropriateness. Oddly, he places here his views on the practice that must follow the inculcation of theory if the student is to be an effective speaker. That practice takes the form of reading, writing, and speaking and so leads to his review of Greek and Roman authors who have something to teach the orator. While Quintilian offers some judgments that go beyond this brief, his purpose is, as ever, instructional. It is also explicitly not exhaustive (10.1.44–45). So, standard authors in Greek and Roman literary history may be omitted completely, as is Sappho, or oddly classified, as is Catullus, who is treated solely as an author of invective iambics (10.1.96).

Quintilian's remarks on genres, however, are a window into ancient literary criticism, while his comments on individual authors, as famous as they are brief, have continued to illumine and amuse. Much of his material, especially on the Greek side, is traditional.

disagrees. This procedure is standard and is an important part of what makes his compendium invaluable for historians of rhetoric. In this fundamental case Quintilian disagrees with all authorities who have defined rhetoric as the art of persuasion, a group that includes Cicero in his works *On Invention* and *On the Orator*. Quintilian further rejects Aristotle's definition (which he slightly garbles) of rhetoric as the facility for discovering the available means of persuasion. Instead, Quintilian's rhetoric, following a Stoic definition, is simply the science of speaking well. The persuasion-based definitions are unacceptable to him because he thinks it is necessary for his ideal orator to be morally good, and such goodness might lead to failure to persuade an audience that is less good. Quintilian later points out that Socrates was not persuasive but was true to his own character. This moral virtue was not useful to gain Socrates an acquittal but was good for him as a person, a fact that is more important (11.1.11). Quintilian's "science of speaking well" means not only speaking effectively but doing so with good moral intentions, whatever the outcome.

After the preliminaries of book 2, Quintilian's presentation of rhetoric follows the traditional five

On the Latin side, he shows more originality. Quintilian begins by noting the importance for the orator of reading poetry, history, and philosophy; he then reviews worthwhile authors by genre in Greek, then Latin. Poetry can teach inspiration in choice of material, sublimity in choice of words, emotional power, and effective character depiction. It also can refresh one tired from the law courts. It is like the oratory of display rather than that of the senate or the courts. It aims only at pleasure, and its style is not to be confused with the more varied and serious business of the practicing orator (10.1.30). The style of history (10.1.31–34) is like poetry without meter, and its proper excellence is in narrative rather than proof. It is designed not for the courtroom but for recording past events and winning glory for its author. Focused as he is upon style, Quintilian recognizes the value of history for supplying examples in arguments but notes that history is outside his present scope. Philosophers treat subjects that originally belonged to orators but that have now been left to those of lesser speaking ability. This attitude is the rhetorician's standard view of the so-called quarrel between rhetoric and philosophy, one that Quintilian expresses at greater length elsewhere in the work (1. pref. 10ff.; 12.2.5ff.) and that the much more philosophical Cicero had expressed before him (for example, *On the Orator*, 3.15). Quintilian suggests that the orator read Stoic discussions of what is just, honorable, and expedient and turn to the Socratics for the techniques of exchanges with opposing counsel and the examination of witnesses (10.1.35).

Among individual authors, Homer is of course supreme among epic poets, and he has given at once the origin and the examples for all parts of eloquence (10.1.46–51). In the canon of nine lyric poets, Pindar is supreme, with his magnificence of inspiration, his maxims, his figures, his exquisite abundance of material and words, and his virtual river of eloquence (10.1.61). In tragedy, Euripides excites greater pity than Sophocles (10.1.68). In history, Thucydides is dense and brief and always urgent; Herodotus is sweet and clear and full (10.1.73). Among the orators, Demosthenes is the first and almost the pattern of speaking—so great is his force and his compactness, so focused with a kind of muscular tension, with nothing otiose, so that there is neither anything lacking nor anything redundant in him (10.1.76). As for philosophers, Plato is supreme not only in acuity but also in his virtually divine and Homeric capacity for eloquence (10.1.81).

Among Roman authors, Virgil is the greatest poet, second only to Homer. And as Domitius Afer had said, Virgil is closer to first than to third (10.1.86). Oddly, given Quintilian's goal of finding models for imitation, he mentions Lucretius as a poet worth read-ing, while explicitly excluding him as a model of style because he is "difficult," presumably in his subject matter rather than his diction (10.1.87). Ennius, in a famous description, Quintilian reverences like an ancient grove of oaks—more venerable than beautiful (10.1.88). Ovid is playful, even in writing epic, and is too much a lover of his own talent, but he is praiseworthy in parts (10.1.88). Lucan is passionate and excited and most outstanding for his pithy phrases but (a bizarre criticism, given Quintilian's goals) is more to be imitated by orators than by poets (10.1.90). In elegy, Quintilian asserts, Romans also challenge the Greeks. Tibullus seems to him especially terse and elegant, although "There are those who prefer Propertius" (10.1.93). Satire is completely Roman (10.1.93). Of Roman lyric poets Horace is almost the only one worth reading. He raises his tone from time to time, is full of charm and grace, varied in his figures, and happily bold in his word choice (10.1.96). In comedy Quintilian finds the Romans "especially lame" (10.1.99). In history, on the other hand, the immortal rapidity of Sallust compares well with Thucydides. Quintilian had already noted Livy's milky richness (10.1.32) and here compares Livy to Herodotus (10.1.101–102).

Above all it is in oratory that Romans equal the Greeks. Cicero is as much to be studied as Demosthenes. Quintilian treats this statement as controversial and is at pains to note that Demosthenes' works should be not only studied but also memorized. Demosthenes and Cicero have in common their judgment; effective arrangement; method of dividing, preparing, and proving; and all gifts concerned with the invention of arguments (10.1.106). Their styles contrast, for nothing can be taken from Demosthenes, nothing added to Cicero (10.1.106). Cicero is superior in wit and in exciting pity. Demosthenes is clearly superior in coming first in time so that Cicero could use him as a model. The ensuing praise of Cicero is well summarized with the famous tag that his is the name not of a person, but of eloquence (10.1.112). Although Quintilian follows the custom of declining to mention authors who are still living, clearly he is not a mere antiquarian reactionary. The best advocates of his own time rival the ancients, and the youth hold great promise for the future (10.1.122).

Turning to Roman writers on philosophy, Quintilian finds that Cicero stands out again, his style rivaling that of Plato (10.1.123). While Quintilian tries to be generous to Seneca, he finds that much in the philosopher's writing is "corrupt in expression and to this extent the more pernicious, because it is rich in pleasant vices. If only he had spoken his own mind but followed the stylistic judgment of others, had not lusted after what was incorrect, had not loved all his own productions, and had not shattered the gravity of his material with pithy little maxims, he would have been approved by the judgment of the wise rather than by the love of students" (10.1.130).

Although these judgments make book 10 the most famous part of Quintilian's work, he makes his own greatest claim to originality for his detailed description of the practices of his "good man skilled in speaking" after this ideal orator has left the school. Even Cicero, his sole predecessor, had only characterized the speech of the perfect orator. Quintilian tries to give the perfect orator a certain character and to assign his duties (12.pref.4). He includes a discussion of what cases to take, whether or not to accept payment, the need to retire before one's powers have diminished too far, and how to spend that retirement (not surprisingly, in instructing the young). He insists at the outset, as he has from the beginning of the work, that the ideal orator must be morally good or else he cannot be perfectly eloquent. This unswerving moral position is Quintilian's hallmark. It stands at variance with the life experience of many of his readers, ancient and modern, and with the perceived moral inconsistencies that mark the lives of his great models, Demosthenes and Cicero. Quintilian insists, however, that he is aiming at an ideal and that just because that ideal has not been attained is no reason to think that it cannot be.

In light of Quintilian's work and times, his ideal orator raises two principal problems. The first is that by endorsing deception in the practice of oratory he seems to undercut his absolute insistence on the speaker's integrity. Quintilian tackles this problem head-on, arguing at length (12.1.36ff.) that there are circumstances in which what is right and good can be served only by deception, defending a would-be tyrannicide before his intended victim, for example. The key seems to be that the orator knows what is right and will use the process to insure a right outcome. Unlike Cicero, who might defend a guilty man because "the populace desires it, custom demands it, human feeling permits it" (*On Moral Duties,* 2.51), Quintilian's ideal orator will defend the guilty, or otherwise deceive his hearers, only if he feels that a greater good is served by doing so.

A second common criticism of Quintilian concerns his choice of arena for his ideal orator, who will devote only a small part of his energy to the law courts but will shine when the senate must be swayed and the errors of the common folk corrected and when troops must be rallied for battle (12.1.26ff). Some have called his view the vision of an ivory-tower academic, an anachronism in a world where Caesar rather than the Senate is the decision-maker in the state and where the orator's scope, like that of Quintilian as a practicing speaker, is simply confined to the law courts. His later contemporary Tacitus, in his *Dialogue Concerning Orators,* had argued that eloquence had declined because its preconditions had disappeared. And Tacitus had given up oratory for the writing of history.

One might reply that Quintilian was first and foremost a teacher. He believed that progress in eloquence was possible and desirable. If he set an unrealistic goal for the political conditions of his time, his was not a vicious error. His pupils, then and later, have perhaps been better served by his apparent naïveté than they could have been by the relentless, brilliant cynicism of a Tacitus.

References:

Stanley Frederick Bonner, *Education in Ancient Rome: From the Elder Cato to the Younger Pliny* (London: Methuen / Berkeley: University of California Press, 1977);

Bonner, *Roman Declamation in the Late Republic and Early Empire* (Liverpool: University Press of Liverpool, 1949);

M. L. Clarke, "Quintilian on Education," in *Empire and Aftermath: Silver Latin II,* edited by T. A. Dorey (London & Boston: Routledge & Kegan Paul, 1975), pp. 98–118;

Clarke, *Rhetoric at Rome* (London: Cohen & West, 1953);

Jean Cousin, *Etudes sur Quintilien* (Paris: Boivin, 1936);

George A. Kennedy, *The Art of Rhetoric in the Roman World* (Princeton, N.J.: Princeton University Press, 1972), pp. 487–514;

Kennedy, "An Estimate of Quintilian," *American Journal of Philology,* 83 (1962): 130–146;

Kennedy, *Quintilian* (New York: Twayne, 1969);

A. D. Leeman, *Orationis Ratio: The Stylistic Theories and Practice of the Roman Orators, Historians, and Philosophers,* 2 volumes (Amsterdam: Hakkert, 1963), pp. 287–310;

Michael Winterbottom, *Problems in Quintilian, Bulletin of the Institute for Classical Studies,* Supplement 25 (1970);

Winterbottom, "Quintilian and Rhetoric," in *Empire and Aftermath,* pp. 79–97.

Winterbottom, "Quintilian and the *Vir Bonus,*" *Journal of Roman Studies,* 54 (1964): 90–97;

Sallust

(ca. 86 B.C. – 35 B.C.)

Robert W. Ulery Jr.
Wake Forest University

MAJOR WORKS: *Catilina* (The War of Catiline, ca. 42 B.C.);

Jugurtha (The War with Jugurtha, 40 B.C.);

Historiae, survives in fragments (Histories, ca. 35 B.C.).

Editio princeps: [*Catilina* and *Jugurtha*] (Venice: Vindelinus de Spira, 1470); [fragments of the *Histories*], edited by Ludovicus Carrio (Antwerp, 1573–1574).

Standard editions: *Catilina, Iugurtha, Fragmenta Ampliora,* edited by Alfons Kurfess (Leipzig: Teubner, 1957); *Catilina, Jugurtha, Fragments des Histoires,* edited and translated by Alfred Ernout, third edition (Paris: Les Belles Lettres, 1958); *Catilina, Iugurtha, Historiarum Fragmenta Selecta, Appendix Sallustiana,* edited by L. D. Reynolds (Oxford: Clarendon Press, 1991); *Historiae,* edited by Bertold Maurenbrecher (Leipzig: Teubner, 1891–1893); *Appendix Sallustiana: Epistulae ad Caesarem, Invectivae,* edited by Kurfess (Leipzig: Teubner, 1962); *Pseudo-Salluste: Lettres à César, Invectives,* edited by Ernout (Paris: Les Belles Lettres, 1962); *Invektive und Episteln,* edited and translated with commentary by Karl Vretska (Heidelberg: C. Winter, 1961).

Translations in English: *Sallust,* edited and translated by J. C. Rolfe, Loeb Classical Library (Cambridge, Mass.: Harvard University Press, 1931; revised, 1965); *The Jugurthine War; The Conspiracy of Catiline,* translated by S. A. Handford (Harmondsworth, U.K. & New York: Penguin, 1963); *The Histories,* translated by Patrick McGushin (Oxford: Oxford University Press, 1992–1994).

C. Sallustius Crispus, Rome's first great historian, entered public life in the crisis of Rome's external expansion and internal revolution; he retired from that public life to write history that survived, in part, the fall of the Empire and achieved a fame that remained virtually intact through the Renaissance. In antiquity Sallust was considered on a par with Thucydides, and during

Sallust (medallion in the Museo Nazionale Romano, Rome)

the Renaissance he was seen as a worthy member of a *quadriga* of Roman historians, with Caesar, Livy, and Tacitus. He was distinguished for the distinctive voice and style he established for himself, an historiographical art of immediate appeal and a moral/political passion that both enlivens the narrative and helps to justify inclusion in the canon.

No ancient biography of Sallust survives (although Q. Asconius Pedianus is said by an ancient commentator on Horace to have written one), and the many *testimonia* are not always trustworthy, as his political and literary reputation inspired early polemics that alleged a life at variance with the moral tone of his writings. Alfons Kurfess's edition of the monographs provides selected *testimonia* (pp. xxii–xxxi); they include (for the biographical details) Asconius's commentary on Cicero's *Pro Milone,* the *Bellum Africanum,* Suetonius, Aulus Gellius, Dio Cassius, Appian, pseudo-Acron on Horace, and Orosius. Information from what purports to be an invective against Sallust by Cicero (probably false and of Augustan date) is not reliable. These references and the autobiographical comments Sallust makes in the proems to his works provide a rather sketchy outline of his political and military career.

Sallust was born in, or at any rate hailed from, Amiternum, a town in the mountainous Sabine region north and west of Rome; the year was 87 B.C. (Jerome) or 86 B.C. *(Chronicon Paschale)*. Nothing further is known of his early life, but presumably he was educated at Rome. He states that already in his youth he was (like many) eagerly drawn to a political career (*Cat.* 3.3: *sed ego adulescentulus initio sicuti plerique studio ad rem publicam latus sum*). That career could have begun as usual with a quaestorship (there is no attestation), for which 55 B.C. is a possible year, or, as Sir Ronald Syme says in *Sallust* (1964), Sallust could have entered the Senate when he became tribune of the plebians in 52 B.C. In the latter year, evidence from several sources places him in the troubled political environment of the period; Asconius says that with his fellow plebeian tribunes Sallust delivered hostile speeches about Milo (on trial for the murder of Clodius) and Cicero (his defender).

Sallust was expelled from the Senate in 50 B.C. (by the censor Appius Claudius Pulcher), probably in retaliation for actions as tribune in the party strife of that period, rather than for sexual misconduct as reported in the *testimonia*–for example, ps.-Acron (on Horace, *S.* 1.2.47 and 49):

> Sallustius Crispus is said to have been caught by Annius Milo committing adultery with Fausta, Sulla's daughter, and beaten with whips, as indicated by Q. Asconius Pedianus in a biography of him. . . . This was raised in objection by the censors to Sallust himself in the senate. At that point he swore that he was a pursuer not of married women but of freedwomen, and for that reason he was expelled from the senate, something for which he defends himself in the *Catiline*.

Gellius (17.18) on M. Varro's authority repeats part of this story and contrasts the incident with the high moral tone Sallust adopts in his monographs, adding that he paid to have the charge of adultery dismissed. Sallust's own statement is vague and fixes the blame (apparently for his expulsion) elsewhere (*Cat.* 3.3–4):

> . . . (in political life) many things worked against me. For in place of propriety, self-control, courage, it was rash behavior, payoffs, greed that flourished. And although my mind held aloof, being unaccustomed to bad morals, nevertheless in the midst of such vices my defenseless youth was corrupted and held captive to political ambition. . . .

The *Invective* (Cicero, *Sal.* 6) speaks of the expulsion from the Senate being followed by his entry into military service under Caesar (*in ea te castra coniecisti, quo omnis sentina rei publicae confluxerat*). Orosius (6.15.8) attests Sallust's command of troops in Illyricum in 49 B.C.: "Dolabella of Caesar's party, defeated in Illyricum by Octavius and Libo and stripped of his troops, fled to Antonius. Basilus and Sallust with the single legions they commanded advanced against Octavius and Libo and were defeated."

Sallust next appears as praetor-designate in 47 B.C., trying to mollify Caesar's mutinous troops in Campania: Dio (42.52.1–2) and Appian (2.92.387) report that the troops nearly killed him, but he fled to Rome to report to Caesar. Dio adds that Sallust had been named praetor in order to be readmitted to the Senate.

More successful must have been his service in supply and transport as praetor in Caesar's African campaign. This success is attested by several passages of the *Bellum Africanum* (8.3; 34.1; 34.3: "Meanwhile the praetor Sallust filled transport ships and sent them to Caesar in his camp"); in 1993 Walter Schmid again asserted the possibility that Sallust is the unnamed author of this *commentarium*. His reward from Caesar was to be named in 46 B.C. as first governor of the new province of Africa Nova (*B. Afr.* 97.1: "Having made a province out of the kingdom, and having left Sallust there as proconsul with *imperium,* he departed from Zama and went to Utica"; cf. Appian 2.100). Dio mentions Sallust's misuse of that position and its aftermath (43.9.2–3):

> . . . and taking over the Numidians, he [Caesar] reduced them to the status of subjects, and delivered them to Sallust, nominally to rule, but really to harry and plunder. At all events this officer took many bribes and confiscated much property, so that he was not only accused but incurred the deepest disgrace, inasmuch as after writing such treatises as he had, and making many bitter remarks about those who fleeced others, he did not practice what he preached. Therefore, even if he was completely exonerated by Caesar, yet in his history, as upon a tablet, the man himself had chiselled his own condemnation all too well. (translated by E. Cary)

Whether in fact he returned to Rome a wealthier man, rich enough to own the Horti Sallustiani (Sallustian Gardens) between the Quirinal and Pincian hills, among other properties of note, is uncertain; the evidence is solely from the *Invective* (Cicero, *Sal.* 7.19). Having reentered the Senate, Sallust seems to have escaped prosecution for extortion thanks to Caesar's intervention on his behalf.

Whatever Sallust's aims and ambitions for the ensuing period, he changed them after the assassination

Victories with a shield (early first century B.C.) commemorating Sulla's capture of Jugurtha in the conflict that is the subject of Sallust's The War with Jugurtha *(Rome, Museo de Conservatori 2750)*

of Caesar in 44 B.C. and devoted the rest of his life to the writing of history. Again, his own statement of this decision is in the most general terms (*Cat.* 4.1–2):

> Therefore, when my mind rested from its many miseries and risky situations and I determined that the rest of my life should be kept far from the world of politics. . . . I returned to the pursuit I had begun, from which evil ambition had kept me, and I decided to write the history of the Roman people selectively, whatever subjects seemed worth recording; all the more, since my mind was free of hope, fear, partisanship.

Similarly, in *Jug.* 4.3, Sallust states: "I decided to live my life at a distance from politics."

Earlier in the *Cat.* (3.1–2) Sallust argues that the service rendered by the historian is equivalent to that of the political leader even if the historian gains less glory. His motivation for the choice of subject is, in the case of the *Catilina,* the unprecedented crime and threat of the conspiracy and, in the case of *Jugurtha,* the conflict's magnitude, ferocity, and variability of outcome, but even more importantly that it was the first example of opposition to the arrogance of the political elite. For Sallust, historiography is the continuation of his political career by other means (*Jug.* 4.4):

> If they [those who may criticize him for abandoning public life to write history] will consider (1) what sort of men were unable, in the period when I achieved public office, to do the same, and (2) what kind of persons later entered the Senate, they will surely think that it was justifiable rather than lazy for me to have changed my mind, and that greater good from my leisure than from others' employment will accrue to the Republic.

His personal crisis had its cause in the crisis of state and society that had reduced Roman political life to a stage of corruption threatening the fabric of contemporary Rome and for which he saw no remedy. All of Sallust's writings are directed at illuminating salient points of this social and political turmoil and revealing as far as possible how deeply rooted its symptoms were. (Patrick McGushin, *Bellum Catilinae: A Commentary,* p. 15)

After the two monographs, Sallust turned to annalistic history beginning with the year 78 B.C. (*Hist.* 1.1: "The history of the Roman people from the consulship of Marcus Lepidus and Quintus Catulus onward, military and domestic, I have written up"), a work that may not have been complete when he died. Suetonius (*Gram.* 10.6) says that L. Ateius Philologus aided Sallust by providing him with a compendium of all Roman history.

Sallust composed an oration for P. Ventidius (suffect consul for 43 B.C.) to deliver at his triumph over the Parthians in November of 38 B.C. (evidence from Fronto). Sallust's death came in 35 or 34 B.C. (Jerome says 36, but "four years prior to the Battle of Actium").

Thucydides was the principal influence on Sallust's historical writing, although his education included the reading of Demosthenes, Isocrates, Plato, Xenophon, and others whose influence may be seen in certain ideas or passages. For a man determined to create for himself a style that did not follow Ciceronian principles and to write recent and contemporary history from a critical point of view, Thucydides was a natural choice, even if Sallust could not claim the intellectual depth of the Greek historian. In his digressions, on the other hand, Sallust seems to be under Herodotean influence. Of later Greek writers connected to Rome, Polybius and Posidonius were part of his intellectual formation. On the Latin side, his influences were those who had contributed to the development of Roman history writing over the past century, in particular Coelius Antipater, the originator of the historical monograph on a limited subject, and among the annalistic historians, Cornelius Sisenna, whose work Sallust chose to continue in his *Histories*. But the Roman who looms largest in Sallust's work is the elder Cato, for the archaism of his style and the similarly old-fashioned strictness of the moral stance.

Sallust remarks tellingly on the underdeveloped nature of Roman historical writing as compared with that of the Greeks (*Cat.* 8.2):

> The achievements of the Athenians, in my opinion, were great and grand enough, but rather smaller than they are reputed to have been. But because there emerged there great writers' talents, throughout the world the deeds of the Athenians are celebrated to the highest degree. Thus the excellence of those who have been active is valued as highly as outstanding talents have been able to give it verbal praise. But the Roman people has never had such an abundance of talent, because all the most sagacious were very greatly burdened with employment, no one trained the mind to the exclusion of the body, all the best men had rather act than speak, rather their own good deeds be praised by others than to tell of others' deeds themselves.

According to McGushin (1992), the *Histories* appear to have begun with an enumeration of Sallust's predecessors from Cato to Sisenna and an evaluation of their style and content.

Syme has suggested that Sallust, from an aversion to the stylistic ideals for history and oratory of Cicero, came to Thucydides late (after an education that was stronger in selected works of Isocrates, Plato, and Xenophon), and chose to emulate him in Latin by using a remote and old-fashioned style derived from Cato. Sallust does not explicitly mention the emulation, but it was evident already to the ancients (Velleius Paterculus 2.36.2: "Sallust, the rival of Thucydides"; Quintilian, *Inst.* 10.101–102: "nor would I scruple to set Sallust over against Thucydides"), and Thomas Francis Scanlon in *The Influence of Thucydides on Sallust* (1980) has recently analyzed the two writers in theme, style, and similarity of passages.

Suetonius says that Asinius Pollio, to whom Ateius Philologus was connected after Sallust's death and whom he aided in matters of style, averred that Ateius had compiled archaic words and figures for Sallust. Suetonius (*Gram.* 15, *Aug.* 86) and other *testimonia* mention the historian's predilection for such archaisms.

The monograph as form, initiated on the Roman side by Coelius Antipater a century earlier, Syme says, had been characterized by Cicero in 56 B.C. in his notorious letter to L. Lucceius (*Fam.* 5.12), suggesting his own career as subject. It would have "drama, colour, concentration [upon one person], and a theme of high politics," qualities achieved by Sallust in his *Catilina* and *Jugurtha*. What Cicero had not yet done at the time of his execution in 43 B.C., the writing of history in Latin to rival Greek historiography, Sallust at that time essayed.

Sallust composed his first monograph, the *Catilina* (The War of Catiline), ca. 42 B.C., on the events related to Catiline's conspiracy to overthrow the government of Rome in the year 63 B.C. It begins with an *exordium,* or prologue, rather long in proportion to the work but based upon the traditional topics (praise of history, how the author came to the writing of it, and the present subject), in passages of decreasing length; then a character sketch of the villain at the center of the monograph is followed by a digression on the rise and moral decline of Rome. Sallust then sketches the background of the formation of the conspiratorial group, and the narration of events begins only to be interrupted by a sketchy account of a supposed prior conspiracy of the year 66 B.C. These preliminaries take up nearly a third of the whole.

Four extensive speeches shape the remaining narrative of the present conspiracy: at the beginning and end, the speeches of Catiline in June of 64 B.C. to his conspirators in the city and in January of 62 B.C. to his soldiers in the field; and at the high point between these speeches, the pair of speeches by Caesar and Cato on opposite sides of the issue of the punishment of those conspirators arrested in the city. A famous comparison and contrast of the characters of the two speakers follows and further emphasizes this latter pair of lengthy speeches (nearly a sixth of the whole).

Page from the most complete manuscript of Sallust's works (ninth or tenth century). This page includes the close of The War of Catiline *and the beginning of* The War with Jugurtha *(Paris, Codex Parisinus 16024).*

Before that debate, Sallust gives two letters as documents in the account of internal and external events leading up to a digression on the decline of political character at Rome that marks the turning point before the conspiracy is discovered. After the debate the consul Cicero carries out the decision and the final military action follows swiftly, with Catiline's speech to his troops and his heroic death. Despite the finality of this dramatic end the actual conclusion is abrupt and open-ended, leaving the reader with little sense of closure and the student of history with a poor sense of chronology but a strong sense of moral decline exemplified by Catiline's conspiracy.

For the second monograph (which appeared perhaps two years later, in 40 B.C.) Sallust took as his subject the political and military conflict with the Numidian ruler Jugurtha in North Africa in 112–105 B.C., using it as an example of the deleterious effect of corrupt and venal "nobles" on Rome's relations with other states. The subject was more ambitious, involving a longer span of time and a complex interaction of domestic and military affairs, but it was also more traditional, and Sallust's control of the material appears more confident. He again delays the beginning of the actual narrative with extensive prefatory material and uses speeches and digressions to break the otherwise continuous flow of the narrative.

The prologue again provides a philosophical basis for the praise of history and his personal choice of that path to glory. In it Sallust announces the subject and follows it with a look backward to Jugurtha's youth and character and his relationship to the Numidian ruler Micipsa. The background continues with events leading up to the division of Numidia between Jugurtha and Adherbal: Jugurtha comes into contact with the Romans for the first time in Spain, and Micipsa adopts him after his excellent performance there; then follows the ruler's deathbed speech to him. Jugurtha's murder of Hiempsal and attack on Adherbal lead to an appeal to Rome, with the speech of Adherbal given in full and Jugurtha's given in summary; the Senate's response in making a division of Africa then necessitates a digression on the geography of Africa.

The narrative proper thus begins only in the twentieth chapter (as in the *Catilina*), with Jugurtha's aggression against Adherbal, the Senate's legation to him, and the attack on him at Cirta and with his letter to the Senate leading to their corrupt response and Adherbal's execution at Jugurtha's order. These actions in turn lead to Rome's limited intervention: Calpurnius Bestia is assigned to Africa as consul and begins recruiting as Jugurtha attempts to buy off the Romans; the army crosses into Africa and forces Jugurtha's surrender. A new section seems to begin with the debate at

Rome, the extensive speech of C. Memmius, and the acceptance of his proposal to have Jugurtha brought to Rome. During that visit Jugurtha accomplishes the murder of his rival Massiva. Spurius Albinus renews the war but soon returns to Rome for elections; his brother Aulus, left in command, is defeated and the Romans are forced to leave. Then the scene shifts back to Rome and the proposal of the tribune C. Mamilius Limetanus to set up tribunals manned by the equestrian order to investigate charges of collaboration with Jugurtha. As in the *Catilina,* a digression, this time on the history of factions at Rome, precedes the turning point.

The narrative of the actual war then begins and is divided into the campaign of Caecilius Metellus and that of C. Marius; in each the general first acts alone, then is joined by another (Marius joins Metellus and Sulla joins Marius). Near the end of the first campaign there is a digression on Carthage and Cyrene; the latter campaign begins with an extensive speech by Marius to recruit soldiers at Rome from the lower classes. Marius captures Capsa and moves to take a fort near the Muluccha River; then L. Sulla appears, and Sallust gives him a background sketch. Sulla fights against Jugurtha and Bocchus and negotiates with the latter (the narration is framed by speeches, Sulla's at the outset, Bocchus's at the close). Bocchus surrenders Jugurtha, and war ends; Marius is reelected and sent to Gaul. Like the first monograph, the *Jugurtha* ends abruptly, as though the reader were being invited to think forward to events yet to come, rather than linger on the tragic fall of the principal figure. Throughout the narrative, the villainy of the foreign adversary is matched by the corruption of the political process at Rome through the venality of the noble elite.

Sallust then begins on a larger scale the annalistic *Historiae,* beginning with the year 78 B.C. after the death of Sulla, and brings that narrative down to the year 67 B.C. in five books (which survive in excerpts and fragments) by the time of his death. Evidence from the fifth-century Fleury palimpsest shows that "Sallust followed the annalistic tradition with a statement on consuls and an annual organization of events in their chronological order. Wars extending over several years were not dealt with in a continuous narrative; their narration was sometimes interrupted by the changeover to a new year" (McGushin, 1992).

Book 1 (78–77 B.C.) included a personal preface and general introductory material on Rome's history, of which a significant passage on political decline survives, and the events prior to 78 B.C.; the account of the revolt of Lepidus included the speeches of Lepidus and Philippus, which survive; the background of Sertorius and the early stages of the Sertorian War; and operations in Cilicia and Macedonia, including the campaign against Cilician pirates. Book 2 covered from late 77 to early 74 B.C., alternating between external wars (Spain, Sertorian War, the East from Illyria to Asia) and internal politics; it included a digression on Sardinia and Corsica, the extant speech of Cotta to the people, and the letter of Pompey to the Senate. A piece of narrative survives on the operations of Servilius at Isaura Vetus and Nova. Book 3 (74–72 B.C.) related the campaigns of Antony against the pirates and, in Crete, the beginning of the Third Mithridatic War and of the slave rebellion under Spartacus, with two portions of the latter narrative surviving; included were a digression on Pontus and the extant speech of Licinius Macer in 73 B.C. Book 4 covered from 72–68 B.C., including the Mithridatic War; the end of the war with Spartacus (with a digression on southern Italy); and campaigns in Thrace and Armenia, with the extant letter of Mithridates. Book 5 (68–67 B.C.) covered the end of the Armenian campaign and the Gabinian Law to counter the pirate threat.

Throughout the *Histories* Sallust was influenced by Thucydides in chronological arrangement of military campaign seasons and in the inclusion of speeches and letters, and by both Hellenistic historiography and Herodotus in the inclusion of geographical and other digressions. Sallust followed Sisenna's lead, however, according to M. L. W. Laistner in *The Greater Roman Historians* (1947), in departing from strict chronological arrangement to group conflicts by region.

All of these works concern in one way or another the revolution that had dominated Rome during the historian's life and brought his political career to an end; moreover, Sallust's account of it is vehemently moralistic from the outset, with his strong opinions developing in the course of the writing. Donald C. Earl relates in *The Political Thought of Sallust* (1961): "He saw that political life had become a sordid scramble for power and social life a desperate search for pleasure, and set himself to record the state to which Rome had fallen and the processes which had brought her to it."

Other works are attributed to Sallust—two letters, *Epistulae ad Caesarem senem de republica* and an *Oratio (invectiva) in Ciceronem*—all of which, if genuine, would have preceded the historical writing. Their genuineness has been debated since the Renaissance and is not decisively rejected even now, though the latter speech has few supporters.

Any just assessment of the writings of Sallust must consider him in three ways: as a literary stylist, as a narrator of history with a moral and political persuasion, and as a source of historical information. In all three aspects he invites comparison with his model Thucydides and his emulator Tacitus and is found to

be of less significance. As a literary stylist, however, the most useful comparisons are with the Elder Cato (Sallust's other model) and Cicero (Sallust's opposite) and against the background of the still inchoate development of prose writing at Rome, upon which Sallust had a profound impact.

His significance as a source of historical information is, of course, dependent upon the meaning given to "historical"; but, if the question is whether the reader gains a better understanding of what actually happened, then Sallust is not as significant as Thucydides or Tacitus. The faults of inconsistency and inaccuracy in the narrative, the apparent willfulness of his selection of material, and Sallust's lack of detachment and historical perspective, as F. R. D. Goodyear points out, work against the reader more than they do in the works of the other historians. However, as Laistner suggests, many of the faults attributed to Sallust are common to all ancient historians—imperfect command of chronology and topography, for example, and a tendency to sacrifice accuracy for dramatic effectiveness. The larger view of the "historical" must in fact include such faults as integral parts of what happened in antiquity.

As a narrator of history with a moral and political persuasion, Sallust clearly takes on a heightened significance. Scanlon points out that the reader should take into account that Sallust emulated Thucydides not merely because the Greek historian had qualities of objectivity, brevity, and accuracy, but also because Sallust wanted himself and Rome to be compared to Thucydides and Athens, so that the readers of his narrative could explore the pathology of Rome's decline as readers of Thucydides had the decline of Athens.

Equally significant is the attitude taken toward Sallust by Tacitus, who read and imitated him as perhaps no one before or since and who refers to him, with apparent sincerity, as "a most outstanding authority on Roman history" (*Ann.* 3.30). Tacitus deliberately borrowed both style and substance, repeating on a deeper level the relation that Sallust had established between himself and his model Thucydides. According to Goodyear, Tacitus not only adopted the merits of his predecessor's literary style but also adopted and adapted for his own subject Sallust's manner and passion, his "skeptical and disenchanted view of Roman political life."

Some of Sallust's ancient critics made a point of setting his moral passion against his (alleged) personal (see the *testimonia* in Kurfess's edition): Lactantius, after quoting the mind/body dichotomy from the prologue to the *Catilina*, adds "this would be rightly said, had he lived as he spoke"; and Symmachus refers to him as "a writer worthy of approbation solely for style, for the detriments of his character do not allow one to seek from him authority for living"; and according to Mac-

Engraved title page for the 1665 edition of Sallust's complete
extant works

robius in a cutting remark, he is "a most serious critic and censor of other men's luxury." But for others he is worthy of superlatives for accuracy (which may of course be nothing but "political correctness"): to Augustine "a most eloquent man . . . a historian of ennobled truthfulness," and to Isidore "a most accurate source." Augustine found significance in Sallust's moral and political analysis for his much later account of Rome's meaning for the human condition, and the historian's place in later curricula was determined more by such judgments than on the grounds of literary style.

The earliest reactions to Sallust's work, however, seem to have focused upon his style, though of course the reactions may have been politically motivated; in the modern era his monographs are appreciated more as literary texts from antiquity than as historical documents or analyses. The distinctive features of his works, which could better be judged if the *Histories* had survived intact, are the prologues, the speeches and letters,

the digressions, and the narratives of events—elements woven together in an almost novelistic fashion and colored throughout by his highly individual style.

His style was similar for Latin to what Thucydides had fashioned for his Greek, described by Dionysius of Halicarnassus as having four qualities: "poetical language, variety of grammatical turns, disharmony, rapidity." Syme suggests that Sallust matched Thucydides' style with his "selective vocabulary ('poetical' and old-fashioned), the abnormal grammar, the broken structure, the impatient omission of words or ideas."

Suetonius (*Gram.* 10) refers to a book of Asinius Pollio "in which he criticized the writings of Sallust as smeared with an excessive affectation toward archaic vocabulary" and writes that Ateius Philologus consistently urged Pollio "to use language in its familiar, unpretentious, and proper sense and to avoid, above all, Sallust's obscurity and his boldness in metaphors" (trans., Kaster). Suetonius reports that a freedman of

Pompey retaliated for Sallust's treatment of his patron (in the *Histories*) by lashing him "with an extremely harsh satire, calling him . . . in addition an unsophisticated thief of Cato's archaic vocabulary." Similar accusations are attributed to Augustus (again by Suetonius) and expressed in an anonymous epigram quoted by Quintilian.

These *testimonia* show that Sallust was immediately read and reacted to. Aulus Gellius noted (4.15.1) that although there were many critics of Sallust who were unknowledgeable and biased, still there were some things in his style that were not unworthy of criticism. He is probably thinking primarily of the unusual grammar and broken sentence structures with which Sallust avoided the smoothness of political rhetoric in his time. The grammatical peculiarities, along with the unusual vocabulary, made Sallust a prime source for the ancient grammarians, and their citations of examples from his works have preserved many fragments of the lost *Histories*.

The elder Seneca asserted that Sallustian brevity (he thinks of it as a virtue) surpassed that of his model Thucydides (though the example he cites is mistaken, being actually from Demosthenes). This quality and the archaism became popular in the second century and help to account for the collection made of the speeches and letters from Sallust's works (which saved those from the *Histories*). Fronto, for example, writes to Marcus Aurelius: "you have translated the maxims with distinction; indeed, this one I received today you translated almost perfectly–it might be put in a book of Sallust." Among Quintilian's many references to Sallust's qualities, this is the most notorious (*Inst.* 4.2.45):

> . . . an orator must avoid as well that famous Sallustian brevity (although it counts as a virtue in the writer himself) and his abrupt mode of speech: it may perhaps be less deceptive to a leisurely reader, but flies right past the listener, nor does he wait until it be repeated, especially since there is almost no reader who is not sophisticated, whereas most of the judges on juries are sent by the rural districts.

Elsewhere (10.1.102) Quintilian hyperbolically praises Sallust's *immortalis velocitas* (divine speed). The younger Seneca (*Ep.* 114.17) says that "while Sallust was flourishing, there was a fashion of truncated sentences, and words falling sooner than anticipated, and obscure brevity" and notes an historian, L. Arruntius, who imitated Sallust in this characteristic to a fault. Tacitus took all of these aspects of Sallust's Latin style and developed them into his voice.

Matters of literary technique appear as well in the ancient reaction to Sallust's writing. Justinus reports that Pompeius Trogus (in the Augustan era) criticized

both Livy and Sallust for exceeding the bounds of history by inserting *contiones* (direct speeches) in their works in place of their own *oratio* (prose). The most comprehensive ancient critical statement on literary matters other than style may be that of Granius Licinianus (in the Hadrianic era): "They write that Sallust is to be read not as an historian but as an orator, for he not only attacks his own times but also censures crimes and inserts speeches and gives an account of places and mountains and rivers and suchlike pleasant and cultivated things and compares them in his narrative." The moralizing prologues, the speeches, and the digressions have been the most memorable aspects of his writing, other than the Latinity itself, from antiquity to the present.

Martial's epigram predicts the future regard for Sallust (14.191): "This Crispus will be, so say learned men's hearts, first in Roman history." Like much of Sallust's prose, this statement may be more epigrammatic than true, but he remains Rome's first great historian and the major influence on her greatest.

References:

Michael von Albrecht, *A History of Roman Literature,* volume 1 (Leiden: E. J. Brill, 1997), pp. 433–463;

C. Becker, "Sallust," in *Aufstieg und Niedergang der römischen Welt,* 1, no. 3 (Berlin: de Gruyter, 1973), pp. 720–754;

G. Bianco, "Sallustio," in *Enciclopedia Virgiliana,* volume 4 (Rome, 1988), pp. 658–663;

K. Büchner, *Sallust* (Heidelberg, 1960; second edition, 1982);

L. Canfora, "L'autobiografia intellettuale," in *Lo spazio letterario di Roma antica,* volume 3, edited by G. Cavallo and others (Rome: Istituto della Enciclopedia Italiana, 1990), pp. 11–51;

Gian Biagio Conte, *Latin Literature: A History,* translated by Joseph B. Solodow (Baltimore & London: Johns Hopkins University Press, 1994), pp. 234–245;

Donald C. Earl, *The Political Thought of Sallust* (Cambridge: Cambridge University Press, 1961);

Earl, "Sallust," in *Ancient Writers: Greece and Rome,* volume 2, edited by T. James Luce (New York: Scribners, 1982), pp. 621–641;

G. Funaioli, "C. Sallustius Crispus," *PW,* I A, 2, columns 1913–1955;

Funaioli, "Sallustio," in *Enciclopedia Italiana di Scienze, Lettere ed Arti,* volume 30 (Rome: Istituto della Enciclopedia Italiana, 1949), pp. 537–539;

F. R. D. Goodyear, in *Cambridge History of Classical Literature,* volume 2: *Latin Literature,* edited by E. J. Kenney and W. V. Clausen (Cambridge: Cambridge University Press, 1982), pp. 268–280;

C. S. Kraus and A. J. Woodman, *Latin Historians,* Greece & Rome: New Surveys in the Classics no. 27 (Oxford: Oxford University Press, 1997), pp. 10–50;

M. L. W. Laistner, *The Greater Roman Historians* (Berkeley: University of California Press, 1947), pp. 45–64;

Antonio La Penna, *Sallustio e la "rivoluzione" romana* (Milan: Feltrinelli, 1968);

Kurt Latte, *Sallust* (Leipzig: Teubner, 1935);

A. D. Leeman, *A Systematical Bibliography of Sallust, 1879–1964* (Leiden: E. J. Brill, 1965);

A. H. McDonald, in *Fifty Years (and Twelve) of Classical Scholarship,* edited by Maurice Platnauer, second edition (Oxford: Blackwell, 1968), pp. 472–474;

Patrick McGushin, *Bellum Catilinae: A Commentary* (Leiden: E. J. Brill, 1977);

McGushin, trans. and comm., *The Histories,* 2 volumes (Oxford: Oxford University Press, 1992–1994);

Domenico Musti, "Il pensiero storico romano," in *Lo spazio letterario di Roma antica,* volume 1 (Rome: Instituto della Enciclopedia Italiana, 1989), pp. 177–240;

Virgilio Paladini, *Problemi Sallustiani* (Bari, n.d.);

G. M. Paul, *A Historical Commentary on Sallust's Bellum Jugurthinum* (Liverpool: Cairns, 1984);

C. B. R. Pelling, "C. Sallustius Crispus," in *Oxford Classical Dictionary,* edited by Simon Hornblower and Antony Spawforth, third edition (Oxford: Oxford University Press, 1996), pp. 1348–1349;

Viktor Pöschl, *Grundwerte römischer Staatsgesinnungen in den Geschichtswerken des Sallust* (Berlin: de Gruyter, 1940);

Pöschl, ed., *Sallust* (Darmstadt: Wissenschaftliche Buchgesellschaft, 1970);

Thomas Francis Scanlon, *The Influence of Thucydides on Sallust* (Heidelberg: C. Winter, 1980);

Scanlon, *Spes frustrata: A Reading of Sallust* (Heidelberg: C. Winter, 1987);

Walter Schmid, *Fruehschriften Sallusts im Horizont des Gesamtwerks* (Neustadt: Ph. C. W. Schmidt, 1993);

P. L. Schmidt, "Sallustius," in *Der kleine Pauly,* edited by Konrat Ziegler and Walther Southeimer (Stuttgart: Druckenmuller, 1964–1975), IV: columns 1513–1517;

Werner Schur, *Sallust* (Stuttgart: W. Kohlhammer, 1934);

Wolf Steidle, *Sallusts historische Monographien* (Wiesbaden: F. Steiner, 1958);

Sir Ronald Syme, *Sallust* (Berkeley: University of California Press, 1964).

Seneca the Elder

(ca. 54 B.C. – ca. A.D. 40)

William Seaton
Long Island University, Brooklyn Center

WORKS–EXTANT: *Oratorum et rhetorum sententiae divisiones colores* (after A.D. 34);
Controversiae (5 books of 10 survive);
Suasoriae (1 book of 7 survives).

WORKS–LOST:
History from the beginning of the civil wars to his own day.

Editio princeps: *Opera philosophica. Epistolae–Suasoriae. Controversiae* (Venice: Bernardinus de Choris, de Cremona, & Simon de Luere, 1490).

Standard edition: *L. Annaei Senecae patris scripta,* edited by H. J. Muller (Vienna: F. Tempsky, 1887).

Translation in English: *The Elder Seneca Declamations,* 2 volumes, Loeb Classical Library, translated by Michael Winterbottom (Cambridge, Mass.: Harvard University Press, 1974).

Commentary: *The Suasoriae of Seneca the Elder,* edited by W. A. Edward (Cambridge: Cambridge University Press, 1928).

The importance of Lucius, or Marius Annaeus Seneca (called Seneca the Elder to distinguish him from his son, Seneca the Younger), for literary criticism is largely historical. He represents his age in taste and opinions, and he has preserved for posterity records of many passages of oratorical works that would otherwise be lost. He gives the reader an idea of what was appreciated by a connoisseur shortly after Cicero's time and an anthology of texts embodying those values, but he also represents a particular attitude toward literature that is not limited historically. For Seneca the word is characterized by its potential categories that passed so naturally through St. Augustine into the Christian Middle Ages and that continue to be taken seriously by many twentieth-century critics: it may delight and also instruct.

The elder Seneca–sometimes called Seneca Rhetor (though he was not a professional orator) to distinguish him from his more prominent son–was a philosopher and tragedian, born to an equestrian family in Cordoba in Spain ca. 54 B.C. Cordoba was thoroughly Romanized, the most important city in the province, and supported a high level of cultural life, but Seneca was sent to Rome to study. Rhetoric and literary studies formed the basis of the educational system, and as a young man Seneca had the opportunity to hear most of the leading orators of the day, anecdotes and specimens of whose work he was to record much later in his life. He seems to have spent most of his career tending his estates in Spain, though little is known of his life. His son describes him according to the conventional ideals of Roman manhood after the model of Cato (whom the father spoke of as an oracle): Seneca the Elder is said to have been old-fashioned and stern, a pious man and a patriot. The remaining fragment of his lost historical work and several passages in his rhetorical text indicate that he regarded Roman society as much degenerated from earlier times, even from the days of his youth, but this belief, too, is commonplace moralizing and does not necessarily reveal any personal attribute beyond respectability. Seneca the Younger also tells of his father's dissuading him from vegetarianism, and the elder does seem to have been distrustful of philosophy, though less so of Stoicism, in the history of which his son was to play an important role.

Seneca's rhetorical work was composed toward the end of his life putatively as instructional material for his sons. Though this claim is yet another conventional topos, the place of the volume in the school context is clear–it reproduces, after all, the author's own education. The proper title for the whole is *Oratorum et rhetorum sententiae divisiones colores* (after A.D. 34), an apt description of the work. It consists of a chrestomathy of passages (of a sort popular until quite recently) from declaimers of Seneca's youth whom he thinks to be superior to those of later times and thus especially valuable examples for imitation by the young. Both the prodigious feat of memory implied by this task and the didactic intent are intrinsic to Seneca's concept of the work. He approached it, however, with the nostalgia of an old man for his school days and the affection of a

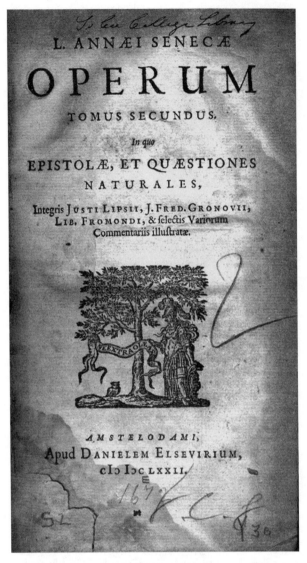

L. ANNÆI SENECÆ

OPERUM

TOMUS SECUNDUS.

In quo

EPISTOLÆ, ET QUÆSTIONES
NATURALES,

Integris JUSTI LIPSII, J. FRED. GRONOVII,
LIB. FROMONDI, & selectis Variorum
Commentariis illustratæ.

AMSTELODAMI,
Apud DANIELEM ELSEVIRIUM,
cIↃ IↃc LXXII.

*Title page for a 1672 Amsterdam edition of Seneca the Elder's works
(courtesy of Special Collections, Thomas Cooper Library, University
of South Carolina)*

connoisseur for his collection, though the tone sometimes shifts to condescension, as he notes at one point that the topic has become tedious to him and that it is in any event "no serious matter."

Each volume of the book—more commonly today regarded as two separate works, the *Controversiae* and the *Suasoriae*—begins with a preface that may touch on many topics but that generally tells something of the style and personalities of the speakers, followed by the anthology of excerpts from their speeches.

The *Controversiae* consisted originally of ten books, each of which included passages from speeches dealing with six to nine hypothetical legal cases. These cases were often of a curious and sensational nature. For example, the law provided that a rape victim could require that her attacker marry her or that he be put to death. What, then, of the case of a rapist who has two victims, one of whom demands his execution and the other his hand? Another case concerns a soldier who, having lost his own weapons, takes those that had been dedicated at a hero's tomb. Having fought bravely with the weapons, should he still be convicted of sacrilege? A third case supposes that a youth was disinherited by his father for aiding his uncle financially. Later, the father himself falls into distress and the son offers him aid as well, thus angering the uncle and causing him, too, to disinherit his loyal relative. Should this filial son indeed lose all rights to inheritance? For each case, Seneca gives the relevant law, then the "theme" or case particulars, and then lines or passages detailing each side of the case. These particulars are followed by possible *divisiones,* called by Seneca the "bare bones" of the case—that is, principles for arrangement of material (often conventional, for instance, by contrasting true equity and law). Next are examples of *colores,* ways of approaching the facts that are favorable to the speaker's point of view. Last comes a section of miscellaneous material. Such fanciful legal cases had been used in schools at least since the time of Aeschines' academy in Rhodes in the fourth century B.C. The aim of the cases was not so much to develop legal acumen as ingenuity. In fact, Seneca decries the replacement of the "glorious art" of declamation by sordid business—which is to say, more pragmatically focused discourse. The *sententiae* are sometimes pithy, moralizing epigrams, but more often they are simply lines that are striking for their wit, their wordplay, and their novelty—little verbal firecrackers. The reader may then understand why Seneca offers such brief one-liners for the most part: he was interested in good lines, not great thought.

The *Suasoriae* seem to have been written somewhat later. They are excerpts from persuasive speeches (related to deliberative oratory as the *Controversiae* are to forensic) of advice to or analysis by historical or legendary figures, often allowing picturesque or exotic material. Such examples as the *Suasoriae* had also been used in schools for centuries, especially for younger students. Such exercises are discussed in Aristotle's *Rhetoric* and in the *Rhetorica ad Alexandrum.* Some of them were already classic set pieces, some to be used into the twentieth century in traditionally minded German and English institutions. These exercises included such situations as Alexander debating whether to sail the ocean in search of further conquests and the three hundred Spartans who opposed Xerxes debating whether they should retreat with the other Greeks. In this volume the description of the theme is followed only by *sententiae.*

To appreciate these texts, one must understand the place of rhetoric and of that form of rhetoric called declamation in ancient culture. To an extent little appreciated today, rhetoric provided the vocabulary and many of the assumptions and values of literary theory, not only in antiquity but through the Renaissance, virtually until the Romantic revolution. Now, of course, the term *rhetoric* suggests either the pedagogy of composition or public speaking, narrowly conceived. That oratory to Seneca was merely the central genre of literature as a whole (as tragedy was to Aristotle) is evident in his willingness to cite examples from comedy, poetry, and even history as declamatory models.

Declamare originally meant simply to speak loudly or emphatically, but the verb came to indicate speech in which rhetorical display was cultivated for purely aesthetic ends, where it needed to answer the practical ends of deliberative speech (as practiced in the assembly or the senate), forensic speech (from the law courts), or epidictic speech. This last type is the clearest antecedent of declamation, but it had earlier been used specifically for "praise and blame," generally with a clear aim of moral edification, if not a clearer one of patriotism or piety. Epidictic speech, though, evolved to a species of "art oratory," appreciated for its own sake under the name *declamation*. Seneca was intimately familiar with declamation, for as he tells his readers, it had been "born after him." Though similar exercises had been part of education centuries earlier in Greece and Rome, declamation became a popular form of public entertainment in the time of Seneca's youth. Figures of speech and thought, Georgianic sound effects, and "Asiatic" excesses became highly prized for their own sake (as well as attacked), and such prominent Romans as Ovid, Maecenas, and even Augustus took the declamatory stage. Competitions became the rage, and "stars" such as those Seneca describes arose.

One factor in this trend toward artistic rather than functional uses of rhetoric is surely political. The emergence of the Empire brought about a situation in which to risk offending the ruler by voicing controversial opinions might prove unwise. Further, court reforms had made the old style of speeches in legal cases impossible. Some of Seneca's regret for the grand old days of oratory may be republican sentiments prudently camouflaged. Nevertheless, the same sort of suspicion with which the old Greeks such as Aristophanes regarded the sophists and rhetoricians of an earlier age persisted in conservative circles of the Roman world. The professors of rhetoric had at one point been banished (most were Greeks, for the profession had been thought rather an improper calling for a Roman citizen). In spite of the ambivalence with which declamation was still regarded, it came to be at the core of the

educational curriculum, a means of continuing education for adults (this trend, too, was still alive through the nineteenth century with institutions such as athenaeums and chatauquas), as well as a pleasurable pastime in itself.

These are the kinds of speeches Seneca records and comments on. He reproduces the social ambivalence toward his subject: in one preface he comments that academic pursuits such as declamation are amusing when lightly touched but become tiresome when dwelt upon and analyzed. He is a curious blend of the dilettante and moralist as he insists both on self-fulfilling amusement and character building as proper ends of declamation.

Many of Seneca's offhand comments support the frivolous view of literature as escapist entertainment. At the outset of the *Controversiae* he compares himself to a producer of shows, noting that novelty is a virtue in theatrical productions, gladiatorial exhibitions, and declamation. His own critical method is far from technical or theoretical. Rather it is descriptive and digressive. Seneca never passes up an opportunity to note odd or interesting personal characteristics of his speakers, often giving attention to foibles that seem irrelevant to their work. His inquiring curiosity, while universal, is desultory rather than systematic, somewhat similar to the sensibilities of Montaigne or Robert Burton. Seneca is unfailingly attracted to individualism; the qualities of style in a given speaker are what render his work unusual and what draw Seneca's interest, not excellence in a traditional mode.

The same equation of character and style, however, can also lead to a moralistic view of rhetoric. Seneca's impatience with his own project, which he calls at one point "trivial dallying," is consistent with his attacks on scholasticism and excesses of style. In this spirit he sees speakers of his own day as too devoted to verbal luxury; for him the tricolor is "this new sickness," and he cites with approval Cicero's condemnation of artificial rhetorical display. He contrasts declamation as an art form with oratory and calls the former insubstantial, though he feels that the skills gained in the practice of declamation can heighten one's abilities not merely in speaking but in all other arts as well. This notion has been assumed for centuries in the placement of linguistic skills as the foundation of education.

This educational role is linked with the positive side of Seneca's equation of style and character. He quotes with reverence Cato's famous definition that gives morality primacy: "An orator is a good man, skilled in speaking." Thus, while the decline in declamation corresponds to a more profound deterioration in society, the educational remedy is available. Seneca supports memory training as a healthy discipline and thinks of its neglect as a symptom of a general softness. Luxury, Seneca declares, destroys intellectual capacity. Bad character brings not only laziness but also an inevitable inability even to select worthy models, models both for writing style and for behavior.

Seneca's influence is difficult to trace. There are few direct mentions of him in the centuries following his own time, and it is often impossible to distinguish what may derive from Seneca from what derives more generally from the rhetorical tradition in which he participated. In his arguments for a more tempered classical style he anticipates Quintilian and neoCiceronianism. For all his fondness for rhetorical ornament he advises moderation and condemns the wilder excesses of declamation and the cultivation of labored ingenuity as the basis for rhetorical education. As anecdotes the *Controversiae* have an independent history, many of them gaining popularity as miniature short stories for their strange and ironic twists of plot. Eleven of the narratives in Giovanni Palazzi's influential collection the *Gesta Romanorum* (1687–1690) are identical with stories in Seneca's *Oratorum et rhetorum sententiae divisiones colores,* though many were told by various ancient authors. Among later writers who imitate Seneca or acknowledge his influence are Montaigne, Ben Jonson, and Abraham Cowley.

Seneca's greatest importance in literary history consists in his preserving evidence of the literary opinions of his time and class. The samples of declamation he regarded as highly entertaining are little read today, but his psychological theories are much like one current today in educational policy making and in popular attitudes toward literature. As a critic Seneca was highly impressionistic, taking no position in the controversies of his day and eschewing technical labels for stylistic characteristics, preferring rather to use terms like "tumultuous," "solid," and "excited." For all his cautions against excessive scholasticism in literature, he dwells today almost exclusively in academe. He vividly records both the now-faded taste for verbal ornament and the sober Roman morality that were characteristic of his day.

References:

Janet Fairweather, *Seneca the Elder* (Cambridge: Cambridge University Press, 1981);

George A. Kennedy, *The Art of Rhetoric in the Roman World, 300 B.C.–A.D. 300* (Princeton, N.J.: Princeton University Press, 1972);

L. A. Sussmann, *The Elder Seneca* (Leiden: Brill, 1978).

Seneca the Younger

(ca. 1 B.C. – A.D. 65)

A. J. Boyle

University of Southern California

MAJOR WORKS–EXTANT:

PROSE WORKS: Dialogues (ca. A.D. 37–41): *Ad Marciam de consolatione* (Consolation to Marcia, ca. A.D. 39/40);

Dialogues (A.D. 41–49): *Ad Helviam matrem de consolatione* (Consolation to His Mother Helvia);

Ad Polybium de consolatione (Consolation to Polybius, ca. A.D. 43);

De ira, books 1–2 (On Anger);

Dialogues (A.D. 49–62): *De ira,* book 3 (On Anger, by A.D. 52);

De brevitate vitae (On the Brevity of Life, by A.D. 55);

De constantia sapientis (On the Firmness of the Sage);

De providentia (On Providence);

De vita beata (On the Happy Life, ca. A.D. 58);

De tranquillitate animi (On Peace of Mind);

De otio, only 8 chapters extant (On Leisure);

PROSE WORKS (A.D. 55–62): *De clementia,* books 1–3 (On Mercy, A.D. 55/56, book 1 and beginning of book 2 extant);

De beneficiis, books 1–7 (On Favors);

PROSE WORKS (A.D. 62–65): *Epistulae Morales ad Lucilium* (Moral Epistles, 124 letters in 20 books extant);

Quaestiones naturales, 8 books (Natural Questions, 2 books now fragmentary);

VERSE: *Epigrams* (Over 70 ascribed to Seneca, some definitely spurious, date uncertain);

Eight Extant Tragedies (listed in the following order by the *Codex Etruscus,* date uncertain): *Hercules [Furens]; Troades; Phoenissae; Medea; Phaedra; Oedipus; Agamemnon; Thyestes;*

MENIPPEAN SATIRE (Prose-Verse Mélange): *Apocolocyntosis* (Pumpkinification, late A.D. 54).

WORKS–ATTRIBUTED (BUT SPURIOUS): *Hercules Oetaeus; Octavia.*

WORKS LOST: Biography of Seneca the Elder, speeches, letters, and treatises.

Editiones principes: Philosophical Prose Works (Naples: 1475); Tragedies (Ferrara: ca. 1484);

Seneca the Younger (bust in Staatliche Museen, Berlin, 371)

Quaestiones naturales (Venice: 1490); *Apocolocyntosis* (Rome: 1513).

Standard editions: *L. Annaei Senecae De Beneficiis Libri VII, De Clementia Libri II,* edited by Carl Hosins, second edition (Leipzig: Teubner, 1914); *Divi Claudii Apokolokyntosis,* edited by Carlo Ferninando Russo, second edition (Firenze: La Nuova Italia, 1955); *L. Annaei Senecae ad Lucilium epistulae morales,* 2 volumes, edited by L. D. Reynolds (Oxford: Oxford University Press, 1965); *L. Annaei Senecae dialogorum libri duodecim* (Oxford: Oxford University Press, 1977); *Anthologia Latina,* volume I, edited by D. R. Shackleton Bailey, 1 (Stuttgart:

Teubner, 1982– , for *Epigrams* attributed to Seneca); *L. Annaei Senecae tragoediae,* edited by Otto Zwierlein, (Oxford: Oxford University Press, 1986); *L. Annaei Senecae naturalium quaestionum libri,* edited by Harry M. Hine, (Stuttgart and Leipzig: Teubner, 1996).

Translations in English: *Seneca: His Tenne Tragedies,* translated by Thomas Newton (London: 1581; reprinted, 1927); *The Workes of Lucius Annaeus Seneca both Morall and Naturall,* translated by Thomas Lodge (London: 1614); *Seneca,* 10 volumes, translated by John W. Basore, Thomas H. Corcoran, Richard M. Gummere, and Frank Justus Miller, Loeb Classical Library (Cambridge, Mass.: Harvard University Press, 1917–1971); *The Stoic Philosophy of Seneca,* translated by Moses Hadas (Garden City, N.Y.: Anchor, 1958); *Four Tragedies and Octavia,* translated by E. F. Watling (Harmondsworth, U.K.: Penguin, 1966); *Seneca's Oedipus,* translated by Ted Hughes (London: Faber & Faber, 1969); *Letters from a Stoic,* translated by Robin Campbell (Harmondsworth, U.K.: Penguin, 1969); *Satyricon and Apocolocyntosis,* translated by J. P. Sullivan (Harmondsworth, U.K.: Penguin, 1977); *Three Tragedies,* translated by Frederick Ahl (Ithaca, N.Y.: Cornell University Press, 1986)–includes *Seneca Medea, Phaedra, Trojan Women; Seneca's Phaedra,* translated by A. J. Boyle (Liverpool: Francis Cairns, 1987); *Seneca's Troades,* translated by Boyle(Leeds, U.K.: Francis Cairns, 1994); *Four Dialogues,* translated by C. D. N. Costa (Warminster, U.K.: Aris and Phillips, 1994); *Moral and Political Essays,* translated by John M. Cooper and J. F. Procopé (Cambridge: Cambridge University Press, 1995); *Dialogues and Letters,* translated by Costa (Harmondsworth, U.K.: Penguin, 1997).

Commentaries: Carlo Prato, *Gli epigrammi attribuiti a L. Anneo Seneca* (Bari: Adriatica Editrice, 1955); C. D. N. Costa, *Medea* (Oxford: Oxford University Press, 1973); R. J. Tarrant, *Agamemnon* (Cambridge: Cambridge University Press, 1976); Maria Grazia Cavalca Schiroli, *Lucio Anneo Seneca: De Tranquillitate Animi* (Bologna: CLUEB, 1981); Harry M. Hine, *An Edition with Commentary of Seneca, Natural Questions, Book Two* (New York: Arno, 1981); C. E. Manning, *On Seneca's Ad Marciam* (Leiden: Brill, 1981); Elaine Fantham, *Seneca's Troades: A Literary Commentary* (Princeton, N.J.: Princeton University Press, 1982); Ivano Dionigi, *De otio* (Brescia: Paideia Editrice, 1983); Bruno W. Häuptli, *Seneca Oedipus* (Frauenfeld: Huber, 1983); P. T. Eden, *Apocolocyntosis* (Cambridge: Cambridge University Press, 1984); R. J. Tarrant

Seneca's Thyestes (Atlanta: Scholars Press, 1985); John G. Fitch, *Seneca's Hercules Furens* (Ithaca, N.Y.: Cornell University Press, 1987); A. J. Boyle, *Seneca's Phaedra* (Liverpool: Francis Cairns, 1987); Costa, *Seneca: 17 Letters* (Warminster U.K.: Aris and Phillips, 1988); Dionigi Vottero, *Questioni naturali di Lucio Anneo Seneca* (Torino: Unione Tipografico-editrice Torinese, 1989); Michael Coffey and Roland Mayer, *Seneca Phaedra* (Cambridge: Cambridge University Press, 1990); Boyle, *Seneca's Troades* (Leeds, U.K.: Francis Cairns, 1994); Costa, *Four Dialogues* (Warminster, U.K.: Aris and Phillips, 1994); Thomas Kurth, *Seneca's Trostschrift an Polybius, Dialog II: ein Kommentar* (Stuttgart: Teubner, 1994); Marcia Frank, *Seneca's Phoenissae: Introduction and Commentary* (Leiden: Brill, 1995).

Seneca the Younger is the principal Stoic philosopher, essayist, and tragedian of imperial Rome. Undoubtedly the most brilliant literary figure of his day, he was also its most complex and most enigmatic. Orator, Stoic philosopher, epistolary, natural scientist, satirist, poet, tragedian, statesman, financier, courtier, sycophant, wealth-encrusted eulogist of the simple life–Seneca requires from the modern reader an unusual complexity of response. Few readers today have stared into the face of a Caligula or experienced the paralyzing nightmare of a tyrant's court. Seneca had; and he became part of the nightmare and its victim. In A.D. 65 at a villa outside Rome he killed himself on instructions from the emperor Nero, whose tutor and chief minister he had been. Seneca's dialogues, treatises, and tragedies are products and indices of an age of moral and cultural crisis. The style of the tragedies is that of shock. Their declamatory form, spectacle, ideological structure, and overt theatricality mirror the spectacular, histrionic, and self-consuming world of late Julio-Claudian Rome.

Lucius Annaeus Seneca was born in 1 B.C., or shortly before, in Corduba (modern Cordova) in southern Spain, the second of three sons of the cultivated equestrian, Annaeus Seneca (ca. 55 B.C.–ca. A.D. 40–*praenomen* probably also Lucius), author of a lost history of Rome, *Controversiae,* and a surviving (but badly mutilated) work on Roman declamation, *Suasoriae.* The youngest son, Mela, was the father of the epic poet Lucan. Brought to Rome as a young child and given the standard education in rhetoric, Seneca had become by the early years of Tiberius's principate (A.D. 14–37), while still in adolescence, a passionate devotee of philosophy. The focus of his ardor was an ascetic, locally taught form of Stoic-Pythagoreanism with a strong commitment to vegetarianism. Before long he had been dissuaded from this practice by his father (*Epistle* 108. 17–

Page from a letter by Seneca, copied by Walfrid Strabo, Abbot of Reichenau, in the early ninth century (St. Gall, Stiftsbibliothek 878, f. 348)

22). During his youth and throughout his life Seneca suffered from a tubercular condition and on one occasion contemplated suicide when he despaired of recovery. He records that only the thought of the suffering he would have caused his father prevented his death (*Epistle* 78.1f.).

Ill health presumably delayed the start of Seneca's political career, as did a substantial period of convalescence during the A.D. 20s in Egypt under the care of his maternal aunt. He returned to Rome from Egypt in A.D. 31 (surviving a shipwreck in which his uncle died) and entered the Senate by way of the quaestorship shortly afterwards, as did Gallio, his elder brother. By the beginning of Claudius's principate (A.D. 41) Seneca had also held the aedileship and the office of tribune of the people. During the A.D. 30s, too, he married (although whether this woman was his wife of later years who survived him, Pompeia Paulina, is uncertain), and he achieved such fame as a public speaker as to arouse the attention and jealousy of the emperor Gaius (Suetonius, *Gaius* 53.2, Dio 59.19.7f), better known as Caligula. By the late A.D. 30s, C. J. Herington writes, Seneca was clearly moving in the circle of princes, among "that tiny group of men on which there bore down, night and day, the concentric pressure of a monstrous weight, the post-Augustan empire." Only one literary product, however, survives from this period, the *Ad Marciam de consolatione* (To Marcia on Consolation, ca. A.D. 39/40), a politically motivated work purporting to console the daughter of the historian Cremutius Cordus for the premature death of her son. Like Seneca's two later consolations this work is packed with generic *topoi* (such as the universality and inevitability of death, the fragility of life, the inappropriateness of excessive grief, the fleeting nature of time, and the therapeutic power of time).

Seneca's presence in high places was initially short lived. He survived Caligula's brief principate (A.D. 37–41) only to be exiled to Corsica in the first year of Claudius's reign (A.D. 41). The charge was adultery with Caligula's sister, Julia Livilla, brought by the new empress, Claudius's young wife, Messalina.

Seneca's exile came at a time of great personal distress—both his father and his son had recently died (*Ad Helviam matrem de consolatione,* (To His Mother Helvia on Consolation) 2.4f.)—and lasted eight tedious years. He devoted much of this time to literary composition. Some scholars wish to assign the composition of some of the tragedies to this period; others dispute this claim. Certainly many of the epigrams mention the Corsican exile. Two consolations are also securely dated to this period, *Ad Helviam matrem de consolatione,* in which Seneca tries to console his mother for the shame and anxiety brought by his exile, and *Ad Polybium de consolatione* (To Polybius on Consolation, ca. A.D. 43), a thinly disguised attempt at imperial flattery, addressed to Claudius's powerful freedman-minister on the death of the freedman's brother, in an endeavor to secure his own return. Also to this period seem to belong all or most of the important treatise *De ira* (On Anger). Stoics regarded emotions as deleterious effects of the unnatural condition they called "vice." In this elaborate, at times repetitive, exposition Seneca defines and analyzes anger as "the burning desire to avenge a wrong," and visualizing its physical effects and (with vivid historical *exempla*) the horrors it generates, he represents anger as the most hideous, frenzied, and inhuman of all the emotions. The professed purpose of the treatise is curative, and Seneca offers prescriptions on how anger may be forestalled, alleviated, and extinguished. The reader may be excused from thinking that many of Seneca's prescriptions are addressed not to the dedicatee of the work, his brother Novatus (governor of Achaea, A.D. 51–52), but to the irascible Claudius and himself.

In A.D. 48 Messalina was executed. In the following year Seneca, through the agency of Agrippina, Claudius's new wife, was recalled to Rome and designated for a praetorship (the political office just beneath the consulship) in A.D. 50. His literary and philosophical reputation was now well established (Tacitus, *Annals* 12.8.3), and he was appointed tutor to Agrippina's son, Nero. This appointment as Nero's tutor not only placed Seneca again at the center of the Roman world but brought him immense power and influence when Agrippina poisoned her emperor-husband, and Nero acceded to the throne (A.D. 54). Throughout the early part of Nero's reign Seneca (suffect consul in A.D. 56) and the commander of the praetorian guard, Afranius Burrus, acted as the chief ministers and political counselors of Nero, whose policies they shaped and substantially controlled. Between Seneca's return from exile in A.D. 49 and his effective retirement in A.D. 62 belong the composition of the remaining philosophical dialogues, infused to a greater or lesser extent with Stoic ethical ideas: the advocacy of virtue, endurance, self-sufficiency, and true friendship; the condemnation of evil, emotions, and the false values of wealth and power; the praise of reason, wisdom, and poverty; and contempt for the fear of death. To this period too are dated *De clementia* (On Mercy, A.D. 55/56), *De beneficiis* (On Favors), and the satire *Apocolocyntosis* (Pumpkinification, A.D. 54). Also at this time Seneca seems to have been active in the theater (Quintilian, *Institutio* 8.3.31), and at least some of the tragedies are best located in this period, especially *Hercules Furens,* probably parodied in *Apocolocyntosis.* The latter, a Menippean satire written in a mélange of prose and verse, is a humorous skit on the "pumpkinification," that is, deification, of the emperor Claudius, and, composed like *On Mercy* in the opening years of Nero's reign, displays a transparent political purpose—eulogy of the young emperor. It achieves this purpose by debunking Claudius's recent apotheosis through having the gods (in particular, his divine predecessor, Augustus) reject it on the grounds of Claudius's unjust execution of senators and knights and appropriation of Roman law. Claudius is escorted to the underworld where he is judged and condemned for mass murder. The prospective rule of Nero, who promised a return to the enlightened principate of Augustus is thereby praised.

De clementia, written a year or so later than *Apocolocyntosis*, delivers a similar political message in an entirely different manner. The first extant example of a "mirror of princes," the treatise presents its addressee, Nero, with a model of the ideal king he has already become, praising mercy as the virtue and protection of monarchs, for leniency in punishing inferiors augments not only a monarch's honor but also his safety. The image in the work of the ideal prince was never realized. Indeed, even when *On Mercy* was published, it glossed over a singular horrific fact—Nero's murder early in A.D. 55 of his stepbrother Britannicus in full view of the imperial court. As Nero's principate evolved, Seneca became increasingly subject to criticism for the gap between his Stoic exhortations and Nero's practice, and for his own hypocrisy (Seneca's praise of poverty did not prevent him from amassing a huge fortune from usury). *De vita beata* (On the Happy Life, ca. A.D. 58), in which wealth is justified as (when properly used) an instrument of virtue, was probably written as a personal *apologia* after a public attack on Seneca launched in A.D. 58 by Suillius (Tacitus, *Annals* 13.42). By this time Seneca's ability to control his protégé was becoming less evident. Nero's matricide in A.D. 59—to which no one knows whether Seneca or Burrus were privy, but for which Seneca wrote a *post factum* justification (Tacitus, *Annals* 14.11)—demonstrated the weakening of their power. Ironically in the same year a palace literary coterie was formed, which included Seneca's nephew, the poet Lucan, and later Petronius, the author of *Satyricon*. Nero (born in A.D. 37) was no longer a malleable teenager. Moreover, when Burrus died—perhaps was poisoned (Tacitus, *Annals* 14.15.1)—in A.D. 62, Seneca went into semi-retirement. *On Favors,* a large work in seven books examining in detail the social and moral issues surrounding acts of kindness by one individual to another, probably belongs between the deaths of Agrippina and Burrus. Since favors lay at the heart of Roman social cohesion, "more than anything they hold society together" (1.4.2), Seneca's extensive discussion offers important illumination of Roman social and moral codes. Its composition on the eve of Seneca's retirement, as the monstrous acts of his former pupil

began to breach all Roman codes, is but one of many ironies defining Seneca's life. To this period too are plausibly dated *De otio* (On Leisure), in which Seneca advocates "leisure" or retirement for the opportunity afforded for cultural and philosophical pursuits, and *De tranquillitate animi* (On Peace of Mind), perhaps earlier than the former, since in it Seneca does not satisfactorily resolve the conflict between public commitment and private contemplative leisure.

Seneca's unofficial retirement (Nero initially refused his request) was only from the political arena. His literary composition continued apace and includes the eight-book "scientific" treatise *Quaestiones naturales* (Natural Questions), an examination of natural phenomena (such as meteorology, terrestial waters, the Nile, earthquakes, and comets—in which inevitably Stoic ethics impinges on Stoic physics), and the 124 letters (originally more were available) addressed to his friend Lucilius (the younger Gaius Lucilius, not the second-century-B.C. satirist) known as the *Epistulae Morales ad Lucilium* (Moral Epistles). The latter became Seneca's most popular prose work from antiquity to the present day, and its popularity is easy to understand. The fictive pose of correspondence enables Seneca to cover an enormous range and variety of subject matter and to treat that subject matter in the kind of informal manner that readers often associate with "authenticity." Topics include friendship, grief, ill health, virtue, travel, suicide, lawsuits, death, civic duty, retirement, old age, gladiatorial bloodsports, literary style and life, and pain—all explored discontinuously within a letter and over a series of letters (hence, the analogy with the modern essay is only partly apt—Seneca wrote an essay series) and treated with a variety of styles and tones. The mood of the epistles shifts from humorous to serious, excited to grave, and protreptic to quietly and thoughtfully analytical, but throughout there is the sense of a mind thinking through issues and problems, reflected in a style calculated to keep the reader focused (hence, the use of short, pointed sentences, asyndeton instead of connectives, powerful imagery, historical anecdotes, poetic and colloquial diction, sharp juxtapositions, epigrammatic phraseology, paradox, ambiguity, and point). Caligula is said to have criticized Seneca's style from the beginning as "sand without lime" (to bind it), and others have echoed this thought. The modern reader, however, like ancient and Renaissance readers, is likely to find Seneca's staccato style both in the treatises and the letters more appropriate to the representation of thinking and feeling than the more conjunctive style of a Cicero. With the *Moral Epistles,* Seneca was writing his way to death. In A.D. 65 he was accused of involvement in the Pisonian conspiracy against the emperor, organized by Seneca's nephew Lucan and

Page from a thirteenth-century manuscript, probably from Waltham Abbey in England. The illuminated capital shows Nero enthroned and Seneca in his bath, having his veins opened (Princeton University Library)

others, and was ordered to kill himself. This he did, dying in a highly theatrical manner with self-conscious allusions to the death of Socrates and to his own place in history. He left to his friends "his one remaining possession—and his best—the pattern of his life" (Tacitus, *Annals* 15.62.1).

Seneca also left to his friends and the world something else—his tragedies, which reflect more vividly than the philosophical works the cultural and moral turbulence of early imperial Rome. Born under Augustus and committing suicide three years before Nero's similar fate, Seneca was encompassed by the Julio-Claudian principate and the social and moral convolution it brought. Throughout Seneca's lifetime—despite the preservation of the political, legal, moral, social, and religious forms of Rome—power resided essentially in one man, the *princeps* or emperor, sometimes (as in the case of Caligula) a vicious psychopath. Political and personal freedom were nullities. In Rome and especially at the court itself, on which the pressure of empire bore, nothing and no one seemed secure; controlling forms of the Roman world were used, abused, and nullified by the power of the *princeps*. Servility, hypocrisy, and corrupting power indexed this Julio-Claudian world. Thus at least the ancient historians reported it, especially Tacitus, whose *Annals,* written in the first decades of the second century A.D., documents the hatreds, fears, lusts, cowardice, self-interest, self-abasement, abnormal cruelty, extravagant vice, violent death, inversion, and perversion of Rome's values and institutions—and, more rarely, the nobility and the heroism—which to his mind constituted the early imperial court. The author of *Annals* had experienced at first hand, the human degradation at the center of the early principate; as had Seneca. As with Tacitus, Seneca's works reflect his experiences. The themes of Seneca's tragedies—vengeance, madness, power-lust, passion, irrational hatred, self-contempt, murder, incest, hideous death, vicissitudes of fortune, and savagery—were the stuff of his life. Seneca's is the theater of a man who had witnessed absolute evil (compare with *On Anger* 3.18–19.5).

At least seven complete tragedies can be assigned to Seneca: *Hercules, Troades, Medea, Phaedra, Oedipus, Agamemnon,* and *Thyestes.* Such are their titles in the E branch of the MS tradition recorded in the *Codex Etruscus.* In the A branch, *Hercules* is given the augmented title *Hercules Furens* (now generally used), *Troades* is called *Tros,* and *Phaedra* is called *Hippolytus.* An eighth play, *Phoenissae* (*Thebais* in A) is also accepted by most modern scholars as Senecan, but it includes no choral odes and is either an experimental drama without chorus or (as most think) incomplete. A ninth play, *Hercules Oetaeus,* is almost twice as long as the average Senecan play and is generally agreed to be—at least in its present form—non-Senecan. A

tenth play, the *fabula praetexta* or historical drama *Octavia,* in which Seneca appears as a character and seems to refer to events that took place after Seneca's death, is missing from A and is certainly not by Seneca.

The date of the composition of the plays is not known. Most modern commentators accept that *Hercules Furens* was probably written by A.D. 54, since *Apocolocyntosis* (securely dated to A.D. 54) seems to parody it. The first unambiguous reference to any of Seneca's plays, however, is by Quintilian (*Institutio* 9.2.8), writing a generation after Seneca's death. Seneca in fact makes no mention of his tragedies in his prose works. Many commentators consequently allocate them to the period of exile on Corsica (A.D. 41–49); others regard as more likely that their composition, like that of the prose works, was spread over a considerable period of time, including the period from A.D. 49 onward, when Quintilian notes Seneca as being active in theatrical debate (*Institutio* 8.3.31). Recent stylometric studies of the plays seem to support the latter position and also suggest that *Thyestes* and *Phoenissae* were his final dramatic compositions.

Seneca, reflecting the nature of his life and world, fills his tragedies with compelling and (on the whole) despairing themes: the failure of reason; the determinism of history; the genealogy and competitive cyclicity of evil; the fragility of social and religious forms; the fragility of epistemological forms; civilization as moral contradiction; man as appetite, as beast, as existential victim; power, impotence, delusion, and self-deception; the futility of compassion; the freedom, desirability, and value-paradox of death; man, god, nature, guilt, and unmerited suffering; the certainty of human pain, the terror of experienced evil; the inexorable, paradoxical, amoral—even morally perverse—order of things; the triumph of evil; and in one play *(Hercules Furens)* the possibility of human redemption, in all the gap between language and the world. Despite the thematic continuity of the tragedies, their ideological worlds differ markedly. Neither *Phaedra* nor *Medea* asserts the moral order implied in *Agamemnon;* nor is the order of nature as presented in *Phaedra,* where all suffer and human impotence seems total, identical with the cosmic order of *Medea,* in which one of the human figures (Medea), working with the divine forces of the cosmos, triumphs. *Thyestes* differs radically from all three plays. In it nature and the gods are reduced to shocked, impotent observers of human bestiality and sin. No life-destroying storm punishes *scelus* (evil) as in *Agamemnon* (465ff.); there is no monster from the sea that punishes evil as in *Phaedra* (1007ff.); no Hecate-generated fire that feeds on its natural antagonist, water, as in *Medea* (885ff.). Evil is unpunished, and prayers are unfulfilled. "The gods are fled," cries Thyestes (*Thy.* 1021), and he is right, as is Oedipus in asserting the existence of mendacious gods

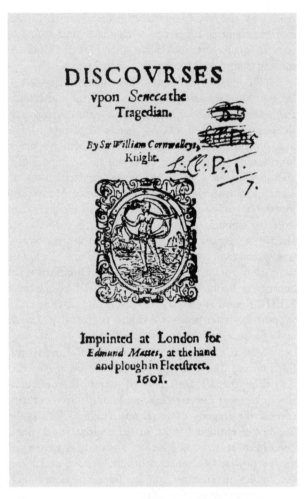

DISCOVRSES
vpon *Seneca* the
Tragedian.

By S[r] *William Cornwalleys*,
Knight.

Imprinted at London for
Edmund Mattes, at the hand
and plough in Fleetstreet.
1601.

Title page for the first English book devoted entirely to Seneca's works

(*Oed.*, 1042ff.) in a world where those who use reason to escape crime and guilt compound both. Senecan moral and metaphysical tragedy investigates distinct and distinctive worlds. The world of *Oedipus* is not that of *Thyestes,* nor is it that of *Medea.*

The ideological complexity of the plays is mirrored in that of form. Some critics have denied that Seneca's tragedies were written primarily for performance but see them instead as created for reading or recitation. The historical evidence indicates not only the performance of high tragedy on stage during Seneca's lifetime but also the recitation of tragedy by a single speaker in a private house or recitation-hall, both for its sake and as a preliminary to theatrical performance and/or publication (Pliny, *Epistles* 7.17.11). In the theater, virtuoso individual recitals of tragic speeches, episodes, or monodies were common. Nero's own performances of "the tragedies of heroes and gods wearing the tragic mask" (Suetonius, *Nero* 21.3) probably belong to this category. The contemporary practice of *recitatio* affected

the form of Seneca's plays. Many believe it unlikely, though, that his plays were written solely or even primarily for recitation (although, appropriately edited, they could be so used) and most improbable that they were written primarily to be read. Their stagecraft is too developed and accomplished for such hypotheses: the careful shaping of dramatic action; the structural unfolding of dramatic language and imagery; the blocking of scenes and acts; the disposition of roles; the handling of actors and of the chorus; the interrelationship between chorus and act; the use of ghosts, messengers, extras, and mutes; the dramatic and thematic use of stage-setting and props; the equivalent of stage directions in the text itself (especially entrance and exit cues, identification cues, and implicit directions for stage business); the essentially theatrical nature of the pace of Senecan tragedy; its movement, violence, spectacle, and closure. The considerable variation evidenced in such standard matters as prologue design and integration, choral length and sequence, techniques of choral identification, the number of choruses and actors, the messenger's speech, verse-dialogue composition, choral lyric, and dramatic structure seem to signal a dramatist interested in dramatic experimentation and innovation. The use of the sword in *Phaedra,* for example, is likely an innovative move; so perhaps is the lyric opening of *Phaedra,* the use of the messenger for closure in *Troades,* and even Seneca's most unvarying dramaturgical device—the ending in dialogue rather than chorus—which seems to depart from standard tragic practice.

A signal constituent of the formal intricacy of all Senecan drama is its sub- and inter-textual dimension, its use of palimpsests (texts written over other texts) to which it deliberately alludes. *Troades,* for example, recycles a multitude of texts from Homer's *Iliad* and the cyclic epics, through Attic and Republican tragedy, to works of Lucretius, Catullus, Horace, Virgil, Ovid, and (possibly) Seneca's own *Agamemnon.* Overt textual allusion and metaliterary language make of Senecan tragedy a self-reflexive, multi-referential body of work that engages in a constant and pervasive counterpoint with the dramatic and poetic tradition. This recycling of the tradition has resonances within and without the text. It underscores one of the recurrent themes of Senecan tragedy, the recycling of the past as the present; it also serves as the product and index of, and metaphor for, the palimpsestic world of late Julio-Claudian Rome, dominated by the forms of its own past—political, social, religious, and legal—which Seneca attempts to *represent* in the play. Senecan tragedy is not simply a quintessential example of the literature of lateness; it reflects and critiques through form and meaning a society of lateness—a palimpsestic world, a theatricalized world. Augustus's deathbed request (Suetonius, *Augustus* 99.1)

288

to be applauded for the part he had acted in "life's mime" indexes the tenor of the times. For both Suetonius and Tacitus, acting seems the emblematic metaphor of the age. The play literally is the thing. Nero's initial "mimicries of sorrow" (Tacitus, *Annals* 13.4) at the funeral of his stepfather Claudius lead in Tacitus's works to insistent attention not only to the emperor's own appearances on the stage but also to the political and social imperatives of role-playing in the theatricalized world of imperial Rome, where citizens mourn what they welcome (*Annals* 16.7), applaud what they grieve (*Annals* 14.15), offer thanksgivings for monstrous murder (*Annals* 14.59, 64), and celebrate triumphs for national humiliation (*Annals* 15.18) or horrendous and impious sin (*Annals* 14.12f.). "This drama of life," Seneca observes at *Epistle* 80.7, "assigns parts for us to play badly."

Inevitably in this theatricalized world Senecan tragedy becomes metatheatrical and draws attention to its own theatricality. Medea requires Jason as audience in order for her own murderous play to have meaning (*Medea* 894, 993); the dead Tantalus is forced to become audience to his descendants' cannibalistic drama in *Thyestes* (66); and the Trojan dead are summoned as "spectators" to Cassandra's recited play in *Agamemnon* (758). The recurrent focus on action as spectacle and on behavior as self-dramatization or role-playing, in which characters become actors before other characters as audience—for example, Phaedra before Theseus (*Phaedra* 864ff.), Medea before Jason (*Medea* 551ff.), Clytemestra before Aegisthus (*Agamemnon* 239ff.), and Atreus before Thyestes (*Thyestes* 491ff.)—the staging in *Medea* and *Thyestes* of a character's own staging as character, actor, and dramaturge of the climactic evil itself, signal a conspicuous metatheatrical dimension to Senecan tragedy, a concern to draw attention to its own conventions and artifice, its own theatricality. *Troades* is especially important in this regard. The play features extensive scenes of role-playing before another character as audience, and the metaphor of the theater pervades the whole of the final act, where the Messenger is not only the narrator of spectacle but also its producer, its presenter, its editor. His description of the gathering and positioning of the crowd to watch the death of Astyanax (1075ff.) is modeled on the audience of the amphitheater and includes its own "callous spectator" (1087). For the death of Polyxena the model is the theater itself (1118–1131). Her death creates a fitting image of theatricalized Rome.

Part of what made imperial Rome theatrical was its rhetoricity, and Senecan tragedy, like Senecan philosophical dialogues, is appropriately rhetorical. Seneca is a master of both declamatory structure and the "pointed" style, with its compression, antithesis, paradox, and counterpoint. Seneca's tragedies and prose works are the product of a sensibility informed by rhetoric at a time

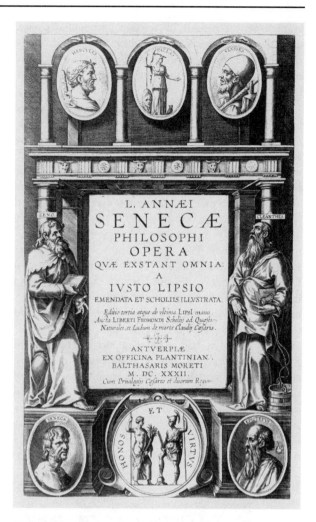

Engraved title page for a 1632 edition of Seneca's works (courtesy of the Lilly Library, Indiana University)

when rhetoric was the controlling principle of both education and literary composition. They are in accord with a contemporary passion for and fullness of response to rhetoric, to pointed discourse, declamation, and dialectical and verbal ingenuity. Senecan tragedy is rhetorical, as Elizabethan tragedy is rhetorical; both are the product and index of an age. In Seneca's case the age is one of grandiose, almost strident aesthetics, the age of fourth-style Roman painting, the baroque in Roman architecture and sculpture, the avalanche of display in political, military, and religious congregation. The early imperial theater—its concrete structures adorned with marble and travertine, its stage curtains ornately decorated, its revolving scenery stands, massive flying devices and collapsible sets, its baroque stage buildings resplendent with statues, scenepaintings, masks, and garlands—was spectacle informing spectacle. Senecan rhetoricity is the verbal correlative of spectacle. In his tragedies the astonishing fusion of spectacle, bombast, paradox, epigram, brevity, plenitude, abstraction, grandeur, violence, disjunction, allusion, and sensuousness is no arbitrarily chosen mode; it is the product of a baroque, post-classical sensibility grounded in the semiotic forms of contemporary Roman life.

The relationship between the tragedies and the philosophical works continues to be a subject of debate. Although the tragedies are not mentioned in the prose works, they used to be commonly regarded as the product of Stoic convictions and the dramatization of a Stoic worldview. Certainly they abound in Stoic moral ideas, and their preoccupation with emotional pathology and with the destructive consequences of passion, especially anger, is deeply indebted to the Stoic tradition (compare with *De ira*). This Stoicism, however, is no outer ideological clothing but part of the dramatic texture of the plays. To many the worldview of most of the plays is decidedly un-Stoic, since the Stoic ideology seems critically exhibited within a larger, more profound, and more disturbing vision. Both the philosophical works and the tragedies had a deep impact on subsequent European letters and thought, influencing in Renaissance England and Europe the formation not only of drama, tragic and otherwise, but of the literary and intellectual essay and treatise. Although his moral philosophy was often appropriated by Christian writers, to all who cared to look, Seneca offered profoundly non-Christian forms of thinking.

References:

K. Abel, "Seneca: Leben und Leistung," *Aufstieg und Niedergang des römischen Welt II,* 32, no. 2 (1985): 654–775;

Richard C. Beacham, *The Roman Theatre and its Audience* (Cambridge, Mass.: Harvard University Press, 1992);

Margarete Bieber, *The History of the Greek and Roman Theater* (Princeton, N.J.: Princeton University Press, 1961);

A. J. Boyle, ed., *The Imperial Muse,* volume I: *To Juvenal Through Ovid* (Berwick, Australia: Aureal, 1988);

Boyle, ed., *Seneca Tragicus: Ramus Essays on Senecan Drama* (Berwick, Australia: Aureal, 1983);

Boyle, *Tragic Seneca: An Essay in the Theatrical Tradition* (London: Routledge, 1997);

Gordon Braden, *Renaissance Tragedy and the Senecan Tradition: Anger's Privilege* (New Haven, Conn.: Yale University Press, 1985);

Francis-Regis Chaumartin, *Le De Beneficiis de Sénèque: Sa signification philosophique, politique et sociale* (Paris: Belles Lettres, 1985);

C. D. N. Costa, ed., *Seneca* (London: Routledge & Kegan Paul, 1974);

Peter J. Davis, *Shifting Song: The Chorus in Seneca's Tragedies* (Hildesheim Ger.: Olms-Weidmann, 1993);

T. A. Dorey and D. R. Dudley, eds., *Roman Drama* (London: Routledge & Kegan Paul, 1965);

T. S. Eliot, "Seneca in Elizabethan Translation," in his *Selected Essays,* third edition (London: Faber & Faber, 1951), pp. 65–105;

Janine Filliou-Lahille, *Le De Ira de Sénèque et la philosophie stoïcienne des passions* (Paris: Klincksieck, 1984);

John G. Fitch, "Sense-pauses and Relative Dating in Seneca, Sophocles and Shakespeare," *American Journal of Philology,* 102 (1981): 289–307;

Miriam T. Griffin, *Seneca: A Philosopher in Politics* (Oxford: Oxford University Press, 1976);

Pierre Grimal, *Sénèque ou la conscience de l'empire* (Paris: Belles Lettres, 1979);

Denis and Elisabeth Henry, *The Mask of Power: Seneca's Tragedies and Imperial Rome* (Warminster, U.K.: Aris & Phillips, 1985);

C. J. Herington, "Senecan Tragedy," *Arion,* 5 (1966): 422–471;

Herington, "The Younger Seneca," in volume II: *Latin Literature, The Cambridge History of Classical Literature,* edited by E. J. Kenney and W. V. Clausen (Cambridge: Cambridge University Press, 1982), pp. 511–532;

Eckard Lefêvre, ed., *Senecas Tragödien* (Darmstadt: Wissenschaftliche Buchgesellschaft, 1972);

Robert S. Miola, *Shakespeare and Classical Tragedy: The Influence of Seneca* (Oxford: Oxford University Press, 1992);

Marc Rozelaar, *Seneca: Eine Gesamtdarstellung* (Amsterdam: Hakkert, 1976);

Thomas G. Rosenmeyer, *Senecan Drama and Stoic Cosmology* (Berkeley: University of California Press, 1989);

Charles P. Segal, *Language and Desire in Seneca's Phaedra* (Princeton, N.J.: Princeton University Press, 1986);

Bernd Seidensticker, *Die Gesprächsverdichtung in den Tragödien Senecas* (Heidelberg: Carl Winter Universitätsverlag, 1969);

Villy Sørensen, *Seneca: The Humanist at the Court of Nero,* translated by W. Glyn Jones (Edinburgh: Canongate, 1984);

J. P. Sullivan, *Literature and Politics in the Age of Nero* (Ithaca, N.Y.: Cornell University Press, 1985);

Dana Ferrin Sutton, *Seneca on the Stage* (Leiden: Brill, 1986);

R. J. Tarrant, "Senecan Drama and its Antecedents," *Harvard Studies in Classical Philology,* 82 (1978): 213–263;

M. J. Wilson, "Seneca's Epistles to Lucilius: A Revaluation," in *The Imperial Muse,* volume I: *To Juvenal Through Ovid,* edited by A. J. Boyle (Berwick, Australia: Aureal, 1988), pp. 102–121.

Statius

(ca. A.D. 45 – ca. A.D. 96)

Stephen T. Newmyer
Duquesne University

WORKS: *Thebaid,* epic poem in twelve books (ca. A.D. 91 or 92);

Silvae, occasional poems in five books (A.D. 91–96);

Achilleid, unfinished epic poem in two books.

Editiones principes: *Achilleid,* edited by I. De Colonia (Venice: Gabriel di Pietro, 1472); *P. Pap. Statii Silvarum libri V,* edited by D. Calderini (Rome: Arnoldus Pannartz, 1475).

Standard editions: *Opere di Publio Papinio Stazio,* edited by Antonio Traglia and Giuseppe Aricò (Torino: UTET, 1980); *Thebaid,* 3 volumes, edited by R. Lesueur (Paris: Les Belles Lettres, 1990–1994); *P. Papini Stati Thebaidos Libri XII,* edited by D. E. Hill (Leiden: Brill, 1983); *P. Papini Stati: Thebais,* edited by Thomas C. Klinnert (Leipzig: Teubner, 1973–revision of the edition of Alfred Klotz, 1908); *P. Papini Stati Silvae,* edited by Aldo Marastoni (Leipzig: Teubner, 1970); *P. Papini Stati Achilleis,* edited by Marastoni (Leipzig: Teubner, 1974).

Translations in English: *Thebaid,* translated by A. D. Melville, with an introduction and notes by D. W. T. Vessey (Oxford: Clarendon Press, 1992); *Thebaid,* 3 volumes, translated by J. B. Poynton (Oxford: Shakespeare Head, 1971–1975); *Statius,* 2 volumes, Loeb Classical Library, edited and translated by J. H. Mozley (Cambridge, Mass.: Harvard University Press, 1928).

Commentaries: Heine Melle Mulder, *Publii Papinii Statii Thebaidos Liber Secundus* (Groningen: De Waal, 1954); Harry Snijder, *P. Papinius Statius, Thebaid: A Commentary on Book III with Text and Introduction* (Amsterdam: Hakkert, 1968); J. J. L. Smolenaars, *Statius Thebaid VII: A Commentary* (Leiden: Brill, 1994); Michael Dewar, *Statius: Thebaid IX* (Oxford: Clarendon Press, 1991); R. D. Williams, *P. Papinii Statii Thebaidos Liber Decimus* (Leiden: Brill, 1972); Harm-Jan van Dam, *P. Papinius Statius: Silvae Book II* (Leiden: Brill, 1984); K. M. Coleman, *Silvae IV* (Oxford: Clarendon Press, 1988); O. A. W. Dilke, *Achilleid* (Cambridge: Cambridge University Press, 1954).

In the twenty-first canto of the *Purgatorio,* Dante and his guide Virgil encounter the poet Statius, who introduces himself to the Florentine master (*Purgatorio* 21.91–93):

> Stazio la gente ancor di là mi noma:
> cantai de Tebe, e poi del grande Achille,
> ma caddi in via con la seconda soma.

> (Statius people yonder still call me:
> I sang of Thebes and then of great Achilles,
> but I fell on the way with the second burden.)

Shortly after, Statius acknowledges his reverence for Dante's companion and his own poetic mentor (*Purg.* 21.100–102):

> E per esser vivuto di là quando
> visse Virgilio, assentirei un sole
> più che non deggio al mio uscir di bando.

> (To have lived yonder when
> Virgil lived, I would consent to one more sun
> than I owe to my release from exile.)

In these few verses, Dante provides a summary of the literary career of Statius and incidentally foreshadows the modern scholarly judgment of Statius as a poet in the shadow of a far greater genius. Yet, that Dante deemed Statius a worthy companion and allowed Statius to accompany him and Virgil as far as Paradise reflects the admiration that Statius's poetry enjoyed almost into the twentieth century. The *Thebaid,* the epic of the Theban saga to which Dante's Statius alludes, was esteemed almost as universally as was Virgil's *Aeneid* and has the distinction of being the only extant Latin epic from classical antiquity that seems to have received the finishing touches of its author. Moreover, Statius's occasional poems, the *Silvae,* which are filled with references to incidents in the poet's daily life, offer

couple remained childless themselves, and the death of their adopted son caused the poet intense grief (*Silvae* 5.5.1–13). Statius took great pride in the victory of his poetry at the Alban Games of A.D. 90, but he was deeply disappointed at his defeat in the Capitoline Games in that same year. Toward the end of his life, Statius returned to Naples in retirement, and he seems to have died before the assassination in A.D. 96 of the emperor Domitian (reigned A.D. 81–96).

Statius was seldom referred to by his poetic contemporaries. The satirist Juvenal (ca. A.D. 60–130), who appears to have had contempt for Statius (perhaps because he wrote epic poetry, a genre that the satirist scorned), admits that Statius had a pleasant voice in his public readings of his *Thebaid,* which the satirist acknowledges was popular with Roman audiences (*Satires* 7.82–87). Yet, Juvenal implies that Statius derived no financial gain from his epic poetry and would have starved had he not produced poetic hackwork, an assertion that may well be an exaggeration.

The poems of the *Silvae,* from which the autobiographical details of Statius's life are derived, paint a far rosier picture of the poet's circumstances. Statius mentions as friends many aristocratic personages more or less closely connected to the imperial court, and he took great pride in an invitation to dinner at the palace of Domitian (*Silvae* 4.2). Statius toured the villas of the leisured aristocrats Manilius Vopiscus and Pollius Felix (*Silvae* 1.3; 2.2), and he congratulated various bureaucrats in Domitian's court on their personal successes and professional advancement. While Statius may have enjoyed an acquaintance with persons of high social station, he was hardly their social equal, and he may have exaggerated the degree of his intimacy with them and their circles. Statius's apparently friendly relations with Domitian may also be a literary fiction, since beneath the outwardly easy appearance of his association with the emperor, one may detect a certain degree of unease and caution. If the evidence of such contemporaries of the poet as Pliny the Younger and Tacitus can be trusted, Domitian would not seem to have been the sort of person to encourage intimacy with his courtiers. The poet's desire to win the approval of the emperor led him to flatter Domitian, especially in the *Silvae,* but in his epics as well, in a manner that many readers have found groveling and insincere. At the same time, Statius's portrait in the *Silvae* of happy families, hardworking and honest public servants, and an efficient government, provides a welcome contrast to the generally dark picture of life in Rome in the late first century A.D. that emerges from other writers of the period whose vision of life under Domitian has been more widely accepted.

Statius published his magnum opus, the epic poem *Thebaid,* in twelve books, in A.D. 91 or 92, after

Virgil watching while Statius and Dante sleep, one of William Blake's paintings of scenes in Dante's Divine Comedy *(Ashmolean Museum, Oxford)*

a clearer picture of the poet's life and personality than is available in the cases of most Roman authors.

Publius Papinius Statius was born around A.D. 45 in Naples, a city famous for its Greek culture and learning. His father conducted a successful school in which Greek and Latin literature were taught, and he was his son's first teacher. The elder Statius, himself a poet, composed an epic on episodes of the Roman civil war of A.D. 69, and at the time of his death he was planning a poem on the eruption of Vesuvius in A.D. 79 (*Silvae* 5.3.195–208). The family moved to Rome around A.D. 69, and the elder Statius opened another school in the capital, dedicated to the education of Roman youth destined for public careers (*Silvae* 5.3.176–194). The younger Statius won his first literary prize in the poetic contest called the Augustalia at Naples around A.D. 78, and he notes that he enjoyed the advice and guidance of his father in the early stages of work on what would be his masterpiece, the epic *Thebaid* (*Silvae* 5.3.234–238). Statius's father died around A.D. 79. About this same time, the younger Statius married Claudia, a widow who brought a daughter to the marriage. The

twelve years of hard work on the poem. Around that same time, he began to collect and publish, perhaps in individual books or groups of books, the five books of his occasional poems, the *Silvae*. Book 1 appeared by the end of A.D. 92, books 2 and 3 by the end of 93, book 4 in 95, and book 5 after the poet's death. In some poems of the *Silvae,* Statius refers to working on an epic about the life of the hero Achilles but died after composing only eleven hundred verses of this *Achilleid*. In addition, there survive four verses of a poem dealing with Domitian's campaigns in A.D. 82–83 against the Germans that are quoted in a commentary on the poems of Juvenal, although that epic is otherwise unattested. Juvenal himself (*Satires* 7.87) mentions a now-lost libretto for a pantomime titled *Agave* that the satirist implies brought Statius more financial gain than did his epic productions.

It is clear from the remarkable apostrophe to his epic that closes the *Thebaid* (12.810–819), in which he speeds it on its way before the reading public, that Statius intended his poetic reputation to rest upon the *Thebaid*. He notes that it had met with a favorable reception from the public already, an apparent reference to his public readings from the work during the years of its composition, and that it was already in his own lifetime becoming a textbook for school students. He observes with pride that Domitian had deigned to study it, but he cautions his epic not to challenge the preeminent position of Virgil's "divine *Aeneid*" (*Theb.* 12.816). Statius's allusion to his epic model is an elegant acknowledgment of the artistic burden that all Roman epic poets who worked in the century after the publication of the *Aeneid* felt they bore as writers whose careers followed the appearance of a work generally accepted to be a masterpiece. Epic poets who worked in the early Empire sought to create poems that were not mere slavish imitations of the *Aeneid* while still taking account of the excellences of that work through incorporation of scenes and language bound to recall the earlier epic to readers of their own poems. The solutions to the artistic dilemma of following after an acknowledged masterpiece that the poets of the first century A.D. devised have brought upon their epics charges (from many modern critics) of inferior workmanship and lack of inspiration. Statius and other epic poets of his generation sought to imitate the excellences of the *Aeneid* while at the same time improving upon the earlier poem, if possible, through greater use of pathos and striking language. Statius and his contemporaries Silius Italicus (ca. A.D. 23–101) and Valerius Flaccus (died ca. A.D. 95) reasoned that scenes that moved readers of the *Aeneid* could be reworked in their own epics in ways that rendered them more affecting through exaggeration of details, sometimes at lengths that modern critics have found absurd. If the scene of a soldier falling in battle could move the reader, it could surely move the reader more if the soldier's severed head were portrayed as whirling through the air while still inside its helmet (*Theb.* 8.699).

The type of education that Statius and his poetic contemporaries received in the first century A.D. helped to condition their response to the *Aeneid*. The increased emphasis on rhetorical skill in the education of Roman youth in the first century A.D. and the bizarre and unreal nature of the subject matter of school declamations that Roman students were taught to compose had a decided influence upon the manner of expression employed in imperial epic. The clear and straightforward expression of Virgil was now replaced with an exaggerated and convoluted style of which Statius's poetry is perhaps the most striking example. A tree is described as so huge that when it falls, it "releases vast spaces of heaven" (*Theb.* 9.534). Added to the difficulties of a style at times bordering on the obscure is Statius's fondness for learned mythological allusions of the sort that delighted educated audiences of his day but that cause his poetry to pose a challenge to modern readers. For example, the city of Thebes, the scene of the *Thebaid,* is referred to by many epithets that recall obscure episodes of its mythological past, including "Aonian" (*Theb.* 1.34), "Echionian" (*Theb.* 1.169), "Ogygian" (*Theb.* 1.173), and "Sidonian" (*Theb.* 3.656). In a similarly learned manner, the people of Argos are called "Inachian youth" (*Theb.* 1.619).

The same rhetorical training that fostered exaggeration of language in epic of the Empire period also exercised a negative influence upon the structure of epic poems, encouraging an elaboration of individual scenes over a concern for the structure of the poems as a whole and resulting in epics that some critics charge amount to less than the sum of their parts. Critics have charged as well that the subject Statius chose for his *Thebaid* was intrinsically unsuitable for epic treatment on the grounds that it is by nature episodic and lacks a clear-cut hero and sympathetic characters. Such shortcomings did not deter poets before Statius from using the tale of Thebes as the subject for epic poems.

The earliest-known epic treatment of the subject that Statius chose for his poem is the *Thebaid* that formed part of the so-called Epic Cycle, a group of Greek poems composed apparently in the seventh and sixth centuries B.C., giving a continuous narrative of mythological history from the creation down to the end of the Trojan War. The *Thebaid* of the Epic Cycle, of uncertain authorship, is now lost, although ancient critics held it in high esteem. The *Thebaid* of Antimachus of Colophon (ca. 400 B.C.) extended to twenty-four books and was known for its Homeric reminiscences and its obscure learning. Because Antimachus's work is also

Page from a manuscript (possibly ca. A.D. 1000) for Statius's epic of the Theban saga, Thebaid *(Chapter Library of Worcester Cathedral)*

lost, its use by Statius cannot be assessed. In addition, many Greek tragedies dealt with episodes included in Statius's *Thebaid;* among those tragedies still extant are the *Seven against Thebes* of Aeschylus (467 B.C.), the *Suppliants* (422 B.C.) and the *Phoenician Women* (409 B.C.) of Euripides, and the *Oedipus at Colonus* of Sophocles (posthumously produced in 401 B.C.). While traces of influence of these tragedies can be detected in matters of plot and treatment, it was Virgil's *Aeneid* that served as Statius's chief poetic model. Many episodes in the *Thebaid* and innumerable verbal reminiscences suggest Statius's close study of his predecessor. As in the *Aeneid,* the hostilities that form the central narrative element of Statius's epic commence with the opening of the seventh book. The earlier poet's scene of the Fury Allecto's hastening the commencement of hostilities between the Trojans and the Latins by inducing Aeneas's son Ascanius to shoot a stag beloved by the locals (*Aeneid* 7.475–539) is reborn in Statius's scene of the Fury Tisiphone's hastening the commencement of hostilities by inducing the Argives to kill two tigers beloved by the priests of Bacchus (*Theb.* 7.564–607).

Although Statius's epic everywhere betrays evidences of Virgil's influence, the dark subject matter of the *Thebaid* afforded little opportunity for the lighter moments and touches of humor that occasionally provide welcome relief to the serious narrative of the *Aeneid.* The *Thebaid* deals with the expedition of Polynices, son of Oedipus, to wrest the throne of Thebes from his hated brother Eteocles. The two brothers had agreed to rule Thebes in alternating years, but Eteocles refused to step down when his first year of kingship ended, thus forcing Polynices to enlist the aid of neighboring kings in his effort to obtain the throne. The first six books of the epic are taken up with Polynices' efforts to organize an army under the leadership of the so-called Seven against Thebes. Adrastus, the aged king of Argos who became Polynices' father-in-law, is the only one of the Seven to return alive from the disastrous expedition. He and Polynices are joined by Tydeus, king of Calydon; Amphiaraus, an Argive seer who foresees his own death on the expedition; Parthenopaeus, the handsome son of the swift-footed heroine Atalanta; and the Argive generals Hippomedon and Capaneus. As the Seven advance toward their fateful encounter at Thebes, they come upon Hypsipyle, former queen of Lemnos, who now serves as a slave to King Lycurgus, whose infant son Opheltes she now tends as nurse. Part of book 4, and books 5 and 6 are taken up with Hypsipyle's narrative of her recent fortunes and the accidental death of the infant while she tells her tale. Hypsipyle's narrative, which many critics have seen as an irrelevant digression that hampers the progress of the epic, illustrates the elaboration of episodes characteristic of epic poetry of the early empire. It causes the commencement of hostilities to be delayed until book 7. While some recent critics, including David Vessey (1973) and William J. Dominik (1994), have argued convincingly that apparently extraneous episodes such as the account of Hypsipyle are in fact closely related to the dominant themes of the epic as a whole; such passages unquestionably give the impression that Statius has temporarily forgotten his main narrative while lavishing excessive attention on individual scenes.

The latter half of the *Thebaid* includes Statius's "war books," in the manner of the second half of the *Aeneid,* and he enlivens the grim account of the fall of the defenders of Polynices by spectacular death scenes. Amphiaraus finds himself hurtling to Hades as the ground opens beneath him to swallow him and his chariot, to the consternation of the Lord of the Underworld, who resents the admission of light into his gloomy realm (*Theb.* 7.771–8.161). The fierce warrior Tydeus gnaws on the skull of the man who dealt him his death blow and thereby loses a chance for immortality that the goddess Pallas, disgusted at his savagery, at last denies him (*Theb.* 8.751–766). Hippomedon and Parthenopaeus fall in book 9, the former exhausted in combat with the river Ismenus (*Theb.* 9.404–569) before falling to a hail of arrows, while the gentle Parthenopaeus, fatally wounded, touchingly beseeches his mother to accord him a decent burial. In book 10 Capaneus, scorner of the gods, challenges Jupiter himself to prevent him from scaling the walls of Thebes; the god obliges, setting the hero aflame with his thunderbolts (*Theb.* 10.883–939). The horrifying climax of the poem is reached in the long-delayed single combat of the brothers Polynices and Eteocles, an encounter that their sister Antigone and mother Jocasta sought in vain to prevent (*Theb.* 11.497–579). The grisly details of their deaths and the pathos of the attempts of family members to prevent the deaths are apt to make the remaining scenes of the epic, including the burials of the Seven amidst the lamentations of their widows and the intercession of King Theseus of Athens to ensure the proper treatment of the bodies of the dead, seem anticlimactic to the modern reader, although they serve to afford the epic a peaceful and in some sense noble conclusion.

Some readers might suppose that in choosing the well-worn mythological saga of the Seven against Thebes as the subject for an epic, Statius sought a "safe" and uncontroversial subject for his poetry, but the theme of fratricidal warfare had painful associations for a nation that traced its beginning to the warfare between the brothers Romulus and Remus. Similarly, Statius's epic predecessor Lucan (A.D. 39–65) had recently composed a poem on the conflict between

Julius Caesar and his former son-in-law, Pompey. Indeed, it was rumored at Rome that Domitian and his brother and predecessor on the throne, Titus (reigned A.D. 79–81), were rivals for power, and the Roman biographer Suetonius claimed that Domitian had plotted to overthrow his brother (*Titus* 9). The subject of the expedition of Polynices was therefore not without danger to Statius at the court of a monarch who suspected insults everywhere. Domitian might have had cause to see an allusion to his own family in Statius's reference to Oedipus's "house in disarray" at the beginning of his epic (*Theb.* 1.17). It is difficult not to see serious political commentary in the poet's striking contrast between the ultimately fruitless conflict between Eteocles and Polynices and the just and merciful actions of Theseus of Athens, who secures the burial of the fallen heroes at the close of the *Thebaid*. Before they beseech Theseus for his aid, the Argive widows take refuge at the Altar of Compassion at Athens, beautifully described in one of the most celebrated passages of the epic (*Theb.* 12.481–518). In view of Statius's portrait of the mercy of Theseus and the power of tears and prayer at the Altar, it is difficult to avoid the conclusion that the *Thebaid* is in some sense a political statement on the preferability of justice and kindness in the governance of states and on the ultimate futility of armed conflict that brings down states.

The influence of the *Thebaid* upon later literature was extensive and long lasting and still has not been fully assessed. In the twelfth century the *Thebaid* joined the works of Virgil, Ovid, and Juvenal as a standard school text. Dante's admiration for Statius was enthusiastic, and his epic was the main source for the mid-twelfth-century *Roman de Thèbes*. Statius is mentioned with respect in Geoffrey Chaucer's *House of Fame* (2.1455ff.), and Statius's *Thebaid* was an important source for the English poet's *Troilus and Criseyde* (2.78–112; 5.1478–1519). Chaucer bids farewell to his *Troilus and Criseyde* in terms that clearly recall Statius's final apostrophe to his *Thebaid,* and he ends his stanza with a mention of the Roman poet's name (*Troilus and Criseyde* 5.1786–1792):

> Go, litel book, go litel myn tregedie,
> Ther god thy maker yet, er that he dye,
> So sende might to make in som comedie!
> But litel book, no making thou nenvye,
> But subgit be to alle poesye;
> And kis the steppes, wher-as thou seest pace
> Virgile, Ovyde, Omer, Lucan, and Stace.

John Lydgate appears to have used Statius for his *Siege of Thebes* (ca. 1420). Alexander Pope and Thomas Gray translated portions of the epic into English verse. Thereafter Statius's reputation fell into eclipse as his

exaggerated rhetoric and taste for pathetic and ghastly scenes failed to win the approval of readers attracted by the restrained style of Roman Classicism. In the past few decades, however, Statius and his epic contemporaries have enjoyed a small renaissance of scholarly interest, and the exalted majesty of Statius's style, as well as the meditations on the use and abuse of power that make the *Thebaid* a serious study in kingship, have won the epic renewed respect and admiration.

While the *Thebaid* remained popular through the Middle Ages, Statius's collection of occasional poems, the *Silvae,* fell into obscurity until the chance fifteenth-century discovery by Poggio of a manuscript including the work. The title of the work, meaning "woods, forest," is typical of the names given to Greek and Latin poetic collections of miscellaneous content. Roman rhetoricians employed the singular form *silva* to refer to a literary rough draft composed at great speed. One of the chief claims that Statius makes for the poems included in the *Silvae* is that they were produced quickly, dashed off in the heat of inspiration (*Silvae* 1. pref.3–4). None of the poems, he claims (*Silvae* 1. pref.14–15), took more than two days to compose, and some were turned out in only one day. Statius's great skill as a versifier and his extensive rhetorical training would certainly have enabled him to produce even the longest poem in the collection (*Silvae* 5.3), which extends to almost three hundred verses, in the space of two days, although his claim of rapid composition may be an exaggeration designed to enhance his reputation for virtuosity. Another factor that may lend support to Statius's claim of rapid composition is the striking degree to which the poems of the *Silvae* reflect the prescriptions set down in handbooks for the composition of speeches in the various genres included in the *Silvae.* Study of the handbooks of succeeding centuries, including that of Menander of Laodicea (third century A.D.), shows that rules had been developed by rhetoricians to aid writers in the composition of speeches intended to address the emperor, speeches congratulating persons on a birthday or career promotion, speeches consoling persons on the loss of a loved one, and speeches for other special occasions. Many of the poems included in the *Silvae* commemorate such occasions, and comparison of Statius's techniques of organizing and executing poems on the sorts of occasions for which prescriptions exist in rhetorical handbooks suggests that he may have availed himself of such works in the composition of the *Silvae.* Statius tends to treat a subject in a similar fashion each time it appears in a poem of the collection. Just as the rhetorical handbooks recommend, Statius's poems consoling persons on the loss of a loved one offer generous praise of the deceased followed by commonplaces of consolation. The encomiastic part of Statius's consol-

Bust of the emperor Domitian, whom Statius flattered in his works (courtesy of the Toledo Museum of Art, Ohio)

atory poems normally includes the combination of praise of family connections, youthful accomplishments, adult career, and fine character that the handbooks recommend. This pattern is observable in *Silvae* 2.1; 2.6; 3.3; 5.1; 5.3; and 5.5.

Just as the poems exhibit certain similarities of content, so do they show evidence of similarity in structure. Statius was fond of organizing his occasional poems in a pattern of ring composition (ABCBA). A narrative element of particular importance is thereby "highlighted" by being surrounded by material of balanced if lesser narrative weight. Frequently the central element in the *Silvae* features a charming mythological tale intended to give an explanation for the event or circumstance celebrated in the poem. Such a structural device may likewise have served as an aid to rapid composition.

Twenty-six poems in the *Silvae* are composed in dactylic hexameter, the meter of classical epic poetry and the verse form with which Statius was most familiar, while the remaining poems in the collection employ a variety of lyric meters used by his Roman predecessors Catullus and Horace. In addition to poems offering consolation to the bereaved, the *Silvae* includes examples of an astonishing variety of poetic genres. Poems celebrating recovery from illness (*Silvae* 1.4), marriage (*Silvae* 1.2.), departure for a journey (*Silvae* 3.2), and the birth of a child (*Silvae* 4.8) are joined by a remarkable set of poetic descriptions of buildings and objects (*Silvae* 1.1; 1.3; 2.2; 3.1; 4.3; and 4.6). Everywhere in the *Silvae* Statius maintains a lighthearted manner, in stark contrast to the somber atmosphere of the *Thebaid,* even in those poems in which Statius celebrates the accomplishments of Domitian (*Silvae* 1.1; 4.1; 4.2; and 4.3). Since praise of the tyrannical Domitian is even more blatant than in the *Thebaid,* the *Silvae* has never won the favorable audience that the epic has enjoyed, but the attractive picture of loving families and warm friendships that the poems provide offers the reader many insights into the everyday lives of Romans of comfortable station. Not the least attractive facet of the collection is the glimpse it affords of Statius's personality in his lamentations over the deaths of his father and adopted son (*Silvae* 5.3; 5.5) and in his address to his wife on the occasion of his decision to retire to Naples (*Silvae* 3.5). These references show Statius to have been a devoted and loving family man. His teasing verses to his friend Plotius Grypus, who had sent him a worthless gift, suggest his sense of humor (*Silvae* 4.9). There is nothing else quite like the *Silvae* in Latin literature.

Twice in the *Silvae*, Statius refers to the composition of his epic on the life of Achilles, upon which he had begun to work while still publishing his books of occasional poetry (*Silvae* 4.7.21–24; 5.2.163). In the opening verses of this *Achilleid*, the poet asserts that he intends to cover the entire life of the Greek hero, while Homer had contented himself in the *Iliad* with Achilles' encounter with Hector (*Achilleid* 1.3–4). The conclusion to be drawn from such an assertion is that the *Achilleid* would have been longer than the *Thebaid*, but the poet did not live to carry out his plan. Indeed, he gives the impression in the *Silvae* that work on the new project did not progress well. He confesses that Apollo was slow to visit him, and the fledgling epic "halts at the first turning-post of its course" (*Silvae* 4.7.23–24). In the fragment that Statius did complete, Achilles' mother Thetis hides the young Achilles at the court of King Lycomedes on Scyros to prevent him from being compelled to join the expedition to Troy. The young hero is tricked into accompanying the Greeks to war. While the extant verses display Statius's customary learning and cleverness of expression, the tone of the *Achilleid* is lighter and more playful than that of the *Thebaid*, and on the whole the fragment is less vigorous and brilliant than is the *Thebaid*, a circumstance that may suggest that the poet's powers were failing. Most modern critics do not regret that Statius did not live to complete the epic, although it shared the popularity of the *Thebaid* in the Middle Ages.

Of all the epic successors of Virgil, Statius is most likely to appeal to modern readers. Variety of mood, deftness of expression, and polish of execution amply reward the reader willing to take the time to master the difficulties of a style that at times pushes the Latin language to its limits. If he did not look so deeply into the human heart as did his mentor Virgil, Statius felt sympathy for those who suffered and gladness for those who rejoiced. Small wonder that Dante, who welcomed his companionship on his spiritual journey, believed Statius to have been a Christian (*Purg.* 22.73).

References:

F. M. Ahl, "Statius' 'Thebaid': A Reconsideration," *Aufstieg und Niedergang der Römischen Welt* II, 32, no. 5 (1986): 2803–2912;

William J. Dominik, *The Mythic Voice of Statius: Power and Politics in the Thebaid* (Leiden: Brill, 1994);

Alex Hardie, *Statius and the Silvae: Poets, Patrons and Epideixis in the Graeco-Roman World* (Liverpool: Francis Cairns, 1983);

Philip R. Hardie, *The Epic Successors of Virgil: A Study in the Dynamics of a Tradition* (Cambridge: Cambridge University Press, 1993);

Stephen T. Newmyer, *The Silvae of Statius: Structure and Theme* (Leiden: Brill, 1979);

David Vessey, *Statius and the Thebaid* (Cambridge: Cambridge University Press, 1973);

Gordon Williams, *Change and Decline: Roman Literature in the Early Empire* (Berkeley: University of California Press, 1978).

Suetonius

(ca. A.D. 69 – post A.D. 122)

Richard C. Lounsbury
Brigham Young University

WORK–EXTANT: *De vita Caesarum,* 12 biographies in 8 books (On the Life of the Caesars, A.D. 119–122?).

WORKS–FRAGMENTARY: *De viris illustribus,* parts of *De grammaticis et rhetoribus* and *De poetis* (On Famous Men);

Treatises on various topics in Greek and Latin.

Editio princeps: *Vitae XII Caesarum,* edited by J. A. Campanus (Rome: Joannes Phillippus de Lignamine, 1470).

Standard editions: *C. Suetoni Tranquilli quae supersunt omnia,* edited by Karl Ludwig Roth (Leipzig: Teubner, 1858); *De vita Caesarum: Libri VIII,* edited by Maximilian Ihm (Leipzig: Teubner, editiō maiōr, 1907; editiō minor, 1908); *Peri blasphemin, Peri paidin, extraits byzantins,* edited by Jean Taillardat (Paris: Les Belles Lettres, 1967).

Translations in English: *Suetonius,* edited and translated by John C. Rolfe, 2 volumes, Loeb Classical Library (Cambridge, Mass.: Harvard University Press, 1913–1914; volume 1, revised 1951, 1998; volume 2, revised 1997).

Commentaries: *C. Suetonii Tranquilli Opera,* 3 volumes, edited by D. C. G. Baumgarten-Crusius (Leipzig: G. Fleischer, 1816–1818); *C. Suetoni Tranquilli Divus Augustus,* edited by Evelyn S. Shuckburgh (Cambridge: Cambridge University Press, 1896); *De grammaticis et rhetoribus,* edited by Rodney Potter Robinson (Paris: Champion, 1925); *C. Suetoni Tranquilli Divus Julius,* edited by H. E. Butler and M. Cary (Oxford: Oxford University Press, 1927; reprinted, Bristol: Bristol Classical Press, 1982); *C. Suetoni Tranquilli Divus Vespasianus,* edited by A. W. Braithwaite (Oxford: Clarendon Press, 1927); *C. Suetoni Tranquilli De vita Caesarum libri VII-VIII,* edited by George W. Mooney (London: Macmillan, 1930; reprinted, New York: Arno Press, 1979); *C. Suetonii Tranquilli De vita Tiberii, Chapters I to XXIII,* edited by Mary Johnstone du Four (Philadelphia: n. p., 1941);

Suetonio De poetis e biografi minori, edited by Augusto Rostagni (Turin: Chiantore, 1944); *Divus Augustus, De vita Caesarum: Liber II,* edited by Mario Attilio Levi, second edition (Florence: La Nuova Italia, 1958); *Nero,* edited by B. H. Warmington (Bristol: Bristol Classical Press, 1977); *Suetonius' Life of Nero: An Historical Commentary,* edited by K. R. Bradley (Brussels: Latomus, 1978); *Divus Augustus,* edited by John M. Carter (Bristol: Bristol Classical Press, 1982); *Claudius,* edited by J. Mottershead (Bristol: Bristol Classical Press, 1986); *De grammaticis et rhetoribus,* edited and translated by Robert A. Kaster (Oxford: Clarendon Press, 1995).

There were other Roman biographers besides Suetonius; Suetonius wrote in more genres than biography. The writings that recorded his various, even odd, scholarship have perished, however, and other Roman biographers were little luckier. Some remain as mere names. Most of Suetonius's own *De viris illustribus* (On Famous Men), which surveyed probably more than a hundred Roman authors, is lost; Cornelius Nepos, apart from an abbreviated *Cato* and a laudatory treatment of Cicero's friend Atticus, is represented only in a series of scanty lives of foreign (mostly Greek) generals; and Tacitus's life of his father-in-law, Julius Agricola, an idiosyncratic blend of encomium and history, resisted imitation and was furthermore overshadowed by the *Histories* and *Annals.* Time, however, was kindest where Suetonius was most innovative and most influential. Comprising lives of the twelve Caesars from Julius to Domitian, his *De vita Caesarum* (A.D. 119–122?) survived to share with Plutarch's *Parallel Lives* the preeminent place in classical biography and its tradition.

Sources for the life and career of Gaius Suetonius Tranquillus are four: Suetonius himself; letters to him and references elsewhere written by his friend and patron the younger Pliny; a contemporary or near-contemporary inscription found at Hippo Regius in what is now Algeria; and later, sometimes much later, notices–

especially in a fourth-century collection of imperial biographies called the *Historia Augusta* and in the *Suda,* a Byzantine encyclopedia of the tenth century–which preserve, however undependably, some memory of the Suetonian corpus before most of it was lost and the remainder mangled. Suetonius himself tells us, in passing, something of his family. His grandfather was able to report a likely motive behind Caligula's bridge of boats across the bay at Baiae, since he was at least close enough to the imperial household to gain information *ab interioribus aulicis* (from courtiers of the inner circle; *Gaius Caligula* 19.3). During the civil wars of the year A.D. 69 Suetonius's father, Suetonius Laetus, of equestrian rank, was a military tribune in the army, and possibly on the staff, of the emperor Otho (*Otho* 10.1); after Otho's suicide, the legion in which Laetus served went over to the cause of the ultimately victorious Vespasian. In the reign of Vespasian's son Domitian, Suetonius himself was sufficiently or conveniently placed to be present at a trial for tax evasion supervised by the emperor's financial officer (*Domitian* 12.2). Under Domitian, too, and about twenty years after Nero's suicide in A.D. 68, Suetonius was, as he describes himself, an *adulescens* (young man; *Nero* 57.2). This remark has suggested that he was born ca. A.D. 69, although a year as early as A.D. 61 or as late as A.D. 77 has been proposed.

Pliny's letters give glimpses of Suetonius early in public life, even if–as is typical of persons appearing in that carefully crafted collection–he is more the occasion for than the subject of what is said, with strenuous elegance. He seems to have inherited some money, for Pliny helped him in negotiating the purchase of land for a country retreat near Rome before Suetonius had made much more than a beginning as an advocate. He took a strong interest in the rhetorical culture of the period, perhaps with a view toward the career that he was eventually to follow. By about A.D. 97 Pliny could include him among *scholastici*–that is, those participating and educated in the world of the declamation schools and their concomitant literary activity (1.24); late in their correspondence Pliny asked Suetonius's advice on the etiquette proper to a private reading of one's poetry to friends (9.34). But Suetonius was fussy, too fussy about his work–so Pliny judged–urging his friend in about A.D. 105 or 106 to see some literary projects through to publication: "Perfectum opus absolutumque est, nec iam splendescit lima sed atteritur" (the work is complete and perfect, nor is it now being polished by revision but rather worn away; 5.10). Pliny's patronage offered, besides literary counsel, a military tribunate to be served in Britain, which Suetonius asked to be transferred to a relative (3.8). In language often interpreted to suggest that Suetonius was with him as a member of

his staff, Pliny as governor of Bithynia (ca. A.D. 110–ca. A.D. 112) petitioned successfully the emperor Trajan for the *ius trium liberorum* (tax, inheritance, and other advantages accruing to those with three or more children) to be granted to Suetonius, whose marriage was childless and whose character deserved imperial favor: he was "probissimus, honestissimus, eruditissimus vir" (a most upright, respectable, learned man; 10.94).

Pliny died during the governorship. He had backed a strong horse: Suetonius was able to rise high and rapidly, even after his patron's death. The details of that elevation are partially lost; what survives is largely owing to an inscription, evidently a dedication, discovered at Hippo Regius. (Why that town so honored Suetonius is not known; it may have been his birthplace.) The inscription is itself fragmentary, fruitful of speculation, especially regarding Suetonius's earlier career. There seem to have been one or more honorific priesthoods, maybe an appointment by Trajan to a panel of judicial assessors in Rome; a broad gap in the text leaves space for several more rungs of a ladder dexterously mounted. Text regarding the top rungs escaped mutilation. Whether separately, together, or in some combination, Suetonius held three imperial ministries lofty in the equestrian career that he had chosen to pursue: *a studiis, a bibliothecis,* and *ab epistulis.* The competence of the first of these ministries is obscure; what can usefully be conjectured suggests that its holder advised the emperor in cultural matters, perhaps informally, perhaps also when dispensing patronage or in connection with important public occasions. The second ministry entailed superintendence of the imperial libraries, and chronology further makes it likely that Suetonius was the first director of the Greek and Latin libraries situated on either side of Trajan's new forum, dedicated in A.D. 112. As *ab epistulis* Suetonius was chief of the imperial secretariat under Trajan's successor Hadrian. This office required more than supervision of the enormous correspondence between the emperor and his officials throughout the empire. What the emperor said and how he said it were expected to announce and confirm his worthiness to incarnate Roman culture, a culture extremely sophisticated in the spoken and the written word: in accordance with this expectation the minister *ab epistulis* advised, probably drafted, perhaps composed wholly or in part the emperor's edicts. All three offices, then, which Suetonius held as the culmination of his career, united to promote and facilitate the emperor's guardianship, as the public regarded it, of the nation's cultural inheritance.

If the admittedly unreliable testimony of the *Historia Augusta* is to be believed, Suetonius was dismissed from his post as *ab epistulis* (*Hadrian* 11.3). The testimony is muddled, but consistent with it is the interpre-

Busts of the emperor Hadrian ca. A.D. 117–118 and the empress Sabina (Uffizi Gallery, Florence). Suetonius lost his position as ab epistulis *under Hadrian in A.D. 122 because of a supposed breach of etiquette toward the empress.*

tation that the dismissal occurred in A.D. 122 in Britain, where Suetonius was in attendance upon his indefatigably perambulatory master. The reason, real or professed, was some breach of etiquette toward the empress Sabina, whom, however, Hadrian himself disliked; the praetorian prefect and many others fell from power along with Suetonius. From this outcome it has been only too easy to speculate upon court factions, plots, or a coup d'état detected and demolished. Of Suetonius's later career, if there was one, and of his life afterward, there is no record (though this fact has not discouraged conjecture), nor is anything known for sure about the dating and sequence of Suetonius's writings.

Most of these works are wholly lost or, at best, survive in epitomes, citations, and fragments—themselves open to question: do they represent, and in how contaminated a form, the original text, or a paraphrase, or a translation into Greek? (No one knows for certain which, if any, of his works Suetonius wrote in Greek; there is consensus only on a study of insults in that language, extant in a medieval abridgement itself fragmentary and mutilated.) The lost works seem to have been concerned with lexicographical matters on the one

hand (such as clothes, physical defects, weather-signs, seas and rivers, winds, and "the signs in books"—shorthand and ciphers?) and institutions on the other (such as children's games, games in Greece and spectacles in Rome, the Roman calendar, Roman customs generally, public offices, and a polemic against a commentator on Cicero's *De re publica*); a common ground may have been the usefulness of vocabulary and language to elucidate manners and institutions. There were, moreover, biographical works besides *De viris illustribus* and *De vita Caesarum*—one on kings, another on prominent prostitutes.

Of *De viris illustribus* there is much better, though still inadequate and disputed, information. The work seems to have been much admired (and plundered) by scholars. In the late fourth and early fifth centuries St. Jerome imitated it for his own work of the same title, meant to be a Christian equivalent; and in his translation and supplement of Eusebius's *Chronicle* St. Jerome turned constantly, to all appearances exclusively, to Suetonius as his source for the history of Latin literature. Divided into categories by genre, *De viris illustribus* comprehended poets, orators, historians, and philosophers; it also included—and here Suetonius seems to have had few if any precursors—those contributing to the education and formation of authors, like antiquarians and teachers of grammar and rhetoric. (Grammar among the Romans constituted the learning and the critical skills needed to read literary works.) The list of authors treated was ambitious but not, apparently, exhaustive: while not neglecting the early period and the generation before his own, Suetonius seems to have emphasized the late Republic and the Augustan and (though rather less) the Julio-Claudian ages. None of the biographies of Roman authors in *De viris illustribus* can be said to survive in the form in which they were written; what is extant of them was transmitted by literary critics and scholars, adapting them to introduce editions and commentaries. However, it is generally agreed that among the poets the Suetonian lives of Terence, Virgil, Horace, and Lucan survive substantially, if incompletely; more harshly abbreviated and adapted are the lives of Passienus Crispus among the orators and Pliny the Elder among the historians. These remnants are not much. But the section devoted to teachers of grammar and rhetoric, *De grammaticis et rhetoribus,* has been preserved in large part in a single manuscript together with the minor works of Tacitus. It is introduced with a sketch of the beginnings of grammar at Rome; brief biographical notices follow, none more than a page in length, of twenty teachers of grammar. Thereupon the rhetoricians receive, after a like introduction, sixteen such notices, of which the first five only are extant; hence, missing are biographies of those teachers of rhetoric of whom Suetonius is likely to have had personal experience, above all Quintilian. What is left, then, of *De viris illustribus* is enough to indicate how grave is the loss of the rest. Even *De grammaticis et rhetoribus,* however much readers may regret that it survived when biographies of Rome's great writers did not, permits a detailed, albeit partial, understanding of the education that those writers received. Had the whole of *De viris illustribus* been preserved, Roman literary history would have more than this niggardly residue.

Of Suetonius's writings *De vita Caesarum* has survived best, though it has not survived intact. Its preface, if following the conventions of the form, would declare something of the biographer's intentions, the importance of his undertaking, and any claims to originality; it included a dedication to Septicius Clarus, to whom the younger Pliny had dedicated the first book of his letters and who as praetorian prefect is recorded as having been dismissed along with Suetonius. This preface has disappeared, along with the first pages of the life of Julius Caesar. The remainder survive; after Caesar comes his great-nephew Octavian, who became the first emperor, Augustus; then follow Augustus's successors by blood or adoption, the Julio-Claudians—Tiberius,

Caligula, Claudius, and Nero; after the end of the dynasty come Galba, Otho, and Vitellius, brief rulers who all perished within a few months of civil war, to be succeeded by a new, Flavian dynasty—Vespasian, its founder, and his two sons, Titus and Domitian.

The lives vary in length and, many have said, in quality. The *Julius* and *Augustus* are the longest; the Julio-Claudian biographies are comparable in treatment, though not so long. The succeeding six, however, are much shorter, an understandable fact perhaps for the transient emperors of the year A.D. 69, or for Titus, who reigned only from A.D. 79 to 81; but Vespasian and Domitian are granted no fuller treatment. It has been argued that Suetonius composed the last six lives first and then, recognizing the opportunities afforded by imperial biography, went back to Julius Caesar and investigated these opportunities with the maturity of a master. But most have preferred to blame the diminishing effort and care, as they seem to be, upon Suetonius's disgrace, which excluded him from documents and other sources available to him as *ab epistulis.* Others, noticing a comparable emphasis of choice in *De viris illustribus,* have assigned the cause to Suetonius's own particular interests in the late Republic and early Empire. Besides, perils increased as the biographer approached his own time, nor did autopsy and personal interviews suit the scholar Suetonius, who was more comfortable with documents—those he chose were often odd, quirky, and not the sort of thing that historians would use—and with the writings of earlier researchers.

However the differing scales and details of the lives are to be interpreted, all the lives show a similar pattern, adapted freely but still recognizable in even the briefest life. Each emperor's life is told in three parts. The first part treats in chronological order his life before he became emperor, together with his ancestry and parentage. The second part, according to categories, describes and assesses the emperor's reign. His death occupies the third, followed by a coda. The categories by which the reigns are organized are perhaps the most celebrated feature of Suetonius's biographical technique, signified thus in the *Augustus* (9): "Proposita vitae eius velut summa partes singillatim neque per tempora sed per species exequar, quo distinctius demonstrari cognoscique possint" (having set forth a summation, as it were, of his life, I shall now survey the parts of it one by one and not chronologically but by categories, so that the parts may be demonstrated and understood more distinctly). These categories are broad, subsuming both public and private life, ranging from magistracies, legal administration, and military commands to literary interests and oratorical style, to marriage, family life, and sexual habits. The mass of detail, however, is organized not only by these categories but also by a skein of virtues and vices imposed upon them, which they illustrate and which in turn state the terms of reference by which the material within each category is to be judged. The judgment is sometimes stated explicitly because organizing the whole life, as at *Gaius Caligula* 22.1: "Hactenus quasi de principe, reliqua ut de monstro narranda sunt" (so much for the emperor; the rest must be related of the monster). This statement is unusually blunt. Other emperors, like Claudius and Otho, are presented as puzzling mixtures. In Caesar, Suetonius found an amalgam of splendid abilities and ferocious ambition, but the latter, poisoning the former, compelled posterity's verdict that Caesar had abused his success and been rightly killed (*Julius* 76.1).

As a whole the Suetonian life seems to have been unprecedented. To its parts, models have been assigned. The scene of death–Nero's is the most elaborate in *De vita Caesarum*–had long fascinated historians, and by the early Empire there was almost a fad for dramatic deaths, Tacitus being the supreme artist of these. A separate genre developed, *exitus illustrium virorum* (the last moments of famous men), wherein victims of the regime, such as Seneca, were glorified by disciples. The coda that Suetonius likes to append to the account of death recalls the summaries on Roman epitaphs. For the first part of a biography Suetonius could look to the form of the funeral eulogy, *laudatio funebris,* in which a Roman aristocrat's fitness and accomplishment were memorialized by a kinsman; even more he could draw on the techniques of praise and blame well developed by the early first century B.C. and exemplified in Cicero's senatorial and forensic speeches. These precedents assisted in developing his celebrated categories, too, even if, as once argued but now in large part discredited, Suetonius had recourse, as in his *De viris illustribus,* to the example of (now lost) Hellenistic biographies of poets and other authors. This multitude of influences and antecedents paradoxically illustrates the novelty of Suetonius's achievement in his lives of the emperors. If nobody agrees on whence he derived his models, none disputes that he fashioned from them something peculiarly his.

He created, moreover, a style adapted to accomplish his purposes. *Rebus ipsis data omnia,* said the Renaissance humanist Politian (to the things themselves everything is given). This statement might seem to say that to Suetonius sense was all, style nothing; and indeed he was unusual among Latin authors in his willingness to cite documents in their original (the letters of Augustus, most conspicuously) and to insert short bits of Greek. But Politian meant rather that Suetonius sought a style of extreme severity and concentration, particularly upon the clearest and most

Title page for an early English translation of Suetonius's De vita Caesarum *(courtesy of the Lilly Library, Indiana University)*

vivid description possible, focused solely upon the emperor, so that, for example, he regularly confined the subject of the main verb, and often of subordinate verbs, to the subject of the life. Because for much of each biography he had discarded narrative developed chronologically, Suetonius must instead compose narrative after narrative, each brief–most are no longer than a single sentence–and dense with detail. The detail is telling: the corpse of Julius Caesar lay abandoned, until three slaves took it away in a litter "dependente brachio" (one arm hanging down; *Julius* 82.3); the forces of Vitellius ambushed his opponents on the Capitol and set fire to the temple of Jupiter, while Vitellius himself *et proelium et incendium e Tiberiana prospiceret domo inter epulas* (from the palace of Tiberius watched both battle and blaze–while at dinner; *Vitellius* 15.3). Suetonius is master of disposing always with precise and persuasive emphasis the right detail, although, or because, he narrowed the choices for subordination allowed by the Latin language, avoiding most conjunctions and preferring to manipulate the Latin participle, his use of which in frequency and variety exceeds that of all other Latin authors. This austere intensity, this constant focus on a single object through a deliberately restricted range of techniques, could risk monotony; how then did Suetonius escape it? Just as in the arrangement of material within categories he continually changed order and emphasis, so in the structure of each sentence he varied the length of the members, the placement of verb and other constituents within each member, and above all its rhythm. Guided by classical rhetoric, scholars can recover features of Suetonian prose, can learn how it profits from the resources that his rhetoric supplied, can discover how its rhythmic ingenuity, for instance, even surpasses what Quintilian had advised. The text, however, is a score without much of the context needed for performance; its most remarkable effects remain only a ghost.

What Suetonius achieved was imitated in the next century by a certain Marius Maximus. His work is lost, but sources say that in style at least he fell short. For Suetonius *familiare fuit amare brevitatem* (the love of brevity was second nature); Marius was *homo omnium verbosissimus* (the wordiest of mankind). This judgment is found in the *Historia Augusta* (*Firmus* 1.2). Suetonian influence has been detected, if improbably, among or in reaction to saints' lives written in later antiquity. Used in the seventh century by St. Isidore of Seville in his *Etymologiae, De vita Caesarum* appears to have survived into the ninth century by a single manuscript. Einhard read it and wrote his *Vita Karoli Magni* as if the Frankish king Charlemagne were a thirteenth Caesar. Einhard's biography initiated in the Carolingian Renaissance a passion for Suetonius. Lupus of Ferrières was soon hunting for manuscripts; his pupil Heiric of Auxerre made a collection of excerpts, used by John of Salisbury in the twelfth century (he knew Suetonius's work also at first hand). Suetonian hues are discernible in William of Malmesbury's *Gesta regum Anglorum,* especially in the portrait of William Rufus. The thirteenth century saw further collections of excerpts and a vernacular *Li fait des Romains,* drawing from Suetonius. Petrarch possessed three manuscripts of Suetonius; Boccaccio transcribed long extracts from him. Manuscripts multiplied as Suetonius became an expected tenant of an educated man's library.

Printed editions commenced in 1470, with two; another followed the next year; twelve more followed before 1500. (By 1829 there were more than two hundred.) Politian lectured on Suetonius; Domizio Calderini prepared commentary and a biography, with forged authorities; they and other humanists squabbled over the biographer's text, life, and controversially, alleged obscenity. Erasmus produced an edition in 1518. In *In Suetonium quaedam* (1522) his friend Juan Luis Vives, who in several treatises on education recommended Suetonius for honesty and style, reconstructed the lost beginning of the *Julius* with a skillful imitation of Suetonian Latin. Jean Bodin, Marc-Antoine Muret, Justus Lipsius, and Ben Jonson inserted Suetonius into the persistent quarrels over what was proper prose in Latin and the vernacular. Suetonius's clinical detachment and diagnostic eye were admired by physicians such as Girolamo Cardano, whose autobiography (1576) adopted Suetonian organization by categories, and Philemon Holland, whose English translation of *De vita Caesarum* appeared in 1606. Suetonian biographers abounded. Pier Candido Decembrio, having translated the *Julius,* in 1446 published a life of one of the Visconti rulers of Milan; in 1549 Paolo Giovio published the lives (twelve of them) of the whole dynasty. Erasmus's friend Adrian Barlandus published many Suetonian biographies, including a sequence of the dukes of Brabant in 1526. In 1528 the Holy Roman emperor Charles V's official chronicler, Antonio de Guevara, produced a life of Marcus Aurelius and in 1539 *Una Década des Césares* (from Trajan to Severus Alexander); both claimed Suetonian ancestry, though the *Historia Augusta* was the closer model. Guevara's successor, Pedro Mexía, translated *De vita Caesarum* into Spanish (1547) and turned out a sequence of emperors down to Charles V's father, the series updated and replaced by others at least until 1636. Other arts did not neglect Suetonius. Ordered from Italy, terra-cotta medallions of Suetonius's Caesars decorated Thomas Cardinal Wolsey's palace at Hampton Court. The duke of Mantua commissioned a series of Caesars from Titian (copies were made for Charles V, the dukes of Alva and Parma, and other clients). After a brief sojourn in the collection of Charles I of England—his court painter Anthony Van Dyck restored the *Vitellius,* damaged in transit—all were destroyed in a palace fire in Madrid.

Suetonius's works were always fertile of apt quotations, as when in 1763 the Scottish jurist Sir David Dalrymple wrote to James Boswell in praise of the mild and improving style of Samuel Johnson's *Rasselas:* it was so unlike the savagery of Jonathan Swift, who might have taken as his motto Caligula's order to his executioner, *ita feri ut se mori sentiat* (strike so that he may feel he is dying; *Gaius Caligula* 30.1). Boswell read this quotation to Johnson, who was gratified by it; he knew Suetonius well, adapting his methods to the *Lives of the Poets* (1779–1781). Texts of Suetonius's works boasting the latest scholarship were readily available. Isaac Casaubon's edition, first published in 1595 and revised with commentary in 1610, was reprinted, wholly or excerpted generously, well into the eighteenth century. The edition of Johannes Graevius had appeared in 1672 and was reprinted in 1691, 1697, and 1703; a pupil of his brought out his own edition in 1736. Competing with these editions were three others produced in the last quarter of the seventeenth century. Richard Bentley was at work on an edition of Suetonius from 1713 to 1719, until he laid it aside. If he was discouraged by a flooded market, others later were not–August Wilhelm Ernesti (1748) and Frans van Oudendorp (1751), both soon reprinted. Edward Gibbon protested. What, another edition of Suetonius? This remark indicated no dislike of the author, however. In his 1764 journal Gibbon defended Suetonius against Voltaire's incredulity (could an old man like Tiberius commit the debaucheries attributed to him?) and in the *Vindication* (1779) commended Suetonius's rigorous objectivity as a model for historical investigation. Gibbon was in good company. Pierre Bayle's enormously successful and influential *Dictionnaire historique et critique* (1697) had devoted a long article to Suetonius, assembling in huge footnotes critical reception since the Renaissance and repudiating reservations expressed by ecclesiastical writers toward the biographer's obscenity, which was not obscenity at all but rather an aspect of the utter impartiality and detachment that characterized the whole of Suetonian biography. In his *Émile* (1762) Jean-Jacques Rousseau complained that the tame and hypocritical respectability of his age had killed the candor necessary if biography was to instruct; biographies might proliferate, but "nous n'aurons plus de Suétones" (we shall have no more Suetoniuses).

This praise was the summit. Stricter, or other, standards of evidence began to be applied. Historians became suspicious. Historians of literature became disdainful. The legacy of classical rhetoric, in which Suetonius and his audience had been trained, was being discarded or forgotten. Dumping him into a footnote, Eduard Norden's *Die antike Kunstprosa* in 1898 summed up dominant opinion: "Sueton schreibt farblos" (Suetonius writes colorlessly). The opinion, though tenacious, is no longer dominant. To historians asking different questions, from the minister's career and the biographer's methods can be deduced a precious, indeed unique, unusual awareness of emperors and empire. However much he is to be distrusted for the time that he describes, for his own time Suetonius is recognized as an evocative and convincing voice, while for critics resuming the rhetorical legacy, the question has become: how does that voice evoke, how convince?

Bibliographies:

Perrine Galand-Hallyn, "Bibliographie suétonienne (Les 'Vies des XII Césars') 1950–1988: Vers une

réhabilitation," *Aufstieg und Niedergang der römischen Welt,* edited by Wolfgang Haase, II, 33, no. 5 (Berlin: de Gruyter, 1991), pp. 3576–3622;

D. Thomas Benediktson, "A Survey of Suetonius Scholarship, 1938–1987," *Classical World,* 86 (1993): 377–447.

References:

Aufstieg und Niedergang der römischen Welt, edited by Wolfgang Haase, II, 33, no. 5 (Berlin: de Gruyter, 1991), pp. 3623–3851–comprises eight articles on Suetonius;

Barry Baldwin, *Suetonius* (Amsterdam: Hakkert, 1983);

Tamsyn Barton, "The *inventio* of Nero: Suetonius," in *Reflections of Nero: Culture, History, and Representation,* edited by Jas Elsner and Jamie Masters (London: Duckworth, 1994), pp. 48–63;

D. Thomas Benediktson, "Structure and Fate in Suetonius' *Life of Galba,*" *Classical Journal,* 92 (1997): 167–173;

Glen W. Bowersock, "Suetonius in the Eighteenth Century," in *Biography in the Eighteenth Century,* edited by J. D. Browning (New York: Garland, 1980), pp. 28–42;

Albert Andrew Howard and Carl Newell Jackson, *Index Verborum C. Suetoni Tranquilli* (Cambridge, Mass.: Harvard University Press, 1922; reprinted, Hildesheim: Olms, 1963);

Matthew Innes, "The Classical Tradition in the Carolingian Renaissance: Ninth-Century Encounters with Suetonius," *International Journal of the Classical Tradition,* 3 (1997): 265–282;

Richard C. Lounsbury, *The Arts of Suetonius: An Introduction* (New York: Peter Lang, 1987);

P. Sage, "L'expression narrative dans les *XII Césars* de Suétone: analyse d'une structure de phrase," *Latomus,* 19 (1979): 499–524;

Sage, "Quelques aspects de l'expression narrative dans les *XII Césars* de Suétone," *Revue Belge de philologie et d'histoire,* 57 (1979): 18–50;

G. B. Townend, "Suetonius and His Influence," in *Latin Biography,* edited by T. A. Dorey (London: Routledge & Kegan Paul, 1967), pp. 79–111;

Andrew Wallace-Hadrill, *Suetonius: The Scholar and His Caesars* (New Haven: Yale University Press, 1983);

D. Wardle, "Did Suetonius Write in Greek?" *Acta Classica,* 36 (1993): 91–103.

Tacitus

(ca. A.D. 55 – ca. A.D. 117)

Ronald Mellor
University of California, Los Angeles

MAJOR WORKS: *De vita Iulii Agricolae,* commonly known as *Agricola* (On the Life of Julius Agricola, A.D. 98);

De origine et situ Germanorum, commonly known as *Germania* (On the Origin and Homeland of the Germans, A.D. 98);

Dialogus de oratoribus, survives with lacunae (Dialogue on Orators, after A.D. 100);

Historiae, 12 books; books 1–4, part of book 5, and fragments survive (Histories, ca. A.D. 100–110);

Annales or *Ab excessu divi Augusti,* 16–18 books; books 1–4, part of book 5, book 6, part of book 11, books 12–15, and part of book 16 survive (Annals, after A.D. 116).

Editiones principes: *Germania, Dialogus, Annales I–VI,* edited by Vindelinus da Spira (Venice, ca. 1470); *Agricola,* edited by Puteolanus (Milan, ca. 1475); *Annals I–VI,* edited by Beroaldus (Rome, 1515).

Editions: *Opera Minora,* edited by R. M. Ogilvie and M. Winterbottom (Oxford: Clarendon Press, 1975)—includes *Agricola, Germania, Dialogus; Cornelii Taciti Annalium ab excessu divi Augusti libri: Volume I*—includes *Annales*—and *Historiarum libri: Volume II,* 2 volumes, edited by C. D. Fisher (Oxford: Clarendon Press, 1906–1911); *Historiarum libri,* edited by Kenneth Wellesley (Leipzig: Teubner, 1989); *P. Cornelii Taciti libri qui supersunt,* edited by Heinz Heubner (Stuttgart: Teubner, 1978)—includes *Annales.*

Bilingual editions: *Agricola-Germania-Dialogus,* edited and translated by M. Hutton, W. Peterson, M. Winterbottom, R. M. Ogilvie, and E. H. Warmington, Loeb Classical Library (Cambridge, Mass: Harvard University Press, 1914; revised edition, 1970); *Tacitus,* 5 volumes, translated by Clifford H. Moore and John Jackson, Loeb Classical Library (Cambridge, Mass.: Harvard University Press, 1925–1937)—includes *Histories* and *Annals.*

Translations in English: *The Complete Works of Tacitus,* translated by Alfred John Church and William Jackson Brodribb (New York: Random House, 1942); *Tacitus on Britain and Germany: A Translation of the "Agricola" and the "Germania,"* translated by Harold Mattingly (Harmondsworth, U.K.: Penguin, 1948); *Tacitus' Agricola, Germany, and Dialogue on Orators,* translated by Herbert W. Benario (Norman: University of Oklahoma Press, 1991); *The Histories,* translated by K. Wellesley (Harmondsworth, U.K.: Penguin, 1964); *The Annals of Imperial Rome,* translated by Michael Grant (Harmondsworth, U.K.: Penguin, 1973); *The Annals of Tacitus,* translated by D. R. Dudley (New York: New American Library, 1966).

Commentaries: *De vita Agricolae,* edited by R. M. Ogilvie and Sir Ian Richmond (Oxford: Clarendon Press, 1967); *Cornelii Taciti De origine et situ Germanorum,* edited by J. G. C. Anderson (Oxford: Clarendon Press, 1938); *Kommentar zum Dialogus des Tacitus,* edited by Rudolf Güngerich (Göttingen: Vandenhoech & Ruprecht, 1980); *Die Historien,* edited by Heinz Heubner, 5 volumes (Heidelberg: Carl Winter, 1963–1982); *A Historical Commentary on Tacitus' Histories I and II,* volume 1; *Histories III, IV, and V,* volume 2, edited by G. E. F. Chilver (Oxford: Clarendon Press, 1979, 1985); *Cornelius Tacitus: The Histories, Book III,* edited by Kenneth Wellesley (Sydney: University Press, 1972); *P. Cornelii Taciti Annalium ab Excessu Divi Augusti,* 2 volumes, edited by Henry Furneaux, revised by H. F. Pelham and C. D. Fisher, second edition (Oxford: Clarendon Press, 1896–1907); *Cornelius Tacitus: Annalen,* 4 volumes, edited by Erich Koestermann (Heidelberg: Carl Winter, 1963–1968); *The Annals of Tacitus, Books 1–6,* 2 volumes, edited by F. R. D. Goodyear (Cambridge: Cambridge University Press, 1972–1981); *The Annals of Tacitus,* edited by A. J. Woodman and R. H. Martin (Cambridge: Cambridge University Press, 1996)—includes book 3.

Cornelius Tacitus was perhaps the greatest historian that the Roman world produced. Though his

Annales (Annals, after A.D. 116) and *Historiae* (Histories, ca. A.D. 100–110) are among the most remarkable works of Latin prose, their extraordinary influence derives not from an agreeable style or from an uplifting theme, for his account of the loss of freedom under the Julio-Claudian and Flavian emperors is grim and depressing, but from the psychological penetration, acute political analysis, moral grandeur, and literary genius that have dazzled his readers for five centuries.

What is known of the life of Tacitus comes from his writings–especially his biography of his father-in-law, Agricola. There are almost no contemporary references to him save the correspondence with his friend Pliny. Scholars cannot even be certain whether Tacitus's praenomen was Gaius or Publius.

Early in the reign of Nero (A.D. 54–68), Tacitus was born into a prominent family in heavily Romanized southern Gaul–perhaps in Vasio (Vaison-la-Romaine) in modern Provence. His father was a financial official in northern Gaul, one of the equestrian administrators so important to the running of the Roman Empire, but still a large social step below the senatorial order. Though Tacitus remained proud of his provincial ancestors as more virtuous than the corrupt senatorial nobility, his rise in social status was accompanied by a snobbish contempt for his perceived ethnic and social inferiors: easterners, freedmen, and the Roman masses.

After the terrible Civil War of A.D. 69, the emperor Vespasian (A.D. 69–79) enrolled increasing numbers of Spaniards and Gauls in the Senate. The adolescent Tacitus was among the ambitious provincials streaming to Rome to study rhetoric–the traditional education for the Roman elite. Tacitus soon achieved success in the law courts, and he advanced quickly after his marriage to the daughter of the Gallo-Roman senator Julius Agricola. Tacitus received minor honors from Vespasian and became quaestor under Vespasian's son and successor, Titus (A.D. 79–81). Through this office, Tacitus attained membership in the Senate by the age of twenty-five.

Titus's successor, Domitian (A.D. 81–96), made Tacitus praetor, and he held a high provincial office during the years A.D. 89 to 93. The paranoid emperor then began a terrible persecution reminiscent of those of Caligula and Nero; scholars know nothing of Tacitus during this terror (A.D. 93–96). He survived to reach the consulship in A.D. 97, perhaps even nominated by Domitian before the latter's assassination. Tacitus had an extraordinarily successful career for a young Gallo-Roman of equestrian descent, but he was deeply traumatized by Domitian's persecutions. Since Tacitus had served Domitian loyally for more than a decade and had been rewarded well, to read his emotional claim that fifteen years were blotted out of his life by the

emperor's tyranny is surprising. While no one knows how Tacitus spent those three years, guilt and political frustration drove him to study history. He believed, as did Polybius, that history should be written by experienced politicians. Tacitus had the necessary qualifications: psychological insight, political acumen, access to sources, and a literary facility. Over two decades he produced five books (four of different genres of historical writing) that displayed increasing sophistication and stylistic virtuosity.

In A.D. 98 Tacitus published a brief, admiring biography of his father-in-law, Agricola, long-time governor of Roman Britain and one of the most successful generals of his day. It had long been traditional for Roman aristocrats to deliver a *laudatio* (public speech) at the death of a distinguished relative. Such a speech glorified the entire family by recounting the deeds of their ancestors and by praising the achievements and character of the deceased. Tacitus says that under tyranny traditional virtue (and even praise of virtue) were regarded as subversive; only after the murder of Domitian could he publish this book.

The *Agricola* begins and ends as a sincere and moving eulogy, but the book is much more ambitious than it might at first appear. It goes well beyond the usual contents of ancient biography, for it includes geography, ethnography, historical narrative, and even speeches. In the guise of biography, Tacitus produced an embryonic history–a trial run for his later historical masterpieces. The *Agricola* reveals Tacitus's political agenda, his deep personal resentment, and his literary strategies. The *Agricola* includes the genesis of Tacitus's moral, political, and psychological ideas.

In his narratives of Agricola's campaigns against the Druids on Anglesey and against the rebels in Scotland, Tacitus subordinates military details to the visual and psychological elements of the battle. There are the beginnings of the cinematic approach that Tacitus perfected later in the grand military tableaux of the *Annals* and *Histories*. From the time of Herodotus, all Greek and Roman historians composed speeches for the characters in their histories. Though the speeches are invented, they are appropriate to the occasion. Tacitus includes extended speeches for both Agricola and his British antagonist, the rebel chieftain Calgacus. Calgacus delivers a powerful oration to thirty thousand British troops gathered before the decisive battle at Mons Graupius in Scotland. In this declamation Tacitus projects Roman rhetoric into the mouth of a remote barbarian tribal leader and thus elevates him into an opponent worthy of Agricola. The speech echoes familiar accusations against Rome's greed, cruelty, and arrogance–characteristics that Sallust had earlier attributed to foreign leaders. Calgacus concludes with a famous

*Engraved title page for a 1640 edition of two of Tacitus's works, his
history of the Germans and his biography of his father-in-law
(courtesy of the Lilly Library, Indiana University)*

denunciation of Roman imperialism: "To robbery, to
slaughter, and to theft they give the false name of
'Empire'; where they create desolation, they call it
'peace.'"

Throughout the *Agricola,* Tacitus maintains the
serious tone that Romans thought appropriate to
proper history. Much of the material found in other
biographies is absent—the casual conversations, the trivial details, the jokes of Plutarch, and the coarse anecdotes of Suetonius. Tacitus even adumbrates political
themes that he developed later in greater detail—censorship and the loss of political freedom, the insidious
workings of imperial freedmen, and the corruption of
both language and values. The central theme of the
Agricola is one close to the heart of Tacitus: "even under
bad emperors men can be great." Under tyrannical government, the compromise of Agricola is more effective
than the dramatic resistance of self-appointed martyrs.

Tacitus is perhaps defending himself as well as praising
Agricola.

This laudatory biography is not just a political
tract; it also includes genuine warmth for its subject.
Tacitus praises Agricola both for his military skill and
for his deep family affections. Though the final paragraph abounds with rhetorical commonplaces such as
"great souls do not perish with the body" and "your
spirit will live forever," Tacitus invests these clichés
with a sincerity that makes the conclusion a personal
farewell. The book is an act of piety, but it also heralds
the arrival of a great new historian and provides a blueprint for his future program.

Soon after the *Agricola,* Tacitus wrote the only ethnographic monograph that survives from antiquity.
Since the time of Homer, poets and historians had
incorporated into their books material on the geography, local customs, political organization, and religious
beliefs of foreign peoples. The *Germania* (A.D. 98) briefly
describes the geography and customs of Germany
before providing an historical account of the various
tribes. Tacitus undertook no personal research; he
relied almost entirely on earlier books by Poseidonius,
Julius Caesar, and the elder Pliny. Though Tacitus
sometimes generalized barbarian peoples and transferred characteristics from one to another, much of
what he said in the *Germania* has been confirmed by
archaeology.

The *Germania* is more than an essay written to
inform the Romans about the lands and peoples of Germany. An important function of ancient ethnography
was to provide a contrast with one's own society,
"another perspective from which the writer could ana-
lyze his own state and its customs," so Tacitus's central
purpose is to criticize Roman morality and political life
through the implied comparisons. His anger at the fashionable immorality of contemporary Rome leads him to
idealize German life: "No one there laughs at vice, or
calls it fashionable to seduce or be seduced." Young
Germans are eager to prove their valor as warriors, not
as lovers.

The *Germania* also idealizes the political freedom
of the Germans, who, unlike the Romans, make their
important decisions collectively: the power of kings is
neither absolute nor arbitrary. The statement is a blunt
suggestion that, even in the enlightened reign of Trajan,
Rome remains a monarchy. Amidst his critique of
Rome's moral and political condition, Tacitus also
warns of the threat that a united Germany will pose to
Rome. This admonition is a challenge to the new
emperor to return to Caesar's aggressively expansionist
foreign policy and fulfill the destiny of the Empire.

After its rediscovery in the fifteenth century, Germans viewed this essay as an affirmation of their noble

past and lost national independence. The picture of chaste Germans and corrupt Romans in the work became enormously popular during the Reformation, when the Roman Catholic Church was regarded as the successor of the corrupt and tyrannical Romans. The greatest impact, however, flowed from Tacitus's observation that "the tribes of Germany are free of all taint of intermarriages with foreign nations, and that they appear as a distinct, unmixed race" (*Germania* 4). Looking back on World War II, the great Italian-Jewish historian Arnaldo Momigliano concluded that the *Germania* was among the "most dangerous books ever written."

Soon after his first two books, Tacitus turned his hand to an intellectual dialogue in the tradition of Cicero. It records an imaginary conversation among three historical orators that supposedly took place in Rome in A.D. 75 at the house of Curiatus Maternus. Tacitus skillfully delineates the personalities and their ideas with wit and good humor. Maternus has turned from oratory to the writing of poetic tragedies. Aper chides his friend for wasting time on poetry; would he not prefer to defend a friend in the present than to glorify long-dead Cato in a poem? Aper sees oratory as the path to fame and fortune. Maternus, for his part, believes the political tyranny of the Empire has corrupted oratory; he will not prostitute his rhetorical skills. The late-arriving Messala criticizes the contemporary reliance on rhetorical technique and exercises instead of the deeply humane moral and literary education of earlier orators such as Cicero. The decline of literature from the earlier golden age is a persistent theme in the writing of the time. Though no single speaker serves as a mouthpiece for Tacitus, he certainly sympathizes with Maternus, who forsook oratory for poetry, since Tacitus himself had rejected oratory for history.

The Latin style of the *Dialogus de oratoribus* (Dialogue of Orators, after A.D. 100) is unexpected: its Ciceronian amplitude has led many scholars to reject it as a work by Tacitus, or to see it as a work of his youth. Tacitus, though, was a highly trained rhetorician who could write Ciceronian Latin when appropriate, as the work certainly is in a Ciceronian dialogue. Most scholars now date the *Dialogus* to A.D. 102, since it is dedicated to the consul of that year, Fabius Justus. Tacitus incorporates into this essay on literature his historical analysis of the effects of tyranny. The lasting lesson of the *Dialogus* is that art and society are intertwined, and both depend on the structure of political life.

During the decade after the appearance of his two monographs, Tacitus was hard at work on a major narrative history of the Flavian emperors. The *Historiae* (Histories), a name attached by a Renaissance editor, covered the period between A.D. 69 and 96 in twelve books. Only four complete books and part of a fifth survive—about a third of the whole—in which Tacitus covers less than two of twenty-eight years. The complex events of A.D. 69, with its four emperors and continuous civil warfare, occupy more than three books and constitute the most detailed extant history in all Greek and Roman literature.

Tacitus had lived close to the corridors of power through much of the Flavian era. He had seen and heard much, but he supplemented memory with the Acts of the Senate. In addition to using histories and memoirs, he asked friends for eyewitness accounts, as when he asked Pliny to describe the eruption of Mt. Vesuvius in A.D. 79. Though Tacitus followed the "annalistic" method of organizing his history by the consular year (hence, book 1 begins with A.D. 1 January 69), he sometimes followed a thematic thread across several years since he understood that the consuls were now of little importance.

Tacitus begins with a personal prologue that addresses the difficulty of writing the history of tyrants: there is flattery in their lifetimes and hostility after their deaths. He confesses how much his career owes to Vespasian, Titus, and Domitian; yet, he asserts that he can speak "without partiality and without hatred." After a summary of the causes of the Civil War and a description of the state of the Empire, the narrative begins with the last weeks of Galba. Galba is the right man at the wrong time; his unquestionable integrity becomes an anachronistic priggishness unsuited to a corrupt and selfish age. When a small act of generosity might have won over the troops and prevented civil war, Galba stubbornly refused, and his murder led to the acclamation of Otho by the praetorians and of Vitellius by the German legions.

The second book opens with a brief glance at Vespasian, the Roman commander in the East who was destined to emerge as the victor in the Civil War. The major focus in this book is the conflict between the forces of Otho and those of Vitellius. It was the first civil war since Antony and Augustus fought at Actium a century earlier, but they, like Caesar and Pompey before them, had avoided pitched battles on Italian soil. Otho and Vitellius felt no such scruple. Otho was no commander, and Vitellius, weak but popular with his troops for his generosity, defeated him.

Book 3 is epic in scope. The Flavian forces of Vespasian defeat the Vitellians in northern Italy, where they sack and burn the ancient city of Cremona. Tacitus paints the moods of the legions, praetorians, and civilians as the Flavian army approaches Rome, and the episode culminates with the horror of the capital itself in flames. Tacitus has here achieved the most poetic history yet written at Rome, with Virgil ever present in the reminiscence of burning Troy as both Cremona and Rome are put to the torch. The anticlimactic murder of the pathetic Vitellius closes this masterly book.

Book 4 covers both Flavian dominance in Rome and the revolt of the Batavians. These rebellious Germans are less idealized than those portrayed in the *Germania*. The generals give long speeches defending their political stance—the rebel leader Civilis's denunciation of Roman imperialism and the Roman general Cerialis's justification of the empire. While Vespasian remained in Judaea, his younger son Domitian represented him in Rome. The brief fragment of book 5 begins with a confused and hostile account of the Jewish people and their religion. The *Histories* breaks off in midsentence with the impending collapse of Civilis's rebellion.

The pace of these books is remarkable. Despite the shifting focus of the action from Rome to Judaea to Cremona to Germany, the narrative is rapid and tightly organized. Tacitus's compressed style contributes to the swift progress of the story. Dramatic vignettes, character sketches, and literary digressions enliven the inexorable marches of armies. This history is largely public, with scenes of armies, mobs, and provincials being addressed by public speeches; only later did Tacitus turn to the secret history found in the *Annals*.

Tacitus regarded the Civil War, which dominates the surviving books of the *Histories*, as the greatest calamity ever to befall the Roman people. It destroyed military discipline and allowed provincials to rebel; it brought scoundrels such as Otho and Vitellius to power; and it resulted in the terrible sacrilege of the burning of the temple of Jupiter on the Capitol. The theme of moral decline is ever present. The legions had become cowardly, insubordinate, and corrupt; they even sacked Roman cities. The senators and people were little better; the senators cravenly gave up their freedom of speech, and the Roman mobs were so corrupted that they cheered on soldiers fighting in the streets as though they were in the arena.

In the *Histories*, Tacitus shows for the first time his understanding of imperial politics and the "secret of power": no constitution can ensure the peaceful transfer of power if the army chooses to ignore it. Tacitus, writing under Trajan, who had been adopted by Nerva, sees the adoptive monarchy as a means of avoiding hereditary despots such as Caligula, Nero, and Domitian. Thus, the historian puts such ideas into the speech Galba delivered on the occasion of his adoption of Piso. Despite the impending demise of Galba and Piso, the speech (which is more than likely pure Tacitus) articulates well the new theory of succession by adoption, which in fact did ensure competent government at Rome from A.D. 96 to 180.

The *Histories*, published about A.D. 108, is a masterpiece of a mature historian. In it Tacitus has forged a powerful narrative in an individual style. On reading it, Pliny told his friend, "your histories will be immortal."

In the preface to the *Histories*, Tacitus announced that in his old age he would write the happier history of the reign of Nerva and Trajan. Yet, he never did so; instead, he chose to look further into the past, finding in Tiberius the origin of imperial tyranny. Thus, Tacitus devoted his last decade to the history of the Julio-Claudian emperors who ruled from A.D. 14 to 68. His public career was crowned when he held the prestigious governorship of the province of Asia in A.D. 112.

This penetrating exposé of imperial politics under the Julio-Claudians represents the pinnacle of Roman historical writing. The *Annals* survives in two long blocks: the first six books cover A.D. 14–37, though the fifth book is largely missing. The second block runs from book 11 to the middle of book 16 (A.D. 47–66). Thus, Tacitus's treatment of Caligula (A.D. 37–41) is unfortunately completely lost. The eighteen books of the *Annals* concluded at the end of A.D. 68, since the *Histories* begins on 1 January 69.

The *Annals* is built of three "hexads" of six books each. The first hexad covers the reign of Tiberius, while the fragmentary second went from the accession of Caligula in A.D. 37 to the death of Claudius in A.D. 54. The third hexad begins with the accession of Nero (13, 1), "The first death of the new regime . . . ," with Tacitus explicitly referring to the accession of Tiberius (1, 6), "The first crime of the new regime was the murder of Postumus Agrippa." Tacitus clearly divides the reigns of Tiberius and Nero into positive and negative phases and probably followed ancient convention in doing the same for Caligula. While this pattern follows the ancient biographical practice of gradually revealing the character, many rulers in quite different societies in fact come to power amid high hopes—a period called a "political honeymoon"—and later crush those expectations.

The *Annals* did not begin with a prologue setting out the goals of the author, such as those found in the *Agricola* and the *Histories*. The opening chapters instead sketch the decline of the Roman Republic and the triumph of Augustus. With an assertion of his own impartiality, Tacitus quickly embarks on his story. In fact, the first words, *urbem Romam* (the city of Rome), define his focus from the outset—the city and its rulers. Tacitus recounts foreign wars and military mutinies to shed light on the emperors and their court. His interest never wandered far from the imperial palace and the senate house.

Tacitus began his history a century before his own time, so he could no longer rely on personal experience and the testimony of contemporaries. He read histories, memoirs, autobiographies of emperors such as Tiberius and Claudius, collections of speeches, and the Acts of the Senate, but he also resorted to other archival material. This archival research may have been a significant innovation in the historical writing of the time. Though he mentions the memoirs of the general Corbulo and the elder Agrippina, Tacitus makes clear that he only cites sources when they disagree: "When the sources are unanimous, I will follow them; when they provide different versions, I will record them with attribution" (*Annals* 13.20). The ancient reader looked for style and intelligence in a book; he did not expect the author to provide evidence of research.

In his few paragraphs on the reign of Augustus, Tacitus shows his skill at innuendo: "He seduced the people with grain, the army with bonuses, and everyone with the sweetness of peace" (1.2). While admitting that Augustus had restored peace after a century of civil conflict, Tacitus uses the word "seduced" to make a remarkable achievement seem tawdry. At the funeral of Augustus, the historian uses the rhetorical device of having groups of spectators speak for or against the dead emperor. By adopting the gloomy Tiberius as his successor, some conclude, Augustus hoped to ensure his own future glory by an invidious comparison. In a few pages Tacitus provides a grim backdrop for Tiberius's entrance.

In tracing the reign of Tiberius—the most complex character in Roman historical writing—Tacitus presents natural diffidence as dissimulation, shyness as haughtiness, and acts of generosity as hypocrisy. There is often a conflict between what Tacitus reports—a hundred treason trials in twenty-three years (with many found innocent)—and his tendentious description, "continual slaughter." As a modern politician may deceive with statistics, an ancient politician or historian used rhetoric. Despite these innuendos, Tacitus does acknowledge that the Empire was well administered and the laws were duly enforced until the emperor fell under the evil spell of Sejanus in A.D. 23. With complete faith in Sejanus, who had once saved his life in a cave-in, Tiberius withdrew to the privacy of the lovely island of Capri for the final ten years of his life. While Tacitus paints a picture of Tiberius's paranoia and moral depravity, he also allows his reader to see Tiberius as a bullied son, a wounded husband, a distraught father, and a lonely old man. Sejanus consolidated his power and even had the emperor's son murdered to further his imperial ambitions. Tiberius's sudden, preemptive strike against Sejanus in A.D. 31 falls in the missing section of book 5, but Tacitus's account of the aftermath amply displays the increased bitterness of the aging emperor. The brief obituary is a classic account of the corrupting effect of absolute power.

Engraved title page for a 1637 edition of Tacitus's works

After a lacuna of ten years, books 11 and 12 cover the last seven years of the reign of Claudius (A.D. 41–54). Perhaps Tacitus presented a more positive image of Claudius in his early years when he conquered Britain, but by A.D. 47 the emperor is portrayed as under the control of his freedmen and his women. While Livia's formidable presence was only sensed in the background of Tiberius's court, Messalina and the younger Agrippina now step confidently into the spotlight. Messalina uses imperial power to satisfy her lust and her whims, but Agrippina is the more dangerous: she uses her sexuality to gain and increase political power. The traditionalist Tacitus certainly believes a man must keep his wife under control, and his contempt for Claudius is withering. Suetonius gives Claudius some wit and charm; Tacitus does not.

Books 13–16 cover the first twelve years of Nero's reign and include the matricide of Agrippina and the great fire of Rome. The accession of the handsome young emperor was promising, with the philosopher Seneca guiding his intellectual and political development. Nero soon turned to sexual license, however, and shocked respectable Romans by performing on the stage as a singer. Book 14 begins with the murder of Nero's mother and ends with the killing of his wife Octavia. Nero's tutor Seneca prudently retires but is soon forced to commit suicide in a dramatic scene. Throughout the *Annals*, Tacitus provides characters ready to be dramatized, and they have been in tragedies, opera, and film. The surviving text ends in A.D. 66 with Nero's reign of terror against the Senate; the absence of Tacitus's account of the emperor's ludicrous singing tour of Greece and the revolt in Judaea are especially regrettable.

The *Annals* is far more than a narrative history. Tacitus examines the early Empire through several analytical themes: senatorial cowardice, the growth of tyranny, the decline of Roman morality, and the corruption of language. He repeatedly contrasts Roman weakness with the stalwart courage of Rome's barbarian enemies, who fight and die to preserve their freedom. In Rome, though, tyranny is not only a political condition but also a psychological state. It is accompanied by informers, manipulative freedmen, treason trials, and universal paranoia; despotism, sycophancy, and treachery form the web that ties together the whole of the *Annals*. Tacitus saw Rome's moral decline not only in the orgies of the emperors but also in the consequent collapse of political morality. In his mind, there was a moral weakness in the passive foreign policy recommended by Augustus and followed by Tiberius. If the armies did not fight abroad, they would turn on each other and bring civil war to Rome itself.

A peculiarly modern element in the *Annals* is Tacitus's fascination with the political misuse of language. Language creates illusions to conceal political realities, and the historian is determined to expose the lies that form the basis of imperial rule. When he says "The titles of the officials remained the same," he makes clear that the powers have changed. He is particularly concerned with the censorship of free speech. In the Republic, politics had been conducted in public but had now become secret. Tacitus understood well the connection between word, thought, and political power, and those links lie at the heart of his genius.

The *Annals* finds Tacitus at the acme of his stylistic powers. The force of the work lies in the relentlessness of its compressed prose. It is less smooth and more concentrated than the *Histories;* even the speeches are shorter and more intense. Despite the roughness of the style, the narrative is remarkably swift. Tacitus is a master of epigram, and he does not lack a sense of humor, though his jokes are bitter and ironic. He said of Caligula, who fawned on the aging Tiberius: "There has never been a better slave or a worse master" (6.20). The historian has

created a personal style appropriate to his message. The *Annals* is a literary masterpiece in which the abrasive style perfectly suits its unsettling content.

In his final work Tacitus reflects more profoundly on his role as an historian. He is scornful of historians who merely record banal facts, and he makes clear his belief that the function of history is both utilitarian and commemorative. The recording of virtuous and evil deeds will not only teach future generations; it will also reward the good and punish the bad. While Tacitus's intentions in writing the *Annals* were moral and political, his passion stemmed from a deeper psychological source—perhaps the need to vindicate himself and his friends who collaborated in the reign of Domitian.

The *Annals* must have been completed about A.D. 117—probably not long before the death of Trajan and the accession of Hadrian. It is likely that Tacitus himself died soon after. His masterpiece is a brilliant and creative expression of political frustration, shame, political paranoia, and deep personal suffering. In it the historian appears as a psychologist, a political theorist, a moralist, and a literary artist. Like Sallust before him and Ammianus and Augustine after him, the moralist in Tacitus looked at the dark side of history. His trenchant, ironic voice has found its most responsive audience in difficult times. Yet, not all Tacitus's writing is bleak; it also celebrates the art of survival and commemorates those who maintain integrity under tyranny. Both his denunciations and celebrations have transcended his own purposes in the enormous influence he has had on later writers, philosophers, and politicians.

Tacitus's slurs on both Christians and Jews made him anathema to early Christian writers, and he was relatively ignored by medieval scribes (hence, the fragmentary survival of his works). Since the Renaissance, however, Tacitus has been accorded a central role in shaping the western intellectual tradition. When Machiavelli's work was prohibited, his ideas could often be attributed more safely to Tacitus. Though his sayings were collected into handbooks for courtiers, Tacitus was usually viewed as an enemy of tyrants, and thus he appealed to John Milton and Thomas Jefferson as much as he displeased Charles I and Napoleon. Tacitus's psychological analysis was an important influence as Michel Eyquem de Montaigne and Francis Bacon developed the language of introspection. Called by the playwright Jean Racine "the greatest painter of antiquity," Tacitus gave dramatic material to Ben Jonson, Racine, and Monteverdi. Though positivist historians of the nineteenth century regarded Tacitus's picture of tyranny as exaggerated, he has found growing popularity in more recent times, which have had their own monstrous tyrants and political persecutions.

Bibliographies:

F. R. D. Goodyear, *Tacitus,* Greece and Rome: New Surveys in the Classics, no. 4 (Oxford: Oxford University Press, 1970);

Herbert W. Benario, *Classical World,* 71 (1977): 1–32.

References:

T. D. Barnes, "The Significance of Tacitus' *Dialogus de Oratoribus,*" *Harvard Studies In Classical Philology,* 90 (1986): 225–244;

T. A. Dorey, ed., *Tacitus* (London: Routledge & Kegan Paul, 1969);

Judith Ginsburg, *Tradition and Theme in the Annals of Tacitus* (New York: Arno, 1981);

C. S. Kraus and A. J. Woodman, *Latin Historians,* Greece and Rome: New Surveys in the Classics, no. 27 (Oxford: Oxford University Press, 1997), pp. 88–118;

T. J. Luce, "Ancient Views on the Causes of Bias in Historical Writing," *Classical Philology,* 84 (1989): 16–31;

Luce and A. J. Woodman, eds., *Tacitus and the Tacitean Tradition* (Princeton, N.J.: Princeton University Press, 1992);

Ronald H. Martin, *Tacitus* (Berkeley: University of California Press, 1981);

Ronald Mellor, *Tacitus* (New York: Routledge, 1993);

Mellor, *Tacitus: The Classical Heritage* (New York: Garland, 1995);

Clarence W. Mendell, *Tacitus: The Man and His Work* (New Haven: Yale University Press, 1957);

Mark Morford, "Tacitus' Historical Methods in the Neronian Books of the 'Annals,'" in *Aufstieg und Niedergang der römischen Welt,* volume 2, 33.2 (Berlin: de Gruyter, 1990), pp. 1582–1627;

Viktor Pöschl, ed., *Tacitus* (Darmstadt: Wissenschaftliche Buchgesellschaft, 1969);

Patrick Sinclair, *Tacitus the Sententious Historian: A Sociology of Rhetoric in Annales 1–6* (University Park: Pennsylvania State University Press, 1995);

Ronald Syme, *Tacitus,* 2 volumes (Oxford: Clarendon Press, 1958);

Syme, *Ten Studies in Tacitus* (Oxford: Clarendon Press, 1970);

B. Walker, *The Annals of Tacitus: A Study in the Writing of History* (Manchester: Manchester University Press, 1952);

A. J. Woodman, *Rhetoric in Classical Historiography* (London: Croom Helm, 1988);

Woodman, *Tacitus Reviewed* (Oxford & New York: Clarendon Press, 1998).

Terence

(ca. 184 B.C. – 159 B.C. or after)

Charles E. Mercier
University of Southern California

MAJOR WORKS: *Andria,* Megalensian Games, Rome (The Girl from Andros, produced April, 166 B.C.);

Hecyra, first attempt, Megalensian Games, Rome (The Mother-in-Law, produced April, 165 B.C.); *Hecyra,* second attempt, funeral games for L. Aemilius Paullus, Rome (produced 160 B.C.); *Hecyra,* successful performance, Roman Games, Rome (produced September, 160 B.C.);

Heauton Timorumenos, Megalensian Games, Rome (The Self-Tormentor, produced April, 163 B.C.);

Eunuchus, Megalensian Games, Rome (The Eunuch, produced April, 161 B.C.);

Phormio, Roman Games, Rome (produced September, 161 B.C.);

Adelphoe, funeral games for L. Aemilius Paullus, Rome (The Brothers, produced 160 B.C.).

Editio princeps: *Comoediae,* edited by A. Rusch (Strassburg: Johann Mentelin, 1470).

Standard editions: Aelius Donatus and Eugraphius, *Commentum Terenti,* 3 volumes, edited by Paul Wessner (Leipzig: Teubner, 1902–1908); *Térence: Comédies,* 3 volumes, edited and translated into French by Jules Marouzeau, Association Guillaume Budé (Paris: Les Belles Lettres, 1942–1949; revised 1947, 1956); *Comoediae,* edited by Robert Kauer, Wallace M. Lindsay, and Otto Skutsch (Oxford: Clarendon Press, 1958).

Translations in English: *Terence,* 2 volumes, edited and translated by John Sargeaunt, Loeb Classical Library (Cambridge, Mass.: Harvard University Press, 1912); *The Complete Comedies of Terence,* edited by Palmer Bovie (New Brunswick, N.J.: Rutgers University Press, 1974); *Terence. The Comedies,* translated by Betty Radice (New York: Penguin, 1976)–includes Suetonius's *Life of Terence.*

Commentaries: *P. Terenti Afri Phormio,* edited by R. H. Martin (London: Methuen, 1959); *P. Terenti Afri Andria,* edited by G. P. Shipp (Melbourne: Oxford University Press, 1960); *Adelphoe,* edited

by Martin (London: Cambridge University Press, 1976); *Phormio, A Comedy by Terence: Manuscript Reproduction, Facing Transcription, Edited Latin Text, Notes, Vocabulary,* edited by Elaine M. Coury (Chicago: Bolchazy-Carducci, 1982); *The Brothers,* edited by A. S. Gratwick (Warminster, U. K.: Aris & Phillips, 1987); *The Self-Tormentor,* edited by A. J. Brothers, (Warminster, U.K.: Aris & Phillips, 1988); *The Mother-in-Law,* edited by S. Ireland (Warminster, U.K.: Aris & Phillips, 1990); *P. Terenti Afri Eunuchus,* edited by John Barsby (London: Cambridge University Press, 1999).

By composing six popular comedies, Terence became pivotal in the development of Latin literature and, because his plays have never ceased to be read, eventually of European drama. Writing toward the beginning of Rome's engagement with Greek culture, Terence pioneers both accurate literary translation and creative competition with his original while setting linguistic standards for the classical Latin style to come. His comedy–written at the end of a living tradition of Greco-Roman comedy–though still in touch with its origins in the grotesque and fantastic, represents the mediocre lives of realistic characters and transmits to a Europe that had no Menander possibilities for comedy at work not only in comic drama but, in time, also in the novel and the situation comedy. As a working professional of the theater Terence gave early witness to the tension between artistic ambition and the commercial demands of a popular art form.

Publius Terentius Afer, called Terence in English, lived in the years between the second and third Punic wars (201–149 B.C.). As a young man befriended by an influential political elite, he won a reputation for his comedies in Latin based on sources from Greek New Comedy (third-century-B.C. comedy based on the lives of average citizens), produced for Roman festival occasions in the years 166–160 B.C. All six have survived. Provocation characterized Terence's dramaturgy; he challenged his older professional colleagues and the

Terence (miniature by Adelricus; Vatican Library, Cod. Vat. Lat. 3868, fol. 2 r)

expectations of his audience. After an engagement of seven seasons in the theatrical life of Rome, he traveled to Greece and did not return. This much can be said with assurance about the life and death of Terence.

Three sources provide materials for constructing a more detailed biography: first, the commentary on Terence by the scholar Aelius Donatus (fourth century A.D.) includes Suetonius's *Life of Terence,* a section of his *On Poets,* written about A.D. 100; second, *didascaliae* (production records) with dates and sequence of plays, on which the production chronology is based, head the manuscripts of the plays; and third, remarkably, the prologues of the plays claim to reveal some of the production histories, making the audience seemingly privy to behind-the-scenes controversy and conspiracy.

Suetonius's *Life of Terence* reports the following: born in Carthage and brought to Rome as a slave, Terence was liberally educated by his master Terentius Lucanus, who eventually manumitted him for his talent and good looks (medium height, graceful build, dark

skin). A group of young Roman aristocrats—identified as Scipio Aemilianus, C. Laelius, and L. Furius Philus—befriended Terence for his eloquence (or his beauty and sexual availability, according to Porcius Licinus). Laelius and Scipio were rumored to be collaborators in the writing of the comedies; Terence never definitely squelched this rumor because he knew it pleased his friends. The approbation of the authoritative old comic master Caecilius Statius launched Terence's career, when the commissioning aediles arranged for him to assess Terence's first comedy, *Andria* (The Girl from Andros, 166 B.C.). Invited to dinner, the young poet, dressed in rags, began to read the play while sitting on a stool, but was soon asked to continue while now reclining at an admiring table. After 160 B.C., when he was not yet twenty-five years old (or thirty-five: the manuscripts give both numbers), Terence sailed for Greece—either for pleasure, to escape the pressure of the accusations that his plays were written by others, or to study Greek society, in order to represent it more accurately in his comedy. He died at Stymphalus in Arcadia or at Leucas. Q. Cosconius (first century A.D.) says Terence was lost at sea returning with 108 new adaptations of Menander, or alternatively, died of a broken heart when he heard the plays shipped before him were lost. He left a daughter, who married a Roman knight with an estate of fourteen acres near the villa of Mars.

In fact, since ancient biographies of dramatists often consist mainly of formulaic fictions and imaginative inferences from the plays, and since Suetonius's sources, presumably Varro and six or so others he cites by name, did not agree among themselves, there is likely little of truth in the *Life*. The African origin and the name of his not-otherwise-known master may be inferences from the name Terentius Afer. If Terence did come from Carthage, his stylistic mastery of an acquired language is the more remarkable, though he could have descended from someone captured in a previous Punic war. The *Life* teems with commonplaces of ancient literary biography: a poet's servile origin and the *fuscus* (dark) skin color and physical appearance of a Carthaginian. Menander, too, is said to have drowned and to have written 108 plays. Chronology is impossible or suspiciously appropriate: a Terence born in 184 B.C. was born the year his predecessor Plautus died and became an age mate to Scipio Aemilianus and Laelius. Caecilius died in 168 B.C., before the production of *The Girl from Andros* in 166 B.C. Is twenty-four too young an age to have produced six plays? Must some years be allowed for a considerable bulk of work lost before he died?

What is most vivid in the *Life* is most suspect, and so readers are left to balance a desire to know something plausible, if false, with an admission that little is known for sure of Terence's life. Still, biographical fiction has always been a part of readers' experience with this author, providing ample material for mythmaking. Montaigne in "Considering Cicero" (*Essay* 2.40, 1580) remarked that if eloquence truly brought glory, Scipio and Laelius would not have allowed the honor due their comedies to be claimed by an African slave. That "one of the greatest geniuses in the history of Rome" was a slave becomes, for Diderot in "On Terence" (1765), emblematic of the need for creative freedom. In an age avid to identify African contributions to the classical achievement Terence can be construed as an exceptionally multicultural figure—an African translating Greek comedy into Latin. Was a foundational Western playwright an African? Possibly.

Didascaliae, by contrast, more or less reliably preserve the basics of Terence's theatrical career. *Ludi scaenici* (stage games) in Rome during the time of Terence were produced regularly in the genres of tragedy, *praetexta* (historical drama), *togata* (comedy set in Rome), and *palliata* (comedy set in Greece) as part of the celebration of annual religious festivals that comprised a season from April to early November (though in Terence's time, due to errors in intercalation, these months were falling in winter through summer). Elected officials, aediles and praetors, contracted for the performance of a play with the producer of a theatrical company, who controlled teams of artists and owned the materials for the wooden temporary stage, props, masks, wigs, and costumes. The Terentian stage was not a huge stone Greek theater; the Romans were reluctant to commit to dramatic performance as a permanent part of Roman life until a hundred years after Terence. As he had been for Caecilius, L. Ambivius Turpio was Terence's producer. A man of sufficient business success and confidence to champion challenging new works by young playwrights before festival audiences, Turpio also played the lead in all the plays teamed with Lucius Hatilius of Praeneste—except in the successful showing of *Hecyra* (The Mother-in-Law, 160 B.C.), when Sergius Turpio replaced Hatilius with Flaccus, slave of Claudius, accompanying the sung parts on the reed *tibia*.

Terence's *palliatae* are versions of originals from Greek New Comedy. *Vortere* (turning an original), as Roman comedians called it, involved both translating and innovatively adapting a Greek play to its Roman context. Menander and his follower Apollodorus of Carystus were Terence's sources, an option for Greek models restrained and neatly constructed and against the tradition of his great predecessor Plautus, who died in 184 B.C. Plautus had often drawn from more-farcical sources by such playwrights as Diphilus and Philemon, but by Terence's time Plautus seemed old-fashioned, with his reliance on physical routines, flamboyant singing, linguistic pyrotechnics, and digressive plotting, though when Terence wanted to add a fistfight to his version of Menander's *Adelphoe* (The Brothers), he did draw a scene from Diphilus's *Synapothnescontes* (Dying Together). Terence, whose titles are in Greek, preferred to present a more realistic Athens in his plays to an audience for whom, as their empire grew, Greece was becoming less and less a faraway fantasy land.

In the prologues the contentious voice of Terence the performer and artist is heard through the character of an actor or of Turpio representing the company: "the poet spends his time writing prologues not to set out the circumstances of the plot, but to respond to accusations . . ." (*And.* 5–6). To give the prologue to an actor playing an actor who defends the playwright from attack is (as far as is known) highly original, with a distant antecedent in Aristophanic parabasis, and necessitates rewriting the exposition, one aspect of Terentian adaptation. The prologues, however, are neither critical essays nor straightforward autobiography; they are part of the showmanship of the Roman festival grounds, where comedy had to compete for an audience with simultaneous entertainment in parallel venues, a somewhat hazardous way of making a popular appeal for a sophisticated play.

Two controversies, one arising out of Terence's aristocratic connections and another out of distance from at least one professional colleague, dog the prologues: the accusation that he did not write his plays himself and the accusation that he "ruined" Greek originals by bringing scenes from one comedy into his version of another. According to the first accusation, noble friends supplemented Terence's inadequate skills, using him as a front man for the unrespectable dramatic pursuits prevented them by their status. Cornelius Nepos (cited in the *Life*) claimed that Laelius one evening in his Puteoli villa came late for dinner rather than interrupt his composition of a speech in *Heauton Timorumenos* (The Self-Tormentor, 163 B.C.)–"Those damn promises of Syrus sure tricked me here . . . " (723 ff.). Explaining exactly what lies behind this charge was guesswork in antiquity and remains so. Terence did not refute it, mentioning his friendships only with pride.

A "nasty old poet," whom Donatus identifies as Luscius of Lanuvium, is the author of the second accusation: "it is wrong to ruin plays" (*Andria,* prologue 16). (It is interesting that Terence need respond to critics already in his first play.) *Contaminatio* (ruination), as it is called by modern critics coining a noun from Terence's verb *contaminari,* evidently offended against what was now established practice, or at least Luscius's practice, of using up only one original at a time. As the prologue of *The Self-Tormentor* reports the charge, "he ruined many Greek plays while writing few Latin ones . . . " (178). There is no single way in which Terence mixed his sources: *The Girl from Andros,* adapted from Menander, adds material from Menander's *Perinthia* (Girl from Perinthos); *Eunuchus* (The Eunuch), from Menander, adds material from Menander's *Kolax* (Flatterer), which had already been adapted by Naevius and Plautus; *The Brothers,* from Menander, adds material from *Synapothnescontes* (Dying Together) by Diphilus. The story that new composition occasioned Terence's travel to Athens can imply that Greek originals were a commodity now growing scarce.

Terentian drama comprises the world of New Comedy, representing with some realism the marital and financial problems of families and neighborhoods, and figured in the conventional characters of stern fathers, young lovers, cynical prostitutes, greedy slave dealers, gluttonous parasites, and slaves both tricky and dutiful. Its myth allows hierarchy to be overturned for a time–slaves assist sons with love affairs in defiance of the father–and inversions to be put right in the end: misunderstandings are resolved; family relationships restored, lovers joined, slaves freed or forgiven. Terence highlights relations between the father and son,

failures of self-awareness and of communication, and his characters' everyday approach to what it means to be a human being. *The Girl from Andros* has a conventional plot–the young lover's hetaera is discovered to be the marriageable lost daughter of a citizen–but Terence handles the Menandrian model with originality: he replaces the prologue of the father speaking alone as exposition with a conversation between the father and his freedman and adds two new characters, a second young lover and his slave. This doubling is the first example of Terence's characteristic use of complementary second plots. His next play, *The Self-Tormentor,* is closer to Menander's original but also experiments in a complicated manner with the dualities of two love affairs and three sets of paired characters. Turpio speaks the prologue in the character of a wise old veteran supporting a worthy, struggling young poet (perhaps an upshot of the first failure of *The Mother-in-Law* two years before).

Phormio (161 B.C.), based on *Epidicazomenos* (The Litigant) and featuring citizen involvement in the technicalities of litigation, and *The Mother-in-Law* are close versions of originals by Apollodorus of Carystus. The two failures of *The Mother-in-Law* before the successful performance in 160 B.C. attest to the challenge of presenting drama at a Roman festival; the "stupefied" audience of the first performance booed it off the stage, their attention diverted to boxers, tightrope walkers, and gladiators. Terence's opponents could have been involved in the interference, as his enemy is said in the prologue to *The Eunuch* to have interrupted a preliminary performance of *The Eunuch* for the aediles. Introducing the third showing of *The Mother-in-Law,* Turpio recalls his difficult experience in producing Caecilius's play and asks vindication for Terence, too. The third performance succeeded, but one can easily see why success came hard to a quiet drama, unusual for representing the young lover's life after marriage rather than before and the family tensions that follow when the young husband finds his wife pregnant–not, it seems, by him. By contrast, *The Eunuch* (161 B.C.) won 8,000 sesterces for a second performance, the highest fee ever paid for a comedy. This sum rewarded Terence's concession to those who liked their comedy more boisterous and action packed: the play has two love plots, the definitive yes-man parasite, a display of exotic slaves, the infiltration of a brothel by a young lover in disguise, and an attack on the brothel led by the blustering soldier whose name gives English the word *thrasonical.*

Whatever else Terence's connection with Scipio Aemilianus was, he and his brother Q. Fabius Maximus Aemilianus commissioned *The Brothers* in 160 B.C. for the funeral games honoring their father L. Aemilius Paullus, the victorious general in the battle of Pydna eight years before and a philhellene who had educated

Page from a ninth-century manuscript for Terence's Adelphoe *with a depiction of Aeschinus and his slave Syrus seizing the prostitute Bacchis from her owner Sannio (Vatican Library, Cod. Lat. 3868)*

his sons in Greek culture. Scholars have been tempted to find topicality in *The Brothers,* construing the clash of two fathers over proper values for child-rearing—one indulgent, one traditional and strict—as embodying contemporary Roman concern over the threat to the traditional education emphasizing law and physical endurance that was posed by the new Greek education, which emphasized philosophy, rhetoric, and art. However, if Terence is proud to acknowledge in the prologue his friendship with those the whole city admires, this mention need not be evidence for membership in a formal philhellenic Scipionic group. The whole of the Terentian project is appropriate to a Rome whose elites now had more time and opportunity for Greek culture and impulse to literary sponsorship.

The prologues articulate explicitly a dramatic aesthetic. Locating himself confidently within his tradition even in his first play, Terence prefers a creative *neglegentia* (carelessness) to an *obscura diligentia* (fussy accuracy) (*And.* 20–21). Naevius, Plautus, and Ennius give authoritative precedent for *contaminatio;* how else can one write but within one's tradition? "There is nothing now that hasn't been said before" (*Eun.* 41). Language is "pure" (*pura oratio; Heaut.* 46): it is restrained; consistent with character; confident in its use of moral abstraction; avoiding obscenity, coinages from Greek, and the exuberance of anything-for-a-joke. Comedy can be *stataria* (quiet, *Heaut.* 36) and need not depend on cliched routines like that of the *servus currens* (a slave running too fast to notice his master). Plotting should be realistic, and scenes should follow by logical consequence uninterrupted by irrelevant buffoonery. The prologue of *The Eunuch* counterattacks Luscius for a scene in his *Thesaurus* (Treasure) in which a defendant absurdly addresses the court before the plaintiff. So "by translating well and writing badly" Luscius turns "a good Greek play into a bad Latin one" (*Eun.* 7–13).

Terentian treatment of music is consonant with the other aspects of his dramaturgy. The Roman audience heard two kinds of delivery in performance: *diverbium* (speech) composed in iambic *senarii,* a rhythm to approximate everyday speech, and *canticum* (song). *Cantica* could be written in two kinds of rhythms—in long iambic or trochaic lines whose rhythmical scheme can be repeated indefinitely and of which whole scenes can be constructed (sometimes called "recitative"), or in shorter lyrics with varying rhythms (polymetric). Ever more frequent polymetric songs were among the crowd-pleasing aspects of Plautine comedy; Terence elides them, a striking refusal to continue development of musical comedy that in late Plautus was verging on the operatic. While Terence could compose as much as a third of a play in recitative, aside from another brief passage in *The Girl from Andros,* he did only two poly-

metric *cantica,* distressed songs for the young lovers of his first and last plays (*The Girl from Andros,* 625–638, and *The Brothers,* 610–617).

In the mid first century B.C. Varro judged Caecilius best of *palliata* comedians in plot, Plautus best in dialogue, and Terence best in characterization. Given a traditional comic vocabulary of figures and situations, character comes of giving a new twist to conventional elements. The title character of *Phormio,* for example, the only play to feature a single dominant character, combines elements of the tricky slave and the parasite. While the *leno* (dealer in young slave women) is stereotypically evil in comedy, Sannio in *The Brothers* suffers beating and theft unjustly and can articulate the double standard to which he is subject: citizens will buy slaves from him, yet hold him in contempt and deny him legal recourse because he sells slaves. The trickiness of the slave Syrus in *The Brothers* consists not so much in wild fiction as in subtle negotiation to fix a family scandal quietly. If Plautine slaves joke elaborately about crucifixion and as one preposterous lie is exposed move boldly to the next, Terentian slaves, liable at all times to threats of casual violence, can, as at the beginning of *Phormio,* chat grimly about the difficulty in keeping their personal savings intact when their rich masters insist that their slaves buy them wedding presents. Parmeno, a slave in *The Eunuch,* is demoralized in realistic ways: living in a small cell, being fed insufficiently, and being susceptible to punishment for eating the food his young master tempts him with.

Terence is famously sententious: *quot homines tot sententiae* (as many men so many opinions, *Phor.* 454) and *homo sum; humani nil a me alienum puto* (I am a man; I think nothing human foreign to me, *Heaut.* 77), pulled from their contexts, are practically household words. In their contexts, *sententiae* can be made ironic, their wisdom undermined. The first recognizes that most people simply ignore legalities not in their interest; the second, a motto of Renaissance humanism, is an invitation less to universal learning than to being a nosy neighbor. In *The Brothers,* generous Micio suggests to his frugal brother Demea "friends hold all in common" when he wants something from him. Demea throws the motto back in Micio's face for cynical revenge. Terentian drama sometimes asks if virtue is ever entirely devoid of self-interest.

The objection to Terence reported in the prologue to *Phormio, tenuis oratio . . . scriptura levis* (thin speech and lightweight writing, *Phor.* 5) is echoed by Caesar's famous judgment, preserved in the *Life,* of the one he called "half a Menander": "if only vigor *(vis)* had been joined to your gentle diction, so that your comic excellence could be potent with honor equal to the Greeks." Terence recognizes the choices to be made in the literary comic myth Rome inherits from Greece and

VENVS AFRA   SCIPIO AFR

PVB.
TERENTII
COMŒDIÆ
SEX
Ex recensione
Heinsiana.

Cornel. Cl. Dusend Sculpsit

AMSTELODAMI,
Ex Officina Elzeviriana. *Aº 1661.*

*Engraved title page for a 1661 edition of Terence's comedies (courtesy of
the Lilly Library, Indiana University)*

Roman religious life, subject to repetition with the whole of the festival if ritual was in some way defective. Terence does not disinherit himself from the comedian's traditional capacity to critique civic forms through parody and metatheater; he even occasionally breaks the dramatic illusion he creates.

For example, *palliata* represents slaves and slave life with greater elaboration than Greek comedy, and this adaptation enacts the concerns of a Roman audience who only recently were holding greater numbers of slaves. Whether or not Terence himself was a freedman, performers came from a servile class and when performing would portray a slave society to an audience of slaveholders. That Terence adds the freedman character to the opening scene of Menander's *Andria* is characteristic. At the close of *The Brothers,* Demea, arguing for the festive manumission of his brother's slave, parodies an element of Roman slaveholding ideology, that slaves be manumitted after a certain time for good service: "Buying party supplies, procuring prostitutes, preparing daylong dinners: these are the duties of a distinguished man. Free him; the other slaves will be the better for it" (*Ad.* 964–968). To represent frankly the slave trade at all, as whenever the *leno* is a character, comes of a holiday license, but does an audience enjoy the festival inversion of slaves mastering their masters and then accept uncritically their return to their place when comedy is done?

Terentian characters can be cynical; hypocrisy can be punctured. *The Mother-in-Law* opens with the professional talk of two prostitutes who expertly distinguish love and marriage and conflate love and greed. Pamphilus, the young husband, goes on to castigate the rapist of his wife before learning that he actually was the rapist. In *The Eunuch,* young lover Phaedria beats up his slave eunuch to keep him quiet about a young prostitute's rape perpetrated by his brother Chaerea disguised as the eunuch. Phaedria explains to the audience: "I couldn't see any other way of getting out of it without compromising my reputation" (716). The question of how a eunuch could commit a rape causes hilarity before slave Parmeno poses another moral conundrum: what sexual crime is actually possible in a whorehouse? While subject to a double standard regarding prostitutes, Thaïs can express the most humane view of love in this play, in which erotic rivalries are resolved in a menage.

More subtle with his metatheater than Plautus, who boasts overtly in his drama that he has surpassed his Greek models, Terence can question the comic tradition. While Chaerea contemplates taking the girl he lusted for, a mural painting of Jupiter carrying off Ganymede inspires the young rapist in *The Eunuch*. If the morality of imitating wicked Greek models is made

reworks: literary comedy could occasion both wild fantasy free of the boundaries of necessity and the realistic representation of the domestic situations and problems of citizens unprivileged in other genres. When Terence avoids, rather than celebrates, the grotesque and inconsistent, when he avoids polymetric musical numbers, linguistic exuberance, silly jokes, and buffoonish characters, he is far from the original carnival theme of the world for a time upside down. This choice, though, at the expense of comic fantasy, allows him a greater degree of social realism.

Terence's holiday audience may have wished to leave their mental faculties at home; yet, dramatic performance still represented community concerns before the assembled community and was conditioned by

to seem dubious, what of this adaptation of a comedy by Menander? At the end of *The Brothers,* Demea offers a moral for the comic closure he has done so much to bring about: "I wanted to demonstrate to you that what our children think is easy-going and festive in you doesn't come from sincerity or from what is right and just, but from telling people what they want to hear, from indulgence, from wasting money . . . " (*Ad.* 986–988). Yet, if that moral were in fact unproblematic, critics would not be perennially exercised to decide upon the sincerity of Demea's striking change of mind. Pamphilus, unwitting rapist of his wife in *The Mother-in-Law,* dismisses a traditional comic denouement and decides to suppress the truth: "No need to tell my father. I wouldn't like this to end up the way it does in comedies, where everybody finds out everything. Those who should have found out know already. Those who shouldn't know won't find out and won't know . . ." (*Hec.* 865–868). The audience's enjoyment of a "happy," comic ending is in this play overtly a complicity in violent secrets: Terentian drama can acknowledge the false comfort of easy comic closure. Terence is among the ambitious comedians who emphasize the complexities of their endings, a critical self-awareness itself drawn from Greek models.

A kind of comedy that denied a holiday audience legitimate fun marks the end of the development of *palliata* in Rome: the last sixty years of *palliata* ignore Terentian innovation. By 100 B.C. Volcacius Sedigitus ranked Terence only sixth on his list of the top ten Roman comedians. Yet, Terence soon became a literate rather than a theatrical pleasure. Alone of all poets of Republican Rome he is acknowledged for his contribution to classical Latin style. Caesar and Cicero, whose judgments are preserved in the *Life,* praise not Terence's theatrical merit but his *purus, lectus sermo* (pure, choice language). Terence achieved first what became hallmarks of classical Latin: skilled use of syntactic subordination, use of metrical patterns to clarify thought, and disciplined concision and clarity amid grammatical complexity. The *purus sermo,* then, is a considerable achievement, making possible in drama realistic characterization, irony, and sophisticated verbal play, an important resource for future European literary comedy, the roots of which are in Plautus and Terence.

Terence remained a standard school author—read, commented on, and sometimes performed—into the fourth century A.D. If Augustine, who read *The Eunuch* in school in Madauros in the A.D. 360s, objected to the immorality of Jupiter giving divine authority for Chaerea's rape, Jerome read Terence for recreation while translating the Vulgate. Terence inspired the moralizing comedy of the tenth-century nun Hrotswitha of Gandersheim and the sixteenth-century

Dutch authors of "Christian Terence," a genre in which *palliata* meets parables from the Bible. Terence was widely copied in the Middle Ages; more than 100 manuscripts before the fourteenth century carry the tradition for more than 440 complete printed editions before 1600 following the *editio princeps* in 1470. Terence most directly influenced the Italian humanist *commedia erudita*: Ariosto did a *Phormio* (1506), Machiavelli, an *Andria* (1517). From the ironic fertility of the marriage of Nicia and Lucrezia that ends Machiavelli's *Mandragola* (1520) to the domestic acrimony of the *Honeymooners* of 1950s American television, whenever bitter human truth intelligently expressed emerges from popular and commercial comedy, the legacy of Terence is alive.

Bibliographies:

H. Marti, "Terenz 1909–1959," *Lustrum,* 6 (1961): 114–238; and *Lustrum,* 8 (1963): 5–101, 244–264;

Sander M. Goldberg, "Scholarship on Terence and the Fragments of Roman Comedy: 1959–1980," *Classical World,* 75 (1981): 77–115;

Giovanni Cupaiuolo, *Bibliografia terenziana (1470–1983), Studi e testi dell' antichità,* 16 (Naples, 1984); and "Supplementum Terentianum," *Bolletino di studi latini,* 22 (1992): 32–57.

References:

W. Geoffrey Arnott, *Menander, Plautus, Terence,* Greece and Rome: New Surveys in the Classics, no. 9 (Oxford: Oxford University Press, 1975);

Richard C. Beacham, *The Roman Theatre and its Audience* (Cambridge, Mass.: Harvard University Press, 1992);

George E. Duckworth, *The Nature of Roman Comedy* (Princeton, N.J.: Princeton University Press, 1952);

Walter E. Forehand, *Terence* (Boston: Twayne, 1985);

Charles Garton, *Personal Aspects of the Roman Theater* (Toronto: Hakkert, 1972);

Sander M. Goldberg, *Understanding Terence* (Princeton, N.J.: Princeton University Press, 1986);

A. S. Grantwick, "Drama," in *The Cambridge History of Classical Literature,* volume 2: *Latin Literature* (Cambridge: Cambridge University Press, 1982), pp. 77–137;

R. L. Hunter, *The New Comedy of Greece and Rome* (Cambridge: Cambridge University Press, 1985);

David Konstan, *Roman Comedy* (Ithaca, N.Y.: Cornell University Press, 1983);

John Wright, *Dancing in Chains: The Stylistic Unity of the Comoedia Palliata,* Papers and Monographs of the American Academy at Rome, 25 (Rome: American Academy, 1974).

Tibullus

(ca. 54 B.C. – ca. 19 B.C.)

David F. Bright
Emory University

WORK: Two books of poems in elegiac couplets.

Editio princeps: Edition without title page, pagination, or signatures (Venice: Vindelinus da Spira, 1472), ff. 188–includes Tibullus, Propertius, Catullus, and the *Silvae* of Statius.

Standard editions: Josephus J. Scaliger, *Catulli Tibulli Properti nova editio* (Amsterdam: Hieronymus Commelin, 1600); Ludolph Dissen, *Tibulli carmina ex recensione Lachmanni passim mutata* (Göttingen: Dieterich, 1835; reprinted, Hildesheim: Gerstenberg, 1969); F. W. Lenz and G. Karl Galinsky, *Albii Tibulli aliorumque carminum libri tres,* third edition (Leiden: Brill, 1971); Georg Luck, *Albii Tibulli aliorumque carmina* (Stuttgart: Teubner, 1988).

Translations in English: *The Poems of Tibullus,* translated by Constance Carrier with introduction, notes, and glossary by Edward W. Michael (Bloomington: Indiana University Press, 1968); *The Poems of Tibullus with the Tibullan Collection,* translated by Philip Dunlop (Baltimore: Penguin, 1972); *Catullus, Tibullus, and Pervigilium Veneris,* Loeb Classical Library, second edition revised by G. P. Goold, translated by F. W. Cornish, J. P. Postgate, and J. W. Mackail (Cambridge, Mass.: Harvard University Press, 1988; corrected edition, 1995); *Tibullus: Elegies,* third edition, translated by Guy Lee (Leeds: Francis Cairns, 1990).

Commentaries: *The Elegies of Albius Tibullus. The Corpus Tibullianum,* edited by Kirby Flower Smith, with introduction and notes on books 1, 2, and 4.2–14 (New York: American Book Company, 1913); *Tibullus. A Commentary,* edited by Michael C. J. Putnam (Norman: University of Oklahoma Press, 1973); Paul Murgatroyd, *Tibullus I: A Commentary on the First Book of the Elegies of Albius Tibullus* (Pietermaritzburg: Natal University Press, 1980); *Elegies II,* edited by Murgatroyd (Oxford: Clarendon Press, 1994).

Among the small but remarkable company of Roman elegiac poets of the first century B.C.–including Catullus, Gallus, Propertius, and Ovid–Albius Tibullus is often underestimated. He is treated as the least distinctive personality, writing the least dramatically confessional poetry in a genre that relies on the illusion of personal confession. His two books of poems also constitute the shortest body of work of the three elegists whose work has survived *in extenso*. But it was precisely his controlled, "bas-relief" style that won him Quintilian's approval as *tersus atque elegans maxime* (especially polished and discriminating). Quintilian was not alone in assessing Tibullus so highly.

Tibullus's work is characterized by purism in language and meter, a varied repertory of erotic and nonerotic themes presented as personal experience, a view of national events through the lens of personal friendship rather than public patriotism, and spare use of mythological topoi in a tradition that was awash in clever mythological allusions. Above all, his poems are marked by a fluidity of thought that moves from apparent fact to confessed dream, present to past, with little transition or clarification. What ties these topics and musings together is the skilled depiction of the poet's feelings. Guy Lee puts the matter succinctly: "If Propertius is the poet of passion and Ovid of wit, Tibullus is the poet of feeling."

Tibullus has none of the slashing obscenity or strident tone of Catullus; he resists the caustic exuberance and flamboyant innovations of Propertius; and although he makes skilled use of the irony for which Ovid became famous, Tibullus weaves it in among other effects rather than making it his chief characteristic. Yet, his poems share crucial features of style, theme, and tone with all three of his fellow elegists (no one can tell how his work compared with Gallus, whose poetic corpus is lost except for a single piece of a quite different type). Tibullus drew on the Hellenistic tradition of elegy and epigram, especially the works of Callimachus and Euphorion, and developed it in a distinctively Roman way. Without his work, scholars and students would have a far harder time seeing the Roman elegists as forming a coherent tradition.

As is often the case with ancient writers, the biographical information about Tibullus is sparse and difficult to evaluate. He constantly speaks of personal experiences, but one should exercise much caution in treating such professions as even approximately autobiographical. Horace and Ovid provide the most extensive contemporary statements, but for the most part they are reflecting on a fellow poet's situation in love and lamenting his passing rather than reporting information. A *vita* from at least a century after Tibullus's death, accompanied by an epigram of his contemporary Domitius Marsus, apparently draws on Suetonius's lost work *On the Lives of the Poets,* but the information may be accurate. The epigram and vita are both brief (quotations are from Guy Lee's translation):

Inequitable Death sent you, Tibullus, also
as Virgil's comrade young to Elysian Fields,
lest any live to weep soft loves in elegiacs
or sing of royal wars in brave rhythms.

Albius Tibullus, Roman knight, noted for good looks and remarkable for personal adornment, beyond others loved Corvinus Messalla the orator, as whose aide also in the Aquitanian War he was awarded military decorations. In the judgment of many he occupies first place among the elegiographers. His amatory epistles, too, though short, are thoroughly useful. He died young, as the epigram quoted above testifies.

Other poets, critics, and grammarians from the first to the fifth century give further useful snippets. From these sources, and from Tibullus's own work, a plausible, if hazy, picture emerges. Tibullus's family home was in the region of Pedum, a town in Latium a few miles east of Rome (Horace, *Epist.* 1.4, addressed to Albius), a location that makes Tibullus one of relatively few Latin authors who were genuinely Latin. He was an *eques,* a Roman knight. He speaks of lost prosperity and pressing circumstances in passages such as the following:

You, O Lares, also receive your gifts as guardians
of a property once prosperous, now poor:
once a slaughtered heifer purified uncounted steers;
now my little acres offer a ewe-lamb. (1.1.19–22)

Horace's summary is more encouraging: "the gods made you handsome, and gave you wealth and the skill to enjoy it" (*Epist.* 1.4.6–7). This comment, as well as other depictions of his life by Tibullus himself, suggest that he lived a comfortable existence encompassing property in both town and country.

At the same time there is no reason to dismiss Tibullus's statement that the family's prosperity had diminished. Many families endured such losses in the civil wars and the accompanying confiscations. Tibullus often uses terms such as "ancient" or "ancestral" in referring to his family's holdings, and it is likely that his ancestors had lived there for several generations. He was then a scion of the country gentry, and this conservative, settled background shows up in his views on religion, the city, and the land.

The date of Tibullus's birth must be cautiously inferred from the information in the epigram and vita. His death came close after that of Virgil (who died 21 September 19 B.C.): it is unlikely that he would be called Virgil's traveling companion to the next world if their deaths occurred more than a year apart. Tibullus then presumably died by 19 B.C. and possibly sooner. Moreover, he died "young" (*obiit adulescens* in the vita, *iuvenis* in Domitius Marsus)–a flexible term at best. While Varro says extreme usage of *iuvenis* stretched up to age forty-five, that age seems ill-suited to laments for the untimely loss of a poet working in the genre of young lovers, as expressed by his contemporaries. Tibullus was probably not past thirty-five at his death.

In that case he was born ca. 54–50 B.C.; he was a young boy when the die was cast and Caesar crossed the Rubicon in 49 B.C., and he grew up in the climactic and terrifying years of civil war. The assassination of Caesar in 44 B.C. was followed by more than a decade of shifting fortunes and loyalties until Octavian gained the victory at Actium in 31 B.C. In light of these facts it is hardly surprising that longing for the serenity of country life, dread of war and travel, nostalgia for simpler and more pious times, and anxiety over the perils of the urban scene figure prominently in Tibullus's poems.

Of his parents nothing is known directly. Tibullus never even alludes to his parents, and it is evident that the poet was responsible for management of the family estate even at a relatively young age. In all probability his father died when Tibullus was quite young (there is no evidence to assist those people who want to speculate on whether his father was responsible for the poet's reduced circumstances by squandering the family fortune). Ovid's touching tribute (*Amores* 3.9) says that Tibullus's mother and sister attended his funeral. There is no evidence of other siblings nor of any offspring.

Tibullus's most important and lasting association–including amatory liaisons–was with his literary patron. M. Valerius Messalla Corvinus was an exact contemporary of Octavian, later known as Augustus (born 64 B.C.). Although Messalla took an independent path in the early years of the struggle for power after

Julius Caesar's assassination on the Ides of March, his loyalties eventually settled on Octavian. Messalla was consul in 31 B.C. and fought beside Octavian at Actium.

Messalla was given a military command in Syria (ca. 30–29 B.C.) and also governed in Gaul, where he subdued the Aquitani. Tibullus alludes to both these campaigns in his poems (1.3 and 1.7). For this latter service the victorious general was awarded a triumph celebrated in Rome in September 27 B.C. Messalla's public career continued for another thirty years, but he continued to show an independent streak: for instance, he was named *praefectus urbi* (Prefect of the City of Rome) in 26 or 25 B.C., but according to St. Jerome he resigned the office after less than a week on the grounds that it gave unsuitable powers to a mere citizen.

Of greatest significance to Tibullus was Messalla's role as a man of letters. He was a noted orator and wrote poems, memoirs, and treatises on grammar and philosophy. But his largest contribution to culture was his patronage of a circle of poets that included Tibullus, Ovid in his early years, Lygdamus, and his own niece Sulpicia (as well as some lesser talents, one of whom wrote the fawning and clumsy *Panegyric of Messalla*). Despite his relationship with one of Augustus's major military supporters and appointees, Tibullus never directly mentions the Princeps Augustus. The poets who were most aggressive in their remarks on the leader of the Roman world were under the aegis of the greatest patron of the day, Maecenas. The independence of spirit that characterized so much of Messalla's career seems to have attracted poets of a similar bent.

Tibullus's career coincided with the greatest poets Rome ever knew. His contemporaries included Horace, Propertius, Ovid, and Virgil as well as minor figures such as Valgius Rufus (addressed in 1.10) and Domitius Marsus. In this luminary company it is all the more remarkable that Tibullus was singled out as the most polished and discriminating poet in his chosen genre.

Tibullus published his first book around 26 B.C. (Propertius had published his *Monobiblos* a year or so earlier and published his second book a year or so after Tibullus's first.) It presents a surprisingly broad array of themes and characters, and even of styles, ranging from drifting dreams of country living to an amusing professorial lecture on winning the affections of young boys. The main characters are his mistress, Delia, the boy Marathus, both objects of his love, and the great general Messalla. The discontinuity among these three possible worlds is what gives the book its texture, keeps the reader wondering what the next poem will bring, and shows Tibullus's sure hand in depicting several realities at once.

The last poem in the book, 1.10, has generally been regarded since at least the early nineteenth century as the earliest in date of composition, although this view reflects little more than the observation that Tibullus professes no experience of either war or love while all his other poems present a figure with greater experience. Some scholars have cast a skeptical eye on this position, but no one has suggested another poem as being earlier. In this poem the reader meets a callow youth whose thoughts are divided between the horrors of war, to which he is being dragged away, and the blessings of a simple rustic life centered on the old-fashioned piety of his fathers before him.

Already the characteristic features of Tibullus's art are clear. He moves from one theme to the next with few overt transitions but often by a kind of mental bridging of opposites. The flow of thoughts in 1.10 might be summarized as follows: war is linked to wealth, death awaits me in a distant place / O household gods save me, I am devoted to a simple pious life / war destroys the countryside / let peace attend the fields / the farmer in such peace comes home to his loving wife / love too brings its own wars.

Despite the discontinuous feel of the subject matter, there is a strong sense of stanzaic structures created by repeated words to begin or end successive lines, rhyme patterns, and strongly contrastive word placement. These signs of formal structure seem at times to be virtually independent of the thoughts that move through them.

Love in this poem is not linked to a specific mistress or even to Tibullus himself: it is an ideal, set in opposition to war, of which he likewise has no experience. The dimension he knows firsthand is tending the ancestral fields and worshiping the ancestral gods. This poem offers a kind of baseline for the book, as each element gains vividness and relevance to the poet's professed experience in the other poems.

Book 1 was known in antiquity as *Delia,* named for the mistress who dominates it and appears in half of the poems (1, 2, 3, 5, and 6). Apuleius (*Apology* 10) says her real name was Plania. This assertion fits the general pattern among the Roman poets (Apuleius gives a half-dozen examples) of Greek pseudonyms having the same metrical shape as the real Latin name. The name is probably an allusion to the goddess Diana, of whom Delia was an epithet—as was Cynthia, the name that Propertius uses for his mistress, whose real name, according to Apuleius, was Hostia.

Delia is as variable as the settings in which Tibullus places her. The only constant is that she does not fulfill his dream. In 1.1 his first words are a rejection of wealth and war and a declaration of his love for the simple country life:

> Wealth let others gather for themselves in yellow gold
> and occupy great acres of cultivated land—
> scared on active service, in contact with the enemy,
> their sleep put to flight by the blare of trumpet-calls.

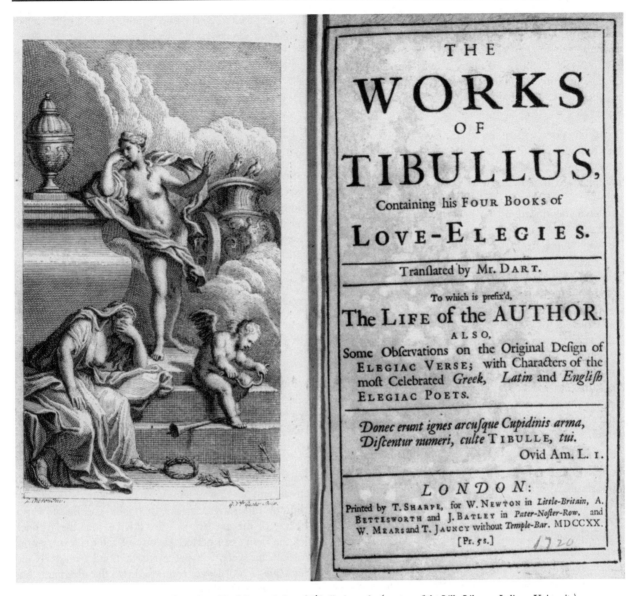

Frontispiece and title page for a 1720 English translation of Tibullus's works (courtesy of the Lilly Library, Indiana University)

But let my general poverty transfer *me* to inaction,
so long as fire glows always in my hearth. (1.1.1–6)

Yet, by the time the narrator addresses Delia for the first time, fifty lines later, the rustic reverie is lost, and he sees himself locked out of her house, presumably in the city. Then, just as abruptly, he hopes she will tend to him when he dies. The interlocking of his dreams of love in the country and death in the city is distinctively Tibullan.

The second poem is clearly set in the city, which is the usual mise-en-scène for the elegists. Roman elegy uses the excitement, the crowds, and the treachery of the

city as its backdrop; only Tibullus adds an elegiac version of the pastoral world of the eclogue (Virgil's *Eclogues* are also a collection of ten poems nearly identical to Tibullus 1 in length and surely served as one of the elegist's models). This poem is a specimen of the *paraclausithyron* (lament outside the locked door), a theme also explored by Propertius and Ovid. The Delia Tibullus now loves but cannot reach (she is under the control of a *coniunx,* who may be a husband or a lover) is quite unlike the independent, rural Delia of the previous poem or the idealized, rustic wife he dreams of in the next elegy.

The background of the third poem is Messalla's campaign in Syria. Tibullus depicts himself as stranded by illness on Corcyra and thus prevented from accompanying his patron on the expedition to Asia. As noted, the eastern campaign came shortly after Actium, probably in 30 or 29 B.C., and offers a rare clue to chronology. Apparently Tibullus was to accompany Messalla—he does not say in what capacity—but was prevented by illness.

The poem is striking for the way in which Tibullus combines two of his major characters, Messalla and Delia, who seem to occupy disparate worlds. They are not pictured together in this poem but play separate roles in a remarkable vision. Adopting a commonly accepted identification, the poet speaks of Corcyra as Phaeacia, the island where Odysseus was stranded on his way home from the war in Troy, and turns this entire elegy into a dream-echo of the *Odyssey* with himself in the lead role. In the opening lines Messalla, like Agamemnon, is leading his troops to fight in far-away Asia, and as the picture develops, Delia is asked to be the Penelope of the piece, waiting patiently and faithfully at home for her man's return. Complete with an imagined tour of the Underworld as in the Homeric model and a sudden, unexpected homecoming of the hero, this elegy is a tour de force of literary homage and personal imagination as the poet brings together Messalla's real exploits and the wish that Delia might refrain from exploits in her own realm.

Needless to say, the relationship with Delia is doomed and consists mainly of laments over lost opportunities, broken promises, and shattered dreams. The last two Delia elegies (5 and 6) convey this harsh realization, and yet 1.5 not only involves both Messalla and Delia again but this time brings them together in a dream of rural bliss. While excoriating Delia for her faithlessness, Tibullus describes his lost hopes of a perfect rustic life with her as his wife. He imagines the great general, now "my Messalla," visiting Tibullus's modest estate and Delia as the one to welcome him. Tibullus does not want to put Messalla where Delia is seen in a harsh light, lest it reflect badly on his patron, but takes the risk of bringing them into the same dream scene, imbedded in a poem of stern chastising.

After one more elegy (1.6), again set in the city and featuring only recrimination, hardening of hearts, and dismissal, Delia is gone from his story; but Messalla advances from supporting actor to leading man. In 1.7, on the occasion of Messalla's birthday, Tibullus pays tribute to the general's triumph over the Aquitani, celebrated in September 27 B.C. This reference is the one datable event in all of Tibullus's work. Not surprisingly, the homage to Messalla is free of any references to Tibullus's amatory escapades, real or imagined. The poem tells of Messalla's successes in Gaul and includes

what appears to be the poet's modest claim to have participated: *non sine me tibi partus honos . . .*

Not without me was your glory gained: witness the Tarbellian
Pyrenees and shore of the Santonic Ocean;
witness Saône and rapid Rhone and great Garonne
and Loire, blue stream of flaxen-haired Carnutes. (7. 9–12)

Even though the *vita* also asserts that Tibullus served in this campaign and was decorated for it (a statement that certainly appears to confirm his claim), some think that for such a majestic catalogue of rivers to bear witness to the poet's modest role is too heavy-handed and would have him say *non sine Marte ibi . . .* (not without warfare was your glory gained there). This change unfortunately would remove the only direct statement of Tibullus's personal experience in war.

The interweaving of the Delia and Messalla motifs is remarkable enough, but there is a third major thread in the book. Poems 4, 8, and 9 are concerned with Tibullus's professions of passion for a young boy named Marathus. These poems are unique in Roman elegiac poetry (though there are some parallels in Greek) in depicting the poet as engaged in homoerotic passion. Indeed, Tibullus's first book is unique in developing two separate loves. The combination sets Tibullus apart from the rest of the tradition. Tibullus owes much to Callimachus both for the theme and for its treatment in this poem. It is brimming with elegant humor and irony. He asks the phallic god Priapus, protector of the garden, to offer advice, and the wooden statue delivers a perfect parody of the professorial lecture. The piece is a precursor to Ovid's masterly *Ars amatoria* (Art of Love) composed two decades later—one of the most amusing specimens of didactic poetry in Latin. Then, as Priapus finishes his lecture, Tibullus says he was actually trying to learn how he could console and instruct his friend Titius (whose wife forbids his learning such things), and sets himself up as a teacher of love; but, in a further twist in the closing couplets, Tibullus suddenly admits he is wracked by unrequited passion for a boy named Marathus.

This same Marathus reappears in 1.8, hopelessly in love with a typical elegiac mistress named Pholoe, while Tibullus pines for the boy. This combinatorial world is likewise rare in the elegiac tradition and allows Tibullus to tackle both the standard poet-mistress theme once more, as observer rather than participant, and also to revive the surprising confession of his passion for Marathus that ended 1.4. The result is complex and highly entertaining. The plot thickens further in poem 9, where Tibullus is still frustrated, but Marathus is now depicted as in the clutches of a gouty old man, who in turn is married. Readers are not required (or perhaps even able) to take this series of poems as a plot or a unified story but as a set of dazzling variations on a complex theme.

Thus, in this book Tibullus takes his readers through several possible realities, overlapping and diverging, dreamed and professed as real. A chronology is not only unattainable but is carefully demolished. The simplicity of language and steady discipline of meter are offset by a daunting complexity of imagination and theme.

Book 2 is not without its own surprises and novelties. Tibullus introduces a third love interest, this time a hard, materialistic girl named Nemesis (after the Greek goddess of Retribution), who appears in four of the six elegies (2, 3, 4, and 6). No ancient source suggests a "real" identity for this character, although in his account of Tibullus's funeral (*Amores* 3.9), Ovid has Nemesis and Delia squabble over the bier as they lament their loss. Nemesis declares she was Tibullus's love at the time of his death. The poems hardly give grounds for such optimism, but even in the last of them, 2.6, Tibullus sings—albeit somewhat bitterly—of the goddess Spes (Hope).

The book is unexpectedly brief—six poems extending to about 432 lines (lacunae make the exact figure uncertain) as compared with ten poems in *Delia,* which runs to 814 verses. Moreover, the last poem ends abruptly, and some believe it has been truncated. This view has prompted the conjecture that the book is incomplete, lacking the end of 2.6 and whatever should have followed (the loss might have been caused by later damage to a published book or imposed by the poet's death). Others see sufficient structure in both 2.6 and the book as a whole to show that book 2 received the poet's final touches.

Book 2 shares several features with *Delia:* a struggling affair with a mistress; the interweaving of erotic and nonerotic poems, and of city and country; and the presence of Messalla at ritual moments. The generalized country rituals of 1.10 become the vividly real observance of the *Ambarvalia* (the blessing of the fields) in 2.1. Two poems are addressed to Tibullus's friend Cornutus (2, which like 1.7 is a birthday poem, and 3): this young man may be the author or at least the subject of a sequence of poems in the third book.

Most of the book is impossible to date, but one poem offers a hint. Not long before 17 B.C., Messalla's eldest son Messalinus was elected to the *XV viri sacris faciundis* (priestly College in charge of the Sybilline books), and in 2.5 Tibullus pays tribute to this honor. The poem probably belongs shortly before the poet's death. This tribute to Messalinus plays the same role in book 2 as the tribute to his father in 1.7, a foray into themes of public significance as seen through his association with the House of Messalla.

Since Tibullus's theme goes back to the fall of Troy and Aeneas's travels to Latium, it is inevitable that this poem should be scrutinized in light of Virgil's *Aeneid.* Scholarly opinion is strongly divided on the question of the relationship between 2.5 and any version of the *Aeneid,* especially the finished poem that was only published after Virgil's death by his literary executors.

While there are moments in the two poems that coincide, Tibullus's poem has different emphases. Tibullus dwells more nostalgically than Virgil on the pastoral life in Italy that preceded the arrival of Aeneas, while looking ahead to the later foundation of Rome; he speaks of the dire portents following the assassination of Caesar (his own losses in the civil wars may yet be haunting him) and then returns to the joys of the rustic life in his own day, thereby resuming the festive note on which he began. Praise of Messalinus begins and ends the poem, and Messalla is also toasted at the end, thus emphasizing the true purpose of this poem.

The two books of elegies by Tibullus are joined to a third book, including twenty poems by possibly as many as five other authors, to form the Corpus Tibullianum. The third book includes six competent but bland love elegies by an otherwise unknown Ovidian poet named Lygdamus, addressed to his mistress Neaera (both names may be pseudonyms); the mawkish *Panegyric* mentioned above; the so-called *Garland of Sulpicia,* five poems telling of the pseudonymous Cerinthus's love for Messalla's niece Sulpicia (that Tibullus himself is the author is sometimes wistfully surmised, and Cerinthus is often identified with Cornutus of book 2); six short, personal, and quite appealing poems by Sulpicia, the only Latin poetry by a woman from the classical period; a brief elegy of Tibullan quality that purports to be his work (even using his name in the text, which, however, Tibullus never does elsewhere) but may belong after Ovid, whose *Ars amatoria* it apparently quotes; and an epigram.

All these works emanated from the Messallan circle and were associated with the work of that circle's leading light, probably in the generation after Tibullus's death. In the Renaissance Lygdamus's six poems were separated as book 3 and the rest relabeled book 4. There is some recent tendency to reverse that act: for example, F. W. Lenz and G. Karl Galinsky (1971) use a double numeration system, numbering poems both simply as 3 and as broken into 3 and 4, and G. P. Goold's Loeb Classical Edition explicitly rejects the Renaissance division of 3.

For a poet who prompted such admiration in his contemporaries, Tibullus fared modestly in succeeding ages. From Ovid to Quintilian–that is, from his own day until the end of the first century after Christ–he is referred to with respect and with some frequency by writers of such different tastes as Horace, Martial, Statius, Velleius Paterculus, and Quintilian, but is almost never directly quoted, thus coming perilously close to Mark Twain's definition of a classic: "a book which people praise and don't read."

Tibullus then glides in near silence through the next millennium, on the slightest of manuscript traditions, until the Renaissance offers a sensibility more receptive to his work. The first printed edition (in a volume including several other poets) appeared in Venice in 1472, and there has been a steady if not always abundant stream of editions and commentaries for the past five centuries. Kirby Flower Smith's 1913 edition was the first scholarly American edition of any Latin author. In the introduction Smith surveyed the poet's reception through the centuries and noted that the eighteenth century was especially responsive to Tibullus: "In this age of Pope, Watteau, and Voltaire, of Dresden shepherdesses and pastoral operas, of *petit-maîtres* and *coeurs sensibles,* the prominence of Tibullus in the literatures of Europe was more marked than it has ever been except in his own time."

Tibullus is a fine example of the precept *ars est celare artem:* the essence of art is in concealing artistry. The smooth, classical purity of his language and meter and the even tenor of his imagery draw the reader into his poetic world and provide ready, almost unsuspecting access to an imagination that is actually startlingly inventive. Yet, at still another level, Tibullus presents variations on a strongly traditional vision: a nature that rewards honest toil in the fields; gods who expect proper reverence but respond to piety; love that gives and waits and hopes, even when evidence runs convincingly to the contrary; and a public sphere sustained by admirable and valiant warriors who also appreciate art and love.

For all his artful haziness, Tibullus makes the Roman world accessible to the modern reader in ways that his fellow elegists do not attempt. His pictures of country life have a gentle, idealized quality, while his city is suitably dangerous and unpredictable: these characteristics are familiar and reassuring. At the same time, there is something almost postmodern about his drifting among alternative worlds, depicted in and seen through three lovers, all crossing between the urban and rural, between the specific and the impressionistic, until no event or person, even Messalla, offers a sure point of reference in the poet's world.

Tibullus's precision and skill in language and the sure exercise of his imagination made him the favorite of many Roman readers; they have likewise secured him an admired place among modern readers. Quintilian's judgment has been reaffirmed over a span of two millennia.

Bibliography:
Hermann Harrauer, *A Bibliography to the Corpus Tibullianum* (Hildesheim: Gerstenberg, 1971).

References:
Atti del convegno internazionale di studi su Albio Tibullo, Roma-Palestrina, 10–13 maggio 1984 (Rome: Centro di studi ciceroniani, 1986);

Robert J. Ball, *Tibullus the Elegist: A Critical Survey* (Göttingen: Vandenhoecht & Ruprecht, 1983);

David F. Bright, *Haec mihi fingebam: Tibullus in his World* (Leiden: Brill, 1978);

Francis Cairns, *Tibullus. A Hellenistic Poet at Rome* (Cambridge: Cambridge University Press, 1979);

Frank O. Copley, *Exclusus Amator: A Study in Latin Love Poetry,* Philological monographs, 17 (Madison, Wis.: American Philological Association, 1956);

Archibald A. Day, *The Origins of the Latin Love Elegy* (Oxford: Blackwells, 1938; reprinted, Hildesheim: Olms, 1972);

Gilbert Highet, *Poets in a Landscape* (New York: Knopf, 1957);

Georg Luck, *The Latin Love-Elegy,* second edition (London: Methuen, 1969);

J. K. Newman, *Augustus and the New Poetry,* Collection Latomus, 88 (Brussels: Latomus, 1967);

Edward N. O'Neil, *A Critical Concordance of the Tibullan Corpus* (American Philological Association, 1963);

Maurice Platnauer, *Latin Elegiac Verse,* second edition (Cambridge: Cambridge University Press, 1951);

Mauriz Schuster, *Tibull-Studien* (Vienna: Hölder, 1930);

F. Solmsen, "Tibullus as an Augustan Poet," *Hermes,* 90 (1962): 295–325;

B. L. Ullman, "Tibullus in the Mediaeval Florilegia," *Classical Philology,* 23 (1928): 128–174;

Gordon Williams, *Tradition and Originality in Roman Poetry* (Oxford: Clarendon Press, 1968);

Walter Wimmel, *Kallimachos in Rom, Hermes* Eizelschriften, 16 (Wiesbaden: F. Steiner, 1960);

Wimmel, *Der frühe Tibull* (Munich: Fink, 1968).

Valerius Flaccus

(fl. ca. A.D. 92)

Andrew Zissos
University of Texas at Austin

WORK: *Argonautica,* 8 books unfinished, probably due to poet's death (The Argonauts, A.D. 92/93).

Editio princeps: *Argonautica* (Bologna: Ugo Rugerius & Doninus Bertochus, 1474).

Standard editions: *C. Valeri Flacci Argonauticon Libri Octo,* edited by Edward Courtney (Leipzig: Teubner, 1970); *Gai Valeri Flacci Setini Balbi Argonauticon Libros Octo,* edited by Widu Wolfgang Ehlers (Stuttgart: Teubner, 1980).

Translations in English: *Valerius Flaccus,* Loeb Classical Library, translated by J. H. Mozley (Cambridge, Mass.: Harvard University Press, 1934); "Valerius Flaccus *Argonautica* Book 7," translated by F. Raphael and K. McLeish, in *Roman Poets of the Early Empire,* edited by A. J. Boyle and J. P. Sullivan (London & New York: Penguin, 1991), pp. 278–296.

Commentaries: *Valerii Flacci Argonauticorum Libri VIII,* edited by Peter Langen (Berlin: S. Calvary, 1896–1897; reprinted, Hildesheim: Olms, 1964); *Valerius Flaccus, Argonautica 4, 1–343: ein Kommentar,* edited by Matthias Korn (Hildesheim: Olms, 1989); *Valerius Flaccus, Argonautica VII: Ein Kommentar,* edited by Hubert Stadler (Hildesheim: Olms, 1989); *Valerius Flaccus Argonautica Book II. A Commentary,* edited by H. M. Poortvliet (Amsterdam: Free University Press, 1991); *Argonautiche Libro VII,* edited by Annamaria Taliercio (Rome: Gruppo Editoriale Internazionale, 1992); *Valerius Flaccus, Argonautica, Book V: A Commentary,* edited by H. J. W. Wijsman (Leiden: Brill, 1996); *Argonauticon, Liber 7,* edited by Alessandro Perutelli (Firenze: Le Monnier, 1997); *Argonautiques, Chants I–IV,* edited by G. Liberman (Paris: Les Belles Lettres, 1997–?); M. *La teichoscopia e l'innamoramento di Medea: Saggio di commento a Valerio Flacco Argonautiche 6, 427–760,* edited by Marco Fucecchi (Pisa: Edizioni ETS, 1997).

The *Argonautica* (The Argonauts, A.D. 92/93), Valerius Flaccus's only known poem, is one of the last important epics of imperial Rome. It is one of three large-scale epics to have survived from the Flavian era (the other two are Statius's *Thebaid* and Silius's *Punica*) and perhaps the one most closely identified with the spirit and ideology of the Flavian dynasty. Valerius turns to myth rather than history for his subject, but a complex system of allusions to Roman history affords the epic a contemporary flavor and relevance. The *Argonautica* is an ambitious poem that reveals a genuine poetic talent, perhaps at a relatively early stage, a talent that was cut off by an untimely death.

Valerius is one of the most elusive literary figures of the imperial Roman period: virtually nothing certain is known about him. Uncertainty extends even to his full name and place of origin. That Gaius Valerius Flaccus was at least the initial part of his name is clear enough. The Vatican manuscript has appended *Setinus Balbus* to this name (and in some places *Babus Sentinus*), though it is not certain that these cognomina really belong to the author. If Sentinus is a cognomen of the author, it might suggest that he was a native of Setia in Campania or, less probably, a native of one of the two Spanish towns of that name. (There is nothing in his writing that would indicate a Spanish origin; if he was indeed a *quindecemvir,* a question addressed below, then he was probably not Spanish.)

For the life and career of Valerius, there is no external evidence beyond a brief obituary notice by the rhetorician Quintilian: "We have a good deal recently in [the death of] Valerius Flaccus" (*Inst. Orat.* 10.1.90). This reference has enabled scholars to fix the death of Valerius at some point before A.D. 96 (the year of Domitian's death and hence the *terminus ante quem* for publication of Quintilian). Because of the extreme paucity of external evidence, scholars have sought autobiographical clues from the *Argonautica* itself. Of such internal clues, the most compelling is a reference in the proem to the "Cymaean prophetess" and the mention of the Sibyl's tripod residing in the poet's own house (1.5-7). These lines have led to the conjecture that Valerius was one of the priests in charge of the Sibylline

Bust of the emperor Vespasian, to whom Valerius Flaccus dedicated his work Argonautica *(The Argonauts), A.D. 92/93 (from Christine Longford,* Vespasian and Some of His Contemporaries, *1928)*

books, the *quindecemviri sacris faciundis*. This hypothesis gains some marginal support from the allusion to the Bath of Cybele at 8.239–241, a rite that was supervised by the *quindecemviri*. If Valerius was a *quindecemvir*, then he was a Roman citizen of considerable means and social standing, perhaps of the senatorial order. Many scholars, however, have pointed out the danger of taking these lines as autobiographical: Valerius may merely be adopting the persona of a Roman priest for artistic effect (compare the use of the *vates*-figure in Augustan poetry).

Valerius was probably an important member of a flourishing literary community at Rome, a group that included fellow poets Statius, Martial, and Silius Italicus. Although none of these writers mentions Valerius explicitly in their extant work, his influence upon them is clear. It is likely that, rather than waiting for completion of the whole opus, Valerius published some of the early books of the *Argonautica* soon after they were composed; this scenario is the simplest explanation for the verbal reminiscences of the *Argonautica* found in the works of both Statius and Silius. The practice of publishing individual books was common enough: earlier in the century, Lucan had done the same with his epic

De bello civili, and Valerius's (presumably younger) contemporary Silius would do likewise with the *Punica*. It is also probable that individual books of the poem were performed in recitation as they were written. Juvenal (*Satires* 1) mentions the adventures of the Argonauts among the recitations making the rounds in Rome: this mention is thought by some to be a specific allusion to Valerius's poem.

If Valerius was a *quindecemvir,* he was probably not dependent upon a literary patron. Nevertheless, he may have enjoyed the political patronage of the Flavians and perhaps in particular Domitian, whose literary aspirations are mentioned in the proem to the *Argonautica*. There Valerius makes reference to an epic poem by Domitian on the conquest of Jerusalem by his older brother Titus. Whether Valerius is referring to an intended literary project or one already undertaken by Domitian is not clear: no such poem has survived. In his praise of Domitian's literary talents, Valerius is in line with Martial, Statius, Silius Italicus, and Quintilian (though he exercises considerably more restraint).

Valerius's poem has been transmitted to the present day unfinished. It breaks off abruptly in the eighth book, as the Argonauts, after acquiring the Golden Fleece, are fleeing their Colchian pursuers. The broad consensus among modern scholars is that Valerius died before finishing the *Argonautica*. Another possibility (most recently advocated by Widu Wolfgang Ehlers) is that the poem was completed by Valerius but subsequently lost its ending when the manuscript was damaged in transmission. This hypothesis has been consistently rejected by the majority of scholars since it was first proposed in the late nineteenth century. Internal evidence points to an unfinished work. In particular, Valerius's narrative is at times inconsistent or disconnected, and there are many passages that seem lacunose or incomplete. Perhaps most notoriously, in 7.398 Iris is said to disappear, although she was never said to be present. Against this omission it must be remembered, a probable explanation is that Valerius almost certainly wrote his poem over several years and might never have addressed such inconsistencies.

Whether *Argonautica* was never finished or was damaged in transmission, an issue of some importance is the intended length of the poem. On this matter scholarly opinion is divided. It is not impossible that the work would have been continued to ten or twelve books, the latter matching the book total of the *Aeneid*, which exerted a strong influence on Valerius's epic. More likely, however, in the light of recent scholarship by B. E. Lewis is that Valerius intended the poem to comprise eight books. Since book 8 breaks off at line 467, and none of the other books exceeds 850 lines, it follows that fewer than 400 lines of text would have been added by the poet to complete the opus.

The precise dates of composition of the *Argonautica* is yet another unresolved issue. The poem was unquestionably written under the Flavian dynasty (A.D. 69–96) and quite possibly under more than one emperor: arguments for composition under all three emperors have been advanced. The most plausible hypothesis is that Valerius was writing during the reigns of the last two Flavian emperors, Titus and Domitian. A period of composition from A.D. 80 or 81 to A.D. 92, with the poem left unfinished because of an unexpected death, seems to tally best with the evidence. This theory suggests that Valerius was writing his epic at roughly the same time that Statius was writing the *Thebaid,* probably slightly before, in view of Valerius's influence on the latter.

The argument for a starting date of A.D. 80 or 81 is based largely on the evidence of the proem (1.1–21), which for various reasons appears to have been written early in the period of composition. In the proem, Valerius addresses Vespasian and mentions both his sons; the textual proximity and coordinated purposes of the three figures is meant to stress familial solidarity, an important point of Flavian propaganda in the wake of the civil wars of A.D. 68–69. The poet places considerable emphasis on the martial exploits of Titus in the Jewish war (at 1.13–14 Jerusalem is clearly described as fallen, offering a *terminus post quem* of A.D. 70 for the start of composition). Treated with somewhat less prominence is Domitian, whose role is merely to write poetry in celebration of his older brother's exploits.

The address to Vespasian is crucial for pinpointing the time of composition, and dating hinges on whether the address is made to a living or a dead emperor. Some scholars (most recently, P. R. Taylor) have argued that the proem is addressed to a still living Vespasian, but significant objections to this theory persist. The mention of "a shrine in honor of" Vespasian's "gens" (*delubra gentis,* 1.15), suggests that Vespasian is already dead. Ronald Syme, for example, takes the phrase as a reference to the Templum Flaviae Gentis. R. J. Getty and other scholars have suggested that *delubra gentis* refers to the Temple of the Divine Vespasian, the construction of which Titus began in A.D. 80 and which was ultimately dedicated by Domitian as the Templum Vespasiani et Titi. Either interpretation of the phrase *delubra gentis* suggests a recently deceased addressee. Likewise the application to Vespasian of the phrase *cultus deum* (divine rites, 1.15) appears to refer to the rites of the college of *Sodales Flaviales,* a priesthood set up by Titus after the death of Vespasian.

Philological arguments lend further support to the theory of a recently deceased imperial addressee. In particular, the language of the address seems more appropriate to a dead emperor about to undergo deification. The adjective *serenus* is fitting for an addressee whose apotheosis is already under way. Likewise, the poet's plea *eripe me* (snatch me away, 1.10) appears in the context more like an entreaty to a god than to a mortal (compare with Jason's plea to the goddess Minerva at 1.88, a rather pointed repetition). These and other phrases lend credibility to the theory that the proem was composed shortly after Vespasian's death. Since that death occurred in A.D. 79, a start of composition in A.D. 80 or 81 is plausible. This hypothesis is further supported by the mention at 3.208–211 of the eruption of Vesuvius (24 August A.D. 79), a reference that again suggests a good deal, if not all, of the poem was written after A.D. 79.

The concluding year of composition probably coincides with the poet's own death. As mentioned earlier, the poet's death can be fixed by Quintilian's obituary notice as occurring *nuper* (recently) with respect to Quintilian's own date of composition. But since Quintilian also uses "recently" regarding the death of Caesius Bassus in A.D. 79, Valerius's death may have occurred some years before. How much earlier, then, is the poet's death likely to have occurred? Again, scholars have turned to internal evidence. In a complex argument, Syme has suggested that the detailed descriptions of Sarmatian warriors at 6.161–162 and 6.231–238 are likely to have been prompted by Domitian's Danube campaigns, which took place in A.D. 89 and A.D. 92. Assuming the earlier date to be true, Valerius was working on book 6 no earlier than A.D. 89 or A.D. 90 and then proceeding to the final two books of the poem in the next few years–making A.D. 92 a reasonable estimate for his death.

The story of the Argonauts' expedition was one of the best-known myths of antiquity, and Valerius stands late in a long and rich poetic tradition. His reworking of the myth was an ambitious undertaking that involved inscribing himself within a literary heritage that included the Greek writers Euripides, Pindar, and Apollonius Rhodius and the Roman poets Catullus, Ovid, and Seneca. Valerius was not the first Roman poet to attempt this epic project: an adaptation of Apollonius's *Argonautica* had been written in the previous century by the neoteric Varro of Atax, but this work has not survived. While Valerius's primary model is undeniably Apollonius, it is also likely that Valerius was drawing upon Varro's adaptation, which may have diverged significantly from Apollonius's work at various points. Other intriguing lost works that may have influenced Valerius are tragedies by Ennius, Accius, Ovid, and Lucan.

.C.VALERII FLACCI SETINI
BALBI ARGONAVTI
CON.

LIBER PRIMVS

RIMA DEVM MAGNIS
canimus freta peruia nautis,
Fatidicamᖢ ratem, scythici quæ phasi
dis oras
Ausa sequi, mediosᖢ interiuga concí
ta cursus

p

Rumpere, flammifero tandem consedit olympo.
Phœbe mone, si cumeæ mihi conscia uatis
Stat casta cortina domo, si laurea digna
Fronte uiret. Tuᖢ ò pelage cui maior aperti
Fama, caledonius postquam tua carbasa uexit
Oceanus, phrygios prius indignatus Iulos.
Eripe me populis, ᖢ habenti nubila terræ
Sancte pater, ueterumᖢ faue ueneranda canenti
Facta uirum. uersam proles tua pandit Idumen,
(Namᖢ potes) solymo nigrantem puluere fratrem
Spargentemᖢ faces, ᖢ in omni turre furentem.
Ille tibi cultusᖢ deum, delubraᖢ genti
Instituet, cum iam genitor lucebis ab omni
Parte poli, neqᖢ in tyrias cynosura carinas
Certior, aut graiis Elice seruanda magistris.
Seu tu signa dabis, seu te duce græcia mittet
Et Sidon, Nilusᖢ rates. Nunc nostra serenus
Orsa iuues, hæc ut latias uox impleat urbes.

b

Page from a 1503 Florence edition of Valerius Flaccus's Argonautica *(courtesy of the Lilly Library, Indiana University)*

Valerius's poem is distinguished by its strikingly innovative treatment of such a well-known myth. Although most of the major episodes are taken from Apollonius's epic, a fresh approach to the material is found throughout. The political suicide of Jason's parents at the end of book 1 (which evokes the suicides of the senatorial opposition under the early principate), the novel handling of the Lemnian women in book 2, the rescue of Hesione in the same book, the deliverance of Prometheus in book 5, and above all the Colchian civil war in book 6 all attest to an innovative poetic articulation of an extremely familiar story.

Valerius owes a considerable debt to Virgil. Just as the *Aeneid* was a mythological narrative written in support of Augustus and his family, so the *Argonautica* creates an explicit analogy to the Flavian dynasty: like the Argonauts, Vespasian expanded geographical knowledge and opened up sea routes for *commercia*. The link between Jason and Vespasian, though, appears not to be sustained consistently during the course of the poem. Valerius "Romanizes" his subject matter throughout: Jupiter predicts a succession of great world empires that will culminate with Rome, and the mention of Troy strongly foreshadows the rise of Rome. Similes invoking the eruption of Vesuvius, Roman civil war, and other events contribute to an overall "Romanization" of the Greek myth. All of these touches suggest a poem that is at once more Roman and more Virgilian. Significant is Valerius's presentation of a cosmos that is overseen by a rational and providential Jupiter who has carefully laid-out plans for the human race. This treatment of the divine machinery represents a reinstatement of the Virgilian worldview in Roman epic in the wake of Lucan's subversive treatment of the gods in the *Bellum Civile*.

In thematic terms, Valerius emphasizes the sailing of the *Argo* as a foundational act, an epochal event in human history. In Roman poetry, the *Argo* was generally presented as the first ship and thus a potent symbol of the birth of technology and man's conquest of nature. Apollonius had forsaken this aspect of the myth: for him the voyage of the Argonauts represented merely an extraordinary application of existing technology rather than an essential innovation. Valerius thus deviates sharply from his Hellenistic model in making the *Argo* the first ship. In the Flavian epic, the Argonauts must open up the seas to navigation so that the various parts of the world can be in contact, an act resulting in the advancement of human civilization and the development of great empires.

Little of the literary reception of Valerius Flaccus is known today. Aside from the obituary of Quintilian, which suggests genuine regret at a lost poetic talent, no certain references have survived. It is striking that neither Martial nor Statius nor Silius ever makes an explicit reference to Valerius. The scant mention suggests that Valerius

had not yet attained widespread renown; the poet himself seems subtly to condemn the indifference of the contemporary Roman public to epic poetry at the close of book 1 (1.841–845). Many scholars have suggested that Juvenal's *Satire* 1 includes a veiled allusion to Valerius's epic. There may also be an indirect engagement of the Flavian *Argonautica* in Martial, *Epigram* 7.19. It is certainly the case that Valerius supplied Statius with much linguistic inspiration. Indeed, Statius must have been deeply impressed with the *Argonautica,* given his extended imitation of Valerius's Lemnian episode in *Thebaid* 5. Walter C. Summers has noted a more muted but still traceable influence of Valerius on the poetry of Silius Italicus.

In general, the influence of Valerius on later Roman poets is not substantial, perhaps because Latin epic declines after the Flavian period. There are, however, many parallels in language and theme in the so-called Orphic *Argonautica,* a Greek poem of the fifth century A.D. Valerius's postclassical reception is likewise limited: he is not mentioned by subsequent writers until Geoffrey Chaucer cites his list of crew members in the *Legend of Good Women*–probably through an intermediary, since it is unlikely that Chaucer had direct access to a text of the *Argonautica.* After a lengthy period of obscurity, Valerius's poem resurfaced in 1417, when Poggio Braeciolini discovered at St. Gaul a manuscript including *Argonautica* 1.1–4.317. By 1429 a manuscript of the entire extant poem (that is, 1.1–8.467) had been recovered. The editio princeps appeared in Bologna in 1474.

References:

D. C. Feeney, *The Gods in Epic* (Oxford: Oxford University Press, 1991);

R. J. Getty, "The Date of Composition of the *Argonautica* of Valerius Flaccus," *Classical Philology,* 31 (1936): 53–61;

Philip Hardie, *The Epic Successors of Virgil* (Cambridge: Cambridge University Press, 1993);

Debra Hershkowitz, *Valerius Flaccus' Argonautica: Abbreviated Voyages in Silver Latin Epic* (Oxford: Oxford University Press, 1998);

Matthias Korn and Hans J. Tschiedel, eds., *Ratis omnia vincet. Untersuchungen zu den Argonautica des Valerius Flaccus* (Hildesheim: Olms, 1991);

B. E. Lewis, "The Significance of the Location of Valerius Flaccus' Second Proem," *Mnemosyne,* 40 (1987): 420–421;

Walter C. Summers, *A Study of the Argonautica of Valerius Flaccus* (London: Deighton, Bell, 1894);

Ronald Syme, "The *Argonautica* of Valerius Flaccus," *Classical Quarterly,* 23 (1929): 129–137;

P. R. Taylor, "Valerius' *Flavian Argonautica,*" *Classical Quarterly,* 44 (1994): 212–235.

Valerius Maximus

(fl. ca. A.D. 31)

Hans-Friedrich Mueller
Florida State University

WORK: *Dicta et facta memorabilia,* 9 books (Memorable Deeds and Sayings, A.D. 31–32).

Editio princeps: *Facta et dicta memorabilia* (Strasbourg: Johann Mentelin, ca. 1470).

Standard editions: *Valerii Maximi Factorum et dictorum memorabilium libri novem,* second edition, edited by Karl Kempf (Leipzig: Teubner, 1888; reprinted, Stuttgart: Teubner, 1982); *Actions et paroles mémorables,* 2 volumes, edited and translated by Pierre Constant (Paris: Garnier, 1935); *Valerius Maximus,* 5 volumes (Pisa: Giardini, 1986–1987); *Detti e fatti memorabili Valerio Massimo* (Turin: Tascabili degli Editori Associati, 1988); *Faits et dits mémorables,* volumes 1 and 2 of 3, edited and translated by R. Combès (Paris: Les Belles Lettres, 1995–); *Facta et Dicta memorabilia,* edited by John Briscoe (Stuttgart & Leipzig: Teubner, 1998).

Translation in English: *Romae antiquae descriptio,* translated by Samuel Speed (London: J. C. for Samuel Speed, 1678; microfilm, Ann Arbor, Mich.: University Microfilms, 1976).

Commentaries: *Valerii Maximi novem libri factorum dictorumque memorabilium,* edited by Abraham Torrenius (Leiden: Samuel Luchtmans, 1726); *De dictis factisque memorabilibus,* 3 volumes, edited by C. B. Hase (Paris: Lemaire, 1822–1823); *Valerii Maximi Factorum et Dictorum Memorabilium libri novem,* edited by Karl Kempf (Berlin: Reimer, 1854; reprinted, Hildesheim: Olms, 1976); *Memorable Deeds and Sayings, Book I,* edited by D. Wardle (Oxford: Clarendon Press, 1998).

What is in a name? Valerius Maximus, author of the *Factorum et dictorum memorabilium libri novem* (Memorable Deeds and Sayings, A.D. 31–32), possesses a name that provides no small proportion of what little is known about him. Although the *praenomina* (first names) Marcus and Publius found attached to various inferior manuscripts are discounted as later inventions, what remains of his name sounds the tones of an illustrious patrician ancestry stretching back to the beginnings of the Roman Republic. Whether or not, however, these echoes of the great, aristocratic *gens Valeriana* (related families of Valerii) record a legitimate son or an upstart shadow and fraud remains in dispute. During the early imperial period, it was after all in fashion to revive ancient and glorious names without necessarily having legitimate claim to them. Moreover, although the *nomen* (family name) Valerius was conspicuously borne by legitimately aristocratic exemplars in the day of the author Valerius, the optional cognomen (additional surname) Maximus had not been used for centuries. An anonymous life prefixed to the 1494 Venice edition of Valerius's work adds that Maximus was a name Valerius inherited from his mother's side—specifically the *gens Fabia*—as well as from his father's side. The source, however, is suspect, and there is no corroborating evidence. On the other hand, although the context leads to the conclusion that he likely is speaking only metaphorically, Valerius in 5.5.*init.* seems to identify with those of the name who claim aristocratic descent: *ex maiorum imaginibus gloriam traxi* (I derived glory from the busts of my ancestors; only those people whose ancestors had held higher political office were allowed to display such busts). Arguing against patrician descent is Valerius's self-confessed poverty (although here again, whether 4.4.11 is truly autobiographical is open to question).

Genuinely autobiographical is the gratitude Valerius expresses toward his benefactor Sextus Pompeius, whom Valerius compares to Alexander the Great in 4.7.*ext.*2 and credits with an active interest in his literary work: *studia nostra ductu et auspiciis suis lucidiora et alacriora reddidit* (his authority and guidance illuminated and inspired my studies). This Sextus Pompeius (who was likewise a friend of the poet Ovid) is identified with the consul of A.D. 14 and the later proconsular governor of Asia ca. A.D. 27. Valerius in 2.6.8 also says that he accompanied Sextus Pompeius to Asia. While en route Sextus, Valerius, and Sextus's entourage formally witnessed a woman who was more than ninety years old commit suicide in accordance with the ancient laws of the island of Ceos. The entire entourage was deeply touched and reduced to tears. Because it is autobiographical, this anecdote is especially noteworthy as a sincere example of the emotional effects (some might call it sentimentality) for which Valerius's rhetoric in general strives.

Some scholars also argue, however, that Valerius could not be an aristocrat because he employs the language of the client. He is obsequious toward those in authority, particularly the emperor Tiberius. Valerius's preface, for example, contrasts his own *parvitas* (insignificance) with the emperor Tiberius's *divinitas* (divinity). Was it likely that an aristocrat of a proud and ancient line would abase himself in this manner before the emperor Tiberius? Answers have varied. Throughout the work, however, Tiberius, Augustus, and Caesar are in fact treated as gods. Although usually dismissed as insincere, this alien religion has helped provide justification for many to deprive Valerius of patrician status and to ignore him as an author. It may be stated safely, however, that although little definite is known about him, Valerius had friends among the powerful and accepted the ruling order enthusiastically. (Further details regarding Valerius's nomenclature and identity with references to other arguments may be found in Clive Skidmore's 1996 study.) Valerius's denunciation of Sejanus in 9.11.*ext*.4 suggests that Valerius's work belongs to the latter half of Tiberius's reign and that it was likely published sometime after A.D. 31.

From the language of his work one may also safely infer that Valerius was the beneficiary of a standard Roman, rhetorical education. In fact, Valerius's Silver Age rhetoric has in the last century been dismissed with contempt by critics as "sententious," "bombastic," "unendurably tasteless," and even "disgusting." Valerius's rhetoric is evidently still capable of arousing emotions. Before, however, inquiring too closely into these charges, one might ask more generally of what the work consists, how it is arranged, and to what ends it was composed. There are also disputes over interpretations in these areas. Valerius compiles more than one thousand anecdotes taken from Greek and Roman history (systems of numbering Valerius's text vary, and thus exact counts vary). They are arranged in nine books, not chronologically but rather according to eighty-five categories of virtue and vice, such as *fortitudo* (bravery) and *libido* (lust). Anecdotes are further subdivided within chapters according to whether they serve as domestic, that is to say, Roman, examples, or foreign, usually Greek, examples. One finds approximately eight Roman and five foreign examples per category, though numbers vary considerably from chapter to chapter. A treatise on names, *De praenomini-*

Valerius Maximus at work on his Dicta et facta memorabilia (Memorable Deeds and Sayings), *illumination from a fifteenth-century Italian manuscript (Rome, Bibl. Vaticana, Reg. Lat. 939, fol. 1)*

bus, was attached to many manuscripts as a "tenth" book, and it is reprinted as a separate treatise in both of Karl Kempf's editions. The tenth book is generally considered the unrelated work of an unknown author, though some have argued that it represents part of, or at least part of a substitute for, a lost tenth book. Valerius's extant work lacks a formal conclusion. Two epitomes of his *Memorable Deeds and Sayings* also survive and, besides attesting to the popularity of the original, are usually employed to fill a gap in the manuscripts that occurs in the first book (1.1.5–1.4.*ext*.1).

A brief conspectus of the work gives a clearer picture of its contents, illustrates its structure, and provides a context for the current debate regarding the intended audience and purpose of the work. The subject matter of book 1 is unified through the relation of the individual and the state to religious matters. In book 1 there are chapters on the scrupulous observance of religion, the neglect of religion, religious observations that were feigned or imitated, superstitions, auspices, omens, prodigies, dreams, and miracles. Book 2 expands the view to other institutions of public life with depictions of ancient customs, military discipline, issues regarding the right to celebrate a triumph, and political prestige. Book 3 narrows the focus to the individual. Chapter topics include character, bravery, endurance, self-confidence, steadfastness, those men of humble birth who achieved great things, those of high birth who did not, and those whose personal grooming and attire was inappropriate. Book 4 focuses even more narrowly on personal virtues, with chapters on moderation, overcoming differences with one's opponents, self-denial and self-control, poverty, modesty, conjugal love, friendship, and generosity. Book 5 begins to expand the focus once again by moving from personal virtues to personal relations. The shift, however, is from the individual to the family, and thus generally the subject matter remains in the realm of private relations. There are examples of kindness and mercy; gratitude and ingratitude; loyalty to parents, brothers, and country; parents' love and indulgence toward their children; fathers' strictness with their children; fathers' moderation toward children who have given grounds for suspicion; and parents' brave acceptance of the deaths of their children. Book 6 continues to expand the social context in which virtue operates, treating the topics of chastity; free speech and freedom of action; severity; harsh words or actions; justice; the good faith of the state; the faithfulness of wives to their husbands; the faithfulness of slaves; and, finally, changes in character, habit, or fortune. As the work progresses, topics become less unified. Book 7 expands the realm of action once more. There are examples of luck, wise words or actions, clever words or actions, stratagems, electoral defeats, hardship, wills that were abrogated, wills that were upheld when there were grounds for their abrogation, and wills that named unexpected heirs. Book 8 begins with a continuation of legal themes. Valerius provides examples of dishonorable defendants who were either acquitted or condemned, noteworthy civil cases, women who pleaded cases either on their own behalf or on behalf of others, judicial inquiries by torture, the testimony of witnesses, and those who themselves committed what they had condemned in others. Book 8 concludes, however, with the more general themes of enthusiasm and hard work, leisure, the power of eloquence, the power of timing in speaking and movements of the body, the power of artifice as well as what skill cannot accomplish, how the most skillful are their own best critics, old age, the desire for glory, and what great things happened to individuals according to their merits. And finally, after so much virtue (although there are some negative examples), book 9 collects examples specifically devoted to vice—such as luxury and lust, cruelty, anger and hatred, greed, arrogance and violence, treachery, sedition and armed rebellion,

mistakes, vengeance, wicked words and criminal behavior, uncommon deaths, the desire to live at any cost, and base-born people who attempted to claim places in noble households through fraud.

Although the earlier books show more unity than later books, one is immediately struck by the great variety of material. Because of the convenient organizational principles of the work, one quickly understands why the work became a ready reference. Indeed, scholars have labeled the work a "mere" compendium for rhetoricians and schoolboys. Valerius's preface can be employed to support this assertion as well:

> Urbis Romae exterarumque gentium facta simul ac dicta memoratu digna apud alios latius diffusa sunt quam ut breuiter cognosci possint, ab inlustribus electa auctoribus digerere constitui, ut documenta sumere uolentibus longae inquisitionis labor absit.

> (Deeds and sayings belonging to the history of the city of Rome as well as to the histories of foreign nations, and worthy of remembrance, were far too dispersed among various authors for anyone to become quickly and efficiently well-versed. I therefore resolved to assemble from the best authorities the choicest part so that those who were interested in obtaining instructive precedents would be spared the effort of long research.)

Whether or not Valerius intended his work simply as a reference tool, it certainly proved convenient to later authors as evidence that is readily demonstrated by the works of Pliny the Elder, Pseudo-Frontinus, Aulus Gellius, Lactantius, Augustine, Priscian, and even the Greek author Plutarch. Nevertheless, even if greater lights make use of it, a compendium "designed" to make the lives of "rhetoricians and schoolboys" easier is hardly likely to gather high praise from scholars. Moreover, Valerius is a master of Silver Age Latin figures and conceits. (The evenhanded 1980 study of Brent W. Sinclair provides a judicious view of Valerius's rhetorical techniques.) One should thus not be amazed that the author of a "sententious," "bombastic," "unendurably tasteless," and "disgusting" "handbook" (to conflate the charges of many) long failed to arouse the attention of literary critics.

Martin W. Bloomer in his 1992 study shows that Valerius's work is more than merely a handy compendium. Bloomer convincingly argues that the work was in its own day certainly intended for performance. Dramatic readings were popular entertainment among the literate elite in both formal and informal settings, and, no matter what Valerius's actual personal status, given his demonstrable social circle, this culture was the one to which Valerius belonged. Closer attention to Valerius's text also reveals that his highly dramatic anecdotes do not just follow one another as self-contained and completely independent excerpts. He reworked the anecdotes he collected. Within chapters, Valerius employs a variety of organizational principles, arranging material, for example, sometimes in chronological order, sometimes in reverse order, and sometimes on the basis of the social status of those people he describes. Valerius also writes introductions to the individual books as well as to many of the individual chapters. He employs transitional devices between anecdotes as well as between chapters. These transitional devices are admittedly often tenuous. For example, in the anecdote concerning the suicide that Valerius and Sextus Pompeius together witnessed, Valerius introduces the anecdote by remarking that there is a similarity between customs in the city of Massilia in Gaul and those in the city of Iulis on Ceos. This connection is indeed tenuous (though actually stronger in this case than in many other cases), but an organic connection is present. Valerius invites his readers to pass from one anecdote to the next and to read his text as a continuous narrative. There is great variety. On a purely formal level, Valerius's methods invite comparison with Ovid's *Metamorphoses*. Both works combine disparate material; neither could be read comfortably in one sitting; and both employ transitional devices that have not always won universal approval. Nevertheless, both remain unified literary creations. (Bloomer provides a closer analysis of such formal elements of arrangement.) In short, Valerius was not an excerptor. He was an author.

Others, however, seeing that Valerius took his material from history, have, despite there being little chronological arrangement, classified him as an historian. In fact, much of the scholarly work during the nineteenth century focused on determining what sources Valerius used and how accurately he reproduced them. The results have shown that Valerius's sources were among the best—especially Livy, Cicero, and Varro. Because much of this source material is lost, Valerius's work constitutes an important source for the history of Republican Rome. Valerius the "historian" is thus often cited when other ancient authorities fail. Where, however, Valerius's versions can be checked against his sources, he may sometimes be justly charged with oversimplification and careless inaccuracies. Valerius thus falls short as an historian and in this area, too, has been roundly and routinely condemned.

The present age disdains verbal artifice and prizes logic, consistency, and accuracy. One does not turn to Valerius for these things. In spite of his current obscurity, however, Valerius has in the past experienced great popularity. More than 350 complete manuscripts survive, testifying to his popularity throughout the Middle Ages. Many editions and commentaries demon-

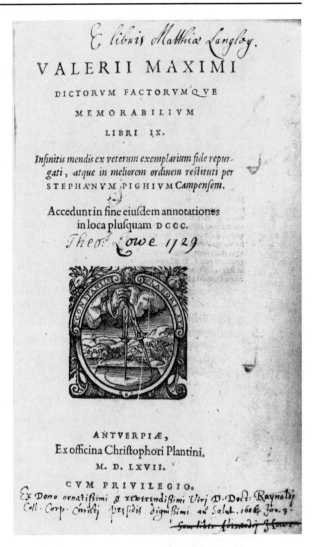

Title page for an eighteenth-century edition of Valerius Maximus's Dicta et facta memorabilia *(courtesy of the Lilly Library, Indiana University)*

strate his popularity during the Renaissance. (D. M. Schullian mentions particulars.) Part of Valerius's popularity lay with the convenience provided by the arrangement of his material, but a more significant reason for it is to be found in his genre. Valerius, although frequently mined for historical data, does not write history. Although his work proved convenient as a reference, Valerius does not paste together an anthology of quotations. He writes exempla.

Examples, according to Aristotle in the *Rhetoric*, are the second of two types of rhetorical proof: the first type, the enthymeme, or rhetorical syllogism, appeals to reason and was thus preferred by Aristotle, but examples appeal to the emotions and are thus preferred by those who want to convince an audience. Exempla are

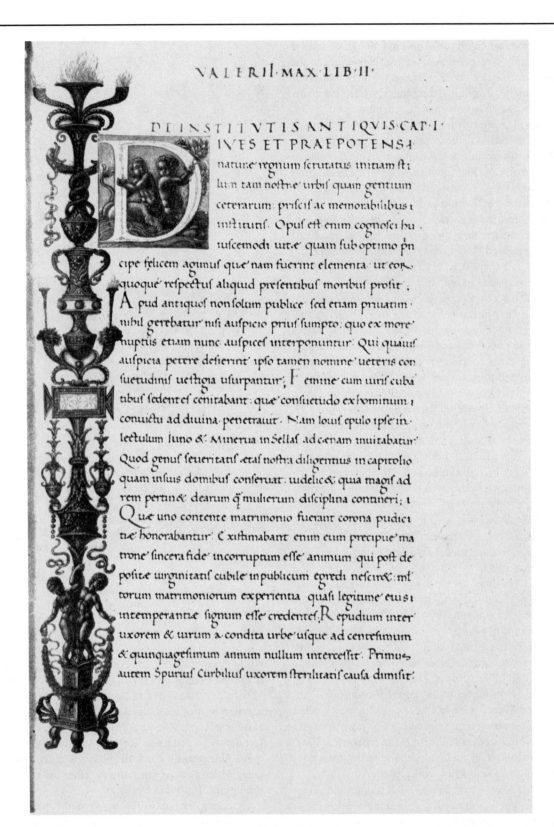

Illuminated page from a fifteenth-century manuscript of Valerius Maximus's Facta et dicta memorabilia *(The Walters Art Gallery, Baltimore, Maryland)*

also especially useful in political discourse, because anecdotes can portray a whole political and moral concept with an immediacy impossible in a discourse of rational analysis. Rational discourse can discuss only one item at a time in linear fashion. Anecdotes overcome this limitation of language both by conveying deeply held convictions in a way that others can intuitively grasp and by presenting material the way people tend to think—that is, not in terms of formal logic but in terms of actual situations and concrete events. As Valerius's contemporary in Roman Palestine also understood, examples are more than merely a powerful means of persuasion. They can illustrate patterns of behavior, patterns to imitate. Romans looked to the authority of ancestral usage, the *mos maiorum*, not only when judging whether or not an action was done rightly or wrongly but also when learning how to conduct themselves. A short survey from Livy's preface to Augustus's *Res gestae* (2.12–14)—as well as Augustus's monumental architecture (especially the Forum of Augustus with its *eulogia*, or praises of famous men), his efforts at religious renewal, his moral legislation, and the punctilious Tiberius's carrying on of Augustus's policies with scrupulous care—is enough to demonstrate that the age was determined to set examples aimed at improving the conduct (or moral behavior) of its citizens. Valerius's *exempla* likewise aimed at moral instruction, and moral improvement was once quite popular.

Valerius's genre is thus fundamental to understanding his work on its own terms—that is, not as a "mere" handbook or reference work and not as a history but as a unified literary creation with a moral agenda in the political context of Tiberian Rome. With this proviso, one may understand why Valerius employs every possible rhetorical device. Not only is he using the literary language of the times, but he is also striving to appeal to the emotions of his audience in order to convince, perhaps even to convert, them to the moral (or, more objectively stated, ideological) values of Augustan and Tiberian Rome. (Skidmore provides an illumination of Valerius's general moral purposes.) Whether or not one shares the values extolled and exalted, Valerius's work provides a rare literary voice from the age of Tiberius. In it the curious can find much of interest.

References:

Francis Royster Bliss, "Valerius Maximus and His Sources: A Stylistic Approach to the Problem," dissertation, University of North Carolina at Chapel Hill, 1951;

W. Martin Bloomer, *Valerius Maximus and the Rhetoric of the New Nobility* (Chapel Hill: University of North Carolina Press, 1992);

Clemens Bosch, *Die Quellen des Valerius Maximus. Ein Beitrag zur Erforschung der Literatur der historischen Exempla* (Stuttgart: Kohlhammer, 1929);

C. J. Carter, "Valerius Maximus," in *Empire and Aftermath: Silver Latin II,* edited by T. A. Dorey (London & Boston: Routledge & Kegan Paul, 1975), pp. 26–56;

Giovanni Comes, *Valerio Massimo* (Rome: A. Signorelli, 1950);

Robert Guerrini, *Studi su Valerio Massimo (con un capitolo sulla fortuna nell'iconografia umanistica: Perugino, Beccafumi, Pordenone),* Biblioteca di Studi Antichi, 28 (Pisa: Giardini, 1981);

R. Helm, "Valerius Maximus (239)," in *RE,* 8 A.1 (1955): columns 90–116;

Alfred Klotz, *Studien zu Valerius Maximus und den* Exempla (Munich: C. H. Beck, 1942);

G. Maslakov, "Valerius Maximus and Roman Historiography: A Study of the *Exempla* Tradition," in *ANRW* II, 32, no.1 (1984): 437–496;

Hans-Friedrich Mueller, "Exempla tuenda: Religion, Virtue, and Politics in Valerius Maximus," dissertation, University of North Carolina at Chapel Hill, 1994;

D. M. Schullian, "Valerius Maximus," in *Catalogus translationum et commentariorum,* volume 5, edited by Paul Oskar Kristeller and F. Edward Cranz (Washington: Catholic University of America Press, 1984), pp. 287–403;

Brent W. Sinclair, "Valerius Maximus and the Evolution of Silver Latin," dissertation, University of Cincinnati, 1980;

Clive Skidmore, *Practical Ethics for Roman Gentlemen: The Work of Valerius Maximus* (Exeter, U.K.: University of Exeter Press, 1996).

Varro

(116 B.C. – 27 B.C.)

Daniel J. Taylor
Lawrence University

MAJOR WORKS–EXTANT: *Saturae Menippeae,* 150 books, of which 90 titles and 600 fragments survive (Menippean Satires, 80–67 B.C.);

De lingua Latina, 25 books, of which 5–10 survive (On the Latin Language, ca. 43 B.C.);

De re rustica, 3 books (On Farming, 37 B.C.).

SELECTED WORKS–LOST (DATED): *De antiquitate litterarum,* at least 2 books (On the Antiquity of Letters, before 86–84 B.C.);

Ephemeris navalis (A Naval Almanac, 77 B.C.);

Eisagogikos ad Pompeium (Advice to Pompey, 70 B.C.);

De utilitate sermonis (On Linguistic Usage, 56–47 B.C.);

Peri kharakteron, at least 3 books (On Distinctions, 56–47 B.C.);

De origine linguae Latinae (On the Origin of the Latin Language, 56–47 B.C.);

De similitudine verborum (On the Similarity of Words, 56–47 B.C.);

De sermone Latino, 5 books (On Latin Speech, ca. 46 B.C.);

Antiquitates rerum humanarum et divinarum, 41 books (Antiquities, 46 B.C.);

Epitome antiquitatum, 9 books (Antiquities: Abridged Version, after 46 B.C.);

Quaestiones Plautinae, 5 books (Plautine Questions, after 45 B.C.);

De lingua Latina, 9 books (On the Latin Language, abridged version, after 43 B.C.);

De gente populi Romani (On the Roman People, 43–42 B.C.);

Imagines vel Hebdomades, 15 books (Illustrated Biographical Dictionary or The Sevens, 39 B.C.);

Imagines vel Hebdomades, 4 books (Illustrated Biographical Dictionary, abridged version, after 39 B.C.);

Disciplinae, 9 books (The Liberal Arts, 35–32 B.C.).

SELECTED WORKS–LOST (UNDATED): *De vita sua,* 3 books (An Autobiography);

Annales, 3 books (Annals);

De iure civile, 15 books (Civil Law);

De ora maritima (Coastal Geography);

De descriptionibus, 3 books (Descriptions);

Logistorici, 76 books (Dialogues);

Legationes, 3 books (Embassies);

Epistolicae quaestiones (Epistolary Questions);

Suasiones, 3 books (Exhortations);

De principiis numerorum, 9 books (Foundations of Numbers);

De bibliothecis, 3 books (Libraries);

De vita populi Romani, 4 books (Life of the Roman People);

Poemata, 10 books (Poems);

Pseudotragoediae, 6 books (Pseudotragedies);

Saturae, 4 books (Satires);

Orationes, 22 books (Speeches);

De proprietate scriptorum, 3 books (On Distinctive Features of Writers);

De scaenicis actionibus, 3 books (On Dramatic Productions);

De originibus scaenicis, 3 books (On the History of Drama);

De poematis, 3 books (On Poetry);

De lectionibus, 3 books (On Recitations);

De actis scaenicis, 3 books (On Theatrical Performances);

De forma philosophiae, 3 books (Outline of Philosophy);

De Pompeio, 3 books (Pompey: A Biography);

De personis, 3 books (Stage Masks);

De aestuariis (Tidal Inlets);

De familiis Troianis, at least 2 books (Trojan Families);

Res urbanae, at least 3 books (Urban Affairs).

Editiones principes: *M. Terenti Varronis De Lingua Latina,* edited by Pomponio Leto (Rome: Georgius Lauer, ca. 1471); *M. Terenti Varronis Rerum Rusticarum Libri III,* edited by Georgius Merula, in *Scriptores Rei Rusticae* (Venice: Nicolaus Jenson, 1472).

Standard editions: *M. Terenti Varronis De Lingua Latina Quae Supersunt,* edited by Georg Goetz and Fritz Schoell (Leipzig: Teubner, 1910); *M. Terenti Varronis Rerum Rusticarum Libri Tres,* edited by Goetz (Leipzig: Teubner, 1912; second edition, 1929); *M. Terenti Varronis Saturarum Menippearum Fragmenta,* edited by Raymond Astbury (Leipzig: Teubner, 1985).

Translations in English: *Varro on Farming,* translated by Lloyd Storr-Best, Bohn Classical Library (London: G. Bell, 1912); *Marcus Porcius Cato: On Agriculture; M. Terentius Varro: On Agriculture,* edited and translated by William Davis Hooper, revised by Harrison Boyd Ash, Loeb Classical Library (Cambridge, Mass.: Harvard University Press, 1934); *Varro: On the Latin Language,* 2 volumes, edited and translated by Ronald G. Kent, Loeb Classical Library (Cambridge, Mass.: Harvard University Press, 1938; revised edition, 1951).

Commentaries: *Scriptorum rei rusticae veterae Latinorum tomus primus,* edited, with commentary, by J. G. Schneider (Leipzig: C. Fritsch, 1794)—only full agricultural commentary; *Varro De Lingua Latina Buch VIII,* edited, with commentary, by Hellfried Dahlmann (Berlin: Weidmann, 1940); *De Lingua Latina Livre V,* edited and translated into French, with commentary, by Jean Collart (Paris: Les Belles Lettres, 1954); *Varron, Satires Ménippées: Edition, traduction, et commentaire,* 11 volumes, edited and translated into French, with commentary, by Jean-Pierre Cèbe (Rome: École Française, 1972–); *Varro the Farmer: A Selection from the Res Rusticae,* edited, with commentary, by Bertha Tilly (London: University Tutorial Press, 1973); *Opere di Marco Terenzio Varrone,* edited and translated into Italian by Antonio Traglia (Turin: Unione Tipografico-Editrice Torinese, 1974); *La Langue Latine Livre VI,* edited and translated into French, with commentary, by Pierre Flobert (Paris: Les Belles Lettres, 1985); *De Lingua Latina,* edited and translated into Spanish by Manuel-Antonio Marcos Casquero (Barcelona: Editorial Anthropos / Madrid: Ministerio de Educación y Ciencia, 1990); *De Lingua Latina X: A New Critical Text and English Translation with Prolegomena and Commentary,* edited and translated, with commentary, by Daniel J. Taylor (Amsterdam: Benjamins, 1996).

Early in his literary career Marcus Terentius Varro urged his readers to forge out their lives by reading and writing, and for the next half century he followed his own advice so successfully that he became a prolific polymath and the most highly acclaimed intellectual figure of ancient Rome. It was Varro who established 753 B.C., by present-day calculations, as the conventional date for the founding of Rome. Varro also determined the canonical list of twenty-one comedies indubitably authored by Plautus, and he contributed long-lasting, influential accounts of the nine liberal arts (the usual seven—grammar, dialectic, rhetoric, arithmetic, geometry, astronomy, and music—plus medicine and architecture). The loss of his *Antiquitates rerum humanarum et divinarum* (Antiquities, 46 B.C.) is one of the most lamented losses in all of Latin literature, for it was a de facto encyclopedia of Roman religious and cultural institutions and customs. Varro's *Imagines vel Hebdomades* (Illustrated Biographical Dictionary or The Sevens, after 39 B.C.), about seven hundred illustrious Greeks and Romans, published by Atticus, was the first illustrated book and circulated throughout the entire Roman world, and *De lingua Latina* (On the Latin Language, ca. 43 B.C.) became an immediate scholarly classic. His corpus included at least 74 works consisting of 620 books (modern chapters). The sheer quantity of Varro's published works has amazed even productive ancient scholars: Cicero terms Varro "the most polyprolific" author; Jerome transmits with awe a lengthy but incomplete catalogue of Varro's works; and Augustine remarks, "Varro read so much that we are amazed he had any time for writing, and yet he wrote so many things that we can hardly believe anyone could read them all." Varro's productivity is best explained by envisioning him dictating or writing one book after another as rapidly as possible without revising or maybe even rereading: by his own admission he worked hastily. Not surprisingly, Varro's style has been severely criticized by ancients and moderns alike. The quality of Varro's scholarship, however, has received nothing but praise throughout the centuries. Cicero, Vitruvius, Quintilian (his phrase "the most learned of the Romans" has become formulaic), Augustine, and assorted late- antique and medieval Christian authors are uniformly effusive in lauding Varro as a scholar. Varro is Petrarch's "third great light of Rome" (after Virgil and Cicero); to Montaigne he is "the most subtle and most learned Latin author"; and today he enjoys a virtually unparalleled scholarly reputation.

Varro did not live in an ivory tower: his lengthy lifetime spanned one of the most violent periods in Roman history, and he was not immune to the vicissitudes of the times. Born in Reate in the Sabine country northeast of Rome in 116 B.C., he maintained a lifelong fondness and respect for the traditional morals and conservative customs of rural Italy. As a young man Varro studied under Lucius Aelius Stilo Praeconinus, Rome's first scholar of note, and the Greek philosopher Antiochus of Ascalon before embarking on a military and political career, which he pursued with considerable distinction for more than half his life. He rose to the ranks of general and admiral, earning a coveted naval crown as an award for his conduct in a major war against pirates (67 B.C.), and he served the Republic in a series of offices: superintendent of public prisons and police (ca. 90 B.C.), quaestor (ca. 85 B.C.), proquaestor (76–71 B.C.), tribune of the plebs, praetor, land commissioner (59 B.C.), and probably others. In the course of his lengthy career Varro traveled widely, amassed great wealth, and acquired vast knowledge; he finally retired to what he surely thought would be a life

I

NONII MARCELLI PERIPATETICI TI-
BVRTICENSIS COMPENDIOSA DOC-
TRINA AD FILIVM DE PROPRIETATE
SERMONVM.

ENIVM Est tædiũ & odiũ
dictũ a senectute cp senes oĩ
bus odio sint & tædio. Ce
cilius in Epheftiõe: Tum i
senectute hoc deputo mi-
serrimũ:sentire ea ætate eũ
ipsum esse odiosũ alteri.Nã
ætatẽ malam senectutẽ ue-
teres dixerũt Plautus i Me
næchmis:Consitus sũ sene
ctute:onustũ gero corpus:uires reliquere ut ætas
mala é ergo Actius i Amphitryone
An mala ætate maius male mulctari exẽplis oĩ
bus?Turpilius in Philopatro:Miser puto:si eti
am istuc ad malã ætate accessit mali.Pacuuius in
Peribœa:par é cp te ætas male habet:ni et hic ad
malã ætatẽ adiungas cruciatũ reticẽti. Affranius
in uopisco:Si possent hoies delinimẽtis capi:oẽs
haberent nunc amatores anus.Aetas etiam corpus teneg & morigeratio:hæc sunt uenena for-
mosæ muliep:Mala ætas nulla delinimenta in
uẽit.Bonã ætatẽ quog dicimus adolescentiã uel
iuuentutẽ.M.Tullius de senectute:Quod si ipis
uoluptatibus bona ætas fruitur libentius primũ
paruulis fruitur rebus.Nã prudentissime noster
Maro diem parties:primas partes quasi eius æta
tem pubere dixit nono libr.Nunc adeo
melior:qñ pars acta diei est. Seniũ ipsum positũ.
Sic Titinnius i Veliterna:Quod petissẽ ia & iur
gia sesemet diebus emigrarũt.Neuius i Gallina-
ria:Opere q actor cantor cursor seniũ sonticum.
Actius in Epinausimache.Mors amici subigit cp
mihi é seniũ multo acerrimũ:Põponius i scone
posteriore: Calue apportas nũciũ nobis disparẽ
diuisũ huic seni seniũ & metũ.Luc.satyrap libro
xy.In nũero quog nũc primus Trebellius mĩtos
Tiros lucios marcescebat febris seniũ uomitum
plus.Turpil.i Demiurgo: Quia.n.odio ac senio
mihi nuptiæ.Pacuuius ipibœa:Mœtus egeitas:
mœror:seniũ exiliũg & senectus & sitis ppetua.
Velitatio dicit uelis contẽtio dicta ex cõgressione
uelitũ.Plautus i Asinaria:Verbis uelitatione fieri
cõpẽdio uolo.Idẽ i Menæchmis : Nescio qd uos
uelitati estis iter uos duos.Turpil.i Lidia:Cõpce
uerbis uelitare:ad rẽ redi Affraius i Priuigno ite
rea uerba iactai & labris iter se uelitari uelificarieĩ
Toga dicta é a tegẽdo.& é toga sicut i cõsuetudine
habet uestimẽtũ quo in foro amicimur cuius &
Cice.meminit i Catilina:Velis amictos ñ togis.
Titinnius i Fullonibus:Quæ iter decẽ ãnos neq
sti unã togã detexere.dicit & tectũ:Titinius i Ge
mina:Syrus cũ scorto cõstituit ire:clauis ilico ab
strudi iubeo rusticæ togæ.ne sit copia tecti.

ollei occidi. uc.li.xxyi.Adiui quẽ febris una at
q una ania uini nũquã hiat° unus potuit tollere
Tollere mittere.Vir.ænei.li.ii.Vnius in miseri exi
tium conuersa tulere.

Tollere iferre.Vir.Geor.li.iii.Tollẽtemg minas:
& sibyla colla tumẽtem.
Tollere eleuaĩ.Vir.æne.li.i.Et mulcei dedit fluct°
& tollere uẽto:Idẽ i.xi.Tollit se ad rectũ qdrupes
M.Tul.Philippicap li.xi.Vel i cælũ uos si fieri po
tuerit:hũeris ñis tollemus.Luc.li.xxyiii.Tutius
& tẽnẽt.mortes:& fœdera tollẽt.M.T.i Hortẽsio
Nihil tamẽ eẽ in quo se animus excellẽs tollat.
Tollere ostẽdere erigere & tollere:Virg.ænei li.i.
Cui mater media sese tulit obuia silua.Idẽ.li.yii.
Laborũ prima tulit finem.
Tollere occidei.Var.sexagesimo:Nũquis patrẽ.x.
annog natus non mõ fert seu tollit nisi ueneno.
Tollere est.& differre:Plau.in penullo:Omnis ex
tollo ex hoc die in alium diem:
Tollei pati sustiere.Vir.æne.li.iii.Iuuenẽg supbũ
Seruitio enixe tulim°:Idẽ li.xii.ñ tulit istãtẽ phe
geus:aisg fremẽtẽ:Terẽ.i Phor.Ego te cõplures
aduersũ igeniũ meũ mẽses tuli.M.T.i Verrẽ diui
natõe.Tuli grauiter & acerbe iudices.Idẽ de off.
li.ii.Nisi.n.multog ipunita scelera tulissemus.
Tenacia é pseuerantia & duricia.Ennius Hectoris
lustris.ducet quadrupedũ iugo inuitam doma i
frẽa & iuge ualida:quog tenacia isfrenari nimis.
Tenacia parsimonia:Affranius in Priuigno:Vixi
sti tristis durus difficilis tenax.
Tẽpestas tẽpus.Salu.i Iugurtha:Ea tẽpestate in ex
ercitu ñõ fuere cõplures:noui atg ignobiles.Iu
ca.li.xxyii.iamg tẽpestate uiuo certe fine ad me
recipio.Pacu.i Teucro:Quã te post mĩtis habeo
tẽpestatib°.M.Tulli.de senectute : Cũrsus é cer
tus ætatis:& una uia naturæ : eag simplex suag
cuig parti ætatis tẽpestiuitas é data:Varro i Edi
mionibus:Dum sermone cœnulã uariamus:ite
rea tonuit bene tempestate serena.
Trepidare metuere.Virg.li.xi.Dũ trepidãt it ha
sta tago per tẽpus utrũg.Luca.lib.xxx.Sed quid
hoc aio trepidante dicta profundo.
repidare festinare:Vir.lib.xi.Ne trepidare mea
teucri defendere nauis:Et Geor.li.iii.Tunc trepi
dæ inter se coeunt:pẽnisg coruscant.
Tangere ferire cõmouei.Vir.li.xi.Nec solos tãgie
atridãus iste dolor.M.T.i Frumẽtaria uerrinap.
Nũg tua me cura tuag fortunap cogitatiog tan
get.Luc.Nec bene.p meritis capi:neg tãgit ira.
Tãgere é cõtingere.Luc.li.i.Tãgere.n.& tãgi nul
la potest res nisi corpus:Terẽ.in adeĩ.Nũquã dũ
ego adero hic te tanget.
Tãgere ispicere:Lucil.li.yi.Nequã potius q uenas
hominis tetigit ac præcordia.
Tãgere é circũuenire.Turpil.i Demetrio : At etiã
ineptus meus é mihi pater iratus:qa se talẽto ar
gẽti tetigi:ueteri exẽplo armãti:Lu.li.xxx.Et mu
sconis manu pscribere posset aiacẽ.Põpo.a leoni
bus:At ego rusticatim tangã:urbatim nescio.
Tãgere cõtingere.M.T.in Verrẽ actiõe.ii.uerres
simul ac tetigit prouinciã:Vir.li.xi.Sat satis uene
riag datũ tetigere cp arua Fertilis ausoniæ troes.
Triste crudele imite.Vir.ænei.li.ii.illi mea tristitia
facta Degenerẽg neoptolemũ narrare memẽto
Luc.li.xxx.Itag tuis sæuis factis& tristib° dictis.

b

devoted exclusively to learning and scholarship. Unfortunately the great civil war between Caesar and Pompey forced him back into action and took him to Spain, where he and Caesar opposed each other; Varro, realizing his cause was hopeless, wisely surrendered without a fight. Caesar pardoned Varro, and in 46 B.C. Caesar set him the task of organizing and acquiring books for the library he intended to build in Rome; that library did not materialize, but when one did, it contained a statue of Varro, the only living Roman so honored. During the ugly period of proscriptions that followed Caesar's assassination, Varro had to go into hiding in 43 B.C. and escaped death only through the intervention of Fufius Calenus, a powerful friend, but Marcus Antonius destroyed Varro's extensive private library at his villa near Casinum south of Rome. In time Varro resumed his literary and scholarly pursuits. The many and diverse subjects on which he wrote encompassed all the liberal arts and more, but he concentrated deeply on his favorite topics, chief among which were the Latin language (at least ten works dealt with what today is called linguistics), Roman religious and cultural history, and Roman comedy. A late Roman wit pointed out the obvious when he described Varro as "the most learned man on just about any subject." Varro died in 27 B.C., probably with pen in hand.

The six hundred extant fragments and ninety titles of Varro's *Saturae Menippeae* (Menippean Satires, 80–67 B.C.) are nothing if not enigmatic, for their witty and lively sketches of Roman life provide scant evidence for literary judgments: they are too short, too textually problematic, too lexically bizarre, and too difficult to understand. It is often impossible to determine who is speaking, and even when an authorial voice is present, whether it is serious or ironic is sometimes unclear. The genre itself, named after Menippus of Gadara, the third-century-B.C. Cynic philosopher who originated it, is usually rather vaguely defined as a somewhat more philosophical version of verse satire but composed in a mixture of prose and poetry. Yet, Cicero criticizes the philosophical content of the satires as inspiring but not instructive, and Varro himself emphasizes the jocularity with which he has infused his literary hybrid. *Menippean Satires* therefore seems intended as much for entertainment as for edification. Also intriguing is the sheer size of Varro's Menippean corpus—150 books, according to Jerome's catalogue, a staggering number—and the awesome variety of topics that must have figured in all those lost vignettes, parodies, and extravagant narratives.

Some Menippean satires present a Varro who does the expected: he vividly contrasts the moral degeneracy and irreverence of the city with the upright, religious, patriotic piety of the country; the decadent urbanity of the city slicker with the simplicity of the open and honest rustic; and antique virtue with contemporary vice. He

subjects pompous philosophers and pedants, but not philosophy and learning per se, to ridicule; parodies Cynic diatribes (his virtues are quintessentially Roman, not Greek); lambastes dogmatic systems of all sorts; moralizes; and of course takes dead aim at that most Roman of vices, gluttony. Varro the verbal connoisseur is ubiquitous in the *Menippean Satires:* he commences a lifelong habit by indulging in etymologies, some fanciful and others insightful; utilizes elegant oxymorons as titles; puns frequently (and like most punsters is oblivious to their quality); shifts rapidly from colloquial to recondite vocabulary, from archaisms to neologisms, and from clichés to purple prose; and everywhere manifests his love for the language. But the *Menippean Satires* also introduce to the reader a self-conscious and self-parodying author. This Varro is inordinately preoccupied with literary matters; knows his *Menippean Satires* are both different and difficult but aspires to literary fame nonetheless; discourses knowledgeably on the craft of writing and the nature of poetry; understands that his moralistic and stylistic purposes are sometimes at odds with each other; and demonstrates, as Cicero recognized, an amazing ability to versify in a dazzling variety of metrical patterns. He also pokes fun at himself as a representative of those pedants who misapply their encyclopedic learning, whose displays of academic opinion ultimately mock their authors more than inform their readers, and whose technical advice is sometimes of suspect validity. Varro is obviously having fun with matters dear to his heart and facetiously exploiting his own knowledge for the purpose of providing entertainment, not instruction. The general impression of the *Menippean Satires* is that the author adopts a pose that abuses precisely such poseurs and engages in mockery that mocks the mocker himself, and if he sometimes writes in a patently transparent tongue-in-cheek manner or occasionally waxes a bit risqué, then so much the better. The Menippean satires are as tantalizing as they are enigmatic, and if more of them had survived, a great deal more would be known about their author.

On the Latin Language is Varro's magnum opus. It originally consisted of twenty-five books: one of introduction followed by six on etymology (theory in books 2–4, practice in 5–7), six on morphology also arranged into theoretical (8–10) and practical (11–13) triads, and the remaining ones (14–25) on syntax. Only books 5–10 survive. Varro's programmatic statements and some fragments suggest that the books on etymological theory pursued the question of whether etymology was a principled intellectual endeavor, that those on morphological practice surveyed inflectional processes and displayed the nominal and verbal paradigms he discovered or created in book 10, and that the second half of *On the Latin Language* dealt heavily with Stoic logic and the structure of propositions, which are what passed for syntax in Greco-Roman antiquity. The books on morphological practice are the most serious loss. Books 5–7 offer a parade of hundreds of etymologies. Most are correct but rather obvious; some are best left unmentioned; but all are important cultural artifacts testifying to what Romans thought about lexical relationships in their native language. These etymological books incorporate a wealth of information on all sorts of topics—for example, Roman money and the topography of Rome—and book 7 is particularly valuable because it concentrates on poetry and transmits fragments of otherwise lost poems. Books 8 and 9 ask respectively whether anomaly or analogy—that is, irregularity or regularity—reigns supreme in the morphological sphere, and the arguments adduced on either side range from the naive to the sophisticated. Traditionally these two books are thought to document an analogy-anomaly quarrel in ancient (primarily Greek) intellectual discourse, but more-recent opinion inclines to treat the arrangement as more of a rhetorical or literary disposition of the linguistic data and arguments. In any case Varro states clearly in book 10, the contents of which he claims as his own and as unprecedented, that both analogy and anomaly are facts of language and that the issue is therefore one of determining exactly what linguistic similarity is, where it occurs, and how it is to be described; he thereby renders the quarrel, if ever it existed, passé. Reductively book 10 is a search for paradigms in the Latin language, and historiographically it is the key to understanding Varro's version of language science, because in it he charts an innovative and independent course.

Varro's accomplishments in *On the Latin Language* are many. By deriving Latin words from other Latin words and privileging Latin semantics rather than positing Greek origins and relations, he sets Roman etymology on the right track. He uses "root" in a quasi-modern sense, cites obsolete words from archaic documents, reconstructs unattested forms in order to explain otherwise inexplicable or aberrant contemporary forms, and generally behaves as scientifically as possible for a first-century-B.C. etymologist. Within linguistics proper and mainly in book 10 Varro distinguishes, for the first time in ancient grammar, between derivational and inflectional morphology; discovers the first embryonic declensions and conjugations in either Greek or Roman language science, which subsequently become the centerpiece of Latin grammatical theory and practice; is the first and only ancient grammarian to apply abstract arithmetical models to the solution of linguistic problems, a heuristic procedure that, along with his creative adaptation of the Stoic analysis of verbal aspect, allows him to identify the future perfective indicative, a tense missing from all of ancient Latin grammar and not rediscovered until the Renaissance; predicates his unique system of four parts of speech on a strictly morphological rather than semantic basis (there are words with case,

words with tense, words with both, and words with neither); and articulates the most sophisticated and advanced account of linguistic regularity up to his time, an account that looks forward to modern structural linguistics as much as or even more than it looks backward to Greek language science. Varro's overall approach to language science is rigorously formal; he asks linguistic questions for their own sake and requires linguistic answers, and he treats language science as an autonomous endeavor. Thus Varro makes of grammar the first of the liberal arts and bequeaths to posterity a distinctly Roman language science that becomes one of ancient Rome's most long-lasting contributions to intellectual history. *On the Latin Language* is therefore a seminal text in the history of linguistics.

The *De re rustica* (On Farming, 37 B.C.) masks itself as a technical treatise but manifests literary pretensions everywhere. Varro treats agriculture proper—that is, tilling the fields—in book 1; livestock—primarily cows, swine, and sheep—in book 2; and smaller, mainly winged, farm stock, such as poultry, game birds, and bees, in book 3. All three books are composed in dialogue form with epistolary introductions, elaborately articulated dramatic settings, and skillfully drawn characters. The dialogue imparts an air of homely informality, spontaneity, and verisimilitude to the work as speakers come and go, interrupt one another, shift topics, and digress. The subject matter is congenial to its author, whose love for the land, its products, and its animal and human inhabitants is on display from start to finish. The author's enthusiasm is contagious, but his knowledge ranges from the expert to the inaccurate as science and pseudoscience compete for space throughout the text. Varro is a socially conscious gentleman farmer who recommends hired hands (rather than slaves), educated overseers, merit pay, and enlightened management of human resources, but he is also keen to turn a profit. The specialized vocabulary and Varro's mania for seemingly endless division and subdivision of topics detract somewhat from the charm and appeal of the whole, but both are to be expected in a work masquerading as a practical manual on husbandry. Varro is writing for his fellow landed gentry and trying "to create, in effect, an agreeable illusion that there was mud on their boots." *On Farming* has been influential, and not simply because it has been quoted often or its contents reproduced by later writers. Virgil's *Georgics* owes much to Varro's work, as many parallels attest, and it has been ingeniously suggested that the map of Italy that Varro places on a temple wall in *On Farming* may have provided Virgil with the inspiration for the famous scene in the *Aeneid* in which Aeneas and Achates gaze at carvings on the temple door at Carthage. Renaissance villas borrow many of the architectural details from Varro's descriptions, and architects and builders alike have attempted to replicate the intricately designed aviary in book 3.

The linguistic style or expression of *On Farming* has engendered both criticism and praise. Syntactic difficulties make some passages virtually impossible to translate; technical or lexical obscurities render the meaning of others opaque; and the ever-present etymologies are not to every reader's liking. On the other hand, the humor with which Varro infuses the work is admirable even if most of his puns and witticisms do require either a knowledge of Latin or good footnotes. The names of the dedicatees and speakers are a case in point. In book 1, dedicated to Varro's wife Fundania, who has just bought a country estate, readers meet not only Fundanius (Varro's father-in-law), Fundilius (the host who never actually appears because he is being murdered), Agrius and Agrasius, whose names derive from *fundus* (farm) and *ager* (field) respectively, but also an expert on *stolones* (shoots, suckers) named Stolo. Book 2, in which Vaccius and Scrofa discuss exactly what their names denote—that is, cows and sows—is dedicated to Varro's friend Turranius Niger, and in book 3 addressed to Mr. Feathery (Varro's neighbor Pinnius), Messrs. Blackbird, Peacock, Magpie, and Sparrow converse about winged creatures with Appius, who of course waxes knowledgeable when the topic turns to *apes* (bees). One example of wordplay may suffice to demonstrate how Varro mixes style and meaning: workers should be encouraged by *verbis* (words) rather than disciplined by *verberibus* (blows). *On Farming* can therefore be read with both profit and pleasure, especially if the reader is interested in gentlemanly farming and/or Latinate humor.

The three extant Varronian texts constitute only 3 percent of Varro's vast but lost corpus of literary and scholarly works, and even they have managed to survive by only the slightest of margins. Most fragments of the *Menippean Satires* are preserved in a late antique encyclopedic dictionary with a notorious manuscript tradition ultimately descending from a single common archetype. The extant text of *On the Latin Language* derives from a manuscript now deposited in the Biblioteca Medicea-Laurenziana in Florence but originally transcribed at the monastery of Monte Cassino in the late eleventh century. *On Farming* also bears a Florentine pedigree, for all the manuscripts derive from one exemplar, now lost but collated on separate occasions in Florence by two distinguished Renaissance scholars. Readers and scholars today are therefore lucky to have the little that survives. If, however, the *Menippean Satires, On the Latin Language,* and *On Farming* are typical representatives of Varro's prose and poetry, then their author was not only a scholar of distinction but also a man of character. He was also witty, able to laugh at himself as well as with others, caustic on occasion, humane, insatiably curious, hardworking, independent, and Roman to the core. More than anything else, however, Varro was a man

in love with language, his language, the Latin language, no matter how strangely he may have used it at times.

Concordances:

Ward W. Briggs Jr., ed., *Varro: Concordantia in Varronis Libros, De re rustica* (Hildesheim: Olms, 1983);

Marcello Salvadore, ed., *Concordantia Varroniana I: Concordantia in M. Terenti Varronis Libros de Lingua Latina et in Fragmenta Ceterorum Operum,* 2 volumes (Hildesheim: Olms-Weidmann, 1995).

References:

Luigi Alfonsi, "Le 'Menippee' di Varrone," *Aufstieg und Niedergang der Römischen Welt* I, 3 (1973): 26–59;

Gaston Boissier, *Étude sur la Vie et les Ouvrages de M. T. Varron* (Paris: Hachette, 1861);

Franco Cavazza, *Studio su Varrone Etimologo e Grammatico: La Lingua Latina come Modello di Struttura Linguistica* (Florence: La Nuova Italia, 1981);

Jean Collart, *Varron Grammairien Latin* (Paris: Les Belles Lettres, 1954);

Hellfried Dahlmann, *Varro und die hellenistische Sprachtheorie* (Berlin & Zürich: Weidmann, 1932);

Francesco Della Corte, *Varrone il Terzo Gran Lume Romano* (Genoa: Istituto Universitario di Magistero, 1954);

Detlev Fehling, "Varro und die grammatische Lehre von der Analogie und der Flexion," *Glotta,* 35 (1956): 214–270; 36 (1957): 48–100;

Jacques Heurgon, "L'effort de style de Varron dans les *Res rusticae,*" *Revue de Philologie, de littérature et d' histoire ancienne,* 24 (1950): 57–71;

Eric Laughton, "Observations on the Style of Varro," *Classical Quarterly,* 54 (1960): 1–28;

Wilhelm Pfaffel, *Quartus Gradus Etymologiae: Untersuchungen zur Etymologie Varros in De Lingua Latina* (Königstein: Hain, 1981);

Charles S. Raymont, "Varro Versutus," *Classical Journal,* 40 (1945): 349–357;

Joel C. Relihan, *Ancient Menippean Satire* (Baltimore & London: Johns Hopkins University Press, 1993);

Jens Erik Skydsgaard, *Varro the Scholar: Studies in the First Book of Varro's De Re Rustica* (Copenhagen: Munksgaard, 1968);

Daniel J. Taylor, *Declinatio: A Study of the Linguistic Theory of Marcus Terentius Varro,* Studies in the History of Language Sciences, volume 2 (Amsterdam: Benjamins, 1974);

K. D. White, "Roman Agricultural Writers I: Varro and his Predecessors," *Aufstieg und Niedergang der Römischen Welt* I, 4 (1973): 439–497;

Erich Woytek, *Sprachliche Studien zur Satura Menippea Varros,* Wiener Studien, supplement 2 (Vienna: Böhlau, 1970).

Velleius Paterculus

(ca. 20 B.C. – ca. A.D. 30)

David Potter
University of Michigan

WORK: *Histories to the Consulship of Marcus Vinicius,* 2 books; book 1 is partly missing; book 2 is complete (A.D. 30).

Editio princeps: *P. Velleius Paterculus Historiae Romanae duo volumina,* edited by Beatus Rhenanus (Basel: J. Froben, 1520).

Standard editions: *C. Vellei Paterculi Ex historiae Romanae libris duobus quae supersunt,* edited by Kurt Stegmann von Pritzwald (Stuttgart: Teubner, 1965); *C. Velleius Paterculus* (Pisa: Giardini, 1976); *Histoire romaine,* 2 volumes, edited by Joseph Hellegouarc'h (Paris: Les Belles Lettres, 1982); *Vellei Paterculi Historiarum ad M. Vinicium consulem libri duo,* edited by W. S. Watt (Leipzig: Teubner, 1988); *Ad M. Vinicium consulem libri duo,* edited by Maria Elefante (Hildesheim: Olms, 1997).

Translation in English: *Compendium of Roman History* (with *Res Gestae Divi Augusti*), translated by Frederick W. Shipley, Loeb Classical Library (Cambridge, Mass.: Harvard University Press, 1917).

Commentaries: *Storia romana Velleio Patercolo,* edited by Felicita Portalupi (Turin: Giappichelli, 1967); *The Tiberian Narrative (2.94–131),* edited by A. J. Woodman (Cambridge: Cambridge University Press, 1977); *The Caesarian and Augustan Narrative (2.41–93),* edited by A. J. Woodman (Cambridge: Cambridge University Press, 1983); *Historia Romana-Römische Geschichte,* edited, with German translation, by Marion Giebel (Stuttgart: Reclam, 1989).

Gaius Velleius Paterculus, the author of a short history of Rome, was probably born in 20 or 19 B.C. He died sometime after A.D. 30, the year in which he presented his history to the consul Marcus Vinicius. At the end of the second book of that history Velleius includes a summary of the *novi homines* (new men), who had come from outside of the traditional governing aristocracy to help shape Roman history (2.127–128). The ostensible point of this passage was to praise Aelius

Sejanus, the praetorian prefect who was then the most influential man in Rome. In doing so, however, Velleius was also praising himself. His life and the history of his family, to which he alludes at various points in his history, were paradigmatic of the process through which Italy was unified under Roman rule and of the process that ultimately unified the Mediterranean world as it had never been unified before. Indeed, the fusion of family and cultural history, the linking of cultural developments with politics, make his history one of the critical documents of the early Roman Empire.

Velleius was the model Augustan loyalist, with roots in both camps during the civil wars that shaped the Roman society in which he lived. His grandfather had supported the losing side with remarkable consistency as a supporter of Pompey, whom Julius Caesar defeated in the civil war of 49–48 B.C. Velleius's grandfather served as a senior staff officer first with Caesar's assassin Marcus Brutus in 44–42 B.C. and then committed suicide in 40 B.C. after siding with Tiberius Nero in a revolt against Augustus (2.76.1). Velleius's uncle, a member of the senate, had participated in the prosecution of Cassius, another of Caesar's assassins, in 43 B.C. (2.69.5). The family had long been prominent in Velleius's native Campania before its members moved on to the political stage at Rome. An ancestor was the Decius Magius who had fought for Rome against Hannibal in the second Punic War (218–201 B.C.); a great-great-great (?) grandfather, Minatius Magius, had remained loyal to Rome in the Social War of 90–88 B.C. (2.16.2).

Velleius himself entered public life as a military tribune in the Balkan campaigns of Marcus Vinicius (the father of the recipient of his history) in 1 B.C. and continued to serve in the region under the command of M. Silius during the next year (A.D. 1). In A.D. 2 Velleius joined the staff of Gaius Caesar, then heir designate of the Emperor Augustus, for Gaius's expedition to the provinces of the eastern frontier (2.101.3). Velleius relates that he visited all the eastern provinces while under Gaius's command and that he witnessed

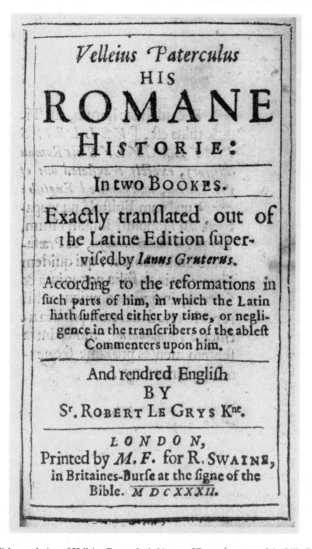

Title page for a 1632 English translation of Velleius Paterculus's history of Rome (courtesy of the Lilly Library, Indiana University)

the negotiations carried out by Gaius with the king of Parthia on the banks of the Euphrates River (2.102.1). He probably accompanied Gaius to Armenia at the end of the year and may have been present when Gaius was wounded during negotiations with the king of Armenia.

It seems likely that Velleius remained with Gaius until his death at Limyra in southern Turkey in the spring of A.D. 4. Velleius returned to Rome immediately thereafter and was dispatched to Germany as a tribune in command of a cavalry unit serving under the future emperor Tiberius Caesar (2.104.3). At the end of A.D. 6 Velleius returned to Rome to take up the office of quaestor. A holder of this office, the first position in a senator's career, was ordinarily assigned as a financial assistant to a senior magistrate. He was assigned to assist Tiberius himself in Germany. He continued to

serve under Tiberius throughout the campaigns in the Balkans that lasted from A.D. 7–12 (2.115.5). In A.D. 14 he received the praetorship, along with his brother, as the personal nominees of Augustus (2.124.4). The praetorship was the penultimate rank in a senatorial career and quite often the senior office to which a man whose father had not been a senator could aspire.

Service as Tiberius's quaestor and appointment to the praetorship by Augustus mark Velleius as a favored servant of the regime. Indeed, another member of his family, Marcus Magius Maximus, rose to the office of prefect of Egypt in A.D. 11–14, suggesting that Velleius had good connections at court. These connections were enhanced in the next generation as Velleius's eldest son rose to the rank of consul in 60 A.D. (the highest annual office in the senate). Velleius himself appears to have been content with his career and writes with evident pride of his services with members of the imperial house.

It is not known if Velleius wrote anything other than the short history that has come down under his name. He says he intended to move on from this book to a larger history, perhaps modeling his cultural aspirations upon the career of Sallust, the great historian of his grandfather's generation, who had taken to literary pursuits after a public career that had ended after his praetorship. It is not known if he lived to write it, and as a man in his fifties (Velleius was at least fifty in 30 A.D.), he was already old by Roman standards. He also appears to have been relatively old when he started a family. Roman consuls were ordinarily in their early forties, suggesting that Velleius was in his mid-thirties when his eldest son was born.

The extant work appears to have been based upon a scheme of world empires–Assyria, Persia, Macedon (or Greece), and then Rome–that offered a popular organizing principle in the first centuries B.C. and A.D. The first book (much of which was lost in transmission) opened with the emergence of the Assyrian kingdom under the legendary king Ninus and ended in 146 B.C., a year that, in the minds of many Romans, marked the point at which Rome achieved world domination and began to suffer from the consequences of having acquired an empire. The second book opens with the tribunate of Tiberius Gracchus in 133 B.C. and ends in A.D. 29, the year before the consulship of Vinicius, though the treatment of the reign of Tiberius in the final seven chapters (2.124–131) takes the form of a panegyric rather than a narrative. The second book, which is preserved intact, thus tells of Rome's descent into the horrors of civil war that culminate with the tragedy of the proscriptions in the period of Marcus Antonius's preeminence after the creation of the triumvirate in 43 B.C. From the depths of the proscriptions and the murder of Cicero (2.66), which occupies an important position at the center of the book–as measured by pages rather than the chapter divisions imposed by Renaissance editors–Velleius shows how the state was restored through the efforts of Augustus when he emerged from the shadow of Antony to achieve supreme power after the battle of Actium in 31 B.C. The virtues of Augustus are compared implicitly with those of other powerful figures–Marius, Sulla, Pompey, and Caesar–who dominate the first half of the book.

A notable feature of Velleius's history is the inclusion of synchronisms between cultural developments and political history. Thus at 1.5.1 he places the lifetime of Homer in the context of the foundation of Greek cities in western Turkey (which he places well after the time of the Trojan War). At 1.7.1 he makes Hesiod a contemporary of Dido, and at 1.11.4–5 he says that the first marble building at Rome was constructed after Metellus Macedonicus defeated Andriscus in 146 B.C. In chapters 14 and 15 of book 1 Velleius offers a list of Roman colonial foundations in Italy, which he rightly sees as the key to the unification of the peninsula under Roman rule (even if he gets many of the dates wrong). The list of colonial foundations is followed in chapter 17 by a description of the evolution of Greek literature–crucial evidence for the evolution of a canon of "classical" authors–and then states that Roman literature had developed as well in the second century B.C. The point he wants to make is that cultural developments need to be seen in the context of the development of states.

Short histories combining cultural with political events appear to have become popular at Rome in the middle of the first century B.C. Cicero's friend Atticus wrote a history of the world in three books; Cornelius Nepos, friend to both Atticus and the poet Catullus, wrote a similar history in two books; and Terentius Varro, the preeminent scholar of the generation of Cicero, also wrote such a history (also in two books). What is not known is whether these other histories devoted as high a proportion of their whole content to recent history as Velleius's did. It appears that just a little more than a quarter of the whole history (assuming that book one was about the same length as book two) is devoted to the lifetime of Augustus. The effect is to suggest that the creation of the principate by Augustus is the culmination of world history.

Velleius's overt admiration of Augustus and Tiberius is at the center of the debate over his quality as an historian. By ancient standards Velleius may well be representative of that sort of historian whom Tacitus said wrote out of too great a partisanship for a living emperor (*Annals* 1.1.2). The concluding section of his history might well have been condemned by critics in the tradition that is most significantly represented in Lucian's *How to Write History*–critics who believed that history should not degenerate into encomium (*Hist.* 7). Since Cicero himself had distinguished between proper historical description and encomiastic treatments that were written to praise rather than to be proper history (*Ad Att.* 1.19.10), readers of today can be certain that this distinction was well known at Rome. According to such standards, Velleius fell well short of the critical facility demanded of history.

Modern scholars have long tended to be dismissive of Velleius on precisely these grounds. Ronald Syme has written of Velleius as a "poisoned fountain" who often got his facts wrong (even when not writing about Augustus) and has traced patterns of distortion that can be attributed to the tastes of Tiberius. The omission of Horace from the list of great poets under Augustus and the hostile treatment of Marcus Lollius, the adviser of Gaius Caesar who had been contemptuous of Tiberius while the future emperor was living in self-imposed exile on Rhodes, may be taken as cases in point (2.36.3, 2.97.1, 2.102.1). In other cases, crimes committed by Augustus are glossed over. Velleius says that Augustus killed only a few enemies who surrendered at Actium in 31 B.C. (2.86.2) and that none died by Augustus's order after the capture of Alexandria the next year (2.87.2). Other sources suggest rather more bloodshed. Augustus's accomplishments as a general are inflated; those of important subordinates are ignored; and the record of the troubled relationship between Tiberius and Augustus is concealed (2.90.2, 2.99.1).

In response to Syme, A. J. Woodman has argued that the standards of objectivity in ancient historiography were less stringent than those of the modern age. This view considerably understates the force of ancient historiographic theory but is valuable in drawing attention to Velleius's considerable rhetorical skill. Judged simply as a writer of Latin, Velleius deserves attention for the power of his expression and for his ability to paint memorable verbal pictures: the description of a party presided over by Marcus Antonius at Alexandria during which the notable senator Munatius Plancus stripped himself naked and painted his body blue to play the role of a sea god is a classic piece of Roman invective (2.83.2). Woodman has also shown that concentration on the errors of Velleius obscures much that is of value and that historians of the reign of Augustus ignore his testimony at their peril.

Recent discoveries have enabled present-day readers to understand the message of Velleius with greater clarity than ever before. He was writing at a time when the memory of the civil wars was still powerful and felt that the greatest evil of all was a return to the chaos of the recent past. In his view, the civil wars were a result of the general immorality of the Roman people (2.1.1–2). The end of the wars, after nearly a century of bloodshed, stemmed from the virtues of one man. Velleius's view was shared by many and helps readers today to understand the pressures on Roman society that led to the rise of the principate from the ruins of the Republic. If Velleius is seen as a man to whom the political myths of the Augustan Age are crucial for the preservation of order in Roman society, the distortions isolated by Syme may seem more comprehensible and explicable.

While he certainly is not the greatest of all ancient historians, Velleius emerges from his writings as a comprehensible human figure, a person of his times who wanted to believe that Rome could properly fulfill what he saw as its destiny–the preservation and enhancement of the culture inherited from the past.

References:

Werner Eck, Antonio Caballos, and Fernando Fernández, *Das Senatus consultum de Cn. Pisone patre* (Munich: Beck, 1996);

R. J. Starr, "The Scope and Genre of Velleius' History," *Classical Quarterly,* 31 (1981): 162–174;

Ronald Syme, *The Augustan Aristocracy* (Oxford: Oxford University Press, 1986);

Syme, "Mendacity in Velleius," *American Journal of Philology,* 89 (1978): 45–63;

Syme, *The Roman Revolution* (Oxford: Oxford University Press, 1939);

A. J. Woodman, "Questions of Date, Genre and Style in Velleius: Some Literary Answers," *Classical Quarterly,* 25 (1975): 272–306.

Virgil

(70 B.C. – 19 B.C.)

Nicholas Horsfall

WORKS–EXTANT: *Bucolica,* 10 poems (Bucolics, 42/
41–39/38 B.C.);

Georgica, 4 books (Georgics, 36–29? B.C.);

Aeneis, 12 books; incomplete (Aeneid, 29?–19 B.C.).

WORKS–ATTRIBUTED: *Appendix Vergiliana;* only
Catalepton 5 and 8 might possibly be by Virgil,
though it is most unlikely.

Editio princeps: *Opera* (Rome: Conradus Sweynheym
& Arnoldus Pannartz, ca. 1469).

Standard editions: *P. Vergili Maronis Opera,* edited by
R. A. B. Mynors (Oxford: Clarendon Press,
1972); *P. Vergili Maronis Opera,* edited by Marius
Geymonat (Turin: Paravia, 1973).

Translations in English: *Virgil,* 2 volumes, translated
by H. Rushton Fairclough, Loeb Classical
Library (New York & London: 1934–1935);
Eclogues, translated by C. Day Lewis (London:
Cape, 1963); *Virgil's Eclogues,* translated by Guy
Lee (Liverpool: Cairns, 1980); *The Georgics of
Vergil,* translated by Day Lewis (London: Cape,
1941); *The Georgics,* translated by L. P. Wilkinson
(Harmondsworth, U.K. & New York: Penguin,
1982); *The Aeneid of Virgil,* translated by Day
Lewis (London: Hogarth Press, 1952; Oxford:
Oxford University Press, 1986); *The Aeneid,* trans-
lated by David A. West (London & New York:
Penguin, 1990).

Commentaries: *The Works of Virgil with a Commentary,* 3
volumes, edited by John Conington, revised by
Henry Nettleship, volume 1, revised by F. Haver-
field, fifth edition (London: Bell, 1883–1898);
Eclogues: Vergil, edited by R. Coleman (Cambridge
& New York: Cambridge University Press, 1977);
A Commentary on Virgil, Eclogues, edited by Wendell
Clausen (Oxford: Oxford University Press,
1994); *Georgica,* edited by Will Richter (Munich:
M. Hueber, 1957); *Georgics,* 2 volumes, edited by
Richard F. Thomas (Cambridge: Cambridge Uni-
versity Press, 1988); *Georgics,* edited by R. A. B.
Mynors (Oxford: Clarendon Press, 1990); *Geor-
gics I and IV,* edited by H. H. Huxley (London:
Methuen, 1963); *P. Vergili Maronis Aeneidos, Liber
Primus,* edited by R. G. Austin (Oxford: Claren-
don Press, 1971); *P. Vergili Maronis Aeneidos, Liber
Secundus,* edited by Austin (Oxford: Clarendon
Press, 1964); *P. Vergili Maronis Aeneidos, Liber ter-
tius,* edited by R. D. Williams (Oxford: Claren-
don Press, 1963); *P. Vergili Maronis Aeneidos, Liber
Tertius,* edited by Arthur Stanley Pease (Cam-
bridge, Mass.: Harvard University Press, 1935);
P. Vergili Maronis Aeneidos, Liber Quartus, edited by
Austin (Oxford: Clarendon Press, 1955); *P. Vergili Maronis Aeneidos, Liber Quintus,* edited by Williams (Oxford: Clarendon Press, 1960); *Aeneis
Buch VI,* edited by E. Norden, third edition
(Leipzig: Teubner, 1934); *P. Vergili Maronis Aeneidos, Liber Sextus,* edited by Austin (Oxford: Clarendon Press, 1977); *Aeneid 7,* edited by N. M.
Horsfall (Leiden, 1999); *P. Vergili Maronis Aeneidos,
Libri VII–VIII,* commentary by C. J. Fordyce,
edited by John D. Christie (Oxford: Oxford University Press, 1977); *A Commentary on Virgil, Aeneid
VIII,* edited by P. T. Eden (Leiden: E. J. Brill,
1975); *Aeneid Book VIII,* edited by K. W. Grans-
den (Cambridge: Cambridge University Press,
1976); *Virgil Aeneid Book IX,* edited by Philip Hardie (Cambridge: Cambridge University Press,
1994); *Virgil Aeneid 10,* edited and translated by S.
J. Harrison (Oxford: Clarendon Press, 1991); *Virgil Aeneid Book XII,* edited by W. S. Maguinness
(London: Methuen, 1953).

The so-called *Appendix Vergiliana* represents a collection of minor poetry (some of it most attractive) of
the fifty years (or more) after Virgil, attributed to him
to gain credit and ensure their survival. Just possibly
(though unlikely) two or three of the short pieces called
Catalepton may be authentic. The remainder certainly
are not. Much of Virgil's biography (*Vergil* with an *e* is
the classical Roman spelling, normal in Germany, and
thence adopted by some in the United Kingdom and

Bust of Virgil in the Virgilian Park in Naples

the United States, contrary to traditional literary usage) has been discredited: while the lives of the saints and the biographies of Greek poets have been subjected to ever more severe criticism, the biographies of Latin poets have been almost immune to skeptical analysis. The ancient lives of Virgil, however, have now been challenged with vigor: they include much material that has been believed only because it was applied to Virgil. Now we have to choose between clinging immobile to credulity and eliminating almost all the information transmitted about the poet. Virgil almost without a biography turns out to be no less great a poet than he was before, and a stern critical approach to the tales about his life sets the readers of his text no new problems at all.

Publius Vergilius Maro was a northern Italian, from Mantua, whose *nomen,* Vergilius, shows distant Celtic origins. Even his earliest poetry reveals a formidable literary training; that fact suggests that his parents

must have had some means, but where he studied before finding congenial sympathy amid Epicurean sympathizers on the Bay of Naples is not at all clear. Two of the *Bucolics* (1 and 9) are concerned with shepherds who have lost land in the confiscations (43/42 B.C.). Did Virgil himself lose land, and was it in some way restored to him through the intervention of one or other of the addressees of the *Bucolics*–that is, Asinius Pollio, Alfenus Varus, and Cornelius Gallus? No one knows. Just possibly when Virgil talks (*Georgics* 2.198) about the land Mantua has lost, beside the river, where the swans fed, he means "swans" as "poets," that is, himself. However, the rustic tragedies of *Bucolics* 1 and 9 are the stuff of life in Italy during the First Triumvirate (Julius Caesar, Pompey, and Crassus) and the Second Triumvirate (Mark Antony, Lepidus, and Octavian) and not necessarily autobiographical. Already in *Bucolic* 1 Virgil writes with admiration of the young Octavian, whom Cicero at the same time dismissed as a teenage butcher. How Virgil actually came into contact with Maecenas, early Octavian's adviser in matters of cultural politics, no one knows. About 38 B.C., however, Virgil was already well enough placed to be able to introduce Horace to Maecenas (Horace, *Satires* 1.6.54f.), and perhaps in the spring of 37 B.C. both Virgil and Horace accompanied Maecenas and various other public figures on their journey from Rome to Brundisium (Horace, *Satires* 1.5). The *Bucolics* were a huge popular success: the poems were performed onstage, and more than four hundred years after publication they were recited in the streets of Rome by Christian priests who should have been reciting psalms. This success made Virgil's next poetic undertaking a matter of public moment. He says (*Georgics* 3.41) that the *Georgics* were "your ungentle orders, Maecenas." "Ungentle," though, is typically elusive: does Virgil mean that the orders were stern or that the subject-matter of the new poem was not gentle? Certainly the words he uses, *haud mollia,* suggest clearly enough a rejection of that *mollitia* (softness, gentleness), which is so characteristic of the world of the *Bucolics.* "Orders" is a crude way of rendering *iussa,* which Peter White says in *Promised Verse* (1993) is a word used for many kinds of literary suggestions, invitations, or requests. The text does not suggest that Virgil is the willing (or unwilling) servant of a vast and coercive propaganda machine. Maecenas had seven years to wait for the *Georgics,* and the poem reflects the political changes of the period of composition. Octavian stopped near Naples for four days in 29 B.C., while returning to celebrate his triumph over Antony and Cleopatra, in order to listen to Virgil and Maecenas recite the newly completed *Georgics.* Virgil had become a major national figure, as well as a rich man: his estate came to be worth twenty-five times the property qualification of a Roman knight, but crude cash handouts in properly behaved circles at Rome were entirely unthinkable, and it would be unjustified cynicism to suppose that Maecenas secured the poet's loyalty with a series of handouts. The date Virgil actually began the *Aeneid* is equally uncertain: the proemium to the third *Georgic* (verses 21–39) suggests that he was thinking of writing an epic long before he actually began it, though he may not even have finished the *Georgics* before beginning the *Aeneid.* Virgil died in 19 B.C., before the *Aeneid* was altogether finished, and formal imperfections have indeed been detected. Just as Propertius was excited by the thought of the forthcoming epic (2.34.61–66), Augustus was urgent to hear something of it before "publication" of the whole; that Virgil read the imperial family three books (2, 4, and 6, though that is not certain) in 22 B.C. seems probable. It is related that Virgil wanted to spend three years in Greece to perfect the text, but Augustus, on his way

back from the East, met him at Athens, and the poet decided to return to Italy with Augustus. Heatstroke incurred at Megara led to Virgil's death at Brindisium. Some of this sequence of events may be true; there are objections to almost all of it, however, and various ancient accounts of what Virgil had laid down in his will as to what should be done in case he died with the poem unfinished are strikingly inconsistent. The tale that Augustus saw to the posthumous publication of the epic that the poet himself had wished should be burned if he could not see to its completion is moving but may well be rather a long way from the facts. Virgil's tomb is in Naples; it was recently vandalized.

In many modern books *Bucolics,* a collection of ten pastoral poems, is called *Eclogues* (chosen pieces), not *Bucolics* (poems about ox herds). Ancient usage is clear: the poems were called *Bucolica,* in obvious homage to the collection's model, the bucolic poems of Theocritus (fl. ca. 270 B.C.); individual poems within Virgil's collection could be called *Eclogae.* Any deviation from that simple distinction seems a sacrifice of ancient facts to modern fancies.

Although the *Bucolics* were a popular triumph, modern studies have revealed a text of extraordinary difficulty and complexity. If present-day readers let themselves be seduced by the singular melody of Virgil's lines, by the charm of his pastoral landscape, by the humor of his characters and situations, then those readers have been captivated by his Arcadia (4.58f., 10.26, a region of the Peloponnese whose shepherds were famed in antiquity for their musical skills) and are in the best literary and artistic company. Intense pleasure, though, is perhaps not enough as a critical reaction. There are, first, all sorts of formal problems crucial to understanding *Bucolics:* poem 1 has none of the characteristics of an opening poem, while poem 6 has them all. Was 6 the first poem of an earlier, shorter collection, as Aelius Donatus, a great Virgil and Terence scholar who lived about A.D. 350, thought? The order in which the poems stand has nothing to do with the order of composition: poems 2 and 3 are quoted in 5, and 5 alludes to the posthumous celebration of Julius Caesar's birthday in 42 or 41 B.C. Poem 4 is firmly dated to 41/40 B.C. by the reference to Asinius Pollio's consulship, and poem 8 is dated to 39 B.C. by his proconsulship, while poem 6 talks of its dedicatee, Alfenus Varus, on campaign (verse 7)—that is, apparently in 38 B.C. The redistribution of land continued for some years after 42 B.C. and cannot be used to date *Eclogues* 1 and 9 precisely. The present order is clearly the result of much precise thought, even if present-day scholars cannot follow all of it. If poem 10 is regarded as a sort of epilogue and the rest revolve around the death of Caesar (poem 5), then the obvious similarities between

INPOSVITNATVRALOCISQVOTEMPOREPRIMVM
DEVCALIONVACVVMLAPIDESIACTAVITINORBE
VNDEHOMINESNATIDVRVMGENVSERGOAGETERRae
PINGVESOLVMPRIMISEXTEMPLOMENSIBANNI
FORTESINVERTANTTAVRIGLAEBASQIACENTIS
PVLVERVLENTACOQVATMATVRISSOLIBAESTAS
ATSINONFVERITTELLVSFECVNDASVBIPSVM
ARCTVRVMTENVISATERITSVSPENDERESVLCO
ILLICOFFICIANTLAETISNEFRVGIBVSHERBAE
HICSTERILEMEXIGVVSNEDESERATVMORHARENam
ALTERNISIDEMTONSASCESSARENOVALIS
ETSEGNEMPATIERESITVDVRESCERECAMPVM
AVTIBIFLAVASERESMVTATOSIDEREFARRA
VNDEPRIVSLAETVMSILIQVAQVASSANTELEGVMEN
AVTTENVISFETVSVICIAETRISTISQLVPINI
SVSTVLERISFRAGILISCALAMOSSILVAMQSONANtem
VRITENIMLINICAMPVMSEGESVRITAVENAE
ERVNTLETHAEOPERFVSAPAPAVERASOMNO
SEDTAMENALTERNISFACILISLABORARIDATANtum
NESATVRAREFIMOPINGVIPVDEATSOLANEVE

Page from an incomplete fourth-century manuscript for Virgil's Georgics, one of the earliest fragments of the poet's works (Vatican Library, Codex Vaticanus 3256)

1 and 9 (redistributions of land), between 2 and 8 (monologues on hopeless love), and between 3 and 7 (contests of pastoral song) give a certain formal solidity to the whole. Therefore, that *Eclogues* 4 and 6 together include 149 verses while 1 plus 9 includes 150, and both 3 plus 7 and 2 plus 8 include exactly 181, is interesting (or crucial, depending on one's approach).

In Virgil's hands, pastoral turned into a poetic genre in which the author could use humble characters to talk about public figures and current affairs. Because shepherds are the poet-musicians of the countryside, Virgil can also talk about poetry on their lips and can lard their conversation with poetic allusions to predecessors and contemporaries, both Greek and Latin. He does so notably in *Eclogues* 6 (Gallus, v. 64) and 10 (Gallus the dedicatee); that ten fragmentary lines of Cornelius Gallus's (rather disappointing) poetry have now been discovered on a scrap of papyrus has not helped to clarify the situation. Particularly in the prologue to *Eclogue* 6, Virgil is at pains to underline the modesty of pastoral poetry: didactic and epic were definite steps up the hierarchy of poetic dignity, but humble pastoral turns out to be a singularly pliable literary form: its meter is epic (hexameter); its theme (love, often) suggests elegy or lyric; its use of refrains is decidedly lyric; and the dialogues, contests, and touches of jolly fun suggest mime. Virgil's pastoral poetry, however, is not just a literary construct, inasmuch as there are striking touches of realism in the descriptions of country life (1.34f., 3.94ff.), and the names of rustic deities and their festivals (3.76f., 5.35, 10.94) suggest familiar Italy and not the distant world of Theocritus, though the landscape, however important an element it is in the various poems as the setting for personal love and public tragedy, and as a consolation for both, never attains that degree of specificity that makes the descriptions in the works of Lucretius and in the *Georgics* so fascinating at times.

Problems do not end there; the *Bucolics* are enigmatic in so many ways that the excitement of finding new puzzles and the dream of solving them have done much to reduce the delight the collection once gave and still should. Many readers, from a really very early period, have seen the text as allegorical; the obvious starting point is the equivalence between the Tityrus of *Eclogue* 1 and the poet himself (compare Virgil as Menalcas in *Eclogue* 9). Was the Daphnis of *Eclogue* 5 Julius Caesar? If so, what of the Daphnis in poem 7? And so it goes on; enthusiasts, ancient and modern, just have not known where to stop. That is not to say that allegory should be dismissed out of hand: many thought that Simichidas in Theocritus's seventh *Idyll* represented the poet. Whether, though, imposing rigorous and systematic identifications between the pastoral

figures in certain *Eclogues* and historical personages of the time is proper is quite another matter. It is far from clear that this is a legitimate way of reading ancient pastoral poetry. Allegory interacts with another problem, the consistency of characterization both between Theocritus and Virgil and within Virgil: how far is the Menalcas of Theocritus's ninth poem going to reemerge in the Menalcas of *Eclogue* 3? And how far is Virgil's Corydon (or Menalcas, or Melibocus, or Amaryllis) going to be the same from one poem to another? He is not, at least to judge from Corydon, a Sicilian shepherd as in *Eclogue* 2 but a goatherd in 7; however, both use the same Theocritean model (*Idyll* 11) to sing of their respective loves (Alexis, Galatea).

Wendell Clausen's commentary on *Bucolics* sets out (pp. 109–119) to demystify the fourth *Eclogue*: it becomes "a brilliant little poem. Brilliant and playful, with overtures of grandeur . . . " (p. 119), essentially Hellenistic in character like all the rest of the collection. In this poem, not on the same level as the others (so Virgil says in the first line), a new golden age is about to begin, and this restoration of human felicity coincides with the birth of a *puer* (male child). Who? Any commentary will list the five historical possibilities, of whom a child to be born of the marriage between Mark Antony and Octavia, Octavian's sister, is the least unlikely (though they never did produce a son). In later times, the poem was thought to prefigure Augustus (not a good idea, except in the loosest of terms) or indeed Christ: Lactantius noted some parallels between prophecies of the coming of the Messiah and the language used by Virgil; the emperor Constantine was convinced that Virgil really did prophesy the coming of Christ (while St. Jerome was quite clear that he did not), and St. Augustine hedged his bets, saying that Virgil was, after all, quoting the Cumaean Sibyl, and she, not the poet, had prophesied Christ's coming. More to the point are the abundant close parallels in imagery between the fourth *Eclogue* and, notably, the book of Isaiah. That is not to suggest that Virgil read the Old Testament, but he must inevitably have had some contact with Alexandrian Jewish prophetic literature (as represented for us by the so-called *Oracula Sibyllina*). It is not even absolutely clear that Virgil had the real birth of a real child in mind; though he speaks of pregnancy, of the goddess of childbirth, and of the smiling infant, even so the child may be imagined as the symbol of a new age of hope, rendered more human and more concrete than in any other obviously political poem. Of all the *Bucolics,* the fourth is the most puzzling.

The proemium of the first *Georgic* announces the subject matter of all four books of the *Georgics:* crops, vines, cattle, and bees. It is a didactic poem, then, about agriculture, but that is something different from a poem

FELICESOPERVMQVINTAMFVGEPALLIDVSHORCVS
EVMENIDESQVESATAETVMPARTVTERRANEEANDO
COEVMQVELAPETVMQVECREATSAEVOMQVETYPHOEA
ETCONIVRATOSCAELVMRESCINDEREFRATRES
TERSVNTCONATIINPONEREPELIOOSSAM
SCILICETATQOSSAEFRONDOSVMINVERTEREOLYMPVM
TERPATEREXTRVCTOSDISIECITFVLMINEMONTIS
SAEPTIMAPOSTDECIMAMFELIXETPONEREVITEM
ETPRENSOSDOMITAREBOVESETLICEATELAE
ADDERENONAFVGAEMELIORCONTRARIAFVRTIS
MVLTAADEOGELIDAMELIVSSENOCTEDEDERE
AVTCVMSOLENOVOTERRASINRORATEOVS
NOCTELEVESMELIVSSTIPVLAENOCTEARIDAPRATA
TONDENTVRNOCTISLENTVSNONDEFICITVMOR
ETQVIDAMSEROSHIBERNIADIVMINISIGNES
PERVIGILANTFERROQVEFACESINSPICATACVTO
INTEREALONGVMCANTVSOLATALABOREM
ARGVTOCONIVNXPERCVRRITPECTINETELAS
AVTDVLCISMVSTIVVLCANODECOQVITVMOREM
ETFOLIISVNDAMTEPIDIDESPVMATAENI
ATRVBICVNDACERESMEDIOSVCCIDITVRAESTV
ETMEDIOTOSTASAESTVTFRITARFAERVGES
NVDVSARASERENVDVSHIEMPSIGNAVACOLONO

Page from the first book of Virgil's Georgics *in a fourth- or fifth-century manuscript for Virgil's works (Vatican Library, Codex Palatinus 1631)* intended to teach its readers how to farm–a fundamental distinction that has caused much confusion and needs to be cleared up. The imagined audience of the *Georgics* is indeed composed of farmers (whom Virgil addresses, for example, at 1.100), but the intended readership of this same poem is necessarily at a far higher cultural level. That is not to say that farmers could not read. They could and did, and a little bit is known about the rough manuals that existed for them, but the literary texture of the *Georgics* is exceptionally dense and complicated, and to get into them to any depth, the reader (ancient or modern) needs ample grounding in a great body of Greek literature, both prose and verse, and not all of it, by any means, about farming. There is a fair bit of apparently instructional material in the poem, but it is unsystematic, incomplete, and at times positively inaccurate, as later Roman writers realized. Nor is it quite clear about what sort of farm Virgil is writing; indeed, he may actually have preferred to leave the issue open. Usually he writes about the smallholder, the farmer who does most of the work himself: that sort of agriculture had most appeal to poet and reader, and it also rested on a long poetic tradition, going back to Hesiod's *Works and Days*. But just sometimes (1.286; possibly 1.343, 2.230, 259) he writes about slaves, and occasionally too he talks about agricultural techniques and situations only appropriate to a large-scale landholder (2.177–258: only on a large farm are there many varieties of soil; 1.49: barns full of grain). So Virgil writes about farming, but not for farmers, and in a precise historical context: he began during the time when the Civil War had wrought great damage to farming in Italy–plunder and destruction, conscription, confiscation, redistribution, and neglect of land while its owners were on active service; all played harmful roles. Sextus Pompeius, son of Pompey the Great, had blocked much of the regular grain supply from Egypt, and famine was a serious prospect. It is too easy to say that Virgil–once Sextus Pompeius was defeated (3 September 36 B.C.) and it became more likely that Octavian, not Antony, would become undisputed master of Italy–began to map out a poetic design for a mass return to the land on the basis of traditional smallholdings, in keeping with an official policy (of sorts) of agricultural renewal. There is no historical evidence for such a policy, though the beneficent effects of peace (after 31 B.C., that is) upon farming were recognized. A return to an agricultural economy based upon smallholdings made no sort of practical sense, but Virgil wrote at a time when "restoration" and "return" were notions dear to Octavian and his advisers (for example, Maecenas and Cicero's old friend Atticus). The spirit of traditional farming (as symbolized by the figure of the elder Cato, both as he had spoken and written and as Cicero had

presented him in his "On Old Age") was a very different matter from the long-gone reality. As a moral and ethical ideal, "the farmers of old" and a style of life that could credibly be attributed to them were eminently suitable and attractive matter for a didactic poem–and not only formally didactic, but also widely and brilliantly descriptive. Not, that is, just "how to" but also "see how it is." That way of looking at nature had come to Virgil, above all, from Lucretius, whose Epicurean didactic poem had appeared when he was sixteen or so years old: to Lucretius, minute observation of the visible world served by analogy to explain what the eye could not see. The infinite poetic possibilities of the detailed observation of nature were perfectly suited to Virgil's talents and purpose, as becomes clear to anyone who reads, for instance, the list of weather signs, (*Geo.* 1.351–423). Even though there survive two Greek texts and two Latin translations used by Virgil, one would never imagine that much of this wonderful precision is literary and derivative. Just how well Virgil himself knew the details of farmwork is not clear: scholars learn more and more both about his Greek sources, in prose and verse, and about the mass of detail compatible with prose farming manuals in Latin of such writers as Cato, Varro, Columella, and Palladius. The *Georgics* are brilliant as didactic poetry precisely because they are so admirable in their descriptions. When Virgil from time to time abandons the (relatively) narrow detail of the matter in hand to turn to an excursus (digression), his reason is not that nature and farming are so dry and dull that they need relief or alleviation but that the poet is well aware that a change of tone and perspective is called for. The digressions comment on and illustrate in ampler terms the more strictly didactic text; their role in some ways is not unlike that of the choruses of Greek tragedy.

The end of the fourth *Georgic* presents a set of particular problems that cannot be dodged. If a swarm of bees dies out (281ff.), it can be reconstituted by an Egyptian system called *bougonia* (birth from an ox), for it was believed that a new swarm could be born by spontaneous generation from the corpse of a bullock. Who, asks Virgil (4.315), invented this system? The mythical culture-hero Aristaeus, who had lost his bees and went to ask his divine mother, Cyrene, for advice. Cyrene sends Aristaeus to consult Proteus, an Old Man of the Sea, capable of infinite metamorphoses (as in Homer's *Odyssey* 4) and endowed with supernatural wisdom (387ff.). Proteus says (453ff.) that it is all Aristaeus's fault: Orpheus has sent the bees' death, for it was in flight from the lustful Aristaeus that Orpheus's beloved Eurydice was bitten by a snake. There follows (464ff.) the story of the inconsolable Orpheus's visit to the underworld to try to recover Eurydice; he was nearly successful, but at the last moment (488ff.) and from excess of love, all was in vain. Orpheus returns to earth to lament his loss with irresistible melancholy, until his own violent death. Aristeus, on the other hand (528ff.), performs expiatory sacrifices to Orpheus and performs the *bougonia* swiftly and successfully. The idea of interlocking narratives came to Virgil above all from Catullus, poem 64, but the problems this text offers are not just of structure and message. What have bees to do with Orpheus? And what is the place of a complex mythological narrative in a didactic poem? These are good questions, and they were put at least sixteen hundred years ago. A strange answer emerged, in the form of a story that Virgil had originally written in praise of his friend Cornelius Gallus (the same poet and public man whom Virgil addresses in *Eclogue* 10), but when Gallus, governor of Egypt (4.287ff.), passed from megalomania to disgrace to suicide, Augustus "made" Virgil change the end of *Georgic* 4. The ancient commentators to the *Georgics* were quite right to see that there were serious questions to be asked about the end of *Georgic* 4; their answer was not necessarily good or acceptable. We need to remember that their grasp of the fine points of Roman history for over four hundred years before their own day was very slender and that they naturally tended to look for biographical solutions to literary problems. To make the panegyric of a provincial governor (who was also a friend and fellow-poet) the climax of a didactic poem, begun with Maecenas's encouragement and moral support (*Georgics* 3.41–42), and once completed, read to Octavian (not yet called Augustus) does not make sense in a great public poem. In the two years, between the completion of *Georgics* and Gallus's disgrace, such a text must have been copied and distributed on a huge scale; that all copies of this panegyric were successfully called in and burned is not credible. Virgil reused some passages from *Georgic* 4 when he was writing the *Aeneid;* those who claim that he reused bits of the *Aeneid* when revising *Georgic* 4 in a hurry did not look at the texts too carefully and never charted the clear and steady growth in Virgil's skillful adaptation of ever-longer passages of Homer. The problem has been settled, to general if not total satisfaction, though even scholars who do not believe the Gallus story often reveal that they have a sense that there is something not quite right about the end of *Georgic* 4? by their hunt for alleged traces of Gallus or of his poetry within the text as it is today. More seriously, the present text does offer a sort of double ending–the tragedy of Orpheus and the oddly banal success of Aristaeus. That ambiguity lies at the heart of a passionate discussion in recent years of the theological, philosophical, or political sense to be attributed to the poem. *Georgic* 1 ends with an extraordinarily powerful evocation of the horrors of civil war (486–511) and an image (512–514) of the world as out of control; *Georgic* 3 ends with a description (478–566) of the irremediable cattle plague in Noricum. Work on the farm is represented (for example, 1.197–203) as a continuous and not hopeful struggle. Does that then mean that all the rest of the text, like it or not, has to be read in the same key? Are even the praises of Italy (2.136–176) "lies"? (The word is used in a well-known recent study.) Or are those rather rhetorical and openly exaggerated praises to be understood as hopeful or ideal, and is the idealization of the countryman's life (2.475–540) to be read as consolation for the long hard toil of work on the land? "The best poem of the best poet" is how Joseph Addison characterizes the *Georgics* in the opening of his introduction to John Dryden's translation (1697). His is not an isolated view, and perhaps the passionate enthusiasm that the *Georgics* has roused makes sense if it is, really and truly, a meditation upon the hopelessness of the human condition and the impossibility of successful and happy farming.

Virgil, in the course of his literary career, undertook steadily larger projects, moving also up the scale of stylistic and generic grandeur. To say that this progression was calculated and inevitable is too easy; already at the time of *Bucolics,* Virgil was thinking about epic (6.1ff.), and when he was writing *Aeneid,* he still remembered *Bucolics* (7.483ff.). Alongside the formal and perfect growth of his literary career, Virgil's relationship with Augustus developed. That an ancient life says that Augustus proposed the topic of the *Aeneid* to Virgil does not matter. More important are the repeated observations, made by ancient readers of the epic to whom a clear perception of rhetorical structure and intent came far more naturally than it does today, that Virgil's purpose was to relate (and praise) the origin of the city of Rome and of Augustus's own family. That from the late second century B.C. onward the family of the Julii Caesares claimed descent from Aeneas is central to Virgil's choice of the story of Aeneas as the plot for his epic. Julius Caesar made much of this genealogy in the image that his publicity projected, and his great-nephew and adopted son Octavian followed this lead–in art, ritual, and coins. However unwelcome such facts are to most modern students of Virgil, who is normally seen as a poet of doubt, suffering, and criticism of Roman and imperial values, they do remain facts; some further details can be found in *Vergilius,* 32 (1986). The crude question "But did Augustus tell Virgil to write the *Aeneid?*" is best not asked, not least because Augustus and Maecenas in their best years did not do things that way. Augustus's repeated involvement in the development and publication of the poem (fragments of the correspondence between poet and emperor are actually available) has inevitably some bearing on modern read-

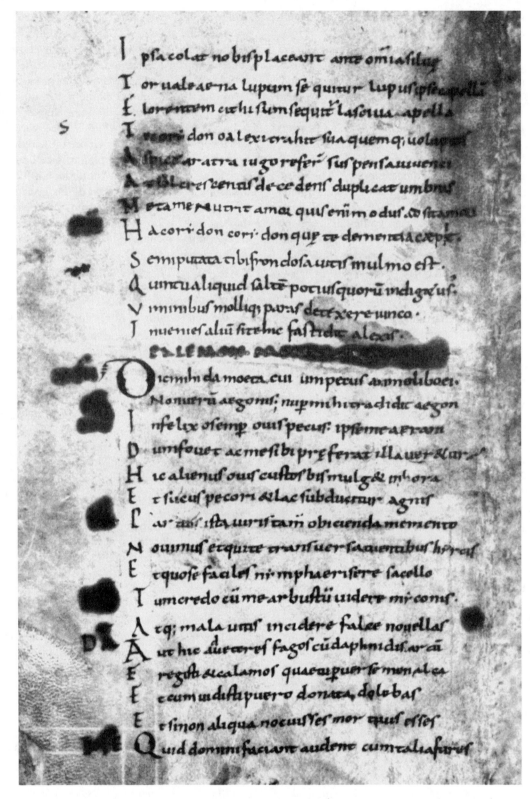

Page from a tenth-century manuscript fragment of Virgil's Eclogues *(British Library, Harley MS 3072 f. 1b)*

ers' judgment if they look at the epic at least in part in its historical context. Of course, a reading of the epic in terms of a modern, liberal, antimilitarist ethic will come up with wildly different answers; indeed, much current discussion of the *Aeneid* is violently politicized.

It is necessary to look at the *Aeneid* in terms that did, demonstrably, make sense in Virgil's own time: that is not to deny that today's Virgil too has a right to exist, but it is best to get to know the text really well before deciding not only what its moral issues are but also what stand the poet takes on them. For there is no room for doubt: while Virgil tells a remarkable story (and St. Augustine as a schoolboy was fascinated by books 2 and 4, as he says in *Confessions,* book 1, ch. 13), which army officers carried on campaign, schoolboys wrote on the walls of Pompeii, and crowds heard read in the theater, the *Aeneid* is also a vehicle for profound meditations on the human condition, on character and moral judgment, on war and peace, on conflict of duties, on the state, on the gods, and on Roman history; see St. Augustine's reading of *Aeneid* in his *City of God.* Such a multiple, complex, non-narrative content may seem a long way from epic as a heroic narrative, but the extraordinary moral depth and grandeur of the last book of the *Iliad* and the various strands of scholarship and geography woven into Apollonius of Rhodes's *Argonautica* should be cases enough to show that Virgil was only developing options already open and not, in this respect, innovating. Some aspects of this enriching of the narrative texture deserve comment. Virgil is fascinated by such causes and explanations. Why, for example, is Juno angry with Aeneas (1.8)? Why did Rome become great (1.1–7)? Why did war break out in Italy (6.93, 7.482, 553)? Why (at a rather different level) were horses not allowed in the precinct of Diana at Nemi (7.778)? This last instance belongs to what is called etiological poetry, the poetry of explanations, dear to the learned Alexandrians, and is less trivial than it might seem, for it is very important to Virgil that the Roman religion of his day shall be seen to have a Trojan origin (12.836–840). Detailed explanations of the hostility between states and individuals belong to historiography (beginning with the first chapters of Herodotus), and the language of Virgil's proemium (7.37–45) to his account of the outbreak of war in Italy shows that he is consciously writing in the historical tradition. The great leap from myth to history, the link between Troy and Rome, and the voyage of Aeneas as necessary preliminary for the foundation and future greatness of Rome probably came to Virgil from the epic poet Naevius, writing (in Latin) in the late third century B.C., about the time of the First Punic War. It looks as though he also told the story of Aeneas's encounter with Dido, and it seems likely that he, like Virgil

(4.622–629), used the disastrous romance between Aeneas and Dido as the cause of an actual, recent war. The full range of literary resources open to the learned epic poet of Virgil's day in fact opened up many possibilities for forging links of real substance between the worlds of epic and history. Apart from etiology (the two most substantial instances are 5.596–602 and 7.601–617), genealogy opened up many possibilities (not just Augustus's Romans were supposed to be descended from Trojans, as indicated by 5.117–123, 12.835–836); by prophecy or curse (1.257–296, 4.622–629, 6.756–886); by the description of works of art made with divine foreknowledge (8.626–728); by the explanation of the history of place-names, or the description either of places yet unnamed that will become great, or of places that do exist but are not yet renowned (like the Rome of Aeneas's visit in book 8); by the use of anachronisms of detail (so the Trojans move in a world in some little ways already Roman); and by the many ways in which Aeneas already behaves like a Roman general, senator, father, or priest, according to Roman ethical standards. His struggle to establish the Trojan settlement on Italian soil in itself anticipates the Romans' struggle to establish their position first in central Italy and then in the Mediterranean. Other readers have taken Aeneas's arrival in Italy as an unwanted irruption upon a calm and idyllic world, prefiguring, inevitably, the Romans' policy of brutal imperialist expansion. Such discord at least demonstrates the suitability of Virgilian epic as, for example, a vehicle for meditations upon history.

It would also be very easy to offer some generalizations about Virgil's language and his narrative skill, but it is much better to read the second book, on the fall of Troy, told by Aeneas at a banquet when he arrives at Dido's palace at Carthage. Just as narrative there is nothing better in the *Aeneid.* No, it is not Homer; Virgil's skills as a narrator are altogether different, and it is no help to say that one is "better" than the other. Readers who are shocked that Aeneas does not stop and reason out the wisest course before wildly seizing his weapons at line 314 are setting unrealistic and inhuman standards for Virgil's hero, though to be sure a philosopher might say otherwise.

Virgil himself narrates Aeneas's journey into exile in *Aeneid,* book 1, until Aeneas arrives at Carthage; for the consequences of that visit, the poet prepares his audience at various levels, both through intimations of the wars to come between Rome and Carthage and through sketches of the origin and character of the Carthaginians, themselves exiles (from Tyre), but, unlike the Trojans, already endowed with riches, given to luxury, and famed for dishonesty. They somehow knew of the Trojan War before Aeneas's arrival, and in

Illuminated capital in a fifteenth-century manuscript for Virgil's works (Vatican Library)

their temple of Juno (the Trojans and Romans' leading enemy on Olympus) had depicted scenes from the Trojan War, including Aeneas, but characterized by unusual brutality on the Greeks' part. When Aeneas is deeply moved by what he sees, readers have to ask whether he should be, and when Aeneas and Dido, Queen of Carthage, actually meet (1.613), history points the careful reader toward a grim outcome, while the extremely complex literary antecedents of the encounter suggest that love and tragedy await the participants. Aeneas's mother, Venus herself, in order to protect Aeneas from the Carthaginians' machinations, sends Cupid, disguised as Aeneas's son Ascanius, to fire Dido with love for Aeneas. This act does not make Dido a boring puppet of Olympian decisions, since Virgil has done much to suggest that Aeneas, though destined to found a great nation in Italy, and Dido, though devoted to the memory of her murdered husband Sychaeus, are necessarily, by similarity and attraction, also destined for each other. At a great banquet for the Trojans, Aeneas tells Dido the story of the fall of Troy (*Aeneid* 2) and of the Trojans' wanderings (*Aeneid* 3, corresponding to Odysseus's account of his own travels at Alcinous's palace in *Odyssey,* books 9–12). Dido is now in love, dangerously (madness, fire, poison, and wound

are the images most often used to characterize her passion), egged on by her rather sinister sister Anna. Juno seizes the moment and proposes to Venus an alliance between Trojans and Carthaginians, but even the cynical Venus knows that would be going too far and (4.110ff.) temporizes. Dido invites Aeneas on a grand hunt. A storm comes up; they take refuge in a cave and consummate their love in a sinister parody of marriage-ritual (166–168). That, comments Virgil, was the beginning of all the trouble; Dido, moreover, used the word *coniugium* (marriage) to cover her *culpa* (fault). As the couple spend the winter in the lap of lust and luxury, forgetful of their missions (4.193–194), rumor personified begins to work, and Dido's rejected African admirer, Iarbas, on hearing the news of Aeneas and Dido's affair, prays indignantly to Jupiter, who sends Mercury to remind Aeneas of his own destiny in the West and its entire incompatibility with his present conduct (4.223–237). The hero is no manipulated puppet: Mercury's message only tells him what he has himself preferred to forget, accelerating, not altering the course of events. Aeneas's behavior is not only contrary to his destiny but altogether improper for him as a model of pre-Roman moral behavior; that his father had died at the end of book 3 is no accident. Aeneas is appalled at the reminder from Mercury, plans to leave at once, and intends (he really does; Virgil leaves no doubt, 4.291–294) to tell Dido of his necessary departure just as soon as the right moment offers. Of course, it does not: Dido hears first, concludes she has been betrayed (though it is not quite that simple), and from then on (4.308) speaks in terms of her own imminent death: her behavior and reaction is that of the classic Greek betrayed heroine (for example, Ariadne), but Aeneas's fault is not so much in leaving her as in having fallen for her in the first place, an emotion that Virgil with brilliant ingenuity suppresses in the narrative. Between Dido's two tremendous outbursts of rage and passion, Virgil gives Aeneas a single speech (4.333–361), in keeping with his general picture of Aeneas as a man of few words and slow, deep emotions. Aeneas loves Dido (4.395); he has not offered marriage (4.337–338); and he has not concealed his destiny (little joy for Dido). Aeneas is like an oak tree buffeted by the storm; he is torn by emotion, and the leaves of the tree fall, as do his tears, to no effect. The tragedy is his, if the text is read sensitively, as much as hers—at least until line 450, when Aeneas passes almost entirely out of the action, but note 554–583, when he is already prepared to depart and Mercury arrives to make him leave even faster. Virgil chooses to focus almost entirely upon Dido, victim of the gods, of Rome's destiny, of her emotions, of the pace of events, of her beauty, and in some degree, of Aeneas. The Aeneas of book 4 has not had a good press among readers and scholars: they have in general failed to realize that the poet prefers complex, balanced, ambiguous emotional situations. To condemn Aeneas as a moral failure and an emotional cripple (as many modern studies of the book do) raises far more problems than it solves. A far more constructive approach is to regard the text as not screaming its moral conclusions from the rooftops. Instead, readers and scholars should look carefully to see what indications Virgil has offered to readers with the sense to see that the poet may also have sketched a tragedy and a justification of Aeneas. Before her suicide, Dido wishes upon the Trojans and their descendants her curse–sufferings for Aeneas, for the Trojans, and for the Romans. Her passion even reaches forward to Hannibal (4.625–626) as Carthage's greatest champion in a panorama of perpetual enmity between Carthage and Rome.

Once Aeneas has escaped (or fled) from Carthage, he touches at the western end of Sicily to celebrate games in commemoration of the first anniversary of his father Anchises' death, in a perfect combination of Roman ritual usage with the vocation of the games in *Iliad* 23, celebrated by Achilles for the death of Patroclus. Even here Juno succeeds in inducing the Trojan women to burn part of the fleet. They are (almost all) left behind, and Aeneas arrives on the coast of Campania. He consults the Sibyl, who gives him (6.83–97) a typically riddling and alarming account of his future travails before accompanying him into the Underworld in accordance with his father's orders. Odysseus had gone to speak with the dead in *Odyssey* 11, but Virgil takes the fullest advantage of seven centuries of poetry, philosophy, and religious thought to offer a remarkably dense, difficult, and at times remarkably moving vision of the other world. Doves sent by Aeneas's mother lead him to find the talismanic golden bough, essential to his passage below. Just what the bough "means," no one honestly knows, though certainly it does not help to explain its meaning in terms of northern mythologies that Virgil could not have known. Sibyl and hero enter the Underworld (6.268–272) in lines of terrible and majestic indirection (see W. R. Johnson, 88ff.). She takes Aeneas past not just a rich and complex gallery of mythological monsters and of personages once familiar to any reader well-grounded in epic and tragic poetry, but also past Palinurus (his steersman, lost on the voyage from Sicily); past Dido herself (utterly irreconcilable); and past Deiphobus, killed the night Troy was sacked–further and further back into Aeneas's experience. In Tartarus, Sibyl shows Aeneas both the great sinners of the world of myth and evildoers who belong not only to Greek religious poetry in the Orphic tradition but also to the Rome of the civil wars. Only at verse 637 do the pair reach Elysium, the realm of the

blessed, inhabited by the virtuous (in Orphic terms) with a marked emphasis on poets and seers (notably Orpheus himself), and at 679ff. meet Anchises, who explains to Aeneas (724–751) the theology of death, punishment, purification, and rebirth, in Stoic and Platonic terms, but with touches of Lucretian (that is, Epicurean) language. Anchises reveals to his son the future of the Roman race, as the Trojans' descendants march past in a review: Virgil selects drastically, on partly understood principles, and does not spare criticisms of flawed heroes from Rome's past. At 6.847–853, Virgil offers the classic contrast of the talents of Rome and Greece and proclaims Rome's destiny of merciful rule. To end on an upward beat would be unlike Virgil, and the last figure in the parade is Marcellus, recently dead when Virgil wrote and therefore the last to come into view in the Underworld. Virgil draws on Augustus's own funeral speech for his nephew and to some tastes overdoes the formal lament; it is said that Marcellus's mother fainted (or burst into loud sobs) during Virgil's own reading. Marcellus therefore joins Virgil's list (for example, Nisus, Euryalus, Pallas, and Lausus) of those who die prematurely, sacrificed to war/fate/Rome/progress. Virgil's belief in Rome's destiny is continuously and profoundly qualified by his pessimism and sense of tragic loss–qualified, not canceled. Virgil expects of his readers the ability to maintain equilibrium between the contrasting and apparently incompatible elements in his worldview. How is Aeneas to leave the Underworld? He can hardly exit through the Gate of Horn, passage for "true shadows"; only the Gate of Ivory is left, passage for *falsa . . . insomnia* (dreams that mislead or dreams that are not dreams at all), as indeed Aeneas's is not. It would be pushing Virgil's sense of doubt and uncertainty to ridiculous limits to suppose (as has been tried!) that the poet was in truth here telling us that his whole vision of Rome's genius and destiny was to be viewed as a misleading dream.

After Aeneas reaches the Tiber mouth and the local king, Latinus, has offered him his daughter Lavinia in marriage, Juno's demonic agent Allecto plays on resentful human reactions to this divinely approved course of events and whips up armed opposition to the Trojans throughout central Italy. Turnus, prince of the neighboring Rutuli, sends for further allies, and the Trojans row up the Tiber to the future site of Rome, currently occupied by settlers from Greece under the benign rule of King Evander, whose people have long been at war with the Latins. Evander offers Aeneas modest reinforcements under his only son, Pallas, and Aeneas leaves the scene of action to acquire help from the Etruscans. Aeneas's visit to Rome (*Aeneid* 8) gives Virgil the chance to involve his hero directly in the past (mythological) and future (religious and historical) asso-

Early commentators on Virgil's works: (clockwise from left) Antonio Mancinelli, Cristoforo Landino, Marius Servius Honoratus, Tiberius Claudius Donatus, and Domizio Calderino; from the 1499 Lyon edition of Virgil's works (courtesy of the Lilly Library, Indiana University)

ciations of the city. While book 6 introduced Aeneas to the future heroes of his people, book 8 introduces him to their capital, not to be founded, on the standard chronology, for another 450-odd years. Evander is represented as an old man: his account of Rome's even earlier past is cast in the mode of personal reminiscence, and Virgil seems to set up a sequence of "villains" in Rome's pre-history–such as Cacus, Turnus, and Mark Antony (to select drastically)–opposed by a sequence of heroes–such as Hercules, Aeneas, and Octavian/Augustus. But too much concentration upon book 8 leads to a simplification of the historical and moral intentions of the *Aeneid:* a more measured reading shows both Hercules and Aeneas prone to anger, just as not all of the great figures in the Parade of Heroes were flawless in thought and action. So readers may wonder how much of Augustus Virgil may want them to see in Aeneas. There are isolated moments in book 8 when the well-informed reader certainly is meant to react with

"but that's just what happened in 29 B.C.," but that is not to say that the whole poem is to be read as an historical allegory, though the reader may in the end feel that there might be just enough identification between Aeneas and Augustus to make the sort of reading out of which Aeneas emerges as some sort of brutal killer, a living reproach to the best Roman (and modern) moral values, just a bit unconvincing. Augustus and his advisers, after all, knew the poem before publication and did not suppress it; in the case of a posthumous publication presumably they could have done so with ease. Imperial assent, even approval, does not rule out serious, critical thinking about ethical problems. Criticism was most definitely not forbidden in Augustus's earlier years. But in the case of a poet intensely committed to both sides of a moral or emotional issue, who expresses fervent Roman patriotism for two or three lines at a time, the strictly allegorical reading of book 8 (and of other passages) has lost much of the appeal it once had.

While Aeneas is absent from the Trojan camp, Turnus attempts an assault upon it; Aeneas's son Ascanius and the senior Trojans keep him (just) at bay. Two young Trojans, Nisus and Euryalus, represented as homosexual lovers, offer to ride to Aeneas for help; they are distracted by the chance to slaughter and plunder the sleeping Latin besiegers, and this delay leads to their deaths, in terms both romanticized and brutal (book 9). There has been heated discussion of this episode. Were Nisus and Euryalus right to deviate from their mission? Were they carried away by blood lust? Was their attack on a sleeping enemy morally deplorable? Does Virgil express condemnation? Just how blameless were the Latins? The young pair are sporadically criticized, but not strongly, and a careful reading suggests careful attempts to explain and justify their conduct.

The whole question of the ethics of warfare reappears with increased force in the next book, when Aeneas returns with many Etruscan allies to even up the lines of battle. Turnus kills Pallas, who is no match for him (10.459). Aeneas hears the news and bursts into violent Homeric battle rage, compared even to the monstrous giant Aegaeon (565ff.). He emerges as a brutal and effective warrior, a fact which is altogether too much for readers who want Aeneas to be an updated, morally correct, righteous hero, who draws his sword only when all else fails, to whom right thinking is even more important than action. Turnus's ally Mezentius, the exiled king of the Etruscans, one of the most robustly convincing figures in the poem in his commitment to blood and brutality, meets Aeneas in fair fight and is wounded. Mezentius's son Lausus (clearly a Latin counterpart to Pallas) rushes to his father's aid and is also killed (before Mezentius dies) by a distressed and reluctant Aeneas (821ff.). Such a sequence of events leaves the poet ample scope for moral comment and judgment, but Aeneas has, in the last forty years, incurred the strongest criticism for "lapsing" into Homeric battle-rage, and Virgil is said to make his criticism entirely plain by comparing Aeneas to the giant Aegaeon. The careful reader, though, learns that in Virgil's work, the bigger the issue, the less simple it is likely to be. Aeneas, after all, had fought at Troy and *Aeneid* 7-12 is an epic of warfare in the Iliadic tradition. Does Virgil expect his audience to judge Aeneas by the highest philosophical standards of his day? Or as a Roman warrior? Or as a real Homeric hero, rather more successful now than Homer made him in the *Iliad,* when he was seven or eight years younger? And what of Aegaeon? Certainly he fought against Zeus in the works of Homer and Hesiod (*Aeneid* 10.567), but not in all versions. Aegaeon is a remote, archaic, violent figure, but the Aeneas of book 10 is not a respectable,

moderate, Stoic hero. He fights with passion, above all when Pallas, whom he had undertaken to protect by a solemn commitment to old Evander, is killed. Readers might wonder whether they are quite simply applying the wrong criteria if they hastily condemn the bloodthirsty Aeneas of book 10. Although today's audience may have lost the taste for gory heroes, by Homeric standards the Aeneas of book 10 has done nothing monstrous.

Rather the same issue arises, but on a grander scale, at the end of book 12. Clearly, the *Aeneid* can only end by a battle between Aeneas and Turnus to decide who shall marry Lavinia, who shall succeed Latinus, and who shall found the new city that will one day lead to the founding of Rome. Turnus is not Aeneas's equal on the battlefield (compare with Juno's words at 12.149) and does not enjoy the favor of Jupiter or, ultimately, the benevolence of destiny. However, his end means the end of the poem, and though Virgil gives many hints about what will happen next, the plot of book 12 is aimed (as is that of book 10) at keeping Aeneas and Turnus apart as long as possible. While Aeneas settles terms with Latinus to decide the future by single combat against Turnus (12.189-194 provides Virgil's political reading of the future), Juno has decided to do all she can to put off her favorite's end, and works, much as in book 7, upon the Latins' emotions. They break the truce; Aeneas is wounded; and for the last time Turnus runs riot on the battlefield. At that point Venus (12.411) has had enough, heals her son miraculously, and he returns with alarming majesty to the battlefield (12.441-495; compare with 10.260ff., his relief of the Trojans' camp). Aeneas cannot run Turnus down and decides to attack (and set fire to) Latinus's city in order to bring the battle to a crisis. Latinus's wife Amata commits suicide. Only at 12.614 does Virgil make Turnus realize that he has let events run out of hand and not until 12.697, with Latinus's city burning down, does Aeneas turn with awful might against his enemy, for whom there is clearly no hope. The result is the strong sympathy of many modern readers, who have not always followed with sufficient care the many indications that Virgil offers his uncommitted reader concerning the flaws of character that make Turnus not a pitiable victim, nor, for that matter, a villain justifiably executed, but a loser who loses for good reason. When one reads the *Aeneid* with care, one learns to distinguish judgments according to who makes them—Virgil in his own voice, or Aeneas, or some other character. In this last case, frequently enough the character in question is a liar, either when talking about him/herself, or when evaluating someone else; this tendency to untruth is particularly characteristic

Virgil's tomb (upper left) near the entrance to the Neapolitan tunnel

marry Lavinia. Turnus pleads too for his life, which Aeneas is even disposed to grant until he sees that Turnus is wearing the swordbelt he had stripped from Pallas in book 10. That memory, for Aeneas, is unbearable: Pallas had become one of his own family (*meorum,* my folk), and Turnus, as a criminal, owes Aeneas a life, which he takes "fired with fury and fearful in his rage" (12.946–947). For many modern readers, Aeneas's action makes Turnus the moral winner and Aeneas the brutal assassin. After the negotiations between Aeneas and Latinus earlier in the book, in the context of the whole elaborate code of single combat established by the *Iliad* and inherited by Virgil, after all that Turnus has done to reveal himself a proponent of confused moral values in a necessarily losing cause, that formally Aeneas has a good right to deal the deathblow is difficult to deny. But in rage, too? Who, though, in the ancient world would have condemned him? Certainly the Stoics would have, and to make out a strong ethical case against Aeneas is easy if one starts from Cicero's Stoic-based treatise, *De Officiis* (On Duties). Virgil, though, does not say that the end of the epic should be read in a Stoic key, and a defense for Aeneas is easy along such other lines (Homeric, Platonic, Aristotelian, traditional Roman, "Augustan," and even Epicurean). Anchises had told his son (book 6, line 853) to beat down the proud in war and spare those who give themselves up. But Turnus had only thought of surrender with Aeneas standing victorious over him. With the killing of Pallas, Turnus might be said to have forfeited his own life. Certainly, the poem could never have made sense at the end in historical and political terms if both Turnus and Aeneas had survived. So the modern reader may not like the end, may not be happy about Turnus's behavior, may wish there had been some other way for the plot to work out, but it was not the first time in Roman literature that the cost, in human terms, of history and empire had been painfully high. There is no real moral ambiguity, but whether the reader is expected to be emotionally easy and happy about the end is something that the present-day reader has to decide after reading and rereading.

of Juno and of characters under her influence. The limping Aeneas now pursues the swordless Turnus round the walls of the burning city, while Juno and Jupiter settle what is to happen when the battle is over (12.791–842). Denis Feeney includes a discussion of them in *The Gods in Epic* (1991, pp. 129–187). They should not be simplified by reducing them to a couple of neat formulations, for Virgil likes to present complex, varied, and often inconsistent aspects of events and systems, both human and divine. The Juno of book 12 has opposed Aeneas since book 1, line 4; only at book 12, line 808, does she admit she has lost; the struggle has been both elemental and personal, both political (for the fate of nations present and future is at stake) and extremely human, for Juno has acted through people whom she has manipulated by means of her agents, without, however, turning them into the mechanical puppets of an Olympian mistress. The last combat is almost banal in its narrative simplicity: Turnus is pinned to the ground by Aeneas's spear, an act that allows him to make a last speech (931–937), in which he admits that Aeneas is right, has won, and shall

Bibliographies:

Werner Suerbaum, "Hundert Jahre Vergil-Forschung: Eine systematische Arbeitsbibliographie mit besonderer Berücksichtigung der Aeneisibild," *Aufstieg und Niedergang der römischen Welt,* 2.31.1 (1980): 3–358, with 2.31.2, 1359–1399 (index);

Ward W. Briggs, "A Bibliography of Virgil's 'Eclogues'," *Aufstieg und Niedergang der römischen Welt,* 2.31.2 (1981): 1265–1357;

Suerbaum, "Spezialbibliographie zu Vergils Georgica," *Aufstieg und Niedergang der römischen Welt,* 2.31.2 (1981): 395–499.

Concordance:

Henrietta Holm Warwick, comp., *A Vergil Concordance* (Minneapolis: University of Minnesota Press, 1975).

Biography:

Colin Hardie, ed., *Vitae Vergillianae,* second edition (Oxford: Clarendon Press, 1957).

References:

William S. Anderson, *The Art of the* Aeneid (Englewood Cliffs, N.J.: Prentice-Hall, 1969);

Francis Cairns, *Virgil's Augustan Epic* (Cambridge: Cambridge University Press, 1989);

W. A. Camps, *An Introduction to Virgil's Aeneid* (Oxford: Oxford University Press, 1969);

Wendell Clausen, *Virgil's Aeneid and the Tradition of Hellenistic Poetry* (Berkeley: University of California Press, 1986);

Steele Commager, ed., *Virgil* (Englewood Cliffs, N.J.: Prentice-Hall, 1966);

Domenico Comparetti, *Vergil in the Middle Ages,* translated by Edward F. M. Benecke (London: Sonnenschien, 1895);

T. S. Eliot, *What is a Classic?* (London: Faber & Faber, 1945);

Joseph Farrell, *Vergil's Georgics and the Traditions of Ancient Epic* (Oxford: Oxford University Press, 1991);

Denis Feeney, *The Gods in Epic* (Oxford: Clarendon Press, 1991);

Jasper Griffin, *Virgil's Iliad; An Essay on Epic Narrative* (Cambridge: Cambridge University Press, 1984);

Philip R. Hardie, *Virgil,* Greece and Rome, New Surveys in the Classics, 38 (Oxford: Oxford University Press, 1998);

Hardie, *Virgil's Aeneid. Cosmos and Imperium* (Oxford: Oxford University Press, 1986);

S. J. Harrison, *Oxford Readings in Vergil's* Aeneid (Oxford: Oxford University Press, 1990);

Richard Heinze, *Virgil's Epic Technique,* translated by Hazel and David Harvey and Fred Robertson (Berkeley & Los Angeles: University of California Press, 1993);

Elisabeth Henry, *The Vigour of Prophecy: A Study of Virgil's* Aeneid (Bristol: Bristol Classical Press / Carbondale: Southern Illinois University Press, 1989);

Gilbert Highet, *The Speeches in Vergil's* Aeneid (Princeton, N.J.: Princeton University Press, 1972);

Nicholas Horsfall, *A Companion to the Study of Virgil* (Leiden: E. J. Brill, 1995);

W. R. Johnson, *Darkness Visible: A Study of Virgil's* Aeneid (Berkeley: University of California Press, 1976);

W. F. Jackson Knight, *Roman Vergil* (London: Faber & Faber, 1966);

R. O. A. M. Lyne, *Further Voices in Vergil's* Aeneid (Oxford: Oxford University Press, 1987);

Lyne, *Words and the Poet: Characteristic Techniques of Style in Vergil's Aeneid* (Oxford: Oxford University Press, 1989);

Charles Martindale, ed., *The Cambridge Companion to Virgil* (Cambridge: Cambridge University Press, 1997);

Ian McAuslan and Peter Walcott, eds., *Virgil, Greece and Rome Studies* (Oxford: Oxford University Press, 1990);

James J. O'Hara, *Death and the Optimistic Prophecy in Vergil's* Aeneid (Princeton: Princeton University Press, 1990);

Brooks Otis, *Virgil: A Study in Civilized Poetry* (Oxford: Oxford University Press, 1963);

Viktor Pöschl, *The Art of Vergil; Image and Symbol in the Aeneid,* translated by G. Seligson (Ann Arbor: University of Michigan Press, 1962);

Kenneth Quinn, *Virgil's Aeneid: A Critical Description* (Ann Arbor: University of Michigan Press, 1968);

Hans-Peter Stahl, ed., *Vergil's Aeneid: Augustan Epic and Political Context* (London: Duckworth, 1998);

Peter White, *Promised Verse* (Cambridge, Mass.: Harvard University Press, 1993), pp. 266–268;

L. P. Wilkinson, *The Georgics of Virgil* (Cambridge: Cambridge University Press, 1969);

G. W. Williams, *Technique and Ideas in the Aeneid* (New Haven: Yale University Press, 1983).

Vitruvius

(ca. 85 B.C. – ca. 15 B.C.)

Peter J. Aicher
University of Southern Maine

WORK: *De architectura,* 10 books (On Architecture, ca. 30–20 B.C.).

Editio princeps: *De architectura,* edited by Giovanni Sulpicio (Rome: Eucharius Silber, 1486).

Standard editions: *Vitruvii De architectura libri decem,* edited by Valentin Rose, second edition (Leipzig: Teubner, 1899); *Vitruvii De architectura libri decem,* edited by F. Krohn (Leipzig: Teubner, 1912); *Architectura (dai libri I–VII),* edited by Silvio Ferri (Rome: Palombi, 1960); *De l'architecture,* edited by Philippe Fleury and Pierre Gros (Paris: Les Belles Lettres, 1969–1992).

Translations in English: *Vitruvius Pollio. The Ten Books on Architecture,* translated by Morris Hicky Morgan (Cambridge, Mass.: Harvard University Press, 1914); *Vitruvius, On Architecture,* 2 volumes, translated by Frank Granger, Loeb Classical Library (Cambridge, Mass.: Harvard University Press, 1931–1934).

Commentaries: *Zehn Bücher über Architektur,* edited by Curt Fensterbusch (Darmstadt: Wissenschaftliche Büchgesellschaft, 1964); *Les dix livres dárchitecture de Vitruve,* edited by Claude Perrault (Brussels: P. Mardaga, 1979); *Zehn Bücher über Architektur,* edited by Jakob Prestel, third edition (Baden-Baden: V. Koerner, 1983).

Vitruvius's treatise *De architectura* (On Architecture, ca. 30–20 B.C.), an architectural and engineering compendium in ten books (each about thirty pages long), is the author's only known work and is the only major work on architecture to survive from classical antiquity. The work is important not only for the picture it provides of the theory and practice of architecture and engineering in classical antiquity but also for its pervasive influence on subsequent architectural theory and practice beginning in the early Renaissance and continuing into the nineteenth century.

Most of the little that is known about the life of Vitruvius (only his family name has come down to present-day readers) must be gathered from his treatise, especially in the preface to book 1. He served under Julius Caesar, probably as a military engineer, and his description of conditions in Numidia suggests that he was there with Caesar in 46 B.C. (8.3.23–4). Upon Caesar's death in 44 B.C. Vitruvius transferred his services to Caesar's adopted son, Octavian (soon to be known as Augustus), and received a post to construct and repair artillery machines. Vitruvius credited the emperor's sister Octavia with renewing his appointments and was thankful to the imperial family for the rewards of service that allowed him to retire without financial worries, leaving him the time and leisure to write his treatise on architecture, which he dedicated to Augustus. At some time Vitruvius also must have been employed on Rome's water supply; Frontinus, in his handbook on Rome's aqueducts, attributes to Vitruvius a new system of measuring water pipes in 33 B.C. (*De Aquaeductu* 25.1). Vitruvius also was engaged as an architect, although he reports with some bitterness that he received few commissions to design or construct buildings, and he mentions only one building as his own work, a basilica in Fano (5.1.6–10).

Internal evidence indicates that Vitruvius likely began *On Architecture* between 31 and 27 B.C. and finished it before the decade was out. This period is the same one in which Virgil and Horace were producing some of the greatest works of Roman literature, and although Vitruvius's practical Latin prose, interrupted on occasion by Greek technical terms and rhetorical passages straining for elevation, is far from the polished poetry of Virgil and Horace, his work on architecture shares more than a common date with the poetic masterpieces of his fellow Romans. Each writer shows a strong pride in Italy and Roman culture while referring to the accomplishments of Greece; each ranges for examples over the vast geography of the Roman Empire and beyond, and each is sprinkled with fulsome praise for Augustus, their common patron.

It is not easy to determine the intended audience of the treatise. In the preface to book 1, Vitruvius com-

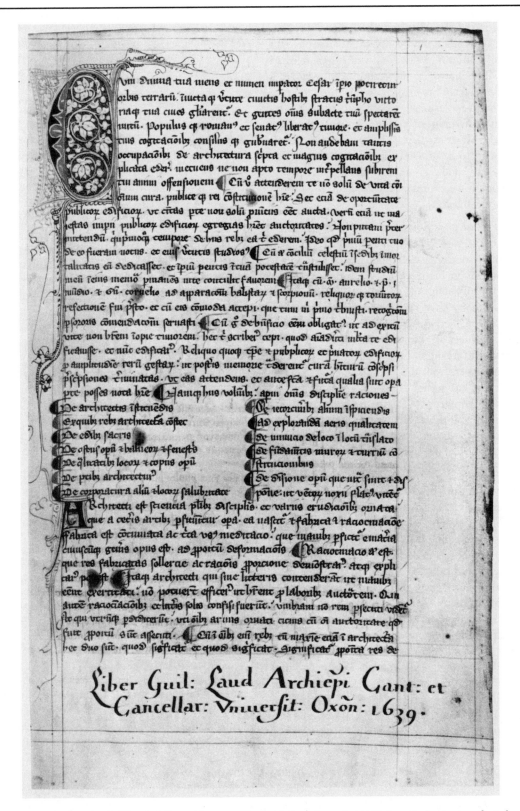

Page from an illuminated manuscript for Vitruvius's De architectura *(On Architecture), transcribed at St. Augustine's monastary, Canterbury, in 1316 (St. John's College, Oxford)*

mends his work to Augustus himself so that the *imperator* (emperor) can judge the quality of the many works taking shape around him now that he had established peace. Elsewhere, however, the author acknowledges a desire both to increase the prestige of the art of architecture and to secure a lasting fame for himself in posterity; clearly he is writing for a larger audience than the imperial circle. Much of what he writes is technical and detailed enough to be of use for an architect and engineer of his day, and yet, in the section on private houses in book 6, he addresses the amateur who hopes to bypass the architect.

As the following summary of the ten books of *De architectura* makes clear, the term architecture as typically used today does not span the broad range of Vitruvius's concerns in his treatise, which includes such matters as city planning and water supply as well as concerns that today devolve upon engineers and construction foremen. Perhaps it is best to think of Vitruvius's ideal architect as someone who could, if called upon, oversee the creation of a complete Greco-Roman city in a wilderness, from the selection of the site and the layout of the city to the design and construction of every type of building, as well as the walls and weapons needed to defend them. In Vitruvius's time the Romans, under the active colonizing policies of Julius Caesar and Augustus, were in fact building scores of cities from scratch in Italy and the provinces.

Vitruvius begins his treatise by laying out the broad training necessary for an architect worthy of the name and argues emphatically for a well-rounded education no less demanding than what Cicero had advised for orators a generation earlier. The architect must learn geometry and drawing, for the drafting of accurate plans and the figuring of proportions; optics, for the calculation of natural lighting; history and myth, for the iconographic significance of ornament (such as pedimental sculpture); philosophy, for its elevation of character (the architect must especially guard against avarice) and for its inquiries into physical properties; music, for fine-tuning catapults and adjusting theater acoustics; medicine, for an awareness of healthy and unhealthy sites and waters; law, for questions concerning property rights and contractual obligations; and astronomy, for the construction of sundials.

Also included in book 1 is the short but highly influential portion of the treatise devoted to architectural theory; this section is where Vitruvius lays out the fundamental principles of his art. At the heart of it are the famous benchmarks of *utilitas, firmitas,* and *venustas* (a triad best known in Henry Wotton's rendering as "commodity, firmness, and delight"). Building

. . . must be carried out with consideration for strength, utility, and beauty. The condition of strength will be assured when the foundations are taken down to a solid base and each of the materials is carefully selected without cutting corners. Utility will be assured when the layout of the building is faultless and presents no hindrance to its use, and its arrangement is suited and conducive to its particular purpose. The condition of beauty will be met when the structure has a pleasing and elegant appearance, and the proportions of its component parts have been calculated with due regard for the correct principles of symmetry (1.3.2).

The first book closes with the more practical considerations of determining a site for a city, how to build its walls, and how to lay out its streets.

Book 2 is a valuable discussion of ancient Roman building materials and their relative merits; the book covers brick, sand, lime, pozzolana (a volcanic sand of remarkable properties that was one of the keys to the strength of Roman concrete), and various stones and timbers. There is also a lengthy section on the varying ways to construct the walls of buildings.

Books 3 and 4 are devoted to the design and building of temples, for which the observance of symmetry and proportion are especially important, not only for the enduring prominence of temples but also because the resultant harmony is expressive of the divinity such buildings house. Vitruvius also links his theory of symmetry in temples to the proportions of the human body:

The design of temples depends on symmetry, the principles of which the architect must follow closely. Symmetry in turn arises from proportion (what the Greeks called *analogia*). Proportion is the relation of the parts of the building and the building as a whole to a consistent module—the means by which the principles of symmetry are realized. For a temple to have an orderly design it must have such symmetry and proportion, with a precise relationship of parts that is characteristic of a well-proportioned body (3.1.1).

This discussion is also the occasion for the famous description of the "Vitruvian man," an ideal human figure whose extended limbs can be fit alternately into a square (horizontal arm span equaling vertical height) or a circle (with the navel as the center). After these theoretical preliminaries he classifies the different types of temple arrangements, such as prostyle and peripteral, along with the proportions appropriate for each, followed by a detailed presentation of the proportions and ornamentation suitable for each of the different *genera* (orders) of temple construction (Ionic, Corinthian, and Doric; a Tuscan style and circular temples are also briefly discussed).

Book 5 discusses the design and location of public buildings—including basilicas, a forum, a senate house, a prison, a theater, colonnades, and baths; because of its complex acoustics, the theater receives special attention. Again such descriptions make clear that the architect of Vitruvius's time might be responsible for the design of an entire city. Book 6 then turns to private dwellings and prescribes the location and proportions of the various rooms and quarters of a house. Climate is one influence on the design; other key variables in the plan of a house are the social standing and profession of the owner:

> The houses of bankers and tax-collectors must be larger and more impressive, as well as secure against burglars. The homes of lawyers and professors of rhetoric should be elegant and roomy enough to hold their audiences. The homes of high-ranking politicians in office needing space for public duties must be designed with lofty, regal entrances, spacious atriums and peristyles, and groves and broad walkways suitably landscaped for the high dignity of office (6.5.2).

There is also advice in book 6 on the design of country estates and working farms, with their special needs of storage and shelter.

Book 7 discusses interior finish work and is concerned primarily with the art of stucco, including surface preparation, the composition of the plaster, and its painting; the second half of the book is devoted to the concocting of dyes for paint from various minerals, vegetation, and shellfish. This book finishes the portion of the treatise concerned with buildings. Book 8 is concerned with water supply—how to find wholesome water, how to purify it further, how to conduct it into the city by aqueduct, and how to distribute it. Book 9 provides instruction on the construction of sundials and water clocks, and book 10 gives instruction on the building of various machines—including cranes, water wheels, pumps, and the artillery pieces that had been Vitruvius's specialty when serving in the army for Caesar and Augustus.

Consistent, however, with Vitruvius's belief in the value of a well-rounded education for architects, his concerns in each of the ten books often take him far afield from the topic of each book narrowly considered, and the tangents in his treatise include valuable information about other fields of ancient thought. In book 2, where the subject matter is building materials, Vitruvius first provides an account of the evolution of civilization and the art of architecture. He follows this history with a summary of some early Greek theories on the material constituents of the universe before getting down to the practical business of making bricks and mixing concrete. The discussion of theater design

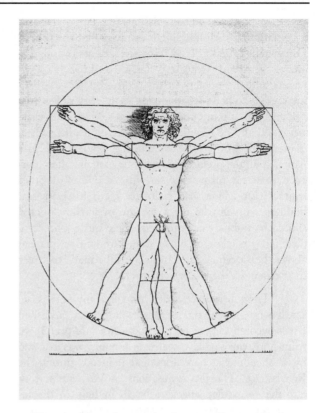

Vitruvian Man, *demonstrating the system of human proportions proposed by Vitruvius, engraving after a ca. 1487 drawing by Leonardo da Vinci*

in book 5 involves a lengthy discussion of music and harmonic theory, since the architect has to "tune" the sounding vessels placed among the theater seats for the amplification of the variously pitched voices of the actors. The discussion of suitable house designs is preceded by a general discussion of the effects of climate on national character (6.1), and the discussion of water supplies occasions a long digression on strange waters of the world (8.3). Fully two-thirds of book 9, ostensibly concerned with the construction of sundials and water clocks, is devoted to astronomical, astrological, and meteorological discussions that have no practical bearing on the solar calculations and geometry needed to construct a sundial. These and other discussions and asides make Vitruvius's work a treasure trove of information for students of antiquity in almost all fields. It is Vitruvius, for instance, who relays the story of Archimedes' bathtub illumination heralded by the cry "Eureka!" (9. pref.).

Also expanding the interest of the work are the passages that reveal something about the author's profession and personality. These segments are primarily grouped in the prefaces to each of the books and are often polemical in tone. Vitruvius is concerned to distinguish himself from poorly educated architects who owe their position and commissions to their good looks; it is thanks to such fraudulent climbers that the profession is in bad repute. To counter the falseness of appearances, Vitruvius writes his book to show his own talents and the nobility of his profession (3. pref.). In the preface to book 5 he defends the brevity of his treatise and the obscurity of some of its subject matter; he worries that if he lengthens his explanations, his subject matter will lose its focus and the reader will lose patience. In the preface to book 7 he explains the difference between plagiarism and his own use of other sources. Elsewhere, bad estimates incur his criticism; builders who do the work for the price they quoted should be publicly commended, while those who complete construction at more than twenty-five percent above their original estimates should be made to cover the extra costs themselves (10. pref.).

"Though little celebrity has come my way, Caesar, it is my hope that once these volumes are published I will become known even to posterity" (6. pref.5). In truth, Vitruvius's relative neglect in antiquity was followed by a phenomenal popularity and influence during the Renaissance. The first translations of Vitruvius's work into the vernacular languages began in Italy in the fifteenth century, and the great early humanist Leone Battista Alberti worked out his own architectural theories with Vitruvius's theories as their starting point. Others began to illustrate and comment upon Vitruvius's treatise; the most famous of the drawings was Leonardo da Vinci's often-reproduced rendition of "Vitruvian man."

Vitruvius's influence reached its zenith in the sixteenth century as the process of translation, commentary, and illustration continued unabated. Among those architects following in his footsteps was Andrea Palladio, whose *Four Books on Architecture* (1570), probably planned as ten books on the model of Vitruvius's treatise, combines Vitruvius's theories and advice with Alberti's theories and his own observations to produce the most celebrated Renaissance book on architecture. It was through the medium of Palladio that Vitruvius's ideals of classicism, proportion, and a well-rounded training inspired subsequent generations of architects and artists, including Thomas Jefferson and Johann Wolfgang von Goethe.

Vitruvius's work is by no means an unerring or comprehensive guide to ancient architecture and its riches. He lived and wrote before the great period of imperial Roman architecture, when so much that was characteristically Roman—the spectacular exploitation of concrete vaulted spaces, for instance—was of necessity beyond his purview. Even his treatment of Republican architecture must be balanced by the archaeological record for an accurate picture of Roman architecture, since much of Vitruvius's advice on building is proscriptive rather than descriptive of actual monuments and practices. Such limitations acknowledged, Vitruvius's treatise is nonetheless an invaluable resource in the understanding of both the principles and the practices of ancient architecture. Furthermore, with its broad range of concerns and digressions, it adds greatly to understanding present-day social conditions, daily life, and intellectual life during one of the high watermarks of ancient civilization. Finally, *On Architecture* played a crucial role in the perpetuation and interpretation of classical ideals in later Western architecture.

Concordance and Index:

Vitruve De architectura concordance, 2 volumes, edited by Louis Callebat, P. Bouet, Philippe Fleury, M. Zuinghedau (Hildesheim: Olms, 1984);

Vitruvius Pollio indices nominum et verborum instruxit, edited by Laura Cherubini (Pisa: Giardini, 1975).

References:

James C. Anderson Jr., *Roman Architecture and Society* (Baltimore & London: Johns Hopkins University Press, 1997), pp. 3–15, 39–45;

Barry Baldwin, "The Date, Identity, and Career of Vitruvius," *Latomus,* 4 (1990): 425–434;

Frank Brown, "Vitruvius and the Liberal Art of Architecture," *Bucknell Review,* 11, no. 4 (1963): 99–107;

Robert Klein and H. Zerner, *Vitruve et le théâtre de la renaissance italienne* (Paris: Editions du centre National de la recherche scientifique, 1964);

Hanno-Walter Kruft, *A History of Architectural Theory from Vitruvius to the Present* (New York: Princeton Architectural Press, 1994), pp. 21–92;

Alexander McKay, *Vitruvius: Architect and Engineer* (Basingstoke, U.K.: Macmillan, 1978);

Hugh Plommer, *Vitruvius and Later Roman Building Manuals* (London: Cambridge University Press, 1973).

Checklist of Further Readings

Albrecht, Michael von. *A History of Roman Literature from Livius Andronicus to Boethius,* 2 volumes, revised by Albrecht and Gareth Schmeling. Leiden: Brill, 1997.

Binns, J. W. *Latin Literature of the Fourth Century.* London: Routledge & Kegan Paul, 1974.

Conte, Gian Biagio. *Latin Literature: A History,* translated by Joseph B. Solodow, revised by Don Fowler and Glenn W. Most. Baltimore: Johns Hopkins University Press, 1994.

Copley, Frank O. *Latin Literature from the Beginnings to the Close of the Second Century A.D.* Ann Arbor: University of Michigan Press, 1969.

Dihle, Albrecht. *Greek and Latin Literature of the Roman Empire from Augustus to Justinian,* translated by Manfred Malzahn. London: Routledge, 1994.

Dorey, T. A., ed. *Empire and Aftermath: Silver Latin II.* London: Routledge & Kegan Paul, 1975.

Duff, J. Wight. *A Literary History of Rome from the Origins to the Golden Age,* third edition, edited by A. M. Duff. New York: Barnes & Noble, 1960.

Duff, *A Literary History of Rome in the Silver Age,* third edition, edited by A. M. Duff. New York: Barnes & Noble, 1964.

Fantham, Elaine. *Roman Literary Culture from Cicero to Apuleius.* Baltimore: Johns Hopkins University Press, 1996.

Feeney, Denis. *Literature and Religion at Rome: Cultures, Contexts, and Beliefs.* Cambridge: Cambridge University Press, 1998.

Goldberg, Sander M. *The Epic in Republican Rome.* New York: Oxford University Press, 1995.

Hadas, Moses. *A History of Latin Literature.* New York: Columbia University Press, 1952.

Hornblower, Simon, and Antony Spawforth, eds. *The Oxford Classical Dictionary,* third edition. Oxford: Oxford University Press, 1996.

Hutchinson, G. O. *Latin Literature from Seneca to Juvenal: A Critical Study.* Oxford: Clarendon Press, 1993.

Kenney, E. J., and W. V. Clausen, eds. *Latin Literature,* volume 2. The Cambridge History of Classical Literature. Cambridge: Cambridge University Press, 1982.

Luce, T. James, ed. *Ancient Writers: Greece and Rome,* 2 volumes. New York: Scribners, 1982.

Rose, H. J. *A Handbook of Latin Literature from the Earliest Times to the Death of St. Augustine,* third edition, supplementary bibliography by Edward Courtney. New York: Dutton, 1966.

Sandys, John Edwin. *A Companion to Latin Studies,* third edition. Cambridge: Cambridge University Press, 1921.

Schanz, Martin von. *Geschichte der römischen Literatur bis zum Gesetzgebungswerk des Kaisers Justinian,* 4 volumes in 5 books, fourth edition, revised by Carl Hosius. Munich: Beck, 1927–1959. Revised as *Handbuch der Altertumswissenschaft,* edited by Reinhart Herzog and Peter Lebrecht Schmidt. Munich: Beck, 1997.

Sullivan, J. P. *Literature and Politics in the Age of Nero.* Ithaca, N.Y.: Cornell University Press, 1985.

Temporini, Hildegard, and Wolfgang Haase, eds. *Aufstieg und Niedergang der Römischen Welt.* Berlin: De Gruyter, 1972– .

Williams, Gordon. *Change and Decline: Roman Literature in the Early Empire.* Berkeley: University of California Press, 1978.

Ziegler, Konrat, and Walther Sontheimer, eds. *Der kleine Pauly.* Munich: Deutscher Taschenbuch, 1979. Five-volume abridgment of *Paulys Realencyclopädie der classischen Altertumswissenschaft,* 51 volumes in 61 books, edited by August F. von Pauly and Georg Wissowa. Stuttgart: Metzler, 1894–1980.

Contributors

Peter J. Aicher . . . . *University of Southern Maine*

William W. Batstone . . . . *Ohio State University*

A. J. Boyle . . . . *University of Southern California*

Ward W. Briggs . . . . *University of South Carolina*

David F. Bright . . . . *Emory University*

Craige B. Champion . . . . *Allegheny College*

Jane Che . . . . *University of Pennsylvania*

Christopher P. Craig . . . . *University of Tennessee*

William J. Dominik . . . . *University of Natal*

Harry B. Evans . . . . *Fordham University*

Richard L. S. Evans . . . . *St. Agnes Academy, Houston, Texas*

Sander M. Goldberg . . . . *University of California, Los Angeles*

Leofranc Holford-Strevens . . . . *Oxford University Press*

Nicholas Horsfall . . . . *Rome, Italy*

F. M. A. Jones . . . . *University of Liverpool*

Tracy Keefer . . . . *University of South Carolina*

Paul T. Keyser . . . . *University of Alabama*

Peter E. Knox . . . . *University of Colorado, Boulder*

Richard C. Lounsbury . . . . *Brigham Young University*

Ralph W. Mathisen . . . . *University of South Carolina*

James M. May . . . . *Saint Olaf College*

Ronald Mellor . . . . *University of California, Los Angeles*

Charles E. Mercier . . . . *University of Southern California*

Timothy J. Moore . . . . *University of Texas at Austin*

Hans-Friedrich Mueller . . . . *Florida State University*

J. K. Newman . . . . *University of Illinois at Urbana-Champaign*

Stephen T. Newmyer . . . . *Duquesne University*

Jeanne Neumann O'Neill . . . . *Davidson College*

David Potter . . . . *University of Michigan*

Kenneth J. Reckford . . . . *University of North Carolina at Chapel Hill*

Gerald Sandy . . . . *University of British Columbia*

Gareth Schmeling . . . . *University of Florida*

William Seaton . . . . *Long Island University, Brooklyn Center*

Botham Stone . . . . *Columbia, South Carolina*

W. Jeffrey Tatum . . . . *Florida State University*

Daniel J. Taylor . . . .*Lawrence University*
Robert W. Ulery Jr. . . . .*Wake Forest University*
David Wray . . . . *University of Chicago*
Andrew Zissos . . . . *University of Texas at Austin*

Cumulative Index

Dictionary of Literary Biography, Volumes 1-211
Dictionary of Literary Biography Yearbook, 1980-1998
Dictionary of Literary Biography Documentary Series, Volumes 1-19

Cumulative Index

DLB before number: *Dictionary of Literary Biography,* Volumes 1-211
Y before number: *Dictionary of Literary Biography Yearbook,* 1980-1998
DS before number: *Dictionary of Literary Biography Documentary Series,* Volumes 1-19

C

D

L

ISBN 0-7876-3105-1

90000